Lecture Notes in Artificial Intelligence 2116

Subseries of Lecture Notes in Computer Science
Edited by J. G. Carbonell and J. Siekmann

Lecture Notes in Computer Science
Edited by G. Goos, J. Hartmanis and J. van Leeuwen

Springer
Berlin
Heidelberg
New York
Barcelona
Hong Kong
London
Milan
Paris
Singapore
Tokyo

Varol Akman   Paolo Bouquet
Richmond Thomason   Roger A. Young (Eds.)

Modeling
and Using Context

Third International and
Interdisciplinary Conference, CONTEXT 2001
Dundee, UK, July 27-30, 2001
Proceedings

 Springer

Series Editors

Jaime G. Carbonell, Carnegie Mellon University, Pittsburgh, PA, USA
Jörg Siekmann, University of Saarland, Saarbrücken, Germany

Volume Editors

Varol Akman
Bilkent University, Department of Computer Engineering
Bilkent, Ankara 06533, Turkey
E-mail: akman@cs.bilkent.edu.tr

Paolo Bouquet
University of Trento, Department of Computer and Management Sciences
38100 Trento, Italy
E-mail: bouquet@cs.unitn.it

Richmond Thomason
University of Michigan, Philosophy Department
2251 Angell Hall, Ann Arbor, MI 48109-1003, USA
E-mail: rich@thomason.org

Roger Young
University of Dundee, Philosophy Department
Dundee DD1 4HN, Scotland, UK
E-mail: r.a.young@dundee.ac.uk

Cataloging-in-Publication Data applied for

Die Deutsche Biblilothek - CIP-Einheitsaufnahme

Modeling and using context : ... international and interdisciplinary conference ;
proceedings. - 1999-. - Berlin ; Heidelberg ; New York ; Barcelona ; Hong Kong ;
London ; Milan ; Paris ; Singapore ; Tokyo : Springer, 1999
  (Lecture notes in computer science ; ...)
  Erscheint jährlich. - Bibliographische Deskription nach 3 (2001)
3. CONTEXT 2001 : Dundee, UK, July 27-30, 2001. - (2001)
  (Lecture notes in computer science ; 2116 : Lecture notes in artificial
intelligence)

CR Subject Classification (1998): I.2, F.4.1, J.3, J.4

ISBN 3-540-42379-6 Springer-Verlag Berlin Heidelberg New York

Springer-Verlag Berlin Heidelberg New York
a member of BertelsmannSpringer Science+Business Media GmbH

http://www.springer.de

© Springer-Verlag Berlin Heidelberg 2001
Printed in Germany

Typesetting: Camera-ready by author
Printed on acid-free paper   SPIN: 10839859   06/3142   5 4 3 2 1 0

Preface

Context has emerged as a central concept in a variety of contemporary approaches to reasoning. The conference at which the papers in this volume were presented was the third international, interdisciplinary conference on the topic of context, and was held in Dundee, Scotland on July 27-30, 2001. The first conference in this series was held in Rio de Janiero in 1997, and the second in Trento in 1999.

Like the previous conferences, CONTEXT 2001 was remarkably successful in bringing together representatives of many different fields, spanning the entire range of the cognitive and informational sciences, and with interests ranging from specific, commercial applications to highly general philosophical and logical theories.

The papers collected here demonstrate well the range of context-related research. While foundational problems remain, and continue to be discussed in many of the contributions collected in this volume, the work shows increased sophistication about what forms of reasoning are important, and what techniques are appropriate in accounting for them. The papers themselves, however, do not convey the lively excitement of the conference itself, and the continuing spirit of cooperation and communication across disciplines that has been the hallmark of these conferences. We are very pleased that the field of context research has shown over four years intense, sustained development while retaining this sense of interdisciplinary cooperation.

We would especially like to thank our keynote speakers: Patrick Blackburn (INRIA, Lorraine, France), Herbert Clark (Psychology Department, Stanford University, California), Jerry Hobbs (SRI International, Menlo Park, California), Alex Lascarides (Division of Informatics, University of Edinburgh, Scotland), and John Perry (Philosophy Department, Stanford University, California) for providing a portrait of the best contemporary work in the field.

We would also like to thank the many people who made CONTEXT 2001 possible. First of all, the program committee members and all the additional reviewers for all they did to ensure the high quality of accepted contributions. We also thank Dr. Nicholas Davey, Head of the Philosophy Department (University of Dundee), Professor Huw Jones, Dean of the Faculty of Arts and Social Sciences (University of Dundee) for help with funding; the Finance Office at the University of Dundee, in particular Mr. Gordon Campbell and his assistants, for help with financial administration; the staff at the West Park Conference Center, co-ordinated by Mrs. Eve Anderson and Mrs. Ann Bishop, for all their work;

Drs. Roy Dyckhoff (University of St Andrews), Nick Taylor, Wayne Murray, and their postgraduate assistants for work on the poster, the Scottish end of the web site and providing support at the conference.

July 2001

Varol Akman
Paolo Bouquet
Richmond Thomason
Roger A. Young

Organization

CONTEXT 2001 was organized by the *Department of Philosophy* at the University of Dundee. CONTEXT 2001 was hosted at the *Conference Center* of the University of Dundee.

Organizing Committee

Conference Chair	Paolo Bouquet (University of Trento, Italy)
Program Co-chairs	Varol Akman (Bilkent University, Turkey)
	Richmond Thomason (University of Michigan, USA)
Local Chair & Treasurer	Roger A. Young (University of Dundee, Scotland)
Publicity Chair	Roy M. Turner (University of Maine, USA)

Program Committee

Daniel Andler (France)
Horacio Arló Costa (USA)
Kent Bach (USA)
Carla Bazzanella (Italy)
David Beaver (USA)
Matteo Bonifacio (Italy)
Cristiano Castelfranchi (Italy)
Jean-Charles Pomerol (France)
Herbert Clark (USA)
Christo Dichev (USA)
Bruce Edmonds (UK)
Paul Feltovich (USA)
Tim Fernando (Ireland)
Anita Fetzer (Germany)
Michael Fisher (UK)
Claude Frasson (Canada)
Chiara Ghidini (UK)
Alain Giboin (France)
Pat Hayes (USA)
Jerry Hobbs (USA)
Lucja Iwanska (USA)

Ruth Kempson (UK)
Ewan Klein (UK)
Yves Kodratoff (France)
Boicho Kokinov (Bulgaria)
Jose Luis Bermudez (UK)
Mark Maybury (USA)
Bernard Moulin (Canada)
John Mylopoulos (Canada)
Rolf Nossum (Norway)
John Perry (USA)
Stefano Predelli (Norway)
Marina Sbisá (Italy)
Carles Sierra (Spain)
Munindar Singh (USA)
Steffen Staab (Germany)
Robert Stalnaker (USA)
Jason Stanley (USA)
Mike Tanenhaus (USA)
Robert Young (USA)
Roger A. Young (UK)

Additional Reviewers

Alpaydin, E.
Avesani, P.
Birmingham, B.
Brézillon, P.
Bucciarelli, M.
Busetta, P.
Castellani, F.
Chella, A.

Radev, D.
Fauconnier, G.
Magnini, B.
Penco, C.
Serafini, L.
Steedman, M.
Turner, R.

Sponsoring Institutions

We thank Arthur Andersen, the British Academy, Dundee and Angus Councils, and the Philosophy Department (University of Dundee) for sponsoring the conference.

Table of Contents

Full Papers

Short Papers

XII

Trade-Offs between Inductive Power and Logical Omniscience in Modeling Context

Horacio Arló Costa

Carnegie Mellon University, Pittsburgh PA 15213, USA
hcosta@andrew.cmu.edu

Abstract. In a series of recent papers the economist Michael Bacharach
[2] has pointed out that most approaches in knowledge representation suffer from two complementary defects. Typically they assume that agents
know all the logical consequences of information encoded in a finite
knowledge base (Cleverness) *and only* these consequences (Cloisteredness). In this article we develop first-order and inductive extensions of
Montague-Scott's semantics in order to tackle both problems at once.
Three desiderata are put forward for representing epistemic context: (1)
expressive adequacy, (2) inductive power, (3) boundedness. An important part of our effort focuses on reconsidering the role of standard formalisms (both logical and probabilistic) in representing the information
of *bounded agents*.

1 Introduction

Several disciplines have recently joined forces trying to develop more realistic
models of bounded and interactive agents. Economics and computer science are
perhaps two salient examples of disciplines engaged in this enterprise, but the
issue has an important pedigree in other areas like philosophy, statistics, logic
and linguistics. As a matter of fact the problem is hardly new in Economics
itself. The economist Ariel Rubinstein makes the point in a nice way in a recent
monograph devoted to modeling bounded rationality in economics [11]:

> Dissatisfaction with classical theory as well as attempts to replace the
> basic model of rational man with alternative decision models are not new.
> Ideas of how to model bounded rationality have been lurking about in
> economics for many years. Many proposals have been inspired from pa-
> pers written by Herbert Simon in the mid-50's. Although Simon received
> worldwide recognition for his work in the form of the Nobel prize, only
> recently his call has affected economic theory. Only a few of the tools
> we discuss here have been applied to economic settings. What's more,
> the usefulness of these models is still far from being established. In fact,
> I have the impression that many of us feel that the attempts to model
> bounded rationality have yet to mount the right track. I tend to agree.

Part of the problem is related to the very nature of the enterprise. Logic
or decision theory can be used in order to articulate normative standards or to

describe performance. Even when these tasks are quite different, they are often confused (see [6] for a careful distinction between performance and commitment in knowledge representation).

In the first part of this article we will limit ourselves to consider non-numerical representations of epistemic states. Moreover we will focus on a particular aspect of boundedness: logically omnisciency. Omniscient agents, says the economist M.O.L. Bacharach, 'are assumed to know all the logical consequences of their assumed knowledge.' Bacharach's name for logical omniscience is Cleverness.

Of course no real agent can be *described* as obeying Cleverness. But the obvious rebuttal is that Cleverness is a straw man. Most decision theorists and philosophers, understand logical omniscience as the articulation of the normative *commitments* of a rational agent, not as part of a description of his performance. This response is fair for most of types of doxastic attitudes, but not for all of them. For example, it is quite clear that (the commitments associated with) certain doxastic notions, like 'it is likely' (in the sense of it is probable above a threshold) cannot be represented as obeying Cleverness. The problem is one of the consequences of Cleverness, called *Adjunction*. In this context Adjunction mandates that if P is likely and Q is likely, then their conjunction P ∧ Q should also be likely. But, it is, of course, clear that even when the probability of propositions P and Q surpasses a threshold t, their conjunction might bear a probability below t. A qualitative construal of likelihood or high probability *should not* obey Adjunction as well as other forms of Cleverness usually assumed in epistemic logic. And this is so on normative grounds.[1]

Even when this situation has been well known for many years the development of logical tools for representing attitudes like likelihood has progressed at a relatively slow pace. One the reasons for this is perhaps the fact that the dominant semantic tool in epistemic logic is the so-called Kripke semantics. Roughly the idea of this semantics is to add to a set of worlds (understood as primitives or points) an *accessibility relation*. A *frame* F is a pair $\langle W, R \rangle$ where W is a set of worlds and R an accessibility relation over W. A Kripke model $\mathcal{M}$ is a triple $\langle \langle W, R \rangle, \models \rangle$ where $\langle W, R \rangle$ is frame and $\models$ is a *valuation*, i.e. a relation between worlds and propositional letters. The valuation is extended beyond the propositional letter level in a standard manner for Boolean connectives. Then, if we focus on some attitude, say knowledge, a proposition P is declared known at a certain point $\Gamma \in W$ in a model $\mathcal{M} = \langle \langle W, R \rangle, \models \rangle$ as long as P comes out true in all points accessible from Γ – in the frame $\langle W, R \rangle$. Relevant properties of the resulting knowledge operator will then be correlated with relevant properties of the accessibility relation. For example, the idea that knowledge entails truth would correspond to reflexivity, etc.

But according to this semantic account all epistemic operators (representable via the semantics) obey Cleverness. First notice that since a tautology holds true

---

[1] This is so quite independently of the separate issue related to the adequacy and interest of the *acceptance rules* used in order to link high probability to a qualitative notion of likelihood. Arguments against can be found in [6], while arguments for have been offered in [4] and [5].

in every world we have that any tautology is known at every world. Secondly, if P is known and Q is known, then their conjunction P ∧ Q is also known. The latter property is the one we called above *Adjunction*. Thirdly, if P ∧ Q is known, both P and Q should be known. Finally, if P is known and P entails Q, then Q should be known as well. From now on we will say that an epistemic representation obeys Cleverness (logical omnisciency) as long as it obeys *all* the properties just mentioned.

A well know alternative is the semantic framework independently developed by R. Montague and D. Scott [9], [7]. A frame in *neighborhood semantics* is a pair ⟨W, N⟩ where W is a set of worlds and N a function from elements of W to sets of sets of worlds. When we have a world Γ and an associated neighborhood N(Γ) there is a very simple manner of determining if a proposition P ⊆ W is known at Γ in the corresponding model. We just check whether P is in N(Γ). If the answer is yes, then P is indeed known. Otherwise it is not known. But then it is rather simple to see that none of the forms of logical omniscience previously considered is now obligatory.[2] Nothing requires that the set of worlds W is part of N(Γ). On the other hand if a proposition P is in a neighborhood, and Q is a superset of P, Q need not be in the neighborhood. Finally even if both P and Q are in N(Γ) P ∩ Q need not be in the neighborhood.

It is a rather contentious issue from the philosophical point of view whether a knowledge operator should or should not obey (all or some of) the properties that determine logical omniscience (under a normative point of view). With some provisos some authors think that none of these properties should be required, others think that all of them should be imposed and, finally, some think that only a subset of these properties are required. More importantly these judgements vary considerably depending on the studied attitude (knowledge, belief, likelihood, etc) and depending on whether the formalized concept intends to capture either *epistemic attributions* made about a third agent or *epistemic claims* made by the agent himself. It is perhaps less controversial that *some* of the properties in question are problematic for *some* epistemic notions, under *all* interpretations of the operator. For example, Adjunction is an inadequate property for a monadic epistemic operator of 'high probability'.

In addition neighborhoods can be used in order to describe *explicit knowledge* (belief, etc), rather than commitments to knowledge (belief, etc). This is a descriptive task. A rational agent can conclude that she is committed to hold all the logical consequences of her assumed knowledge, but at each instant there is only a handful of propositions that the agent is aware of. Neighborhoods can also be used in order to describe states of awareness or transitions between them [1].

As the British economist M.O.L. Bacharach has made clear [2], the use of representations eschewing (some or all aspects of) Cleverness cannot be the sole

---

[2] A weak form of logical omniscience, not considered above, continues to hold. When A and B are logically equivalent, A should be known if and only if B is known. The status of this form of logical omniscience will be discussed below

4

response to the development of adequate models of bounded agents.[3] In fact, according to the standard model of rationality agents are described as being committed to all the logical consequences of their assumed knowledge (Cleverness) *and only* these consequences (Cloisteredness).[4] The second problem is as pressing as the first. In fact, even if our goal is purely descriptive, real agents not only have far less deductive powers than the one assumed by classical (modal and Bayesian) theories; they also have far greater inductive powers. Therefore the standard solutions to Cleverness tend to make Cloisteredness worse. Bacharach's proposed solution is to extend bounded representations of epistemic states with non-monotonic and inductive methods. In this paper we will implement such proposal. In order to do so we will first make some observations about the use of the Montague-Scott's approach as a representational tool in epistemic logic. Then, we will consider *autoepistemic* extensions of epistemic contexts not necessarily constrained by Cleverness.

The final sections of the paper will be devoted to discuss first order extensions of the previously considered models. We will study necessary and sufficient conditions under which the full force of Cleverness is regained from the adoption of standard first order axioms. When formulated in its more general form, the result only holds in the presence of structural constraints on the neighborhoods frames. In a nutshell, we will show that as along as an agent is capable of discerning at least as many objects as beliefs he is capable to entertain, the representation of his epistemic state should obey (all aspects of) Cleverness when the so-call Barcan schemas are imposed.

2 Neighborhoods revisited

2.1 Propositional modal logic

We will introduce here the basis of the so-called *neighborhood semantics* for propositional modal logics. We will follow the standard presentation given in Part III of [3].

---

[3] The view of bounded rationality defended by Herb Simon throughout the second part of the last century does not mesh well with the view of the enterprise as defended by economists like Bacharach or Rubinstein. See [11], chapter 11 (in the MIT version of [11]) for a comparison. Simon has always insisted on procedural aspects of boundedness and in the need to develop models for predicting behavior. The Rubinstein-Bacharach view seems to focus instead on normative models and the need to establish 'conceptual linkages' between concepts that appear in our daily thinking on economic situations. When it comes to develop economic agents each approach might have its merits. This paper discusses some proposals presented by Bacharach and therefore is less concerned with procedural and predictive aspects of boundedness. For the sake of brevity the reader is invited to consult [11], chapter 11, for an account of boundedness which fits well the account tacitly used by Bacharach (and, therefore, the one discussed here).

[4] See section 2.3 for a technical definition. 'Assumed knowledge' here means a finite set of axioms, which Bacharach calls the knowledge base.

DEFINITION 21 $\mathcal{M} = \langle W, N, \models \rangle$ *is a neighborhood model if and only if:*

(1) W is a set
(2) N is a mapping from W to sets of subsets of W
(3) $\models$ is a relation between possible worlds and propositional letters.

Of course the pair $\mathcal{F} = \langle W, N \rangle$ is a *neighborhood frame*. The notation $\mathcal{M}$, Γ $\models$ A is used to state that A is true in the model $\mathcal{M}$ at world Γ. The following definition makes precise the notion of truth in a model.

DEFINITION 22 Truth in a neighborhood model: *Let Γ be a world in a model* $\mathcal{M} = \langle W, N, \models \rangle$. $\models$ *is extended to arbitrary formulas in the standard way for Boolean connectives. Then the following clauses are added in order to determine truth conditions for modal operators.*

(1) $\mathcal{M}, \Gamma \models \Box A$ if and only if $|A|^{\mathcal{M}} \in N(\Gamma)$
(2) $\mathcal{M}, \Gamma \models \Diamond A$ if and only if $|\neg A|^{\mathcal{M}} \notin N(\Gamma)$

where, $|A|^{\mathcal{M}} = \{\Gamma \in W : \mathcal{M}, \Gamma \models A\}$

$|A|^{\mathcal{M}}$ is called A's *truth set*. Intuitively $N(\Gamma)$ yields the propositions that are necessary at Γ. Then $\Box A$ is true at Γ if and only if the 'true set' of A (i.e. the set of all worlds where A is true) is in $N(\Gamma)$. If the intended interpretation is epistemic $N(\Gamma)$ contains a set of propositions understood as epistemically necessary. This can be made more precise by determining the exact nature of the epistemic attitude we are considering. $N(\Gamma)$ can contain the known propositions, or the believed propositions, or the propositions that are considered highly likely, etc. Then the set P $=\{A \in W : \models \Diamond A\}$ determines the space of epistemic possibilities with respect to the chosen modality - knowledge, likelihood, etc.

Clause (2) forces the duality of possibility with respect to necessity. It just says that $\Diamond A$ is true at Γ if the denial of the proposition expressed by A (i.e. the complement of A's true set) is not necessary at Γ. As we said above, $N(\Gamma)$ is called the *neighborhood* of Γ.

2.2 Augmentation

The following conditions on the function N in a neighborhood model $\mathcal{M} = \langle W, N, \models \rangle$ are of interest. For every world Γ in $\mathcal{M}$ and every proposition (set of worlds) X, Y in $\mathcal{M}$:

(m) If $X \cap Y \in N(\Gamma)$, then $X \in N(\Gamma)$, and $Y \in N(\Gamma)$.
(c) If $X \in N(\Gamma)$, and $Y \in N(\Gamma)$, then $X \cap Y \in N(\Gamma)$.
(n) $W \in N(\Gamma)$

When the function N in a neighborhood model satisfies conditions (m), (c) or (n), we say that the model is *supplemented*, is *closed under intersections*, or *contains the unit* respectively. If a model satisfies (m) and (c) we say that is a *quasi-filter*. If all three conditions are met it is a *filter*. Notice that filters can also be characterized as non-empty quasi-filters - non-empty in the sense that for all worlds Γ in the model $N(\Gamma) \neq \emptyset$.

DEFINITION 23 *A neighborhood model* $\mathcal{M} = \langle W, N, \models \rangle$ *is* augmented *if and only if it is supplemented and, for every world Γ in it:*
$$\cap N(\Gamma) \in N(\Gamma).$$

It is important to remark that the notion of augmentation bridges Kripke semantics with the scott-Montague approach. Augmented models are pointwise equivalent to corresponding Kripke models (see [3] for details). Therefore any epistemic representation via augmented neighborhoods will also impose *all* forms of Cleverness on the representation. Now we can present an observation (established in [3], section 7.4), which will be of heuristic interest in the coming section.

Observation 21 $\mathcal{M}$ *is augmented just in case for every world Γ and set of worlds X in the model: (BS) $X \in N(\Gamma)$ if and only if $\cap N(\Gamma) \subseteq X$.*

2.3 Epistemic interpretation of augmentation

It is well known that neighborhood (otherwise called *minimal*) models of epistemic modalities provide a 'very flexible approach' when it comes to develop sophisticated models of attitudes in areas like the theory of games and decisions or multi agent-systems. This is recognized quite openly in [2], section 2.8, pages 316-17. Nevertheless the use of neighborhood models in epistemic logic is fairly recent and some important features of it are still not perfectly understood. One of our goals here is to have a fresh look at the role of neighborhood semantics as an epistemic and doxastic tool.

Notice that in many non-trivial applications the corresponding models need to include a rich set of non-logical axioms. For example in game theory Bacharach proposes what he calls a *broad* theory of a game, encompassing special axioms detailing the payoff structure, facts about player's rationality etc. So, a *broad theory* of a standard game[5] is parametrized as an ordered pair $\langle \Theta, NL \rangle$, where Θ is what Bacharach calls the *formal theory of rational play* and NL is a set of non-logical axioms for Θ. Then a *knowledge base for a player i* at state Γ, is defined as (and where $\square_{i,\Gamma} A$ abbreviates A is known at state Γ):

$$K(\square_{i,\Gamma}) = \{A : \square_{i,\Gamma} A \in NL\}$$

A *knowledge set for player i* at state Γ, $K(S_{i,\Gamma})$ is the set of sentences A such that i knows that A according to Θ. The *base closure* of $Cn(K(\square_{i,\Gamma}))$ are the logical consequences of the knowledge base $K(\square_{i,\Gamma})$. Then, Bacharach articulates Cleverness as follows:

(Clev) $Cn(K(\square_{i,\Gamma})) \subseteq K(S_{i,\Gamma})$

Bacharach points out that when Θ is articulated in terms of a classical Kripkean theory, Cleverness is imposed. No less important for applications in the theory of games and decisions is Cloisteredness:

---

[5] A game is called standard, if it is a simultaneous-play non-cooperative, complete information game.

(Cloi) $\mathrm{K}(S_{i,\Gamma}) \subseteq \mathrm{Cn}(\mathrm{K}(\square_{i,\Gamma}))$

The property says that the players 'have no knowledge about the situation other than that which is derivable from a finite set of items, often very small, the knowledge base'. As we explained above, the explicit knowledge of real players might not include items included in the logical closure of the knowledge base. On the other hand it might include as well inductive conclusions that are not part of $\mathrm{Cn}(\mathrm{K}(\square_{i,\Gamma}))$.

Now the situation varies when Θ is a Montague-Scott model. In fact, at each state Γ, the set of propositions in the neighborhood $\mathrm{N}(\Gamma)$ is a natural representation of the propositions expressed by the sentences in the agent's *knowledge base*, at Γ. In fact, for every fixed model $\mathcal{M}$ and point Γ in $\mathcal{M}$:

$$\mathrm{N}(i, \Gamma) = \{|A|^{\mathcal{M}} : A \in \mathrm{K}(\square_{i,\Gamma})\}$$

Neither (Clev) nor (Cloi) need to be satisfied as long as the neighborhood is not augmented. In fact, when a neighborhood frame is augmented we have the guarantee that, for every world Γ, its neighborhood $N(\Gamma)$ contains a smallest proposition, composed by the worlds that are members of every proposition in $N(\Gamma)$. In other words, for every Γ we know that $N(\Gamma)$ always contains $\cap N(\Gamma)$ and every superset thereof (including W).

We will propose to see the intersection of augmented neighborhoods as (propositional representations of) knowledge sets obeying the rationality constraints required by logical omniscience (and Cloisteredness). The following results help to make this idea more clear.

Observation 22 *If $\mathcal{M}$ is augmented, then for every Γ in the model: (1) $\Gamma \models \square A$ iff and only if $\cap N(\Gamma) \subseteq |A|^{\mathcal{M}}$.*

But, models containing non-augmented neighborhoods behave in a different manner. For example, say that $|A|^{\mathcal{M}} \subseteq |B|^{\mathcal{M}}$. Nevertheless, we can have that only the proposition expressed by A is in the agent's knowledge base. Then $|B|^{\mathcal{M}}$, need not be in $\mathrm{N}(\Gamma)$. In other words the logical consequences of the sentences in the agent's knowledge base need not be in the agent's knowledge set. Of course, augmentation precludes this possibility.

We will show in section 3 that the agent's knowledge set might be represented also as containing information that goes beyond what is representable as logical consequences of the agent's knowledge base.

3 Stable neighborhoods

One of the concrete proposals made by Bacharach in [2] is to use representations where Cleverness is avoided and where there is enough inferential force, nevertheless, to 'jump to conclusions' in the face of new evidence. More precisely, Bacharach suggested the use of some *non-monotonic* notion of inference mounted over a representation where Cleverness is avoided.

8

In the previous sections we sketched a semantic approach where Cleverness can be avoided. At a given point a neighborhood can contain representations of attitudes like belief or likelihood, where, either in virtue of normative or descriptive reasons, the neighborhood might fail to be augmented. Is it possible to extend the previous account in order to mitigate Cloisteredness as well? We will consider one of the possible ways of achieving this, namely the one proposed in [2], section 6.2. The idea is to extend knowledge sets of agents with the *atoepistemic consequences* of the their knowledge bases.

Many of the examples used in [2] are drawn from the theory of games, but they are easily adaptable to similar situations in multi-agent systems or similar settings. The knowledge base of an agent can contain some operators depending on different forms of distributed or shared knowledge. For example, if we focus on a game played between two agents i and j, the operator Bp can be used to indicate that the proposition p is shared belief between both players.

Say that agent i is represented in a non-augmented neighborhood and that in his knowledge base the agent has the proposition BN $\rightarrow$ N, indicating that if it is shared belief that a Nash equilibrium is played then N is played. One can, in addition consider an atoepistemic extension of the neighborhood in question, such that:

(A1) $|A|^{\mathcal{M}} \in N(\Gamma)$ iff $|BA|^{\mathcal{M}} \in N(\Gamma)$
(A2) $|A|^{\mathcal{M}} \notin N(\Gamma)$ iff $|\neg BA|^{\mathcal{M}} \in N(\Gamma)$

Any extension of the (eventually non-augmented) neighborhood obeying (A1-2) represents an apistemic situation where the agent's beliefs are in mutual equilibrium. A given knowledge base (encoded in a neighborhood) can be embedded in different autoepistemic extensions. Some of these extensions can contain information that goes beyond what explicitly appears in the knowledge base. For example, the base that only contains the proposition expressed by BN $\rightarrow$ N, can be embedded in two extensions closed under A1-2. One of these extensions contains (the propositions expressed by) both BN and N (call it AE1), while the other contains none of them (AE2).

As long as the knowledge set of the agent collects the sentences (whose respective propositions figure) in one of the possible autoepistemic extensions of the knowledge base, it is clear that (Cloi) might be avoided. In fact, if for example, the knowledge set collects the contents of AE1, it is clear that this set goes beyond what can be deduced from the base only containing BN $\rightarrow$ N. In fact, the knowledge set of the agent will contain N, a fact that does not follow (neither classically nor modally) from a knowledge base only containing BN $\rightarrow$ N.[6]

---

[6] Of course some decisions concerning risk have to be made here. One can construct the knowledge set of the agent by focusing only on *some* AE extensions (say grounded or ungrounded extensions), or one can adopt a less skeptical approach. Some game theorists have argued recently in favor of adopting approaches where ungrounded extensions are permissible - see below.

Theories corresponding to neighborhoods closed under A1-2 are usually called *stable* in computer science.[7] and the study of such theories is considered part of *autoepistemic logic*, a branch of intensional logic introduced by Robert Moore (see[8] for a foundational introduction to the subject). The main intuition in autoepistemic logic is as follows: one starts with a *premise set*, which typically is not closed. Then the idea is to capture the final states that an agent might reach by reflecting on his beliefs and by making inferences from them and about them. As Stalnaker explains in [10] these final states must meet two intuitive conditions: first they must be stable, in the sense that no further conclusions can be drawn from them; and secondly they should be *grounded* in the initial (usually not closed) premise set. Intuitively a belief B is grounded in a set Σ of further beliefs if B is justified by Σ and Σ is justified in a way which does not depend on B. Interestingly the 'creative' extension AE1 is not grounded in $\{BN \rightarrow N\}$. But some game theorist adopt epistemological views for which groundedness is not of the essence:

> Game theories are indeterminate when players have, in them, too few beliefs. A Coherentist position permits us to expand player's beliefs with few questions asked [...] A player's beliefs need only be in equilibrium with each other and include the base. It may therefore be conjectured that there are expansions of classical belief sets satisfying Coherentist requirements which embody generalizations of Nash equilibrium and, in case the beliefs are conformable across players, Nash equilibrium itself. [2], page 334.

Bacharach then uses the aforementioned example in order to show how agents holding Nash equilibrium beliefs can be represented in terms of ungrounded autoepistemic extensions of a classical knowledge base (the extension AE1 of BN $\rightarrow$ N). So, for the purposes of this analysis, we can just focus on neighborhoods that are doxastically stable (grounded or not), in the sense that they represent the final states that an agent might reach by reflecting about his beliefs. Although all stable neighborhoods are doxastically stable, they need not be augmented. In other words we are considering agents who are not necessarily omniscient under a logical point of view, but whose beliefs are in reflective equilibrium.

Stability has different applications. Here we are interested in representing agents capable of *ampliative* inferences. Some pragmatic implicatures, for example, can be captured in this setting. For example, it is well known that when $\Box$ is interpreted as a doxastic operator of belief the schema:

(B) $\Box A \wedge \neg A$

is pragmatically incoherent, even when such incoherence cannot be cashed out in terms of logical inconsistency. But it is easy to see that the proposition expressed by (B) cannot belong to any stable neighborhood (where A1-2 are

---

[7] The terminology was probably introduced by Stalnaker in [10].

formulated in terms of the operator $\Box$). This can be articulated in a different manner by noticing that the proposition expressed by the schema:

(T) $\Box A \to A$

should belong to every stable neighborhood. In other words, (M) is logically consistent but unbelievable ($\Box M$ is true in all stable models).[8]

The propositions expressed by several of the axioms of the modal system S5 (like the schema T, and the axioms usually known as positive and negative introspection) belong to all stable neighborhoods, but crucial properties related to logical omniscience need not belong to every stable neighborhood. An example is the schema:

(K) $\Box(A \to B) \to (\Box A \to \Box B)$

4 First order extensions

Most of the work in knowledge representation presupposes that the expressive power of first order logic is available. Even when such power is not explicitly used, it is tacitly assumed that first order extensions are achievable while preserving the salient features of the propositional model. This is so at least when particular first order axioms reflect natural properties of the notion that is being represented. In this section we will extend the Montague-Scott's approach presented before to the first order case. Then we will verify that there are surprising connections between the adoption of well-known first order axioms and logical omniscience. All results will be constructed in the framework of *constant domain* first order models where the domain of objects remains constant across models.[9]

DEFINITION 41 *A constant domain neighborhood frame* $\langle W, N, D \rangle$ *is augmented if* $\langle W, N \rangle$ *is augmented.*

---

[8] Going back to the previous example in terms of shared belief, where the extensions are constructed in terms of the operator B, the previous result indicates that no consistent AE extensions are such that the proposition 'it is shared belief that N is played, but N is not played' is part of the extension. By the same token, even if BN $\to$ N is not part of the knowledge base, every extension of a knowledge base containing BN (it is shared belief that some Nash equilibrium is played) should contain N (the equilibrium is played). This is a further example of how non-deductive inferences are performed via AE extensions. Of course, as long as the *knowledge set* of the player i collects items in the AE extensions of neighborhoods (which, in turn, encode i's knowledge base at state Γ) $\Box_i N$ will hold at Γ.

[9] It would be interesting to study varying domain models, but this issue is beyond the scope of this paper. It should be remarked in passing that aside from the purely formal interest in the study of those models, it would be equally (or perhaps more) interesting to determine whether relaxing the assumption of constant domains is of any relevance in epistemic applications. Most of the arguments pro and are usually carried our for ontological (rather than epistemic) interpretations of modal operators – or for Kripkean epistemic operators.

CDN will stand from now on for 'constant domain neighborhood'. Now we can move from frames to models by introducing the classical notion of interpretation:

DEFINITION 42 $\mathcal{I}$ *is an interpretation in a CDN* $\langle W, N, D \rangle$ *if* $\mathcal{I}$ *assigns to each n-place relation symbol R and to each point (in W), some n-place relation on the domain D of the frame.*

DEFINITION 43 *A CDN model is a structure* $\langle W, N, D, \mathcal{I} \rangle$, *where the triple* $\langle W, N, D \rangle$ *is a CDN frame and* $\mathcal{I}$ *is an interpretation in it.*

DEFINITION 44 *Let* $M = \langle W, N, D, \mathcal{I} \rangle$ *be a CDN model. A valuation in the model M is a mapping v that assigns to each variable x some member v(x) of D. w is a x-variant of a valuation v if w and v agree on all variables except possibly the variable x.*

Now we can introduce the notion of truth in neighborhood models. The last two conditions deal with (a classical characterization of) quantification. For the moment we will not modify the standard definition of possibility. After presenting two central results about the conditions imposed by Barcan schemas in neighborhood frames, we will consider the impact of reforming the characterization of epistemic possibility (via the adoption of Definition 4.1 (Poss)).

DEFINITION 45 (Truth in a model) *Let* $\mathcal{M} = \langle W, N, D, \mathcal{I} \rangle$ *be a CDN model. For each* Γ *in W and valuation v in the model:*

(1) If R is an n-place relation symbol, $\mathcal{M}, \Gamma \models_v R(x_1, ..., x_n)$ provided $\langle v(x_1), ..., v(x_1) \rangle \in \mathcal{I}(R, \Gamma)$.
(2) Standard valuations for negation and binary connectives.
(3) $\mathcal{M}, \Gamma \models_v \Box A$ if and only if $|A|^{\mathcal{M},v} \in N(\Gamma)$
(4) $\mathcal{M}, \Gamma \models_v \Diamond A$ if and only if $|\neg A|^{\mathcal{M},v} \notin N(\Gamma)$
(5) $\mathcal{M}, \Gamma \models_v (\forall x)\phi$ if and only if for every x-variant w of v in $\mathcal{M}$; $\mathcal{M}, \Gamma \models_w \phi$
(6) $\mathcal{M}, \Gamma \models_v (\exists x)\phi$ if and only if for some x-variant w of v in $\mathcal{M}$; $\mathcal{M}, \Gamma \models_w \phi$

We make explicit only some basic extensions of the notion of truth set used above in the propositional case.

$$|R(x_1, ...,x_n)|^{\mathcal{M},v} = \{\Gamma \in W: \mathcal{M}, \Gamma \models_v R(x_1, ...,x_n)\}$$

The following schemas have an interesting pedigree in first-order modal logic. They implement some basic forms of quantifier/modality permutability.

DEFINITION 46 *All formulas of the following form are Barcan formulas:*
$(\forall x)\Box\phi \rightarrow \Box(\forall x)\phi$.
$(\exists x)\Diamond\phi \rightarrow \Diamond(\exists x)\phi$

The implications going the other way give us:

DEFINITION 47 *All formulas of the following form are Converse Barcan formulas:*

$\Box (\forall x)\phi \rightarrow (\forall x)\Box \phi$

$(\exists x)\Diamond\phi \rightarrow \Diamond(\exists x)\phi$

Now we can state some results on first order doxastic logic, which will be relevant immediately. Call *non-trivial* a frame whose domain contains more than one object.

Observation 41 *A non-trivial constant domain neighborhood frame is supplemented if and only if every model based on it is one in which the Converse Barcan formula is valid.*

A frame is *consistent* if and only if for every Γ in W, $N(\Gamma) \neq \emptyset$ and $\{\emptyset\} \notin N(\Gamma)$. In other words a frame is consistent as long as the agent represented by the frame does not believe the falsity - and the neighborhoods of the frame are not empty. Call *regular* any frame that is consistent and non-trivial.

Observation 42 *A regular constant domain neighborhood frame is closed under finite intersections if every model based on it is one in which the Barcan formula is valid.*

The last result can be generalized. A frame $\langle W, N, D \rangle$ is *monotonic* if and only if the number of objects in its domain is as large as the number of sets in the neighborhood with the largest number of sets in the model. The intuitive idea behind monotonicity is that an agent represented by a monotonic model is capable of discerning at least as many objects in the universe as beliefs he is capable of entertaining. Let B-schema-$\Diamond$ be the schema in terms of $\Diamond$.[10]

Observation 43 *A monotonic constant domain neighborhood frame is closed under infinite intersections if and only if every model based on it is one in which B-schema-$\Diamond$ is valid.*

Therefore we can conclude[11]:

----

[10] The following characterization of possibility is adopted in order to prove Observation 43:

DEFINITION 48 *(Poss)* $\mathcal{M}, \Gamma \models \Diamond A$ *if and only if for every* X *in* $N(\Gamma)$, $|A|^{\mathcal{M}} \cap X \neq \emptyset$

The idea is that A is possible as long as the proposition expressed by A overlaps *every* proposition in the neighborhood, independently of whether the neighborhood is augmented or not. When this definition of possibility is adopted, necessity and possibility cease to be duals in general. See [1] for details.

[11] The proofs offered in [1] can be easily adapted to prove all results presented in this section.

Observation 44 *A regular and monotonic constant domain neighborhood frame is augmented if and only if every model based on it is one in which the Barcan-schema-◊ and Converse Barcan schemas are valid.*

In a nutshell all aspects of Cleverness are established by the adoption of the Barcan schemas and by requiring a purely structural condition on the *quantity* of beliefs an agent is capable of having in conceivable situations.

5 Expressive adequacy

There is no unified account of epistemic context. At most there are reductive programs where a notion is assumed as an epistemic primitive and all other epistemic dimensions are derived from it. Radical probabilism, for example, proposes to assume standard probability as the sole primitive. But even if one is a radical probabilist there are degrees of freedom when it comes to represent qualitative attitudes. For example, one can either focus on the highly likely propositions derivable from primitive probability, or one can focus on measure one propositions. Under a normative point of view, it is the latter notion which requires the full force of Cleverness, while, as we explained above, the former notion only requires the imposition of *some* aspects of Cleverness - all of them except Adjunction.

At the propositional level the different dimensions of Cleverness can be treated modularly. For normative or descriptive reasons different aspects of logical omniscience can be added or dropped depending on parametrical requirements. Epistemic contexts can then be represented as including all tautologies, or they can be represented as being closed under consequence or as obeying Adjunction. The use of neighborhood models allows for this discriminatory power. And as we saw in section 3 the resulting representations can, in turn, obey or not Cloisteredness.

When the expressive power of representations is increased and quantifiers are added, the situation is slightly different. We studied the role of the Barcan and Converse-Barcan schemas. For finitary representations we showed that (modulo some minimal provisos) the Barcan schema behaves as a quantified version of the principle of Adjunction. The use if the schema should therefore be avoided in first order extensions of propositional representations where Adjunction is not adequate.[12]

---

[12] For example, in virtue of normative considerations, first order qualitative models of likelihood should not be constrained by the Barcan schema. Most other doxastic notions seem to require it, and with it closure as well, again on normative grounds. In order to see this consider the schema $(\forall x)\,\Box\phi \rightarrow \Box\,(\forall x)\phi$, and interpret ϕ as the unary predicate 'ticket x does not win'. When $\Box$ is understood as an operator of likelihood, this instance of the Barcan schema carries a paradoxical content. It says that if every ticket is likely to be a loser then it is highly likely that the lottery has no winning ticket (see [4]). Such situation does not arise, say, for certainty. If you are certain that no ticket will win the lottery, you had better be certain that no ticket will win.

When finitary requirements are lifted, the imposition of the Barcan schemas brings back the full force of Cleverness, not just some aspects of it. This is done by guaranteeing augmentation. In other terms, the imposition of the Barcan schemas erases the distinction between Kripke models and neighborhood models - as long as domains are constant. In fact, all neighborhood models where the Barcan schemas are imposed are pointwise equivalent to corresponding Kripke models. At least this is so, when purely structural conditions are imposed on infinite frames. These conditions (regularity and monotony) only establish structural (rather than inferential) links between the size of the underlying ontology and the size of the doxastic representation. Monotony, in particular, demands an intuitive correlation between the number of beliefs and the number of discernable objects in the domain.

Notice, nevertheless, that the satisfaction of Cleverness in first order stable neighborhood models where the Barcan schemas are validated does not force the satisfaction of Cloisteredness. In the extended version of this paper we argue that most of the interesting extensions of the standard representational methods (both Bayesian and the ones based on the use of Kripke semantics) can be implemented as extensions of the Montague-Scott approach where the epistemic contexts encoded in neighborhoods are endowed with more structure, and where the agent is capable of *inducing* and *abducing* information from given data.

References

1. Arló-Costa, H., First order extensions of classical systems of modal logic: the role of the Barcan schemas, forthcoming in *Studia Logica*.
2. M.O.L. Bacharach. 'The epistemic structure of a theory of a game,' in M.O.L. Bacharach, L.-A. Gérard-Varet, P. Mongin and H.S. Shin (eds.), *Epistemic Logic and the theory of Games and Decisions*, Boston, Dordrecht, London, 303-345, 1997.
3. B. F. Chellas. Modal logic: an introduction. Cambridge University Press, Cambridge, 1980.
4. H.E.Jr. Kyburg. *Probability and the logic of rational belief* Wesleyan University Press. Middletown, 1961.
5. H. E. Jr. Kyburg. 'Probabilistic inference and non-monotonic inference,' *Uncertainty in Artificial Intelligence*, R.D Schachter, T.S. Evitt, L.N. Kanal J.F. Lemmer (eds.), Elsevier Science (North Holland), 1990.
6. Isaac Levi. *The Enterprise of Knowledge.* The MIT Press, Cambridge, Massachusetts, 1980.
7. R. Montague. 'Universal Grammar,' *Theoria 36*, 373-98, 1970.
8. Robert Moore. *Logic and Representation*, CSLI Lecture Notes No. 39, 1995.
9. D. Scott 'Advice in modal logic,' K. Lambert (Ed.) *Philosophical Problems in Logic* Dordrecht, Netherlands: Reidel, 143-73, 1970.
10. Robert Stalnaker. 'A note on non-monotonic modal logic,' *Artificial Intelligence* 64, 183-196, 1993.
11. Ariel Rubinstein. *Lectures on Modeling Bounded Rationality*, Core Lecture Series, Louvain-La-Neuve, Universite Catholique de Louvain, reprinted by MIT Press (1998), 1996.

Uncertainty and Conflict Handling in the ATT-Meta Context-Based System for Metaphorical Reasoning

John A. Barnden

School of Computer Science, The University of Birmingham
Birmingham, B15 2TT, United Kingdom
J.A.Barnden@cs.bham.ac.uk

Abstract

At CONTEXT'99, the author described the ATT-Meta context-based system for (a) reasoning uncertainly about agents' beliefs and (b) performing some of the uncertain reasoning needed for the understanding of metaphorical language. ATT-Meta's handling of uncertainty is qualitative, and includes provisions for adjudicating conflicts between different lines of reasoning. But most of the detail on conflict-handling given in the earlier paper concerned conflicts arising for the special requirements of (a). Furthermore, there have been major recent changes in the conflict-handling approach. The present paper provides a detailed account of major parts of the current approach, stressing how it operates in metaphorical reasoning. In concentrating on uncertainty-handling, this paper does not seek to repeat the justifications given elsewhere for ATT-Meta's approach to metaphor.

Acknowledgment

The research is being supported by grant GR/M64208 from the Engineering and Physical Sciences Research Council of the U.K.

1 Introduction

Various types of uncertainty and conflict are important in the understanding of metaphorical utterances. They have crucially affected much of our detailed theoretical and implementational development of the ATT-Meta approach and system (see Barnden references, Barnden *et al.* references and Lee & Barnden 2001). As explained in Barnden & Lee (1999), some contexts in ATT-Meta serve as belief spaces within which to simulate alleged reasoning of agents, while others serve as spaces within which to conduct reasoning conforming to "pretences" set up by metaphorical utterances. For instance, in the case of

"In the far reaches of her mind, Anne believes that Kyle is unfaithful."

(slighlty edited version of a real-discourse example) the context is one in which Anne's mind is taken actually to be a physical space that has far reaches. Some consequences of this are teased out by reasoning that is typically uncertain, and then operated on by mapping rules (context-bridging rules) to create hypotheses about Anne's mind, outside the pretence context. This process should become clearer below. Thus, our approach is heavily context-based, especially as contexts can be nested within each other in several different ways (Barnden 1998). The uncertainty and conflict-handling included in our approach and system operates both within individual contexts and "across" contexts in the sense that flow of information across context boundaries can cause conflict with other information within contexts. It is plausible that our provisions can be adapted for use in context-based reasoning systems that have nothing to do with metaphor.

In our approach metaphor in general is the phenomenon of thinking or communicating about something X in a way that relies on or is motivated by seeing it as something qualitatively different from it. Thus, in the Anne/Kyle example X is Anne's mind, which is being seen as a physical space of a sort that allows for "far reaches." This metaphorical view (conceptual metaphor—Lakoff 1993) of MIND AS PHYSICAL SPACE is very commonly used in English natural language discourse, and we will assume that a normal user of English is accustomed to its use, and possesses a suitable mapping between aspects of physical space and aspects of mind. Nevertheless, we do not assume that in the Anne/Kyle example the understander is able to map the concept of "far reaches" of a physical region to something to do with the mind. Rather, the understander must be able to connect this concept to other source-domain concepts that *are* mapped. The connecting is the within-pretence-context reasoning mentioned above. We will also assume that the metaphoricity is not "sidelined" by a mind-domain lexical sense for the phrase "in the far reaches" that permits the understander to avoid mapping from the source domain to the target domain.

Some of the types of uncertainty and conflict that ATT-Meta handles, at least to a useful extent, are:

1. Inferential links within the target domain of a metaphorical view can be uncertain, and there can be conflict between different inference chains in that domain.
2. Similarly for the source domain.
3. Reasoning within source-domain terms sometimes needs to interact with facts imported from the target domain, and conflict can arise as a result.

Explanation of (3) will be deferred until Section 7. Concerning point (2), understanding of the type of metaphor addressed in this paper requires possibly-substantial reasoning in the terms of the source domain, as we will see below. Assuming that the source domain is a commonsense one (e.g., the commonsense domain of physical space and physical objects), reasoning within it will be full of uncertainty and conflict. Consider "One part of Mike was insisting that Sally was right, but another part believed she was wrong." This rests on a metaphorical view of MIND PARTS AS PERSONS, in which the mind (or a person) is viewed as having parts that are sub-persons, able themselves to have mental states, communicate in natural language, etc. When someone insists something, they generally believe it. So the understander can infer, in source-domain terms, that the first "part" mentioned in the sentence probably believed that Sally was right. The reasoning process rests purely on general knowledge about verbal communication and related mental states, which are aspects of the source domain of the metaphor. As for possible conflict in the source domain, this arises simply because commonsense domains generally contain exceptions to general rules or principles.

As for (1), equally, when the target domain is a commonsense one, reasoning within it is likely to be uncertain and conflictful. This applies just as much to reasoning episodes in the target domain that are triggered by transfers of information from the source domain as to reasoning episodes arising independently in the target domain. Handling of the three types of uncertainty listed, and others, is seamlessly integrated in ATT-Meta.

2 Main Operations in Metaphor Understanding in ATT-Meta

Our approach encapsulates the proposed source-domain reasoning within a special computational context called a *pretence cocoon*. A pretence cocoon is akin to the more familiar idea of a belief space. In general there can be more than one pretence cocoon (e.g., because of metaphor compounding: Lee & Barnden 2001), but this article will assume just one. Use of the cocoon is tantamount to the understander pretending to take the source-domain scenario alluded to in the utterance as a true statement. The propositions inside the pretence cocoon can be thought of as forming a description of an imaginary, pretend world. Propositions outside are about reality as the understander sees it, and will include, but not be restricted to, propositions about the target domain of the metaphorical utterance. Metaphorical mapping acts operate between the inside of the pretence cocoon and outside.

Thus, for the Anne/Kyle example, the reasoner pretends, within the cocoon, that Anne's mind *really is* a physical space and that the believing really does occur in the far reaches of this space. Consequences of this, using knowledge about physical space, can be inferred in the pretence cocoon, possibly by substantial amounts of reasoning, and *some* consequences may (hopefully) then be able to be transformed, via mapping rules forming part of the relevant metaphorical views, to become propositions about the Anne's state of mind that are outside the cocoon. We will call the reasoning within the cocoon "within-pretence reasoning." Within-pretence reasoning is similar to the *simulative reasoning* used or proposed by many researchers for reasoning about agents' beliefs and reasoning (see, e.g., Creary 1979, Davies & Stone 1995).

In the Anne/Kyle example, within-pretence reasoning could infer that the idea that Kyle is unfaithful cannot be physically operated upon (more than to a very low degree) by the Anne's conscious self (metaphorically viewed as a person within the mind-region), because that self is in a *central* part of the mind-region, not in the far reaches. This proposition is, we assume, part of the understander's knowledge of the MIND AS PHYSICAL SPACE metaphorical view. Then, if part of the understander's knowledge of the IDEAS AS PHYSICAL OBJECTS metaphorical view is that ability to engage in (pretended) physical operation on an idea corresponds to ability to engage in (real) conscious mental operation on the idea, then the understander can infer that Anne cannot consciously operate, mentally, on the idea that Kyle is unfaithful. More detail of the reasoning performed by ATT-Meta on the example is given in Figure 1 (at end of paper) and below.

We can summarize the main types of processing activity that we claim should take place in understanding of the type of metaphorical utterances of interest as follows:

- construction of the direct meaning of the utterance, i.e. the meaning it has by taking only the source-domain senses of the metaphorical words/phrases in the utterance.[1]
- placing of the direct meaning in the *pretence cocoon*, which is a special computational context
- usually, performance of (predominantly) source-domain reasoning within the pretence cocoon, using that direct meaning together with general knowledge about the source domain
- possibly, application of *ancillary assumptions* associated with the relevant metaphorical views to create further propositions within the pretence cocoon (an example of this is the assumption in the Anne/Kyle discussion above that Anne's conscious self is in the central part of the mind-space)
- source-to-target or target-to-source mapping acts, including at least one that goes from source to target (e.g. mapping of inability to operate on an idea physically to inability to consciously, mentally operate on it).

This listing does not imply any particular temporal ordering of the types of processing. Indeed in ATT-Meta the reasoning works backwards from queries and can involve any intertwining of the above types of reasoning.

3 Irreality of Domains

Any non-fact rules pertaining to any domain (including even the target domain) can be considered for application inside the pretence cocoon. One reason for allowing this, despite the fact that the pretence cocoon is mainly for conducting reasoning in source-domain terms, is that the source domain and target domain in a metaphor can overlap. The possibility of overlap is not often discussed in the literature, but is pointed out by Kittay (1989) for example, and we see in the MIND PARTS AS PERSONS example in Section 1 that the source and target domains there overlap – they both involve people, mental states and (often) natural language communication.

---

[1] This is a highly simplified statement, ignoring ordinary lexical ambiguity, mixing of metaphor with other figurative phenomena, and other complications.

But quite apart from overlap, there is no convincing way of dividing knowledge up into domains anyway. The often-implicit claims about domains being different in the metaphor literature are often self-serving, context-sensitive and without independent justification. For instance, in a metaphorical portrayal of a person as a fox, the presumption (by someone who wanted to distance source domains from target domains) would have to be that foxes and people are in different domains. But, although we certainly do qualitatively distinguish sometimes between animals and people in common sense, we would lump them together in the case of some types of metaphor. For instance, in the IDEAS AS ANIMATE BEINGS metaphorical view, the animate beings could be either people or animals, and sometimes there may be no clue as to which or importance in making the decision (consider, e.g., "The idea was lurking in the back of his mind"). In any case, the domain of ideas presumably involves people, because people are the (main or only) beings that have ideas, so the source and target domains would overlap.

Moreover, the boundaries of a domain are extremely difficult to determine. What should be in the domain of people, for instance? Should electrons be, because they are parts of people? Should for that matter foxes be, because people hunt foxes? Questions like these have led the design of ATT-Meta to shy away from any requirement to label particular rules, predicates, etc. as belonging to particular domains. Therefore, there is no way for the system to control, on the basis of domains, what rules, etc., can be used in a particular pretence cocoon.

However, the matter goes deeper than this. It is incorrect to think of a pretence cocoon as being tied in principle to the source domain of the metaphor at hand: it is just that in practice, because of the action of source-to-target rules associated with metaphorical views, subqueries that are in source-domain terms are placed in the cocoon, and in practice most, but not necessarily all, of the resultant backwards reasoning might be *theoretically* labelled, by an observer who ascribes to a particular set of domains, as being within the source domain.

4   What ATT-Meta Does Overall

ATT-Meta itself has no knowledge of any specific metaphorical view or any particular domain. It is merely a reasoning engine. It does, however, include some built-in rules about pretence, beliefs, qualitative degrees, and some other matters. The user supplies, as data for ATT-Meta, whatever target-domain knowledge, source-domain knowledge, metaphorical mapping relationships and ancillary assumptions the user wants to try out for handling examples. These pieces of information are expressed as rules (with fact-rules as a special case). The rules are applied by ATT-Meta. In the illustrative syntax used in this article, a simple rule about birds might be

```
IF bird(X) AND alive(X) THEN {presumed} can-fly(X).
```

The symbol presumed is a qualitative certainty qualifier (see below), and can also be read as "by default." Rules with this qualifier are intuitively similar to "normal" rules in Default Logic (Reiter 1980). If-then rules with a special, essentially null IF part count as fact-rules. We will write a fact-rule without any IF or THEN part, as in

{certain} is-person(Anne).

The user supplies fact-rules that are intended to couch the logical forms of the direct meanings of one utterance or a small set of utterances that form a (real or imaginary) chunk of discourse. Utterances may or may not be metaphorical. In the metaphorical case, the fact-rule contains a special feature (see Barnden & Lee 2001) that causes the factual hypothesis arising from it is placed in the pretence cocoon, not the top reasoning context. Such factual hypotheses can be seen at the top of the cocoon box in Figure 1.

The user supplies a top reasoning query that ultimately drives all the reasoning. For example, the query could be *"Anne is consciously aware to degree at least D of the idea that Kyle is unfaithful?"* In reality, we suppose that surrounding discourse has the effect of posing such queries (or queries for which they are indirect subqueries). For instance, it may be that surrounding discourse makes Anne's conscious mental state about Kyle be of interest.

When the top query does not contain a variable (such as the D just above), ATT-Meta tries to find evidence for and against the top query, using the user-supplied knowledge and the user-supplied logical forms of utterances. In cases of conflict, a conflict-resolution mechanism attempts to favour one side or the other. When the top query contains variables, ATT-Meta tries to find values for the variables such that the thereby instantiated versions of the query are supported.

5   Hypotheses and Rule Application

The information dynamically manipulated by ATT-Meta consists of *hypotheses*. Hypotheses are reasoning queries or propositions created by rule applications. A query is either the top query supplied by the user or a subquery created by ATT-Meta in the course of backwards reasoning in relation to the top query. One simple way a query can be supported is if it matches a user-supplied fact-rule. The query hypothesis is then called a *factual hypothesis* or just a *fact*. Queries can contain variables, and these are regarded implicitly as existentially quantified. Thus, intuitively, the query can-fly(X) is asking whether there is at least one entity that can fly. The system tries to find all possible values for X for which can-fly(X) is supported.

At any time, any particular hypothesis H is tagged with a qualitative certainty level, one of certain, presumed, suggested, possible or certainly-not. The last one just means that the negation of H is certain. Possible just means that the negation of H is not certain but no evidence has yet been found for H itself. Presumed means that H is a *default*: i.e., it is taken as a working assumption, pending further evidence. Suggested means that there is evidence for H, but the evidence is not (yet) strong enough to enable H to be a working assumption. When a hypothesis is created (as a query), it is immediately given a certainty value of `possible`. Of course, reasoning may sooner or later downgrade it to `certainly-not` (i.e., impossible).

When a rule is applied, the certainty it contributes to its result is the minimum of its own certainty qualifier and the certainty levels assigned to the hypotheses picked up by the condition part. Multiple rule applications can support a given hypothesis. In this case, the maximum of the certainty values contributed by the different applications is used. When there is evidence to level `presumed` for both a query and its complement (complement hypotheses being negations of each other), then at an appropriate point the conflict-resolution mechanism steps in and tries to adjudicate the relative evidence strength.

Hypotheses are annotated as to which reasoning contexts they exist in. In this article, we need consider only two contexts: a single pretence cocoon and the reasoning environment outside the pretence cocoon, which we call the "top" context. The top context is the system's own reasoning context, in which the hypotheses are about reality as the system sees it. A hypothesis can be replicated in different contexts, but if so the different copies are handled entirely separately, as if they were unrelated hypotheses. This is because even if a hypothesis is supported in two different contexts, the lines of reasoning supporting it can differ radically, and the level of certainty can differ.

Except in the case of metaphor-related rules (including source-to-target mapping rules), when a rule is applied to a query in a specific reasoning context, the subqueries emanating from its condition part are set up in the same reasoning context except when special rule features dictate otherwise (Barnden & Lee 2001). All rules are available for use in any context, but rules can contain special conditions that can prevent the application of the rule if the context is inappropriate (Barnden & Lee 2001).

6 Basic Conflict Resolution

Here we describe the basic conflict-resolution provisions. There are additional provisions concerning pretence cocoons that are in Section 7 below, and they are our main target in this paper, given its orientation towards contexts. The provisions in the present section apply to rules of any sort, in any context. However, for simplicity we will explicitly talk about them being applied only to adjudicate conflicts between reasoning chains arising in the top reasoning context. Various complications in basic conflict resolution will not be addressed in this paper:

- The question of exactly when conflict resolution should happen, in cases where the derivation network for hypotheses contains cycles. There is a complex algorithm for postponing conflict resolution until all hypotheses around a cycle can be treated together and fairly.
- The fact that `presumed` hypotheses can be non-downgradable because they depend via `certain` rules on `presumed` hypotheses whose certainly level has already been finalized.

- Back-propagation of downgrading through applications of `certain` rules, to help maintain consistency of certainty levels.
- Dealing with the point that facts can sometimes also be derivable from other facts. Normally, in such cases the derivable facts should be treated as non-facts for the purpose of conflict-resolution.

Recall that conflict resolution steps in when both a hypothesis H and its complement are supported to level `presumed`. The final result of the resolution attempt will be that one or both hypotheses will be downgraded to `suggested`. They are both downgraded if neither can be determined to be the winner. On the other hand, when one is the winner, it stays at `presumed`, and the `suggested` level that is given to the other one records the fact that there *was* some strong evidence for it. Fundamentally, conflict resolution *specificity-based* and is to that extent traditional (cf. exception handling in semantic networks, and see, e.g., Loui 1987). That is, the system tries to see whether one of the hypotheses relies on a more specific situation than the other one does. This comparison is based on the sets of facts employed by the arguments supporting the hypotheses, combined with some consideration of the precise way the hypotheses depend on those facts. We now describe the core of the specificity comparison.

6.1 Core of the Fact-Based Specificity Comparison

The main intuition of the fact-based specificity comparison is that if one of the conflicting hypothesis relies on more facts, in a set-theoretic rather than numerical sense, then it is more specifically supported. For instance, if the hypothesis that Ralph is not tidy follows only from the fact that he is a student, whereas the hypothesis that he *is* tidy follows from the combination of the facts that he is a student and is elderly, then the latter hypothesis wins. To be more precise, suppose ATT-Meta contains the following rules, where `at-least-m-a` means at-least-middle-aged:

```
IF student(X) THEN {presumed} NOT(tidy(X)).
IF student(X) AND at-least-m-a(X) THEN {presumed} tidy(X).
IF elderly(X) THEN {certain} at-least-m-a(X).
```

```
{certain} student(ralph).      {certain} elderly(ralph).
```

It is clear that there is one argument for the hypothesis RNT that Ralph is not tidy, and that this argument relies on the set of facts { `student(ralph)` }. There is also one argument for the hypothesis RT that Ralph is tidy, and it relies on the factset { `student(ralph), elderly(ralph)` }. Both facts in that set are necessary for the argument. Now, in other examples, there could be alternative arguments for either hypothesis, giving alternative factsets. ATT-Meta therefore calculates the *factset-set* (set of factsets) for each of the conflicting hypotheses. In our example, because there is just one argument for each hypothesis, we have just:

factset-set for RNT: { {student(ralph)} } factset-set for RT: { {student(ralph), elderly(ralph} }.

This will make RT win, because of the factset-set comparison method detailed below. Here, it is tantamount to noting that the single factset for RNT is a subset of the single factset for RT, but the factset for RT is not a subset of the factset for RNT. The single argument for RNT relies on a situation that is at least as unspecific (actually, strictly less specific) than the single argument for RT; but the reverse is not true.

When a hypothesis can be supported by more than one rule application, these applications are parts of alternative arguments for the hypothesis. They are therefore also parts of alternative arguments for other hypotheses depending on that hypothesis. When there are alternative arguments for a hypothesis, where the alternatives rely on different facts, it generally has more than one supporting factset. We see a simple illustration of this in our Ralph example augmented with the following rules:

```
IF musician(X) THEN {presumed} NOT(tidy(X)).
{certain} musician(ralph).
```

The two factset-sets are now

factset-set for RNT: { {student(ralph)}, {musician(ralph)} }
factset-set for RT: { {student(ralph), elderly(ralph} }.

In this case, there is no winner because there is no clear sense in which one of the hypotheses has more specific support overall than the other. The reason RT won before was that its single factset was not a subset of any factset for RNT. This is still true, but the converse is now also true: the new factset for RNT is not a subset of any factset for RT. Intuitively, there is no support for RT that is at least as specific as the new argument for RNT. It seems reasonable to say that for there to be a losing hypothesis, *every* argument for it must rely only on facts that are also used by *some* argument for the winner. To respect this principle, the actual specificity comparison on factset-sets is as follows.

Definition: Let the two factset-sets for a hypothesis and its complement be FSS1 and FSS2. Then FSS2 is deemed to be more specific than FSS1 if and only if

– for every member FS of FSS1, FS a subset of some member of FSS2
– the reverse is not true.

An abstract example of FSS2 being more specific than FSS1 is

FSS1 = { {a,b}, {b,c,d}, {a,b,e,f}, {k} }
FSS2 = { {a,b,e}, {a,b,e,f,g}, {b,c,d}, {k,l}, {m} }

Even though one member of FSS2, namely {a,b,e}, is a (proper) subset of a member of FSS1, the conditions for FSS2 being more specific still hold, because at least one member, in fact three members, of FSS2 are not subsets of any member of FSS1. Notice also that FSS1 and FSS2 can intersect: {b,c,d} is a member of both. In fact, an extreme case of this, which can arise in practice, is that FSS2 is more specific than FSS1 even when FSS1 is just a proper subset of FSS2, i.e. they contain the same factsets except that FSS2 has at least one more. An example:

FSS1 = { {a,b}, {b,c,d} }
FSS2 = { {a,b}, {b,c,d}, {a,c} }

even though the unshared fact-set {a,c} in FSS2 happens not to introduce any facts that do not appear in the shared factsets. But it is still reasonable for FSS2 to be deemed more specific, because it uses facts a and c in an extra way that is not paralleled by any factset in FSS1.

The factset-set comparison provision is quite a powerful technique, but there is a widespread type of phenomenon it fails on. Consider the question of whether penguins can swim underwater. If we have

```
IF bird(X) THEN {presumed} NOT(swim-uw(X)).
IF penguin(X) THEN {presumed} swim-uw(X).
IF penguin(X) THEN {certain} bird(X).
IF says(mary, penguin(X)) THEN {presumed} penguin(X).
{certain} says(mary, penguin(peter)).
```

then both conflicting hypotheses (that Peter can swim underwater, and the negation) have just one factset, {{p}}, where p is the fact that Peter is a penguin. The way ATT-Meta handles this situation is given in the next subsection.

6.2 Removal of Derivation Links and Use of "Even-Though" Conditions

Before the factset-set comparison in the previous subsection, *derivation-link removal* occurs in the derivation network for the two conflicting hypotheses. (A derivation network is a network of hypotheses and supporting rule applications, such as that shown in Figure 1.) This is designed to cope with the problem noted above for situations like the penguin-swimming-underwater case, and more complex cases where a fact fails to provide a specificity advantage for one hypothesis because the other hypothesis also makes use of it in a way that is intuitively less specific but is not caught by the factset-set comparison above. Link removal replaces the derivability-based analysis briefly referred to in previous papers on ATT-Meta.

The intuition in the penguin case is that we want the Peter-swim-uw hypothesis to win *even though* Peter is a bird. So, the evaluation of the specificity of the support for the Peter-swim-uw hypothesis should somehow take into account the proposition that Peter is a bird, not just the fact that Peter is a penguin. We achieve this effect in ATT-Meta by (a) imposing a particular discipline on the writing of rules and (b) deleting shared derivation links in a way to sketched. We will not fully describe the process as the complications noted in the next section concerning cocoons are more important for this paper.

The discipline (a) is that the user must think, in designing a rule, whether the rule is *meant* to apply *even though* some proposition will hold that could cause another, conflicting, rule to be enabled. What it amounts to in the penguin example is that the penguins-swim-underwater rule must be written as

```
IF penguin(X) AND bird(X) THEN {presumed} swim-uw(X).
```

The "AND is a bird THEN ..." is to be intuitively interpreted as "THEN EVEN THOUGH X is a bird ...." Indeed, in later versions of ATT-Meta we plan to introduce an explicit EVEN-THOUGH connective for use in rules, as then they become more intuitively palatable. However, the AND approach is computationally adequate for present purposes. The even-though condition technique is intuitively related to the familiar idea of rules being able to cancel other specific rules, but has the advantage that rules refer only to content, not to other rules.

In this example the effect of derivation-link removal will be to delete the link going from penguin(peter) to bird(peter). As a result, the factset-set for NOT(swim-uw(peter)) will contain just the empty set, whereas the factset-set for swim-uw(peter) will be unchanged, allowing the latter to win the conflict, as desired.

The link deletion happens because of an analysis of the way in which the conflicting hypotheses depend on facts. This analysis looks at shared prefixes (maximal shared initial portions) of derivation paths going up from facts to the conflicting hypotheses. In addition, the analysis determines which shared prefixes are "independent" for a hypothesis in the sense of not being a shared prefix as a mere result of being an initial portion of some other shared prefix for that hypothesis. The following are the sets of independent shared prefixes for the conflicting hypotheses in the examples :

for NOT(swim-uw(peter)): {(m,p,b)}

for swim-uw(peter): {(m,p), (m,p,b)}.

where m is says(mary, penguin(peter)), p is penguin(peter) and b is bird (peter). Although {(m,p)} is a shared prefix, it is not independent for hypothesis NOT(swim-uw(peter)) because the only supporting path for that hypothesis that contains that prefix also contains the more extensive shared prefix {(m,p,b)}.

The next step is find the intersection of the two sets of independent shared prefixes, namely {(m,p,b)} in our example. For each prefix in the intersection, the last link in the prefix is removed from the derivation network.

The technique is quite robust, in the sense that extra hypotheses can interrupt the links on the original derivation network without changing the specificity comparison. In addition, arguments for NOT(swim-uw(peter)) that do *not* pass through the bird(peter) hypothesis are not affected by the particular manipulations above, as is intuitively correct, as it allows NOT(swim-uw(peter)) then possibly to win. The technique also copes easily with iterated defeat, as arises. for instance, if sick penguins cannot normally swim underwater (even though they are penguins), but pregnant sick penguins can (even though they are sick penguins). We do not have space to demonstrate this here.

7 Matters of Pretence: Rules, Fact Importation and Pretence Bias

We noted in Section 3 that any non-fact rule possessed by the system can be considered for application inside the pretence cocoon. But, because of the unreal situations that can arise in pretence, rules that have strength `certain` are downgraded to strength `presumed` when used inside the pretence cocoon, to allow more intuitive conflict-resolution. The reason for not allowing fact-rules to be used in the pretence cocoon, unless they are specially written to specify this, is that typically such rules describe the specific circumstances holding in a real situation or holding within the pretence. However, because of the possible overlap of source and target domains in a metaphor, and because of the blending that happens in any case by virtue of the initialization of the pretence (by a fact saying, for instance, that Anne's mind has far reaches), ATT-Meta provides for *importation* of facts holding in the top context into the pretence cocoon. Note that this is importation of factual hypotheses, not a use of fact-rules within the pretence, so that what happens is that two copies of the fact arise, one in the cocoon and one outside, and the former depends on the latter via an *importation link*. One is shown in Figure 1.

Also, importation can support the inner copy only to level `presumed`, much for the same reason as that non-fact rule certainties are capped at `presumed`. But this capping of fact certainty is not enough to avoid unintuitive conflict resolutions, and imported facts need to be given lower priority in the conflict-resolution process inside the cocoon than facts that are inside the cocoon, or than facts that are outside the cocoon and support within-cocoon hypotheses via the action of target-to-source rules (such as ancillary assumption rules). Both these types of facts should be more powerful in providing specificity, because they are to do with special features of the metaphor at hand, whereas importation is a completely general act insensitive to the particular metaphor at hand. An illustration is given by the Anne/Kyle example, as follows.

There is an argument inside the cocoon that Anne's mind is presumably a physical space. The fact this argument rests on is that Anne's mind has far reaches, as illustrated in Figure 1. This fact arises directly in the cocoon by a fact-rule—it is not the result of an importation. But in the Anne/Kyle example (and of course others) we provide rules saying that minds are certainly *not* physical spaces, and that for, any person X, `mind-of(X)` is a mind; and in the example we have the fact-rule that Anne is a person. Thus, by virtue of the importation of that fact that Anne is a person into the cocoon, an argument arises in the cocoon that Anne's mind is presumably not a physical space. (This is not shown in the Figure.) We therefore have conflict. Because the importation would have been available no matter what the metaphorical utterance had been, what the metaphorical views in play had been, or what specific situation had been under consideration, we wish to make the importation-based argument look less specific to the conflict-resolution than the non-importation-based argument for the hypothesis that Anne's mind is a physical space.

In more complex situations, it can be that in a given factset supporting a hypothesis there are both imported facts and non-imported ones. Different factsets for a hypothesis can differ on whether they contain imported facts or not. Both hypotheses in the conflict can have factsets containing imported facts. And, an imported fact might have independent, non-importation-based support within the cocoon. The general handling of anti-importation bias takes these complexities into account by first ignoring the contribution of imported facts, and only using them in the specificity comparison if the conflicting hypotheses are otherwise equal in specificity (i.e., have equal factset-sets). One desirable effect of this is that a hypothesis that is partly, but only partly, dependent on importation will win against its complement if the latter is entirely dependent on importation. Also, importation cannot upset a winning situation that arises from the special circumstances arising within the pretence.

In more detail, ATT-Meta's factset-set comparison happens in (possibly) two phases. In the first phase, importation is ignored. That is, the derivation network is slimmed down by removing all links that represent importation acts; any hypotheses therefore deprived of all support are also removed, and so on. A rule application is only removed from the derivation network when all its condition nodes are removed. After this slimming process, the factset-sets are determined and compared. If one hypothesis wins, the conflict resolution is complete and there is no second phase.

Otherwise, if the two factset-sets are unequal, so that the two hypotheses have *incomparable* specificity, the conflict resolution attempt is again complete and there is no second phase, but this time there is failure to find a winner. However, if the two factset-sets are the same, so that the two hypotheses are *equally* specific, the second phase is executed, and a winner then possibly found. In the second phase, the original derivation network from before the slimming process is reinstated, and factset-sets again calculated and compared.

In the Anne/Kyle example, the hypothesis that Anne's mind is not a physical space only has one fact in its pre-slimming factset, and this fact is the imported one that Anne is a person. Therefore, in the first phase this factset-set becomes empty. On the other hand, the hypothesis that Anne's mind is a physical space relies on the non-imported fact that it has far reaches, and the slimming therefore does not affect this factset-set. The latter hypothesis therefore wins in the first phase and there is no second phase.

The two-phase process as described here is actually a special case of a more general process that caters for nesting of cocoons within each other (Lee & Barnden 2001) by given preference for deeper importations over shallower ones, but this is beyond the scope of the present paper.

8 Conclusion

We have argued that ATT-Meta can robustly handle conflict and uncertainty in both the reality and pretence contexts, and in particular can cope with conflicts in the pretence cocoon between source-domain reasoning based on special pretence circumstances and conclusions depending partly on non-pretence information. ATT-Meta can handle other types of uncertainty and conflict (such as conflict between intrinsic target information and the results of metaphorical reasoning), but this will be presented in detail elsewhere.

References

1. Barnden, J.A. (1998). Combining uncertain belief reasoning and uncertain metaphor-based reasoning. In *Procs. Twentieth Annual Meeting of the Cognitive Science Society*, pp.114–119. Mahwah, N.J.: Lawrence Erlbaum Associates.
2. Barnden, J.A., Helmreich, S., Iverson, E. & Stein, G.C. (1996). Artificial intelligence and metaphors of mind: within-vehicle reasoning and its benefits. *Metaphor and Symbolic Activity, 11*(2), pp.101–123.
3. Barnden, J.A. & Lee, M.G. (1999). An implemented context system that combines belief reasoning, metaphor-based reasoning and uncertainty handling. In P. Bouquet, P. Brezillon & L. Serafini (Eds), *Lecture Notes in Artificial Intelligence, 1688*, pp.28–41, Springer. (CONTEXT'99.)
4. Barnden, J.A. & Lee, M.G. (2001). Understanding usages of conceptual metaphors: An approach and artificial intelligence system. Technical Report CSRP-01-05, School of Computer Science, The University of Birmingham, U.K.
5. Creary, L. G. (1979). Propositional attitudes: Fregean representation and simulative reasoning. *Procs. 6th. Int. Joint Conf. on Artificial Intelligence* (Tokyo), pp.176–181. Los Altos, CA: Morgan Kaufmann.
6. Davies, M. & Stone, T. (Eds) (1995). *Mental simulation: evaluations and applications.* Oxford, U.K.: Blackwell.
7. Kittay, E.F. (1989). *Metaphor: its cognitive force and linguistic structure.* (Paperback ed.) Oxford, U.K.: Clarendon Press.
8. Lakoff, G. (1993). The contemporary theory of metaphor. In A. Ortony (Ed.), *Metaphor and Thought,* 2nd ed., pp.202–251. Cambridge, U.K.: Cambridge University Press.
9. Lee, M.G. & Barnden, J.A. (2001). Reasoning about mixed metaphors with an implemented AI system. *Metaphor and Symbol, 16* (1&2), pp.29–42.
10. Loui, R.P. (1987). Defeat among arguments: a system of defeasible inference. *Computational Intelligence, 3,* pp.100–106.
11. Reiter, R. (1980). A logic for default reasoning. *Artificial Intelligence, 13,* pp.81–132.

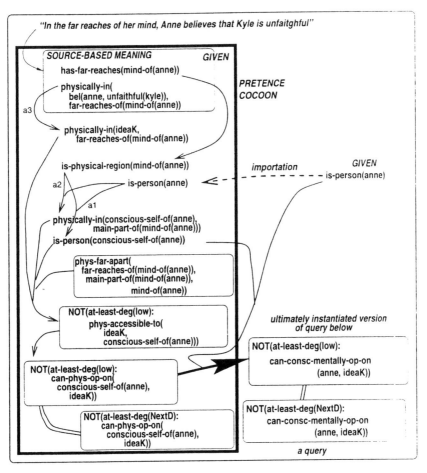

Fig. 1. Showing the main features of ATT-Meta's metaphor-based reasoning in a particular application that was performed on the Anne/Kyle example. The logical notation is an illustrative, simplified form of that used in the system. The symbol ideaK is an abbreviation for the-idea-that(unfaithful(kyle)). The third argument of the phys-far-apart hypothesis specifies that the far-apartness (of the far reaches and the main part) is relative to the scale of Anne's mind as a whole. The heavily outlined box depicts the pretence cocoon. Facts are marked as GIVEN; both hypotheses in the small box at top left are facts. All facts in the example are certain. All other hypotheses shown attain a certainty qualifier of presumed. The fat arrow depicts the application of source-to-target metaphorical mapping rule. Applications of ancillary-assumption rules are numbered a1–3. Double lines connect general queries with their instantiations. The depiction of some rule applications is simplified (i.e., links omitted), and many hypotheses and reasoning steps are omitted, including the within-pretence hypothesis that ideaK is a physical object. This hypothesis is supported within the pretence by the hypothesis that ideaK is in a physical region. The query at bottom right is a subquery arising from the actual top query used, which was "Can Anne consciously operate mentally on IdeaK to exactly degree D?"

WordSieve:
A Method for Real-Time Context Extraction*

Travis Bauer and David B. Leake

Computer Science Department
Lindley Hall, Indiana University
150 S. Woodlawn Avenue
Bloomington, IN 47405, U.S.A.
{trbauer,leake}@cs.indiana.edu
http://www.cs.indiana.edu/~{trbauer,leake}

Abstract. In order to be useful, intelligent information retrieval agents must provide their users with context-relevant information. This paper presents WordSieve, an algorithm for automatically extracting information about the context in which documents are consulted during web browsing. Using information extracted from the stream of documents consulted by the user, WordSieve automatically builds context profiles which differentiate sets of documents that users tend to access in groups. These profiles are used in a research-aiding system to index documents consulted in the current context and pro-actively suggest them to users in similar future contexts. In initial experiments on the capability to match documents to the task contexts in which they were consulted, WordSieve indexing outperformed indexing based on *Term Frequency/Inverse Document Frequency*, a common document indexing approach for intelligent agents in information retrieval.

1 Introduction

Intelligent information retrieval agents are an emerging class of software designed to aid computer users in various aspects of their work. By observing the user's interaction with the computer to determine contextual cues, these agents can suggest information that is likely to be useful in the current context. Much research has studied the formalization of context (e.g., [2, 5, 4])), and rich context representations have been proposed (e.g., [18, 19]). However, the circumstances in which information retrieval agents function strongly constrain the context extraction methods and representations that are practical for them to use. In order to provide robust support, information retrieval agents must automatically generate context descriptions in a wide, unpredictable range of subject areas; in order to provide information when it is most useful, they must make context-related decisions in real time, as rapidly as possible.

* Travis Bauer's research is supported in part by the Department of Education under award P200A80301-98. David Leake's research is supported in part by NASA under awards NCC 2-1035 and NCC 2-1216.

Because of their need to handle unpredictable subject areas, intelligent information retrieval agents generally forgo carefully-crafted, pre-specified context representation schemes in favor of representations gathered implicitly by observing the user working in some task context. In systems that seek to aid a user by retrieving documents relevant to the user's current context, a common approach is to analyze the content of the current document being accessed and retrieve similar documents, under the assumption that documents with similar content will be useful in the current context.[1] These systems often index documents based on Term Frequency/Inverse Document Frequency [17], a term-based approach which focuses on the relationship of the document to the corpus. In particular, TFIDF does not take into account another contextual cue, the order in which the documents were accessed. Our goal is to develop a practical method for using information about document access patterns to help improve on standard techniques for selecting context-relevant documents.

We are developing a context extraction algorithm, called WordSieve, to take advantage of implicit contextual information provided by considering the user's document access patterns over time. By considering information developed from the order in which the documents are accessed, the algorithm is able to make suggestions that reflect not only the content of documents, but also when documents with that content tend to be consulted. WordSieve has been implemented in an intelligent information retrieval agent, CALVIN, which observes users as they browse the world wide web, indexes the documents they access in a given context, and suggests those documents in similar contexts in the future [13]. The success of this approach can be measured by whether it selects documents that are appropriate to the user and task context, even when no explicit description of the task is available to the system. In initial experiments, with CALVIN monitoring users who were given two browsing tasks, WordSieve outperformed TFIDF at matching documents to the tasks in which they were accessed.

This paper is organized as follows. We first discuss issues involved in selecting a context model for intelligent agents. Next we describe the WordSieve algorithm and its performance in our initial experiments. Finally, we discuss some issues raised by this work and its relationship to previous research.

2 Content or Context?

One of the issues addressed by context theory is disambiguating sentence meanings with respect to a specific context (such as disambiguating the sentence "Now I am here") [15]. Similar issues arise in determining the relevant content of documents in context. For example, the explicit content of a document written in the middle ages by a Benedictine monk about food preparation is a constant in any context, but its relevant content changes depending on the context in which it is used. A person interested in finding out about the Benedictine order would use the document in a different context from a person interested in cooking, and

---

[1] For a contrasting view, see [8].

in each context, there would be a different answer to the question "What is this document about?"

Information retrieval agents generally retrieve based on document content [3, 6, 7, 14, 16], and commonly treat a document as an independent entity, taking into account its relationship to the entire corpus but not to the immediate group of recently-consulted documents within which it was accessed. For example, in TFIDF-based indexing, an index vector is created for each document; the magnitude of each element indicates how well that term represents the contents of the document, based on its frequency within the document and the inverse of the frequency of documents in the corpus containing that term. Thus if a term occurs very frequently in some document, but rarely occurs in the corpus as a whole, it will be heavily weighted in the term vector. In practice this approach provides robust results for many collections. However, it does not reflect potentially-useful information about access context: it considers only the relationship between documents and a corpus, not the context in which those documents are used.

Our research on WordSieve is guided by the hypothesis that the relevant features of a document depend not only on what makes it different from every other document (which is captured by TFIDF), but what makes it similar to the documents with which it was accessed. In other words, the context of a document is not reflected only in its content, but in the other documents with which it was accessed.

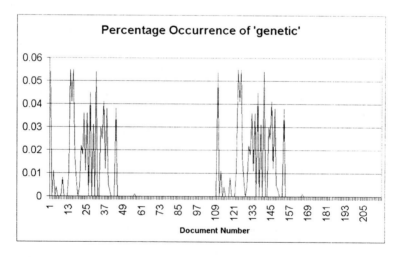

Fig. 1. Percentage occurrence of the term 'genetic' during a user's search session.

As an illustration, consider figure 1. The graph represents the occurrence of the word 'genetic' in web pages during the course of a web search. This access pattern shows four clear partitions, distinguishable by the occurrence pattern of the word "genetic." When the word 'genetic' occurred frequently the user was searching for pages about "the use of genetic algorithms in artificial life software." Our hypothesis is that terms with this type of access pattern are useful indicators of the context of a user's browsing task.

TFIDF works by exhaustively analyzing the corpus, extracting and comparing word occurrences. There are two reasons why this can be undesirable. First, it is time consuming. In an information agent, the system needs to respond and learn in real time. Second, in an information agent, it is not desirable to store an entire full-text library of all the documents a user has accessed. WordSieve overcomes both of these weaknesses by being able to learn these terms in real time, and building up information incrementally rather than requiring the entire corpus to analyze at one time.

3   The WordSieve Algorithm for Context Extraction

WordSieve's goal is to find terms associated with document access patterns. The WordSieve algorithm finds groupings of documents which tend to be accessed together, and indexes documents according to frequently occurring terms which also partition the documents. Our hypothesis is that these terms are good indicators of task context. We evaluate this hypothesis in section five.

Because WordSieve automatically extracts terms associated with sets of document accesses, rather than using explicit task descriptions, WordSieve does not require a user to specify when one task is finished and another has begun. Thus there is no need for the user to artificially limit browsing behavior to provide task-related information (which a user would be unlikely to do in practice).

WordSieve's context representation and its system design reflect several constraints affecting real-time information retrieval agents that assist users as they perform other tasks:

1. The system must be relatively compact and should consume only limited resources. It should not, for example, require storing and re-processing previously accessed documents, and consequently must accumulate its contextual information along the way.
2. The system must run in real time. It must make its suggestions while the user is performing the task for which they are relevant.
3. The system should develop a user profile, reflecting the access patterns of the particular user, in order to provide personalized recommendations likely to be useful for that user.
4. The system should be able to use the user profile to produce a context profile when the user is accessing documents, reflecting both the user and the current task.

4   The WordSieve Architecture

The WordSieve network consists of three small, interdependent levels of nodes. Their function is analogous to a sieve, "trapping" partitioning words that reflect a user's context. Each of the nodes in each level contains a small number of attributes: a word and one or two real number values. The word associated with any node can change over time.

The architecture of the current version of WordSieve is shown in figure 2. WordSieve processes documents by first passing each word through the Most-FrequentWords level as the words are encountered in a document. Levels 2 and 3 then get their information solely from what survives in the MostFrequentWords level. We will examine each level individually, then consider how well the system performs.

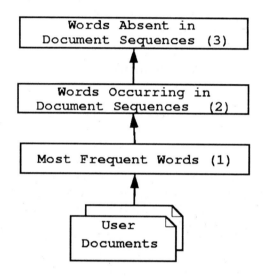

Fig. 2. Word Sieve Diagram

4.1   Level 1: MostFrequentWords

The MostFrequentWords level (level 1) learns which words are currently occurring frequently in the stream of text passing through it, without needing to refer to a database of pre-indexed documents. It will trap any word that occurs frequently, including non-discriminators, such as "and," "or," and "not." The intention is for this layer to select a small number of common terms; in our experiments, this level contains 150 nodes, each of which is associated with a single term.

Nodes in this level do not directly record how many times their words occur. Instead, each occurrence of a word in the text stream increases the excitement of its associated node. To control growth, at each processing step the excitement of the nodes in level 1 decreases by $r = \frac{b}{100}$ where r is the rate of decay per word passed into the sieve and b is a base rate for decay. In short, for every 100 words presented to the sieve, the excitement of every node is decreased by b.

The desired effect is that the excitement of a node will be related to the frequency of occurrence of its corresponding word in recent texts. More precisely, node activation levels are characterized by a threshold of frequency, the "rate goal" g, $0 < g < 1$, representing the percentage occurrence of a term at which the excitement of that term's associated node should increase. If a word occurs with a frequency of g, its node will tend to maintain the same level of excitement. If a word occurs with a frequency less than g, then its node will decay more than it is excited, and over time, its excitement will decrease. If a word occurs with a frequency greater than g, the opposite occurs: its node will be excited more than it decays, and its excitement level will tend to increase.

When a word enters level 1, WordSieve does one of two things, depending on whether there is already a corresponding node for it in level 1.

1. If there is a node corresponding to that word, its excitement is increased by $e = \frac{b}{g}$ where b and g are as defined above.
2. If there is no node corresponding to that word, the word gets a chance to "take over" a node already assigned to another word. In this process, a node is randomly chosen from the sieve. Then, that node will be re-assigned to the new word with a probability of $.0001 * (E - 100)^2$. This way, a word with a high excitement value is unlikely to be replaced. A word with a low excitement value has a greater chance of being replaced.

The proper operation of this level depends on g. If g is too low, then too many terms will have increasing values in level one, and the network will be unable to distinguish the ones occurring frequently. If g is too high, then the words will decay too fast, resulting in the decay of even the frequently occurring words. The correct value of g depends on the distribution of word frequencies in the incoming text stream. Level 1 continuously adjusts the value of g to keep the excitement levels of about 10% of the nodes increasing, and the rest decreasing. After every document, g is reset to a new value g', given by the following equation.

$$g' = \frac{\left(o - \frac{N}{10}\right)}{\frac{N}{10} * 0.1} \tag{1}$$

In this equation, o is the number of nodes with excitement values greater than the initial value given to the nodes when they are assigned to a word, and N is the number of nodes in level 1.

The result is that level 1 can identify an approximation of the most frequently occurring words in the stream of text, without keeping track of all the words occurring and without keeping a database of the documents which have been accessed. In return for this, WordSieve sacrifices absolute precision and complete determinism. Because of the probabilistic element in the algorithm, the system will produce slightly different values each time it is run. However, as will be shown later, it is sufficiently precise that the system as a whole produces reliably similar results each time it is run.

4.2 Level 2: Words Occurring in Document Sequences

The nodes in level 2 identify words that tend to occur together in sequences of document accesses. In our experiments, this level contained 500 nodes. Because this level does not have direct access to the stream of text, it is only sensitized to words corresponding to nodes in level 1.

Each node in this layer is associated with a word and two real values, excitement and priming. The excitement of the node increases as a word continues to have high excitement values in level 1. Priming determines how fast the excitement of the node can change. Both excitement and priming are allowed to have values between 0.0 and 1.0. At each pass, all the words in the word sieve are presented to this level sequentially. For each word presented to this level, every node's excitement decays by 0.5% and each node's priming decays by 0.1%. Then, if a node is already sensitized to the given word, its priming is increased by 1.75 × the decay amount.

The node's excitement is increased as a function of its priming. If the given word has not yet been trapped by this level, it probabilistically replaces a node in a manner similar to that described above.

While level 1 is sensitized to the terms that are currently frequent in the text stream, level 2 keeps a record of the words that have tended to occur frequently at different times. Level 2 remembers words even after they stop occurring in the text stream, and only slowly forgets them. Nodes for non-discriminators will get high values at this level, as will nodes for terms which partition the set.

4.3 Level 3: Words Absent in Document Sequences

The function of level 3 is similar to that of level 2. However, its nodes achieve high excitement when they correspond to words that occur infrequently for periods of time. Specifically, its nodes are automatically sensitized to exactly the same words as level 2. However, the nodes keep a low level of excitement until the word stops occurring and increase the excitement value for as long as the word does not occur. Non-discriminators will not get a high level of activation in this level, although nodes will exist for them. The partition words which reflect the user's context will achieve higher activation levels here.

4.4 WordSieve Output

The last two criteria for our architecture specified that user and context profiles should be generated by the system. These are derived from the nodes in the three levels as follows.

User Profiles We define the user profile to be the set of words which tend to partition the user's document accesses into groups. These are words that have occurrence patterns such as that shown in figure 1. Once WordSieve has experienced a reasonably diverse set of document accesses, the user profile can be extracted from the nodes of levels 2 and 3. The user profile consists of the set of words corresponding to nodes in those levels, each word associated with the product of its excitement values in levels 2 and 3. Words with high products tend to have the desired occurrence patterns.

Note that this user profile will be different for every user, because it depends on the user's patterns of document access. These profiles enable the system to learn about the kinds of documents the user accesses as a group, and use them to identify terms which indicate the context in which a user is working. Having identified the context, the system can index a document by that context for suggestion later, and can identify previously indexed documents which may be helpful to the user, aiding personalization of recommendations.

Context Profiles While the user is accessing documents, we can use WordSieve to build a profile of the current context. Intuitively, the context profile should consist of the words which are frequent in that particular document stream and have high values in the user profile. We achieve this in WordSieve by multiplying the excitement values of words in level 1 and their values in the upper levels. These words should be characteristic of the sets of document sequences.

5 Evaluation

We have evaluated the performance of the algorithm for the ability to index documents according to a search task given to the user, where the context is defined as a topic given to the users, but unavailable to WordSieve. In our tests, WordSieve is able to more strongly match documents to task context than TFIDF. The software used for data collection in our experiment is CALVIN, an Intelligent Agent for research assistance [13]. This system is designed to observe a person using a computer and suggest resources that have been helpful in similar contexts in the past. CALVIN uses WordSieve to index documents.[2]

5.1 Experiment

This experiment examined the comparative performance of WordSieve and TFIDF at matching a document, when seen out of context, to its original search task, described by a term vector representation of the search phrase. The search phrase vectors were compared to the vectors produced by WordSieve profiles and TFIDF.

Seven subjects separately searched the WWW for 20 minutes each. During that time, they were asked to perform two tasks. For the first ten minutes, they were told to load into their browser pages about "The use of Genetic Algorithms in Artificial Life Software." After ten minutes, they were asked to search for information about "Tropical Butterflies in Southeast Asia." Every document they

---

[2] Some of the classes used in Calvin and WordSieve are released as an open source Java package, IGLU, available at http://www.cs.indiana.edu/~trbauer/iglu.

accessed through the browser was automatically recorded. The HTML tags were stripped, as well as punctuation, but no filtering was done on the pages accessed. "PAGE NOT FOUND" pages and pages which contained advertisements were not filtered out. Thus the data collected represents a realistic sampling of the kinds of pages that an Intelligent Agent must handle when observing a user accessing the WWW. To provide an evaluation criterion, documents which did not pertain to the user's search (such as "PAGE NOT FOUND" documents) were then hand-tagged as "noise" documents, and the other documents were hand tagged as either belonging to the genetic algorithm or the butterfly task. These tags were not available to WordSieve.

Users accessed an average of 124 documents per 20 minute session. On average, they accessed 69 "noise" documents and 54 relevant documents. A total of 590 different documents were accessed, 381 of which were determined to be relevant. There were 135 documents which were accessed by more than one user, 88 of which were determined to be relevant documents.

During the user's browsing, the documents were stored. This data was then run through the WordSieve in a series of "simulated" browsing sessions. The sessions were simulated only in the sense that the user was not actually at the browser; the data was processed by WordSieve in the same order in which the user accessed it, and no pages were omitted. To simulate multiple task changes, a single simulated browsing session consisted of passing data from one user session through WordSieve three times. Thus information presented to the system was as if the user alternated searching for information about genetic algorithms, and information about butterflies three times, for ten minutes each.

Having built up a context model with WordSieve, a vector for each relevant document in each simulated run was computed by running the document through an empty level 1 and multiplying the resulting node values by their values in the other two levels. The vector for the TFIDF was computed as per Salton [17]. For each word in the document, the weights of each word in the vector were defined by equation 2.

$$w_{ij} = tf_{ij} \cdot \log \frac{N}{df_i} \tag{2}$$

Then, each resulting vector was compared to the original query. Similarity to the original query was calculated via the cosine similarity metric shown in equation 3 [17].

$$\frac{\sum_{i=1}^{t} x_i \cdot y_i}{\sqrt{\sum_{i=1}^{t} x_i^2 \cdot \sum_{i=1}^{t} y_i^2}} \tag{3}$$

In all cases, when computing vectors and doing comparison, the algorithms only had access to the documents in one user's session. Each user's session was treated independently.

5.2 Consistency of Results

Because WordSieve is a probabilistic algorithm, it does not produce exactly the same results every time it is run. To test its performance variation, all simulated user sessions were run through WordSieve four times and the results were compared. Although there was variation among individual rankings of documents, the variation was not statistically significant according to a repeated measures ANOVA test $(F(3, 1146)=2.26, p<.05)$. This suggests that although WordSieve works probabilistically, it is consistent across even a relatively small set of data (in our experiment, 60 minutes worth of browsing). This also suggests that the results of the experiment are not the results of "lucky" runs of the simulation, but that our data set is large enough to faithfully represent the abilities of the algorithm.

5.3 Performance vs. TFIDF

On the whole, when viewing a document in isolation, WordSieve is better able to match the document to its original context than TFIDF. Using a repeated-measures analysis of variance shows that these findings are statistically reliable. $F(1, 382)=91.03, p<.05$.

The overall comparison of WordSieve and TFIDF are shown below. The following table reports the average similarity of all relevant documents of all users to their original context as measured by TFIDF and WordSieve. WordSieve's mean performance at this task surpassed that of TFIDF by 54%.

	TFIDF	WordSieve
Mean	0.145	0.224
Standard Deviation	0.142	0.170

As shown in figures 3 and 4, the overall patterns generally hold true when breaking down the comparisons by context and user. WordSieve outperformed TFIDF in all cases except for users 2 and 3 where it performed almost as well. Without a larger set of users, it is difficult to determine why it did not do as well in those cases. However, it may be significant that both had accessed relatively small number of relevant documents (only user 7 accessed fewer). Overall, these analyses show that the results are reproducible across diverse subsets of the data.

5.4 Discussion

WordSieve extracts context information from documents in the form of keywords. This is standard for many intelligent information agents, and for the purposes of document retrieval, seems to be a natural approach. However, the results of these experiments suggest the benefit of taking into account extra contextual information available in user document access patterns, and the effectiveness of

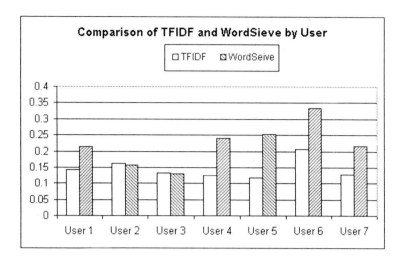

Fig. 3. Comparisons by User

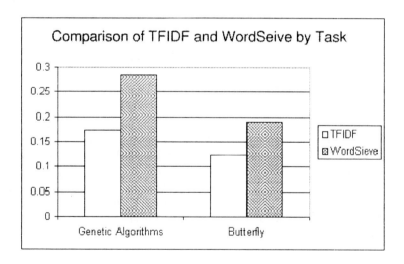

Fig. 4. Comparisons by Query

the WordSieve algorithm for this task. The experiments suggest that keyword occurrence patterns exist in user document accesses over time, and that those patterns can help characterize the context within which the document was accessed, compared to a method such as TFIDF that is unable to capitalize on this information. The results also suggest the viability of using a small, short term memory (the MostFrequentWords level) and probabilistic networks in learning about the user's context, though more experiments and long-term studies are needed.

This research also raises the issue of what constitutes the context of a given instance of a web search. For this experiment, we defined the context as the relevant terms from the topic for which the users were asked to search. However, a number of comments we received from users after they had performed the experiment question those assumptions. The users all seemed to have more trouble with the butterfly query than with the genetic algorithm query.[3] Two users commented that they had found much information about a particular kind of butterfly, but not about Asian butterflies in general. This suggests that the user's perception of the context was informed both by the explicit task given the user and the kind of information the user actually found, and suggests that perhaps the context should be defined not only as what the users were asked to find, but what they were asked to find plus what they actually did find. That type of context description could be generated by asking the users to write five keywords that they thought characterized the web pages they actually found, but that were not in the original question, and using those to augment the task description. However, we expect that both TFIDF and WordSieve would benefit from these expanded queries, so that the comparative performance patterns for the two algorithms would still hold.

We believe we can improve this algorithm's performance. We have not yet sufficiently explored the values assigned to the free parameters in the system to see how we can increase the accuracy of this model and decrease the variance in its performance. Also, another level could be added which would become sensitized to only non-discriminators. These words could then be banned from the upper two levels, or perhaps from the lower levels altogether, assuring that space in the profile is reserved for useful words only.

Obviously, there are many forms of contextual information that WordSieve does not yet take into account. For example, WordSieve does not take into account the location of a term on a page, nor is it able to treat a document differently if a user keeps returning to it. For example, consider a situation where a user performs a web search, then clicks on many links from that page, returning frequently to make another choice. That page is probably useful in determining the context, but WordSieve would not treat it in any special way (other than re-reading it many times). Thus we see WordSieve as a useful tool to reflect one aspect of context, to be augmented with others for richer descriptions.

---

[3] Figures 3 and 4 shows that documents for the butterfly query tended to rank lower on average. That may indicate a lack of web pages which clearly map to that context.

Another interesting question concerns how to account for the quality of a document in the subject domain being searched. WordSieve's analysis does not address this. In Calvin, users can set up customized filters to stop certain documents from being indexed (e.g., to filter out advertisements and error pages), but this increases the need for user configuration.

6 Relationship to Other Work

Calvin is an intelligent agent for learning about a user's context and making suggestions based on that information. Perhaps the best known agent in this class is the Microsoft Office Assistant [12]. Using a Bayesian network, the office assistant infers what a user's goals might be from the user's behavior, and makes suggestions based on those inferences. However, the Office Assistant has a very specific model of how the underlying application works, and its suggestions deal with how to use the software. Thus, this agent's understanding of context is tailored to its special-purpose task. The advantage of this approach is the ability to give very specific advice. However, the advantage is gained at the cost of generality. (See [11] for comments on the potential difficulty of applying a problem-specific notion of context to form a broader theory.) CALVIN could potentially make suggestions based on the documents loaded into any application. Although it does not claim a formal theory of context, its architecture is easily transferred across document access applications.

Margin Notes [16] is another agent that suggests previously accessed documents. Unlike Calvin, which indexes documents accessed at runtime, this system pre-indexes documents and email stored on the user's computer. Then, while the user is accessing information on the WWW, the user's web pages are automatically annotated with references to related pre-indexed files. Margin Notes uses TFIDF for pre-indexing documents, so its understanding of context is based purely on the content of a set of documents and not on how the user accesses them. Other approaches also index documents in isolation from the context in which they were accessed [10].

Watson [6] observes uses of standard software tools, such as browsers and word processors, and generates queries to WWW search engines for context-relevant information. Watson, like Calvin, uses a vector representation of the context. However, it focuses on information about the immediate task context, rather than information about the user's task sequence. Its method of document parsing helps it find significant words without a larger corpus, in a spirit similar to WordSieve, and its automated use of WWW search engines gives it an advantage over both Calvin and Margin Notes in that it can suggest documents which system users have not yet seen. In should be noted, however, that as document indices are generated by WordSieve for multiple users, those indices can enable cross-user retrievals, providing an individual user with new documents expected to be of interest in the current context.

Other techniques, such as data mining with rule learning, have been employed to record user profiles [1]. Rule learning methods would be well-suited to finding the kinds of terms that WordSieve learns. However, rule learning usually requires a database of user activity to analyze in order to find the rules, while WordSieve works incrementally in real time.

Finally, the idea of learning user profiles for making suggestions has been applied to areas other than text document indexing and retrieval, such as recommending television programs [9]. The PTV system builds a user profile using information such as explicit descriptions of preferences, as well as user watching practices. This system also makes use of the preferences of other users who have similar profiles. One design challenge facing such systems is that the actual contents of the television programs are opaque to the system, unlike the contents of text documents for systems such as WordSieve.

7 Conclusions

In this paper, we have presented WordSieve, a new algorithm for characterizing a user's context by analyzing documents which the user is accessing. The algorithm builds a user profile during document access to reflect the range of user interests, and generates context profiles to reflect the user's current context. WordSieve outperforms TFIDF in initial experiments on associating documents to the contexts in which they were accessed. This performance gain does not seem to be specific to some subset of the overall data, but appears to generalize well over various subsets of the data which we have examined. Research on WordSieve and its application suggests a number of questions for context studies research, especially concerning the use of context in Intelligent Information Agents and the kinds of information about a user's context that can be learned automatically from implicit feedback.

References

1. Gediminas Adomavicius and Alexander Tuzhilin. Using data mining methods to build customer profiles. *Computer*, 34(2):74–82, February 2001.
2. V. Akman and M. Surav. Steps toward formalizing context. *AI Magazine*, 17(3):55–72, 1996.
3. Marko Balabanović. An interface for learning multi-topic user profiles from implicit feedback. In *AAAI-98 Workshop on Recommender Systems*, 1998.
4. M. Benerecetti, P. Bouquet, and C. Ghidini. Contextual reasoning distilled. *Philosophical Foundations of Artificial Intelligence*, 12(3), July 2000.
5. Bruno Bouzy and Tristan Cazenave. Using the object oriented paradigm to model context in computer go. In *Proceedings of the First International and Interdisciplinary Conference on Modeling and Using Context*, 1997.
6. J. Budzik and J. K. Hammond. Watson: Anticipating and contextualizing information needs. In *Proceedings of the Sixty-second Annual Meeting of the American Society for Information Science*, Medford, NJ. 1999. Information Today, Inc.
7. J. Budzik, K. Hammond, and L. Birnbaum. Information access in context. In *Knowledge based systems*, 2001.

8. J. Budzik, K. Hammond, L. Birnbaum, and M. Krema. Beyond similarity. In *Working Notes of the AAAI-2000 Workshop on AI for Web Search*. AAAI Press, Menlo Park, 2000.

9. P. Cotter and B. Smyth. PTV: Intelligent personalised tv guides. In *Proceedings of the 12th Innovative Applications of Artificial Intelligence (IAAI-2000) Conference*. AAAI Press, 2000.

10. Marti A. Hearst. *Context and Structure in Automated Full-Text Information Access*. PhD thesis, University of California at Berkeley, 1994.

11. Graeme Hirst. Context as a spurious concept. In *Proceedings, Conference on Intelligent Processing and Computational Linguistics*, pages 273–287, Mexico City, February 2000.

12. Eric Horvitz, Jack Breese, David Heckerman, David Hovel, and Koos Rommelse. Inferring the goals and needs of software users. In *Proceedings of the Fourteenth Conference on Uncertainty in Artificial Intelligence*, pages 256–265, 1998.

13. David Leake, Travis Bauer, Anna Maguitman, and David Wilson. Capture, storage and reuse of lessons about information resources: Supporting task-based information search. In *Proceedings of the AAAI-2000 Workshop on Intelligent Lessons Learned Systems*, Menlo Park, CA, 2000. AAAI Press.

14. Henry Lieberman, Neil Van Dyke, and Adriana Vivacqua. Let's browse: A collaborative web browsing agent. In *Proceedings of the 1999 international conference on Intelligent user interfaces*, pages 65–68, 1999.

15. Carlo Penco. Objective and cognitive context. In Paolo Bouquet, Luigi Serafini, Patrick Brézillon, Massimo Benerecetti, and Francesca Castellani, editors, *Modeling and Using Contexts: Proceedings of the Second International and Interdisciplinary Conference*, pages 270–283. Springer-Verlag, 1999.

16. Bradley J. Rhodes. Margin notes: Building a contextually aware associative memory. In *Proceedings of the 2000 international conference on Intelligent user interfaces*, pages 219–224, Jan 2000.

17. Gerard Salton. *Automatic Text Processing: The Transformation, Analysis, and Retrieval of Information by Computer*. Addison-Wesley Series in Computer Science. Addison-Wesley Publishing Company, Inc., 1989.

18. Roy Turner. Context-sensitive reasoning for autonomous agents and cooperative distributed problem solving. In *Proceedings of the IJCAI Workshop on Using Knowledge in its Context*, Chambery, France, 1993.

19. Roy Turner. Context-mediated behavior. In J. Mira, A.P. del Pobil, and M. Ali, editors, *Lecture Notes in Artificial Intelligence 1415: Methodology and Tools in Knowledge-Based Systems*, pages 538–547, Benicassim, Spain, June 1998. Springer, New York.

Pragmatic Reasoning
Pragmatic Semantics and Semantic Pragmatics

John Bell

Applied Logic Group
Department of Computer Science
Queen Mary, University of London
London E1 4NS
jb@dcs.qmw.ac.uk

Abstract. This paper is concerned with the conceptual foundations of *pragmatic reasoning* (context-dependent reasoning). A general *pragmatic semantics* (a semantic analysis which includes a pragmatic parameter) is given for pragmatic reasoning, the logical properties of the various forms of pragmatic reasoning are discussed, as are many examples. The *semantic pragmatics* (the general study of choosing or inferring appropriate contexts) for pragmatic reasoning is then discussed, with illustrations from common sense reasoning and scientific reasoning.

1 Introduction

This paper is concerned with the conceptual foundations of pragmatic reasoning, or context-dependent reasoning. This is a very general notion which includes reasoning with explicit contexts; such as McCarthy's formalization of context [28], Buvac and Mason's propositional logic of context [11], and Giunchiglia and Ghidini's local models semantics for contextual reasoning [13]. However, in this paper the emphasis is on reasoning with an implicit context or contexts. Reasoning of this kind is ubiquitous, and its analysis and formalization has been undertaken in linguistics and the philosophy of language, the philosophy of science, and in the formalization of common sense reasoning in artificial intelligence.

Pragmatic reasoning is defined in the next section. A pragmatic semantics (a semantic analysis which includes a pragmatic parameter) is given in Section 3, and semantic pragmatics (general methods for choosing or inferring contexts) are discussed in Section 4.

2 Pragmatic reasoning

Traditionally, reasoning is divided into theoretical reasoning, reasoning about what is the case, and practical reasoning, reasoning about what to do. Theoretical reasoning is then subdivided into deductive reasoning and inductive (non-deductive) reasoning. Inductive reasoning thus includes enumerative induction (or rule-based induction), the nonmonotonic logics which have been developed in order to represent common sense reasoning, implicature, abduction, and para-consistent reasoning.

Instead, I suggest that reasoning should be classified on the basis of context dependence or independence. Consequently, I distinguish between *semantic reasoning*, or context-free reasoning, and *pragmatic reasoning*, or context-dependent reasoning. According to this classification, semantic reasoning is just deductive reasoning, while all of the remaining forms of reasoning mentioned above are forms of pragmatic reasoning. Thus, for example, enumerative induction takes place in the partial epistemic context consisting of the relevant current hypotheses and observational evidence to-date, and practical reasoning takes place in a context of action which may include the agent's beliefs, desires, intentions, obligations, capacities, etc.

Semantic reasoning is concerned with valid inference, with establishing conclusions with certainty, with what follows from the premises regardless of the context in which they occur, with what follows from the semantic (or literal) interpretation of the premises. The context-free nature of semantic reasoning is reflected in the fact that it is monotonic. If a sentence ϕ is a semantic consequence of a set of premises Φ, then ϕ is also a semantic consequence of any larger set of premises $\Phi \cup \Psi$; enlarging the premise set in an arbitrary way does not lead to the loss of conclusions. So if enlarging the premise set involves a change to a context in which the new premises are true, then conclusions which were established earlier remain true.

By contrast, pragmatic reasoning is concerned with establishing conclusions which are reasonable or appropriate in particular contexts, with what follows from the premises in particular contexts, with what follows from the pragmatic (or appropriate) interpretation of the premises. If the context can be explicitly represented in the premises, then they can be interpreted semantically, and semantic reasoning suffices. However, it is typically impractical or impossible to represent the context explicitly. Consequently the pragmatic interpretation of the premises depends on the choice of an appropriate implicit context.[1] The context-dependent nature of pragmatic reasoning is reflected in the fact that it is defeasible, or nonmonotonic. If a sentence ϕ is a pragmatic consequence of a set of premises Φ, then it need not be a pragmatic consequence of a larger premise set $\Phi \cup \Psi$; thus enlarging the premise set may well lead to the loss of conclusions. Thus if the sentences in Ψ conflict with the implicit context used in the pragmatic interpretation of Φ, then the addition of these sentences results in a shift to a new context in which some of the formerly appropriate conclusions are no longer appropriate.

3 Pragmatic semantics

But if pragmatic reasoning is context-dependent, how is a semantic analysis of it possible? The answer lies in the approach adopted by those giving formal seman-

---

[1] As several choices of context may be appropriate, pragmatic interpretation may be ambiguous. This further complication is discussed in the next section.

tic analyses of other context-dependent phenomena, such as Kaplan's analysis of indexicals [19], Kripke's possible-worlds semantics for modalities [22], Montague's Intensional Logic [29], and the theories of counterfactual conditionals of Stalnaker, Thomason, and Lewis [34, 36, 24]. Thus Stalnaker argues is that it is possible to draw a clear distinction between the semantics of counterfactual conditionals and their pragmatics by constructing a semantic theory of counterfactuals, in which they are given fixed truth conditions, and treating their ambiguity pragmatically; that is, as a parameter of the interpretation whose value is to be determined by pragmatic considerations. This is justified because:

> The grounds for treating the ambiguity of conditional sentences as pragmatic rather than semantic are the same as the grounds for treating the ambiguity of quantified sentences as pragmatic: simplicity and systematic coherence. The truth conditions for quantified sentences vary with a change in the domain of discourse, but there is a single structure to these truth conditions which remains constant for every domain. The semantics for classical predicate logic brings out this common structure by giving the universal quantifier a single meaning and making the domain a parameter of the interpretation. In a similar fashion, the semantics for conditional logic brings out the common structure of the truth conditions for conditional statements by giving the connective a single meaning and making the selection function a parameter of the interpretation. [p. 176]

The selection function of Stalnaker's analysis is a function f which, for possible world w and proposition ϕ, selects the closest possible world to w in which ϕ is true; that is, the world in which ϕ is true and which otherwise differs minimally from w. Stalnaker imposes a number of general, semantic, conditions on f in order to ensure that an appropriate world is selected; for example, if ϕ is true at w, then $f(\phi, w) = w$. However, Lewis argues that there is not always a single closest world to a given world, and so he generalizes Stalnaker's analysis by introducing a selection function which returns a set of worlds; thus the intention is that, for possible world w, $f(\phi, w)$ should be the set of worlds in which ϕ is true and which are otherwise as similar to w as possible, all things considered. Accordingly, Lewis's semantic conditions for the selection function are weaker than Stalnaker's. He also gives an alternative semantics which uses a comparative similarity relation on worlds as a parameter. This use of selection functions or comparative similarity relations as parameters of the truth conditions for conditionals makes it possible to define semantic notions such as validity and consequence, and to give sound and complete axiomatizations for conditionals.

The same strategy can be used in order to give a pragmatic semantics for pragmatic reasoning; as the implicit context in which a pragmatic argument occurs can be represented by a pragmatic parameter. The following formal definition of pragmatic reasoning is very general, and is formulated in terms of context-dependent reasoning with structures; where a structure may be any organized collection of "objects", and may thus include individual sentences, sets of sentences, texts, semantic nets, inheritance hierarchies, visual images, sequences of images, etc. Having given the general case, the discussion shifts to pragmatic reasoning with sentences, as pragmatic reasoning in this form is best under-stood, and various specializations of the general definition are considered and illustrated.

The definition begins with the very general notion of the interpretation of an object occurring in a structure. The semantic interpretation of the object should produce its semantic meaning. The interpretation may thus take account of the syntactic structure of the object, but should ignore the remainder of the structure in which the object occurs. By contrast, the pragmatic interpretation of the object should produce its pragmatic meaning or meanings, and this typically involves taking account of the remainder of the structure in which the object occurs. Let $\mathcal{O}$ be a set of objects, $\mathcal{R}$ be a set of relations on $\mathcal{O}$, and $\mathcal{S}$ be a set of structures which are defined in terms of $\mathcal{O}$ and $\mathcal{R}$. It is assumed that these sets are such that meaningful definitions can be given for the following relations:

- $In(o, \Sigma)$, which is true if and only if object o occurs in structure Σ.
- $Remove(o, \Sigma, \Sigma')$, which is true if and only if Σ' is the structure which results from removing an instance of object o from structure Σ; thus, if $In(o, \Sigma)$ is false, then $Remove(o, \Sigma, \Sigma)$ is true.
- $Compose(\Sigma, \Sigma', \Sigma'')$, which is true if and only if the structures Σ and Σ' can be composed to form the structure Σ''.
- $Substructure(\Sigma, \Sigma')$, which is true if and only if Σ is a substructure of Σ'.

Thus if $In(o, \Sigma)$, then structure Σ is said to be the *syntactic context* of object o. For example, the structures in question may simply be sets of first-order sentences; $\mathcal{O}$ is the set of all such sentences, $\mathcal{S}$ is the powerset of $\mathcal{O}$, In is set membership, $Remove$ is set difference, $Compose$ is set union, and $Substructure$ is the subset relation. Alternatively, the structures in question may be English texts or discourses; $\mathcal{O}$ is a set of English sentences (say those defined by a GPSG), $\mathcal{S}$ is the set of all sequences of sentences in $\mathcal{O}$, In is sequence membership, $Remove(o, \Sigma)$ denotes the result of deleting an instance of the sentence o from Σ, $Compose$ is concatenation, and $Substructure$ is the subsequence relation.

It is further assumed that the objects in $\mathcal{O}$ can be interpreted semantically. Thus it is assumed that there is a set I of semantic interpretations of the objects in $\mathcal{O}$ and that the notion of semantic truth in an interpretation (the relation $\models$ such that $i \models o$ if and only if object o is true in interpretation i) is defined. Given this notion, a semantic interpretation function can be defined: for each object $o \in \mathcal{O}$, let $[\![o]\!] = \{i \in I : i \models o\}$. Thus the semantic meaning of o, $[\![o]\!]$, is the common meaning that o has in all interpretations in which it is semantically true. For example, if $\mathcal{O}$ is the language of classical first-order logic, then I is the set of Tarski interpretations of $\mathcal{O}$, the truth relation $\models$ is that defined by Tarski and, for each sentence o, $[\![o]\!]$ is the proposition expressed by o. Alternatively if, as in Ullman's object recognition system [37], each $o \in \mathcal{O}$ is a 2-D representation of an object to be recognized, then I is a collection of stored 3-D representations of objects ("models"), and $i \models o$ if and only if object o can be matched with object i by Ullman's sequence-seeking process, using only what can be considered to be semantic interpretation methods; that is, using initial classification and bottom-up transformations only.

Definition 1. *A semantics* for $\mathcal{S}$ *is a pair* $S = \langle I, [\![\cdot]\!] \rangle$ *where:*

I is a set of interpretations of $\mathcal{O}$, and
$[\![\cdot]\!] : \mathcal{O} \to \mathcal{P}I$ is a semantic interpretation function.

For each $o \in \mathcal{O}$, $[\![o]\!]$ is the set of semantic models *of o, the set of interpretations in which o is* semantically true. *For each structure $\Sigma \in \mathcal{S}$, $[\![\Sigma]\!] = \bigcap \{ [\![o]\!] : In(o, \Sigma) \}$.*

The intuition that $[\![o]\!]$ represents the semantic, or literal, or context-free meaning of object o is captured by the extension of $[\![\cdot]\!]$ to structures; which has the consequence that, for any structure Σ and object o such that $In(o, \Sigma)$, $[\![\Sigma]\!] = [\![o]\!] \cap [\![Remove(o, \Sigma)]\!]$. The semantic interpretation of o is thus independent of the structure (the syntactic context) in which it occurs.

Each semantics determines a semantic logic.

Definition 2. *Let $S = \langle I, [\![\cdot]\!] \rangle$ be a semantics for $\mathcal{S}$. The* semantic logic determined by S, L_S, *is defined by its semantic entailment relation. For any $\Sigma, \Sigma' \in \mathcal{S}$:*

$$\Sigma \models_S \Sigma' \quad \text{iff} \quad [\![\Sigma]\!] \subseteq [\![\Sigma']\!].$$

Thus Σ semantically entails Σ' in L_S if and only if all semantic models of Σ are also semantic models of Σ'.

As the semantic interpretation of a sequence is independent of its syntactic context, it follows that any semantic logic is monotonic: if $\Sigma \models_S \Sigma'$ then, for any structure Σ'' such that $Substructure(\Sigma, \Sigma'')$, $\Sigma'' \models_S \Sigma'$.

In order to define a pragmatics for $\mathcal{S}$ it is necessary to have a representation of contexts. A simple and general solution is to represent contexts as sets of interpretations.[2] If I is the set of interpretations of $\mathcal{O}$ and $c \subseteq I$ is a context then a structure Σ is semantically true in c if and only if $c \subseteq [\![\Sigma]\!]$; that is, Σ is semantically true in c if and only if Σ is semantically true in all interpretations in c.

The semantic context for a structure Σ can thus be taken to be the context $[\![\Sigma]\!]$. Clearly $[\![\Sigma]\!]$ represents the semantic, literal, context-free meaning of Σ. In particular, if Σ is semantically ambiguous and several semantic interpretations of it are possible, then $[\![\Sigma]\!]$ represents those aspects of the meaning of Σ that the interpretations have in common. The term 'semantic context' might seem slightly paradoxical as semantic contexts are representations of unchanging, invariant, meanings, and we are accustomed to thinking of contexts in association with changing meaning. However the terminology is useful in that it emphasises the strangeness of semantic reasoning. In order to obtain conclusions which are certain from some given structure Σ it is necessary to eliminate all but the invariant and universal aspects of its meaning. Thus semantic reasoning can be

---

[2] Similarly, Stalnaker [35] suggests and defends the view that contexts can be represented as sets of possible worlds; in effect as sets of interpretations of classical logic.

seen as the process of determining the semantic context of Σ, by stripping away any context-dependent aspects of its meaning in order to obtain the semantic context for Σ, and then concluding that a structure Σ' semantically follows from Σ if Σ' is semantically true in this context.

Intuitively then, a pragmatic context for a structure Σ is a context in which a pragmatic interpretation of Σ is semantically true. If Σ is pragmatically ambiguous, then there may be several pragmatic contexts for it; one for each pragmatic interpretation. Thus a pragmatic interpretation function, $[\cdot]$, should be such that, for each structure Σ, $[\Sigma]$ is the set of all pragmatic contexts for Σ. Initially, in the interests of generality, no restrictions are imposed on the pragmatic interpretation function; thus the following definition requires only that it is of the correct type.

Definition 3. *A pragmatic semantics for $\mathcal{S}$ is a triple $P = \langle I, [\![\cdot]\!], [\cdot] \rangle$ where:*

$\langle I, [\![\cdot]\!] \rangle$ *is a semantics for $\mathcal{S}$, and*
$[\cdot] : \mathcal{S} \to \mathcal{PPI}$ *is a pragmatic interpretation function.*

Each $c \in [\Sigma]$ is called a credulous pragmatic context *for Σ, while $\bigcup [\Sigma]$ is called the* sceptical pragmatic context *for Σ.*

The distinction between sceptical and credulous pragmatic contexts in this definition allows us to keep an open mind regarding what counts as pragmatic reasoning. Note that there need be no connection between the semantic and the pragmatic interpretation functions. For example, it may be the case that Σ has the sceptical pragmatic context $[\![\Sigma']\!]$ and that $[\Sigma] \cap [\![\Sigma']\!] = \emptyset$. Note also that it is not possible to start with a pragmatic function of type $\mathcal{O} \to \mathcal{PI}$ as it is not assumed that, for any structure Σ, $[\Sigma] = \bigcap \{[o] : In(o, \Sigma)\}$. Indeed it may well be the case that, for structure Σ and object o such that $In(o, \Sigma)$, $[\Sigma] \neq [o] \cap [Remove(o, \Sigma)]$. The pragmatic interpretation of o may thus depend on the structure (the syntactic context) in which it occurs.

The possibility of pragmatic ambiguity and the aim of formalizing reasonable, if defeasible, context-based reasoning suggests (at least) two notions of pragmatic entailment.

Definition 4. *Let $P = \langle I, [\![\cdot]\!], [\cdot] \rangle$ be a pragmatic semantics for $\mathcal{S}$. The* credulous pragmatic logic *determined by P, L_{PC}, is defined by its credulous pragmatic entailment relation. For any $\Sigma, \Sigma' \in \mathcal{S}$:*

$$\Sigma \approx_P^C \Sigma' \text{ iff for some } c \in [\Sigma], \ c \subseteq [\![\Sigma']\!].$$

Thus Σ credulously entails Σ' in L_{PC} if and only if Σ' is semantically true in some pragmatic context for Σ.

The sceptical pragmatic logic *determined by P, L_P, is defined by its sceptical pragmatic entailment relation. For any $\Sigma, \Sigma' \in \mathcal{S}$:*

$$\Sigma \approx_P \Sigma' \text{ iff for every } c \in [\Sigma], \ c \subseteq [\![\Sigma']\!].$$

Thus Σ sceptically entails Σ' in L_P if and only if Σ' is semantically true in every pragmatic context for Σ.

Note that, as the definition of the pragmatic interpretation function typically depends on syntactic context, it need not be the case that, for structures Σ and Σ' such that $Substructure(\Sigma, \Sigma')$, $[\Sigma'] \subseteq [\Sigma]$. Thus both forms of pragmatic inference may be nonmonotonic; extending the syntactic context may result in the loss of previously established pragmatic conclusions. Note also that it is the determination of pragmatic contexts which distinguishes pragmatic reasoning from semantic reasoning. Given a credulous (the sceptical) pragmatic context for a structure Σ, credulous (sceptical) pragmatic reasoning reduces to semantic reasoning.

All pragmatic interpretation functions satisfy the following conditions:

(Tautologies) For any structure Σ and structure of tautologies $\top$:
$$\bigcup [\Sigma] \subseteq [\![\top]\!].$$
(Weakening) For any structures Σ and Σ' and Σ'', and context c:
if $c \in [\Sigma]$ and $c \subseteq [\![\Sigma']\!]$ and $[\![\Sigma']\!] \subseteq [\![\Sigma'']\!]$, then $c \subseteq [\![\Sigma'']\!]$.

All tautologies of $\mathcal{O}$, if indeed there are any given its semantics,[3] are pragmatically inferable, so is any semantic consequence of what is pragmatically inferable.

Sceptical entailment also satisfies the following condition:

(Scepticism) For any structures Σ, Σ' and Σ'':
if $\bigcup [\Sigma] \subseteq [\![\Sigma']\!]$ and $\bigcup [\Sigma] \subseteq [\![\Sigma'']\!]$ and $Compose(\Sigma', \Sigma'', \Sigma''')$, then $\bigcup [\Sigma] \subseteq [\![\Sigma''']\!]$.

This condition may fail for credulous entailment. Indeed, if $\mathcal{O}$ is a logical language which contains negation, then it may be the case that $\Sigma \approx_P^C o$ and $\Sigma \approx_P^C \neg o$. Consequently it seems that the sceptical form yields a better notion of entailment than the credulous form. It is perhaps better to read $\Sigma \approx_P^C \Sigma'$ as claiming that Σ suggests Σ', or that Σ' is credible or plausible given Σ. Thus, in the following discussion, the consideration of the sceptical form predominates and consequently it is usually referred to simply as 'pragmatic entailment'.

The above conditions on pragmatic interpretation functions can be restated as general properties which any pragmatic entailment relation satisfies. For example the property corresponding to Scepticism is:

(Scepticism) For any sequences Σ, Σ' and Σ'':
if $\Sigma \approx \Sigma'$ and $\Sigma \approx \Sigma''$ and $Compose(\Sigma', \Sigma'', \Sigma''')$, then $\Sigma \approx \Sigma'''$.

In the sequel the emphasis will be on pragmatic reasoning with sets of sentences, or simply sentences. Thus, for sets of sentences Φ and Ψ, the definition of (sceptical) pragmatic entailment reduces to the following: $\Phi \approx_P \Psi$ if and only

---

[3] There are, for example, no tautologies given Kleene's three-valued semantics [20].

if $\bigcup [\Phi] \subseteq [\![\Psi]\!]$. This use of sets provides an elegant way of stating general properties of pragmatic entailment. Thus all pragmatic entailment relations (defined on pairs of sets of sentences) satisfy the following familiar properties:

(Tautologies) For any set Φ and set of tautologies T: $\Phi \mathrel{\mid\!\!\sim} \mathsf{T}$.
(Weakening) For any sets Φ, Ψ and Ξ:
  if $\Phi \mathrel{\mid\!\!\sim} \Psi$ and $\Psi \models \Xi$, then $\Phi \mathrel{\mid\!\!\sim} \Xi$.
(Scepticism) For any sets Φ, Ψ and Ξ:
  if $\Phi \mathrel{\mid\!\!\sim} \Psi$ and $\Phi \mathrel{\mid\!\!\sim} \Xi$, then $\Phi \mathrel{\mid\!\!\sim} \Psi \cup \Xi$.

Many other conditions can be imposed on pragmatic interpretation functions, resulting in corresponding properties of pragmatic entailment relations. The following are of particular interest:

(Identity) For any set Φ: $\Phi \mathrel{\mid\!\!\sim} \Phi$.
(Cut) For any sets Φ, Ψ and Ξ:
  if $\Phi \mathrel{\mid\!\!\sim} \Psi$ and $\Phi \cup \Psi \mathrel{\mid\!\!\sim} \Xi$, then $\Phi \mathrel{\mid\!\!\sim} \Xi$.
(Cautious Monotony) For any sets Φ, Ψ and Ξ:
  if $\Phi \mathrel{\mid\!\!\sim} \Psi$ and $\Phi \mathrel{\mid\!\!\sim} \Xi$, then $\Phi \cup \Psi \mathrel{\mid\!\!\sim} \Xi$.

Identity and Weakening together imply:

(Reflexivity) For any sets Φ and Ψ: $\Phi \cup \Psi \mathrel{\mid\!\!\sim} \Phi$.
(Semantic Inclusion) For any sets Φ and Ψ: if $\Phi \models \Psi$, then $\Phi \mathrel{\mid\!\!\sim} \Psi$.

Adding Identity thus has the effect of making the pragmatic entailment relation *ampliative*; the pragmatic consequences of a set Φ include the semantic consequences of Φ. Identity is appropriate for much of common sense reasoning and scientific reasoning, as discussed below. In general, ampliative reasoning is appropriate for reasoning with incomplete or partial information. By contrast, reasoning with inconsistent information should be *restrictive*; as an inconsistent premise set semantically entails any sentence. The aim of paraconsistent reasoning is to extract useful information in such circumstances, and consequently Identity should not be a property of it.

Cut and Cautious Monotony taken together have the effect that if the pragmatic interpretation of Φ pragmatically entails Ψ then the pragmatic interpretations of Φ and $\Phi \cup \Psi$ are equivalent. Proof-theoretic counterparts of these conditions were introduced by Gabbay [12] and have been investigated further by Makinson [25, 26].

The conditions Weakening, Identity, Cut and Cautious Monotony together imply:

(Equivalence) For any sets Φ, Ψ and Ξ:
  if $\Phi \models \Psi$ and $\Psi \models \Phi$ and $\Phi \mathrel{\mid\!\!\sim} \Xi$, then $\Psi \mathrel{\mid\!\!\sim} \Xi$.

Weakening, Identity, Cut and Cautious Monotony together also imply Scepticism.

If $\mathcal{L}$ contains suitable connectives, then the pragmatic entailment relation can be defined on sentences. Thus if $\mathcal{L}$ contains conjunction and $[\![\phi \wedge \psi]\!] = [\![\phi]\!] \cap [\![\psi]\!]$, then, for example, Cautious Monotony can be restated as:

(Cautious Monotony) For any sentences ϕ, ψ and χ:
if $\phi \approx \psi$ and $\phi \approx \chi$, then $\phi \wedge \psi \approx \chi$.

Moreover, if $\mathcal{L}$ contains disjunction and negation, and $[\![\phi \vee \psi]\!] = [\![\phi]\!] \cup [\![\psi]\!]$ and $[\![\phi]\!] \cap [\![\neg\phi]\!] = \emptyset$, then it is possible to state two further conditions:

(Disjunction) For any sentences ϕ, ψ and χ:
if $\phi \approx \chi$ and $\psi \approx \chi$, then $\phi \vee \psi \approx \chi$.
(Rational Monotony) For any sentences ϕ, ψ and χ:
if $\phi \not\approx \neg\psi$ and $\phi \approx \chi$, then $\phi \wedge \psi \approx \chi$.

The proof-theoretic counterparts of properties such as these have been studied by Kraus, Lehmann, and Magidor [21, 23]. Their systems **C**, **P** and **R** consist of axioms and rules corresponding to the sentential versions of the properties of pragmatic entailment; thus, for example, the axiom corresponding to Identity is $\phi \hspace{1pt}\vdash\hspace{-6pt}\sim \phi$ and the rule corresponding to Cautious Monotony is:

$$\frac{\phi \hspace{1pt}\vdash\hspace{-6pt}\sim \psi, \quad \phi \hspace{1pt}\vdash\hspace{-6pt}\sim \chi}{\phi \wedge \psi \hspace{1pt}\vdash\hspace{-6pt}\sim \chi}.$$

The names will be used here to refer to the corresponding properties of pragmatic entailment, thus **C** consists of the sentential versions of Identity, Equivalence, Weakening, Cut and Cautious Monotony.[4] Then **P** consists of **C** together with Disjunction, and **R** consists of **P** together with Rational Monotony. Kraus, Lehmann and Magidor describe **C** as having "the rockbottom properties without which a system should not be called a logical system". However a weaker system, which will be called **D**, which satisfies all of the properties of **C** except perhaps Cautious Monotony, is also of interest.

These sets of properties can be thought of as rationality postulates which constrain the definition pragmatic entailment. It is easily shown that the conditions in **D** do not imply Cautious Monotony, that the conditions in **C** do not imply Disjunction, and that the conditions in **P** do not imply Rational Monotony. So **D**, **C**, **P** and **R** form a hierarchy of increasingly strong conditions on pragmatic entailment.

The pragmatic semantics given here should be contrasted with Shoham's Preference Logics [32]. The definition of these can be seen as a more restricted, but attractively simple alternative. Given the set of models I of a logic L and an arbitrary partial ordering $\prec$ on I, the preference logic $L_\prec$ is determined by its preferential entailment relation. A model $i \in I$ is said to be a preferred model of a sentence A iff i is a model of A and there is no model j of A such that $j \prec i$.

---

[4] Note that Equivalence is now needed as a basic condition. Alternatively, Permutation (for any sentences ϕ, ψ and χ, if $\phi \wedge \psi \approx \chi$ then $\psi \wedge \phi \approx \chi$) can be added and Equivalence derived.

Then a sentence A preferentially entails a sentence B (written $A \models_\prec B$) iff the preferred models of A are all models of B. Clearly Predicate Circumscription [27] is a preference logic; the preferred models of A are just the P-minimal models of A. Clearly also any preference logic is a (sceptical) pragmatic logic; $\bigcup[A]$ is just the set of preferred models of A. It is also clear that the converse is not true. A notable case is Default Logic [31], which resists preferential treatment, [33, Sec. 3.3.4], but which is readily shown to be a pragmatic logic in [3]. Indeed, any preference logic which satisfies the additional, natural, condition that if a chain of descending models $M_0 \succ M_1 \succ M_2 \succ \ldots$ contains a model of A, then the chain also contains a minimal model of A, satisfies the conditions **P**. However, Makinson [25] shows that Default Logic does not satisfy Cautious Monotony; although it does satisfy the conditions **D**. It is also worth noting that pragmatic entailment is sceptical, but that a credulous form can be defined by supplying an appropriate equivalence relation on the set of preferred models. Intuitively the models in an equivalence class are those in which the same pragmatic assumptions are made. For example in the case of the circumscription of a predicate P given an axiom A, put $i \sim j$ if i and j are P-minimal models of A and, for any name a, $i \in [\![P(a)]\!]$ iff $j \in [\![P(a)]\!]$.

4   Semantic pragmatics

While the semantic conditions discussed in the previous section constrain the choice of a pragmatic interpretation function, they generally do not determine it. Stalnaker makes a similar point regarding the pragmatic semantics for conditionals:

> [T]he *pragmatic problem of counterfactuals* ... [arises because] ... the formal properties of the conditional function, together with all of the *facts*, may not be sufficient to determine the truth value of a counterfactual. ... The task set by the problem is to find and defend criteria for choosing among these different valuations. [pp. 165-6]
>
> ... Just as we communicate effectively using quantified sentences without explicitly specifying a domain, so we can communicate effectively using conditional sentences without explicitly specifying ... [a selection] ... function. This suggests that there are further rules beyond those set down in the semantics, governing the use of conditional sentences. Such rules are the subject-matter of a *pragmatics* of conditionals. Very little can be said, at this point, about pragmatic rules for the use of conditionals ... [p. 176]

The pragmatic problem for pragmatic reasoning is thus that of choosing an appropriate pragmatic function. Indeed, as the pragmatic semantics shows, once the pragmatic interpretation function is given, pragmatic reasoning reduces to semantic reasoning; for example, if it is known that the pragmatic interpretation of the premises Φ, $\bigcup[\Phi]$, is $[\![\Phi']\!]$, then the pragmatic consequences of Φ are just the semantic consequences of Φ'.

However, while putting the matter this way may be enlightening from a theoretical viewpoint, it is unenlightening from a practical one. As suggested in

[3], pragmatic reasoning is better viewed as the *process* of *inferring* the appropriate context or contexts when interpreting the given. Interpreting a syntactic structure may involve both semantic and pragmatic interpretation rules. But while semantic interpretation rules can be applied in isolation and incrementally, pragmatic rules depend on a context of application, on an existing, partial, pragmatic context. Thus, for ampliative pragmatic reasoning at least, inferring a pragmatic context can be thought of as a bootstrapping process which may involve backtracking if a pragmatic rule is used inappropriately. During the process the existing partial pragmatic context and the current object of interpretation are used as the basis for the selection of an appropriate pragmatic rule with which to continue the interpretation, and the application of this rule results in the further extension of the pragmatic context. Backtracking may occur if the interpretation process does not result in a consistent, or perhaps even a coherent, interpretation of the structure. Examples of pragmatic rules are: Grice's maxims of cooperative conversation [15]; Kamp and Reyle's construction rule for pronouns, (CR.PRO), [18]; the enumerative induction rule (All observed P's are Q's, therefore all P's are Q's); Reiter's default rules [31]; the defeasible change and inertia axioms used in the formalization of common sense causal reasoning, for example those used in [4]; and the use of an inertia axiom in the representation of the changing mental states of rational agents [7–10]. Examples illustrating the inference process are: the incremental construction of Kamp and Reyle's discourse representation structures (each of which represents the evolving interpretation of an English discourse), Hempel's syntactical definition of enumerative induction [17]; the quasi-inductive definition of an extension of a default theory [31], and the chronological construction of preferred models in a causal theory [2, 4, 38].

The problem of the justification of formal pragmatic reasoning is, of course, a large one, so I will simply add a few remarks on the use of an empirical, example-based methodology. The identification of pragmatic rules and providing a means for applying them correctly is largely an empirical study. The aim is that the contexts which are generated by the formal theory correspond to the appropriate interpretations. However, there can be no foundational formal definition of appropriateness; for if there were, then the question of its appropriateness would arise. Consequently investigations in semantic pragmatics can at best result in *theses* (relating an intuitive notion of appropriateness for a species of pragmatic reasoning and the proposed formalization of it), rather than *theorems* (relating two formal theories). Semantic pragmatics is thus unlike pragmatic semantics.[5]

But theses are always open to counter-examples. A notorious case is Goodman's grue paradox [14], which led to the abandonment of the attempt to develop a qualitative definition of enumerative induction. Similar problems arose with formalizations of common sense causal reasoning, where conflicting pragmatic rules led to unintended models; for example, the Yale Shooting Problem [16] and its ilk. As a result, work in this area has appeared to outsiders (and even to

---

[5] A more extensive discussion along these lines, for the case of common sense causal reasoning, is given in [4].

56

insiders) to be obsessed with the correct formalization of a few "toy" examples; or, as McCarthy puts it, with drosophila. But, as Goodman put it, the study of problematic examples is significant from the standpoint of theory because they present "clinically pure cases that ... display to best advantage the symptoms of a widespread malady" [14, p. 80]. Indeed the difficulties raised by such examples have led some philosophers to go so far as to dismiss the possibility of a logical formalization of inductive inference, and consequently the attempt to automate it. For example, Putnam is doubtful that work in artificial intelligence will provide the answer: "in many ways the history of artificial intelligence is a repeat of the history of logical positivism (the second time perhaps as farce)" [30, p. 281].

However, it seems that there is every reason to be optimistic. The lesson of the Yale Shooting Problem was that instances of the inertia axiom have to be applied chronologically; thus Shoham proposed a preference relation based on the principle of chronological minimization [33]. In order to be able to represent both inertia and defeasible change, I propose that the preference relation is refined to what might be called prioritized chronological minimization [4]. This has the effect that if, at any time point, there is a conflict between instances of the change axiom and the inertia axiom, then the change axiom should be applied, and reflects the intuition that if there is a choice between an event succeeding and a fact persisting, the event should succeed. Moreover, in [6] I give a formal solution to Goodman's paradox, or, more accurately, to the difficult metaphysical version of the paradox which is concerned with objects changing colour over time. Informally, we conclude that emeralds first observed at time t or subsequently will be green rather than grue (that is, blue) by reasoning that emeralds observed to be green before t will remain green at t, and only then reasoning that emeralds first observed at t or thereafter will, by similarity, be green also. The persistence part of the argument depends on the fact that nothing about the evolving context of emerald observations before t leads us to expect that those emeralds which have been observed to be green will turn blue subsequently; we know of no events which will cause this to happen and so conclude by inertia that it will not. The similarity part of the argument then takes place at t in the partially extended context in which it has been concluded that the emeralds which were observed to be green beforehand are still green. In this context it is reasonable to conclude, by past and present similarity, that all emeralds are green, and it is inconsistent to conclude that all emeralds are grue (and hence now blue) because some emeralds are now green. In order to formalize the argument a defeasible induction axiom is added to the theory of common sense causal reasoning referred to above, and the principle of prioritized chronological minimization is refined further, with the effect that the induction axiom only applies if its use does not conflict with the change or inertia axioms, reflecting the intuition that we should reason about observed instances before speculating about unobserved ones. In addition, the implicit asymmetry underlying Goodman's Paradox is made explicit in the syntactic representation of the paradox and is reflected in the pragmatic interpretation of the theory; models in which emeralds remain green at t are preferred to those in which emeralds turn blue at t because additional events occur in the latter which turn green emeralds blue. A further application of the theory of common sense causal reasoning is its use in providing a formal pragmatics for a species of causal counterfactuals [5].

The general moral, if there is one, seems to be that although a great deal of unsuspected complexity lurks behind apparently simple pragmatic inferences, it seems that with enough attention to detail this complexity can be exposed and that formal theories can be developed which are capable of representing it faithfully. The process starts with the detailed analysis of problematic examples and, if the story is to have a happy ending, results in the uncovering not only of the asymmetry which underlies the intuitive interpretation of each particular example but also of the general principles used in the interpretation.

References

1. J. Bell (1991) Pragmatic Logics. Proc. *KR'91*, Morgan Kaufmann, San Mateo, California, pp. 50-60.
2. J. Bell (1995) Pragmatic Reasoning; A Model-Based Theory. J. Bell. In: *Applied Logic: How, What, and Why?*, L. Pólos and M. Masuch (Eds.), Kluwer Academic Publishers. Amsterdam, pp. 1-28.
3. J. Bell (1999) Pragmatic Reasoning: Inferring Contexts. Proc. *Context'99*. P. Bouquet et al. (Eds.), Lecture Notes in Artificial Intelligence 1688, Springer, Berlin, pp. 42-53.
4. J. Bell (2000) Primary and Secondary Events. Submitted to *Electronic Transactions on Artificial Intelligence.*[6]
5. J. Bell (2001) Causal Counterfactuals. To be presented at *Common Sense-2001.*[7]
6. J. Bell. (Forthcoming) Goodman's paradox and inductive logic.
7. J. Bell and Z. Huang (1997) Dynamic Goal Hierarchies. In: *Intelligent Agent Systems: Theoretical and Practical Issues.* L. Cavedon, A. Rao, W. Wobcke (Eds.), Lecture Notes in Artificial Intelligence 1027. Springer, Berlin, pp. 88-103.
8. J. Bell and Z. Huang (1999) Dynamic Obligation Hierarchies. In: *Norms, Logics and Information Systems: New Studies in Deontic Logic and Computer Science*, P. McNamara and H. Prakken (Eds.), Ios Press, Amsterdam, 1999, pp. 231-246.
9. J. Bell and Z. Huang (1999) Dynamic Belief Hierarchies. In: *Formal Models of Agents*, J.J. Meyer and P-Y. Schobbens (Eds.), Lecture Notes in Artificial Intelligence 1760, Springer, Berlin, pp. 20-32.
10. J. Bell and Z. Huang (1999) Seeing is believing: A common sense theory of the adoption of perception-based beliefs. *Artificial Intelligence for Engineering Design, Analysis and Manufacturing* 13, pp. 133-140.
11. S. Buvac and A. Mason (1993) Propositional logic of context. Proc. *AAAI-93*.
12. D.M. Gabbay (1985) Theoretical foundations for non-monotonic reasoning in expert systems. In: K.R. Apt (Ed.) *proceedings of the NATO Advanced Study Institute on Logics and Models of Concurrent Systems*, Springer, Berlin, 1985.
13. F. Giunchiglia and C. Ghidini (1998) Local models semantics, or contextual reasoning = Locality + compatibility. Proc. *KR'98*, pp. 282-289.

---

[6] Available at: www.ida.liu.se/ext/etai/rac/.
[7] Available at: www.cs.nyu.edu/cs/faculty/davise/commonsense01/.

14. N. Goodman (1955) *Fact, Fiction and Forecast*, 4th Edition, Harvard University Press, Cambridge, Mass.
15. P. Grice (1989) *Studies in the Way of Words*, Harvard University Press, Cambridge, Mass.
16. S. Hanks and D. McDermott (1987) Nonmonotonic logic and temporal projection. *Artificial Intelligence* 33, pp. 379-412.
17. C.G. Hempel (1943) A Purely Syntactical Definition of Confirmation, *Journal of Symbolic Logic*, 8 pp. 122-143.
18. H. Kamp and U. Reyle (1993) *From Discourse to Logic; Introduction to Modeltheoretic Semantics of Natural Language, Formal Logic and Discourse Representation Theory*, Kluwer Academic Publishers, Dordrecht.
19. D. Kaplan (1978) On the logic of demonstratives. *Journal of Philosophical Logic* 8, pp. 81-98.
20. S.C. Kleene (1952) *Introduction to Metamathematics*. North-Holland, Amsterdam.
21. S. Kraus, D. Lehmann and M. Magidor (1990) Nonmonotonic reasoning, preferential models and cumulative logics. Artificial Intelligence 44, pp. 167-207.
22. S. Kripke (1963) Semantical considerations on modal logic. *Acta Philosophica Fennica* 16, pp. 83-94.
23. D. Lehmann and M. Magidor (1992) What does a conditional knowledge base entail? *Artificial Intelligence* 55, pp. 1-60.
24. D. Lewis (1973) *Counterfactuals*. Basil Blackwell, Oxford.
25. D. Makinson (1989) General theory of cumulative inference. In: M. Reinfrank, J. de Kleer, M. Ginsberg and E. Sandewall (Eds.) *Non-Monotonic Reasoning*, Springer LNAI 346, Berlin.
26. D. Makinson (1994) General Patterns in Nonmonotonic Reasoning. In: *Handbook of Logic in Artificial Intelligence and Logic Programming*, D.M. Gabbay, C.J. Hogger and J.A. Robinson (Eds.), Vol. 3, pp. 35-110.
27. J. McCarthy (1980) Circumscription–A Form of Nonmonotonic Reasoning, *Artificial Intelligence* 13, pp. 27-39.
28. J. McCarthy (1993) Notes on formalizing context. Proc. *IJCAI'93*, pp. 555-560.
29. R. Montague (1970) Pragmatics and intensional logic. *Synthese* 22, pp. 68-94.
30. H. Putnam. Much Ado About Not Very Much (1988) In: *The Artificial Intelligence Debate*, S.R. Graubard (Ed.), MIT Press, Cambridge, Mass.
31. R. Reiter (1980) A logic for default reasoning. *Artificial Intelligence* 13, pp. 81-132.
32. Y. Shoham (1987) Nonmonotonic Logics: Meaning and Utility. In: Proc. *IJCAI'87*, pp. 23-28.
33. Y. Shoham (1988) *Reasoning About Change*, M.I.T. Press, Cambridge Mass.
34. R.C. Stalnaker (1975) A theory of conditionals. In *Causation and Conditionals*, E. Sosa (Ed.), Oxford University Press, Oxford, 1975, pp. 165-179. First published in N. Rescher (Ed.) *Studies in Logical Theory*, Basil Blackwell, Oxford, 1968.
35. R.C. Stalnaker (1998) On the Representation of Context, *Journal of Logic, Language and Information*, 7(1), 1998, pp. 3-19.
36. R.C. Stalnaker and R.H. Thomason (1970) A semantic analysis of conditional logic. *Theoria* 36, pp. 23-42.
37. S. Ullman (1996) *High-Level Vision; Object recognition and Visual Cognition*, MIT Press, Cambridge, Mass.
38. G. White, J. Bell and W.Hodges (1998) Building models of prediction theories. Proc. *KR'98*, pp. 557-568.

On the Dimensions of Context Dependence: Partiality, Approximation, and Perspective

Massimo Benerecetti[1], Paolo Bouquet[2], and Chiara Ghidini[3]

[1] Department of Physical Sciences – University of Naples,
Via Cintia, Monte S. Angelo – I-80126 Napoli, Italy
[2] Department of Computer and Management Sciences – University of Trento
Via Inama, 4 – I-38100 Trento, Italy
[3] Department of Computer Science – University of Liverpool
Liverpool L69 7ZF, U.K.
bene@na.infn.it   bouquet@cs.unitn.it   chiara@csc.liv.ac.uk

Abstract. In this paper we propose to re-read the past work on formalizing context as the search for a logic of the relationships between partial, approximate, and perspectival theories of the world. The idea is the following. We start from a very abstract analysis of a context dependent representation into three basic elements. We briefly show that all the mechanisms of contextual reasoning that have been studied in the past fall into three abstract forms: *expand/contract*, *push/pop*, and *shifting*. Moreover we argue that each of the three forms of reasoning actually captures an operation on a different dimension of variation of a context dependent representation, *partiality*, *approximation*, and *perspective*. We show how these ideas are formalized in the framework of MultiContext Systems, and briefly illustrate some applications.

1 Introduction

In the last twenty years, the notion of context has become more and more central in theories of knowledge representation in Artificial Intelligence (AI). The interest in context is not limited to AI, though. It is discussed and used in various disciplines that are concerned with a theory of representation, such as philosophy, cognitive psychology, pragmatics, linguistics. Despite this large amount of work, we must confess that we are very far from a general and unifying theory of context. Even if we restrict the focus to theories of representation and language, it is very difficult to see the relationship between different works on contextual reasoning. As an example, there are good pieces of work on utterance contexts, belief (and other intensional) contexts, problem solving contexts, and so on, but it is not clear whether they address different aspects of the same problem, or different problems with the same name.

In this paper we propose to re-read the past work on context as the search for a logic of the relationships between partial, approximate, and perspectival theories of the world. The idea is the following. We start from an very abstract analysis of a context dependent representation into three basic elements: a collection of parameters (the contextual dependencies), a value for each parameter, and a collection of linguistic expressions (the explicit representation). Then, we briefly show that all the mechanisms of contextual reasoning that have been studied in the past fall into three abstract forms, *expand/contract*, *push/pop*, and *shifting*, each corresponding to an operation on one of the basic elements of the representation. Then, we argue that each of the three forms of reasoning actually captures an operation on a different dimension of variation of a context dependent representation, *partiality*, *approximation*, and *perspective*. This leads us to the conclusion that, at a suitable level of abstraction, *a logic of contextual reasoning is precisely a logic of the relationships between partial, approximate, and perspectival theories of the world*. We show how these ideas are formalized in the framework of MultiContext systems, and briefly illustrate some applications.

2   Contexts as boxes

In general, a representation is called context dependent when its content cannot be established by simply composing the content of its parts. In addition, one has to consider extra information that is left implicit in the representation itself. In [13], this notion of a context dependent representation is illustrated by introducing the so-called metaphor of the box (figure 1). A context dependent representation has three basic elements: a collection of parameters $P_1, \ldots, P_n, \ldots$, a value V_i for each parameter P_i, and a collection of linguistic expressions that provide an explicit representation of a state of affairs or a domain. The intuition is that the content of what is inside the box depends (at least partially, and in a sense to be defined) upon the values of the parameters associated with box. For example, in a context in which the speaker is John (i.e. the value of the parameter 'speaker' is set to John), the content (the intension, if you prefer) of the pronoun 'I' will be John, but this is not the case in a context in which the speaker is Mary.

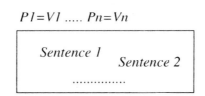

Fig. 1. Contexts as boxes.

Starting from the metaphor of the box, it is quite easy to see that a theory of contextual reasoning is faced with a number of philosophical problems. A partial list includes: What features of context should be included among the parameters? Is it possible to specify *all* the relevant parameters, or the collection is always incomplete? How is the representation affected when the collection of parameters or their values changes? Can we get rid of parameters and get a context independent representation of the contents of a box? What is the relationship between the parameters of different boxes? How does this relationship affect the relationship between the contents of different boxes?

Since the goal of this paper is not to provide a general foundation for a theory of context, we will not propose an answer to the issues above. Indeed, the analysis of the patterns of contextual reasoning is meant to hold no matter what solutions one adopts to these fundamental issues.

3 Forms of contextual reasoning

Mechanisms for contextual reasoning have been studied in different disciplines, though with different goals. A very partial list includes:*reflection* and *metareasoning* [22, 14], *entering and exiting context, lifting, transcending context* [16, 20, 5], *local reasoning, switch context* [12, 4], *parochial reasoning* and *context climbing* [7], *changing viewpoint* [1], *focused reasoning* [17]). As a matter of fact, it is very difficult to see the relationship between these different works. We try to put some order in this situation by addressing the problem of identifying the general patterns of contextual reasoning, namely the general mechanisms that people use to reason with information (i) whose representation depend on a collection of contextual parameters, and (ii) which is scattered across a multiplicity of different contexts.

Our proposal is that all the forms of contextual reasoning that are discussed in the literature fall into three basic patterns, according to the element of the box that they affect: the representation, the collection of parameters, and the parameters' values.

Expand/Contract. A first general form of contextual reasoning (depicted in Figure 2) is based on the intuition that the explicit representation associated with a specific context does not contain all the facts potentially available to a reasoner, but only a subset of them. As a consequence, depending on the circumstances, the subset which is explicitly taken into account can be expanded (typically because some new input from the external environment makes it necessary to consider a larger collection of facts), or contracted (typically because the reasoner realizes that some facts are not relevant on a given occasion). An example of expansion is the Glasgow-London-Moscow (GLM) example [19, 4]: when reasoning about traveling from Glasgow to Moscow via London, we normally do not include in the problem solving context the precondition that one must be dressed to get on a plane; however, if one's clothes are stolen at London airport, being clothed becomes a relevant precondition for the success of the travel plan, and therefore the original problem solving context must be expanded with facts about social conventions and buying clothes.

In general, expansion and contraction are used to adjust a particular representation to a problem or to a given goal. The way problem solving contexts are built in CYC (using the strategy of lift-and-solve [16]), the mechanism of building appropriate mental spaces [8] or partitioned representations [7], and the process

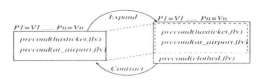

Fig. 2. Expand/Contract.

of selecting the relevant facts to interpret an utterance [21] are typical examples
of this pattern of contextual reasoning.

Push/Pop. The content of a context dependent representation is partly encoded
in the parameters outside the box, and partly in the sentences inside the box.
Some authors propose reasoning mechanisms for altering the balance between
what is explicitly encoded inside the box and what is left implicit (i.e. encoded
in the parameters). Intuitively, the idea is that we can move information from
the collection of parameters outside the box to the representation inside the box,
and vice versa. We call these two mechanisms *push* and *pop* to suggest a partial
analogy with the operations of adding (pushing) and extracting (popping) elements from a stack. In one direction, *push* adds a contextual parameter to the
collection outside the box and produces a flow of information from the inside to
the outside of the box, that is part of what was explicitly encoded in the representation is encoded in some parameter. In the opposite direction, *pop* removes
a contextual parameter from the collection outside the box and produces a flow
of information from the outside to the inside, that is the information that was
encoded in a parameter is now explicitly represented inside the box.

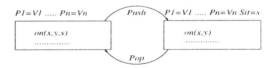

Fig. 3. Push/Pop.

Consider, for instance, the well known AboveTheory scenario, introduced
in [20]. The fact that block x is on block y in a situation s is represented as
$on(x, y, s)$ in a context c with no parameter for situations. This is because in
some cases we want to leave implicit the dependence on the situation s (typically,
when we don't want to take situations into account in reasoning). This means
that the situation can be encoded as a parameter, and the representation can
be simplified to $on(x, y)$. Push is the reasoning mechanism which allows us to
move from $on(x, y, s)$ to $on(x, y)$ (left-to-right arrow in figure 3), whereas pop is
the reasoning mechanism which allows us to move back to $on(x, y, s)$ (right-to-
left arrow in figure 3). Hence, push and pop capture the interplay between the
collection of parameters outside the box and the representation inside the box.

It is worth noting that the mechanism of entering and exiting context proposed by McCarthy and others can be viewed as an instance of push and pop.

63

Suppose we start with a sentence such as $c_0c : p$, whose intuitive meaning is that in context c_0 it is true that in context c the proposition p is true. The context sequence c_0c can be viewed as the reification of a collection of parameters. Exiting c pops the context sequence, and the result is the formula $c_0 : ist(c, p)$, where the dependence on c is made explicit in the representation $ist(c, p)$ ($ist(c, p)$ is the main formula of McCarthy's formalism, asserting that a p is true in context c); conversely, entering c pushes the context sequence and results in the formula $c_0c : p$, making the dependence on c implicit in the context sequence. Other examples of push/pop are: *reflection up* to pop the collection of parameters and *reflection down* to push it in [14]; the rule of *context climbing* to pop the collection of parameters, and the rule of *space initialization* to push it in [7].

Shifting. Shifting changes the value of one or more contextual parameter, without changing the collection of parameters. The name 'shifting' is inspired to the concept of shifting in [18]. The intuition is that changing the value of the parameters shifts the interpretation of what is represented inside the box.

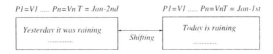

Fig. 4. Shifting.

The simplest illustration of shifting is again indexical expressions. The fact that on January 1st it is raining is represented as 'Today is raining' in a context in which time is set to January 1st, but it is represented as 'Yesterday it was raining' if the value of time changes to January 2nd. As it is shown in figure 4, *shifting* is the reasoning mechanism which allows us to move from one representation to the other by changing the value of the parameter time, provided we know the relationship between the two parameter's values. Another very common example of shifting is when the viewpoint changes, e.g. when two people look at the same room from opposite sides (what is right for the first will be left for the other). A third case is categorization. For the supporters of team A, the members and the supporters of team B are opponents, and vice versa for the supporters of team B. And the examples can be multiplied.

In the literature, we can find different instances of shifting. Kaplan's notion of *character* is the semantical counterpart of this reasoning mechanism with indexical languages; Guha and McCarthy formalize a form of shifting using the notion of *lifting* [16]; Dinsmore introduces the notion of *secondary context*.

4 Dimensions of context dependence

Our next step is to show that the three forms of contextual reasoning actually operate each on a fundamental dimensions of a context dependent representation: *partiality*, *approximation*, and *perspective*. We start with a more precise characterization of partiality, approximation, and perspective.

Partiality. We say that *a representation is partial when it describes only a subset of a more comprehensive state of affairs.* We observe that the notion of partiality can be analyzed from two different perspectives: metaphysically, a theory is partial if it does not cover the entire universe; however, cognitively, a representation is partial if it does not cover the totality of what an agent can talk about. For our present purposes, either perspective is acceptable, even though our general attitude is in favor of the cognitive view.

Perhaps the more intuitive example of partial theories are domain specific theories. For instance, a theory about the theory about the Italian cuisine is partial because it does not provide information about Indian or French cuisine, about soccer, about quantum mechanics. A different usage of partial theories is in problem solving. Given a problem, people seem to be capable of circumscribing what knowledge is relevant to solve it, and disregard the rest. In this case, assumptions on what is relevant act as contextual parameters. Partial theories are also used in theories of linguistic communication. When a speaker says something to a hearer, it is assumed that the latter interprets what the speaker said in some context. According to [21], '[a] context is a psychological construct, a subset of the hearer's assumptions about the world'. Such a context includes the set of facts that the hearer takes to be relevant in order to assign the correct interpretation to what the speaker said. In this sense, it is a partial theory.

Partiality is a relative notion. Intuitively, there is a partial order between partial representations. Therefore a representation can be more or less partial of another one. Two partial representations may also overlap. We do not further discuss these aspect here. We only need to make clear the idea that partiality is a dimension along which a representation may vary.

Approximation. We say that a *a representation is approximate when it abstracts away some aspects of a given state of affairs.* A representation of the blocks world in terms of the binary predicates $on(x, y)$ e $above(x, y)$ is approximate, because the time (situation) is abstracted away.

As for partiality, approximation is a relative notion: a representation is approximate because it abstracts away details that another representation takes into account. The representation $on(x, y)$ and $above(x, y)$ is more approximate than the representation $on(x, y, s)$ and $above(x, y, s)$ because the first abstracts away the dependence on the situation. Of course, an open point is whether there is such a thing as a non approximate representation of a state of affairs. This would be a sort of least approximate representation, namely a representation which is less approximate than anyone else. We avoid committing to one position or the other; here we are interested in the reasoning mechanisms that allow us to switch from a more to a less approximate representation (and vice versa), and not in the epistemological status of representations.

Perspective. A third dimension along which a representation may vary is perspective. We say that *a representation is perspectival when it encodes a spatio-temporal, logical, or cognitive point of view on a state of affairs.*

The paradigmatic case of spatio-temporal perspective is a given by indexical languages. A sentences such as 'It's raining (here)(now)' is a perspectival representation because it encodes a spatial perspective (i.e. the location at which the sentences are used, the speaker's current 'here') and a temporal perspective (i.e. the time at which the sentences are used, the speaker's current 'now'). The philosophical tradition shows us that some sentences (e.g. 'Ice floats on water') encode a logical perspective as well, because they implicitly refer to 'this' world, namely the world in which the 'here' and 'now' of the speaker belong (the same sentence, if uttered in a world different from our world, might well be false). Thus Kaplan includes a world among the features that define a context, and uses this world to interpret the propositional operator 'actually'.

Indexicals are not the only type of expressions that encode a physical perspective. Suppose, for example, that two agents look at the same object (for example the magic box of figure 5). Because of their different viewpoints, the representation of what they see is completely different, and the same ball can be described as being on the right by **Side** and as being on the left by **Front**.

A subtler form of perspective is what we call cognitive perspective. It has to do with the fact that many representation encode a point of view which includes a collection of beliefs, intentions, goals, and so on. Cognitive perspective is very important in the analysis of what is generally called an *intensional context*, such as a belief context. John and Mary may have dramatically different beliefs about Scottish climate, even if they represent the same universe of discourse (or portion of the world) at the same level of approximation. We don't see any other way of making sense of this difference than that of accepting the existence of a cognitive perspective, which is part of what determines the context of a representation.

At this point, we are ready to justify our claim that the three forms of contextual reasoning are precisely mechanisms that operate on the dimensions of partiality, approximations, and perspective:

- Expand/Contract is the reasoning mechanism that allows us to vary the degree of partiality by varying the amount of knowledge which is used in the representations of the world.
- Push/Pop is the reasoning mechanism that allows us to vary the degree of approximation by regulating the interplay between the collection of parameters outside and the explicit representation inside a box.
- Shifting is the reasoning mechanism that allows us to change the perspective by taking into account the 'translation' of a representation into another when the value of some contextual parameter is changed.

As a consequence of our claim, a logic of contextual reasoning must formalize the reasoning mechanisms of expand/contract push/pop, and shifting and use them to represent the relationship between partial, approximate, and perspectival representations. Our final step is to show that MultiContext systems satisfy this requirement, and to validate this assertion by analyzing in detail some applications of MultiContext systems.

5 A logic of contextual reasoning: MultiContext Systems

In the past, various logics have been proposed which formalize one aspect or the other of such a logic of contextual reasoning. For example, Kaplan's logic of demonstratives is a logic which allows only for a multiplicity of perspectival representations (partiality and approximation are left unchanged from one context to the other) and, consequently, provides only mechanisms for shifting (in the form of the semantic notion of character). Buvač and Mason's propositional logic of context allows for a multiplicity of partial, approximate, and perspectival representations, and provides the machinery for expand/contract, push/pop, and shifting; however, it formalizes a quite weak form of partiality (via the use of partial functions for interpreting a global language) and only a special form of push/pop (i.e. making explicit or implicit the context itself).

MultiContext systems (MCS) [14], and their *Local Model Semantics* (LMS) [9], provide a logic for contextual reasoning based on the principles of *locality* and *compatibility*. These principles impose that:

1. each context c_i is associated with a different formal language L_i, used to describe what is true in that context. The semantics of L_i is *local* to the context itself. Therefore each context has its own set of local models M_i, and local satisfiability relation $\models_i$;
2. the relations between different contexts are modeled by means of *compatibility* relations between (sets of) local models of the different contexts.

We believe that principle of locality and principle of compatibility provide LMS and MCS with the capability of being a suitable logic of the relation between partial, approximate, and perspectival representations. For lack of space, we focus the discussion of our claim on LMS. A similar analysis applies to the axiomatic system MCS.

By associating distinct languages and local semantics to different contexts, LMS allows for different partial, approximate, and perspectival representations. The most intuitive case is partial representations. Simple examples are: the language might contain only a subset of a more comprehensive set of symbols, the class of models might satisfy only a subset of a more comprehensive set of axioms, or rules of well-formedness. Second, approximate representations. A simple case is the AboveTheory example: a context might contain the binary predicate $on(x,y)$ or the ternary predicate $on(x,y,s)$ depending on the fact that the it abstracts away or represents the dependence on the situation. Third, perspectival representations. An example is the fact that the truth value of a formula in a context might depend on the perspective from which the world is represented. The truth value of the formula might change in different contexts, depending on the corresponding shift of perspective.

By modeling compatibility relations between different contexts as relations among the (sets of) local models of the different contexts LMS allows one to represent the relations existing between a multiplicity of partial, approximate, and perspectival representations of the world. For instance, if the relation contains a pair $\langle models(c_1), models(c_2) \rangle$ composed by a set $models(c_1)$ of models

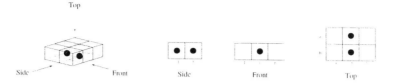

Fig. 5. The magic box and its partial views.

of context c_1 and a set $models(c_2)$ of models of context c_2, and all the models in $models(c_1)$ are obtained as the expansion of a model in $models(c_2)$, then it is easy to observe that c_2 describes a portion of the world which is a subset of the portion described by c_1. By studying and classifying the different relations existing among the (sets of) local models of the different contexts we might. in principle, try to classify the many different relations existing among different partial, approximate, and perspectival representations. Unfortunately, even if we restrict ourselves to model each context c_i by mean of a first order language and the classical semantics. we must admit that we are still far from having a (even partial) classification of these many different relations. Although some of them are very easy to identify, as the relation of expansion mentioned above, relations between partial, approximate and perspectival representations may be, in general, much trickier. Nonetheless, by analyzing existing applications of LMS and MCS we are able to show that LMS and MCS have been used to represent context-based representation and reasoning in terms of the relations among partial, approximate, and perspectival representations. In the rest of the section briefly show the result of our analysis. This provides a first evidence of the fact that LMS is a logic of the relations between partial, approximate and perspectival representations. This provides also a fist motivation for a future work on studying and classifying the many different relations existing among different partial, approximate, and perspectival representations.

Viewpoints. A paradigmatic example of reasoning with viewpoint is the Magic Box (MB) example, developed in [3].

> There are three observers, **Top**, **Side**, and **Front**, each having a partial view of a box as shown in the top part of Figure 5. **Top** sees the box from the top, and **Side** and **Front** see the box from two different sides. The box consists of six sectors, each sector possibly containing a ball. The box is "magic" and **Side** and **Front** cannot distinguish the depth inside it. The bottom part of Figure 5 shows the views of the three agents corresponding to the scenario depicted in the top part. **Top**, **Side**, and **Front** decide to test their new computer program ϵ by submitting the following puzzle to it. **Side** and **Front** tell ϵ their partial views. Then they ask ϵ to guess **Top**'s view of the box.

[3] describes a formalization of the reasoning process of ϵ in solving the puzzle, by mean of the four contexts depicted in figure 6. Contexts **Side** and **Front** contain the program's representation of **Side**'s and **Front**'s knowledge:

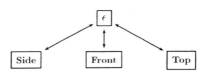

Fig. 6. The four contexts in the MB example.

context **Top** contains the program's representation of **Top**'s knowledge, and is the context in which it will try to build the solution; context ϵ contains the knowledge that the computer program has about the game, namely what the relations among the other contexts are.

According to our classification of dimensions of a context dependent representation, the representations of the different contexts **Side** and **Front**, **Top**, and ϵ may vary along three dimensions: partiality, approximation, and perspective. Focusing on partiality, the different contexts are related to different specific domains. For instance, **Side** can only talk about the (non) presence of a ball in the left or right sector it sees, **Front** can talk about the (non) presence of a ball in the left, or the central or right sector it sees, **Top** can talk about the presence of a ball in each one of the six sectors, while ϵ needs only to talk about how the pieces of knowledge contained in each one of the contexts above are related to each other. Focusing on approximation, we notice that the description of (a portion of) the world in **Side**, **Front**, and **Top** is given in terms of balls and sectors of the box, whereas the description in context ϵ concerns how to relate the information coming from the different observers. In order to do this, context ϵ needs to make explicit some information that was implicit in the observers' contexts. In particular, it needs to make explicit what information comes from what observer. This is an example of push/pop and is related to the different levels of approximation of the different contexts. In this case we say that the representation in **Side**, **Front**, and **Top** is more approximate than the one in ϵ, because the first ones abstract away what information comes from what observer. Focusing on perspective, each of the observer's contexts expresses knowledge about the box which depends on the observer's physical perspective. For example, the fact that **Side** sees a ball in the left sector (from his point of view) is different from **Front** seeing a ball in the left sector (from his point of view). Since their perspectives are different, the same description (e.g., 'A ball is in the left sector') may, thus, have a different meaning in different contexts.

Formally, the specific domains of **Side**, **Front**, and **Top** are described by three different propositional languages $L_{\textbf{Side}}$, $L_{\textbf{Front}}$ and $L_{\textbf{Top}}$ built up from the sets $AP_{\textbf{Side}} = \{l, r\}$, $AP_{\textbf{Front}} = \{l, c, r\}$, and $AP_{\textbf{Top}} = \{a1, a2, a3, b1, b2, b3\}$ of propositional constants (where l means that the observer sees a ball in the *left* sector, c means that the observer sees a ball in the *central* sector, and so on) To account for the specific domain of ϵ, and its shift in the approximation level described above, the language L_{ϵ} contains a set $\{Side, Front, Top\}$ of constant symbols for each one of the contexts above, a set of constant symbol "ϕ" for each formula ϕ that can be expressed in the languages $L_{\textbf{Side}}$ or $L_{\textbf{Front}}$ or $L_{\textbf{Top}}$, and a binary predicate $ist(c, ``\phi")$, whose intuitive meaning is that formula $\phi \in L_c$ is true in context c (see [20]). In order to solve the puzzle ϵ needs to relate information contained in different contexts associated with different levels of approximations. In particular [3] needs to formalize the relation denoted as arrows connecting contexts in figure 6. This is done by imposing a compatibility relation between the models of each observers' context c and models of the context ϵ. To state the correspondence between a formula ϕ in each observers' context c and the formula $ist(c, ``\phi")$ (denoting the same fact at a different degree of approximation) in context $\epsilon$, if a formula of the form $ist(c, ``\phi")$ is a theorem in ϵ, then the formula ϕ must be a theorem in c, and vice-versa. The different perspectival representations are formalized in [3] by the different (initial) axioms satisfied in each observer's context and the relations between them are explicitly stated as axioms in context ϵ.

Belief contexts. LMS and MCS have been applied to formalize different aspects of intentional contexts, and in particular belief contexts (see e.g.,[15,6]). An example is a puzzle described in [2], where LMS and MCS are used to solve the problem of the opaque and transparent reading of belief reports.

A computer program ϵ knows that Mr. A believes that the president of the local football team is Mr. M and that Mr. B believes that the president is Mr. C. The computer program knows also that Mr. B knows that A believes that the president of the local football team is Mr. M. Actually, Mr. B is right, and the computer program knows that. Now, B tells ϵ: "Mr. A believes that the president of the local football team is a corruptor". How will ϵ interpret the sentence?

The program is a little puzzled, since the question has two possible answers: (1) Mr. A's belief is referred to Mr. M (since Mr. A is the subject of the belief). This is an instance of opaque reading. (2) Mr. A's belief is referred to Mr. C (since it is Mr. B who is speaking). This is an instance of transparent reading.

We are not interested here in the solution of the puzzle (the interested reader may refer to [2]), but in analyzing the representations of the different contexts involved in the formalization.

The formalization is based on the notion of *belief context*. A belief context is a representation of a collection of beliefs that a reasoner (in this example, the program) ascribes to an agent (including itself) from a given perspective. Possible perspectives are: the beliefs that the program ascribes to itself (e.g., that Mr. B believes that Mr. A believes that the president of the local football team is a corruptor); the beliefs that the program ascribes to Mr. B (e.g., that Mr. A believes that the president of the local football team is a corruptor); the beliefs that the program ascribes to Mr. B about Mr. A (e.g., that the president of the local football team is a corruptor). The belief contexts that the program can build in this example can be organized in a structure like that presented in figure 7.

ϵ represents the context containing the beliefs that the program ascribes to itself, **A** is the context containing the beliefs that the program ascribes to Mr. A.

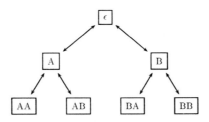

Fig. 7. The structure of belief contexts

B is the context containing the beliefs that the program ascribes to Mr. *B*, **BA** is the context containing the beliefs that the program ascribes to Mr. *A* from Mr. *B*'s perspective, and so on.

The formalization of the different contexts in figure 7 may vary along the three dimensions of contextual dependence. Focusing on partiality, the different contexts are related to different sets of beliefs. For instance, **A** is the context containing the beliefs that the program ascribes to Mr. *A*, whereas **B** is the context containing the beliefs that the program ascribes to Mr. *B*. Focusing on approximation, we notice that each context in the hierarchy must be able to to talk about beliefs contained in each one of the contexts above. In order to do this it needs to make explicit some information that was implicit in the observers' contexts. In particular, it needs to make explicit what beliefs are contained in what context. The relations involving different contexts associated with different degrees of approximations are the one denoted as arrows in figure 6 and are similar to the ones described in the MB example. Focusing on perspective, each of the belief contexts expresses knowledge about the world which depends on the cognitive perspective of the agents, from the point of view of the computer program. For instance, Mr. *B* will refer to Mr. *C* as "the president of the local football team", whereas Mr. *A* will refer to Mr. *C* as Mr. *M*.

Integration of different information sources. LMS and MCS have been applied to formalize the integration of information coming from different information sources. [10, 11] contain the formal definitions and motivating examples. Let us focus on a simple example.

A mediator *m* of an electronic market place collects information about fruit prices from 1, 2, and 3 and integrates it in a unique homogeneous database. Customers that need information about fruit prices may therefore submit a single query to the mediator instead of contacting the sellers.

The formalization of the exchange of information in this example based on the four contexts and the information flows depicted in figure 8. Circles represent contexts associated to the different databases and arrows represent information flow between contexts (databases).

The representations of the different contexts in figure 8 may have different degrees of partiality, as each database is associated to a specific domain. For instance, the sellers might provide different subsets of fruits and therefore the domains of their databases are different. Focusing on approximation, the domain

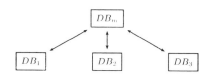

Fig. 8. Contexts in the mediator example.

of fruits can be represented at different level of details by different sellers. E.g., database 1 may contain prices for red apples and yellow apples, while database 2 and 3 abstracts away the dependence on the color and do not make this distinction. Focusing on perspective, prices of the different sellers might be not homogeneous, depending on their particular viewpoint. E.g., prices of database 1 don't include taxes, while prices of database 2, 3 and the mediator do.

Formally, the specific domains of the different databases are described by using different first order languages. Each database is associated with a different interpretation domain. The compatibility relation between the different levels of approximations in the fruit domains is formalized by using *domain relations*, i.e. relations between the interpretation domains of the different databases. A domain relation may, for instance, relate a "more abstract" object (e.g. apple) in the domain of a database to a set of "less abstract" objects (e.g. red−apple, green−apple) in the domain of another database. Compatibility relations between the different perspectival views contained in the databases are formalized by using *view constraints*, i.e. relations between formulae contained in different languages (databases). For instance every time the models of database 1 satisfy the formula $hasprice(x, y)$ (meaning that item x has price y, then the models of the mediator database must satisfy the formula $\exists y' hasprice(x, y') \land y' = y + (0.07 * y)$ (meaning that the same item x has price y' which is obtained adding the amount of taxes to y.

6 Conclusions

In the paper, we have not presented a new theory about partiality, approximation, or perspective. Instead, we have shown that the work on contextual reasoning in AI (and not only in AI) can be re-read as an attempt of providing a logic of the mechanisms that govern the relationship between partial, approximate, and perspectival representations of the world.

In this sense, the paper is only a preliminary step. Indeed, it opens a whole field of research, both philosophical and logical. Our next step will be a formal study of a logic of partiality, approximation, and perspective in the framework of LMS and MCS. In particular, we are interested in finding the compatibility relations (and the relative bridge rules) involved in the corresponding reasoning mechanisms. This, we hope, will be part of a new approach to a theory of knowledge representation, in which context will play a crucial role.

References

1. G. Attardi and M. Simi. A formalisation of viewpoints. *Fundamenta Informaticae*, 23(2–4):149–174, 1995.
2. M. Benerecetti, P. Bouquet, and C. Ghidini. Formalizing Belief Reports — The Approach and a Case Study. In *Proc. of the 8th International Conference on Artificial Intelligence, Methodology, Systems, and Applications*, volume 1480 of *LNAI*, Springer, 1998.
3. M. Benerecetti, P. Bouquet, and C. Ghidini. Contextual Reasoning Distilled. *Journal of Theoretical and Experimental Artificial Intelligence*, 12(3):279–305, 2000.
4. P. Bouquet and F. Giunchiglia. Reasoning about Theory Adequacy. A New Solution to the Qualification Problem. *Fundamenta Informaticae*, 23(2–4):247–262, 1995.
5. S. Buvač and I. A. Mason. Propositional logic of context. *Proc. of the 11th National Conference on Artificial Intelligence*, pages 412–419, 1993.
6. A. Cimatti and L. Serafini. Multi-Agent Reasoning with Belief Contexts: the Approach and a Case Study. In *Intelligent Agents: Proceedings of ATAL '94*, number 890 in LNCS. Springer, 1995.
7. J. Dinsmore. *Partitioned Representations*. Kluwer Academic Publishers, 1991.
8. G. Fauconnier. *Mental Spaces: aspects of meaning construction in natural language*. MIT Press, 1985.
9. C. Ghidini and F. Giunchiglia. Local Models Semantics, or Contextual Reasoning = Locality + Compatibility. *Artificial Intelligence*, To Appear.
10. C. Ghidini and L. Serafini. Distributed First Order Logics. In *Frontiers Of Combining Systems 2*, Studies in Logic and Computation. Research Studies Press, 1998.
11. C. Ghidini and L. Serafini. Information Integration for Electronic Commerce. In *Proceedings of the Workshop on Agent Mediated Electronic Trading (AMET'98)*, volume 1571 of *LNAI*. Springer Verlag, 1998.
12. F. Giunchiglia. Contextual reasoning. *Epistemologia, special issue on I Linguaggi e le Macchine*, XVI:345–364, 1993.
13. F. Giunchiglia and P. Bouquet. Introduction to contextual reasoning. An Artificial Intelligence perspective. In *Perspectives on Cognitive Science*. NBU Press, Sofia, 1997.
14. F. Giunchiglia and L. Serafini. Multilanguage hierarchical logics (or: how we can do without modal logics). *Artificial Intelligence*, 65:29–70, 1994.
15. F. Giunchiglia, L. Serafini, E. Giunchiglia, and M. Frixione. Non-Omniscient Belief as Context-Based Reasoning. In *Proc. of the 13th International Joint Conference on Artificial Intelligence*, pages 548–554, Chambery, France, 1993.
16. R.V. Guha. Contexts: a Formalization and some Applications. Technical Report ACT-CYC-423-91, MCC, Austin, Texas, 1991.
17. J. E. Laird, A. Newell, and P.S. Rosenbloom. Soar: An architecture for general intelligence. *Artificial Intelligence*, 33(3):1–4 64, 1987.
18. D. Lewis. Index, Context, and Content. In S. Kranger and S. Ohman, editors, *Philosophy and Grammar*, pages 79–100. D. Reidel Publishing Company, 1980.
19. J. McCarthy. Overcoming an Unexpected Obstacle. Unpublished, 1991.
20. J. McCarthy. Notes on Formalizing Context. In *Proc. of the 13th International Joint Conference on Artificial Intelligence*, 1993.
21. Dan Sperber and Deirdre Wilson. *Relevance. Communication and Cognition*. Basil Blackwell, 1986.
22. R.W. Weyhrauch. Prolegomena to a Theory of Mechanized Formal Reasoning. *Artificial Intelligence*, 13(1):133–176, 1980.

Context of Utterance and Intended Context

Claudia Bianchi

Department of Philosophy - University of Padua and University of Genoa (Italy)
via Balbi 4 – 16126 Genova (Italy)
cbianchi@vc.unipmn.it
http://www.dif.unige.it/epi/hp/bianchi/

Abstract. In this paper I expose and criticise the distinction between pure indexicals and demonstratives, held by David Kaplan and John Perry. I oppose the context of material production of the utterance to the "intended context" (the context of interpretation, i.e. the context the speaker indicates as semantically relevant): this opposition introduces an intentional feature into the interpretation of pure indexicals. As far as the indexical *I* is concerned, I maintain that we must distinguish between the material producer of the utterance containing *I* and the "intended agent of the context" - i.e. the individual designated by the material producer as the *responsible* for the utterance.

1 Introduction

The aim of this paper is to challenge a distinction well established in semantics since Kaplan's and Perry's works: the distinction between pure indexicals (or automatic indexicals) like *I, now, here,* and demonstratives (or intentional indexicals), like *he, she, that.* To this end, I oppose the context of material production of the utterance to the "intended context" (the context of interpretation, i.e. the context the speaker indicates as semantically relevant): this opposition introduces an intentional feature into the interpretation of the pure indexicals. As far as the indexical *I* is concerned, I maintain that we must distinguish between the material producer of the utterance containing *I* and the "intended agent of the context" - i.e. the individual designated by the material producer as the *responsible* for the utterance.

2 Indexicality

As it is well known, indexicals are referential expressions having a reference only given a context of utterance: different occurrences of the same indexical as a type can have different referents. The conventional meaning of an indexical sentence like

(1) *I am Italian,*

independently of any context whatsoever, cannot determine the truth conditions of the sentence: to evaluate the sentence, the referent of *I* must be identified. The truth conditions of an indexical sentence are thus indirectly determined, as a function of the context of utterance of the sentence, and in particular as a function of the values of the indexicals. According to Kaplan and Perry, a function is assigned to each indexical expression as a type: the *character*, in Kaplan's terminology, or the *role*, in Perry's terminology. Given a context, the character determines the *content* (the intension) of the occurrence – which is a function from circumstances of evaluation (possible world and time) to truth values.

2.1 The Distinction between Indexicals and Demonstratives

In "Demonstratives", Kaplan introduces the distinction between pure indexicals and demonstratives.[1] As I said, the language conventions associate with a pure indexical as a type a rule fixing the reference of the occurrences of the expression in context. The semantic value of an indexical (its content, its truth conditional import) is thus determined by a conventional rule and by a contextual parameter, where the mode of context-dependence itself is determined by this same conventional rule. The character of an indexical encodes the specific contextual co-ordinate that is relevant for the determination of its semantic value: for *I* the relevant parameter will be the speaker of the utterance, for *here* the place of the utterance, for *now*, the time of the utterance, and so on[2]: the designation is then automatic, "given meaning and public contextual facts".[3]

Conversely, the meaning of a demonstrative, like *she* in the sentence

(2) *She is Italian,*

by itself doesn't give an automatic rule individuating, once a context is given, the referent of the expression. The semantics of *she* cannot determine unambiguously its reference: if, in the context of utterance of (2), for instance, there is more than one woman, the expression *she* can identify any woman in the same way. According to Kaplan, the occurrence of a demonstrative must be supplemented by a *demonstration*, an act of demonstration, like a pointing.[4] This could be expressed[5] by saying that a demonstrative as a type, unlike an indexical as a type, doesn't have a character: only an *occurrence* of a demonstrative acquires a character, once it is associated with a

---

[1] [11].

[2] The character is not a component of the proposition, but it determines the reference, which, in turn, is a component of the proposition expressed; cf. [11], p. 497: "The indexicals may have a limited kind of specific descriptive meaning relevant to the features of a context of use... But in any case, the descriptive meaning of a directly referential term is no part of the propositional content".

[3] [24], p. 595.

[4] [11], p. 490: "typically, though not invariably, a (visual) presentation of a local object discriminated by a pointing"; cf. [12], p. 389.

[5] According to the Reichenbachian view, as held by Perry [24] and Garcia Carpintero [9].

demonstration.[6] The relevant semantic unit is then the demonstrative associated with a demonstration.[7]

Consequently, for Kaplan in "Demonstratives", the act of demonstration is *semantically relevant* in order to complete the character of a demonstrative. The act of demonstration that could accompany a pure indexical is, in turn, either emphatic (as when one utters *I* pointing to oneself) or irrelevant (as when one utters *I* pointing to someone else: in this case, the referent of *I* remains the speaker): once the context of utterance is fixed, the linguistic rules governing the use of the indexicals determine completely, automatically and unambiguously their reference, no matter what the speaker's intentions are.

In "Afterthoughts", Kaplan modifies his own theory. He now acknowledges that even a gesture associated with an occurrence of a demonstrative, working as an act of demonstration, may be insufficient to disambiguate the expression. Just imagine the sentence

(3) *I like that*

uttered by someone pointing clearly and unambiguously to a child: the expression *that* could designate the child, or his coat, or a button of the coat, or the colour of the coat or, for that matter, any spatial region or molecule between the speaker's finger and the child. The gesture hasn't then a semantic role anymore; for Kaplan the relevant factor is now "the speaker's directing intention". Every occurrence of the same demonstrative as a type has to be associated not with an act of demonstration but with an intention.[8] Of course an intention, to be semantically relevant, must be made available or communicated to the addressee[9], and for that purpose the speaker can exploit any feature of the context, words, gestures, relevance or uniqueness of the referent in the context of utterance; nevertheless, this exploitation of the context has

---

[6] As it is shown in Kaplan's formal treatment of demonstratives, where every occurrence of a demonstrative has its own character - and it is treated as a different expression: see [6], pp. 101-104, and [9], pp. 552-553.

[7] [11], p. 492: "The referent of a pure indexical depends on context, and the referent of a demonstrative depends on the associated demonstration".

[8] [13], p. 588: "The directing intention is the element that differentiates the 'meaning' of one syntactic occurrence of a demonstrative from another, creating the *potential* for distinct referents, and creating the actuality of equivocation". On the contrary, the speaker cannot associate different intentions to multiple occurrences of a same pure indexical, like *today*: two occurrences of a same pure indexical must be co-referential; cf. [13], p. 587: "It is no part of the meaning of *today* that multiple syntactic occurrences must be associated with different contexts. In contrast, the meaning of a demonstrative requires that each syntactic occurrence be associated with a directing intention, several of which must be simultaneous".

[9] But, in my opinion, not to *any* competent speaker, as Garcia Carpintero proposes; cf. [9], p. 537: "I will take demonstrations to be sets of *deictical intentions* manifested in features of the context of utterance available as such to any competent user". On this point, see [6], ch. X.

only the role of manifesting the intention, of externalising it – a role of pragmatic aid to communication.[10]

Perry draws substantially the same distinction as Kaplan: the distinction between automatic and intentional indexicals. According to Perry, an utterance of *I, here,* or *now* designates respectively the speaker of the utterance, the place of the utterance or the time of the utterance, the speaker's intentions playing no role in the determination of the reference: therefore, Perry calls those expressions *automatic* indexicals. Conversely, as far as a demonstrative is concerned, the determination of the reference is not automatic and the speaker's intentions become relevant: in this sense demonstratives are "intentional".

2.2 The Asymmetry between Indexicals and Demonstratives

As we have seen, Kaplan and Perry underline the asymmetry between pure indexicals and demonstratives. The reference of a pure indexical like *I* or *today* is completely determined once the context of utterance - "brute facts of the context, like location and time", as Kaplan puts it – is given.[11] We may say that pure indexicals are semantically complete because they have an *uniqueness* clause coded in their character; as Kaplan expresses it: "although we must face life one *day* at a time, we are not condemned to perceive or direct our attention to one *object* at a time".[12]

As far as demonstratives are concerned, there are no automatic rules of saturation, but only *constraints* on possible referents: *he* refers to a male individual who is neither the speaker nor the addressee, *she* to a female individual, and so on. The possibility of equivocation – called by Kaplan "an exotic form of ambiguity"[13] – concerns only the demonstratives. The reference of *I* is the object satisfying, in a given context, the condition coded in its own character:

"*I* refers to the speaker";

while the rule associated with a demonstrative is:

"an occurrence of *that* refers to the object the speaker *intends* to refer to".

The condition amounts to saying that demonstratives are different from the non indexical expressions, because they haven't a pre-assigned semantic value and are different from pure indexicals, having no automatic rule of saturation. The semantic value of demonstratives is then fixed according to the speaker's (directing) intentions - as manifested, of course, by features of the context.

---

[10] Cf. [13], p. 582: "I am now inclined... to regard the demonstration as a mere externalization of this inner intention. The externalization is an aid to communication, like speaking more slowly and loudly, but is of no semantic significance".

[11] [13], p. 588.

[12] [13], p. 587.

[13] [13], p. 590.

3 *Here, Now, We*: Small Worries

In what follows, I will examine some objections that can be raised against the classification of *here*, *now* and *we* as pure indexicals. In some cases the difficulties are secondary, often raised by Kaplan and Perry themselves, in other cases the objections force us to reformulate the entire framework and, in particular to rethink the distinction between indexicals and demonstratives.

Kaplan, for example, observes that *here* can be either a pure indexical, as in

(4) *I am here*

or a demonstrative, as in

(5) *I was born here*

uttered pointing to a town on a map.[14]

And Perry underlines that, even if the rule associated with *here* and *now* states that the two expressions refer to the place and time of utterance, the spatial region including the place of utterance (for *here*), and the temporal region including the time of utterance (for *now*) are intuitively countless. Consider, for example, the different places one can refer to uttering the same sentence containing *here*, as in

(6) *It's cold here*

one could refer to this room, Dundee, Scotland, Europe, or to the Earth, and so on. Or consider the different extensions of the temporal region one could refer to with an occurrence of *now*, as in

(7) *The conference starts now*

compared to

(8) *Now men don't live in caves anymore*

Here and *now* seem then to be "intentional" terms in Perry's sense, at least as far as the relevant spatial or temporal extensions are concerned.[15]

Likewise, the indexical *we* refers to a group of individuals including the speaker: the fact that the group must include the speaker is the constraint working as a rule for *we*. Which particular group the speaker is actually referring to isn't coded by a rule,

---

[14] [11]; cf. [12], p. 389: "I will speak of a *demonstrative* use of a singular denoting phrase when the speaker intends that the object for which the phrase stands be designated by an associated demonstration". We can talk then of *demonstrative uses* of an indexical, ruling out some of Smith's examples, namely the utterances of *here* in a "map-reading context" (a context that sounds dangerously *ad hoc* to me); cf. [39], p. 181.

[15] [24], p. 596.

but fixed by the speaker's intention. Therefore, the context allows the addressee to determine which group of people the speaker is referring to, by uttering, for example,

(9) *We are extremely clever*:

the speaker may refer to the people in this room, to philosophers, to women, to Italians, or to human beings, and so on.

A different point is made by Quentin Smith, when he says that with

(10) *I will stop here*

a speaker could mean "I will cease my lecture with these words" or "I will stop reading my book at this passage" or "I will stop playing the music at these bars"; in other words, according to Smith, uttering *here* a speaker could refer to a point in a discourse, or in a book, or in a musical composition - and hence to different kinds of objects and, in particular, to Nonspatial Items.[16] I am inclined to categorise those cases as metaphorical or extended, based on spatial (or temporal) metaphors quite widespread in natural language[17]; therefore I will dismiss them, for nothing essentially "indexical" is involved in their occurrence.

The aforementioned objections - or some variants of them - have often been raised in the literature, and are usually regarded as not alarming. *Here, now* and *we* refer to a spatial region or a temporal region or a group of individuals – where the extension *can* be indeterminate or contextual, but, in order to satisfy their condition of designation, *must* include respectively the place, or the time or the producer of the utterance.[18]

4 *Here, Now, We*: Big Worries

It is possible to raise more serious objections to the indexicals/demonstratives distinction. In particular, it is possible to find cases in which *here* and *now* do not respectively designate the place and time of utterance; or, rather, cases in which *here* does not designate a place that *includes* the place of utterance and *now* does not designate a time that *includes* the time of utterance.[19]

---

[16] Cf. [39], pp. 181-182. Similarly, according to Smith, *now* can refer to Nontemporal Items, like a point in an argument or in a musical composition: [39], p. 175.

[17] On this point, see [15], or [14].

[18] [24], p. 598.

[19] Before turning to the examples, let me observe that most of the cases examined hereafter would be probably rejected by Kaplan - who holds a very abstract notion of context and distinguishes "utterance" from "sentence-in-a-context": now, the first notion belongs to linguistic acts theory and only the second to semantics: see [11], p. 546. According to Kaplan, for example, that utterances take time and that utterances of different sentences cannot be simultaneous - therefore cannot be "in the same context" - is an empirical fact that would make a logic of demonstratives impossible: for, in logics, we must evaluate the premises and the conclusion of an argument "in the same context". Kaplan suggests that we

I will first examine some examples adapted from Stefano Predelli.

First case. Suppose that, before leaving home at 8 'o clock in the morning, Paolo writes a note to his wife Francesca, who will be back from work at 5 'o clock in the evening:

(11) *As you can see, I'm not at home now. Meet me in two hours at our favourite bar downtown.*

Intuitively, the note does not convey the (false) content that Paolo is not at home at the time of utterance (or of inscription) of the note, nor does it ask Francesca to be in the bar at 10 'o clock in the morning – namely two hours after the note was written.

Second case. John, while in his office, writes a note saying:

(12) *I am here,*

and then, arrived home, leaves it in the kitchen, to let his wife Mary know that he is back from work: the note is not informing Mary that John is in his office (the place of utterance or inscription), but rather that he is at home.

In order to account for examples (11) and (12), Predelli suggests that we distinguish between the context of utterance (or inscription) – which I will call *context of* (material) *production* - and a context the speaker considers semantically relevant, the *context of interpretation*[20] - which I will call *intended context*. The characters of *now*, in (11), and of *here* in (12), apply to the intended context and not to the context of utterance/inscription. In (11), the context giving the correct interpretation contains, as the temporal co-ordinate, Francesca's expected time of arrival (5 p.m.) and not the moment Paolo wrote the note (8 a.m.): this intended context provides the correct values for *now* and *in two hours*, namely 5 p.m. and 7 p.m., while keeping the usual characters for the two expressions. Similarly, in (12), the relevant context, the intended context, contains as the spatial parameter Paolo's house and not the place where he actually wrote the note, i.e. his office.

Predelli opposes his own interpretation to two possible alternatives, allowing to remain in a more traditional framework and, in particular allowing to maintain the distinction between the indexicals – semantically complete, automatic, functional – and the demonstratives – semantically incomplete, intentional, pragmatic. The two alternatives are the *Many Characters View* and the *Remote Utterance View*.

(A) According to the Many Characters View, there are two characters associated with the indexical *now*, one for the time of production of the utterance containing *now* (the coding time) and one for the time the utterance is heard or read (the decoding

---

avoid most problems studying "expressions-in-a-context", an idealisation and an abstraction of genuine utterances, for "Logic and semantics are concerned not with the vagaries of actions, but with the verities of meanings" - [13], p. 585. Unfortunately, doing so we run the risk of losing some important features of natural language, which actually deals with the vagaries of actions; that's why I will take Garcia Carpintero's perspective on this point, and take utterances (namely concrete and not abstract events) to be the bearers of the fundamental semantic properties cf. [9], pp. 538-544.

[20] [31], p. 403

time). Just think of the recorded message of an answering machine, or of radio or television programs, recorded one day and broadcast another day, or of written messages as (11) or (12).

(B) According to the Remote Utterance View, written notes and recorded messages allow one to utter sentences "at a distance", so to speak; in other terms they allow to utter sentences at time t and location l without being in l at t. In this line of thought, Paolo "uttered" (11) at 5 p.m., when Francesca came home from work, and John "uttered" (12) at home, and not in his office.

Predelli doesn't provide a knock-down argument against (A). His argument is essentially that to associating two characters with *now* or *here* amounts to multiplying meanings unnecessarily, and to accepting the unpleasant and counterintuitive conclusion that most indexicals have more than one meaning. On the contrary, to rule out (B)., just imagine that Francesca comes home late, and reads the note at 9 p.m.: intuitively she must interpret the message not in relation to her actual time of arrival but to her *expected* time of arrival (the expected decoding time), since Paolo is not inviting her for a drink at 11 p.m. – an intuition the Remote Utterance View cannot account for.

However, both those traditional views are at odds with another group of examples. Predelli examines the following passage from a book on the history of World War II, written in 1996:

(13) *It is May 1940. Germany outflanks the Maginot line. Now, nothing stands between Hitler's troops and Paris.*[21]

Predelli observes that, clearly, the author is not saying that Hitler's troops are on their way to Paris in 1996: (13) must be interpreted with respect to a context containing as the temporal co-ordinate 1940, and not 1996, which is the temporal parameter belonging to the context of production.

According to another Predelli's example (slightly modified), I am in San Diego, watching on television a reporter, located in Los Angeles, who utters

(14) *Let us turn to the weather in New York. Here, the winds are blowing at 50 mph.*

As Predelli writes, "If we desire to be faithful to our pre-theoretic intuitions about the content and truth-value of the reporter's utterance, we must be able to derive from the semantic theory at our disposal the result that the second part of the utterance talks about the weather in New York".[22] Neither A. nor B. allow us to derive the desired conclusion: in particular, A. has as a consequence that *now* in (13) is ambiguous between the coding time (1996) and the decoding time (2000) – none of which is the relevant time for *now* in (13). Similarly, according to A. *here* in (14) could refer either to the coding location (Los Angeles), or to the decoding location (San Diego): this View doesn't succeed in offering the correct interpretation, namely New York.

[21] [30], p. 72.
[22] [30], p. 73.

None of Predelli's examples, as they are, is entirely satisfactory, but I am interested in the intuition behind them, that I regard as correct and attractive. The problem with the examples (13) and (14) is that the occurrences of *now* and *here* appearing in them are not genuine indexicals, but anaphors. What is designated by the expressions *now* and *here* in these examples does not rely on contextual facts, but depends, in a trivial way, on what is designated by another expression (*May 1940* in (13), or *New York* in (14)) in the same sentence, or in the previous portion of the text.[23] Nonetheless, it is easy to think of some examples which are not anaphoric. Suppose that the Los Angeles reporter I am watching on television, while in San Diego, is talking about the weather across United States. A picture of the Golden Gate appears behind him and the reporter utters:

(15) *Here the weather is foggy as usual,*

then a picture of the Statue of Liberty appears, and he utters

(16) *Here, the winds are blowing at 50 mph.*

Or suppose that the passage from the book on the history of World War II, written in 1996, reads simply:

(17) *Germany outflanks the Maginot line. Now, nothing stands between Hitler's troops and Paris.*

In examples (15) and (16), the picture behind the reporter *creates* a context, or *introduces* the addressee into a context, which is distinct from the context of utterance – a new context that the speaker considers as the one semantically relevant - the one providing the contextual parameters and in particular the spatial parameter for *here*. In example (17), it is the first sentence (*Germany outflanks the Maginot line*) that creates or makes salient the intended context, the one providing the temporal parameter for *now*.[24] Or imagine an American guide book of Rome showing on its cover a picture of the Coliseum, but nothing else, or maybe just a general title like "The most beautiful capitals in Europe", and imagine the first sentence in the book being

(18) *Here you can eat the best bucatini all'amatriciana in the world.*

Here in (18) will refer neither to the coding place (let's say Los Angeles) nor to the decoding place (let's say Dundee), but, quite naturally, to a context having Rome as the spatial co-ordinate: the guide book author relies on features of the context of

---

[23] Of course there is a relation between indexicality and anaphora - an issue I won't address in this paper: see [24], pp. 594-595, and [9], pp. 531-532. "As is customary in these discussions, for most of the paper I will be ignoring the sensible desideratum that they [anaphors] should be accounted for in a uniform way with other uses of indexicals".

[24] Cf. [39], pp. 172. "The chronological *description* of this past time... is not what is important for his present purpose: rather it is the temporal relations (of simultaneity, earlier or later) of this past time to the indicated events that is important".

utterance to succeed in making available to the addressee a different context, the intended context.

Following Predelli's suggestion, to interpret *here* and *now*, the addressee should not consider (at least, not directly) the place and time of utterance, i.e. the place and time of production of the utterance; she should instead consider an "intended" place and an "intended" time, taken as semantically relevant by the speaker, and *available as such to the addressee*: this place and this time will be the contextual co-ordinates belonging to the context of interpretation. If we accept this analysis, the reference of a pure indexical like *now* or *here* is no longer a function of the context of utterance (the semantic context), but a function of a context made salient or "created" in the context of utterance. The speaker's intentions direct the addressee to this intended context - which is identified and sorted out by pragmatic means (knowledge of the world, knowledge of the speaker's desires and beliefs, knowledge of social practices, and so on). The rule associated with the aforementioned indexicals seems now to be:

"an occurrence of *now* or *here* refers respectively to the time or the place intended by the speaker in the given context - to the time and place that are the temporal and spatial parameter of a context made salient by the speaker (and which can be different from the context of utterance)".

The semantic value of these expressions is then fixed only once the intended context is fixed - a determination involving encyclopaedic knowledge of the world and of the speaker's desires, beliefs and intentions.

5 *I*

It is now time to analyse the semantic behaviour of *I*.[25] In what follows, I will try to undermine the pure indexical status of *I*. I believe that it is possible to think of examples containing *I* which are analogous to the examples containing *now* or *here* examined in section 4.[26]

Let us consider a first example. Paolo and Francesca have, in their living room, a little Picasso, that their neighbour Alice obsessively desires. Francesca goes out for a

---

[25] I believe that the semantic behaviour of *we* is largely parasitic on the semantic behaviour of *I*. First of all, as I said before, the set of individuals the speaker is referring to with an occurrence of *we* can be under-determined: this fact introduces an intentional element blurring the pure indexical status of *we*. Moreover, it is possible to think of examples in which the "intended" set of individuals the occurrence of *we* refers to doesn't include the speaker: suppose, for instance, that, during a conversation on the cooking skills of Italians, Paolo utters to John: *We are all excellent cooks, but I can't boil an egg*.

[26] I will not consider Predelli's examples, which are both cases of free indirect speech - traditionally treated in terms of pretence; cf. [31], p. 408. Neither will I consider Smith's examples of "The Use of 'I' to Refer to Someone Other than the Speaker" (like *I am in last place*) nor of "The Use of 'I' to Refer to Impersonal Items" (like *I am out of gas*) ([39], pp. 182-185) - which I take to be cases of "transfers of meaning" or predicate transfers *à la* Nunberg rather than cases of reference transfers: see [19], pp. 109-116.

drink with her friends every evening at 7 p.m., and comes back at around 8 p.m. One evening, at about 8 p.m., Alice rings at Paolo's door and to his question "Who's that?", answers:

(19) *It's me,*

or (to stick to *I*),

(20) *I am back,*

relying on the fact that it is Francesca's customary time of arrival, and on the fact that Paolo cannot recognise her voice through the door. Paolo then opens the door, and Alice gets in, ties him up and steals the Picasso.

Predelli's proposal was that, to interpret *here* and *now*, the addressee must consider not the context of utterance, but an intended place and an intended time. Likewise, it is my opinion that a sentence like (19) can be informative: to make the point clear, it is helpful to introduce a new distinction[27] - between the material producer of the utterance containing *I* and the *intended agent*, i.e. the individual the material producer indicates as responsible for the utterance.

Another example will clarify what I mean by "intended producer" or "intended agent" of the utterance. Suppose that, one Monday, Francesca who teaches at Genoa University, is ill and cannot attend her usual meeting with the students. She phones Paolo and asks him to put a note on her office door. Paolo goes to the University and writes a note saying

(21) *I am ill and I am not here,*

sticks it on the door, gets into the office and starts working. The addressee must not interpret (21) with respect to the context of inscription, or production, which identifies Paolo as the speaker (the producer of the utterance), but with respect to a context of interpretation made semantically relevant by the producer, containing Francesca as the parameter for the speaker/agent. This context will provide the intuitively correct content that Francesca is ill and is not in the office, while Paolo is well and is in the office. In this sense the intended agent of the utterance is the one who, even if not the material producer, has to be taken as *responsible* for the utterance, and can be recognised as such by the addressee or the addressees. As a matter of fact, if a student reads the note, she will easily attribute it to Francesca, exploiting the contextual factors available to her (that the note is on Francesca's office door, that it is the day and time of Francesca's weekly meeting with the students, etc.). Those pragmatic factors will allow the student to identify easily and univocally the reference of *I*.

---

[27] Not so new, in fact: the distinction is present in the French linguistic tradition, from Saussure to Benveniste and Ducrot. Actually, the distinction to be made is between "material producer", "author" and "responsible". For the sake of simplicity, I will assume that, in most cases, author and responsible coincide.

6 Conclusion

If we accept the distinction between context of production of the utterance and intended context, and if we extend this distinction to the indexical *I*, we must recognise that, at least in some circumstances, to interpret *I* we have to take into consideration not the material producer of *I* but an intended responsible for the utterance, who is a contextual parameter of the intended context and must be made available to the addressee as semantically relevant by the speaker.

If this analysis is correct, the reference of *I* is not a direct function of the context of utterance anymore (the semantic context): its context of interpretation is fixed by recognising the utterance producer's intentions, hence by relying on pragmatic considerations. The rule associated with *I* seems now to be:

"an occurrence of *I* refers to the individual the producer of the utterance indicates as responsible for the utterance in the given context".

We thus introduce an intentional factor in the very rule associated with *I*. Here too, the reference of *I* is partially determined by the material producer's directing intentions, as manifested by features of the context. To achieve reference, the rule demands a completion by the producer's intentions.

Of course, I am well aware that such a thesis is far more intuitive when written messages are concerned. As for verbal occurrences of *I*, the exotic form of ambiguity that Kaplan restricts to demonstratives, seems ruled out. *I* seems then to be the extreme frontier of the uniqueness clause coded in the character of the indexicals, as Garcia Carpintero writes: "the characteristic relational property... is in the case of pure indexicals one typically satisfied by just one entity in the linguistic contexts where they are produced, it is normally satisfied by more than one entity in the case of true demonstratives".[28] But (and this is essential) it seems that it is so only for contingent reasons, or empirical reasons, as if one uttered the sentence

(2) *She is Italian*

in a world where only one female individual was left. Consequently, it would be better to think of *I* as a case of relevance or uniqueness of the candidate for referent. So we could argue that the semantic behaviour of *I* is special only because, to paraphrase Kaplan, although we can perceive more than one object at a time, we are usually condemned to face life one "I" at a time.[29]

---

[28] [9], pp. 551.

[29] At least if you exclude the cases of multiple personality.

I wish to thank Josep Macia, Ernesto Napoli, Stefano Predelli, François Récanati and two anonymous referees for very helpful comments and remarks on the earlier drafts of this paper.

References

1. Almog, Joseph, Perry, John and Wettstein, Howard (eds.): Themes from Kaplan. Oxford University Press, Oxford (1989).
2. Bach, Kent: Paving the road to reference. Philosophical Studies, 67 (1992) 295-300.
3. Bach, Kent: Intentions and Demonstrations. Analysis, 52, 3,(1992) 140-146.
4. Bar-Hillel, Yehoshua: Indexical Expressions. Mind, 63 (1954) 359-379
5. Bianchi, Claudia: Three Forms of Contextual Dependence. In: Bouquet et al. [8] 67-76.
6. Bianchi, Claudia: La dipendenza contestuale. Per una teoria pragmatica del significato. Edizioni Scientifiche Italiane, Napoli (2001).
7. Bouquet, Paolo: Contesti e ragionamento contestuale. Pantograf, Genova (1998).
8. Bouquet, Paolo et al. (eds.): Modeling and Using Context. Second International and Interdisciplinary Conference, Context'99, Proceedings. Springer-Verlag, Berlin Heidelberg New York (1999).
9. Garcia-Carpintero, Manuel: Indexicals as Token-Reflexives. Mind, 107 (1998) 529-563.
10. Hale, Bob and Wright, Crispin (eds.): A Companion to the Philosophy of Language. Blackwell, Oxford (1997).
11. Kaplan, David: Demonstratives. An Essay on the Semantics, Logic, Metaphysics, and Epistemology of Demonstratives and Other Indexicals (1977). In: Almog et al. [1] 481-563.
12. Kaplan, David: Dthat (1978). In: P. French, T. Uehling & H. Wettstein: Contemporary Perspectives in the Philosophy of Language, (1979) 383-400.
13. Kaplan, David: Afterthoughts (1989). In: Almog et al. [1] 565-614.
14. Lakoff, George and Johnson, Mark: Metaphors We Live By (1980). French tr.: M. Defornel and J.J. Lecercle: Les métaphores dans la vie quotidienne. Minuit, Paris (1985).
15. Langacker, Ronald W.: Foundations of Cognitive Grammar, vol. 1: Theoretical Prerequisites. Stanford University Press, Stanford (1987).
16. Lewis, David: General Semantics. Synthese, 22 (1970) 18-67.
17. Lewis, David: Index, Context, and Content. In: Kanger and Ohman (eds.): Philosophy and Grammar. Reidel Publishing Company (1980) 79-100.
18. Montague, Richard: Formal Semantics. Yale University Press, New Haven (1974).
19. Nunberg, Geoffrey: Transfers of Meaning. Journal of Semantics, 12 (1995) 109-132.
20. Perry, John: Frege on Demonstratives. The Philosophical Review, 86 (1977) 474-97.
21. Perry, John: The Problem of Essential Indexical. Noûs, 13, 1 (1979) 3-21.
22. Perry, John: Thought without Representation (1986). In: Perry [23] 205-225.
23. Perry, John: The Problem of the Essential Indexical and Other Essays. Oxford University Press, New York (1993).
24. Perry, John: Indexicals and Demonstratives. In: Hale and Wright [10] 586-612.
25. Perry, John: Reflexivity, Indexicality and Names. In: W. Kunne, M. Anduschus, and A. Newen (eds.): Direct Reference, Indexicality and Proposition Attitudes. CSLI-Cambridge University Press, Stanford (1997) 1-14.
26. Perry, John: Myself and I. In: M. Stamm (ed.): Philosophie in Synthetisher Absicht. Klett-Cotta, Stuttgart (1998) 83-103.
27. Perry, John: Indexicals, Contexts and Unarticulated Constituents. Proceedings of the 1995 CSLI-Amsterdam Logic, Language and Computation Conference. CSLI Publications, Stanford (1998) 1-16.
28. Perry, John: Rip Van Winkle and Other Characters. European Review of Analytical Philosophy, 2: Cognitive Dynamics (1998) 13-39.
29. Predelli, Stefano: Never put off until tomorrow what you can do today. Analysis, 56, 2 (1996) 85-91.
30. Predelli, Stefano: Talk about fiction. Erkenntnis, 46 (1997) 69-77.

31. Predelli, Stefano: Utterance, Interpretation, and the Logic of Indexicals. Mind and Language, 13, 3 (1998) 400-414.
32. Récanati, François: The Pragmatics of What is Said. Mind and Language, 4 (1989) 295-329.
33. Récanati, François: Direct Reference: From Language to Thought. Blackwell, Oxford (1993).
34. Reichenbach, Hans: Elements of Symbolic Logic. Free Press, New York (1947).
35. Reimer, Marga: Demonstratives, Demonstrations, and Demonstrata. Philosophical Studies, 67 (1991) 187-202.
36. Reimer, Marga: Do Demonstratives Have Semantic Significance? Analysis, 51, 4 (1991) 177-183.
37. Reimer, Marga: Demonstrating with Descriptions. Philosophy and Phenomenological Research, LII, 4 (1992) 877-893.
38. Roberts, Lawrence: How Demonstrations Connect with Referential Intentions. Australasian Journal of Philosophy, 75, 2 (1997), 190-200.
39. Smith, Quentin: The Multiple Uses of Indexicals. Synthese, 78 (1989) 167-91.
40. Stalnaker, Robert: Pragmatics (1970). In: Stalnaker: Context and Content. Oxford University Press, Oxford (1999) 31-46.
41. Travis, Charles: Saying and Understanding. Blackwell, Oxford (1975).
42. Travis, Charles: The True and the False: the Domain of Pragmatics. Benjamins, Amsterdam (1981).

Two Formalizations of Context: A Comparison

P. Bouquet[1] and L. Serafini[2]

[1]Department of Computer and Management Sciences – University of Trento
Via Inama, 5 – 38100 Trento (Italy)

[2]ITC-IRST – Istituto per la Ricerca Scientifica e Tecnologica
Via Sommarive – 38050 Trento (Italy)

bouquet@cs.unitn.it   serafini@itc.it

Abstract. We investigate the relationship between two well known formalizations of context: *Propositional Logic of Context* (PLC) [4], and *Local Models Semantics* (LMS) [11]. We start with a summary of the desiderata for a logic of context, mainly inspired by McCarthy's paper on generality in AI [15] and his notes on formalizing context [16]. We briefly present LMS, and its axiomatization using MultiContext Systems (MCS) [14]. Then we present a revised (and simplified) version of PLC, and we show that local vocabularies – as they defined in [4] – are inessential in the semantics of PLC. The central part of the paper is the definition of a class of LMS (and its axiomatization in MCS, called MMCC), which is provably equivalent to the axiomatization of PLC as described in [4]. Finally, we go back to the general desiderata and discuss in detail how the two formalisms fulfill (or do not fulfill) each of them.

1 Introduction

This paper is an investigation on the relationship between two well-known formalizations of context, namely the *Propositional Logic of Context* (PLC) [4] and *Local Models Semantics* (LMS) [11], axiomatized via Multi Context Systems [14, 13] (MCS)[1].

Both PLC and LMS/MCS address issues that were raised by McCarthy in his papers on generality in AI [15] and in his notes on formalizing context [16]. These issues can be summarized as a list of general desiderata for an adequate logic of context: (i) context should allow a simpler formalization of common sense axioms; (ii) context should allow us to restrict the vocabulary and the facts that are used to solve a problem on a given occasion; (iii) the truth of a common sense fact should be dealt with as dependent on a (possibly infinite) collection of assumptions (which implicitly define its *context*); (iv) there are no absolute, context independent facts, namely each fact must be stated into an appropriate context; (v) reasoning across different contexts should be modeled.

The main results of this paper are two: first, we technically prove that LMS is strictly more general than PLC; second, we argue that PLC only partially fulfills

---

[1] Hereafter, we will refer to the general framework of LMS together with its axiomatization via MCS as LMS/MCS.

88

the general desiderata for a logic of context. Technically, the first conclusion is justified by proving a theorem of equivalence between PLC and a special class of LMS; the second, by arguing that the technical features of PLC in fact prevent it from fulfilling some of the desiderata, as it fails to formalize a strong form of locality. The main representational drawback of PLC is that it does not fulfill the locality of vocabularies. Indeed, we prove that satisfiability and validity in PLC do not essentially depend on the vocabularies of each single context, and that any PLC-structure with partial vocabulary is equivalent to a PLC-structure where the universal vocabulary is associated to each context.

2 Logics for Contexts

In this section we summarize the two formalisms for contexts we will compare. LMS has been presented in [11], while [14, 13] propose a class of proof systems for LMS called Multi Context Systems (MCS). PLC is presented in [4].

2.1 Local Model Semantics and Multi Context Systems

Let $\{L_i\}_{i \in I}$ be a family of languages defined over a set of indexes I (in the following we drop the index $i \in I$). Intuitively, each L_i is the (formal) language used to describe the facts in the context i. We assume that I is (at most) countable. Let M_i be the class of all the models (interpretations) of L_i. We call $m \in M_i$ a *local model* (of L_i).

To distinguish the formula ϕ occurring in the context i from the occurrences of the "same" formula ϕ in the other contexts, we write $\langle \phi, i \rangle$. We say that $\langle \phi, i \rangle$ is a labelled wff, and that ϕ is an L_i-wff. For any set of labeled formulas Γ, $\Gamma_i = \{\phi \mid \langle \phi, i \rangle \in \Gamma\}$[2]

Definition 21 (Compatibility sequence). A *compatibility sequence* $\mathbf{c} = \{c_i \subseteq M_i\}_{i \in I}$ is a family of sets of models of L_i. We call c_i the i-th element of $\mathbf{c}$. A compatibility sequence is *nonempty* if at least one of its components is nonempty. A *compatibility sequence* $\mathbf{c}$ is a *compatibility chain* if all its elements contain at most one model.

A compatibility sequence represents a set of "instantaneous snapshots of the world" each of which is taken from the point of view of the associated context. Such a snapshot may be incomplete, that is the truth value of some of the propositions in a context cannot be inferred from the information contained in the snapshot. This is formalized by associating *sets of models* to each context rather than a single model.

---

[2] As contexts have distinct languages, it is not the case that the same formula can belong to different contexts. However, it is possible that two formulas with the same syntax occur in different contexts. In this is the case, it should be clear that the "same" formula in two distinct contexts is interpreted in different sets of local models, and therefore they have different semantics.

Definition 22 (Compatibility relation and LMS model). A *compatibility relation* is a set of compatibility sequences. A *LMS model* is a compatibility relation that contains a nonempty compatibility sequence.

A compatibility relation formalizes all possible sets of "instantaneous snapshots of the world". Indeed, as contexts are not independent viewpoints, some combinations can never happen. This is expressed via a collection of *compatibility constraints*, namely conditions that say when local models of different contexts can belong to the same compatibility sequence.

Definition 23 (Satisfiability and Entailment). Let $\models$ be the propositional classical satisfiability relation. We extend the definition of $\models$ as follows:

1. for any $\phi \in L_i$, $c_i \models \phi$ if, for all $m \in c_i$, $m \models \phi$;
2. $\mathbf{c} \models \langle \phi, i \rangle$ if $c_i \models \phi$;
3. $\mathbf{C} \models \langle \phi, i \rangle$ if for all $\mathbf{c} \in \mathbf{C}$, $\mathbf{c} \models \langle \phi, i \rangle$;
4. $\Gamma_i \models_{c_i} \phi$ if, for all $m \in c_i$, $m \models \Gamma_i$ implies $m \models \phi$;
5. $\Gamma \models_{\mathbf{c}} \langle \phi, i \rangle$ if, either there is a $j \neq i$, such that $c_j \not\models \Gamma_j$, or $\Gamma_i \models_{c_i} \phi$;
6. $\Gamma \models_{\mathbf{C}} \langle \phi, i \rangle$, if for all $\mathbf{c} \in \mathbf{C}$, $\Gamma \models_{\mathbf{c}} \langle \phi, i \rangle$;
7. For any class of models $\mathfrak{C}$, $\Gamma \models_{\mathfrak{C}} \langle \phi, i \rangle$, if, for all LMS-models $\mathbf{C} \in \mathfrak{C}$, $\Gamma \models_{\mathbf{C}} \langle \phi, i \rangle$.

We adopt the usual terminology of satisfiability and entailment for the statements about the relation $\models$. Thus we say that $\mathbf{c}$ satisfies ϕ at i, or equivalently, that ϕ is true in c_i, to refer to the fact that $c_i \models \phi$. We say that Γ entails $\langle \phi, i \rangle$ in $\mathbf{c}$ to refer to the fact that $\Gamma \models_{\mathbf{c}} \langle \phi, i \rangle$. Similar terminology is adopted for $\Gamma \models_{\mathbf{C}} \langle \phi, i \rangle$ and $\Gamma \models \langle \phi, i \rangle$.

MultiContext Systems (MCS) [14] are a class of proof systems for LMS[3]. The key notion of an MCS is that of bridge rule.

Definition 24 (Bridge Rule). A *bridge rule* on a set of indices I is a schema of the form:

$$\frac{\langle A_1, i_1 \rangle \quad \ldots \quad \langle A_n, i_n \rangle}{\langle A, i \rangle} \ br$$

where $i_1, \ldots, i_n, i \in I$ and $A_1, \ldots, A_n, A$ are schematic formulas. A bridge rule can be associated with a *restriction*, namely a criterion which states the conditions of its applicability.

Definition 25 (MultiContext System (MCS)). A *Multicontext System (MCS)* for a family of languages $\{L_i\}$, is a pair $\mathrm{MS} = \langle \{C_i = \langle L_i, \Omega_i, \Delta_i \rangle \}, \Delta_{br} \rangle$, where each $C_i = \langle L_i, \Omega_i, \Delta_i \rangle$ is a theory (on the language L_i, with axioms Ω_i and natural deduction inference rules Δ_i), and Δ_{br} is a set of bridge rules on I.

MCSs are a generalization of Natural Deduction (ND) systems [18]. The generalization amounts to using formulae tagged with the language they belong to.

---

[3] In this paper, we present a definition of MC system which is suitable for our purposes. For a fully general presentation, see [14].

This allows for the effective use of the multiple languages. The deduction machinery of an MCS is the composition of two kinds of inference rules: *local rules*, namely the inference rules in each Δ_i, and *bridge rules*. Local rules formalize reasoning within a context (i.e. are only applied to formulae with the same index), while bridge rules formalize reasoning across different contexts.

Deductions in a MCS are trees of formulae which are built starting from a finite set of assumptions and axioms, possibly belonging to distinct languages, and by a finite number of application of local rules and bridge rules. A formula $\langle \phi, i \rangle$ is *derivable* from a set of formulae Γ in a MC system MS, in symbols, $\Gamma \vdash_{MS} \langle \phi, i \rangle$, if there is a deduction with bottom formula $\langle \phi, i \rangle$ whose undischarged assumptions are in Γ. A formula $\langle \phi, i \rangle$ is a *theorem* in MS, in symbols $\vdash_{MS} \langle \phi, i \rangle$, if it is derivable from the empty set. The standard notation for deductions can be obtained by drawing a tree of labelled formulas. An example is presented in Appendix 2.

2.2 Propositional Logics of Contexts Revisited

In this section we present a slightly simplified (but provably equivalent) version of the logic PLC as presented in [4]. The simplification concerns both the semantics and the axiomatization. Given a set $\mathbb{K}$ of labels, intuitively denoting contexts, the language of PLC is a multi modal language on a set of atomic propositions $\mathbb{P}$ with the modality $ist(\kappa, \phi)$ for each context (label) $\kappa \in \mathbb{K}$. More formally, the set of well formed formulas $\mathbb{W}$ of PLC, based on $\mathbb{P}$, are

$$\mathbb{W} := \mathbb{P} \cup (\neg\mathbb{P}) \cup (\mathbb{P} \supset \mathbb{P}) \cup ist(\mathbb{K}, \mathbb{P})$$

The other propositional connectives are defined as usual. The formula $ist(\kappa, \phi)$ can be read as: ϕ holds (is true) in the context κ. PLC allows to describe how a context is views from another context. For this PLC introduces sequences of contexts (labels). Let $\mathbb{K}^*$ denote the set of finite contexts sequences and let $\overline{\kappa} = \kappa_1 \ldots \kappa_n$ denote any (possible empty) element of $\mathbb{K}^*$. Intuitively the sequence of contexts $\kappa_1 \kappa_2$ represents how context κ_2 is viewed from context κ_1. Therefore, the intuitive meaning of the formula $ist(\kappa_2, \phi)$ in the context κ_1 is that ϕ holds in the context κ_2, from the point of view of κ_1. A similar interpretation can be given to formulas in sequences of contexts longer than 2. As a consequence, satisfiability is defined with respect to a context sequence. Indeed a model for PLC associates a set of partial truth assignments to each context sequence. In the following definition we use $A \to_p B$ to denote the set of *partial* functions from A to B and $\mathbf{P}(A)$ to denote the powerset of A.

Definition 26. A *PLC-model* $\mathfrak{M}$ is a partial function that maps each context sequence $\overline{\kappa} \in \mathbb{K}^*$ into a set of partial truth assignments for $\mathbb{P}$.

$$\mathfrak{M} \in (\mathbb{K}^* \to_p \mathbf{P}(\mathbb{P} \to_p \{\text{true}, \text{false}\}))$$

Satisfiability and validity are defined with respect to a vocabulary. A *vocabulary* is a relation $\mathsf{Vocab} \subseteq \mathbb{K}^* \times \mathbb{P}$ that associates a subset of primitive propositions with each context sequence $\overline{\kappa}$. Each formula ϕ in a context sequence $\overline{\kappa}$ implicitly defines a vocabulary, denoted by $\mathsf{Vocab}(\overline{\kappa}, \phi)$, which intuitively consists of the minimal vocabulary necessary to build the formula ϕ in the context sequence $\overline{\kappa}$. $\mathsf{Vocab}(\overline{\kappa}, \phi)$ is recursively defined as follows:

$$\mathsf{Vocab}(\overline{\kappa}, p) = \{\langle \overline{\kappa}, p \rangle\}$$
$$\mathsf{Vocab}(\overline{\kappa}, \neg\phi) = \mathsf{Vocab}(\overline{\kappa}, \phi)$$
$$\mathsf{Vocab}(\overline{\kappa}, \phi \supset \psi) = \mathsf{Vocab}(\overline{\kappa}, \phi) \cup \mathsf{Vocab}(\overline{\kappa}, \psi)$$
$$\mathsf{Vocab}(\overline{\kappa}, ist(\kappa, \phi)) = \mathsf{Vocab}(\overline{\kappa}\kappa, \phi)$$

Analogously, a model $\mathfrak{M}$ defines a vocabulary denoted by $\mathsf{Vocab}(\mathfrak{M})$. $\langle \overline{\kappa}, p \rangle \in$ $\mathsf{Vocab}(\mathfrak{M})$ if and only if $\mathfrak{M}(\overline{\kappa})$ is defined and, for all $\nu \in \mathfrak{M}(\overline{\kappa})$, $\nu(p)$ is defined (where ν is a truth assignment to atomic propositions). Satisfaction in a model $\mathfrak{M}$ of a formula ϕ in a context sequence $\overline{\kappa}$ is defined only when $\mathsf{Vocab}(\overline{\kappa}, \phi) \subseteq$ $\mathsf{Vocab}(\mathfrak{M})$. Similarly, validity of a formula is defined only on the class of models that contain the vocabulary of the formula.

Definition 27 (Satisfiability and Validity). A formula ϕ such that $\mathsf{Vocab}(\overline{\kappa}, \phi) \subseteq$ $\mathsf{Vocab}(\mathfrak{M})$ is satisfied by an assignment $\nu \in \mathfrak{M}(\overline{\kappa})$, in symbols $\mathfrak{M}, \nu \models_{\overline{\kappa}} \phi$, according to the following clauses:

1. $\mathfrak{M}, \nu \models_{\overline{\kappa}} p$ iff $\nu(p) = true$;
2. $\mathfrak{M}, \nu \models_{\overline{\kappa}} \neg\phi$ iff not $\mathfrak{M}, \nu \models_{\overline{\kappa}} \phi$;
3. $\mathfrak{M}, \nu \models_{\overline{\kappa}} \phi \supset \psi$ iff not $\mathfrak{M}, \nu \models_{\overline{\kappa}} \phi$ or $\mathfrak{M}, \nu \models_{\overline{\kappa}} \psi$;
4. $\mathfrak{M}, \nu \models_{\overline{\kappa}} ist(\kappa, \phi)$ iff for all $\nu' \in \mathfrak{M}(\overline{\kappa}\kappa)$, $\mathfrak{M}, \nu' \models_{\overline{\kappa}\kappa} \phi$;
5. $\mathfrak{M} \models_{\overline{\kappa}} \phi$ iff for all $\nu \in \mathfrak{M}(\overline{\kappa})$; $\mathfrak{M}, \nu \models_{\overline{\kappa}} \phi$;
6. $\models_{\overline{\kappa}} \phi$ iff for all PLC-model $\mathfrak{M}$, such that $\mathsf{Vocab}(\overline{\kappa}, \phi) \subseteq \mathsf{Vocab}(\mathfrak{M})$, $\mathfrak{M} \models_{\overline{\kappa}} \phi$.

ϕ is *valid* in a context sequence $\overline{\kappa}$ if $\models_{\overline{\kappa}} \phi$; ϕ is *satisfiable* in a context sequence $\overline{\kappa}$ if there is a PLC-model $\mathfrak{M}$ such that $\mathfrak{M} \models_{\overline{\kappa}} \phi$. A set of formulas T is satisfiable at a context sequence $\overline{\kappa}$ if there is a model $\mathfrak{M}$ such that $\mathfrak{M} \models_{\overline{\kappa}} \phi$ for all $\phi \in T$.

The axiomatization of PLC is a Hilbert style calculus with axioms and rules reported in Figure 1. A formula ϕ is derivable from a set of formulas Γ in the context sequence $\overline{\kappa}$, in symbols $\Gamma \vdash_{\overline{\kappa}} \phi$, if and only if there are a finite set $\phi_1, \ldots, \phi_n$ of formulas in Γ, such that the formula $\vdash_{\overline{\kappa}} \phi_1 \supset (\phi_2 \ldots \supset (\phi_n \supset \phi) \ldots)$ is derivable from (PL), (K), and (Δ) by applying the inference rules (MP) and (CS). A set of formulas Γ is consistent in a context sequences $\overline{\kappa}$ if, for every ϕ, it is not the case that $\Gamma \vdash_{\overline{\kappa}} \phi$ and $\Gamma \vdash_{\overline{\kappa}} \neg\phi$.

The proposed axiomatization is simpler than that contained in [4], as we do not introduce the following axiom:

$$(\Delta_-) \quad \vdash_{\overline{\kappa}} ist(\kappa_1, \neg ist(\kappa_2, \phi) \vee \psi) \supset ist(\kappa_1, \neg ist(\kappa_2, \phi)) \vee ist(\kappa_1, \psi)$$

The reason is that it can be derived in PLC as follows:

92

(PL) $\vdash_{\overline{\kappa}} \phi$ If ϕ is an instance of a classical tautology
(K) $\vdash_{\overline{\kappa}} ist(\kappa, \phi \supset \psi) \supset ist(\kappa, \phi) \supset ist(\kappa, \psi)$
(Δ) $\vdash_{\overline{\kappa}} ist(\kappa_1, ist(\kappa_2, \phi) \vee \psi) \supset ist(\kappa_1, ist(\kappa_2, \phi)) \vee ist(\kappa_1, \psi)$

(MP) $\dfrac{\vdash_{\overline{\kappa}}\phi \quad \vdash_{\overline{\kappa}}\phi \supset \psi}{\vdash_{\overline{\kappa}}\psi}$

(CS) $\dfrac{\vdash_{\overline{\kappa}\kappa}\phi}{\vdash_{\overline{\kappa}}ist(\kappa,\phi)}$

Fig. 1. Axioms and inference rules for PLC

$$\vdash_{\overline{\kappa}\kappa_1} ist(\kappa_2, \phi) \vee \neg ist(\kappa_2, \phi) \text{ By (PL)} \tag{1}$$

$$\vdash_{\overline{\kappa}} ist(\kappa_1, ist(\kappa_2, \phi) \vee \neg ist(\kappa_2, \phi)) \text{ By (CS)} \tag{2}$$

$$\vdash_{\overline{\kappa}} ist(\kappa_1, ist(\kappa_2, \phi)) \vee ist(\overline{\kappa}_1, \neg ist(\kappa_2, \phi)) \text{ By (Δ) and (MP)} \tag{3}$$

$$\vdash_{\overline{\kappa}\kappa_1} ist(\kappa_2, \phi) \supset (\neg ist(\kappa_2, \phi) \vee \psi) \supset \psi \text{ By (PL)} \tag{4}$$

$$\vdash_{\overline{\kappa}} ist(\kappa_1, ist(\kappa_2, \phi) \supset (\neg ist(\kappa_2, \phi) \vee \psi) \supset \psi) \text{ By (CS)} \tag{5}$$

$$\vdash_{\overline{\kappa}} ist(\kappa_1, ist(\kappa_2, \phi)) \supset$$
$$(ist(\kappa_1, \neg ist(\kappa_2, \phi) \vee \psi) \supset ist(\kappa_1, \psi)) \text{ By (K)} \tag{6}$$

$$\vdash_{\overline{\kappa}} ist(\kappa_1, \neg ist(\kappa_2, \phi) \vee \psi) \supset$$
$$ist(\kappa_1, \neg ist(\kappa_2, \phi)) \vee ist(\kappa_1, \psi) \text{ From (2) and (6)} \tag{7}$$
$$\text{by PL and MP}$$

Theorem 21 (Completeness [4]). *Any set of formulas Γ is consistent in $\overline{\kappa}$ if and only Γ is satisfiable in $\overline{\kappa}$.*

3 Reconstructing PLC in LMS

The reconstruction of PLC in LMS is based on the observation that PLC is multi-modal K, restricted to a vocabulary, and extended with the axiom (Δ).

In [14], a family of MCS, called MBK, is used to represent multi-modal K; moreover, [11] presents the definition of a LMS for MBK (and the corresponding completeness result). To prove that PLC can be represented in LMS/MCS, we first show that vocabularies in PLC play no logical role. Then we extend MBK for multi-modal K, and we define the MC system MMCC, in which (Δ) is a theorem.

As far as vocabularies are concerned, it is worth remarking that PLC does not make any essential use of them as far as satisfiability and validity are concerned. To argue this, we prove the following theorem of reduction. Proofs of theorems are presented in the appendix.

Definition 31. A *complete vocabulary* is the vocabulary that associates to each sequence of contexts the whole set of propositions.

Theorem 31 (Complete vocabularies). *A formulas ϕ is valid in a context sequence $\overline{\kappa}$ if and only if it is satisfied at $\overline{\kappa}$ by all the PLC-models with complete vocabulary. Similarly, a formula ϕ is satisfiable in a context sequence $\overline{\kappa}$ if and only if there is a PLC-model with complete vocabulary that satisfies ϕ at $\overline{\kappa}$.*

Let us now reconstruct PLC in LMS and MCS. For each (possibly empty) sequence $\overline{\kappa} \in \mathbb{K}^*$, the language $L_{\overline{\kappa}}$ is the smallest propositional language that contains $\mathbb{P}$ and the *atomic formula* $ist(\kappa, \phi)$ for any $\kappa \in \mathbb{K}$ and any formula $\phi \in L_{\overline{\kappa}\kappa}$. Notice that, unlike PLC, the formula $ist(\kappa, \phi)$ is an atomic formula of $L_{\overline{\kappa}}$, and not the application of a modal operator to the formula ϕ.

Definition 32. An MBK($\mathbb{K}^*$)-model is a model for the family of languages $\{L_{\overline{\kappa}}\}_{\overline{\kappa} \in \mathbb{K}^*}$, such that, for any $\mathbf{c} \in \mathbf{C}$ and $\overline{\kappa}\kappa \in \mathbb{K}^*$:

1. $\mathbf{c}$ is a compatibility chain;
2. if $\mathbf{c} \models \langle ist(\kappa, \phi), \overline{\kappa}\rangle$, then $\mathbf{c} \models \langle \phi, \overline{\kappa}\kappa\rangle$;
3. if $\mathbf{c}' \models \langle \phi, \overline{\kappa}\kappa\rangle$ for all $\mathbf{c}' \in \mathbf{C}$ with $c_{\overline{\kappa}} = c'_{\overline{\kappa}}$, then $\mathbf{c} \models \langle ist(\kappa, \phi), \overline{\kappa}\rangle$.

Definition 33. MBK($\mathbb{K}^*$) is an MCS on the family of languages $\{L_{\overline{\kappa}}\}_{\overline{\kappa} \in \mathbb{K}}$, where, for any $\overline{\kappa}$, $\Omega_{\overline{\kappa}}$ is empty and $\Delta_{\overline{\kappa}}$ is the set of propositional natural deduction inference rules, and Δ_{br} is the following set of bridge rule schemas:

$$\frac{\langle ist(\kappa, \phi), \overline{\kappa}\rangle}{\langle \phi, \overline{\kappa}\kappa\rangle} \; \mathcal{R}_{dn\overline{\kappa}\kappa} \qquad \frac{\langle \phi, \overline{\kappa}\kappa\rangle}{\langle ist(\kappa, \phi), \overline{\kappa}\rangle} \; \mathcal{R}_{up\overline{\kappa}\kappa}$$

RESTRICTION $\mathcal{R}_{up\overline{\kappa}\kappa}$ is applicable only if $\langle \phi, \overline{\kappa}\kappa\rangle$ does not depend upon any assumptions in $\overline{\kappa}\kappa$. $\mathcal{R}_{up\overline{\kappa}\kappa}$ and $\mathcal{R}_{dn\overline{\kappa}\kappa}$ are called reflection up and reflection down, respectively.

The soundness and completeness theorems for MBK($\mathbb{K}^*$), with respect to the class of MBK($\mathbb{K}^*$)-models, is given in [11].

Theorem 32 (Soundness and Completeness). $\Gamma \models_{\mathrm{MBK}(\mathbb{K}^*)} \langle \phi, \overline{\kappa}\rangle$ *if and only if* $\Gamma \vdash_{\mathrm{MBK}(\mathbb{K}^*)} \langle \phi, \overline{\kappa}\rangle$.

Definition 34 (MMCC-model). An *MMCC model* is defined as a MBK($\mathbb{K}^*$)-model, with the further condition that:

4 if $\mathbf{c} \models \langle ist(\kappa', \phi), \overline{\kappa}\kappa\rangle$, then $\mathbf{c} \models \langle ist(\kappa, ist(\kappa', \phi)), \overline{\kappa}\rangle$.

Condition 4 of the previous definition characterizes the axiom (Δ).

Theorem 33. *Any* MBK($\mathbb{K}^*$)*-model* $\mathbf{C}$ *is an MMCC-model if and only if* $\mathbf{C} \models \langle (\Delta), \overline{\kappa}\rangle$, *for any* $\overline{\kappa}$.

We now extend MBK($\mathbb{K}^*$) in order to prove the axiom (Δ).

Definition 35 (MMCC). MMCC is an MCS defined as MBK($\mathbb{K}^*$) where the restriction of $\mathcal{R}_{up\overline{\kappa}\kappa}$ is applied only if the premise of $\mathcal{R}_{up\overline{\kappa}\kappa}$, is not of the form $\langle ist(\kappa', \psi), \overline{\kappa}\kappa\rangle$.

Now, we need to prove that the extension of MBK($\mathbb{K}^*$) is the right one, namely that MMCC is sound and complete w.r.t. the class of MMCC-models.

Theorem 34 (Soundness and Completeness of MMCC). *MMCC is sound and complete w.r.t. the set of MMCC-models. In symbols*

$$\Gamma \vdash \langle \phi, \overline{\kappa} \rangle \text{ if and only if } \Gamma \models \langle \phi, \overline{\kappa} \rangle$$

The last step is to state the equivalence between MMCC and PLC, as far as provability is concerned.

Theorem 35 (MMCC is equivalent to PLC). $\vdash_{\overline{\kappa}} \phi$ *if and only if* $\vdash \langle \phi, \overline{\kappa} \rangle$.

4 Discussion

In the introduction, we recalled some of the desiderata for a logic of context that LMS and PLC share. In this section, we discuss if these desiderata are fulfilled by PLC and LMS, and how.

Contexts allow simpler formalization of common sense. LMS and MCS have been successfully used for formalizing important aspects of common-sense knowledge and reasoning. Among others PLC and its extensions have been used to formalize information integration, planning composition and reuse, and discourse representation [17]. LMS has been used to formalize reasoning about beliefs [1, 7, 8, 6, 12], a solution to the qualification problem [3], multiple viewpoints [11], meta-reasoning [9, 10] multi-agent specification languages [2]. A discussion on the above results is beyond the scope of this paper. We only remark that the two formalisms seem to have fulfilled the goal of allowing new formalizations of various domains.

Contexts allow formalizations using a restricted vocabulary. PLC meets this desideratum only in a weak form. First of all, there is no neat way of restricting the language of a context. If, on the one hand, partial truth assignments are introduced as a way of restricting the vocabulary of a context κ, on the other hand the formula $ist(\kappa, \phi)$ is a well-formed formula for whatever ϕ. This observation is formally supported by Theorem 31, which shows that the notion of vocabulary defined in the semantics of PLC does not impact the definition of satisfiability and validity of formulas. Therefore, PLC with different vocabularies for different contexts is essentially equivalent to PLC with a unique global vocabulary shared by all the contexts.

One of the consequences of this formal property of PLC is that we in a context one can always represent what is true in another context. Technically, $ist(\kappa, \phi)$ is a well formed formula in the context $\overline{\kappa}$, if and only if, ϕ is well formed in the context sequence $\overline{\kappa}\kappa$. Furthermore, under the so called "flatness" hypothesis, namely when the context sequence $\overline{\kappa}\kappa$ coincides with the context κ, ϕ is well formed in the context κ, if and only if $ist(\kappa, \phi)$ is well formed in all the other contexts. This property is very strong (perhaps too strong) for a logic of context, as it has two main consequences. First, in every context we can always represent all the propositions that may be true in any other context. For example, in the context of the Sherlock Holmes story we would be able to represent the fact that the sentence "The Millenium bug produced no serious damages" is true in the context of XXI century technology, which seems a little odd. Second, if in a context we state that a proposition is true (or false) in some other context, we force that fact to be expressible in the language of that context. In other words, if in κ we state that ϕ is true (or false) in some other context κ', then ϕ is necessarily a well formed formula of $\kappa\kappa'$. For instance, we cannot say that "Galileo believed that the millenium bug produced no serious damages" is false in the context of XXI century technology without having a formula for the fact "the millenium bug produced no serious damages" in the context of Galileo's beliefs.

Unlike PLC, in LMS we are allowed to associate a distinct language to each context. This means that, if we put the formula $ist(\kappa', \phi)$ in the language L_κ of the context κ, we don't need to have ϕ as a well formed formula in the language $L_{\kappa\kappa'}$ of the context $\kappa\kappa'$ or in the context κ'. Going back to the Galileo example, in the context T of XXIst century technology, we can have the following formula, which states that Galileo believed that the millenium bug produced no serious damages,

$$ist(G, MB) \qquad (8)$$

without forcing MB to be a well formed formula in the context G of Galileo's beliefs. The interpretation of (8) is given by the local models of the language L_T. The fact that MB is not a formula in the language of the context G simply means that one cannot impose any constraint on the interpretation of (8) in T and the interpretation of MB in the context G.

To sum up, it is worth stressing the following difference between PLC and MMCC: in the former, this strong property is part of the logic itself, whereas in the latter it is an additional constraint on the definition of a MMCC model that can be relaxed at any time. This gives MMCC a further degree of flexibility.

Contexts allow to "localize" reasoning. Both LMS/MCS and PLC allow facts to be partitioned into different contexts. The set of facts belonging to a context can be defined in two ways: *directly*, by explicitly enumerating the facts that are in a context (using expressions of the form $\langle\phi, \kappa\rangle$); and *compositionally*, by defining the set of facts of a context from sets of facts in other contexts. In PLC this is done via *lifting axioms*, which are formulas of the form:

$$\langle ist(\kappa_1, \phi) \supset ist(\kappa_2, \phi), \ \kappa_{ext}\rangle \qquad (9)$$

Intuitively, (9) says that, if κ_1 contains the fact ϕ, than this fact is lifted also in the context κ_2. In PLC, lifting axioms are necessarily stated in an external context, which must be expressive enough to represent the truth of facts in both contexts (using *ist*-formulae). In LMS, compositional definition is formalized via compatibility relation, and represented in MCS via bridge rules. For example, the compatibility relation corresponding to the lifting axiom (9) is:

$$\text{for any } \mathbf{c} \in \mathbf{C}, \text{ if } \mathbf{c} \models \langle \phi, \kappa_1 \rangle, \text{ then } \mathbf{c} \models \langle \phi, \kappa_2 \rangle \tag{10}$$

or some equivalent formulation of (10). The corresponding bridge rule is:

$$\frac{\langle \kappa_1, \phi \rangle}{\langle \kappa_2, \phi \rangle} \; br_{(10)} \tag{11}$$

Moreover, LMS/MCS allows us to compositionally define the content of a context via lifting axioms, as in PLC. Indeed, to lift a fact ϕ from κ_1 to κ_2, it is enough to define an external context connected with κ_1 and κ_2 via reflection rules (see Definition 33) and explicitly add axiom (9) to this context. This approach was used in the solution to the qualification problem presented in [3].

The main difference between a bridge rule such as (11) and a lifting axiom such as (9) is that the first case does not require to define an external global context, capable of representing the truth of all the other contexts, the second does. Notice that, in some cases, defining an external context might be very expensive – especially when there are many interconnected contexts –, as the external context essentially duplicates all the information presented in each single context. Still, having a context that contains all lifting axioms may have some advantages, e.g., it allows one to reason about them. This is useful, for instance, to discover whether certain lifting axioms are redundant, or lead to inconsistent contexts. Since in LMS/MCS both approaches are possible, the formalism seems to be more flexible.

The truth of a common sense fact always depends on their context. In PLC this is only partially true. It holds for the formulas that do not contain the *ist* predicate, since a PLC-model associates to each context sequence a set of evaluations for primitive propositions, which defines the truth of facts for that context. However, for *ist* formulas this is not completely true, as the truth of a formula $ist(\kappa, \phi)$ is independent of the assignments of the contexts in which it occurs. Indeed, the following property holds:

$$\text{for any pair of assignments } \nu, \nu' \in \mathfrak{M}(\overline{\kappa}), \mathfrak{M}, \nu \models_{\overline{\kappa}} ist(\kappa, \phi) \text{ if} \\ \text{and only if } \mathfrak{M}, \nu' \models_{\overline{\kappa}} ist(\kappa, \phi) \tag{12}$$

The truth of $ist(\kappa, \phi)$ in $\overline{\kappa}$, is actually defined by the assignments of the context $\overline{\kappa}\kappa$ and the assignments of the context $\overline{\kappa}$ cannot affects such a truth in any way. One of the effects of this definition is that the formula (Δ) is valid. However, in our view, it seems quite hard to argue that such a formula describes a genuine principle of contextual reasoning.

In LMS, the satisfiability of a formula of the type $ist(\kappa, \varphi)$ is local to the context in which the formula is asserted (this is one of the distinguished properties of LMS in general), and therefore such a problem can be avoided. Indeed, in order to prove the equivalence between MMCC and PLC, we had to impose a very strong compatibility relation such as condition 4 of Definition 35. However, it can be easily relaxed, as it is not part of the underlying logic.

There are no absolute, context independent facts. This is true both with PLC and LMS. Indeed we have that each formulas is prefixed by a label that contextualizes it. Neither PLC nor LMS and have absolute external language. In both formalisms we have the two formulas $\langle \phi, \kappa_1 \rangle$ and $\langle \psi, \kappa_2 \rangle$ but there is no formula that represents the conjunction or the implication or any other kind of logical relation between the two formulas.

In PLC, however, the context labelled with the empty string ϵ can represent the facts contained in any other context, and therefore any logical relation between them. For instance the implication between the formulas $\langle \phi, \overline{\kappa}_1 \rangle$ and $\langle \psi, \overline{\kappa}_2 \rangle$, is representable in the root context ϵ, by the formula $\langle ist(\overline{\kappa}_1, \phi) \supset ist(\overline{\kappa}_2, \psi), \epsilon \rangle$.

In LMS and MCS we have that contexts are not necessarily organized in a hierarchy, so that we can consider an MCS composed of two simple contexts κ_1 and κ_2, each of which has its own vocabulary. In such an MCS a logical relation, e.g., conjunction or disjunction of two formulas in κ_1 and κ_2 is not representable in any contexts.

Reasoning "navigates" across contexts. The reasoning systems associated to PLC and LMS are very different. Despite the fact that they both implement reasoning in different contexts, PLC is about *validity*, while LMS is about *logical consequence* between formulas. A reasoning system about validity allows one to prove that a formula is true in the whole class of models, while a reasoning system about logical consequence allows one to prove that a formula is true in the class of models that satisfy a set of formulas called assumptions.

For a formal system for contexts, it is very important to be able to represent logical consequence across different contexts, in order to adequately formalize reasoning across contexts. Logical consequence across different contexts, formalizes the dependence between the truth of formulas in different contexts, which is the basis of the reasoning steps that allow switching from one context to another. While in many (single language) formal system, logical consequence can be reduced to validity of an implication formula (think for instance to the deduction theorem in propositional logic, where $\phi \models \psi$ is equivalent to $\models \phi \supset \psi$), in a logic of contexts, in general this rewriting is not possible. For instance, to represent the fact that ψ in κ is a logical consequence of ϕ in κ', one needs a third context containing the language of κ and κ', where it is possible to express the implication between ϕ and ψ. This of course is not always guaranteed.

5 Conclusions

To the best of our knowledge, this paper is the first attempt to make a technical comparison between PLC and LMS/MCS. Even though the two formalisms are perhaps the most significant attempts to provide a logic of context in AI, so far the comparison between them has been limited to a few lines describing related work in papers by authors of the two proponent groups. We hope that the results provided here will help to clarify the the technical and conceptual differences between the two approaches.

A final remark. In the paper, we only considered PLC and did not discuss the quantificational logic of context proposed in [5]. However, [19] shows that such a logic is provably equivalent to a quantified multimodal logic K45 + T on single modality. Using the results on the reduction of modal logic to MCS presented in [14], the equivalence between Buvač's quantificational logic of context and a suitable MCS is almost straightforward.

References

1. M. Benerecetti, P. Bouquet, and C. Ghidini. Formalizing belief report – the approach and a case study. In F. Giunchiglia, editor, *Artificial Intelligence: Methodology, Systems, and Applications (AIMSA '98)*, volume 1480 of *Lecture Notes in Artificial Intelligence*, pages 62–75. Springer, 1998.
2. M. Benerecetti, F. Giunchiglia, and L. Serafini. Model Checking Multiagent Systems. *Journal of Logic and Computation, Special Issue on Computational & Logical Aspects of Multi-Agent Systems*, 8(3):401–423, 1998.
3. P. Bouquet and F. Giunchiglia. Reasoning about Theory Adequacy: A New Solution to the Qualification Problem. *Fundamenta Informaticae*. 23(2–4):247–262, June,July,August 1995.
4. S. Buvač and Ian A. Mason. Propositional logic of context. In R. Fikes and W. Lehnert, editors, *Proc. of the 11th National Conference on Artificial Intelligence*, pages 412–419, Menlo Park, California, 1993. AAAI Press.
5. Saša Buvač. Quantificational logic of context. In *Proceedings of the Thirteenth National Conference on Artificial Intelligence*, 1996.
6. A. Cimatti and L. Serafini. Multi-Agent Reasoning with Belief Contexts III: Towards the Mechanization. In P. Brezillon and S. Abu-Hakima, editors, *Proc. of the IJCAI-95 Workshop on "Modelling Context in Knowledge Representation and Reasoning"*, pages 35–45, 1995.
7. A. Cimatti and L. Serafini. Multi-Agent Reasoning with Belief Contexts: the Approach and a Case Study. In M. Wooldridge and N. R. Jennings, editors, *Intelligent Agents: Proceedings of 1994 Workshop on Agent Theories, Architectures, and Languages*, number 890 in Lecture Notes in Computer Science, pages 71–85. Springer Verlag, 1995.
8. A. Cimatti and L. Serafini. Multi-Agent Reasoning with Belief Contexts II: Elaboration Tolerance. In *Proc. 1st Int. Conference on Multi-Agent Systems (ICMAS-95)*, pages 57–64, 1996.
9. G. Criscuolo, F. Giunchiglia, and L. Serafini. A Foundation for Metareasoning, Part I: The proof theory. Technical Report 0003-38, IRST, Trento, Italy, 2001. To appear in the Journal of Logic and Computation.

10. G. Criscuolo, F. Giunchiglia, and L. Serafini. A Foundation for Metareasoning. Part II: The model theory. Technical Report 0010-07, IRST, Trento, Italy, 2000. To appear in the Journal of Logic and Computation.

11. C. Ghidini and F. Giunchiglia. Local Models Semantics, or Contextual Reasoning = Locality + Compatibility. *Artificial Intelligence*, 127(2):221–259, 2001.

12. E. Giunchiglia and F. Giunchiglia. Ideal and real belief about belief. *Journal of Logic and Computation*. To appear in 2000.

13. F. Giunchiglia. Contextual reasoning. *Epistemologia, special issue on I Linguaggi e le Macchine*, XVI:345–364, 1993. Short version in Proceedings IJCAI'93 Workshop on Using Knowledge in its Context, Chambery, France, 1993, pp. 39–49. Also IRST-Technical Report 9211-20, IRST, Trento, Italy.

14. F. Giunchiglia and L. Serafini. Multilanguage hierarchical logics (or: how we can do without modal logics). *Artificial Intelligence*, 65:29–70, 1994.

15. J. McCarthy. Generality in Artificial Intelligence. *Communications of ACM*, 30(12):1030–1035, 1987. Also in V. Lifschitz (ed.), *Formalizing common sense: papers by John McCarthy*, Ablex Publ., 1990, pp. 226–236.

16. J. McCarthy. Notes on Formalizing Context. In *Proc. of the 13th International Joint Conference on Artificial Intelligence*, pages 555–560, Chambery, France, 1993.

17. J. McCarthy and S. Buvač. Formalizing Context (Expanded Notes). In A. Aliseda, R.J. van Glabbeek, and D. Westerståhl, editors, *Computing Natural Language*, volume 81 of *CSLI Lecture Notes*, pages 13–50. Center for the Study of Language and Information, Stanford University, 1998.

18. D. Prawitz. *Natural Deduction - A proof theoretical study*. Almquist and Wiksell, Stockholm, 1965.

19. L. Serafini. Quantificational logic of contexts revisited. Technical Report 0105-01, ITC-IRST, 2001.

A Proof of theorems

Proof. of Theorem 31 We prove the theorem by showing that each PLC-model $\mathfrak{M}$ can extended to a PLC-model $\mathfrak{M}_c$ with a complete vocabulary with the following property:

For any formula ϕ and context sequence $\overline{\kappa}$, such that $\mathsf{Vocab}(\phi, \overline{\kappa}) \in$ (13) $\mathsf{Vocab}(\mathfrak{M})$, $\mathfrak{M} \models_{\overline{\kappa}} \phi$ iff $\mathfrak{M}_c \models_{\overline{\kappa}} \phi$

The *completion* of a PLC-model $\mathfrak{M}$, is the PLC-model $\mathfrak{M}_c$ defined as follows. For any $\overline{\kappa} \in \mathbb{K}^*$:

– if $\mathfrak{M}(\overline{\kappa})$ is undefined, then $\mathfrak{M}_c(\overline{\kappa})$ contains all the possible total assignments to $\mathbb{P}$.

– if $\mathfrak{M}(\overline{\kappa})$ is defined, then $\mathfrak{M}_c(\overline{\kappa})$ is the following set of assignments:

$$\left\{ \nu_c : \mathbb{P} \to \{\text{true}, \text{false}\} \,\middle|\, \begin{array}{l} \nu_c \text{ is a completion of} \\ \text{some assignment } \nu \in \\ \mathfrak{M}(\overline{\kappa}) \end{array} \right\}$$

where ν_c is a *completion* of ν if and only if ν_c agree with ν on the domain of ν.

Clearly $\mathfrak{M}_c$ is a PLC-model. To prove property (13) we show by induction on the complexity of ϕ, that for any assignment $\nu \in \mathfrak{M}(\overline{\kappa})$, and for any completion ν_c of ν in $\mathfrak{M}_c$:

$$\mathfrak{M}, \nu \models_{\overline{\kappa}} \phi \text{ iff } \mathfrak{M}_c, \nu_c \models_{\overline{\kappa}} \phi$$

Basis case: $\mathfrak{M}, \nu \models_{\overline{\kappa}} p$ iff $\nu(p) = $ true, since any extension of ν_c agree with ν on its domain, then $\nu_c(p) = $ true.

Inductive case: $\mathfrak{M}, \nu \models_{\overline{\kappa}} \neg\phi$ iff not $\mathfrak{M}, \nu \models_{\overline{\kappa}} \phi$, iff, by induction, not $\mathfrak{M}_c, \nu_c \models_{\overline{\kappa}} \phi$, iff $\mathfrak{M}_c, \nu_c \models_{\overline{\kappa}} \neg\phi$. The case of $\phi \supset \psi$ is similar. Let us consider the case of $ist(\kappa, \phi)$. $\mathfrak{M}, \nu \models_{\overline{\kappa}} ist(\kappa, \phi)$ iff for all $\nu' \in \mathfrak{M}(\overline{\kappa}\kappa)$, $\mathfrak{M}, \nu' \models_{\overline{\kappa}\kappa} \phi$, iff, by induction, for all $\nu'_c \in \mathfrak{M}_c(\overline{\kappa}\kappa)$, $\mathfrak{M}_c, \nu'_c \models_{\overline{\kappa}\kappa} \phi$, iff $\mathfrak{M}, \nu_c \models_{\overline{\kappa}} ist(\kappa, \phi)$. $\square$

Proof. of Theorem 33 Suppose that $\mathbf{c} \models \langle ist(\kappa, ist(\kappa', \phi) \vee \psi), \overline{\kappa}\rangle$. If for all $\mathbf{c}'$, with $c_{\overline{\kappa}} = c'_{\overline{\kappa}}$, we have that $\mathbf{c}' \models \langle \psi, \overline{\kappa}\kappa\rangle$, then by condition 3 of Definition 33 of MBK($\mathbb{K}^*$)-model, we have that $\mathbf{c} \models \langle ist(\kappa, \psi), \overline{\kappa}\rangle$ and therefore that $\mathbf{c} \models \langle ist(\kappa, ist(\kappa', \phi)) \vee ist(\kappa, \psi), \overline{\kappa}\rangle$. If there is such a $\mathbf{c}'$, such that $\mathbf{c}' \not\models \langle \psi, \overline{\kappa}\kappa\rangle$, from the fact that, by condition 2 of Definition 33 of MBK($\mathbb{K}^*$)-model $\mathbf{c}' \models \langle ist(\kappa', \phi) \vee \psi, \overline{\kappa}\kappa\rangle$, we have that $\mathbf{c}' \models \langle ist(\kappa', \phi), \overline{\kappa}\kappa\rangle$. By condition 4 of Definition 34 of MMCC-model, we have that $\mathbf{c}' \models \langle ist(\kappa, ist(\kappa', \phi)), \overline{\kappa}\rangle$. Since $c_{\overline{\kappa}} = c'_{\overline{\kappa}}$, then $\mathbf{c} \models \langle ist(\kappa, ist(\kappa', \phi)), \overline{\kappa}\rangle$, and therefore $\mathbf{c} \models \langle ist(\kappa, ist(\kappa', \phi)) \vee ist(\kappa, \psi), \overline{\kappa}\rangle$.

Vice-versa, suppose that $\mathbf{C} \models \langle(\Delta), \overline{\kappa}\rangle$ and let us prove condition 4 of Definition 34. Since the formula $\langle ist(\kappa, ist(\kappa', \phi) \vee \neg ist(\kappa', \phi)) \supset ist(\kappa, ist(\kappa', \phi)) \vee ist(\kappa, \neg ist(\kappa', \phi)), \overline{\kappa}\rangle$, is an instance of (Δ), and since $\mathbf{c} \models \langle ist(\kappa, ist(\kappa', \phi) \vee \neg ist(\kappa', \phi)), \overline{\kappa}\rangle$,

$$\mathbf{c} \models \langle ist(\kappa, ist(\kappa', \phi)) \vee ist(\kappa, \neg ist(\kappa', \phi)), \overline{\kappa}\rangle \tag{14}$$

Suppose that $\mathbf{c} \models \langle ist(\kappa', \phi), \overline{\kappa}\kappa\rangle$, then $\mathbf{c} \not\models \langle \neg ist(\kappa', \phi), \overline{\kappa}\kappa\rangle$, and by condition 2 of Definition 33, $\mathbf{c} \not\models \langle ist(\kappa, \neg ist(\kappa', \phi)), \overline{\kappa}\rangle$. By property (14), and by the fact that $|c_{\overline{\kappa}}| \leq 1$, we have that $\mathbf{c} \models \langle ist(\kappa, ist(\kappa', \phi)), \overline{\kappa}\rangle$. $\square$

Proof. of Theorem 34 To prove soundness it is enough to prove that the unrestricted version of $\mathcal{R}_{up}$, is sound w.r.t. logical consequence in MMCC-models. Namely that:

$$\langle ist(\kappa', \phi), \overline{\kappa}\kappa\rangle \models_{\text{MMCC}} \langle ist(\kappa, ist(\kappa', \phi)), \overline{\kappa}\rangle$$

This is a trivial consequence of condition 4 of the definition of MMCC-model. Completeness of MMCC can be proved in an indirect way. We have indeed that MBK($\mathbb{K}^*$) is complete w.r.t. the class of MBK($\mathbb{K}^*$)-models. Furthermore, from Theorem 33, we have that, the class of MMCC-models, is the class of MBK($\mathbb{K}^*$)-models that satisfy $\langle(\Delta), \overline{\kappa}\rangle$. Completeness can be therefore proved by showing that (Δ) can be proved in MMCC. Figure 2, we show a deduction of the (Δ) Notationally, $Prem(\Delta)$ and $Cons(\Delta)$ denote the premise and the consequence of (Δ) respectively.

$\square$

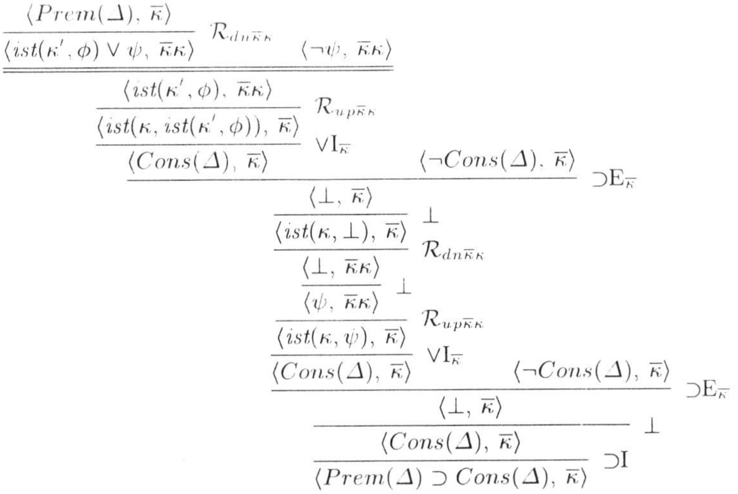

$$
\cfrac{
  \cfrac{
    \cfrac{
      \cfrac{\langle Prem(\Delta),\ \overline{\kappa}\rangle}{\langle ist(\kappa',\phi)\vee\psi,\ \overline{\kappa}\kappa\rangle}\ \mathcal{R}_{dn\overline{\kappa}\kappa}
      \qquad \langle\neg\psi,\ \overline{\kappa}\kappa\rangle
    }{
      \cfrac{
        \cfrac{\langle ist(\kappa',\phi),\ \overline{\kappa}\kappa\rangle}{\langle ist(\kappa,ist(\kappa',\phi)),\ \overline{\kappa}\rangle}\ \mathcal{R}_{up\overline{\kappa}\kappa}
      }{\langle Cons(\Delta),\ \overline{\kappa}\rangle}\ \vee I_{\overline{\kappa}}
      \qquad \langle\neg Cons(\Delta),\ \overline{\kappa}\rangle
    }\ \supset E_{\overline{\kappa}}
  }{
    \cfrac{
      \cfrac{
        \cfrac{
          \cfrac{
            \cfrac{\langle\perp,\ \overline{\kappa}\rangle}{\langle ist(\kappa,\perp),\ \overline{\kappa}\rangle}\ \perp
          }{\langle\perp,\ \overline{\kappa}\kappa\rangle}\ \mathcal{R}_{dn\overline{\kappa}\kappa}
        }{
          \cfrac{\langle\psi,\ \overline{\kappa}\kappa\rangle\ \perp}{\cfrac{\langle ist(\kappa,\psi),\ \overline{\kappa}\rangle}{\langle Cons(\Delta),\ \overline{\kappa}\rangle}\ \vee I_{\overline{\kappa}}}\ \mathcal{R}_{up\overline{\kappa}\kappa}
        }
      }{\langle\perp,\ \overline{\kappa}\rangle}\ \qquad \langle\neg Cons(\Delta),\ \overline{\kappa}\rangle \ \supset E_{\overline{\kappa}}
    }{}
  }
}{
  \cfrac{\langle Cons(\Delta),\ \overline{\kappa}\rangle}{\langle Prem(\Delta)\supset Cons(\Delta),\ \overline{\kappa}\rangle}\ \supset I
}\ \perp
$$

Fig. 2. A proof of Δ in MMCC

Proof. of Theorem 35 Provability in PLC can be defined as provability in multi modal K (denoted by $\vdash_K$) plus the axiom (Δ). For any subset $\mathbb{H}$ of $\mathbb{K}^*$, the notation $ist(\mathbb{H},\phi)$ denotes the set of formulas:

$$ist(\mathbb{H},\phi)=\big\{ist(k_1,ist(k_2,\dots ist(k_n,\phi)))\big\}\mid \kappa_1\kappa_2\dots\kappa_n\in\mathbb{H}\}$$

For any finite set of formulas $\Gamma=\{\gamma_1,\dots,\gamma_n\}$, $\bigwedge\Gamma$ denotes the formula $\gamma_1\wedge\dots\wedge\gamma_n$. If $\vdash_{\overline{\kappa}}\phi$, then there is a *finite* set $\mathbb{H}\subseteq\mathbb{K}^*$, such that

$$\vdash_K \bigwedge ist(\mathbb{H},(\Delta))\supset\phi$$

From the equivalence between multi modal K and $\mathrm{MBK}(\mathbb{K}^*)$ we have that

$$\vdash_{\mathrm{MBK}(\mathbb{K}^*)}\langle\bigwedge ist(\mathbb{H},(\Delta))\supset\phi,\ \overline{\kappa}\rangle$$

Since any formula in $\langle ist(\mathbb{H},(\Delta)),\ \overline{\kappa}\rangle$ is provable in MMCC, then we can conclude that

$$\vdash_{\mathrm{MMCC}}\langle\phi,\ \overline{\kappa}\rangle$$

If $\nvdash_{\overline{\kappa}}\phi$, then we have that $\nvdash_\epsilon\phi$, (where ϵ is the empty sequence). This implies that there is a model $\mathfrak{M}$, such that $\mathfrak{M}\not\models_\epsilon\phi$. We define the MMCC-model $\mathbf{C}_{\mathfrak{M}}$, that contains all the sequences $\mathbf{c}$ such that $c_{\overline{\kappa}}\in\mathfrak{M}(\overline{\kappa})$, and $c_{\overline{\kappa}}$ is empty if $\mathfrak{M}$ is not defined for some $\overline{\kappa}'$, such that $\overline{\kappa}=\overline{\kappa}'\overline{\kappa}''$. It can be easily show that $\mathbf{C}_{\mathfrak{M}}$ is a MMCC-model, and that $\mathbf{C}_{\mathfrak{M}}\not\models\langle\phi,\ \epsilon\rangle$. $\qquad\square$

Consider the Alternatives:
Focus in Contrast and Context

Jocelyn Cohan

UiL-OTS, Universiteit Utrecht, Trans 10
3572 JK Utrecht, Netherlands +31 30 253 6006
jocelyn.cohan@let.uu.nl

Abstract. This paper addresses two proposed properties of the kind of linguistic focus connected to alternatives in discourse: contrast and exhaustiveness. Using data occurring in spontaneous spoken English, it argues that neither contrast nor exhaustiveness is inherent to a particular category of focus. These characteristics can be derived from the contexts in which focus occurs, and thus do not need to be considered an inherent part of the meaning of focus. Contrast and exhaustiveness thus result from pragmatic aspects rather than from linguistic features of focus. They can be understood to arise from the interaction of the meaning of focus with the pragmatics of the context in which it occurs.

1.1 Introduction

Because the linguistic phenomenon of focus involves pragmatics, discourse structure and aspects of grammar ranging from phonetics to semantics, it has interested a broad range of researchers in theoretical and applied linguistics, philosophy and psychology. A number of issues concerning focus remain controversial. The oldest issue concerns the linguistic function of focus, central background to any discussion. A related controversy concerns the issue of contrast: whether contrastive focus can or should be distinguished from other kinds. Also controversial is the status of the exhaustiveness that focus sometimes expresses: this is sometimes claimed to be an inherent aspect of the meaning of a particular type of focus, sometimes an implicature.

Consideration of focus data occurring in spontaneous English, in light of the contexts in which they occur, suggests that neither contrast nor exhaustiveness is inherent to a particular category of focus. Both can be predicted by the contexts in which focus occurs, and thus do not need to be stipulated as part of the meaning of focus or a particular type of focus. Contrast and exhaustiveness are thus argued to be pragmatic results of the interaction of the meaning of focus with context, rather than linguistic features of focus *per se*.

1.1 Perspectives on Focus

The cross-linguistic semantic phenomenon of focus is characteristically connected to words in an utterance that are perceived as emphasized by speakers. In many languages, including English, this perception is tied to sentence accent. H. Paul noted in 1880 that the accented word of a sentence is related to the question that the sentence answers [1]. The constructed question answer pairs appearing in (1)-(2) demonstrate this relationship.

(1) (a) Who is driving to Paris tomorrow?
     (b) ALEX is driving to Paris tomorrow
     (c) % Alex is driving to PARIS tomorrow.

(2) (a) How is Alex getting to Paris tomorrow?
     (b) Alex is DRIVING to Paris tomorrow.
     (c) % ALEX is driving to Paris tomorrow.

The focus of the felicitous answers, represented by the word in capital letters that would be accented in the context in (1a) and (2a), corresponds to the wh-constituent of the question. *Alex* corresponds to *who* (1a) and *driving* to *how* (2a). An answer is pragmatically odd or infelicitous when the pitch accented word of the answer does not correspond to the wh-element of the question ((1b),(2b)). Pierrehumbert ([2],[3]) identifies semantic focus with the obligatory, nuclear pitch accent of an intonation phrase.

The exact nature of the communicative purpose of focus remains problematic. There are two main perspectives on this issue. One is that focus highlights new information in a discourse, information "which is represented by the speaker as being new, textually (and situationally) non-derivable" ([4]; cf. also [5],[6],[7]). The second is the view is that focus signals the existence of alternatives to the item in focus (cf. [8],[9],[10],[11]). These alternatives may appear explicitly in the discourse, and may also be supplied by the context. This second view is reflected in the formal semantic models that attempt to capture the phenomena of focus sensitivity and the link between wh-elements and focus.

1.2 Perspectives on Contrast

Other authors, in considering the insights offered by these two perspectives, have argued for two categories of focus. Although these two kinds of focus have been given a variety of names in different works, there are certain consistencies: one is linked to the discourse (new) status of information (e.g., *i-focus* [12], *information focus* [13], *broad focus* [14]), and the other to alternatives determined by the context (e.g., *contrastive focus* [4],[6], *c-focus* [12], *identificational focus* [13], *narrow focus* [14]).

As the range of terms provided for the second category suggests, there are some differences in the characteristics proposed by different authors. An example that fits all the proposals appears in (3), where *the conversation* stands in contrast to *the meal*.

(3) The meal was delicious,
     but the CONVERSÁTION made the evening worthwhile.

While *contrastive-* or *c-focus* is always associated with discourse contrast, *identificational* and *narrow focus* have been claimed to have both contrastive and non-contrastive interpretations. É.Kiss [13] proposes a [±contrastive] feature for identificational focus, encoding contrast as an inherent semantic property of a sub-category of identificational focus.

Some research has attempted to determine whether there is a phonetic distinction between contrastive and non-contrastive accents, but to date, no clear acoustic differences have been established [15],[16]. Examination of focus data taken from natural English discourse indicates that contrastive interpretation is derivable from context; the evidence for this will be discussed in section 2. Contrast is a general cognitive concept, reflected in the pragmatics of a discourse situation, and the linguistic evidence indicates that it does not need to be understood as a feature of focus.

1.3 Focus and Exhaustiveness

According to the proposal of É.Kiss [13], *identificational focus* may be either contrastive or not. What distinguishes it from focus of the new information type is that identificational focus is exhaustive in meaning. In É.Kiss's proposal, contrastive focus is a subtype of exhaustive focus, resulting in (at least) three types of focus: new information (non-exhaustive) focus and contrastive and non-contrastive exhaustive focus. The focus on *the conversation* in (3') has an exhaustive interpretation because it is interpreted as excluding any alternatives to *the conversation* (here, an explicit alternative is *the meal*) from the set of *x* such that *x made the evening worthwhile*.

(3') The meal was delicious,
      but (it was) the CONVERSÁTION (that) made the evening worthwhile.[1]

É.Kiss is not alone in claiming that focus has an exhaustive interpretation. Other authors, however, partition the categories differently, proposing exhaustiveness as a characteristic of contrastive focus in general. According to some of these proposals, this is a biconditional relationship: all contrastive focus is exhaustive focus and vice versa (e.g., [12]). Other analyses claim exhaustiveness for a subtype of contrastive focus (e.g., *corrective focus* [17]), categorizing contrastive focus as either exhaustive or non-exhaustive. The focus on *Alex* in Speaker B's response in (4), for example, excludes the alternative *Sam* from the set of x such that *x helped me plan the conference*.

(4)   Speaker A: I heard that Sam helped you plan the conference.
      Speaker B: ÁLEX helped me plan the conference.

A further controversy concerns the nature of the observed exhaustive interpretation of focus. Under some analyses, it is a (presuppositional) part of the meaning of focus or a non-cancelable conventional implicature ([12],[13],[18]). I will show in section 4 that exhaustiveness can be treated as a cancelable conversational implicature arising from the interaction of the meaning of focus and Gricean conversational maxims of quality and quantity [20] with alternatives available in the context.

---

[1] É.Kiss claims exhaustiveness only for *it*-clefts in English, represented in this example by the material in parentheses; other evidence suggests that an exhaustive interpretation is not restricted to this context (see [12],[18],[19], also section 2).

2 Contextual Contrast

As discussed in section 1.2, a number of proposals divide focus into two broad categories on the basis of its function – one associated with the discourse status of information, and the other with the existence of alternatives. For the sake of argument, let us assume that the issue of discourse contrast is only relevant for focus of the kind connected to the existence of alternatives. The observations and arguments to be made hereafter will be relevant primarily to this category of focus.

In formal semantic models of focus, a focus constituent is always an alternative to itself; that is, it is always an element of its alternative set. Other alternatives for a constituent in focus can appear explicitly in a discourse, can come from pragmatic context, or both. The source of the additional alternatives to items in focus can thus be divided into three possible categories.

- All alternatives to the focus item provided explicitly in discourse
- No alternatives to the focus item provided explicitly in discourse
- Some alternatives to the focus item provided explicitly in discourse

The data to be discussed below will demonstrate that a focus constituent can be predicted to be "contrastive" or not depending on the source of its potential alternatives[2]. The source of alternatives to a focus is a characteristic of a particular discourse, external to the focus constituent. "Contrast" is thus not a genuine property of focus or a type of focus, but something arising from the context in which it occurs. It is thus unnecessary to posit a linguistic feature like [± contrastive] for focus.

2.1 Explicit Alternatives

First, let us consider some examples drawn from natural spoken discourse where all alternatives to the focus item are explicitly provided. For the moment, we will be concerned with the focus items *actors* in (5b) and *juvenile* in (6d); these are intuitively contrastive with *stuntmen* (5a) and *Freddy Cardoza* (6a), respectively.

(5)   *The producer of a television miniseries is discussing the technical difficulties involved in the production.*
    (a)   It was úsually stúntmen that were actually in the suíts.
    (b)   We had ÁCTORS come down for very specífic scenes
    (c)   so that they would be incórporated into it

(6)   *A parole officer begins a story to help illustrate the effectiveness of a program to reduce juvenile crime:*
    (a)   There was a young mán by the name a Fréddy Cardóza
    (b)   who was caúght with a búllet.
    (c)   He was also caught pássing a gún to a júvenile
    (d)   because the JÚVENILE would get a lesser séntence.

---

[2] Regardless of the type of pitch contour associated with the focus (assuming those as in [2],[3]); pitch contours may also come with additional (primarily pragmatic) meaning (see, e.g., [21]) that will not be addressed here.

In both excerpts, the context explicitly provides all relevant alternatives: here, the focus item and one additional element. The alternative set for *actors* (5b) would include *actors* and *stuntmen*. The alternative set for *the juvenile* (6d) would include *the juvenile* and *Freddy Cardoza*.

These examples also support the view that "contrastive" focus is exhaustive. The focus constituents have an exhaustive interpretation, within the set of alternatives. The predications of the sentences in which the constituents appear – *we had x come down for SPECIFIC scenes* and *x would get a lesser SENTENCE* – apply exhaustively to the focus constituents. The paraphrases in (7) and (8), which make the alternative sets explicit, help demonstrate this.

(7) Of actors and stuntmen, it was ACTORS we had come down for spécific scenes.

(8) Of Freddy and the juvenile, it was the JUVENILE who'd get a lesser séntence.

The meanings these paraphrases convey are compatible with those of the original discourses. The alternative *stuntmen* is excluded from the set of x such that *we had x come down for SPECIFIC scenes* and the alternative *Freddy* is excluded from the set of x such that *x would get a lesser SENTENCE*.

These excerpts provide alternative sets containing only two elements, but the same observations regarding the contrastive and exhaustive character of the focus constituents in question would hold if additional alternatives had been explicitly provided. The adapted discourses in (5') and (6') help establish this:

(5') Equipment technicians had to inspect the suits before a take. It was usually stuntmen that were actually in the suits.
We had ÁCTORS come down for very specífic scenes

(6') There were two fellows, Freddy Cardoza and Alex Weems, who were caught with a bullet. They were also caught passing a gun to a juvenile because the JÚVENILE would get a lesser séntence.

Actors contrasts with explicit alternatives *stuntmen* and *equipment technicians*, and *the juvenile* contrasts with alternatives *Freddy Cardoza* and *Alex Weems*. The focus on *actors* and *the juvenile* remains exhaustive, given the respective alternative sets {*actors, stuntmen, equipment technicians*} and {*Freddy, Alex, the juvenile*}.

(9) Of equipment technicians, stuntmen and actors, it was ACTORS we had come down for spécific scenes.

(10) Of Freddy, Alex and the juvenile, it was the JUVENILE who'd get a lesser séntence.

These data indicate that focus is receives a contrastive interpretation whenever all its alternatives appear *explicitly* in the linguistic context.

2.2 No Explicit Alternatives

Theories of focus that rely on alternatives to help model the contribution of focus to sentence meaning also allow for alternatives to be provided by pragmatic context. An example of focus in a context without explicitly mentioned alternatives appears below; the relevant focus item is the constituent *the stick* in (11d).

(11) *The speaker begins telling a story about a confrontation that he had with some street gang members when he was a child. He explains that he went with his father to attend a college hockey game--*
   (a)   and one of my fávorite cóllege pláyers gave me a stíck
   (b)   and I toók the stick the next day, went out and skáted on a pónd
   (c)   and a groúp of foúr fíve kids came úp to me late in the day
   (d)   they wanted the STÍCK and I wouldn't gíve it to them

The stick in (11d) is clearly not new information: it is introduced as a referent in (11a) as *a stick*, and mentioned again in (11b), *the stick*. It does, however, appear to be a focus constituent, as the felicitous paraphrases in (12) demonstrate. The paraphrase in (12a) shows that *the stick* corresponds to the wh-constituent of the question the sentence answers, a classic test for focus constituents (cf. section 1.1). In (12b), *the stick* appears felicitously in the post-cleft portion of a wh-cleft paraphrase, a test that has also been used to identify the focus constituent of a sentence [19]. Finally, (12c) demonstrates that *the stick* can appear within an *it*-cleft, a position claimed to be syntactically marked focus, [22] even overtly exhaustive focus [13].

(12) I took the stick the next day, went out and skated on a pond, and a group of four, five kids came up to me, late in the day.
   (a)   What did they want? The STICK, and I wouldn't gíve it to them.
   (b)   What they wanted was the STICK, and I wouldn't gíve it to them.
   (c)   It was the STICK they wanted, and I wouldn't gíve it to them.

These paraphrase tests make explicit what is presupposed in the original sentence in this particular context: here, that the group of kids wanted something[3]; what is not presupposed, *the stick*, is the focus.

It also appears to that *the stick* in (10d) has an exhaustive interpretation. Besides the fact that it can felicitously occur in an *it*-cleft, it also passes proposed tests for exhaustiveness. The first test involves coordinating the noun phrase in focus with another noun phrase, and comparing the result with the sentence containing the item whose exhaustiveness is in question [24]. If the sentence containing the item being tested is a logical consequence of the sentence containing the coordinate structure, then it is not exhaustive; if it is not a logical consequence, it is exhaustive.

(13) I took the stick the next day, went out and skated on a pond. A group of four, five kids came up to me, late in the day.
   (a)   They wanted MY WALLET AND THE STICK, and I wouldn't give ' em to them.
   (b)   They wanted THE STICK, and I wouldn't give it to them.

The comparison indicates that, at least in this complete context, (13b) is not a logical consequence of (13a). In the situation described, if it were true that the group

---

[3] It is presupposed that *they wanted x*: this is the *presuppositional skeleton* (Jackendoff [23]) or *background* ([9],[11]). In proposals that employ alternatives, focus has been identified with the variable.

of kids wanted the speaker's wallet and his stick, it would not be true that they wanted the stick alone. Thus, *the stick* passes the first test for exhaustiveness.

It also passes a second proposed test for exhaustiveness [13]. In the follow-up sentence (14a), *No* negates the proposition *they wanted the stick*, which is then replaced with the proposition *they wanted my wallet*.

(14) … A group of four, five kids came up to me, late in the day.
They wanted the STICK
(a) No, they wanted my WALLET (but I gave them the STICK instead).
(b) No, they wanted my WALLET, too (but it was the STICK that I refused to give them).

In (14b), on the other hand, the felicitous presence of *too* indicates that here *No* does not negate the proposition *they wanted the stick,* but serves instead to negate the idea that they wanted the stick and nothing else: evidently, the exhaustiveness of the focus on *stick*. This result also indicates that the focus on *the stick* is exhaustive.

Unlike the examples discussed in section 2.2, however, *the stick* is not an intuitively contrastive item. There is nothing explicit in the discourse with which it might be contrasted. It could be argued that there is an implied contrast with some other item that can be assumed to be present in the context based on pragmatic factors: *they wanted the stick instead of my wallet.* Such an explanation, however, is not intuitively satisfying, in that the original example does not imply such a contrast. This intuition is supported by explicitly spelling out the proposed contrast in the context of the example, as in (15b); a representation of the utterance from the corpus appears again as (15a).

(15) I took the stick the next day, went out and skated on a pond, and a group of four, five kids came up to me, late in the day.
(a) They wanted the STICK, and I wouldn't gíve it to them.
(b) %They wanted the STICK instead of my WALLET, and I wouldn't gíve it to them.

Sentence (15b) is markedly odd in this context. First, it carries an implicature that the speaker would have given the group of kids his wallet if the wallet was what they had wanted (which could be cancelled by a follow-up utterance like *I wouldn't have given them my wallet, either*). The context provides no reason to believe that the speaker intended to communicate this idea, making an implicit contrast between the stick and some other item appropriate to the context unlikely. Second, and perhaps more fatally, the formulation in (15b) presupposes that there is an expectation that the group of kids wanted the wallet. The context simply does not support this presupposition, although, as the paraphrases in (12) suggest, it supports the presupposition that the group of kids wanted something from the speaker. In so far as this intuition can be confirmed, *the stick* is not contrastive.

Without contrast, is it reasonable to conclude that there are alternatives supplied by pragmatic context? The felicitousness of the wh-question in (12a) in this context suggests that – at least for this discourse excerpt – it is. Questions are only felicitous when there is something to question, when more than one possible answer could potentially apply – an idea captured by models of focus that employ alternatives or something like them [10],[11]. The felicitousness of the wh-question in (12a) can be explained if alternatives to *the stick* are supplied by pragmatic knowledge.

Discussion of this example suggests that focus constituents whose alternatives are supplied *only* by pragmatic context are not perceived as contrastive.

2.3 Some Explicit Alternatives

The most typical situation in discourse is one in which some alternatives to the focus item are explicitly given by the linguistic context, and others provided only by pragmatic context. This is frequently the environment for focus constituents in the focus-sensitive contexts that are modeled by semantic frameworks employing alternatives. Indeed, this is almost always the case for sentences involving additive particles like *also* or *too,* which appear felicitously only when the background of the sentence (the part that is not focus) applies to a member of the alternative set other than the focus. It is also frequently the situation for sentences with scalar particles like *even.*

(6)   *A parole officer begins a story to help illustrate the effectiveness of a program to reduce juvenile crime:*
    (a)   There was a young mán by the name a Fréddy Cardóza
    (b)   who was caúght with a búllet.
    (c)   He was also caught PÁSSING A GUN TO A JÚVENILE
    (d) because the júvenile would get a lesser séntence.

(16)   *The creator of an animated television series is explaining the problems that arose during a failed attempt to produce a live-action TV spin-off.*
    (a)   We couldn't get a traíned beáver to gnáw on the woód.
    (b)   A STÚFFED beaver was even gonna cost a lot
    (c)   and forgét about a robótic beaver
    (d)   If it's a cártoon, you can dráw that beáver.

The focus constituent that appears with *also* in (6c), *passing a gun to a juvenile* has a previously identified alternative: *with a bullet* (6b). The focus with *even* in (16b), *stuffed beaver,* has as a previously identified alternative *trained beaver.* Like the examples *actors* in (5b) and *the juvenile* in (6d), these contrast with their explicitly provided alternatives.

What about alternatives that pragmatic context provides? Consideration of the discourse excerpts indicates that implicit alternatives are available. We will see that the focus does not genuinely contrast with these, but does convey exhaustiveness within the set comprised of explicitly mentioned and pragmatically supplied alternatives.

The focus constituent *passing a gun to a juvenile* in (6c) represents a subset of the illegal things that Freddy was caught doing on the occasion in question. The focus, together with the alternative explicitly expressed in the discourse, can be considered to comprise the complete set of illegal things Freddy was in fact caught doing. We understand from the speaker's story that Freddy was not caught, on this occasion, doing anything else that might occur to us, such as *laundering money* or *destroying evidence.* The discourse in (6), however, does not set up a contrast between the focus and such implicit alternatives.

Pragmatic context likewise provides alternatives for the focus in (16b). The focus constituent *a stuffed beaver* represents a subset of the kinds of beavers that were going to cost a lot. Also included in the set of elements x such that x *was gonna cost a lot* is the previously mentioned *a trained beaver,* as well as other kinds of beavers more likely than a stuffed beaver to be expensive, such as a robotic beaver. The alternative *a robotic beaver* is supplied at this point in the discourse only by pragmatic context, but is explicitly mentioned later in the discourse (16c). The focus in (16b) excludes from the set of elements x such that x *was gonna cost a lot* any implicit members of the alternative set even less likely to be expensive than a stuffed beaver. That is, given the context for the example in (16b), we can infer that any kinds of beaver less likely to be expensive than a stuffed beaver are excluded from the set of x such that x *is gonna cost a lot.* These might include, for example, a cartoon beaver (also explicitly mentioned later in the discourse, (16d)) and a paper-maché beaver. Such alternatives only contrast with *a stuffed beaver* once they are mentioned explicitly in (16c) and (16d).

The focus in these examples thus contrasts only with explicitly mentioned alternatives. The focus is also exhaustive, even though the discourses require the inclusion of some additional alternatives in the sets *Freddy was caught x* and *x was gonna cost a lot,* because it continues to exclude other alternatives supplied by the pragmatics of the discourse. The fact that *no* can appear felicitously at the beginning of a continuation including one of these pragmatically supplied alternatives confirms the intuition that the focus conveys exhaustiveness within the remainder of the respective alternative sets.

(17) Freddy was caught with a BULLET, and he was also caught passing a gun to a JUVENILE — (No,) he was caught destroying EVIDENCE, too. (cf. (6))

(18) A STUFFED beaver was even gonna cost a lot — (No,) even a paper-maché beaver would have cost a lot. (cf. (16))

The fact that *no* is optional, however (as it would also be in the test supplied in (14)), indicates that this exhaustiveness is a conversational implicature, rather than a conventional implicature (presupposition), or otherwise inherent part of the meaning of focus. Section 3 addresses how this conversational implicature might arise.

2.4 Proper alternatives

Consideration of these examples from natural discourse indicates that contrast arises only in relation to explicitly specified alternatives to the focus; when alternatives are supplied only by pragmatic context, focus does not contrast with them.

Umbach [17] proposes that the appearance of accent presupposes a "proper alternative," a notion that is useful in describing the contrastive/non-contrastive character of focus as discussed here. A proper alternative is simply a member of the alternative set that is not equal to the focus item in meaning. Umbach's generalization is that accent is infelicitous when this "presupposition of a proper alternative" is not met. This presupposition can be satisfied either by something given in the discourse or by presupposition accommodation. The evidence in sections 2.2-2.4 suggests that focus accent is "contrastive" when the presupposition of a proper alternative is satisfied by a given item, and is not contrastive when the presupposition is pragmatically accommodated.

An evidently non-contrastive example can be converted by specifying a proper alternative explicitly, as in the adapted discourse below (cf. (12)). The phonetic realization of the focus accent on *stick* in (12') would not necessarily be any different from that in (12).

> (12') I took the stick the next day, went out and skated on a pond, and a group of four, five kids came up to me, late in the day. I offered 'em my wallet, but they wanted the stíck, and I wouldn't gíve it to 'em.

Contrast arises from the discourse, then, and is not part of the meaning of a type of focus. The generalization, simply stated, is that focus is contrastive focus if and only if at least one proper alternative is given. If the proper alternative must be accommodated, focus is not contrastive.

Successful accommodation of all presuppositions, including a presupposition of proper alternatives [17], depends on pragmatic context [25]. Definite noun phrases, for example, come with presuppositions of existence and uniqueness. Frequently, these presuppositions can be pragmatically accommodated. In (5a), for example, while there has been no previous mention of suits, the appearance of *the suits* is entirely felicitous. Pragmatic knowledge that a TV series about space travel would include space suits allows *the suits* to be accommodated.

> (5) (a) It was úsually stúntmen that were actually in the suíts.

In other situations, however, the presuppositions of *the N* cannot be satisfied by accommodation, and the use of a definite noun phrase is infelicitous. Similarly, according to Umbach [17], when context does not allow for the accommodation of a presupposition of proper alternatives, focus is not felicitous.

Proportional quantifiers (*most X, every X, half the X,* etc.) provide a good test for the proposed generalization about the accommodation of this presupposition and contrast. They have frequently been observed to be infelicitous in focus, as in example (19) ([13],[18],[24]). The data below demonstrate that once a quantifier is restricted (20) or placed in the right context ((11'),(21)) it becomes felicitous in focus.

> (19) What did the kids want? They wanted %EVERY STICK.

> (20) What did the kids want? They wanted ÉVERY STICK ON THE ÍCE RINK.

> (11')... One of my favorite college players gave me a stick. I took the stick the next day, went out and skated on a pond, and a group of four, five kids came up to me, late in the day. They wanted évery stick, and I wouldn't gíve mine to 'em.

> (21) The kids didn't want some sticks, they wanted ÉVERY STICK.

In isolation, as in (19), presupposition of a proper alternative to *every stick* cannot be satisfied. Restricting the domain of the quantifier, as in (20), also restricts the domain in which alternatives are to be determined, allowing accommodation of the presupposition. In (11'''), context restricts the domain sufficiently for a proper alternative to be accommodated (an additional quantifier including *stick,* e.g., *a few sticks, most sticks*). When the proper alternative is accommodated, as in (20) and (11'''), focus on the quantifier is felicitous but not contrastive. When a proper alternative is explicitly provided by the linguistic context (21), focus on the quantifier is contrastive. These data thus further support the simple generalization that focus is contrastive when its requirement for a proper alternative is satisfied by items that appear explicitly in the linguistic context, and not contrastive when it is pragmatically accommodated.

3 Pragmatic exhaustiveness

Languages typically contain lexical items or constructions that overtly indicate the exhaustiveness of a focus associated with them. Exclusive particles like *only* or the *it-cleft* are examples in English. Even without such items, however, focus connected to alternatives conveys exhaustiveness (cf. section 2.1-2.3). This appears to be a conversational implicature, since it can be cancelled by an appropriate follow-up utterance without resulting in a contradiction. How might this implicature arise?

If, as Umbach [17] proposes, focus comes with the presupposition of a proper alternative, its apparent exhaustiveness can be easily explained by appealing to Grice's [20] cooperative principles. To be invoked are the maxims of quality and quantity.

• Quality: Try to make your contribution one that is true. Do not say what you believe to be false or that for which you lack evidence.
• Quantity: Make your contribution only as informative as is required for the purposes of the exchange.

The mechanism of this pragmatic exhaustiveness can be illustrated with the following, adapted from the naturally occurring example in (6).

(22) Speaker A: Freddy Cardoza was caught Friday night holding a bullet.
  (a) Speaker B:(%Yes/No,) He was caught PASSING A GUN TO A JUVENILE.
  (b) Speaker B:(Yes/%No,) He was also caught PASSING A GUN TO A JUVENILE.

The apparent exhaustiveness in (22a) ("corrective focus";[17]) can be explained as an implicature arising from the maxim of quantity. If speaker B were presupposing speaker's A report, thereby accepting it as accurate, she would have indicated this by including an additive particle (as in (22b)) or *and* in her response (e.g., ... *and passing a gun to a juvenile*). Affirmation with *Yes* alone would not be adequate to indicate agreement, given that *Yes* is infelicitous here; *No* would make rejection explicit and part of the asserted content of B's contribution. In (22a), B does not include elements that would indicate her agreement with A's assertion; since the maxim of quantity requires that speakers make their contributions as informative as required, this omission leads to the implicature that B rejects A's contribution.

Speaker B also adds the proposition *Freddy was caught passing a gun to a juvenile,* with focus on *passing a gun to a juvenile.* The maxims of quantity and quality then lead straightforwardly to an implicature of exhaustiveness. The maxim of quantity requires B to indicate whether the proposition *Freddy was caught x* applies to any other alternatives of the focus in the relevant domain. The maxim of quality, however, dictates that she avoid saying something she believes to be false or for which she lacks evidence. Since B does not indicate that *Freddy was caught x* applies to any focus alternatives, the conversational implicature thus arises that the complete set of x such that (B knows that) *Freddy was caught x* is {*passing a gun to a juvenile*}, with any alternatives excluded.

The felicitous (optional) appearance of *Yes,* and the infelicitous appearance of *No,* demonstrate that the additive particle *also* in (22b) presupposes that the proposition of the sentence applies to an alternative of the focus *passing a gun to a juvenile.* This presupposition is not compatible with presupposed exhaustiveness of the focus, however, since this would exclude from the set of x such that *Freddy was caught x* the alternative *(holding) a bullet.* The presupposition of *also* is, however, entirely compatible with the presupposition that there is a proper alternative to the focus [17].

Speaker B's contribution in (22b) further implies that any other alternatives to *passing a gun to a juvenile* and *holding a bullet* that happen to be around are excluded from the set of x such that *Freddy was caught x,* and in this respect, the focus is exhaustive. This exclusion can also be explained by the maxims of quantity and quality. If B knew that the proposition *Freddy was caught x* applied to any other predicate in the relevant domain, the maxim of quantity would have required B to say so, while the maxim of quality requires B to say only what she knows to be true. Since B does not say that *Freddy was caught x* applies to anything else in the relevant domain, the implicature arises that the complete set of x such that *Freddy was caught x* is {*passing a gun to a juvenile, holding a bullet*}, with any remaining alternatives excluded.

A pragmatic account of exhaustiveness can also deal with the different pattern that emerges with scalar predicates [26]. For each possible x, *Freddy was caught x* is simply true or not true. The set of *x* such that it is possible that *x is gonna cost a lot,* however, can be ranked according to real world expectations about their relative cost: a live, trained beaver is expected to cost more than a stuffed beaver. The adapted examples in (23a) and (23b) maintain the order of the original discourse in (16). "Corrective focus" occurs when this order is reversed, as in (24).

(23) Speaker A: A trained beaver was gonna cost a lot.
    (a)   Speaker B:(Yes/%No,) A STUFFED beaver was <u>even</u> gonna cost a lot.
    (b)   Speaker B:(Yes/ %No,) A STUFFED beaver was gonna cost a lot.

(24) Speaker A: A stuffed beaver was gonna cost a lot.
    Speaker B: (%Yes/ No,) A TRAINED beaver was gonna cost a lot.

In (23a), the scalar particle *even* of B's contribution requires that *x is gonna cost a lot* applies to an alternative of the focus, here, *a trained beaver.* This is confirmed by the felicitous appearance of *Yes.* Speaker B's contribution also implies that any other alternatives to *a trained beaver* or *a stuffed beaver* less likely to cost a lot remain excluded from the set of beaver types x such that *x is gonna cost a lot* (a paper-maché or cartoon beaver, for example). Again, this exclusion can be derived from Gricean maxims of quantity and quality. Quantity requires B to mention whether *x was gonna cost a lot* applied to something less likely to cost a lot than a stuffed beaver, while quality requires her to mention only what she knows to be true. Since B mentions only *a stuffed beaver,* the implicature arises that the complete set of beaver types such that *x was gonna cost a lot* starts with *a stuffed beaver* and ranges upwards, thus excluding all beaver types less likely than a stuffed beaver to cost a lot.

The relevant difference between (23a) and (23b) is that (23b) does not explicitly presuppose that *x is gonna cost a lot* applies to the alternative *a trained beaver;* B's acceptance of A's contribution arises through implicature. Speaker B's contribution is compatible with A's due to the scalar nature of the predicate *x is gonna cost a lot*. In a world like ours, if *a stuffed beaver* costs a lot, *a trained beaver* will cost more, and so the maxim of quantity delivers the implicature that B agrees with A. Alternatives like paper-maché and cartoon beavers remain excluded from the set of *x* such that *x is gonna cost a lot* in (23b) as in (23a), despite the absence of *even*. The discussion concerns the cost of beaver types, so if B knew that *x was gonna cost a lot* applied to something less likely to cost a lot – like a paper-maché beaver – she would have mentioned this instead of *a stuffed beaver*.

The scalar nature of the predicate *cost a lot* pushes in the other direction in (24). Here, B's utterance is not compatible with A's: in our world, *a trained beaver* is more expensive than *a stuffed beaver*. As in (22a), the implicature arises that Speaker B does not accept Speaker A's contribution. Speaker B's contribution carries its own implicature of scalar exhaustiveness, excluding from the set of beaver types *x* such that *x is gonna cost a lot* those less likely to cost a lot than a trained beaver – including *a stuffed beaver*. The interaction of the alternative set with the maxims of quality and quantity lead to an implicature of exhaustiveness as they did in the previous examples.

This analysis argues that exhaustiveness is neither a presupposition nor a property otherwise inherent to focus. Focus presupposes only the existence of alternatives; the exclusion that it typically conveys arises from the interaction of this presupposition with pragmatic principles.

4 Summary

I have argued here that two properties often attributed in the literature to focus arise as a result of the alternatives connected to focus. Evidence from the occurrence of focus in natural spoken English discourse suggests that whether or not a focus constituent is contrastive depends on characteristics of the discourse at large, and is not a feature of the focus itself. If a proper alternative of the focus constituent is explicitly provided by the discourse, the focus will intuitively feel contrastive. When proper alternatives are accommodated, it will not be contrastive. This evidence also suggests that focus connected with alternatives typically conveys an interpretation of exhaustiveness, in that it excludes potential alternatives from the set of items to which the proposition of the sentence applies. This exhaustiveness, like contrast, is not an inherent characteristic of focus, but an implicature that can be derived from the existence of alternatives to the focus item and Grice's maxims of quality and quantity.

The observations and discussion presented here are relevant to focus connected to an alternative set. The literature on focus has also devoted much attention to information focus, typically distinguishing it from contrastive focus and from focus that conveys exhaustiveness. I have argued that these apparent characteristics of focus are due to the existence of alternatives. The more relevant distinction, if there is a distinction, may simply be between focus that is connected to alternatives and focus that is not.

References

1. Krifka, M. *Focus in Grammar and Discourse.* (to appear).
2. Pierrehumbert, J. *The phonetics and phonology of English intonation.* Dissertation, MIT (1980).
3. Beckman, M. & Pierrehumbert, J. Intonational structure in Japanese and English. *Phonology Yearbook* 3 (1986): 255-309.
4. Halliday, M.A.K. Notes on transitivity and theme in English. *Journal of Linguistics* 3 (1967): 37-81.
5. Sgall, P.H., Hajicova, E., Panevova, J. . *The Meaning of the Sentence in its Semantic and Pragmatic Aspects.* Reidel, Dordrecht. (1986)
6. Rochemont, M. *Focus in generative grammar.*: John Benjamins, Amsterdam (1986.)
7. Lambrecht, K. *Information structure and sentence focus.* Cambridge University Press, New York (1994)
8. Rooth, M. A theory of focus interpretation. *Natural Language Semantics* 1 (1992): 75-116.
9. Stechow, A. von. Focusing and backgrounding operators. In W. Abraham, ed., *Discourse Particles.* John Benjamins, Amsterdam (1990)
10. Groenendijk, Jeroen & Stokhof, Martin. *Studies on the Semantics of Questions and the Pragmatics of Answers.* Dissertation, University of Amsterdam (1984)
11. Krifka, M. For a structured account of questions and answers. Proceedings to Workshop on Spoken and Written Text, ed. C. Smith, University of Texas at Austin (1999)
12. Zubizaretta, M-L. *Prosody, focus and word order.* MIT Press, Cambridge, Massachusetts. (1998)
13. É.Kiss, K. Identificational focus versus information focus. Language 74 (1998): 245-273.
14. Ladd , D.R.. *The Structure of Intonational Meaning: Evidence from English.* Indiana University Press, Bloomington (1980)
15. Ladd, D.R. *Intonational Phonology.* Cambridge University Press, Cambridge (1996)
16. van Deemter, K. Contrastive Stress, contrariety and focus. In P. Bosch & R. van der Sandt, eds. *Focus: Linguistic, Cognitive and Computational Perspectives.* Cambridge University Press, Cambridge/ New York (1999)
17. Umbach, C. Non-given definites. Paper at *Sinn und Bedeutung V,* Amsterdam, December 2000 (2000)
18. Bush, R. & M. Tevdoradze. Identificational foci in Georgian. Proceedings of NELS 30 (1999).
19. Cohan, J.B.. *The realization and function of focus in spoken English.* Dissertation, University of Texas at Austin (2000)
20. Grice, H.P. Logic and conversation. In P. Cole & J. Morgan, eds., *Speech Acts,* p. 41-58. Academic Press, New York (1975)
21. Hirschberg, J. & Ward, G. The interpretation of the high-rise question contour in English. Journal of Pragmatics (1995): 407-412.
22. Prince, E. A comparison of it-clefts and wh-clefts in discourse. Language 45 (1978): 883-906.
23. Jackendoff, R. *Semantic interpretation in generative grammar.* MIT Press, Cambridge, MA (1972)
24. Sczabolsci, A. The semantics of topic-focus articuation. In J. Groenendijk, T. Janssen, M. Stokhof, eds., *Formal Methods in the Study of Language.* pp.513-541 Matematisch Centrum, Amsterdam (1981)
25. Beaver, David. Presupposition. In J. van Benthem & A. ter Meulen, eds., *Handbook of Logic and Language.* Elsevier, Amsterdam (1997)
26. Horn, Laurence.. Presupposition and implicature. In S. Lappin, ed., *The Handbook of Contemporary Semantic Theory.* pp.299-319. Blackwell, Oxford (1996)

Context in the Study of Human Languages and Computer Programming Languages: A Comparison

John H. Connolly
Department of Computer Science
Loughborough University

Address: Department of Computer Science,
Loughborough University,
Loughborough, LE11 3TU, UK
Telephone: +44 1509-222943
Fax: +44 1509-211586
Email: J.H.Connolly@lboro.ac.uk

Abstract. Human languages and computer programming languages are very different from one another. Nevertheless, in spite of this, is it possible to accommodate both of them within a single overarching framework? In addressing this question, the various aspects of context are surveyed, in order to facilitate a comparison between context in relation to natural language and context in relation to programming languages. The conclusion is that, at least to a degree, a common framework is feasible.

1   Introduction

Human languages (or natural languages) clearly differ in character from computer programming languages in a number of ways. Nevertheless, one property which both types of language have in common is that they are actualised (or brought into concrete use) within contexts.

If we wish to study the relationship between language and context, then one of the attendant questions concerns the extent to which we require a different framework for the analysis and description of context in relation to human languages, in comparison with computer programming languages. This question forms the theme of the present paper.

2   Context with Reference to Human Languages

Let us begin by identifying some key concepts pertaining to context. These will then serve as a basis for the purposes of comparison when we come to consider context in relation to computer programming languages.

2.1 Linguistic and Situational Context

Typically, units of human language, such as words, phrases or sentences, do not occur in isolation, as self-contained texts, but occur in combination with other units of similar status. Examples are seen wherever two or more words are combined together into a phrase, or wherever a number of related sentences are organised into a paragraph. Within such combinations, if we focus our attention on a particular unit (for instance, the fourth sentence in a five-sentence paragraph), then we can regard the accompanying units as comprising its *linguistic context*. For instance, the present sentence is the fourth sentence of the paragraph in which it stands, while the remaining sentences in this paragraph constitute its linguistic context. Again, if we take the phrase 'the present sentence' and consider any one of the three words of which it is composed, then the two remaining words will be seen to form its context within the boundaries of that phrase.

It is customary to distinguish the linguistic context from the non-linguistic context, or *situational context* as we shall here term it, which consists of the relevant aspects of the environment wherein the text exists, but which is itself non-textual in nature. Thus, the situational context includes the author of the text, the purpose behind its composition, and so forth.

Context should not be thought of as a mere static backdrop to language. Rather, it is dynamic in nature; see Goodwin and Duranti [15]. Moreover, context not only influences the language used on particular occasions, but is also itself changed by language (for instance in the issuing of an instruction, which suddenly imposes a need to take some action). Hence, we can perceive an interactive relationship between language and context.

Next, we need to make some further remarks, in turn, about both linguistic and situational context. Let us begin with linguistic context.

2.2 Matters of Linguistic Context

2.2.1 Co-text and Intertext

Linguistic context is frequently important in the interpretation of texts. For instance, pronouns like 'he' or 'she' often refer to a person mentioned earlier in the discourse, and cannot be properly understood in the absence of the relevant context.

In fact, linguistic context can be divided into two types. The first is called *co-text*, a term which appears to have been coined by J.C. Catford; see Halliday [16]. The co-text of a unit of language is the linguistic context provided by the text in which it occurs, as opposed to any other text. However, it sometimes happens that in order to interpret part of one text, information from some other text may be needed. For example, to understand what is meant when someone is described as a 'Scrooge' requires some familiarity with Dickens' *A Christmas Carol*. Such relationships between one text and another go under the heading of *intertextuality*; and when one text provides the relevant background for another, we classify this type of linguistic context not as co-text but as *intertext*; see Cook [12].

Intertext is internally structured, inasmuch as it is possible (up to a point) to classify texts into categories known as *discourse-types* or *genres*, for example expository texts or narrative texts. Moreover, within each genre it is possible to recognise various *sub-genres*. For instance, expository texts include instruction manuals, academic textbooks, and so on. Admittedly, however, the classes are not watertight, and some texts turn out to be hybrids of more than one genre.

2.2.2 Formal   Context-sensitivity

Another important consideration in Linguistics is a phenomenon known as *context-sensitivity*, whereby certain syntactic constructions are constrained by the co-text. An example is the convention in English that the word 'this' can co-occur with a singular but not a plural noun, which would require the word 'these' instead.

In Formal Linguistics there has been a good deal of interest in the notion of context-sensitivity in respect of the rules in terms of which the description of natural languages may be formalised. This has been an issue at least since Chomsky [11], and has led to developments in Computational Linguistics in which context-sensitive rules are avoided as far as possible, in the interests of computational tractability; see Barton, Berwick and Ristad [4].

2.3   Matters of Situational Context

2.3.1 Situation   Theory

Turning our attention from the linguistic context to the situational context, a useful place to start is with *Situation Theory* (ST). This is a theory of meaning and communication in which situations are recognised as primary (as opposed to derivative) phenomena; see Barwise and Perry [5] and Devlin [13]. As Devlin indicates, in ST various types of situation are recognised, including the following hierarchy:

(1)   (a)   Utterance situation.
       (b)   Discourse situation.
       (c)   Embedding situation.
       (d)   World.

Assuming that a given discourse can be analysed into a series of one or more individual utterances, we can say that the production of each utterance can be regarded as an event (known as an *utterance situation*) which can be described in terms of the following pieces of information.

(2)   (a)   Who is addressing whom, where and when.
       (b)   What utterance is produced.
       (c)   What entities are referred to in the utterance.

Combining the succession of utterance situations together into the whole of which they constitute the parts, we arrive at the *discourse situation*. This, in turn, is part of an *embedding situation*, which also includes that part of the world which is directly relevant to the discourse. The embedding situation may be changed as a result of an utterance. If so, the change represents its *impact*. Finally, the *world* (or, it might be preferable to say, the *universe*) represents the maximal situation.

Devlin's exposition was formulated with the spoken language particularly in mind. However, it is applicable to the written language as well, as long as we allow the place and time of the writing and the reading of any text to be distributed, rather than being necessarily proximal and simultaneous. (In fact, even spoken communication may be spatio-temporally distributed, for instance when it is mediated by a telephone answering machine.)

The interpretation of discourse may depend upon what are called *resource situations*, which are prerequisites for the successful understanding of the message. For instance, if someone refers to 'the country in which the conference Context'99 took place', then in order to work out which country is meant, the reader would have to know that Context'99 took place in Italy. This fact would therefore function as a resource situation. Moreover, if the information was, indeed, known to the reader, then that knowledge, too, would be a resource situation, in addition to the objective fact that constituted the object of that knowledge. Knowing a particular fact is an example of a psychological state, which is designated in ST as a *mental situation*.

If someone writes about some situation, then the latter has the status of a *described situation*. For example, in a biography of Julius Caesar, the events in Caesar's life would feature as described situations.

2.3.2 Analysing and Describing Situational Context

A major problem in dealing with situational context is the fact that it is potentially so vast. Ultimately, as we have already noted, the environment in which any language-use takes place is the whole universe. Consequently, if we wish to analyse and describe situational context, we are faced with the problem of reducing it to some kind of tractable concept.

The first step, which we have already anticipated, is to decide that when we analyse or describe situational context, we shall confine ourselves to what is relevant to the language used within the context concerned. For instance, suppose that someone says or writes the following sentence:

(3)   I hope that you are feeling well.

In that case, the speaker or writer and the listener or reader are relevant to the interpretation of the sentence, and should therefore be regarded as part of the context. On the other hand, the head-of-state in the country in which the sentence is produced, although being part of the wider world at the time, is not to be considered as part of the context of the above sentence, on grounds of lack of relevance.

Next, we need some framework in terms of which to analyse and describe context. A well-known attempt to provide a framework to enable the systematic description of the situational context is that of Hymes [17]. The framework which Hymes proposes is known as the 'SPEAKING' grid, following the initial letters of the categories which it employs:

(4) S: setting/scene.
     P: participants.
     E: ends.
     A: act sequences.
     K: key.
     I: instrumentalities.
     N: norms of interaction.
     G: genre.

The *setting* of a communicative act is comprises its physical circumstances, including its time and place. The *scene*, on the other hand, relates to the way in which the context is mentally perceived, recognised or regarded. For example, in the same physical setting, such as a university sports hall, one might (on different occasions) come across very different scenes, such as a netball match or a written examination.

The *participants* are, in the simplest case, what Cook [12] terms the *addresser* (the speaker or writer) and the *addressee* (the intended listener or reader), subject to the consideration that in dialogue, such as everyday conversation, the roles of addresser and addressee are interchanged at intervals.

Ends are specific communicative purposes, and can be classed as either *goals* or *outcomes*. A 'goal' is an aim which one hopes to achieve, whereas an 'outcome' is a result that actually ensues.

Communicative activity generally consists of a whole series of individual communicative acts (for example, a question followed by a series of statements in reply), which Hymes calls an *act sequence*. It is by performing this sequence of acts that meaning is conveyed from one person to another within a contextual setting. Insofar as such acts are linguistic in nature, they belong to the linguistic rather than the situational context. However, any non-verbal communicative acts, such as gestures, which accompany language are part of the non-linguistic context.

Key refers to the tone, spirit or manner in which communication is conducted. For example, a mocking tone and a serious, respectful tone would represent different 'keys'.

Instrumentalities encompass two sets of choices. One concerns the medium used (for example, the auditory medium of spoken language versus the visual medium of written language). The other relates to attributes such as a person's accent, formality of style, and so on. Selection of medium, degree of formality, and such like, all represent choices of instrumentality. Each instrumentality plays a part in providing a vehicle for the expression of what one wishes to communicate, and thus forms part of the context of one's message. Furthermore, the choice of instrumentalities will depend upon the circumstances, and hence upon other, broader aspects of the context.

Norms of interaction are the rules which govern the conduct of communication among two or more people. An example can be seen in the politeness conventions associated with language use.

Genre has already been mentioned above, in relation to linguistic context. However, genre is also linked to the situational context. For example, if we compare a ceremonial speech with a lecture, we shall find that they have different linguistic properties, which reflect the different intentions of their authors in terms of their overall purpose in speaking or writing. These differences in intention in relation to overall communicative purpose are what give rise to differences in genre.

A distinction is drawn by van Dijk [27] between *local context*, which refers to the immediate circumstances of the verbal activity, and *global context*, which comprises the broader social and cultural surroundings. Members of society can be divided into various groupings, in relation to categories such as gender, age, ethnicity, socio-economic position, geographical provenance, and so forth. Any of these factors can have effects on language. Moreover, social institutions such as the educational system, the legal system or the political system, tend to have particular forms of language associated with them. Furthermore, every society is characterised by one or more culture(s), each of which provides a set of beliefs, values and norms for its adherents. One of the norms of any culture is its language system or systems. In a multi-cultural society there is therefore a tendency towards linguistic diversity.

2.4 Cognitive and Objective Context

A useful distinction is drawn by Penco [21] between the following:

(5)   (a)   *Objective context*. From this perspective, context is regarded as a set of features of the universe.
      (b)   *Cognitive context*. From this perspective, context is regarded as a representation of the universe within an animate or inanimate information-processor.

Clearly, the cognitive aspect of context is important, inasmuch as language is used by humans and, to some extent, by computing systems; and unless the context is somehow internally represented within the minds of the people concerned, or else within the storage components of the computing systems involved, then it is not going to have the opportunity to influence language use. In the case of language use by humans as opposed to machines, the cognitive context may also be termed either the *mental context* or the *subjective context*.

Of particular significance, in the view of a number of scholars, is the notion of *shared knowledge*, common to both addresser and addressee. For example, Clark employs the term *common ground* to denote the mutual knowledge, beliefs and suppositions between those engaged in language-based interaction; see in particular Clark and Carlson [9]. As the interaction proceeds, its content is normally added to the common ground; see Clark and Schaefer [10].

A rather similar standpoint is adopted by Dik [14], who uses the term *common pragmatic information* in a similar sense to Clark's notion of common ground. Dik further proposes the following three-way distinction:

(6) (a) General information.

    (b) Situational information.

    (c) Contextual information.

General information is long-term in nature, and relates to the physical universe, the social and cultural world, and also other possible worlds. *Situational information* derives from the experience of the language users in relation to the local situation in which they find themselves, while *contextual information* derives from the co-text.

It is important not to confuse contextual information with the co-text that acts as its source. Co-text is spoken or written language. However, the interpretation of speech or writing often involves making inferences which the addresser did not actually state. For example, if someone utters (7a), then the addressee is likely to infer (7b), even though it is not overtly expressed.

(7) (a) Helen tries to avoid Bertram. She can't bear show-offs.

    (b) Bertram is a show-off.

The unstated assumptions inferred during the interpretation process form part of the contextual information.

Yet another author who utilises the idea of presumed common knowledge in the definition of context is Stalnaker [24]. According to Stalnaker, the common ground is to be identified with the addresser's presuppositions, which consist of whatever the addresser takes for granted (or pretends to take for granted) in order to communicate with the addressee. This common ground can be represented in terms of the possible worlds compatible with these presuppositions. The set of possible worlds in question is said to constitute the *context set*; see also Stalnaker [25].

3   Context with Reference to Programming Languages

As was stated at the outset, there are various differences between human languages and computer programming languages. These differences include the following.

First of all, because natural languages are normally used for communication among humans, the addresser and addressee are similar in nature, whereas programming languages exist to enable human-computer communication, and therefore involve processing by both human and machine. Obviously the human mind is very different from the CPU (central processing unit) of a computer. However, there is a complication, in that a computer program written in a high-level language (such as Pascal, C or Java) is also readable by its author and by other human beings with the necessary knowledge, and so it may be interpreted by humans as well as processed by computers. All of this suggests that when we come to analyse and describe context in relation to computer programming languages it may be helpful to differentiate between (i) context from the human perspective and (ii) context from the standpoint of the machine.

Another important difference lies in the multi-stage character of the employment of computer programming languages. In order to produce a program, it is usual to go through a development process that begins with a specification and proceeds via a design which is actualised in the form of the program. The program is then either compiled or interpreted in order to run. Clearly, human languages are not employed in such a manner. In the present paper, in order to place some reasonable bounds on the discussion, we shall be concerned only with the program text itself and its execution. We shall not consider the broader context of software specification and design.

When a program is actually in execution, then it may take input from the context external to the system on which it is running, and deliver its output into that context. At this stage we become involved with the whole field of human-computer interaction, and potentially with real-time systems as well. Unfortunately, however, these areas are far too broad to review here.

It is true that, as Berztiss [6] points out, some computations are not affected by the external environment. For instance, the calculation of the cosine of a given angle will be the same in all situations. Such calculations he terms *procedural computations*, as opposed to *transactional computations*, which do vary with the external context.

The particular importance of context for the programming of intelligent agents has been pointed out by several authors. As Wobke [28] emphasises, the contexts of agent programs have (in Penco's terminology) both cognitive and objective aspects. Turner [26] proposes that in order to be able to take context into account when making decisions regarding how they should behave, agents require explicit representations of the contexts in which they find themselves, together with knowledge of how to act in such contexts.

Context is also of great importance for natural language processing (NLP) systems. In fact, NLP programs occupy a special place in relation to the present paper, in that they simulate (to an extent) the NL-based interaction that we normally associate with human-human communication. Not only does this ensure that the contextual framework pertinent to NL-based communication among humans is relevant to NLP systems as well, but also, as with agent programs, it raises the need for representing context within the system. See Allen [3].

4   Comparison

At first sight it may appear that the factors pertaining to context in human languages and the factors relating to computer programming languages in general (leaving aside the special case of NLP systems) are quite different, and that it would be difficult to find a common framework for the analysis and description of context to suit both fields. However, it turns out that certain concepts are, indeed, applicable to both types of context, and could form the basis of an overarching framework accommodating them both.

4.1   Co-text, Intertext and Genre

The concept of *co-text* is applicable to the text of programming languages as well as natural language. For example, a procedure-call statement and the procedure which it invokes are crucial parts of each other's co-text. The same is true of variable definitions and the statements in which the variables in question are used.

The concept of *intertext*, similarly, is applicable to both types of language. In composing a program text, one is always reliant to some extent on other program texts of which one has previous experience. In fact, it is sometimes possible to re-use units of code, drawing for example on libraries of programs or modules. Re-use is particularly well facilitated within the object-oriented programming (OOP) paradigm. Again, the generic familiarity which the graphical user interface (GUI) of a new program is likely to present to its users, despite the fact that they have not encountered that particular program before, is attributable to the intertextual relationship with other, comparable GUIs; and this similarity will inevitably be reflected in the actual program text which serves to display the GUIs concerned.

The notion of *genre*, too, is relevant to program texts. The different genres will reflect the differences in overall purpose between various types of program. Possible genres might include business software, computer games software, and so on. These genres would then be divisible into sub-genres. In the case of business software, sub-genres would include document production software (such as word-processing applications), accounting software, and so on. However, as with human language, any classification into genres is likely to to involve some overlap between categories. For instance, accounts packages will have a document generation facility, though this will be limited in comparison with a sophisticated word-processing package.

Moreover, formal context-sensitivity is relevant to software. For instance, as already pointed out, the inclusion of context-sensitive (as opposed to context-free) production rules in a syntax adversely affects parsing performance.

4.2 Applying Situation Theory

The hierarchy of situations associated with the ST-based approach to human language has a counterpart in relation to computer programming languages, as well. Programming languages are, of course, part of the overarching world situation. As far as the lower levels of the hierarchy are concerned, however, it is useful to distinguish between the program text and the run-time execution of the software.

Let us begin with the program text. At the lowest level of the hierarchy we find units that are somewhat analogous to the utterances of human language, namely the individual statements (the declarations, assignments, and so forth) of which programs are composed. The program text as a whole can be regarded as the counterpart of a discourse. The embedding situation of any one copy of the program is the computer (and perhaps network) on which it is stored. If the program incorporates information about other parts of the world (for instance, the capacity of vessels in a chemical factory), then this information pertains to a described situation. The program may also draw on resource situations. For example, if it contains the representation of a path within the system's file hierarchy, then this representation denotes a situation which is vital for the correct interpretation of the program and therefore acts a resource for this purpose.

When the program is in execution, it becomes a dynamic entity. Within individual statements, variables can have values assigned or reassigned (for instance to initialise and update a running total), input can be accepted and output delivered, and so on. At the next level up, where the program is regarded as a kind of discourse, the whole sequence of events entailed in a run of the program can be treated as a unit. Then at the level of the embedding situation, the impact of the program on its environment becomes relevant. The effects may be observed in changes both to the internal state of the system and to the world outside, for instance in the operation of actuators involved in the control of machinery.

For a more detailed discussion of the application of ST in the field of Artificial Intelligence, see Akman and Surav [1, 2]. These papers deal with the important issue of formalising context, which for reasons of space unfortunately cannot be dealt with here.

4.3 Elements of the Situational Context

A description of the situational context along the lines of Hymes (above) is also possible. Again it helps if we distinguish between the text of the program and its behaviour in execution.

Once more, let us start by considering the program text. The setting and scene will be those in which the program is developed. The addresser will be the programmer and the addressee the system. The goal will normally be to fulfil some kind of functionality, while the outcome may or may not match the goal. If not, there could be various reasons, such as the code not conforming to the specification, or the specification itself being flawed. The act sequence will be the program statements. The key will be serious. The medium will almost certainly be written, and the style formal. However, programming style also covers other factors that do not apply to human languages, for example modular structure. Norms are seen in conventions such as the desirability to comment code in order that it be more readily readable. As for genre, this was dealt with above.

When a program is in execution, the setting and scene may well differ from those in which it was written. The user and the system may be engaged in a dialogue, in which the roles of addresser and addressee are exchanged at intervals. The act sequence will be the execution of the statements, not necessarily in exactly the same order as in the program text, and producing concrete outcomes such as the acceptance of input, the production of output, changes to memory and to backing-store, and so on. A choice of medium is theoretically available (for example, spoken input and/or output), and the style and key will depend on the genre. For instance, game programs are more likely to output colloquial language or ironic remarks than programs to support business activities.

4.4 Cognitive Context

As suggested above, it is useful to distinguish between the human perspective and the machine perspective when dealing with cognitive context. When a program is the object of mental processing by its developer or other any person, then its cognitive context lies in the mind of that individual. However, from the point of view of a computer on which a program is stored or run, it is the internal states and processes of the system that constitute its cognitive context. The latter can be considered to include at least the following:

(8)   (a)   The system software, including the operating system.
        (b)   The internal organisation of the system.
        (c)   The contents of memory and backing-store, which are subject to continual change.

Clearly, this is very different from the cognitive context afforded by the human mind.

However, programs in which an attempt is made to represent context and context-change explicitly within the system do show some degree of parallelism with the activity involving mental context in humans. For example, adaptive systems may make use of internal models of the user, the task, the interaction and the system itself; see Norcio and Stanley [19]. Moreover, software agents may incorporate models of other agents with which they have dealings; see Müller, Pischel and Thiel [18]. NLP systems, too, may incorporate representations of context. Some of these systems produce a discourse *history list* (that is to say, a list of the entities mentioned in the discourse so far), and this can provide contextual information to help in such tasks as deciding the precise interpretation of pronouns like 'he' or 'she'; see Allen [3]. Situational information may also be represented within the system, for instance the characteristics of the current user; see Paris [20], who describes a NL generator whose output is tailored to the person using it. As for general information, for example the (if necessary, approximate) numerical value of particular mathematical constants, this can be incorporated into any type of program, as long as it is relevant to the application.

Simulating computationally the comprehension of natural language by humans is, of course, a difficult challenge. For example, special efforts have to be made in order to enable computers to infer unstated assumptions or implications; see Schank and Abelson [22].

5   Conclusion

In the course of this paper we have seen that:

(9)   (a)   The notions of co-text and intertext, together with associated concepts such as genre, are readily applicable both to human language and to computer programming languages.
        (b)   The ST-based typology of situations and descriptive apparatus can be applied both to human language and to computer programming languages.
        (c)   The situational context can be analysed in terms of the same kinds of category, such as participants and goals, whether we are dealing with human language or computer programming languages.
        (d)   The notion of cognitive context is applicable both to human language and to computer languages.

(e)   The conceptualisation of context which is needed for NLP programs, in particular, has much in common with that which we require for natural language when used to communicate between humans.

On the other hand, it is evident that:

(10)   (a)   The units of human language (such as sentences) and the units of computer programming languages (such as procedure calls) between which co-textual and intertextual relations exist are rather different in character from one another.

(b)   In the case of computer programming languages it is useful to distinguish between the program text and the program in execution. This distinction does not apply to human languages.

(c)   The components of the situational context may differ in content, depending which class of language we are dealing with. For instance, the norms relating to the structure of book-chapters are different from those relating to the structure of computer programs.

(d)   The cognitive context afforded by the human mind is very dissimilar to the cognitive context afforded by the internals of a computer system.

Nevertheless, these difference, important as they are, do not prevent us from recognising the commonalities, outlined in (9), between context in relation to human languages and context in relation to computer programming languages. The conclusion, therefore, is that it is, indeed, possible to apply a high-level common framework to the analysis and description of context with reference to either class of language.

This conclusion represents a gain at the theoretical level, insofar as it contributes to our understanding of context. However, it may also lead to practical benefits. For example, if the potential re-usability of a piece of software is being considered, then the question of the range of contexts in which it may be re-used will need to be addressed. ST may help here, as a possible means of characterising those contexts explicitly; see further [1, 2]. Moreover, Hymes' SPEAKING grid may suggest some ways of classifying the contexts of potential re-use. For instance, in what settings may the software be re-used, and in the context of which instrumentalities (including media of interaction)? Almost certainly, however, additional criteria, for the classification of contexts of re-use will be seen to be necessary as well, and the resulting insights will, hopefully, then lead to further gains at the theoretical level.

References

1.   Akman, V., Surav, M.: Steps towards formalising context. AI Magazine 17 no.3 (1996) 55-72

2.   Akman, V., Surav, M.: The use of situation theory in context modelling. Computational Intelligence 13 (1997) 427-38

3.   Allen, J.: Natural Language Understanding, 2nd edition. Benjamin/Cummings, Redwood City, CA: (1995)

4.   Barton, G.E., Berwick, R.C., Ristad, E.S.: Computational Complexity and Natural Language. MIT Press, Cambridge, MA (1987)
5.   Barwise, J., Perry, J.: Situations and Attitudes. MIT Press, Cambridge, MA (1983)
6.   Berztiss, A.T.: Contexts, domains and software. In [7] 443-446
7.   Bouquet, P., Serafini, L., Brézillon, P., Benerecetti, M., Castellani, F. (eds.): Modelling and Using Context. Springer, Berlin (1999)
8.   Clark, H.H. (ed.): Arenas of Language Use. University of Chicago Press, Chicago (1992)
9.   Clark, H.H., Carlson, T.B.: Context for comprehension. In [8] 60-77. Reprinted from: Long, J., Baddeley, A. (eds.): Attention and Performance IX. Erlbaum, Hillsdale, NJ (1981) 313-330
10. Clark, H.H., Schaefer, E.F.: Contributing to Discourse. In [8] 144-175. Reprinted from: Cognitive Science 13 (1989) 259-294
11. Chomsky, N.: Syntactic Structures. Mouton, The Hague (1957)
12. Cook, G.: The Discourse of Advertising. Routledge, London (1992)
13. Devlin, K.: Logic and Information. Cambridge University Press, Cambridge (1991)
14. Dik, S.C., ed. Hengeveld, K.: The Theory of Functional Grammar, Part 1: The Structure of the Clause, 2nd, revised edition. Mouton de Gruyter, Berlin (1997)
15. Goodwin, C. and Duranti, A.: Rethinking context: an introduction. In: Duranti, A., Goodwin, C. (eds.): Rethinking Context: Language as an Interactive Phenomenon. Cambridge University Press, Cambridge (1992) 1-42
16. Halliday, M.A.K.: The notion of 'context' in language education. In: Ghadessy, M. (ed.): Text and Context in Functional Linguistics. Benjamins, Amsterdam (1999) 1-24
17. Hymes, D.: Models of the interaction of language and social life. In: Gumperz, J.J., Hymes, D. (eds.): Directions in Sociolinguistics: the Ethnography of Communication. Holt, Rinehart and Winston, New York (1972) 35-71
18. Müller, J.P, Pischel, M., Thiel, M.: Modelling reactive behaviour in vertically layered agent architectures. In: Wooldridge, M.J., Jennings, N.R. (eds.): Intelligent Agents. Springer, Berlin (1995) 261-276
19. Norcio, A.F., Stanley, J.: Adaptive human-computer interfaces: a literature survey and perspective. IEEE Transactions on Systems, Man and Cybernetics 19 (1989) 399-408
20. Paris, C.L.: User Modelling in Text Generation. Pinter, London (1993)
21. Penco, C.: Objective and cognitive context. In [7] 270-283
22. Schank, R.C., Abelson, R.P.: Scripts, Plans Goals and Understanding: an Inquiry into Human Knowledge Structures. Erlbaum, Hillsdale (1977)
23. Stalnaker, R.C. (ed.): Context and Content: Essays on Intentionality in Speech and Thought. Oxford University Press, Oxford (1999)
24. Stalnaker, R.C.: Indicative conditionals. In [23] 63-77. Reprinted from: Philosophia 5 (1975)
25. Stalnaker, R.C.: On the representation of context. In [23] 96-113. Reprinted from: Journal of Logic, Language and Information 7 (1998)
26. Turner, R.M.: A model of explicit context representation and use for intelligent systems. In [7] 375-388
27. van Dijk, T.A.: Discourse as interaction in society. In: van Dijk, T.A. (ed.): Discourse as Social Interaction. Sage, London (1997) 1-37
28. Wobke, W.: The role of context in the analysis and design of agent programs. In [7] 403-416

Modeling Context Effect in Perceptual Domains

Mehdi Dastani[1] and Bipin Indurkhya[2]

[1] Institute of Information and Computing Sciences, Universiteit Utrecht
Padualaan 14, De Uithof 3584CH Utrecht, The Netherlands
mehdi@cs.uu.nl
[2] Tokyo University of Agriculture and Technology
2-24-48-305 Nakacho, Koganei, 184-0012, Japan
bipin@cc.tuat.ac.jp

Abstract. In this paper we present a formal approach to modelling context effect in perceptual domains: namely how the perception of an object is effected by other objects. Our approach is operational and perceptually motivated in the sense that we focus on how objects are perceived as being constructed from certain components. Based on a psychological theory of perception, called Structural Information Theory, we develop an algebraic model for context sensitive perception. We illustrate our model by using the domain of alphabetic strings and discuss its extension to the domain of visual objects. Finally, we remark on how this approach can be applied to model context effect in non-perceptual situation, and then make some observations on the general problem of context.

1 Introduction

In this paper, we present our approach to modelling a particular manifestation of context effect — namely how the perception or representation of an object is effected by the presence of other objects. This phenomenon is perhaps best demonstrated by analogy problems. For example, in one experiment Tversky [20] asked the participants to choose a country that is most similar to Austria from a given list of three countries. When the given list was Sweden, Hungary and Poland, Sweden was chosen over Hungary more often. But when the given list was Sweden, Hungary and Norway, Hungary tended to be preferred over Sweden. Another example, motivated by Hofstadter and Mitchell's ([8]) Copycat domain of letter strings, is shown in Figure 1. Here, the same object 'abccba' is perceived differently depending on the context (i.e. analogy) in which it occurs. In the same vein, Figure 2 shows an example of context effect in the domain of analogy consisting of geometric figures (See also [10], p. 52). More recently, Goldstone et. al [7] have also experimentally explored different aspects of context effect in analogy, and proposed a model that is based on weighing the variability and diagnosticity of dimensions.

In this paper we use an operational approach to modelling the context effect in perceptual domain. That is, instead of considering dimensions along which objects are measured or categorized, we focus on how objects are perceived as being

A)   abccba   :   abcabc
B)   abccba   :   ccabbacc

Fig. 1. Examples of analogies based on letter strings.

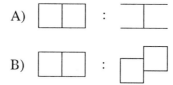

Fig. 2. Examples of analogies based on two-dimensional line-drawings.

constructed from certain components. In this respect, we follow in the footsteps of Leeuwenberg [12] and Leyton [13]. However, both these approaches focus on context-free perception and representation of objects. We, on the other hand, are primarily concerned with modelling context effect in perceptual domains and propose a formal framework in which the interaction between context-free perception of objects can be modelled.

As we take the Structural Information Theory [SIT, henceforth] of Leeuwenberg *et al.* as our starting point, we will present it briefly in Section 2 and describe our algebraic formalization of it. How the context effect can be characterized within our formalization will be explained in Section 3. In Section 4, we will comment on how the framework can be extended to model context effect in other situations — that is, situations that are not perceptual or analogy problems. In Section 5 we discuss some related research. Finally, in Section 6, we present our conclusions and briefly mention further research issues.

2   Structural Information Theory (SIT)

The structural information theory is a general theory of perception which aims to explain and predict the perceived organization of sensory patterns on the basis of a principle related to structural regularity and simplicity of those patterns. This principle is an instantiation of the well-known *minimum description length* principle. According to the structural information theory, the perceptual organization of sensory patterns are determined by certain types of structural regularities in those patterns [23, 22]. These structural regularities are described by means of ISA operators: *Iteration, Symmetry* and *Alternation*.

A sensory pattern can be described in different ways by applying different ISA operators. Each description represents a possible perceptual organization of the pattern. In order to disambiguate the set of descriptions and to decide which perceived organization of the pattern is preferred, a simplicity measure, called *Information Load*, is introduced. It is claimed that the description of a sensory pattern with the minimum information load represents its perceived organization

[21]. It is important to note that SIT is applicable to various domains of sensory patterns such as letter-string, visual and auditory patterns [12].

The notion of information load in SIT provides a criterion for choosing only the context-free organization of an object. In order to model the context effect in perceptual domains, it is necessary to provide some mechanism so that the information loads of different objects can interact. We address this problem by developing an algebraic version of SIT so that perceptual organizations of an object corresponds to the *terms* of an algebra. We then require that when several objects are viewed together, not only the information loads of their context-free organizations should be considered, but the complexity of the algebra that can generate all those organizations must be taken into account as well. These ideas are explained below in more detail.

We introduce an algebraic model of SIT for the domain of string patterns. There are various reasons to focus on this simple domain of sensory patterns. First, it is relatively easy to present the SIT model for this simple domain which is general enough to incorporate the core idea of SIT and yet shows the full complexity of the context effect in perceptual domains. Second, the main aim of this paper is to discuss the context effect in sensory domain rather than modeling SIT for complex domains. Algebraic SIT models for more complex perceptual domains such as two-dimensional visual patterns are introduced elsewhere [2]. Although we do not introduce an algebraic SIT model for two-dimensional visual patterns, we do present some examples from this domain, and hope that the reader can intuitively understand the underlying algebra.

2.1 Algebraic SIT Model for Strings

The algebraic tools we use in our formalization are developed for specifying programming languages and abstract data types ([5, 18]). An algebra is essentially a domain of objects and a number of operators (or functions) defined on these objects. An n-ary operator takes as input n objects and results in another object in the domain. The operators of the algebra allow an object to be decomposed into its component objects. In order to develop an algebraic model of SIT, we define the structural operators of SIT (i.e. ISA operators) as algebraic operators. First, we must define the domain of objects that are of interest to us. We call this the set of string patterns.

Definition 1 *The domain of string patterns D is defined as follows:*
1) If $x \in \{a, \ldots, z\}$ then $x \in D$,
2) If $x_1, \ldots, x_n \in D$ then $x_1 \cdots x_n \in D$,
3) If $x_1, \ldots, x_n \in D$ and $n > 1$ then $(x_1 \cdots x_n) \in D$

The parentheses introduced in the last clause indicate that the enclosed string is an indivisible string. Note that $x_1 \cdots x_n$ is one string and (ab), $ab(cd)$, $(ab)(c(de))fg$, etc. are all in D. Single elements are not allowed to be grouped to avoid cumbersome notations like $(((a)))$ or $(((abc)))$ which are equivalent to a and (abc), respectively. In order to distinguish between divisible and indivisible strings, we define the notion of *unit* object.

Definition 2 *An object x of D is called a unit object if either:*
1) $x \in \{a, \ldots, z\}$, or
2) x is of the form $(x_1 \cdots x_n)$

The SIT operators are structural operators that specify perceptually relevant structural organization of patterns parts. However, pattern parts may also be related to each other by non-structural operators called *domain operators*. In our domain, strings can be related to each other by domain operators such as *successor* and *predecessor* (e.g. $b = succ(a), cd = pred(ab)$). In the domain of two-dimensional visual patterns, examples of domain operators are 90-degree rotation and vertical translation. The set of domain operators is denoted by F_D. The core idea of domain operators is that the perceptually motivated structural regularities are not only defined on patterns parts, but also on the (domain) relations between pattern parts (for more discussion see [2]).

The SIT operators can now be easily defined over $< D, F_D >$. Moreover, beside the ISA operators we will represent the concatenation and group operators, which are tacitly assumed in SIT, explicitly in our algebra by two operators *Con* and *Unit*, respectively. We are now ready to define the *SIT algebra* over the domain D as follows:

Definition 3 *A SIT-algebra over the domain D is a quadruple $< D, \mathcal{N}, \mathcal{F_D}, \mathcal{S} >$, where D is the domain of objects, $\mathcal{N}$ is the set of natural numbers, F_D is a set of one-place domain operators ($f \in F_D : D \to D$), and $\mathcal{S}$ is the set of SIT-operators as defined below. In the following, $X = x_1 \cdots x_k \in D$, where each of x_i is an object; $Y, Y_1, \ldots, Y_m$, with $m > 1$, are arbitrary string patterns from D; and $n \in \mathcal{N}$. We write $f^n(X)$ to indicate that the domain operator f is applied n times to X.*

$$Iter(Y, f, n) \quad \to Y \; f(Y) \cdots f^{n-1}(Y)$$
$$Sym_e(X) \quad \to x_1 \cdots x_k x_k \cdots x_1$$
$$Sym_o(X, Y) \quad \to x_1 \cdots x_k Y x_k \cdots x_1$$
$$Alt_r(Y, f, X) \quad \to Y \; x_1 \; f(Y) \; x_2 \cdots f^{k-1}(Y) \; x_k$$
$$Alt_l(Y, f, X) \quad \to x_1 \; Y \; x_2 \; f(Y) \cdots x_k \; f^{k-1}(Y)$$
$$Con(Y_1, \ldots, Y_m) \to Y_1 \cdots Y_m$$
$$Unit(Y_1 \cdots Y_m) \quad \to (Y_1 \cdots Y_m)$$

Note that because iteration and alternation operators take domain operators as argument, the SIT-algebra becomes a higher order algebra [14, 15]. Below are some examples of how string patterns can be generated by the SIT-algebra.

$$Sym_e(Iter(a, succ, 3)) \hspace{3cm} \to abccba$$
$$Sym_o(Con(a, b), Iter(c, id, 2)) \hspace{2cm} \to abccba$$
$$Con(a, b, Iter(c, id, 2), Iter(b, pred, 2)) \to abccba$$
$$Sym_e(Con(a, Unit(Con(b, c)), d)) \hspace{1cm} \to a(bc)dd(bc)a$$
$$Alt_r(a, succ, Con(f, k, t)) \hspace{2.3cm} \to afbkct$$

Now we can represent the perceptual organizations of a pattern by structural descriptions of that pattern, each of which shows how the pattern is built out of other (sub)patterns. In the above example, three different perceptual organizations for the string *abccba*, used in Figure 1, are given: 1) as consisting of one substring abc, 2) as consisting of two substrings ab and cc, or 3) as consisting of four substrings a, b, cc, and ba. In algebraic formalism, a structural description of an object is called a *term* or an *Ω-word* of an algebra [1](page 116). For lack of space, we omit the definition of SIT-terms and note only that SIT-terms are syntactic expressions for the structural descriptions of strings.

As mentioned in Section 2, SIT assigns a complexity value called information load to each structural description. Below we define information load for SIT-terms, based on the empirically motivated suggestion proposed by Leeuwenberg and Van der Helm [23], that denote possible perceptual organizations of string patterns.

Definition 4 *Let $t \in \{a, \ldots, z\}$, $T_1, \ldots, T_n$ be arbitrary SIT-terms, f_{SIT} be any SIT operator except the Unit operator, and f_D be any domain operator. If we write $f_{SIT}(< T_1, \ldots, T_n >, f_D)$ to capture the arguments (i.e. SIT-terms T_i and domain operator f_D) of the SIT operator f_{SIT}, then the information load, IL, can be defined as follows:*

1. $IL(t) = 1$
2. $IL(f_D) = 1$ if $f_D \neq id$, else 0
3. $IL(f_{SIT}(< T_1, \ldots, T_n >, f_D)) = \sum_{i=1}^{n} IL(T_i) + IL(f_D)$
4. $IL(Unit(T)) = IL(T) + 1$

Note, however, that it is possible to define different measures of information load on the set of structural descriptions by assigning a load to each operator and to each element. Moreover, our formalization allows different operators to be assigned different weights, so that the model can be tuned according to the empirical results obtained from psychological experiments.

3   Modelling Perceptual Context

Consider the string $abccba$ for which the SIT algebra generates a set of SIT terms, each of which represents an alternative perceptual organization of the string. Two possible perceptual organizations of this string are represented by $g_1 = Sym_e(Iter(a, succ, 3))$ and $g_2 = Sym_o(ab, Iter(c, id, 2))$ having information loads 2 and 3, respectively. Applying the minimality principle — which states that the perceived organization for a given pattern, among all its possible organizations, is the one with the lowest information load — predicts that g_1 represents the perceived organization. According to this description, $abccba$ consists of one substring (i.e. abc) followed by its reflection. Note that the string is described by Sym_e operator which takes one single argument that denotes abc.

However, the minimality principle provides the perceived organization of a pattern in isolation and ignores the mutual contextualization effect. This is because the perceived organizations of two individual patterns taken in isolation may be different from when they are seen together. This is due to the fact that each object acts as a context for the other and constraints its perceptual organization. Although each context may impose different constraints on the objects involved, we believe that one general constraint concerns similarity between the objects. We hypothesize that two objects present in a context are perceived as having as much shared substructures as possible. It is this aspect of the context that we aim to formalize. The conjecture that the perceived organization of two simultaneously present objects share most substructures will be called the *simplicity constraint*.

The simplicity constraint is clearly manifested in analogy contexts as illustrated in Figures 1 and 2. For example, consider again the string *abccba* in different analogies as illustrated in Figure 1. In the context of the first analogy (i.e. *abccba : abcabc*), g_1 forms an appropriate structural description since the second string *abcabc* can also be described as consisting of the same substring (i.e. *abc*). In fact, the analogical relation between *abccba* and *abcabc* can easily be formulated in terms of the substring *abc*.

In the context of the second analogy (i.e. *abccba : ccabbacc*) , g_1 does not form an appropriate structural description for *abccba* since the second string (i.e. ccabbacc) can hardly be described as consisting of the substring *abc*. In this context, g_2 represents the perceived organization of *abccba*, even though it has a higher information load than g_1. The reason is that g_2 shares common substructures with the preferred structural description $g_3 = Sym_o(Iter(c, id, 2), Sym_e(ab))$ of *ccabbacc*.

In order to formalize this aspect of the context, we note that the full SIT-algebra, as defined in Definition 3, generates every possible structural descriptions of all strings. However, in any given context, we may want to restrict our attention to only a small subset of the domain elements and a small subset of domain operators that together generate the objects that are present in the context. We will call such a restricted domain as a *representation system*. (See also [9].) In order to define a representation system, we first need to introduce the notion of *closure*.

Definition 5 *Given an algebra $< D, F >$ and a pair $< E, G >$ such that $E \subseteq D$, $G(n) \subseteq F(n)$ for all n, the closure of $< E, G >$ is E' such that $E \subseteq E'$; whenever $e_1, \ldots, e_n \in E'$ and $g \in G$, then $g(e_1, \ldots, e_n) \in E'$; and nothing else is in E'.*

Next we define a representation system for a set of objects.

Definition 6 *Given an algebra $< D, F >$ and set of objects $S \subseteq D$, a representation system of S is a pair $< E, G >$ such that $E \subseteq D$, $G \subseteq F$, E and G are both finite, and S is subset of the closure of $< E, G >$.*

What we would like is that when two patterns are present together, any common substructure between them adds to the information load only once. This is exactly what the simplicity constraint is about. In fact, the simplicity constraint restricts the way we compute the information load of more than one structural descriptions. The simplicity constraint can now be defined as imposing a complexity ordering on representation systems, which is determined by the number of elements in it: the more elements in it, the higher the complexity.[1] This

---

[1] It is also possible to consider the weights of the elements included in the representation systems such that perceptually complex operators are given more weight.

notion of complexity which is defined on representation systems will be called *collective information load*. The underlying idea here is that when two patterns are represented by structural descriptions that overlap, the representation system that generates these two structural descriptions will have a lower complexity. For instance, a minimal representation system that generates structural descriptions g_1 and g_3 for the first two strings of the above analogy (also see Figure 1) is $< \{a, ab, c\}, \{succ\} >$, which has four elements. (In the current version, in keeping with the SIT approach, the SIT operators are given zero weight and are not counted.) But if we consider structural description g_2 for *abccba*, then g_2 and g_3 can be generated by the representation system $< \{ab, c\}, \emptyset >$, with only two elements.

A representation system is now considered as a context for a given set of simultaneously present objects since it generates different descriptions of these objects, their constitutive parts, and the objects in which they are parts of it. Moreover, this SIT based representation system provides perceptually relevant, but not necessarily the perceived, organizations of the involved objects. In order to extend this algebraic notion of context such that it satisfies the simplicity constraint as well, we define the notion of *perceptual context* for a given set of objects.

Definition 7 *Let the collective information load of a representation set be the sum of the information loads of its ingredients as defined above. A perceptual context for a set of objects can now be defined as a SIT-based representation system for that set of objects which has the minimum collective information load.*

Consider again the second example of the string analogies illustrated in Figure 1. The perceptual context for this analogy will be $< \{ab, c\}, \emptyset >$ as it is discussed above.

3.1   Determining a Perceptual Context

In order to determine the perceptual context for a given set of objects, one should note that for a given SIT term T a SIT-based representation system can be constructed, which generates T. This is easily done by defining the representation set based on the constituents of the SIT term. For example, given a SIT term $Sym_e(Iter(a, succ, 3))$, the corresponding representation system will be $< \{a\}, \{succ\} >$. Let now RS_1 and RS_2 be the representation systems that are obtained by two given SIT terms T_1 and T_2 that represent two objects O_1 and O_2, respectively. These two representation systems can be combined into one by taking the union of their corresponding sets of domain objects and domain operators. The resulting representation system will be called a context for the objects O_1 and O_2.

In general, given a set of objects $O_1, \ldots, O_n$, the SIT algebra determines their possible structural organizations. Let $S_{O_1}, \ldots, S_{O_n}$ be the sets of structural organizations of objects $O_1, \ldots, O_n$, respectively. Since for each structural organization a SIT-based representation system can be constructed, each set of structural organizations will induce a set of representation systems. One can now take the Cartesian product of these systems resulting in a set of n-tuples of representation systems. The representation systems in each n-tuple can be combined to generate a context for the original sets of objects $O_1, \ldots, O_n$. Consequently, the set of n-tuples of representation systems corresponds to a set of context. The perceptual context for the set of objects $O_1, \ldots, O_n$ can now be decided as the context which has the minimum collective information load.

Notice that our method can be made more efficient by incorporating the assumption that the context-free structural descriptions that represent the most salient features of objects have the best chance of being the intended descriptions within the context. This assumption can be incorporated by taking the ordered lists (instead of sets) of structural descriptions and their corresponding ordered list of representation systems and start by checking their context in an increasing order of their information loads. Of course, this approach presumes that either the minimum collective information load of the context or an approximation of it can be known beforehand.

In order to illustrate an example of visual context, consider the first analogy between line drawing visual patterns as illustrated in Figure 2. Let the available domain elements for the two-dimensional SIT algebra [2] be those illustrated in Figure 3-A and let *v-trans* and *h-trans* be the available domain operators for two-dimensional vertical and horizontal translations, respectively, as shown in Figure 3-B. In Figure 3-A, the symbols that are attached to different visual parts are used to denote them when we write their structural descriptions. The first

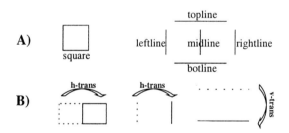

Fig. 3. Examples of A) domain elements and B) domain operators of the two-dimensional SIT algebra.

and the second visual objects in the first analogy from Figure 2 can be described in many different ways, among which, those that are listed below.

- 1a: $Iter(square, h - trans, 2)$
- 1b: $Con(Iter(leftline, h - trans, 3), Iter(topline, v - trans, 2))$
- 1c: $Con(Sym_o(leftline, midline), Iter(topline, v - trans, 2))$

---

[2] A SIT algebra for two-dimensional visual patterns are developed in [2].

- 2a: $Con(midline, Iter(topline, v - trans, 2))$
- 2b: $Con(midline, topline, botline)$

The representations systems that are induced by these structural descriptions are listed below.

- 1a: $< \{square\}, \{h - trans\} >$
- 1b: $< \{leftline, topline\}, \{h - trans, v - trans\} >$
- 1c: $< \{leftline, midline, topline\}, \{v - trans\} >$

- 2a: $< \{midline, topline\}, \{v - trans\} >$
- 2b: $< \{midline, topline, botline\}, \emptyset >$

The Cartesian product between the first three and the last two representation systems results in six pairs of representations systems. When the representation systems in each pair are combined with each other, we get the following six perceptual contexts.

- 1a-2a: $< \{square, midline, topline\}, \{h - trans, v - trans\} >$
- 1a-2b: $< \{square, midline, topline, botline\}, \{h - trans\} >$
- 1b-2a: $< \{leftline, midline, topline\}, \{h - trans, v - trans\} >$
- 1b-2b: $< \{leftline, midline, topline, botline\}, \{h - trans, v - trans\} >$
- 1c-2a: $< \{leftline, midline, topline\}, \{v - trans\} >$
- 1c-2b: $< \{leftline, midline, topline, botline\}, \{v - trans\} >$

Using similar definition of collective information load as defined for string domain, the fifth perceptual context has the minimum collective information load which implies that the perceived structural descriptions of the first and the second visual patterns in the first analogy illustrated in Figure 2 are determined by the description 1c and 2a, respectively. It should be noted that the preferred structural description of the first visual pattern is not the simplest description of that pattern, but the one that results in the simplest collective information load.

4   Extending the Model to the Context Effects in Other Domains

We now speculate how our model could be applied to other kinds of situations, not necessarily analogies, and not necessarily restricted to perceptual phenomena. Consider, for instance, the context effect described in Kokinov [11], where purportedly extraneous information on the problem sheet was found to affect the subjects' problem-solving ability. We could posit a cognitive algebra for any object or situation, containing the cognitive operations that are possible to apply to that object (or situation). Then the 'context-free' cognitive algebra for an object can be seen as providing the context in which the other object must be seen, thereby influencing what operations are seen possible in the second object.

There are two major issues that Kokinov's context effect brings up. One is the separation between the object (or the situation or the process) and its context. In the problem-solving example, the problem was given, so it was the focus, and the 'extraneous' information left on the problem-solving sheet would be considered the context. However, in the analogy situation described above, there is no such clear-cut focus. In describing our model, we tacitly considered the term A to be providing the context for the term B. But it is equally possible to reverse this and consider B to be providing the context for A. Using examples like Tversky [20], one may even be able to demonstrate asymmetry of the context effect. Perhaps the most striking result could be if one could show asymmetry of context effect in analogy relations (which are otherwise symmetric): it may well be that the left to right scanning order imposes a subconscious ordering relation. (In this case it would be interesting to see if the asymmetry is reversed in subjects from a culture where reading is from right to left, as in Persian or Japanese.) The other major issue highlighted by Kokinov's experiments is that the context effect need not be conscious. In fact, the context effect in perceptual analogies may also be largely subconscious, or even partly hard-wired in the neurological structure of the brain.

Now let us try to venture out to other non-analogical situations, and see if we can apply some of our ideas to model the context effect there as well. Consider the communication situations: most of the natural language discourse situations can be characterized as such. Well, if we compare the before and the after situations of a discourse, it is the information content (in the recipient) that is supposed to change. Thus, the impact of the discourse depends on the state of information that the recipient had before the discourse. We are saying 'information', but of course, it includes beliefs, assumptions, biases, and so on. Moreover, there may be various factors that may affect this before-discourse information state: environmental factors such as the place (at a company party, one may expect to hear conversation related to company's politics), and the time (after winter vacation one may expect to hear about holiday travels, perhaps skiing trips); the state of the mind (if one has just broken off a relationship, for example); the educational and the cultural background; and so on and on. Notwithstanding these numerous factors affecting the before-discourse information state, the state itself can be modelled as a list of the events that are considered possible, and a probability distribution for them showing for each event how likely it is according to the subjects beliefs. This distribution can be seen as providing the context for the discourse. After the discourse is assimilated, the changed information state can be expressed in the same formalism as used to describe the before-information state. Thus, the dynamics of context can be modelled: a discourse is interpreted in a context, and the context is changed as a result of the discourse.

5 Related Research

We would now like to make a few remarks in connecting our model with some of the empirical research on context effect in perception. First of all, we draw attention to the fact that most of the empirical work on context uses some version or another of multi-dimensional feature space, with little emphasis on structural aspects. (See, for example, [7, 16, 17, 19]) Some studies that have explored the structural aspects of context have also focused on the alignment and matching of structures — whether relations or attributes are used as a basis of alignment, etc. (See, for example, [6]). As far as we are aware, there has been little effort at studying how complex structures are encoded, how they carry information, and how they affect context.

Now in a general way, we believe that the context effects found by Tversky [20], and more recently elaborated in the experiments of Goldstone et. al. [7], could be explained as shifts from one subalgebra to another. Moreover, how context affects object decomposition ([16]), and how the order in which context is learnt affect their encoding ([17]), can be modelled as a kind of hysteresis effect whereby the representation algebras from the previous context influence the subsequent cognitive tasks. For example, Rodet et. al. [17] found that the subjects who learned concept XY before learning concept X did not possess the feature to distinguish Y, but the subjects who learned concept X before learning XY did possess this feature; even though both groups of subjects performed equally well in identifying exemplars of both concepts X and XY.

Similarly, an explanation can perhaps be put forward for the context effects observed by Stins et. al. [19]. They found that when the subjects were given an integrative task (determining whole-part relationship), they could be influenced by the prime, but not when they were given a non-integrative task (comparing an internal angle of two figures). An integrative task triggers structural decomposition, in which representation systems play a crucial role (which can be influenced by primes).

More importantly, however, our approach does have some non-trivial implications, even for experimental data that is based on multi-dimensional feature space (with essentially no structure). For example, in Experiment 3 by Goldstone et. al. [7], they sought to show non-monotonicity of similarity judgment, where adding a unique feature to one of the two objects being compared results in an increased similarity between the two. The intuition behind this is that the added feature brings to the foreground another dimension, along which the two objects are rather similar. (Consider the objects to be letters 'b' and 'd', for example — we are focusing on the shape of the letters here — and in the added feature part, we make 'd' with slightly thicker line.) Now, in fact, Goldstone and his colleague did not really find non-monotonicity, but they found that the similarity ratings were quite close in the two conditions. In our approach, we could perhaps say that bringing another dimension to the foreground has the effect of increasing the number of elements in the representation system, thereby adding to the collective information load, which counteracts the increased similarity along this new dimension. An interesting fact here is that in the follow up experiment, Goldstone *et al.* asked the subjects to explicitly write down the dimensions along which the two objects were similar, and they were able to find a small non-monotonicity effect. Perhaps explicitly writing down the dimension reduces some of the perceptual information load of the representation system.

6 Conclusions and Future Research

We would like now to take a step back and consider what is context in general and what can be gained from pursuing formal approaches (such as ours) to modelling it. In any cognitive situation, there are many objects and/or processes that interact together, affecting each other, to determine the final outcome of that situation. For example, in analogies, two terms interact with each other, affecting each other's representations, to arrive at a final interpretation. If we consider this process as a whole (and it is not embedded in another situation, as it would be if we were examining the effect of priming on the ability to solve analogies), then there can be no context effect, almost by definition. However, whenever we identify any process, there is always something that is not included in there, there is the before and after of the process, and given proper conditions, one could show that these excluded factors affect the process in some way. Then they seem to become the context for the process.

Also, within a process itself, we can identify some component or sub-process, and focus on it, in which case the remaining components and sub-processes take the role of context, as in the analogy example, when we focus on the representation of one of the terms. So in either case, the notion of context, in our view, presupposes a foreground object or process that is the focus of study. Now there are two ways in which one can go about studying the effect of context. One is to take some factor (or set of factors) that may affect the context, and see what role they play in affecting different kinds of processes. For example, one could focus on the environmental factors (or even more specifically, how does the 'place' where the foreground process is taking place affects its outcome), or the mental factors (how does the emotional state of the cognitive agent affects the foreground's process's outcome). This may be useful in some ways, but we feel that given the wide range of cognitive processes that could be foreground processes, it would put a huge demand on a theory or model of context to be able to explain how that factor affects different kinds of cognitive processes.

Instead, the approach we favor is to consider some class of cognitive processes. The class can be quite large as in, analogy, or problem-solving, or discourse situations. The main thing is that there must be some way to uniformly characterize the cognitive processes in that class. Now to model the context effect, we need to figure out a formalization that is suitable as a background process (or object) for this class of foreground processes. For example, we characterized analogy as a mapping between representations of the terms, so the background object became the representation system for the terms. Similarly, if a discourse situation is characterized as an information-changing process, then the background object becomes the information state containing the possible events and their probability distribution. Note that the distinction between foreground/background process or objects implies different formalisms that are related to each other according to some (possibly hierarchical) structures. In this sense, the work proposed by Giunchiglia et. al. [3, 4] provide the right framework to formalize such concepts.

This formalized background object can be called 'context', and we can then study how the foreground processes interact dynamically with the context: how the context determines the foreground process's outcome and how the foreground processes modify the context. Of course, this still leaves out the problem of how the context is determined, meaning how do various factors affect context settings. For example, how do environmental and emotional factors determine which events are considered possible and with what probability by a subject. To complete the story of context, these issues must be addressed as well.

However, we feel that the approach outlined here offers a methodology that divides the difficult problem of modelling the context effects in two parts. One part lies in figuring out how the context effects (and is affected) by the foreground processes, and the other part lies in figuring out how various other factors affect the context. For example, in the approach outlined in Section 3, we articulated some principles for showing how a representation system affects the representation of an object, and how the object modifies the representation system. But that is only one half of the story. To complement it, one must study how other factors, such as priming, affects the representation system. To sum up, we see the research on modelling of context as providing a way to have an intermediate formal structure that can mediate the effect of various environmental and other internal factors on the foreground processes. In our view, this approach seems most promising for a study of context.

References

1. P.M. Cohn. Universal algebra. Revised edition, D.Reidel, Dordrecht, The Netherlands, 1981.
2. M. Dastani. Ph.D. thesis, University of Amsterdam, The Netherlands., 1998.
3. E. Giunchiglia, F. Giunchiglia, L. Serafini, and M. Frixione. Non-omniscient belief as context-based reasoning. In *IJCAI-93*, 1993.
4. F. Giunchiglia and L. Serani. Multilanguage hierarchical logics (or: how we can do without modal logics). In *Articial Intelligence, 65*, pages 29–70, 1994.
5. J.A. Goguen, J.W. Thatcher, and E.G. Wagner. *An Initial Algebra Approach to the Specification, Correctness, and Implementation of Abstract Data Types*. Prentice Hall, Inc., New York, 1978.
6. R.L. Goldstone. Similarity, interactive activation, and mapping. In *Journal of Experimental Psychology: Learning, Memory, & Cognition 20*, pages 3–28, 1994.
7. R.L. Goldstone, D.L. Medin, and J. Halberstadt. Similarity in context. In *Memory & Cognition, 25 (2)*, pages 237–255, 1997.
8. D. Hofstadter. *Fluid Concepts and Creative Analogies: Computer Models of the Fundamental Mechanisms of Thought*. Basic Books, New York, NY., 1995.
9. B. Indurkhya. On the role of interpretive analogy in learning. *New Generation Computing*, 8:385–402, 1991.
10. B. Indurkhya. *Metaphor and cognition: an interactionist approach*. Kluwer Academic Publishers, Dordrecht, The Netherlands, 1992.

11. B. Kokinov. A dynamic approach to context modeling. In P. Brezillon and S. Abu-Hakima, editors, *IJCAI-95 Workshop on Modeling Context in Knowledge Representation in Reasoning*, Laforia, 1995.

12. E. Leeuwenberg. A perceptual coding language for visual and auditory patterns. *American Journal of Psychology*, 84:307–349, 1971.

13. M. Leyton. *Symmetry, causality, mind.* The MIT Press, Cambridge MA, 1992.

14. K. Meinke. Universal algebra in higher types. In *Theoretical Computer Science, 100*, pages 385–417, 1992.

15. K. Meinke and L.J. Steggles. *Specification and Verification in Higher Order Algebra: A Case Study of Convolution.* Springer Verlag, Berlin, 1993.

16. R. Pevtzow and R.L. Goldstone. Categorization and the parsing of objects. In *Proceedings of the Sixteenth Annual Conference of the Cognitive Science Society*, pages 717–722, Hillsdale, New Jersey, 1994. Lawrence Erlbaum Associates.

17. L. Rodet and P.G. Schyns. Learning features of representation in conceptual context. In *Proceedings of the Sixteenth Annual Conference of the Cognitive Science Society*, pages 766–771, Hillsdale, New Jersey, 1994. Lawrence Erlbaum Associates.

18. T. Rus and T. Halverson. Algebraic tools for language processing. In *Comput. Lang. 20 (4)*, pages 213–238, 1994.

19. J.F. Stins and C. Van Leeuwen. Context influence on the perception of figures as condition upon perceptual organization strategies. *Perception & Psychophysics*, 53 (1):34–42, 1993.

20. A. Tversky. Features of similarity. In *Psychological Review, 84*, pages 327–352, 1977.

21. P. Van der Helm. The dynamics of prägnanz. *Psychological Research*, 56:224–236, 1994.

22. P. Van der Helm and E. Leeuwenberg. Avoiding explosive search in automatic selection of simplest pattern codes. *Pattern Recognition*, 19:181–191, 1986.

23. P. Van der Helm and E. Leeuwenberg. Accessibility: A criterion for regularity and hierarchy in visual pattern code. *Journal of Mathematical Psychology*, 35:151–213, 1991.

Learning Appropriate Contexts

Bruce Edmonds

Centre for Policy Modelling,
Manchester Metropolitan University,
Aytoun Building, Autoun Street, Manchester, M1 3GH, UK.
b.edmonds@mmu.ac.uk http://www.cpm.mmu.ac.uk/~bruce

Abstract. Genetic Programming is extended so that the solutions being evolved do so in the context of local domains within the total problem domain. This produces a situation where different "species" of solution develop to exploit different "niches" of the problem – indicating exploitable solutions. It is argued that for context to be fully learnable a further step of *abstraction* is necessary. Such contexts abstracted from clusters of solution/model domains make sense of the problem of how to identify when it is the content of a model is wrong and when it is the context. Some principles of learning to identify useful contexts are proposed. **Keywords:** learning, conditions of application, context, evolutionary computing, error

1. Introduction

In AI there have now been many applications of context and context-like notions with a view to improving the robustness and generality of inference. In the field of neural networks there have been some applications of context-related notions, but so far the fields of inductive learning, evolutionary computing and reinforcement techniques do not seem to have much use for the notion. There have been some attempts to apply context detection methods to neural networks, so that a network can more efficiently learn more than one kind of pattern but these have been limited in conception to fixes for existing algorithms.

Of course, if one knows in advance that there will be several relevant contexts, the human designer (who is naturally adept at distinguishing the appropriate context) can 'hard-wire' some mechanism so that the learning algorithm can detect and make the sudden change necessary (for example simply switching to a new neural network) to adjust to a new context. But if one does not have such prior knowledge then this is not possible – the appropriate contexts have to be learnt at the same time as the content of the models. In such cases the question is "why does one need separate parts of the model for context and content, why not just combine them into a unitary model?". If one does not combine them one always has the problem of determining whether any shortcoming in the model is due to a misidentification of context or simply erroneous content – a problem that is impossible to solve just by looking at the context & content of a model on its own. Rather the tendency has often been, in the absence of a good reason to do otherwise, to simplify things by combining the conditions of application of a model explicitly into the model content.

This paper seeks to make some practical proposals as to how notions of conditions of applicability and then contexts themselves can be introduced into evolutionary computing. Such a foray includes suggestions for principles for learning and identifying the appropriate contexts without prior knowledge.

2. Adding conditions of applicability to evolving models

2.1 Standard Evolutionary Computing Algorithms

Almost all evolutionary computing algorithms have the following basic structure:
- There is a target problem;
- There is a population of candidate models/solutions (initially random);
- Each iteration some/all of the models are evaluated against the problem (either competitively against each others or by being given a fitness score);
- The algorithm is such that the models which perform better at the problem are preferentially selected for, so the worse models tend to be discarded;
- There is some operator which introduces variation into the population;
- At any particular time the model which currently performs best is the "result" of the computation (usually taken at the end).

There are various different approaches within this, for example, genetic programming (GP) (Koza, 1992). With GP the population of models can have a tree structure of any shape with the nodes and terminals taken from a fixed vocabulary. The models are interpreted as a function or program to solve the given problem, and usually given a numeric measure of their success at this – their "fitness". The models are propagated into the next generation with a probability correlated to this fitness. The variation is provided by "crossing" the tree structures– as shown in figure 1).

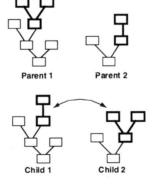

Parent 1   Parent 2

Child 1   Child 2

Fig. 1. The action of crossover in GP

For example, the problem may be that of finding a functional expression, e.g. $2 - 3x^2$, to most closely "fit" a given set of data pairs. In this case the set of models will be trees with terminals being either x or a set of constants, the nodes might be the simple arithmetic operators, and the measure of success the inverse of the error of the resulting function with respect to the data.

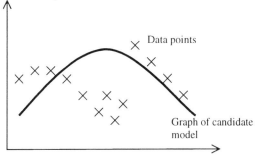

Fig. 2. An illustration of a candidate functional "fit" for some data

One of the key features of such algorithms is that each candidate model in the population has the same scope – that of the problem. In the long run, a model can only be selected if it is successful (at least on average relative to other models) over the *whole* domain. Essentially the algorithm results in a single answer – the model that generally did best. There is no possibility that (in the long run) a model can be selected by doing well at only a small part of the whole problem. The technique is essentially context-free – the only context involved is that implied by the scope of the problem and that is selected manually by the designer.

2.2 Adding Conditions of Application

Thus the first step is to allow each candidate model to specialise in different parts of the problem domain. For this to be possible, success at solving the target problem must be evaluated locally, *without* the model being (unduly) penalised for not being global successful. In evolutionary terms, we allow the problem domain to be the environment and allow different models to co-exist in different "niches" corresponding to particular sub-spaces. This is illustrated in fig. 3 below.

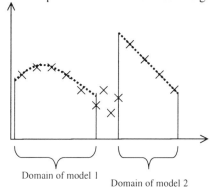

Domain of model 1

Domain of model 2

Fig. 3. Two models specialising in different parts of the problem.

It is well know that allowing "demes", that is separate areas of evolution, acts to preserve the variety in the population. Allowing the problem space itself to structure the evolutionary should allow for clustering and competition according to what makes sense for that problem.

To do this each model in the population needs to indicate its conditions of application as well as its content, and both need to evolve in response to the problem presented within the problem domain. There are many different ways of doing this – perhaps the easiest is to simply *position* each model in the space and allow replication to other positions nearby.

One algorithm for this is:

```
Randomly generate candidate models and place them
randomly about the domain, D
for each generation
   repeat
      randomly pick a point in D, P
      pick n models, C, biased towards those near P
      evaluate all in C over a neighbourhood of P
      pick random number x from [0,1)
      if x < (1 - crossover probability)
         then propagate the fittest in C to new
              generation
         else cross two fittest in C, put result into
              new generation
   until new population is complete
next generation
```

The idea is that models will propagate into the areas of the problem domain where they are relatively successful in (until a model that does even better locally appears).

The main parameters for this algorithm are:

- Number of generations;
- Size of population;
- Initial maximum depth of model;
- Number of models picked each tournament;
- The extent of the bias towards the point, P, picked;
- The size of the neighbourhood that the models are evaluated over;
- Probability of crossover.

Also, more importantly, the following need to be specified:

- The problem;
- The language of the models in terms of their interpretation w.r.t. the problem (usually done in terms of nodes, and terminals if this is an untyped model);
- The space over which the models will propagate (usually a subspace of the domain of the problem).

A disadvantage of this technique is that once the algorithm has finished is does not provide you with a single best answer, but rather a whole collection of models, each with different domains of application. If you want a *complete* solution you have to analyse the results of the computation and piece together a compound model out of several models which work in different domains – this will not be a simple model with a neat closed form. Also there may be tough areas of the problem where ones does not find any acceptable models at all.

Of course, these "cons" are relative – if one had used a standard universal algorithm (that is all models having the same domain as the problem and evaluated over that domain), then the resulting "best" model might well not perform well over the whole domain and its form might be correspondingly more complex as it had to deal with the whole problem at once.

2.3   An Example Application

The example implementation I will describe is that of applying the above algorithm to predicting the number of sunspots (shown in fig 4 below). The fitness function is the inverse of the root mean squared error of the prediction of the model as compared to the actual data. The models are constructed with the nodes: PLUS, MINUS, TIMES, SAFEDIVIDE, SIN and COS, and the terminals: x, x1, x2, x4, x8, x16 (which stand for the current time period and then the number of sunspots with lags 1, 2, 4, 8, and 16 time periods respectively) the along with a random selection of numeric constants.

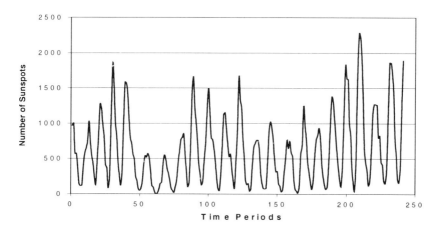

Fig. 4. The problem function – the number of sunspots

The fixed parameters were as follows:
- Number of generations: *50*;
- Size of population: *723*;
- Initial maximum depth of model: *5*;
- Number of models picked each tournament: *6*;
- Locality bias: *10*;
- Size of the neighbourhood: *from 1 to 7 in steps of 2*;
- Probability of crossover: *0.1*.

There were four runs, in each the neighbourhood over which the models were tested was *1*, *3*, *5*, and *7* respectively. The first graph (Fig. 5) shows the average fitness of the models for these runs.

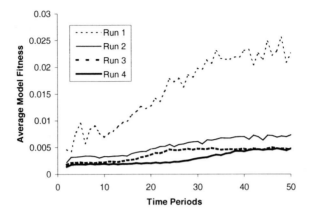

Fig. 5. The Average Fitness of Models in the four runs

The smaller the domain the greater the average model fitness. This is because it is much easier to "fit" an expression to a single point than "fit" longer sections of the graph, with fitting the whole graph being the most difficult. Of course, there is little point in fitting single points with expressions if there is not *any* generalisation across the graph. After all we already have an completely accurate set of expressions point-by-point: the original data set itself. On the other hand, *if* there *are* distinct regions of the problem space where different solutions make sense, being able to identify these regions and appropriate models for them would be very useful. If the context of the whole problem domain is sufficiently restricted (which is likely for most of the "test" or "toy" problems these techniques are tried upon).

Figure 6, below, shows the maximum coverage of the models for the four runs. In each case early on a few models take over from the others in terms of the amount of problem space they occupy. Then as they produce descendants with variations, these descendants compete with them for problem space and the coverage of any particular model equals out.

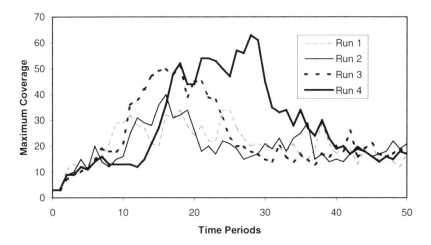

Fig 6. Maximum coverage (in terms of number of positions) of models over the four runs

One individual propagates itself for a while before new models (often its own offspring) start to compete with it. This is illustrated in Fig. 7. Which shows the coverage of the dominant model at each stage of run four, where the different individual models are identified.

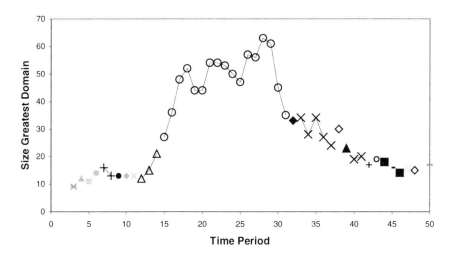

Fig 7. Maximum coverage of individual models in run 4 (the same individual is indicated by the same symbol and are connected)

Thus you get a short-term domination by individual models by propagation and a longer-term effect composed of the domination of closely related but different individuals – what might be called "species". The end of run 4 is analysed below

150

using a very rough division into such species. Those models that start with the same 25 characters are arbitrarily classed as the same species. The 10 most dominant species at the end of run 4 are shown below in Table 1.

Species	Start of model	Size of Domain
1	[MINUS [SAFEDIVIDE [PLUS ...	260
2	[PLUS [PLUS [SIN [TIMES ...	187
3	[PLUS [SAFEDIVIDE [PLUS ...	31
4	[MINUS [MINUS [x1] [TIME ...	24
5	[PLUS [x1] [SIN [PLUS [T ...	22
6	[PLUS [MINUS [x1] [0.641 ...	19
7	[PLUS [MINUS [x1] [0.868 ...	17
8	[SAFEDIVIDE [PLUS [x1] [...	13
9	[MINUS [MINUS [x1] [0.57 ...	12
10	[PLUS [PLUS [SIN [0.5712 ...	9

Table 1. The 10 "species" with the largest domain

As you can see two quite different such "species" dominate. The figure below (Fig. 8.) Indicates the domains of these species.

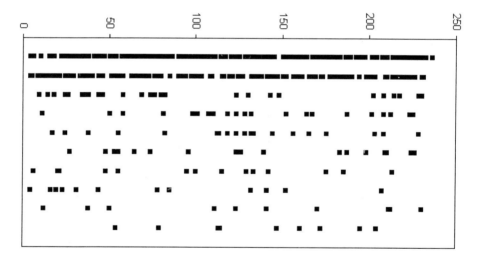

Fig. 8. The domains of the ten most common species (most dominant in the top line) of models at the end of run 4

Simply by inspection, some of these species do seem to have identifiable parts of the problem space in which they apply. This effect could be accentuated by adding a period of "consolidation" at the tail end of the algorithm. During this period there would be no crossover and the locality of the operation of the propagation process kept to a minimum. This would allow individual models to have a chance to "dominate" contiguous sub-spaces of the whole domain. Such a consolidation period has obvious parallels with the technique of "simulated annealing", and I guess a similar technique of slowly lowering the "temperature" (the distance models can jump around) of the algorithm towards the end might have similar effects.

3. The move to really learning and using contexts

Given the picture of "context" as an abstraction of the background inputs to a model, implicit in the transfer of knowledge from learning to application (that I argued for in Edmonds, 1999). There is still a step to take in order for it to be truly "context" that is being utilised – a collection of conditions of application become a context if it is sensible to abstract them as a coherent unit. Now it may be possible for a human to analyse the results of the evolutionary algorithms just described and identify context – these would correspond to niches in the problem domain that a set of models competes to exploit – but the above algorithm *itself* does not do this.

Rather the identification of context in a problem reveals something about the problem itself – it indicates that there are recognisable and distinct sub-cases where different sets of models/rules/solutions apply. In other words that there is a sufficient *clustering* or *grouping* of the conditions of applications of relevant models that it makes sense to abstract from this set of domains to a *context*. This is what a biologist does when identifying the "niche" of an organism (or group of organisms) – this is not highly detailed list of where this organism happened to live, but a relevant abstraction from this taking into account the *way* the organism survives. This idea of abstracting a context from clusters of model domains is illustrated in Fig. 9. below.

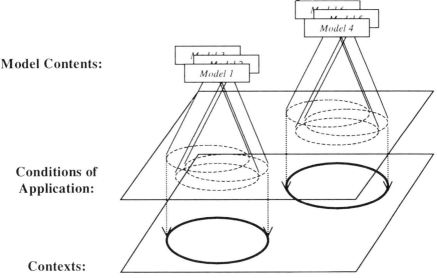

Fig. 9. Contexts abstracted from models with different, but clustered, domains of application

Of course, it is not necessarily the case that the model domains *will* be clustered so that it is at all sensible to abstract them into explicit contexts. Rather this is a contingent property of the problem and the strategy, resources and limitations of the learner. The existence of meaningful *contexts* arises out of the fact that there *happen to be* heuristics that can do this clustering, otherwise even if all the relevant models are not universal in scope context, as such, might not arise.

Such an abstraction requires a further level of learning not present in the above algorithm. Extra levels of learning require resources and so must be justified – so why would one need to cluster and identify *contexts* rather than directly manipulate the model domains themselves? In the natural world organisms do not usually bother to explicitly identify where they live. A simple answer is that an abstracted context is a far more compact and elegant representation of the conditions under which a whole collection of models might hold, but this is not a complete answer because the overhead in retaining the detail of the source models domains may not be an advantage compared to the advantage of knowing *exactly* when a model applies. A partial answer to this question will be offered in the next section.

4. Knowing whether it is the context or the content that is wrong

There is a fundamental difficulty is in attributing the source of error displayed by a model. Perhaps this, more than anything else, characterises different strategies for learning. Given that a model displays an unacceptable level of error in a situation, what are the options? They include:

1. Changing the model content (either by a minor elaboration or parameter adjustment or by a more radical restructuring);
2. Adjusting the conditions of application so as to exclude the domain where the model did not work;
3. Making the predictions of the model less precise so as to allow for the error;
4. Finally, and most radically it may be necessary to change the language/basis of the model formulation itself.

The problem is to determine which is appropriate in each case. In this paper I am particularly focusing of the decision between (1) and (2) above (for a wider discussion see Moss and Edmonds 1998).

The point is that *in isolation* there is no principled way of telling whether it is the model content or context that is wrong. However, given that the problem or circumstances *is* such that there are meaningful clusterings of the domains of models into *contexts* there is a way, namely: *to check the predictions of other models with the same context*. If other models associated with the same context are also in error, then it is probably the context that is wrong; if the other models associated with the same context are correct then it is most likely the original model content that is in error. This collective view of model building suggests the following principles of context identification:

1. (*Formation*) A cluster of models with similar or closely related domains suggests these domains can be meaningfully abstracted to a *context*.
2. (*Abstraction*) If two (or more) contexts share a lot of models with the same domain, they may be abstracted (with those shared models) to another context.

In other words, by dropping a few models from each allows the creation of a super-context with a wider domain of application.

3. (*Specialisation*) If making the domain of a context much more specific allows the inclusion of many more models (and hence useful inferences) create a sub-context.

4. (*Content Correction*) If one (or only a few) models in the same context are in error whilst the others are still correct, then these models should either be removed from this context or their contents altered so that they give correct outputs (dependent on the extent of modifications needed to "correct" them)

5. (*Content Addition*) If a model has the same domain as an existing context, then add it to that context.

6. (*Context Restriction*) If all (or most) the models in a context seem to be simultaneously in error, then the context needs to be restricted to exclude the conditions under which the errors occurred.

7. (*Context Expansion*) If all (or most) of the models in a context seem to work under some new conditions, then expands the context to include these conditions.

8. (*Context Removal*) If a context has only a few models left (due to principle 2) or its domain is null (i.e. it is not applicable) forget that context.

These conditions are somewhat circular – context are guessed at from clusterings of model domains, and model contents are changed in models who disagree with a majority of models in the same context. However, I do think that these principles should allow the "bootstrapping" of meaningful contexts. A starting point for this process can be the assumption that models learnt in similar circumstances (situations) share the same context – that the relevant contexts are defined by the similarity of experience. Later these assumption based contexts can be abstracted, refined and corrected using the above. Any bootstrapping learning process depends upon the possibility of starting with simple models and situations and working upwards (compare Elman 1993).

5. Related Work

5.1 Evolutionary Computation

The obvious technique from evolutionary computation which employs ideas of model domains are Holland's "Classifier" (Holland 1992) and descendent techniques. Here each model is explicitly divided into the conditions and action of a model. Such models are not designed to evolve in parallel as in the above algorithm, but to form computational chains.

Eric Baum has developed this idea by applying more rigorous property rules to govern the chaining of models and the apportionment of reward. Thus in his model each model has an implicit domain, in that it is only applies when it out-bids other models in order to be applied (Baum and Durdanovic, 2000b). In the most recent version of his algorithm (called Hayek 4) he also introduces explicit conditions of application as each model is a Post production rule (Baum and Durdanovic, 2000a).

5.2 Machine Learning

There has been more attention to context-related ideas in the effort to improve inductive and neural network learning techniques. Some techniques require the explicit identification of what the contextual factors will be and then augment the existing machine learning strategy with a meta-level algorithm utilising this information (e.g. Turney 1993 or Widmer 1997). Others look to augment strategies using implicit information about the context to adjust features of the learning such as the weightings (Aha 1989), or normalisation (Turney and Halasz 1993). These usually utilise a clustering algorithm and thus are closest to the evolutionary technique I have described (e.g. Aha 1989).

Peter Turney surveys the various heuristics tried to mitigate the effects of context on machine learning techniques in (Turney 1996). He keeps an extensive bibliography on context-sensitive learning at URL:

    http://extractor.iit.nrc.ca/bibliographies/context-sensitive.html

6. Conclusion

If one abandons the myopic view of focusing on *single model* solutions and models, and looks at their *group dynamics* instead, then further learning heuristics become available. These allow one to distinguish when it is the identification of the content or the context that is at error. Indeed it is only by considering *groups* of models that contexts themselves make sense.

7. References

Aha, D. W. (1989). Incremental, instance-based learning of independent and graded concept descriptions. In *Proc. of the 6th Int. Workshop on Machine Learning*, 387-391. CA: Morgan Kaufmann.
Baum, E. and Durdanovic, I. (2000a). An Evolutionary Post-Production System. http://www.neci.nj.nec.com/homepages/eric/ptech.ps
Baum, E. and Durdanovic, I. (2000b). Evolution of Co-operative Problem Solving. http://www.neci.nj.nec.com/homepages/eric/hayek32000.ps
Edmonds, B. (1990). The Pragmatic Roots of Context. CONTEXT'99, Trento, Italy, September 1999. *Lecture Notes in Artificial Intelligence*, **1688**:119-132.
Elman, J. L. (1993). Learning and Development in Neural Networks - The Importance of Starting Small. *Cognition*, **48**:71-99.
Gigerenzer, G and Goldstein, D. G. (1996). Reasoning the fast and frugal way: Models of bounded rationality. *Psychological Review*, **104**:650-669.
Harries, M. B., Sammut, C. and Horn, K. (1998). Extracting Hidden Contexts. *Machine Learning*, **32**:101-126.

Holland, J. H. (1992). *Adaptation in Natural and Artificial Systems*, 2nd Ed., MIT Press, Cambridge, MA.

Koza, J. R. 1992. *Genetic Programming: On the Programming of Computers by Means of Natural Selection.* Cambridge, MA: MIT Press.

Moss, S. and Edmonds, B. (1998). Modelling Economic Learning as Modelling. *Cybernetics and Systems*, **29**:215-248.

Turney, P. D. (1993). Exploiting context when learning to classify. In *Proceedings of the European Conference on Machine Learning*, ECML-93. 402-407. Vienna: Springer-Verlag.

Turney, P. D. (1996). The management of context-sensitive features: A review of strategies. *Proceedings of the ICML-96 Workshop on Learning in Context-Sensitive Domains*, Bari, Italy, July 3, 60-66.

Turney, P. D. and Halasz, M. (1993). Contextual normalisation applied to aircraft gas turbine engine diagnosis. *Journal of Applied Intelligence*, **3**:109-129.

Widmer, G. (1997). Tracking Context Changes through Meta-Learning. *Machine Learning*, **27**:259-286.

Context and Relevance: A Pragmatic Approach

Hamid R. Ekbia[1] and Ana G. Maguitman[2]

[1] Center for Research on Concepts and Cognition
[2] Center for Research on Artificial and Natural Intelligence
Computer Science Department, Indiana University
Bloomington, IN 47405-7104
Phone: (812) 855-6965/Fax: (812) 855-6966
{hekbia,anmaguit}@cs.indiana.edu

Abstract. In recent years, AI research has started to take seriously the role of context in developing models. This trend is heralded by a departure from logic-based views and their over-emphasis on the formal aspects of thought processes. The departure, however, has not been complete—some fundamental assumptions of formal logic are still maintained in the new approaches. Similarly, "relevance" remains a major challenge for AI research. This paper outlines an alternative proposal that takes context and relevance as intertwined aspects of thought and intelligence. We argue for a pragmatic approach, which shows better promise than formal logic in dealing with such issues.

1 Introduction

Issues of context and relevance arise repeatedly in science and philosophy. Most often, however, they are dealt with separately as unrelated topics, or, if treated together, within the general framework of logic. This paper brings the two together under the assumption that they are not only conceptually linked, but also co-constituted. Furthermore, we shall argue, all the alternative approaches taken within the logical tradition fail to address context and relevance for fundamentally similar reasons—namely, what we call "formality assumptions" of logic.

We begin with an outline of a pragmatic approach to context and relevance inspired by the views of Dewey in section 2. In sections 3 and 4 we provide a synopsis of logical approaches to these issues, and explain why the logical tradition cannot support the criteria suggested by the pragmatic view. The last section points out some of the implications of this view for AI.

Our main goal in this paper is to discuss the limits of the logical approach rather than to abandon or rebuke logic-oriented views more generally. It needs to be stressed that the view that we advocate here, far from being an elaborated comprehensive scheme, is meant to suggest an alternative way of thinking about context and relevance. As these issues are propounded in many places in science and philosophy, a multidisciplinary approach strongly suggests itself. Thus, throughout, we have also mentioned similar intuitions in other areas that seem to be close to our own.

2 The Pragmatic View of Context and Relevance

> We grasp the meaning of what is said in our language not because appreciation of context is unnecessary but because context is inescapably present. [9]

Dewey looked upon modern philosophers as moving between two extremes: those who claim that knowledge and reality are constructed out of discrete and independent elements, and those who claim that everything is so interrelated that reality and knowledge are ultimately a single whole. Arguing against both extremes, Dewey believed that they suffer from the same fallacy, neglect of context—"the greatest single disaster which philosophic thinking can incur" [5]. More than fifty years of AI practice demonstrates the aptness of a similar assertion about AI: neglect of context is the greatest single disaster that AI practice has incurred thus far.

As a remedy for this situation in philosophy, Dewey proposed a notion of context, which, for ease of reference, we call the "pragmatic" view. Context, according to him, has two components (see Figure 1): (i) background, which is both spatial and temporal, and is ubiquitous in all thinking; and (ii) selective interest, which conditions the subject matter of thinking. The background is that part of context that "does not come into explicit purview, does not come into question; it is taken for granted" [9]. According to Dewey, this is because background context, or rather some part of it, cannot be an object of examination: "If everything were literally unsettled at once, there would be nothing to tie those factors, that being unsettled, are in process of discovery and determination" (ibid).

This simple argument highlights a major difference between the logicist and pragmatist views. Formal logic, let us recall, is strictly constrained to "explicit" forms of knowledge representation. Nothing in logic, in other words, could be taken for granted as such, whether it is part of the context or part of the subject matter. This is one explanation of why traditional AI (GOFAI) models have a hard time dealing with context. In these models, every fact with a remote chance of relevance has to be codified and explicitly represented. Since there is, in principle, no limit to relevant facts, one is always susceptible to land on one of the two extremes: incorporating too many or too few facts about the situation—hence the "problem of relevance" in AI. To complicate matters even further, it is not clear which facts remain unchanged as a result of interaction with the environment—hence the notorious "frame problem" of AI.

2.1 Background Context

Background context, as we said, has both spatial and temporal aspects. The spatial aspect, according to Dewey, "covers all contemporary setting within which a course of thinking emerges" (ibid). The temporal aspect, in turn, is intellectual as well as existential. The existential background is an important notion for Dewey—it is part of the material means that contribute to the possibility of a

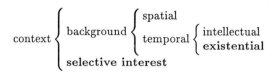

Fig. 1. The aspects of context

thought process. A full grasp of this notion requires a discussion of "situations",
which we will take up shortly.

The intellectual background, on the other hand, can be social (traditions),
individual (mental habits), theoretical (science), etc. Thinking, in other words,
always take place in a background of social and cultural setting, and within an
individual frame of mind. In physical science, for instance, Aristotelian physics
and Ptolemaic astronomy were for centuries the taken-for-granted background
of all special inquiries. Next came the Newtonian background, then relativity
and quantum mechanics, ... and so on.

This much about background context may be old hat in AI, as in other
places. Philosophers of language, in discussing *indexical* content, have taught
us that any speech act happens within a context that crucially belongs to *here*
and *now* [37, 44]. The meaning of the sentence "I have to finish the book in two
months before I leave town" is as much dependent on who utters it as it is on
the time and place of the utterance. Similar issues have been addressed in AI,
especially in knowledge representation and language processing, although, as we
shall see later, the recognition of the issues has not always resulted in the most
feasible solutions. Part of the reason for the failure, we believe, is the neglect
of the *existential* aspect of context mentioned above. More important, however,
is the neglect of the second major component of context in Dewey's account—
namely, "selective interest" (or bias). Both of these are related to Dewey's notion
of "situation".

2.2 Situations, Selective Bias, and Relevance

The notion of a *problematic* or *indeterminate* situation plays a central role in
Dewey's thought. Thinking, according to Dewey, is a process of inquiry in which
a confused, obscure, or conflicting situation is transformed into a determinate
one. While this claim might be agreeable to many, the core idea behind it might
not necessarily be so—namely the idea that situations are not doubtful only in
a "subjective" sense, but also in an "objective" or non-subjective way: "It is
the *situation* that has these traits [confusion, ambiguity, conflict, etc.]. *We* are
doubtful because the situation is inherently doubtful" (ibid). In other words,
the indeterminacy is first and foremost in the situation, not in us—an assertion
that may not find many supporters among the believers in mentalistic theories
of cognition.

Dewey used the notion of "situation" to also talk about relevance: "The existence of the problematic situation to be resolved exercises control over the selective discrimination of relevant and effective evidential qualities as means" [10]. Relevance, Dewey concluded, is not inherent but accrues to natural qualities in virtue of the special function they perform in inquiry. What determines relevance, furthermore, is the impress of the individual inquirer on the context.

> There is selectivity (and rejection) found in every operation of thought.
> There is care, concern, implicated in every act of thought. There is someone who has affection for some things over others; when he becomes a thinker he does not leave his characteristic affection behind. As a thinker, he is still differentially sensitive to some qualities, problems, themes.[9]

"Material considerations", as Dewey calls them, represent the total effect of existential background and selective bias on thought processes. They reveal the close relation between "context" and "relevance" at once. They also happen to be the same considerations that, we claim, have been traditionally ignored in AI. How so?

The answer should be sought in a philosophical and scientific tradition that, in the name of "objectivism", has tended to undermine the individual and "subjective" aspects of thought processes, especially when it comes to scientific inquiry. However, as Dewey notes, there is bad and good subjectivity, and confounding them has been the source of major mistakes in science and philosophy. While "subjectivism" deserves its ill repute and should be avoided as such, being subjective is not entitled to a similar treatment. "Interest, as the subjective, is after all equivalent to individuality and uniqueness", and individuality "is not a part or constituent of subject matter, but as a manner of action it selects subject matter and leaves a qualitative impress on it" [9]. In other words, subjectivity only influences the "context of inquiry", as opposed to the "context of use", which has a rather intersubjective character.

Scientific inquiry, for instance, may be devoid of individual influence as far as its final products are concerned. It is, to be sure, also a product of the social and communal activity of scientists. Nevertheless, the process of inquiry that leads to those products is, at some level, an individual activity. We should, thus, "distinguish between science as a conclusion of reflective inquiry, and science as a ready-made body of organized subject matter" (ibid). Any thought process or linguistic expression, by the same token, involves both a context of inquiry and a context of use. Attending to the latter, as many linguistics and philosophers do, should not come at the cost of the former.

GOFAI, in its pursuit of becoming an "objective" science, tended to neglect "material considerations". We believe that the same attitude still continues, to prevail, by and large, in many parts of AI. In planning, for instance, despite the advent of new models (like interleaved planning), AI research still follows the general scheme of plan generation, execution, and explicit recognition as the main vehicle for interaction between the system and the environment. As Suchman [46] has noted, the problem of interaction between individuals, on this view, is to recognize the actions of others as the expression of their underlying plans, and the research problem is to formulate a set of inference rules for mapping between actions and plans. By the same token, interaction with the environment, according to this view, would involve the ability to detect and recognize the context explicitly and to revise the plans according to some reasoning scheme.

What motivates this approach, we suggest, is a logicist point of view. But what in logic, it might be asked, dictates such views? Why should it not be possible for logic, in other words, to embrace contextual dependence in the sense outlined by Dewey? The answer to the above question is multifarious—e.g., adherence to explicit representations, universal meanings, etc. Such attributes, as we argue elsewhere [13], are not fully characteristic of human behavior. In specific, the pragmatic approach suggests the following:

1. Context, most often, is not explicitly identifiable.
2. There are no sharp boundaries among contexts.
3. The logical aspects of thinking cannot be isolated from material considerations.
4. Behaviour and context are jointly recognizable.

Points 1 and 2 follow from Dewey's discussion of "background" context, and point 3 follows from his notions of "situation" and "selective bias". The fourth point is going to be discussed in more detail. Logic, we are going to argue, fails on all of these accounts. The reason, we believe, is what could be roughly called "formality assumptions" in logic—namely, the requirement of having sharp boundaries among things in a messy world that does not necessarily live up to such mandates.

3   The Logical View of Context

"Environment" is not something around and about human activities in an external sense; it is their *medium*, or *milieu*, in the sense in which a *medium* is *intermediate* in the execution or carrying *out* of human activities, as well as being the channel *through* which they move and the vehicle *by* which they go on. ([11], original emphases)

Setting up *absolute* separations between mind and nature, subject and object, inner and outer,... is another fallacy of modern philosophy to which Dewey referred (ibid). In this section, using the CYC project [26] as an example, we want to show how the above fallacy is manifested in AI practice.

For some time, under the mandates of formal logic, context was either neglected in AI, or considered a triviality that could be given due attention if and when necessary. Occasional concessions as to its significance were also made with a strong residual commitment to formal logic, basically leading to similar outcomes. The continuous challenge and recurring problems that the CYC project has faced in dealing with issues of context could only be understood as such.

As late as 1991, for instance, Lenat and Feigenbaum, responding to Smith's [42] critique of the context-insensitive notion of meaning adopted for CYC, had this to say in rebuttal: "Use-dependent meaning does not imply that we have to abandon the computational framework of logic" [25]. The implied moral was to stick to the "universalized" meanings of logical terms and sentences (as opposed to use-dependent meanings of natural language utterances), and to maintain consistency at the cost of context. This turned out to be an illusive approach to the question of meaning.

It took some years for the CYC group to learn that "it was foolhardy to try to maintain consistency in one huge flat CYC knowledge base" [23]. A new scheme was thus adopted: breaking up the knowledge base into hundreds of contexts and "microtheories", each of which was internally consistent but could, in principle, be in contradiction with other contexts. Presumably, this scheme did not have the difficulties of the previous one, but it suffered from other problems [24].

In consideration of problems like the above, Lenat [24] has proposed yet another approach to context, which he calls "Dimensions of Context Space". This approach, as its name implies, treats context as a space with many dimensions. For reasons that should become clear throughout this paper, though, we doubt that the new scheme has a better chance of success than the previous two. We believe that some of the reservations expressed by McCarthy and Buvač [31], albeit on purely formal grounds, support our suspicion. The main reason, in our opinion, is the thesis that context is either directly given, or else should be inferred in a deductive fashion.

Haugeland [17] calls the view behind the above thesis the "inferential" view of context dependence, which he characterizes as follows:

1. An instance of I, in context C, would be (or count as) an R.
2. Here is an instance of I; and it is in context C.
3. So, here is an R.

As Haugeland notes, however, this presumes "that C and I are identifiable as such independently, and that the recognition of R is then just drawing a conclusion—not really *a recognition* at all". Haugeland argues that this is usually not the case in human cognition. What happens, rather, is that "context-informed phenomena (...) are recognized for what they are, quite apart from any *independent* recognition of the context or of anything which is "in" the context" (ibid, original emphasis). In other words, the phenomenon and the context are recognized jointly, not as separate entities one happening inside the other. A behavior such as a smile, for instance, could be understood either as reassuring or as a cautionary gesture, depending on the circumstances in which it is made. It is not the case that one first recognizes a smile, and then interprets it as either reassuring or cautionary. Nor is it the case that one first detects the context as such, and then interprets the smile accordingly. The context determines what the smile means as much as the smile defines and reinforces the context. Haugeland calls this the "joint recognizability of instance-cum-context" (op. cit.).

Although Haugeland's discussion was focused on pattern recognition, its basic intuitions could be carried over to other domains. Stalnaker [44], for instance,

162

has argued for a similar interaction between content and context in a linguistic environment: "First, context influences content, . . . But second, the contents that are expressed influence the context: speech acts affect the situation in which they are performed." As Stalnaker points out, his account is radical as compared to those which only consider the influence in one direction—namely, from context to content.

A more radical step in this direction should crucially involve dropping the formality assumption with regard to phenomenon and context. It is only then that one could get rid of unbridgeable dichotomies between a behavior and its embedding context, between an utterance and its use, or among different contexts. As an example of such an attempt in another domain, let us mention the work of Oyama [36] in developmental biology. Having picked up the old question of the origin of "form" and "information" in biological systems—usually framed in traditional dichotomies of nature/nurture, genes/environment, adaptation/development, function/structure, instruction/selection, etc.—Oyama has proposed an alternative approach to the question. She finds the so-called "interactionist" approaches, that have been in vogue for some time in developmental biology, unsatisfactory mainly because of their commonly-shared "preformationist" attitude toward information—namely that information "exists before its utilization or expression".

By disposing of old dichotomies, Oyama's "constructive interactionism", we believe, has succeeded in shedding new light on an old question. We are basically advocating a similar approach in AI.

4   The Logical View of Relevance

The issue of relevance repeatedly appears in AI, and its meaning seems to be intuitively clear. Broadly speaking, a piece of information is said to be relevant if it is of consequence to the matter in hand, or if it interferes with some of our beliefs or actions. Thus, we can describe the "problem of relevance" as the problem of identifying and using properly all the information that should exert an influence on our beliefs, goals, or plans.

The problem of relevance has received an admittedly distinct treatment from context in AI. Here, unlike context, the research community has been rather aware of the outstanding issues. Although the challenge is mostly met under the guise of the celebrated "frame problem" (which, by most accounts, is but a subspecies of the relevance problem), it comes up in various other places in AI—e.g., perception and representation [20], analogical reasoning [40], case-based reasoning [21], knowledge and inference [24]). "Relevance" is also ubiquitous in other places in science and philosophy, such as in cognitive psychology—e.g., in perception of similarity [34]—and in philosophy of science—e.g., in theory and explanation [47]. The formal framework of logic has been arguably dominant in most of these places.

In the following subsections, we want to review some of the formal treatments of relevance in AI and the surrounding disciplines. Our goal is to show that these accounts, although they improve upon some aspects of classical logic, are still insufficient for capturing relevance in human cognition. The reason, we believe, is that they are still constrained to explicit representation, and that they solely focus on syntactic aspects of relevance. As we have seen, there are material considerations involved in any thought process, and, we are going to argue, they cannot be captured by pure formal and syntactic considerations.

4.1 The Logic of Relevance

The notion of relevant implication has received special treatment in symbolic logic. It has been suggested, for instance, that in a formal theory of "entailment" some sentences like $A \to B$ should be considered false if A does not have a bearing on the validity of B. Such a notion of relevance is then used to represent a special form of implication, more rigorous than material implication, in which the consequent of a rule is expected to be proved "from" the antecedent. The seminal idea of relevant implication, also known as rigorous implication, was introduced in 1956 by Ackermann [1]. Anderson and Belnap [2, 3] following the lead of Ackermann, proposed "The Calculus of Entailment." In this calculus, implication is constrained by conditions of relevance and necessity. Inferring $A \to B$ means that A is used in the proof of B. For instance, a formula like $A \to (B \to B)$ is always true in classical logic but it is not a universally valid formula in the logic of relevance since A is not a reason to conclude $B \to B$. On the other hand, a formula like $(A \to B) \to ((B \to C) \to (A \to C))$ is valid in the logic of relevance since the step from $B \to C$ to $A \to C$ can be made given the assumption $A \to B$. This gave rise to a technique for keeping track of the steps used in a proof, which restricts the application of the deduction theorem to those cases in which the antecedent is relevant to the consequent.

But "proof" is a purely syntactic notion. The logic of relevance, although it was a move in the right direction (by dispensing with some unintuitive notions of implication), has not addressed the crux of relevance, which is neither always explicit nor necessarily syntactic.

4.2 Default Reasoning

AI has long dealt with the challenge of modeling inferential processes in the face of incomplete or inconsistent information. Default reasoning has emerged as a mechanism for drawing conclusions when there is conflicting information that justifies the derivation of differing conclusions. Default reasoning has also been defined as a mechanism that allows drawing conclusions when more information could prove to be relevant, and therefore when the inference is corrigible. The well known "qualification problem" arises when we need to make explicit the absence of every potentially relevant factor that can interfere with our conclusion.

All approaches to formalizing default reasoning, even when they diverge in other respects, share the basic principle of maintaining tentative conclusions as long as there is no relevant factor that dictates the opposite. Accordingly, in the frame of "defeasible reasoning" proposed by Pollock [38], the acceptance of a belief is based on a mechanism for verifying that a reason that supports the belief remains undefeated after going through a process of justification. In this process of justification the *rebutting defeaters* and *undercutting defeaters* play the role of blocking factors—they are the relevant factors that can drive an agent to retract certain beliefs. In McDermott and Doyle's nonmonotonic logic [32, 33], Reiter's default logic [39] and Moore's autoepistemic logic [35], the consistency test can be seen as the verification of the nonexistence of relevant information interfering with certain inference. In all these logics there is a general pattern of inference that allows to "assume A in the absence of relevant information that dictates the contrary", usually interpreted as "if A can be consistently assumed, then assume A". At the same time, cirumscription (McCarthy [29, 30]) allows to conjecture that "...no relevant object exists in certain categories except those whose existence follows from the statement of the problem and common sense knowledge" [30]. The above approaches are also known as extensional approaches to default reasoning. They are able to go beyond the deductively valid conclusions, but they are also able to determine whether there exists relevant information interfering with the generation of certain conclusions.

In approaches to default reasoning based on conditional or intentional interpretations [15, 16, 8, 28, 22, 6] the notion of relevance appears when the incorporation of some relevant condition to the antecedent of a conditional results in a "more exceptional" (or less normal) situation, in which case the previously maintained conclusion must be retracted, or a conclusion that was omitted before must be incorporated. If a conditional is true, it is natural to expect that a new conditional that results from adding new irrelevant information to the antecedent remains true. However, the basic conditional systems are too cautious, and do not allow to keep conclusions in the presence of new information, even when this information is irrelevant to the conditional. The problem of explicitly adding all properties that are irrelevant to a conditional is known as the irrelevance problem or "inverse qualification problem" [6].

In situational calculus, a special notion of relevance naturally appears in the first attempts to give a solution to the frame problem. The frame problem states the necessity of determining what aspects of a certain state are not changed after an action takes place. In other words, which true facts will remain true, and which false facts will remain false once an action has been completed. The frame problem can be stated as the problem of determining relevance relations between actions and properties of situations. Among the first proposals for representing such relevance relations was the one presented by Sandewall [41] with the introduction of the "unless" primitive.

All of the above schemes are meant to give a more realistic account of reasoning. Each one of them, however, invokes a purely syntactic notion—e.g., "consistency" in the case of extensional systems, and "normality" in the case of intentional systems—in order to do this. Also, they solely rely on explicit representations. For example, an extensional default reasoning system can have rules like "if you reach the front door, and it is consistent to assume (or believe) that you can open the door, then open the door". Obviously, several rules are needed to determine whether the door is open or not, but they are far fewer than an exhaustive enumeration of irrelevant features such as the material of the door, its color, or the patterns of flickering shadows on it. An intentional default reasoning system can represent the same information as follows: "In the normal state of affairs, if you reach the front door, then open the door", where the normal state of affairs is somehow introduced to the system beforehand. It is also assumed that the properties of the objects with which we are dealing remain unchanged unless there is some relevant factor that dictates the contrary.

Default reasoning was meant to address the qualification, inverse qualification and frame problems. It should be noticed, however, that all the proposed methods rely on the assumption that all meaning is context-insensitive, and could thus be fixed a priori in the knowledge base.

4.3 Computational relevance

The notion of relevance has also been analyzed as an efficiency factor, giving rise to what is know as computational (ir)relevance. In automatic problem solving as well as in deductive databases special attention has been paid to the implementation of mechanisms that are guided by principles of computational relevance. In this sense, the traditional mechanisms of inference have been modified to profit from the notion of relevance, pre-selecting from the search space the information that is either useful for certain goals, or is within certain precision limits.

The notion of computational (ir)relevance underlies mechanisms of resolution as simple as the *set of support* strategy, where the resolution is forced to take into account only the resolvents that are relevant to the goal. In some *bottom-up* evaluation techniques, especially used in deductive databases, the computation of an answer is made more efficient by calculating a relevant subset of the database model rather that the complete model. Examples of such techniques are *naïve* evaluation, *seminaïve* evaluation, *magic sets* [7, 4] and other techniques in which the evaluation of the query is done after constructing trees or graphs [27]. These techniques allow the removal of irrelevant formulas and ignore useless resolution paths. It is the incorporation of relevance as an efficiency factor that allows the shift from blind search to a guided search method, as well as the creation of simpler theories with better computational properties.

A theoretical analysis of the notion of computational (ir)relevance has been presented by Subramanian and Genesereth in [45]. In their work, besides introducing definitions of computational (ir)relevance in terms of complexity, they propose a *Logic of (Ir)relevance* focused on the metatheoretic computation of (ir)relevant assertions.

The use of special data structures like indexed list, trees and graphs, which make it possible to organize information, is another manifestation of the notion of relevance as an efficiency factor. In such cases the information is arranged in such a way that the relevant pieces (to a specific plan) can be easily identified and retrieved.

The methods discussed are aimed at improving the performance of an inference mechanism by discarding what is irrelevant or by facilitating the access to relevant information. Computational relevance, as we see, only deals with efficiency but, having stayed within the framework of logic (e.g. resolution), it basically begs the question of determining relevance.

Generally speaking, all of the variations on logic that we have discussed in this section, as important as they are in formalizing thought processes, remain committed to the solely explicit forms of representation and to the formality assumptions of classical logic. In specific, they assume independence of the syntax and semantics in the way understood by Fodor [14]:

> What makes syntactic operations a species of formal operations is that being syntactic is a way of *not* being semantic. Formal operations are the ones that are specified without reference to such semantic properties of representations as, for example, truth, reference, and meaning.

GOFAI systems were famously built on a similar assumption. The idea was to equip the system with enough rules that would make it possible for it to engender the right set of behaviors without paying attention to the embedding environment—whence the dictum: "you take care of the syntax, and the semantics will take care of itself." In most of these systems, the syntactic rules were dictated by the normative constraints of formal logic. Since these systems did not perform well in handling real-world tasks, however, alternative logics of the kind discussed in this section were sought and created.

Formal alternatives have once again demonstrated that logic as a discipline does not deal with the question of how to get the interpretation function; it just *assigns* it. In order to get the interpretation, we suggest, one has to look in other directions. These directions could be as variegate as the number of ways human beings interact with the world—actions, beliefs, emotions, tastes, goals, plans, etc. In this paper, we have tried to show that the pragmatic approach can provide one such direction, that of acting.

5 Conclusion: Implications for AI

The pragmatic tradition highlights the action-oriented nature of intelligence. Despite lay connotations of the word, the term "action" is to be understood in a broad sense that includes reasoning behavior as well. Action understood in such broad terms, we suggest, is the key to dealing with issues of context and relevance. At the heart of intelligence lies the ability to find out what is relevant in any given situation, and to act accordingly. This understanding of intelligence is, in fact, shared by many other writers within AI and cognitive science. Hofstadter, for instance, describes the core of intelligence to be "the ability to adapt to different domains, to spot the gist of situations amidst a welter of superficial distractors" [19].

Our aim in this paper was to discover the limits of the logicist approach in dealing with issues of context and relevance. We have discussed that the existing alternatives to formal logic have not parted company with the formality assumptions of classic logic—e.g., the assumption that there are sharp boundaries between behavior and its embedding context, the assumption that syntax and semantics are independent, ... etc. Because of this, logic-based systems cannot fulfill the pragmatic requirements outlined in this paper. The work of Sperber and Wilson [43], for instance, who have tried to come up with a psychologically plausible account of context and relevance in speech communication, provides one example of the limits of the logicist framework.

In contrast to the logicist framework, the pragmatic approach focuses our attention on aspects of thinking and intelligence that are ubiquitous, but have been traditionally ignored in logic. Most importantly, it highlights the twin aspects of context—namely "background" and "selective bias". In doing so, it also provides a new perspective for dealing with issues of relevance, and shows how context and relevance are co-constituted. Furthermore, by giving rise to an interactive notion of intelligence, it opens up the possibility of the joint recognition of the system and environment. Although some phenomenologists like Dreyfus [12] have also emphasized this point by invoking the notion of "being-in-a-situation," they do not seem to give enough importance to the active role of human judgment in making sense of situations. Dreyfus says: "Human experience is only intelligible when organized in terms of a situation in which relevance and significance are already given."

Other implications of the pragmatic view for AI also suggest themselves. "Coordination management," as Smith [42] has described it, arises in many places in AI, and the pragmatic approach can complement the logicist one by focusing on this aspect of behavior. Take the notion of search, for instance. Inferential and computational relevance might provide useful notions. Compared to classical logic, they allow a more informed and efficient way of doing search (note that it is a common premise that any AI problem is a search problem). Determining the search space, however, has been taken for granted in most formal approaches to AI. Pragmatic relevance, differently from inferential and computational relevance, has mainly to do with "selecting the search space" rather than with the search process itself.

Acknowledgments

The authors wish to thank Brian C. Smith and Rasmus G. Winther for commenting on an earlier version of this paper and an anonymous reviewer for helpful suggestions.

References

1. Ackermann, W. *Begründung einer strengen Implikation.* The Journal of Symbolic Logic 21, pages 113-128. (1956).
2. Anderson, A. R., and Belnap, N, Jr. The Pure Calculus of Entailment. The Journal of Symbolic Logic 1 (27), pages 19-52. (1962).

3. Anderson, A. R., and Belnap, N., JR. *Entailment—The logic of relevance and necessity*. Princeton University Press (1975).
4. Beeri, C., and Ramakrishnan, R. *On the Power of Magic*. Journal of Logic Programming 10, pages 255-299. Elsevier Science Publisher (1991).
5. Bernstein, R. J. On Experience, Nature, and Freedom: Representative Selections (John Dewey), Bobbs-Merrill Co., Indianapolis, (1960)
6. Boutilier, C. *Conditional Logics for Default Reasoning and Belief Revision*. PhD. thesis. Department of Computer Science. University of British Columbia (1992).
7. Das, S. K. *Deductive Databases and Logic Programming*. Addison-Wesley Publishing Company (1992).
8. Delgrande, J. P. *A Logic for Representing Default an Prototypical Properties*. IJCAI-87, pages 423-429. Milan, Italy (1987).
9. Dewey, J. *Context and Thought*. In Richard Bernstein (ed. 1960), pages 88-110 (1931).
10. Dewey, J. *Logic: The Theory of Inquiry*. In John Dewey: The Latter Works, 1925-1953, vol. 12. J. A. Boydston (ed.) Southern Illinois University Press, Carbondale (1991).
11. Dewey, J. *Common Sense and Science*. In John Dewey: The Later Works, 1925-1953, vol. 16. J. A. Boydston (ed.) Southern Illinois University Press, Carbondale (1991).
12. Dreyfus, H. L. *What Computers Still Can't Do: A Critique of Artificial Reason*. MIT Press, Cambridge (1992).
13. Ekbia, H. R. Forever On the Threshold: The Case of CYC. Forthcoming (2001)
14. Fodor, J. A. *Methodological Solipsism considered as a research strategy in cognitive psychology*. Brain and Behaviour Sciences 3, 63-109 (1980).
15. Gabbay, D. *Theoretical Foundations for Non-monotonic Reasoning*. Expert Systems, Logics and Models of Concurrent Systems, pages 439-459. Springer Verlag (1985).
16. Ginsberg, M. L. *Counterfactuals*. Artificial Intelligence 30, pages 35-79. Elsevier Science Publisher (1986).
17. Haugeland, J. *Pattern and Being*. In his *Having Thought: Essays in the Metaphysics of Mind*. Harvard University Press, Cambridge (1993/98).
18. Haugeland, J. *Mind Design II: Philosophy, Psychology, Artificial Intelligence*. A Bradford Book, MIT Press, Cambridge (1997).
19. Hofstadter, D. R. *Le Ton beau de Marot: In Praise of the Music of Language*. Basic Books, New York (1997).
20. Hofstadter, D. R., and Fluid Analogies Research Group. *Fluid Concepts and Creative Analogies*. Basic Books, New York (1995).
21. Kolodner, J. L, and Leake, D. B. *A Tutorial Introduction to Case-Based Reasoning*. In David Leake (ed.) (1996): Case-Based Reasoning: Experiences, Lessons, and Future Directions. AAAI Press/MIT Press, Menlo Park/Cambridge (1996).
22. Kraus, S., Lehmann D., and Magidor, M. *Nonmonotonic Reasoning, Preferential Models and Cumulative Logics*. Artificial Intelligence 44,pages 167-207. Elsevier Science Publisher (1990).
23. Lenat, D. B. *From 2001 to 2001: Common Sense and the Mind of HAL*. In David G. Stork (ed.) *Hal's Legacy: 2001's Computer As Dream and Reality*. MIT Press, Cambridge, Mass. (1997)
24. Lenat, D. B. *The Dimensions of Context Space*. CYCORP Web Page at www.cyc.com (1998)
25. Lenat, D. B., and Feigenbaum, E. A. *On the Thresholds of Knowledge*. Artificial Intelligence 47, 1-3, Jan. 1991, pages 185-250 (1991)

26. Lenat, D. B., and Guha, R. V. *Building Large Knowledge-Based Systems*. Addison Wesley, Reading (1990).
27. Levy, A. Y. *Irrelevance Reasoning in Knowledge Based Systems*. PhD thesis. Computer Science Department. Stanford University (1993).
28. Makinson, D. *General Theory of Cumulative Inference*. Proceedings of the Second International Workshop on Non-Monotonic Reasoning, Lecture Notes in Artificial Intelligence 346, pages 1-18. Springer-Verlag (1989).
29. McCarthy, J. *Circumscription—A Form of Non-Monotonic Reasoning*. Artificial Intelligence 13, pages 27-39. Elsevier Science Publishers (1980).
30. McCarthy, J. *Applications of Circumscription to Formalizing Common-Sense Knowledge*. Artificial Intelligence 28 (1), pages 89-116.Elsevier Science Publishers (1986).
31. McCarthy, J., and Buvač, S. *Formalizing Context (Expanded Notes)*. Technical Note STAN-CS-TN-94-13, Stanford University (1994).
32. McDermott, D., and Doyle, J. *Non-Monotonic Logic I*. Artificial Intelligence 13, pages 41-72. Elsevier Science Publishers (1980).
33. McDermott, D. *Non-Monotonic Logic II*. Journal of Association for Computing Machinery 29 (1), pages 33-57. ACM (1980).
34. Medin, D. L., Goldstone R. L, and Gentner D. *Respects for Similarity*. Psychological Review 100 (2,) pages 254-278 (1993).
35. Moore, R. C. *Semantical Considerations on Nonmonotonic Logic*. Artificial Intelligence 25 (1), pages 75-94. Elsevier Science Publishers (1985).
36. Oyama, S. *The Ontogeny of Information: Developmental Systems and Evolution* (2nd ed.). Duke University Press (2000).
37. Perry, J. *Indexicals, Contexts and Unarticulated Constituents*. Available at http://www-csli.stanford.edu/ john/context/context.html (1998).
38. Pollock, J. L. *Defeasible Reasoning*. Cognitive Science 11, pages 481-518. (1987).
39. Reiter, R. *A Logic for Default Reasoning*. Artificial Intelligence 13, pages 81-132. Elsevier Science Publishers (1980).
40. Russell, S. J. *The Use of Knowledge in Analogy and Induction*. Morgan Kaufmann Publishers (1989).
41. Sandewall, E. *An Approach to the Frame Problem and its Implementation*. Machine Intelligence 7, pages 195-204. Edinburgh University Press (1972).
42. Smith, B. C. *The Owl and The Electric Encyclopedia*. Artificial Intelligence 47, 1-3, Jan. 1991, pages 251-288 (1991).
43. Sperber, D., and Wilson, D. *Relevance: Communication and Cognition*. Harvard University Press, Cambridge, MA. (1986)
44. Stalnaker, R. C. *Context and Content*. Oxford Cognitive Science Series, Oxford University Press (1999)
45. Subramanian, D, and Genesereth M. R. *The Relevance of Irrelevance*. In Proc. IJCAI-87, pages 423-429. Milan, Italy (1987).
46. Suchman, L. *Plans and Situated Actions*. Cambridge University Press, UK (1987).
47. van Fraassen, B. C. *The Scientific Image*. Clarendon Press, Oxford (1980).

Counterfactual Reasoning

Roberta Ferrario

Département de Philosophie – Université Marc Bloch de Strasbourg
Dipartimento di Filosofia – Università degli Studi di Milano
Via Festa del Perdono, 7 - Milano (Italy)
Email: ferrix@cs.unitn.it

Abstract. Primary goal of this paper is to show that counterfactual reasoning, as many other kinds of common sense reasoning, can be studied and analyzed through what we can call a cognitive approach, that represents knowledge as structured and partitioned into different domains, everyone of which has a specific theory, but can exchange data and information with some of the others. Along these lines, we are going to show that a kind of "counterfactual attitude" is pervasive in a lot of forms of common sense reasoning, as in theories of action, beliefs/intentions ascription, cooperative and antagonistic situations, communication acts. The second purpose of the paper is to give a reading of counterfactual reasoning as a specific kind of contextual reasoning, this latter interpreted according to the theory of MultiContext Systems developed by Fausto Giunchiglia and his group.

1 Introduction

Counterfactuality has been the focus of a multitude of works, in philosophy [20, 25, 13, 16, 2, 23, 24, 19], in psychology [3, 22, 15], in artificial intelligence [9, 14, 4, 17] and in the cognitive sciences in general [8, 18]. In most approaches the study of counterfactuality is related to the problem of causality, and there is a wide agreement in describing counterfactuals as a powerful tool in explaining past events and predicting future outcomes.

In the literature, it is possible to find two different approaches to a theory of conterfactuals: a *metaphysical approach*, in which the problem is mainly to define the relationship between the actual world and a counterfactual world; and a *cognitive approach*, in which the emphasis is on the properties of counterfactual reasoning from the perspective of an agent in a given situation. In this paper we assume the cognitive approach to argue that counterfactual reasoning can be treated as a specific kind of contextual reasoning. This will be done as a preliminary step toward our long term goal, that is to build a formal system based on the logic of MultiContext Systems [12].

Our main interest is how agents reason when they face scenarios in which actions can be influenced by the presence of other agents and have consequences for the other agents involved. We believe this is a dimension of counterfactual reasoning that has not been satisfactorily investigated in the literature. So, for example, an interesting typology of counterfactual reasoning, namely counterfactuals of the form: "If I were you ..." (that are usually defined *counteridenticals*), has been almost neglected, even though it seems to be extremely useful to ascribe reasoning processes to other agents in multi-agent scenarios (e.g. in cooperative and antagonistic reasoning and, even more importantly, in communication acts).

The paper goes as follows. After a brief introduction on cognitive approaches, the main section of the paper is dedicated to an analysis of possible applications of counterfactual reasoning to other forms of common sense reasoning, showing how many of them has a (sometimes hidden) counterfactual dimension. Then we present our main thesis, namely that counterfactual reasoning can be studied as a type of contextual reasoning. In order to do this, we sketch the definitions of context and contextual reasoning as they are given in [12]. In the final part of the paper we present some preliminary ideas on a possible connection between counterfactual reasoning and contexts on one side and Game Theory on the other.

2   Cognitive approaches to counterfactual reasoning

As a general definition, we call *counterfactual reasoning* all those reasoning processes that an agent performs starting from a set of assumptions she believes to be *true*, with the addition of an hypothesis that she believes to be *false*, but that she treats as true *for the sake of the argument*. A simple example is the sentence *"If I could turn back time, I would study economics"*. In a cognitive approach, the stress is not on how reality is, but on the way agents can inquire it. In a sense, it isn't of a great importance to know whether there is an "objective" reality or not: the cognitive analysis will be directed towards the cognitive tools that agents display while reasoning about what they call reality.

On the "cognitive front", there are two theories that are extremely relevant for our approach to counterfactual reasoning: the theory of *mental spaces* by Gilles Fauconnier [7], and the theory of called *partitioned representations*, proposed by John Dinsmore in AI [5]. Both theories share the intuition that the cognitive state of an individual is better described as divided into multiple portions, called mental spaces in one case, partitioned representations in the other. Agents carry on reasoning processes locally to these portions of their mental state, trying to build a representation of reality. Dinsmore calls these processes *simulative reasoning* [6]:

> "Simulative reasoning requires a partitioning of knowledge into distinct spaces and additionally assumes that the contents of each space effectively simulate or model a possible reality, or a part of a possible reality, and therefore represents a meaningful domain over which normal reasoning processes work."

There are some elements in the language that work as *space builders*, because they introduce new partitions in the cognitive state. Counterfactuals are one of these space builders. In particular, in Fauconnier's view, they open a peculiar kind of hypothetical space, whose structure is *analogical* [8], and not truth functional, as in Lewis' and Stalnaker's approach [20, 25]). According to Fauconnier, it is a *projection* of the structure of the base space.

Fauconnier calls *base space* the mental space from which the counterfactual space has originated , through an analogy-based mechanism. This mechanism requires that some *matching conditions* are met by a counterfactual space in order to be related to a given base space. Fauconnier makes this point as follows:

> "[...] a counterfactual sets up an imaginary situation which differs from the actual one in one fundamental respect, expressed in the antecedent part (A, the protasis) of the *if A then B* construction. [...] In spite of appearances, the structure of counterfactuals is not truth functional (entailment from an alternative set of premises); it is analogical: projection of structure from one domain to another. [...] What is the use of C [the counterfactual space] in the discourse? It does not give direct information about actual situations, and it does not represent existing frame configurations. However, besides being counterfactual, C is also *conditional*. The semantics linked to C includes the general *matching* conditions on hypothetical spaces. The matching condition (an extended form of modus ponens) specifies in general that a space matching the defining structure of a conditional space fits it in all other respects." [8]

The *projection of structure* called for is the analogous of what Dinsmore calls the *default inheritance*:

> "The content of one space can depend crucially on the content of another as a function of the semantics of the respective contexts and yet not exhibit absolute inheritance. This is the case for counterfactual [...] spaces. [...] The kind of inheritance involved in this case cannot be absolute. [...] Such cases require a weaker form of inheritance, *default inheritance*." [6]

3 The counterfactual dimension of common sense reasoning

Our next step is to argue that there are many forms of common sense reasoning that involve reasoning processes with a counterfactual structure. Some of them, as practical reasoning, have already been mentioned in literature; however, there are many more that haven't been explored yet and that can reveal very useful applications.

3.1 Counterfactual reasoning and theories of action

In the philosophical tradition many authors stress the strong connection between counterfactuality and causality (see for instance [21, 2, 24]), whereas in AI people have widely investigated the role of counterfactual reasoning in the diagnosis of artificial systems' failures and in the planning of future actions ([9] is a paradigmatic reference in this area). However, from our perspective, we can identify two general types of applications: one directed to reason about the past and the other one focused on reasoning about states of affairs. Each type can then be divided into two sub-categories, depending on the outcome of the reasoning. So we have four cases:

- **Past strategies to be changed**: the agent has previously planned an action that didn't reach the goal; she has to figure out different scenarios in which she alters one of the elements of the plan with the purpose of understanding what has gone wrong and has to be changed. The general schema is the following: "If I had performed that different action, I would have reached my goal". An instance of the schema is: "If I had come before, I would have met the President".
- **Past strategies to be confirmed**: the agent has previously planned a successful action; she can try to guess which elements of the plan were decisive for success, to be able to use them again in other plans. What she has to do is simply to imagine altered situations in which the lack of one or more of the elements influence negatively the outcome of the plan. The general schema is: "If I hadn't performed that action, this result wouldn't have been possible". A possible instance is: "If I hadn't waken up so early, I wouldn't have been able to arrive at the station on time".
- **State of affairs to be changed**: the agent can realize that she lacks some means to an end or some essential characteristics to obtain what she's looking for by imagining a situation in which she would have these means or characteristics. The general schema is: "If I were that way, I would do this thing". An example is: "If I were more courageous, I would ask my boss for a raise".
- **State of affairs to be confirmed**: the agent figures out a situation in which she lacks something (a means, a characteristic) she actually has and she realizes that she would not be able to do something she actually can do. The general schema is: "If I didn't have this property, I wouldn't be able to do this thing". An example is: "If I hadn't these mobility funds, I would not be able to travel so often".

The intuitive picture of counterfactual reasoning processes and of how they work in presence of plans and strategies is the following:

1. the agent wants to reason about a particular fact, event or problem. Thus she *selects*, inside her global knowledge base, a set of relevant assumptions which, in her opinion, are necessary and sufficient for the reasoning process at hand;
2. she builds a working context for the reasoning process, in which are contained all the assumptions she has previously selected and the effect that has been reached;

3. finally, a counterfactual context is constructed by:
   - importing all the assumptions from the working context, but changing the truth-value of one of them, or
   - importing all the assumptions from the working context and adding a new assumption that wasn't previously selected (this possibility is very important to show that counterfactual reasoning is a form of non monotonic reasoning).

   In both cases, the result of the reasoning performed inside the counterfactual context will be the negation of the one reached in the working context.

The final purpose of the reasoning process performed inside the counterfactual context is not only to show the relevance of the datum that has been changed (the counterfactual hypothesis), but also to show the importance of keeping all the other data unchanged. What the agent is trying to check with the counterfactual reasoning is the correctness of the choice she has made about the most relevant assumptions.

If we reconsider the classification given above about satisfactory/unsatisfactory strategies or states of affairs and the consequent strategy confirmation or revision, we can reformulate it and define a goal for counterfactual reasoning.

Counterfactual reasoning can be interpreted as a mechanism of verification and control of the selection function: counterfactual reasoning checks if the assumptions selected are *all* there is that is relevant for the reasoning and if they are *the only* that are relevant.

Strategy confirmation The agent has elaborated a strategy that has reached the expected goal. Still, she wants to check if all the assumptions she has considered were necessary to the achievement of the result and if there was something else that she has not considered which could have prevented the outcome of the plan.
   - In order to understand if all the assumptions were necessary, she can try to negate one or the other and verify if this change influences the result.
   - In order to understand if she has considered a sufficient set of assumptions, she can try to add some other assumption that could look relevant and see which is the result. If it doesn't change, this new assumption is redundant, if it does, this has to be added to the set of the relevant ones.

Strategy revision The strategy hasn't reached the goal. The agent wants to understand if her statement of the problem was correct, if something she has done or thought has been an obstacle to the realization of the plan or if she has neglected some important assumption.
   - Analogously as in the case of strategy confirmation, the agent verifies if the change of truth-value of an assumption affects the result of the reasoning. If it does, this assumption can be considered responsible of the failure of the plan.
   - Similarly, the agent tries to guess if there was some unexpected obstacle she hasn't considered.

We can try to make these ideas clearer with an example.

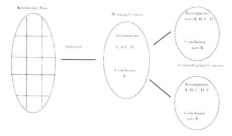

Fig. 1. The process of counterfactual strategy confirmation

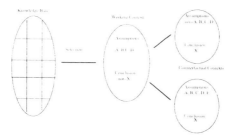

Fig. 2. The process of counterfactual strategy revision

Example: the flight to Paris The situation is the following: we have an agent, Anna, who wants to take a flight to Paris. She lives in a small town near Milan and she has selected certain assumptions in order to take the flight at 10 o'clock in the morning at the airport of Milan Malpensa. These are the assumptions she has selected. She has to:

- Pack the suitcase the evening before
- Close all the windows and back doors the evening before
- Check if there is a bus at 8 o'clock that arrives at the airport at 9
- The alarm must ring at 7 o'clock

1. **Strategy confirmation** In this case, we can imagine that all the conditions have been fulfilled and in the end Anna has taken her flight to Paris. Now we have the two possible counterfactuals:
   - Alteration of the truth-value of a selected condition: "If the alarm hadn't rung, I wouldn't have caught the plane"
   - Addition of a new relevant condition: "If there had been a strike of the bus drivers, I wouldn't have caught the plane"
   Anna wants to show that, assuming that all the other conditions hold, the ringing of the alarm or the strike are very relevant elements.
2. **Strategy revision** In this case the situation is that the alarm actually didn't ring and Anna didn't catch the plane. Here are the two counterfactuals:

- Alteration of the truth-value of a selected condition: "If the alarm had rung, I would have caught the plane"
- Addition of a new relevant condition: "If I had set two alarms, instead of one, I would have caught the plane"

Anna is trying to show not only that the fact that the alarm didnt't ring is the cause of the failure of her plan, but also that it was the only reason why the plan failed: all the other important assumptions have been taken into consideration.

What the agent is interested in is to discover if her plan was correctly settled, if she has forgotten anything or if she has considered something that was inessential. The counterfactual reasoning is a tool to analyze the relevance of the assumptions previously selected from the global knowledge base.

There are a lot of other forms of counterfactual reasoning that are not so strictly connected with plans and actions that must be examined in more detail and this is undoubtedly a direction in which this analysis has to be deepened.

As we have seen, there are many situations in which a single individual is involved that require a counterfactual form of reasoning. What we are going to show next is how counterfactuality (and in particular a peculiar kind of counterfactual reasoning) can be considered a very important element in the processes of reasoning typical of multiagent situations.

3.2 Counterfactual reasoning and beliefs/intentions ascription

Before presenting our own suggestion, we have to set a preliminary fact: we think we can take for granted that when agents have to interact with each other, everyone of them has to ascribe beliefs and intentions to others and, since none of them has direct access to the cognitive state of the others, they have to find some means to figure out how others reason.

Each agent has two direct sources to detect to guess how other minds work: one external and the other internal.

Externally, an agent can listen to the descriptions other agents give of their own reasonings, hoping that they are sincere; moreover, she can observe their behavior and try to deduce their internal processes of reasoning from their *"modus operandi"*.

Internally, an agent can try to be "selfconscious" of her own reasoning schemes and assume that all minds work in a similar way, i.e. like her own does.

Putting together these two amounts of data, the agent can perform a "mental act" consisting in her "walking in somebody else's shoes"; she constructs a new cognitive context containing knowledge, beliefs and intentions that she ascribes to the other agent and, from this context, she begins a process of reasoning using her cognitive tools as a substitute of those belonging to the other agent.

To make it clearer, here are the schema and an example:

"If I were X, knowing what he knows and having that particular belief, I would perform this action".

"If I were Giovanni, I would invite Anna to the party"

All reasonings of this kind have the purpose of predicting the actions and opinions of other agents in order to accomodate our behavior as to obtain the best result from the interactions with others.

There are three important applications of this "counterfactual ascription of beliefs/intentions": cooperative reasoning, antagonistic reasoning and, maybe the most interesting case (because in a way it applies to the others), communication.

Cooperative reasoning The first application we are going to consider is cooperative reasoning. Cooperative reasoning is essential for agents, because they often cannot execute with success what they have planned unless they ask the help of other agents.

But, before deciding whom to ask, the agent must consider capabilities and knowledge of the possible candidates and guess if they can be, directly or indirectly, interested in her plan.

To do this, once again, the agent has to perform the reasoning process "If I were X...". If the result of the reasoning is that the candidate is suitable and would probably agree to join the plan, she can proceed and ask the help of this agent; otherwise, she has to activate the same process "If I were X..." to think about something that the other would find appealing to propose as a "payoff" of the requested cooperation.

Another application in the domain of cooperative reasoning is when an agent considers retrospectively a plan (both individual and cooperative).

If the plan has failed, she can think about an alternative situation (that didn't take place) in which, with the help of some agent (or of a different agent if the plan was cooperative), it could have ended successfully.

Instead, if the plan was successful, she can try to imagine how things could have been without the cooperation of that particular agent (virtually substituting that agent with another one, or imagining an individual action instead of the cooperative) in order to understand how profitable the cooperation was.

Antagonistic reasoning The situation is dual to that of cooperative reasoning: the agent has settled a plan, but she realizes that there is an obstacle to overcome: the opposition of another agent.

To begin with, what she has to do is try to guess why the other agent is against her plan. To do it, once again she has to think "Why would I be against this plan, if I were this agent?".

The first possibility is that the other agent has misunderstood some of her intentions, so she only has to try to explain her reasons to show the other that his opposition is not actually justified.

The other possibility is that the other agent has a strong and justified reason to oppose the plan. In this case the agent must "walk in the shoes of the other" ("If I were X...") and figure out what she can offer in exchange as to make him give up his opposition.

Both cooperative and antagonistic reasoning and in general all reasoning processes including multiagent scenarios are based upon the possibility for the agents to communicate.

As we are going to argue in the next paragraph, we think that the important function of communication rests on the capability of agents to ascribe to each other certain ways of reasoning; counterfactual reasoning of the form "If I were X..." is an important tool in this direction.

Counterfactual reasoning in communication When an agent is to begin a communication, she has to check the conditions that will make her communication act effective. She has to elaborate a kind of *communication strategy*.

The first element to be considered is the form of the language that will be used. This language must not be too complicated or too simple relatively to the capabilities of the receiver: if it is too complicated, there is the risk of a lack of understanding; if it is too simple, it could be judged inappropriate by the receiver.

The language must match not only the cultural and cognitive features of the agent receiving the communication, but it also has to fit the situation (in some cases it must be technical, in others informal and so on and so forth).

Second, the agent has to consider the degree of interest that the content of the communication can arise in the listener and she has to evaluate if the receiver has a minimal competence in the subject, otherwise the communication act would be pointless.

Finally, when agents communicate, they usually have the purpose of persuading the other agent to perform an action, to share the same opinion about something or to behave in a particular way. The goal of persuasion can be obtained only mixing together the right form with the right content, producing the convincing arguments.

All these evaluations can be stated thanks to counterfactual processes of reasoning of the kind "If I were X..." and through the ascription of certain beliefs and cognitive capabilities to other agents, that are fundamental to predict other agents' reactions to our communication acts.

Now we can think about an example that can summarize a series of situations in which an imaginary agent is involved in various sequences of counterfactual thoughts.

Mr.1 is a wealthy middle-aged man, who lives in a small villa with a little but beautiful garden, in common with his neighbour.

Last year, in this season, he had an accident with a tree that was in his garden: after a storm, the tree fell against the house, damaging the roof.

Now Mr.1 is in the garden looking at another tree of the same species that looks similarly ill; he looks also at the sky and notices that the weather is getting worse. Then he thinks: **"If last year I had cut the tree before the storm, it wouldn't have damaged the roof"**.

So, his next action is to manage to cut the tree, to avoid to pay for the repairing.

But let's suppose that, after having tryed to do it by himself, he realizes that he's not able to. But then it comes to his mind that his neighbour (Mr.2) was once a lumberjack, now retired, and that he could help him.

Then he thinks that, being the tree situated in a place such that it could fall even against the house of Mr.2, maybe Mr.2 would agree about the convenience of cutting the tree. The thought of Mr.1 will be something like: **"If I were Mr.2, I would be worried about the tree and I would agree to cut it"**.

Before asking Mr.2, Mr.1 has to decide in which way to express his thoughts to Mr.2; this will depend on the idea Mr.1 has about Mr.2: which are his basic beliefs, which is his level of education, which are his prejudices and so on and so forth. This operation is in most cases implicit, but it is expressible in counterfactual terms: **"If I were Mr.2, which argument would I understand and find convincing?"**.

Sometimes it can happen that the evaluation of Mr.1 relative to the thoughts of Mr.2 is not correct. In this case, we suppose the answer of Mr.2 is something like: "I don't think there is a need of cutting the tree, this coming storm won't be devastating like the one of last year."

In this case, Mr.1 has to find another way to persuade Mr.2 to help him, maybe proposing something in exchange. Even in this situation, Mr.1 can think **"If I were Mr.2, I would agree to cut the tree, provided that, after the tree is cut, we would build in the place now occupied by the tree a gazebo"**, because some months ago Mr.2 proposed this thing, that Mr.1 refused.

These are some of the possible examples of common sense reasoning conducted with a counterfactual attitude; we think they show some applications of counterfactual reasoning underestimated, at least untill now.

In our opinion, all these instances of counterfactuality can be studied and analyzed according to a contextual approach in a way that we will try to illustrate in the next paragraph.

4 Contexts and Contextual Reasoning in MultiContexts Systems

There are a great variety of works on contexts and contextual reasoning, but there is a particular interpretation of the notion of contexts and - consequently - of contextual reasoning that we find appropriate for the analysis of counterfactual reasoning that we want to give.

This interpretation is the one given by Fausto Giunchiglia and his research group (MRG: Mechanized Reasoning Group) and the formalization derived from this perspective is called MultiContext Systems.

There is a wide literature on MultiContext Systems [10, 12, 11, 1], so our goal here will not be that of giving precise formal definitions, but we want to give an idea about what contexts are with respect to those definitions that are given somewhere else and how counterfactual reasoning, analogously defined, works.

Firstly, contexts are theories (in the formal sense of the term: each of them has its language, axioms and inference rules).

They have three main features: *partiality, approximation* and *perspective*.

- They are *partial* because each context of reasoning utilizes only a subset of the knowledge base that is actually available to the agent;
- They are *approximate* because the representation expressed by a context can be presented at different and variable levels of detail. In other words, a set of parameters (time, space, agent, ...) defines each context and their number can be varied.
- They are *perspectival* because they always express the epistemic point of view of an agent.

Being contexts these partial objects, we have two forms of contextual reasoning: inside a single context and between different contexts.

- The reasoning performed inside a single context has been termed *local reasoning* and it utilizes only the language, axioms and inference rules peculiar of that specific context;
- The process of reasoning that begins with a premise stated in a context and that ends with a conclusion drawn in a different context needs an appropriate tool to switch from one context to another. This tool has been semantically defined as *compatibility relations*.

The logics of MultiContext Systems has proved very useful in the resolution of some typical philosophical problems, such as the treatment of indexical expressions and the difficulties connected to belief ascription.

Our hope is that some good results could be reached even in the analysis of counterfactual reasoning; the reason that supports our hope is the intuition that countefactual reasoning can be viewed as a specific kind of contextual reasoning. In the next paragraph we will show why it is so.

5   Counterfactual reasoning as a particular kind of contextual reasoning

In this paragraph we will try to give a reading of counterfactual reasoning that could define it as an instance of contextual reasoning. This will be done in order to legitimate the use that we intend to make of MultiContext Systems as a paradigm inside which to develop the analysis of counterfactual reasoning.

Our first step will consist then in showing how we can find the three main features of contexts in what, from now on, we will call counterfactual context:

- it is *partial*: the agent performing a counterfactual reasoning is only interested in relevant information related to the counterfactual premise and this information is only a subset of the global knowledge base of the agent;
- it is *approximate*: the level of detail can be dynamically varied in the course of a counterfactual reasoning and these variations influence the outcome of the reasoning;

– it is *perspectival*: the centrality of the epistemic perspective of the reasoning agent can be deduced from the fact that different agents can reach different counterfactual conclusions starting from the same situation. The features of the counterfactual context built by an agent are strictly dependent on her set of beliefs about the "factual" situation.

Moreover, the two notions of locality and compatibility (the basis of every contextual reasoning) are crucial in the definition of a counterfactual reasoning:

– the core of the counterfactual reasoning is *local*, because it is performed entirely inside the countefactual context;
– but if we consider the whole process of counterfactual reasoning, it switches from the counterfactual context - that is defined by the counterfactual premise - and the working context, which is precisely what the agent performing the reasoning is actually interested in. For this reason, working context and counterfactual context must be *compatible* and all the assumptions that are relevant for the subject of reasoning (except the counterfactual premise) must be imported from the working context to the counterfactual one.

6 Counterfactual Reasoning and Game Theory

After having sketched the main features of the treatment of counterfactuals under a contextual theory, we want to give a hint of some possible connections with another theory emerged in a different discipline.

Another framework in which counterfactual reasoning can demonstrate its importance is a theory developed in economics, that has been widely applied and it is called Game Theory.

We will show how a lot of decision processes in Game Theory could be based upon a counterfactual reasoning and, moreover, we will try to compare the Game Theory framework with the one provided by MultiContext Systems.

When confronted with a decision about her future move in a game, an agent (or player) must consider the previous history of the game to try to guess which could be the future actions of her opponents .

All these considerations about the past history of the game can be used to build a "profile" of other agents. If the strategies played by an agent in the past are useful to reconstruct her profile, we cannot deny that the strategies that the same agent has decided not to follow are nearly as important.

The reasons why an agent has decided to reject the choice of a certain strategy can be very useful in the prediction of which strategies she will accept or reject in the future.

The importance of counterfactual reasoning is even greater in those cases in which the game is of imperfect information (something in the past history of the game is not common knowledge).

In such cases, the agent with the move is not perfectly aware of the precise situation she is in (this state is called in game theory information set, because a set of "situations" are available to the agent and she has to guess which is the one she is in on the basis of the lacking information she possesses).

When a part of the game is uncertain, the importance of the strategies (realized or not) of which the agent is sure of, is increasingly high.

But predicting future actions of the opponents is not the only aim of counterfactual reasoning: the inquiry about the credibility, attitudes, beliefs, intentions of other agents also has the purpose of understanding which of them are fit to cooperate or, to use a more technical locution, to enter into a coalition.

As we have anticipated, the notion of information set (sets of possibilities determined by the lack of information) is very close to the notion of context as partial theory. Being partial, a context is a set of models representing "the possible ways the situation can be".

The use of contexts to represent information sets is promising for another reason: very often (if not in every situation) an agent has to consider not only the opinions and beliefs of other agents about the game, but also the opinions and beliefs these agents have toward her (and what they think she thinks of them and so on).

If we use a formalization based on MultiContext Systems, we have at our disposal all the tools developed within it to switch from one context (representation of the game of an agent) to another.

7   Conclusions

What we have tried to do with this paper is to give a preliminary and intuitive account of a cognitive approach to the subject of counterfactuality.

In doing so, we followed some intuitions coming from cognitive sciences and artificial intelligence, which make evident some points of distinction with the "traditional" works on counterfactuals developed by most philosophers in the study of the subject.

As we have shown, the primary difference has to be found in the goal: while these philosophers have concentrated their analyses on the semantics of counterefactual conditionals (what we have called the *metaphysical approach*), we are mainly interested in the way in which processes of reasoning having a counterfactual dimension develop in human or artificial "minds".

Another topic that we want to deepen is the one of the possible applications of the "counterfactual structure" to other forms of common sense reasoning.

Nevertheless, there are a series of points that are still open, the most important of which is the elaboration of a formal model able to illustrate and integrate counterfactual reasoning.

In this direction, our purpose is to apply the tools of MultiContext Systems and Local Models Semantics with their principles of locality and compatibility, that seem to fit the features of this peculiar kind of reasoning.

183

References

1. M. Benerecetti, P. Bouquet, and C. Ghidini. Contextual Reasoning Distilled. *Journal of Theoretical and Experimental Artificial Intelligence*, 12(3):279–305, 2000.
2. J. Bennett. Counterfactuals and temporal direction. *The Philosophical Review*. XCIII(1):57–91, January 1984.
3. R. Byrne and A. McEleny. Counterfactual thinking about actions. In P. Cherubini, editor, *Human Reasoning: Logical and Psychological Perspectives*. 1999.
4. T. Costello and J. McCarthy. Useful counterfactuals. Technical Report Vol. 3 (1999): nr 2, Linköping University, Articles in Computer and Information Science, 1999. http://ep.liu.se/ea/cis/1999/002/.
5. J. Dinsmore. *Partitioned representations*. Kluwer Academic Publishers, 1991.
6. J. Dinsmore. Mental spaces from a functional perspective. *Cognitive Science*, 1987.
7. G. Fauconnier. *Mental spaces: aspects of meaning construction in natural language*. MIT Press, 1985.
8. G. Fauconnier. Analogical counterfactuals. In G. Fauconnier and E. Sweetser, editors, *Spaces, Worlds, and Grammar*, pages 1–28. The University of Chicago Press, 1996.
9. M. L. Ginsberg. Counterfactuals. *Artificial Intelligence*, 1986.
10. F. Giunchiglia. Contextual reasoning. *Epistemologia, special issue on I Linguaggi e le Macchine*, XVI:345–364, 1993.
11. F. Giunchiglia and P. Bouquet. Introduction to contextual reasoning. An Artificial Intelligence perspective. In B. Kokinov, editor, *Perspectives on Cognitive Science*, volume 3, pages 138–159. NBU Press, Sofia, 1997.
12. F. Giunchiglia and C. Ghidini. Local Models Semantics, or Contextual Reasoning = Locality + Compatibility. In *Proceedings of the Sixth International Conference on Principles of Knowledge Representation and Reasoning (KR'98)*, pages 282 289, Trento, 1998. Morgan Kaufmann.
13. N. Goodman. The problem of counterfactual conditionals. In *Conditionals*.
14. J. Y. Halpern. Hypothetical knowledge and counterfactual reasoning. *International Journal of Game Theory*, 28, 1999.
15. S. J. Hoch. Counterfactual reasoning and accuracy in predicting personal events. *Journal of Experimental Psychology*, 11(4):719–731, 1985.
16. F. Jackson, editor. *Conditionals*. Oxford Readings in Philosophy. Oxford University Press, 1991.
17. C. Ortiz Jr. Explanatory update theory: Applications of counterfactual reasoning to causation. *AI*, 1999.
18. G. Lakoff. Sorry, I'm not myself today: The metaphor system for conceptualizing the self. In G. Fauconnier and E. Sweetser, editors, *Spaces, Worlds, and Grammar*, pages 1–28. The University of Chicago Press, 1996.
19. M. Lange. Inductive confirmation, counterfactual conditionals, and laws of nature. *Philosophical Studies*, 1997.
20. D. Lewis. *Counterfactuals*. Blackwell, 1973.
21. D. Lewis. *Philosophical papers*. Oxford University Press, 1983. Two volumes.
22. M. G. Lipe. Counterfactual reasoning as a framework for attribution theories. *Psychological Bulletin*, 109(3):456–471, 1991.
23. M. McDermott. Counterfactuals and Access Point. *Mind*, 1999.
24. P. Noordhof. Probabilistic Causation, Preemption and Counterfactuals. *Mind*. 1999.
25. R. Stalnaker. A Theory of Conditionals. In F. Jackson, editor. *Conditionals*. Oxford Readings in Philosophy. pages 28–45. Oxford University Press. 1991.

Context-Based Ambiguity Management
for Natural Language Processing

Martin Romacker & **Udo Hahn**

Text Understanding Lab
Freiburg University
Werthmannplatz 1
D-79085 Freiburg, Germany
{romacker|hahn}@coling.uni-freiburg.de

Abstract. We introduce a formal context mechanism, embedded into a description logics framework, which allows to uniformly represent and manage different kinds of natural language ambiguities as they occur in the course of text understanding. Multiple lexical, syntactic and semantic interpretations are separated by assigning each of these alternatives a single context space for local reasoning and incremental disambiguation.

1 Introduction

The vast potential to create ambiguities at all levels of natural language analysis – lexical, syntactic, semantic, referential and pragmatic – constitutes one of the great challenges of natural language processing (NLP). Although formal analyses of ambiguity phenomena in isolation yield truly discouraging results (e.g., Church and Patil [2] give evidence that syntactic ambiguity grows exponentially with the number of genitive or prepositional phrase attachments, noun-noun modifiers, stack relative clauses, etc.), NLP researchers build trustfully on the disambiguating power of the *linguistic context* in which utterances occur. The phrasal and clausal level of language description is then taken to eliminate many of the lexical, syntactic and semantic ambiguities [14], whereas the level of discourse context is believed to help resolve many referential and higher-level pragmatic ambiguities [15, 3].

While a considerable amount of work has been done on disambiguating effects due to the linguistic context, only few proposals have been made with respect to a *general* computational framework how to manage ambiguous language and knowledge structures in NLP systems. One of the most promising approaches to deal with contexts as *formal objects* at the level of knowledge representation and reasoning proper is due to John McCarthy and his co-workers [9, 1]. Despite the fact that language theorists have already tried to incorporate a more rigid representational notion of context into their language models (for a survey, cf. Sowa [12]), a comprehensive attempt to integrate *all* levels of language analysis into a uniform formal framework is still lacking.

In this paper, we aim to combine the representational and reasoning perspective with the needs of ambiguity management for NLP. Given the application framework of the text understanding system SYNDIKATE [6], we propose an extension of its knowledge representation backbone by a formal context mechanism. The way we will use contexts leads to the creation of alternative hypothesis spaces which account for the different levels of ambiguity mentioned above. In order to keep the number of context spaces manageable, we make direct use of constraints for disambiguation purposes that become available by the particular discourse context, i.e., the input text.

Generally, we consider an interpretation to be invalid, if adding an axiom (originating from the semantic interpretation of the input text) to a formal context leads to a set of axioms that are no longer satisfiable [4]. Two perspectives on context can then be distinguished — the *static* context, as given by the a priori domain knowledge, which is further augmented by the *dynamic* context as resulting from the incremental processing of a text [17], thus making new information (in terms of interpretation constraints) continuously available.

2 Overview of the System Architecture

Grammatical knowledge for syntactic analysis is based on a fully lexicalized dependency grammar [7]. Such a grammar captures binary valency constraints between a syntactic head (e.g., a noun) and possible modifiers (e.g., a determiner or an adjective). These include restrictions on word order, compatibility of morphosyntactic features and semantic integrity conditions. For a dependency relation $\delta \in \mathcal{D} := \{specifier, subject, dir\text{-}object, ...\}$ to be established between a head and a modifier, all valency constraints must be fulfilled. Figure 1 depicts a sample dependency graph in which word nodes are given in bold face and dependency relations are indicated by labelled edges.

At the parsing level, these constraint checking tasks are performed by lexicalized processes, so-called *word actors*. Word actors are encapsulated by *phrase*

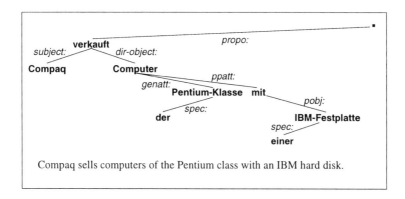

Fig. 1. A Sample Dependency Graph

actors which enclose partial parsing results in terms of a dependency subgraph (e.g., for phrases). Syntactic ambiguities, i.e., several phrase actors keeping alternative dependency structures for the same text segment, are packaged in a single *container actor* (cf. Hahn *et al.* [5] for details on the actor-based model of dependency parsing).

Domain Knowledge is expressed in terms of a concept description language ($\mathcal{CDL}$), which has several constructors combining *atomic* concepts, roles and individuals in order to define the terminological theory of a domain (see Table 1; cf. Woods and Schmolze [16] for a survey of languages based on such a description logics framework). *Concepts* are unary predicates, *roles* are binary predicates over a domain Δ, with *individuals* being the elements of Δ. We assume a common set-theoretical semantics for this language — an interpretation $\mathcal{I}$ is a function that assigns to each concept symbol (from the set $\mathcal{F}$) a subset of the domain Δ, $\mathcal{I}: \mathcal{F} \rightarrow 2^{\Delta}$, to each role symbol (from the set $\mathcal{R}$) a binary relation of Δ, $\mathcal{I}: \mathcal{R} \rightarrow 2^{\Delta \times \Delta}$, and to each individual symbol (from the set $\mathbf{I}$) an element of Δ, $\mathcal{I}: \mathbf{I} \rightarrow \Delta$.

Syntax	Semantics
C	$\{d \in \Delta^{\mathcal{I}} \mid \mathcal{I}(C) = d\}$
$C \sqcap D$	$C^{\mathcal{I}} \cap D^{\mathcal{I}}$
$C \sqcup D$	$C^{\mathcal{I}} \cup D^{\mathcal{I}}$
$\neg C$	$\Delta^{\mathcal{I}} \setminus C^{\mathcal{I}}$
$\forall R.C$	$\{d \in \Delta^{\mathcal{I}} \mid R^{\mathcal{I}}(d) \subseteq C^{\mathcal{I}}\}$
R	$\{(d, e) \in \Delta^{\mathcal{I}} \times \Delta^{\mathcal{I}} \mid \mathcal{I}(R) = (d, e)\}$
$R \sqcap S$	$R^{\mathcal{I}} \cap S^{\mathcal{I}}$

Table 1. Syntax and Semantics for a Subset of $\mathcal{CDL}$

Terminological Axioms	
Axiom	Semantics
$A \doteq C$	$A^{\mathcal{I}} = C^{\mathcal{I}}$
$A \sqsubseteq C$	$A^{\mathcal{I}} \subseteq C^{\mathcal{I}}$
$Q \doteq R$	$Q^{\mathcal{I}} = R^{\mathcal{I}}$
$Q \sqsubseteq R$	$Q^{\mathcal{I}} \subseteq R^{\mathcal{I}}$
Assertional Axioms	
Axiom	Semantics
$a : C$	$a^{\mathcal{I}} \in C^{\mathcal{I}}$
$a\ R\ b$	$(a^{\mathcal{I}}, b^{\mathcal{I}}) \in R^{\mathcal{I}}$

Table 2. $\mathcal{CDL}$ Axioms

Concept terms and *role terms* are defined inductively. Table 1 states corresponding constructors for concepts and roles, together with their semantics. C and D denote concept terms, while R and S denote role terms. $R^{\mathcal{I}}(d)$ represents the set of *role fillers* of the individual d, i.e., the set of individuals e with $(d, e) \in R^{\mathcal{I}}$. By means of *terminological axioms* (cf. Table 2, upper part) a symbolic name can be defined for each concept and role term. We may supply necessary and sufficient constraints (using "$\doteq$") or only necessary constraints (using "$\sqsubseteq$") for concepts and roles. A finite set of such axioms, $\mathcal{T}$, is called the *terminology* or *TBox*. Concepts and roles are associated with concrete individuals by *assertional axioms* (see Table 2, lower part – a, b denote individuals). A finite set of such axioms, $\mathcal{A}$, is called the *world description* or *ABox*. An interpretation $\mathcal{I}$ is a model of an ABox with regard to a TBox, iff $\mathcal{I}$ satisfies the assertional and terminological axioms.

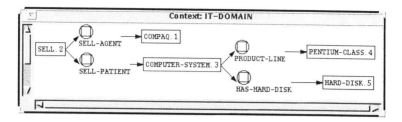

Fig. 2. A Sample Semantic Interpretation

Semantic knowledge accounts for conceptual linkages between instances of concept types according to those dependency relations that are established between their corresponding lexical items. Semantic interpretation processes operate on so-called *semantically interpretable* subgraphs of the dependency graph (cf. Romacker *et al.* [11]). By this, we refer to subgraphs whose bounding nodes contain content words (i.e., words with a conceptual correlate), while all possibly intervening nodes contain only non-content words (such as prepositions, articles). Hence, the linkage between content words may be direct (in Figure 1 between *"Compaq"* and *"verkauft"* via the dependency relation *subject*), or it may be indirect (e.g., between *"Computer"* and *"IBM-Festplatte"* via the preposition *"mit"* and the dependency relations *ppatt* and *pobj*).

When the first word in our sample sentence, *"Compaq"*, is read, its conceptual correlate, COMPAQ.1, is instantiated. The next word, *"verkauft"* *(sells)*, also leads to the creation of an associated instance (SELL.2) (cf. Figure 1 and 2). Syntactic constraints of the transitive verb *"verkauft"* lead to checking the *subject* dependency relation for *"Compaq"*. At the conceptual level, *subject* always translates into AGENT or PATIENT (sub)roles, since we statically link each dependency relation to a set of conceptual relations by a function $i : \mathcal{D} \mapsto 2^{\mathcal{R}}$ (e.g., $i(subject) = \{$AGENT, PATIENT$\}$). To infer a valid semantic relation we incorporate knowledge about the concept types of COMPAQ.1 and SELL.2, *viz.* COMPANY and SELL, respectively. Semantic interpretation then boils down to a search of the knowledge base, checking whether a COMPANY can be interpreted in terms of an AGENT or a PATIENT of a SELL event. For SELL, only SELL-AGENT and SELL-PATIENT are allowed for interpretation as they are subroles of AGENT and PATIENT. Checking sortal restrictions (e.g., SELL-AGENT requires a PERSON, while SELL-PATIENT requires a PRODUCT) succeeds only for SELL-AGENT (cf. Figure 2).

3 Description Logics with Contexts

Lexical, syntactic and semantic ambiguities of an utterance translate into different conceptual interpretations at the ABox level. So we need a uniform representation device *within* description logics to deal with different readings locally. This is achieved by reformulating the notion of context within description logics. We, first, introduce the set of context symbols $\mathcal{H}$. Syntactically, assertional axioms internal to a context $h \in \mathcal{H}$ are enclosed by brackets and are subscripted by the corresponding context identifier. For example, $(a : C)_h$ means that in a context h the individual a is asserted to be an instance of the concept C. We then define the set-theoretical semantics of the *interpretation* $\mathcal{I}_h$ relative to a context h for assertional axioms as summarized in Table 3. The TBox $\mathcal{T}$ and the ABox $\mathcal{A}$ for a context $h \in \mathcal{H}$ is given by $\mathcal{T}_h$ and $\mathcal{A}_h$, respectively.

Syntax	Semantics
$(a : C)_h$	$a^{\mathcal{I}_h} \in C^{\mathcal{I}_h}$
$(a\ R\ b)_h$	$(a^{\mathcal{I}_h},\ b^{\mathcal{I}_h}) \in R^{\mathcal{I}_h}$

Table 3. Context-Embedded Assertional Axioms

We then define the transitive and reflexive relation $subcontextOf \subseteq \mathcal{H} \times \mathcal{H}$ (cf. Table 4) to account for property inheritance in a context hierarchy. We re-

$$subcontextOf(h_1, h_2): \Leftrightarrow$$
$$\forall\ h_1,\ h_2\ \in\ \mathcal{H}:$$
$$\mathcal{T}_{h_1}\ \supseteq\ \mathcal{T}_{h_2}\ \wedge\ \mathcal{A}_{h_1}\ \supseteq\ \mathcal{A}_{h_2}$$

Table 4. Hierarchy of Contexts: The *Subcontext* Relation

quire the TBox and the ABox of a parent context to be inherited by all of its child contexts. Since multiple inheritance may occur, a (directed, acyclic) 'context graph' emerges. We also allow for incremental, context-specific extensions of the TBox or ABox. However, some restrictions apply:

1. Extensions of contexts by additional terminological or assertional axioms have to be monotonic, i.e., neither are redefinitions of concepts or relations, nor are retractions of assertions allowed.
2. Context-specific assertions which assign an individual to a concept type or to conceptual relations are permitted, while context-specific concept definitions are prohibited. If a concept occurs in two different contexts, it must have the same definition.
3. The discourse universe Δ is identical for all contexts. $\top$ denotes the top concept in the TBox, the interpretation of which covers all individuals of the domain Δ, $\top^{\mathcal{I}} = \Delta^{\mathcal{I}}$, so that every individual is an instance of $\top$ in the uppermost context.

Provided these extensions to standard description logics, the basic idea for the application of the *formal context* mechanism is to use a separate context for each assertion added to the text knowledge base during text analysis. Such an assertion contains a statement about the meaning of a word or an utterance. Previous assertions (which constitute the formal counterpart of the *discourse context*) are made accessible by inheritance between contexts. Since, under ambiguity, alternative assertion sets have the status of hypotheses, they may or may not be true. Whenever an assertion in a particular context turns out to be nonsatisfiable for a particular TBox[1] and a dynamically extended ABox, the corresponding reading is treated as erroneous and will be excluded from further consideration. An ABox is nonsatisfiable if there exists an individiual a for which the TBox and ABox imply that it is not in the interpretation of any concept C of the TBox (formally: $\mathcal{T} \cup \mathcal{A} \models a^{\mathcal{I}} \notin C^{\mathcal{I}}$ for all C in the terminology). In this view, contexts provide the representational foundation for managing ambiguities and for computations aimed at their disambiguation.

The linkage between the syntactic dependency level and the evolving text knowledge base, consisting of a context graph (contexts related by *subcontextOf*), is made by assigning these contexts to phrase actors. Let $\mathcal{P}$ be the set of phrase actors. Every instance of a phrase actor $p \in \mathcal{P}$ is linked to a (possibly empty) set of contexts $cont_p \subseteq 2^{\mathcal{H}}$ that hold all of p's alternative semantic interpretations.

4 Managing Ambiguities by Contexts

Contexts account for ambiguities at all levels of language interpretation. We here focus on two forms of *lexical* ambiguity – due to multiple part-of-speech assignments and polysemy —, *structural (syntactic)* ambiguity, as well as sentential *semantic* ambiguity due to compositional interpretation. Four phases of text analysis where ambiguities may arise or, finally, get pruned, have to be considered:

- *Lexical Instantiation*: Different conceptual instances for lexical items contained in the input text are created for polysemous words, each one of them in a separate context. Different part-of-speech categorizations of the same underlying concept, however, are dealt with by different contexts, too.
- *Syntactic Analysis*: Topologically different parse structures (in terms of dependency graphs) for the same text segment yield different semantic interpretations each of which is assigned to a corresponding alternative context.
- *Semantic Interpretation*: Whenever a semantic interpretation relating several conceptual instances is performed, different readings (if they exist) are encapsulated in corresponding alternative contexts.
- *Selection*: The interpretation results at the end of sentence analysis, which are contained in alternative contexts, are finally ranked to select the most plausible reading(s).[2]

Lexical Instantiation — Lexical Ambiguity. Text analysis starts with an empty text knowledge base, one that contains no assertions at all. By default, the empty text knowledge base is assigned as a subcontext to the a priori given domain knowledge base, thus preserving the entire information it encodes for subsequent interpretations. We call the initial text knowledge base

---

[1] We assume this TBox $\mathcal{T}$ to be consistent, i.e., there exist no concept C for which $\mathcal{T}$ implies an empty extension.

[2] We currently extend our context-based ambiguity management system to deal with referential ambiguities within the framework of the centering model [13], too.

190

NEWHYPO. All interpretation contexts created during text analysis are subcontexts of NEWHYPO. As the system incrementally reads the words from an input text, instances are created in the text knowledge base for each content word associated with a concept identifier.

During the instantiation phase, we have to cope with two different sources of *lexical ambiguity*. First, a lexical item in a text may refer to different word classes (*part-of-speech ambiguity*) and, therefore, requires the creation of different contexts for semantic interpretation. Second, a lexical item in a text may relate to more than one conceptual correlate (*polysemy*) for each of which a separate context has to be created and maintained.[3]

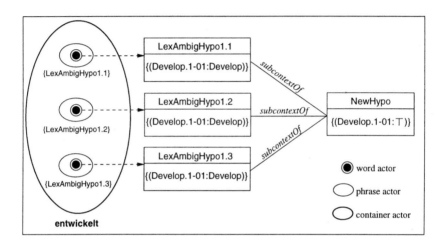

Fig. 3. Context Management for Part-of-Speech Ambiguity

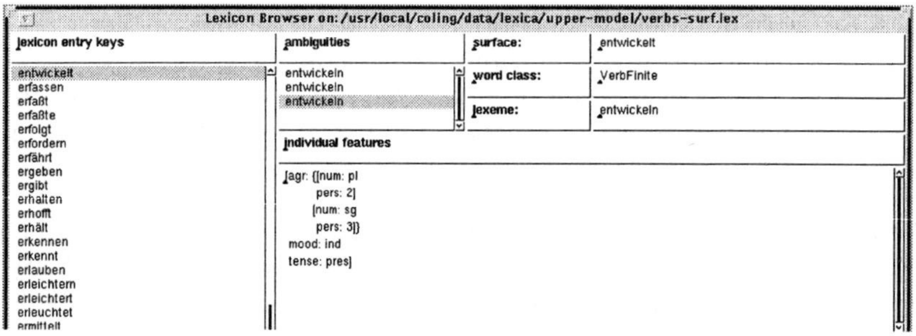

Fig. 4. Fragment of the Lexicon: Lexical Entry for *entwickelt*

---

[3] By convention, these contexts are named LEXHYPO, if no ambiguities occur, and LEXAMBIGHYPO, otherwise.

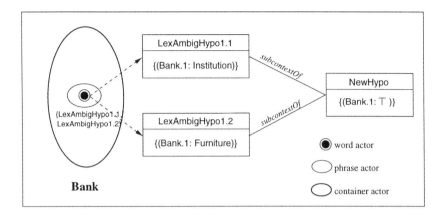

Fig. 5. Context Management for Polysemy

Consider Figure 3 where the instantiation of contexts for the German lexical item *"entwickelt"* (*develop*) is depicted. In the lexicon, it is linked to three different word classes, *viz.* VERBFINITE, VERBPARTPASSIVE, VERBPARTPERFECT (cf. the corresponding three entries in the **ambiguities** field in Figure 4; the corresponding word class, VERBFINITE, is only visible for the highlighted verb entry). Though different parts of speech have to be considered, they, nevertheless, refer to the same (sense of the associated) lexeme (*"entwickeln"*). For each of the three categorial readings a corresponding word actor is created, since the syntactic requirements and behaviors of different word classes have to be accounted for. As the base lexeme is associated with only one concept identifier in the domain knowledge (DEVELOP), each word actor triggers the creation of the same single assertion in a separate context. In Figure 3, e.g., the uppermost word actor initializes the creation of the assertion (DEVELOP.1-01:DEVELOP)$_{LexAmbigHypo1.1}$. Note that the instance symbol is also introduced in NEWHYPO, the uppermost context, by the assertion (DEVELOP.1-01: ⊤)$_{NewHypo}$. The contexts are then linked to the phrase actors enveloping the three word actors.

In case of polysemy (cf. Figure 5), one lexical entry is linked to more than one conceptual correlate. Consider the German noun *"Bank"* which may refer to *'financial institution'* or *'kind of furniture'*. Both meanings are linked to a single lexical item belonging to the same word class. The corresponding word actor causes the creation of two lexical contexts, with the assertions (BANK.1:INSTITUTION)$_{LexAmbigHypo1.1}$ and (BANK.1:FURNITURE)$_{LexAmbigHypo1.2}$. The same instance symbol, BANK.1, receives different interpretations depending on its context. The interpretation alternatives are administrated by the phrase actor which embeds the word actor in terms of a set of contexts.

Semantic Interpretation — Semantic Ambiguity. Semantic interpretation is basically a search for a (composed) conceptual relation in the domain knowledge base, required to hold between the conceptual correlates of the two content words spanning a semantically interpretable dependency subgraph. If the search succeeds, a corresponding assertional axiom is added to the considered context. If more than one conceptual relation can be computed, a case of *semantic ambiguity* is encountered. Each of these representational alternatives is kept in a separate context, and each of the resulting contexts is defined as a subcontext of the contexts containing the two content words. Thus, they inherit the assertions of their parent contexts and contain the interpretation of the dependency graph that emerges after syntactically linking the two content words.

Let p_1 and p_2 be the phrase actors that contain the word actors for the two content words, which negotiate a dependency relation, and let all constraints except the semantic one be fulfilled. Let $cont_{p_1}$ and $cont_{p_2}$ be the sets of contexts attached to p_1 and p_2, respectively. Semantic interpretation applies to all context tuples contained in $cont_{p_1} \times cont_{p_2}$. Note that an instance identifier – the conceptual correlate of a lexical item involved – may belong to different concept types in different contexts (cf. Figure 5), and that the interpretation space holding the assertional axioms necessarily differs for all tuples. All new contexts resulting from semantic interpretation are finally included in the set of contexts acquainted with the phrase actor p_3, which is created after the dependency relation has been established and, thus, encompasses p_1 as well as p_2.

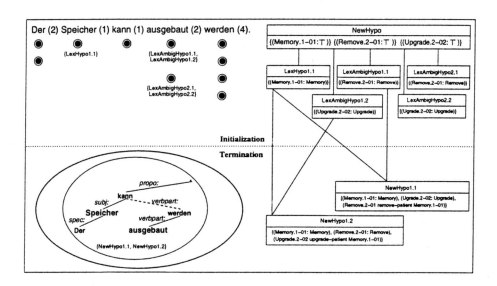

Fig. 6. Context Management for Semantic Ambiguity

Consider an ambiguous sentence such as *"Der Speicher kann ausgebaut werden."*. Due to the lexical ambiguity of the German word *"ausbauen"*, one reading is given by *"The memory can be upgraded"*, while the second reading can be phrased as *"The memory can be removed"*. The left side of Figure 6 depicts the syntactic level, its right side contains the (semantic) context graph. Horizontally, Figure 6 is divided into two layers, initialization and termination.

The number of word actors (reflecting lexical ambiguities) instantiated at the syntactic level is given in brackets behind each word in the sentence. A corresponding number of word actor symbols is depicted beneath each lexical item. Since *"Speicher"* (*memory*) and *"ausgebaut"* (*upgrade, remove*), the sole content words, are linked to a conceptual correlate, each associated word actor initiates the creation of instances in separate contexts. *"ausgebaut"*, e.g., belongs to the word classes VERBPARTPERFECT and VERBPARTPASSIVE. Hence, two word actors are created with two meanings contained in two independent lexical contexts, viz. *LexAmbigHypo1.1 (remove)* and *LexAmbigHypo1.2 (upgrade)* for the word class VERBPARTPASSIVE, as well as *LexAmbigHypo2.1 (remove)* and *LexAmbigHypo2.2 (upgrade)* for the word class VERBPARTPERFECT.

Semantic interpretation starts as soon as the word actor for *"kann"* (*can*) tries to govern its modifier *"werden"* (*be*) – which itself already governs the VERBPARTPASSIVE *"ausgebaut"* (*ugrade/remove*) – by the dependency relation verbpart. Identifying the phrase actor of *"kann"* with p_1 leads to $cont_{p_1} = \{LexHypo1.1\}$; p_2, the phrase actor containing *"ausgebaut"* as VERBPARTPAS-SIVE, results in $cont_{p_2} = \{LexAmbigHypo1.1, LexAmbigHypo1.2\}$. This leads to two different interpretation contexts (two tuples), one with the *upgrade* and the other with the *removal* reading.[4] Since we consider semantic interpretation as a search problem to link the conceptual correlates of the content words spanning the semantically interpretable subgraph – composed of *"Speicher"* (*memory*) and *"ausgebaut"* (*removed/upgraded*) – a search for appropriate conceptual relations is conducted in the domain knowledge base. It retrieves the relations REMOVE-PATIENT and UPGRADE-PATIENT for MEMORY.1-01 with regard to REMOVE.2-01 and UPGRADE.2-02, respectively. The resulting assertions are added to new interpretation contexts, viz. (REMOVE.2-01 REMOVE-PATIENT MEMORY.1-01)$_{NewHypo1.1}$ and (UPGRADE.2-02 UPGRADE-PATIENT MEMORY.1-01)$_{NewHypo1.2}$. These contexts form the context set $cont_{p_3}$ and are linked to the phrase actor p_3 that contains the entire dependency graph for the input sentence (cf. Figure 6, left, lower part). This way, a single syntactic structure is associated with two different semantic interpretations.

Syntactic Analysis — Structural Ambiguity. An example of syntactic ambiguity is given by the German sentence: *"Geliefert wird der Computer von Compaq"*. The different readings it has are reflected by two corresponding English paraphrases: *"The computer will be delivered by Compaq"* vs. *"The computer from Compaq will be delivered"*. The ambiguity is due to alternative PP-attachments which either bind *"Compaq"* to the past participle *"geliefert"* or to *"Computer"*, each of which results in diverging interpretations in the text knowledge base. In Figure 7 three interpretation steps are depicted, the initializa-

---

[4] The initial contexts *LexAmbigHypo2.1* and *LexAmbigHypo2.2* are abandoned because of syntactic reasons. The VERBPARTPERFECT analysis of *"ausgebaut"* is rejected by any of the preceding word actors in the sentence.

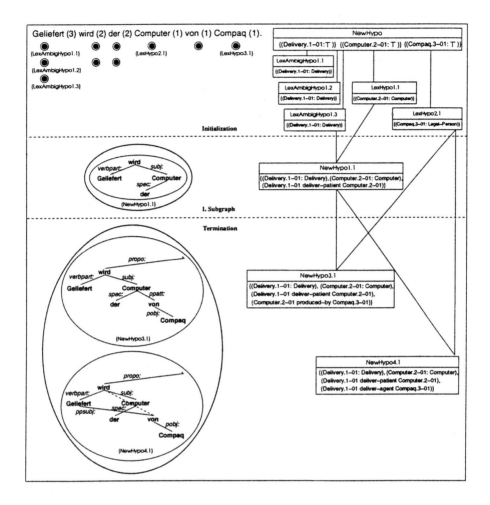

Fig. 7. Context Management for Structural Ambiguity

tion phase (top), the interpretation step for the first semantically interpretable subgraph (centre), and, finally, the termination of the interpretation process (bottom).

At the initialization layer the word actors associated with the lexical items are shown with their corresponding instances and contexts in the text knowledge base. *"Geliefert"*, e.g., relates to three word classes, with three word actors accounting for each part of speech variety (cf. Figure 7, top, left side). As they converge, however, on a single conceptual correlate, *viz.* DELIVERY, just one context is linked to each word actor containing the instance DELIVERY.1-01.

The first interpretation step occurs when *"geliefert"* and *"Computer"* are syntactically bound by a connecting path via *verbpart* – *"wird"* – *subject* (cf. Figure 7, centre, left side). Semantic interpretation of the passive voice results in the relation DELIVER-PATIENT. As a consequence, the assertion DELIVERY.1-01

DELIVER-PATIENT COMPUTER.2-01 is added to the text knowledge base in a separate context, NewHypo1.1. Since no ambiguities arise, the interpretation of the entire sentence analyzed so far is encapsulated in this context (cf. Figure 7, centre, right side).

As soon as the prepositional phrase *"von Compaq"* is parsed two alternative syntactic bindings become possible which are captured by two independent phrase actors. Each of them holds a different syntactic dependency structure. In Figure 7 (bottom, left side), the upper phrase actor contains the attachment of *"von Compaq"* to *"Computer"* via the dependency relation *ppatt*. The lower of these phrase actors encodes the binding of *"von Compaq"* to the past participle *"geliefert"* by the dependency relation *ppsubj*. These diverging syntactic representations yield different semantic interpretations, too. In the first case, the semantic interpretation process results in the relation PRODUCED-BY linking the two discourse entities under consideration. Hence, the interpretation context NewHypo3.1 is augmented by the corresponding assertion, COMPUTER.2-01 PRODUCED-BY COMPAQ.3-01. In the second case, at the conceptual level *"Compaq"* is interpreted as being the agent of the underlying delivery event, i.e., the relation DELIVER-AGENT is determined by the semantic interpretation. Accordingly, a new context, NewHypo4.1, is created in order to represent the semantic interpretation alternative as given by the assertion DELIVERY.1-01 DELIVER-AGENT COMPAQ.3-01. Finally, two contexts, NewHypo3.1 and NewHypo4.1, hold the different hypotheses emerging from the structural ambiguities, with just a single context assigned to the corresponding phrase actors.

Selection. As the input text is incrementally analyzed, each of the interpretation results resides in *terminal contexts*, i.e., ones that have no children. Finally, each sentence is assigned its set of terminal contexts as sentential reading(s). If multiple semantic interpretations exist after the analysis of a sentence has been completed, we apply several assessment heuristics to accumulate different sources of evidence for selecting a preferred reading: syntactic coverage, ranking of semantic interpretations (e.g., PP interpretations receive a higher weight than genitives), and the potential of particular assertions to foster additional, reasonable inferences.

The weight of a context is determined by iteratively adding the weight of the current terminal context and its ancestor contexts in the context graph. Selecting the best reading(s) for a sentence then boils down to the selection of the terminal context(s) with maximal weight. This can be considered as a brute-force mechanism for removing possibly contradictory sets of assumptions from the underlying knowledge base (for more sophisticated ways of dealing with contradiction identification and advanced belief revision using contexts, cf. Martins and Shapiro [8]).

5 Conclusions

We have introduced a formal context mechanism for representing and reasoning about natural language ambiguities which occur at different levels of text analysis. Part-of-speech and structural ambiguities are already handled at the syntax level (by phrase actors) and then get propagated to the context level, while lexical polysemy and sentence-level semantic ambiguities are only dealt with at the context level (by multiple interpretation contexts). The dynamic context extension mechanism which reflects the incremental processing of the input text further constrains the satisfiability of additional assertional axioms and supports the disambiguation of the alternative readings.

A crucial feature of this methodology is its clean embedding into the terminological reasoning mechanisms underlying text understanding. Ambiguities are represented as disjunctions of logical axioms [1], tentatively assumed to hold in their local contexts. This implies that all interpretation alternatives be enumerated explicitly (cf. Reyle [10] for a different approach using semantic underspecification as a technique to cope with scoping ambiguities of quantifiers, an issue not touched upon here). The use of contexts as a formal vehicle for encapsulating alternative readings and reasoning about their resolution distinguishes our work from more ambitious uses of contexts, e.g., to detect contradictory information within or between different contexts for the purpose of belief revision as discussed by Martins and Shapiro [8].

Acknowledgments. We would like to thank our colleagues in the CLIF group for fruitful discussions. M. Romacker was supported by a grant from DFG (Ha 2097/5-2).

References

1. Sasa Buvač, Vanja Buvač, and Ian A. Mason. Metamathematics of contexts. *Fundamenta Informaticae*, 23(3):263–301, 1995.
2. Kenneth Church and Ramesh Patil. Coping with syntactic ambiguity or how to put the block in the box on the table. *American Journal of Computational Linguistics*, 8(3/4):139–149, 1982.
3. Giacomo Ferrari. Types of contexts and their role in multimodal communication. *Computational Intelligence*, 13(3):414–426, 1997.
4. Jeroen Groenendijk, Martin Stokhof, and Frank Veltman. Coreference and modality. In Shalom Lappin, editor, *The Handbook of Contemporary Semantic Theory*, pages 179–213. Oxford: Blackwell, 1996.
5. Udo Hahn, Norbert Bröker, and Peter Neuhaus. Let's PARSETALK: Message-passing protocols for object-oriented parsing. In Harry Bunt and Anton Nijholt, editors, *Advances in Probabilistic and other Parsing Technologies*, volume 16 of *Text, Speech and Language Technologies*, pages 177–201. Dordrecht, Boston: Kluwer, 2000.
6. Udo Hahn and Martin Romacker. Content management in the SYNDIKATE system: How technical documents are automatically transformed to text knowledge bases. *Data & Knowledge Engineering*, 35(2):137–159, 2000.

7. Udo Hahn, Susanne Schacht, and Norbert Bröker. Concurrent, object-oriented natural language parsing: The PARSETALK model. *International Journal of Human-Computer Studies*, 41(1/2):179–222, 1994.

8. João P. Martins and Stuart C. Shapiro. A model for belief revision. *Artificial Intelligence*, 35(1):25–79, 1988.

9. John McCarthy. Notes on formalizing context. In *IJCAI'93 – Proceedings of the 13th International Joint Conference on Artificial Intelligence*, volume 1, pages 555–560. Chambéry, France, August 28 - September 3, 1993. San Mateo, CA: Morgan Kaufmann, 1993.

10. Uwe Reyle. Dealing with ambiguities by underspecification. *Journal of Semantics*, 10:123–179, 1993.

11. Martin Romacker, Katja Markert, and Udo Hahn. Lean semantic interpretation. In *IJCAI'99 – Proceedings of the 16th International Joint Conference on Artificial Intelligence*, volume 2, pages 868–875. Stockholm, Sweden, July 31 - August 6, 1999. San Francisco, CA: Morgan Kaufmann, 1999.

12. John F. Sowa. Syntax, semantics, and pragmatics of contexts. In Gerard Ellis, Robert A. Levinson, William Rich, and John F. Sowa, editors, *Conceptual Structures: Applications, Implementation and Theory. Proceedings of the 3rd International Conference on Conceptual Structures – ICCS'95*, volume 954 of *Lecture Notes in Artificial Intelligence*, pages 1–15. Santa Cruz, CA, USA, August 14-18, 1995. Berlin etc.: Springer, 1995.

13. Michael Strube and Udo Hahn. Functional centering: Grounding referential coherence in information structure. *Computational Linguistics*, 25(3):309–344, 1999.

14. Patrizia Tabossi. What's in a context? In David S. Gorfein, editor, *Resolving Semantic Ambiguity*, pages 25–39. New York: Springer, 1989.

15. Janyce Wiebe, Graeme Hirst, and Diane Horton. Language use in context. *Communications of the ACM*, 39(1):102–111, 1996.

16. William A. Woods and James G. Schmolze. The KL-ONE family. *Computers & Mathematics with Applications*, 23(2/5):133–177, 1992.

17. Gian Piero Zarri. Internal and external knowledge context, and their use for interpretation of natural language. In *Proceedings of the IJCAI'95 Workshop on 'Context in Natural Language Processing'*, pages 180–188. Montréal, Quebec, Canada, August 1995, 1995.

A Connectionist-Symbolic Approach to Modeling Agent Behavior: Neural Networks Grouped by Contexts

Amy E. Henninger[1,2], Avelino J. Gonzalez[1], Michael Georgiopoulos[1], Ronald F. DeMara[1]

[1] Intelligent Systems Laboratory
School of Electrical Engineering and Computer Science,
University of Central Florida
Orlando, FL 32816
{amy, ajg, mge, rfd}@isl.ucf.edu
[2] Soar Technology, Inc.
317 North First Street
Ann Arbor, MI. 48103-3301
amy@soartech.com

Abstract. A recent report by the National Research Council (NRC) declares neural networks "hold the most promise for providing powerful learning models". While some researchers have experimented with using neural networks to model battlefield behavior for Computer Generated Forces (CGF) systems used in distributed simulations, the NRC report indicates that further research is needed to develop a hybrid system that will integrate the newer neural network technology into the current rule-based paradigms. This paper supports this solicitation by examining the use of a context structure to modularly organize the application of neural networks to a low-level Semi-Automated Forces (SAF) reactive task. Specifically, it reports on the development of a neural network movement model and illustrates how its performance is improved through the use of the modular context paradigm. Further, this paper introduces the theory behind the neural networks' architecture and training algorithms as well as the specifics of how the networks were developed for this investigation. Lastly, it illustrates how the networks were integrated with SAF software, defines the networks' performance measures, presents the results of the scenarios considered in this investigation, and offers directions for future work.

1 Introduction

The combination of computer simulation and networking technologies has provided military forces with an effective means of training through the use of Distributed Interactive Simulation (DIS). DIS is an architecture for building large-scale simulation models from a set of independent simulator nodes that represent entities in the simulation [1]. These simulator nodes individually simulate the activities of one or more entities in the simulation and report their attributes and actions of interest to other simulator nodes via the network. DIS nodes simulating combat vehicles, such as M1 Abrams tanks, are crewed by soldiers being trained. The trainees operate the controls of the simulators as they would in the actual vehicles, and the simulators implement actions in the simulated battlefield. Since, in a synthetic battlefield, the trainees need opposing forces against which to train, a type of DIS node known as a Computer Generated Force (CGF) system was developed.

CGFs are computer-controlled behavioral models of combatants used to serve as opponents against whom trainees can fight or as friendly forces with which the trainees can fight. At a minimum, the behavior generated should be feasible and doctrinally correct. For example, behaviors should be able to emulate the use of formations in orders, identify and occupy a variety of tactical positions (e.g., fighting positions, hull down positions, turret down positions, etc), and plan reasonable routes.

Researchers in [2], [3], and [4] have experimented with using neural networks to model battlefield behavior for CGF systems used in military simulations. This technology has been identified as one that "holds the most promise for providing powerful learning models" in a recent National Research Council Report [5]. Also asserted in this report, however, is the need for further research to develop hybrid systems that will integrate the newer neural network technology into the current rule-based paradigms. This investigation considers one such approach by using a framework based on modular decomposition to develop and apply the neural networks generating SAF behavior. Specifically, this research examines the performance improvements made to a neural network based near-term movement model by adopting a modular approach that groups neural networks according to contexts..

2 Modular Decomposition

The use of a modular approach to a modeling task can be beneficial in a variety of ways. For example, it can be used for the purposes of improving performance. In other words, although the task could be solved with a monolithic set, better performance is achieved when it is broken down into a number of expert modules. Once the task is decomposed it is possible to switch to the most appropriate module, depending on the current circumstances or context. Switching has been discussed in the control literature [6][7], as well as the literature on behavior-based robotics [8].

In addition to performance improvement, other motivations for adopting a modular approach to a problem include a reduction in model complexity and construction of the overall system such that it is easier to understand, modify, and extend. Thus the "divide and conquer" principle is used to reduce the complexity of a single net system. This enables the use of different neural net architectures or algorithms to be applied to individual sub-problems, making it possible to exploit specialist capabilities. Moreover, where appropriate, some of these components could make use of non-neural computing techniques. This justification has been noted [9][10] and is common to engineering design in general. Another motivation for adopting a modular approach is the reduction of network training times [11]. Finally, in well-defined domains, the use of a priori knowledge can be used to suggest an appropriate decomposition of a task. This approach complements the knowledge acquisition efforts and knowledge representation paradigms used in current SAF systems [12] and can be easily extended to the acquisition of knowledge and tactics for SAF systems [13].

The decomposition of a problem into modular components may be accomplished automatically or explicitly. When the decomposition of the task into modules is determined explicitly, this usually relies on a strong understanding of the problem. The division into sub-tasks is known prior to training [14], and improved learning and performance can result. An alternative approach is one in which the task is automatically decomposed according to the blind application of a data partitioning technique. Automatic decomposition is typically applied with the intent of performance improvement, whereas explicit decomposition could have the aim of either improving performance or accomplishing tasks that might not be accomplished as easily or as naturally with a monolithic net.

3 Methodology

The synthetic force system used for the prototype development work was ModSAF, a training and research system developed by the Army's Simulation, Training, and Instrumentation Command (STRICOM). ModSAF provides a set of software modules for constructing computer-generated force behaviors at the company level and below. Typically, ModSAF models are employed to represent individual soldiers or vehicles and their coordination into orderly-moving squads and platoons, but their tactical actions as units are planned and executed by a human controller. The human behaviors represented in ModSAF include move, shoot, sense, communicate, tactics, and situation awareness. The authoritative sources of these behaviors are subject matter experts and doctrine provided by the Army Training and Doctrine Command (TRADOC). ModSAF uses finite state machines (FSMs) to represent the behavior and functionality of a process for a pre-defined number of states.

Figure 1 illustrates the scope of a Road March task through a possible representation of its FSM transition formalism. Inherent in this representation, is a temporal logic or sequencing to the state transitions in the formalism. For example, a tank would never reach an "end of road march" state (where it would slow down) before it would reach a "start of road march" state (where it would speed up). The near-term movement models addressed in this research pertain to the "Follow Route" state of the Road March FSM shown in Figure 1. In other words, the model is developed for and evaluated when the M1A2 is in a "Follow Route" state that is not influenced by proximity to the start or the end of the route. This simplifies the modeling task since the model does not have to learn to speed up and slow down at the beginning and end of the route, respectively. Further, it indicates that long-term route planning is not a part of the model's functionality. Lastly, it constrains the model's range of operability to those scenarios where there are no "Halt" states embedded in the Road March behavior.

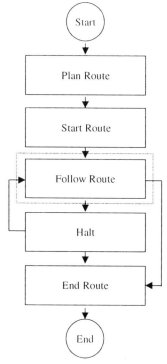

Fig. 1. FSM Representation of Road March Behavior

Figure 2 further illustrates the model addressed in this research and presents it relative to other models that might be required in a "Follow Route" state of the Road March FSM. These models blend low-level decisions with motor skills and environmental feedback. This model is responsible for the physical movement of the tank through the virtual battlefield and is represented by the change in the tank's speed and orientation.

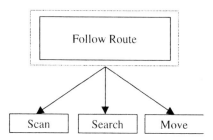

Fig. 2. Skill Models Supporting Follow-Route State

202

The route used for development and testing in the prototype work (see Figure 3) can be found in the section of terrain east of Barstow Road and west of Hill 720 in the NTC-0101 terrain database. In general, the route is represented by 45 route points and is approximately 7 kilometers long. It takes the M1A2 tank about 15 minutes of simulation time to travel at 8m/s. From this route, two similarly constructed segments were selected for detailed work. Each of these segments consisted of 4 route points centered about a turn. These are labeled as segments 1 and 2 in Figure 3 and they were used for purposes of model training and testing.

Eleven scenarios were constructed for purposes for training and testing. In each of these scenarios a single ModSAF M1A2 entity was placed at X,Y position 22579,24328 with an initial heading of 359° and each entity was assigned to perform a Road March with the route boldfaced in Figure 3. These scenarios were created with identical user-supplied parameters.

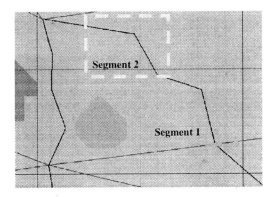

Fig. 3. Segments Used for Model Training Testing

As communicated in Table 1, a preliminary analysis of these graphs resulted in one possible partitioning of the data. These data groupings are considered with the intent to improve model generalization and system performance.

Table 1. Classification of Data According to Approach Type

Scenario Number	Approach Category
DEMO	Nominal
1	Nominal
2	Early
3	Late
4	Early
5	Late
6	Nominal
7	Early
8	Double
9	Nominal
10	Late

where "Approach Category" categorizes the approach types to a curve by distance away from the target waypoint. Specifically, this is defined by:

Early	> 45m to target waypoint
Nominal	45< > 30 m to target waypoint
Late	< 30 m to target waypoint

This categorization can be expressed as a rule-set that represents an explicit decomposition of the task. We refer to the product of this explicit task decomposition as a "context" [15]. The application of this rule results in the generation of six networks for three categories including two networks each. These two networks represent the change in the M1A2 entity's speed and the change in the M1A2 entity's heading.

All of the networks used a feed-forward architecture and were trained with back-propagation according to the delta learning rule using a momentum factor to speed the descent along the error surface. All networks were trained with randomly generated initial weights according to four different random seeds. Also, all networks used 0.01 for the training rate, η, and 0.9 for the initial momentum parameter, α. The momentum parameter was periodically adjusted to speed the rate of descent along the error surface.

Each network used a sigmoid function at the hidden nodes and a linear transformation at the output nodes. Each of these networks had 7 inputs, 20 nodes in the first hidden layer, 5 nodes in the second hidden layer, and a single output. The inputs were derived and normalized according to equations 1 – 18 below. Fundamentally, the inputs for each of the networks were a function of the M1A2 entity's state at the last simulation clock and how this state related to the road characteristics and March Order parameters.

$$S_t = S_{t-1} + \Delta S_t$$
$$\text{where } \Delta S_t = f(Ra_{t-1}, Rb_{t-1}, Rc_{t-1}, Rp_{t-1}, \quad (1)$$
$$Rs_{t-1}, HRab_{t-1}, HRbc_{t-1}, Hz_{t-1})$$

$$\theta_t = \theta_{t-1} + \Delta\theta_t$$
$$\text{where } \Delta\theta_t = f(Ra_{t-1}, Rb_{t-1}, Rc_{t-1}, Rp_{t-1}, \quad (2)$$
$$Rs_{t-1}, HRab_{t-1}, HRbc_{t-1})$$

where

$$Ra_t = S_t / (Da_t + M) \quad (3)$$
$$Rb_t = S_t / (Db_t + M) \quad (4)$$
$$Rc_t = S_t / (Dc_t + M) \quad (5)$$
$$Rp_t = S_t P_t / M \quad (6)$$
$$Rs_t = S_t / M \quad (7)$$

$$HRab_t = Hab_r \times Hxy_t \qquad (8)$$

$$HRbc_t = Hbc_r \times Hxy_t \qquad (9)$$

$$S_t = entity\ speed\ at\ t \qquad (10)$$

$$Da_t = distance\ to\ previous\ waypoint \qquad (11)$$

$$Db_t = distance\ to\ current\ waypoint \qquad (12)$$

$$Dc_t = distance\ to\ next\ waypoint \qquad (13)$$

$$M = march\ order\ speed \qquad (14)$$

$$P_t = perpindicular\ distance\ to\ road \qquad (15)$$

$$Hab_t = direction\ of\ road\ segment\ ab \qquad (16)$$

$$Hbc_t = direction\ of\ road\ segment\ bc \qquad (17)$$

$$Hxy_t = entity\ orientation \qquad (18)$$

As a point of comparison, this scheme of models (i.e., 2 models for each of three categories) was compared with a non-categorized set of the same training data. That is, the experimental baseline model used all of the same model parameters but did not apply the classification rule to partition the training data or control the model execution. As such, the experimental baseline model was trained with roughly 3 times more data than were any of the models in the categorized approach. Thus, by comparing the two methods (i.e., context approach according to rules and mono-lithic approach), the utility of the context approach can be evaluated for this application.

4 Experimental Results

Essential to the task of determining whether one model out-performed another is a metric to make such a comparison. Validating SAF models has typically been performed subjectively by SMEs and the DIS community has no known quantitative performance measure to evaluate the performance of a SAF near-term movement model. Given the level of resolution of SAF maps, it is impractical to assume that a SME could detect a noticeable difference in models due to the addition of a context shift. In other words, even if a human observer could visibly discriminate between two different types of movement models, it is unlikely that he could visibly detect the difference in the same movement model represented by a monolithic neural network versus represented by a module of networks. Because using SME validation to compare the models in this research was susceptible to error, the investigators made use of the DIS entity state synchronization concept to evaluate model performance. This was accomplished by implementing each of the models as DIS dead-reckoning models [16] and then comparing the numbers of ESPDUs generated by each of models 1 and 2. DIS dead-reckoning is a predictive contract of vehicle movement that can be used to reduce network traffic in a distributed simulation. An ESPDU is the protocol data unit used to communicate that an error between the entity's synchronization model and the entity's true position exceeds

205

some threshold value. By communicating the vehicle's location, velocity and acceleration to other DIS simulators, the dead-reckoning models residing on these simulators can predict the physical location of the vehicle. Implicit in this measure of performance is the assumption that the model with the lower PDU count is the model that best fits the source data used to develop the model and from which the PDU count is derived.

As shown in Figure 4, the comparison of the entity's true position and the position according to the dead-reckoning model occurs in the ModSAF *libentity* library. As such, the neural network models used in this investigation replaced the dead-reckoning code in the *libentity* library

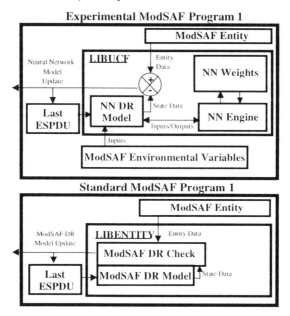

Fig. 4. Functional Relationship of Neural Networks to ModSAF Dead-Reckoning Code

Evaluating the context-based neural network scheme over segment 1 results in the PDU counts indicated in Table 2.

Table 2. Combined Segment 1 Results of Networks Trained According to Approach Type Classification Scheme

	Scenario by Classification of Segment 1 Approach									
Training on	**D**	**1**	**2**	**3**	**4**	**5**	**6**	**7**	**8**	**9**	**10**
Segment1	**N**	**N**	**E**	**L**	**E**	**L**	**N**	**E**	**D**	**N**	**L**
DEMO&1(N)	24	24	45	47	38	41	33	42	56	41	42
2 & 4 (E)	44	42	23	39	19	39	38	27	54	58	40
3 & 5 (L)	52	45	49	18	36	16	46	42	44	68	17
DIS	40	42	41	31	33	35	42	38	41	45	34
% Reduction	40	43	44	42	43	55	22	29	X	9	50

where N – nominal, E – early, L – late, D - double

206

From these results, it is apparent that the same category of networks consistently performs better on like categories of testing. Thus, it appears that the use of a hybrid approach is of some benefit to this problem. Using this approach would yield an average ESPDU reduction of 45% over Scenarios involved in training (D-5) and 28% over the same category scenarios not used in training (6-10).

Evaluating this same combination of networks over segment 2 results in the PDU counts communicated in Table 3.

Table 3. Combined Segment 2 Results of Networks Trained According to Approach Type Classification Scheme

| | Scenario by Classification of Segment 2 Approach | | | | | | | | | |
Training on Segment1	D N	1 N	2 E	3 L	4 E	5 L	6 N	7 E	8 D	9 N	10 L
DEMO&1(N)	91	95	66	101	110	102	105	121	105	108	101
2 & 4 (E)	53	53	47	50	70	50	46	56	45	46	49
3 & 5 (L)	42	43	36	43	72	44	45	51	48	42	44
DIS	42	43	47	32	58	30	43	43	40	38	39

While these models do not consistently reduce PDU counts across all of the Scenarios over Segment 2, a pattern of lower PDU counts in Scenarios whose approach classification correlates with the network classification is apparent. For example, the Scenarios in Segment 2 classified as "L" yield consistently lower PDU counts with the network trained by Segment 1 Scenarios 3 and 5 (also both classified as late). Also, the Scenario in Segment 2 classified as "E" yields a lower PDU count when tested with the network trained by Segment 1 Scenarios 2 and 4 (also both classified as early). So, while the total PDU count for Segment 2 is not reduced through this modeling scheme, there does appear to be a correlation between the type of approach represented by the trained model and the approach classification of the tested segment.

As a means of comparison, the data from the scenarios used to generate the networks for the previously presented modular configuration were used to develop a single, monolithic neural network with the same parameters. That is, the entire, aggregated data set in a single network category (as opposed to three, individual data sets partitioned by Approach Type) was considered. Thus, the results of this network can be compared with the results of previously defined to determine the effects of modularizing the data on the system's performance. The results of this experiment may be seen in Tables 4 and 5, representing the evaluation of the model over Segment 1 and Segment 2, respectively.

The results of this experiment indicate a reduction in ESPDUs on Segment 1 (see Table 4) and seem to suggest an ability to generalize to scenarios not used in training. However, by comparing results in Tables 2 and 4, it is apparent that neither the scenarios used in training nor the scenarios held out from the context-based network scheme outperform the current monolithic network scheme. Correspondingly, as evidenced in a comparison of Tables 3 and 5, when evaluated on Segment 2, the monolithic network scheme did not perform as well as the modularized scheme.

Table 4. Combined Segment 1 Results of Monolithic Networks Trained with Data from all Scenarios DEMO,1,2,3,4,&5

	Scenario by Classification of Segment 1 Approach									
Training on	**D**	**1**	**2**	**3**	**4**	**5**	**6**	**7**	**8**	**9**	**10**
Segment1	**N**	**N**	**E**	**L**	**E**	**L**	**N**	**E**	**D**	**N**	**L**
All (D-5)	32	34	34	32	25	29	36	29	48	55	31
DIS	40	42	41	31	33	35	42	38	41	45	34

Table 5. Combined Segment 2 Results of Monolithic Networks Trained with Data from all Scenarios DEMO,1,2,3,4,&5

	Scenario by Classification of Segment 2 Approach									
Training on	**D**	**1**	**2**	**3**	**4**	**5**	**6**	**7**	**8**	**9**	**10**
Segment1	**N**	**N**	**E**	**L**	**E**	**L**	**N**	**E**	**D**	**N**	**L**
All (D-5)	48	47	41	52	71	52	48	55	48	48	52
DIS	42	43	47	32	58	30	43	43	40	38	30

5 Summary

In summary, a context-based neural-network modeling scheme was empirically developed and then tested in a simulated environment. As part of this effort, the use of explicit model decomposition schemes was considered as a mechanism for improved model performance. The performance of the best modeling combination was evaluated in three ways. First, the models were tested on movement methods that were used in training. Second, the models were tested on movement methods that were not used in training, but similar to those used in training. Third, the models were tested on movement methods on an entirely new part of the route other than that used in training. The modeling scheme in the first case gave an average ESPDU reduction of approximately 45% over current DIS dead-reckoning methods. The same modeling scheme in the second case resulted in an average ESPDU reduction of approximately 28% over current DIS dead-reckoning methods. Lastly, the modeling scheme in the third cases did not result in ESPDU reduction over DIS dead-reckoning methods, but did yield results consistent with the expectations of the classification scheme. These results suggests that the performance of neural networks applied to a low-level SAF reactive-task is improved by the use of the context-based task decomposition scheme. Future work in this aspect of the study includes investigating methods of automating the learning of the task decomposition and hence, the context-shifting rules. Also, the improvement of the neural networks' performance continues to be explored. This includes considering alternative types of architectures, inputs, normalization schemes, and sampling strategies. Since the ModSAF infrastructure to collect data and evaluate models is now in place, more work can be done to improve these preliminary results.

References

1. Smith, S., and Petty, M. (1992). Controlling Autonomous Behavior in Real-Time Simulation. In Proceedings of the Second Conference in Computer Generated Forces and Behavior Representation. Orlando, FL., May, 1992.

2. Crowe, M. (1990). The Application of Artificial Neural Systems to the Training of Air Combat Decision-Making Skills. Proceedings of the 12th Interservice/Industry Training Systems Conference, Orlando, FL. Nov., 1990.

3. Jaszlics, S.L. (1993). Artificial Intelligence in Tactical Command and Control Applications: Architecture and Tools. In Proceedings of the Third Conference on Computer Generated Forces and Behavior Representation. Orlando, FL., March, 1993.

4. Morrison, J.D. (1996). Real-time Learning of Doctrine and Tactics Using Neural Networks and Combat Simulations. Military Operations Research, vol. 2, no. 3, pages 45-60.

5. Pew, R.W., and Mavor, A.S., eds. (1998). Modeling Human and Organizational Behavior: Application to Military Simulations. Washington, DC: National Academy Press.

6. Murray-Smith, R., and Johansen, T.A. (1997). Multiple Model Approaches to Modelling and Control. Taylor and Francis, UK.

7. Narendra, K. S., Balakrishnan, J., and Ciliz, K. (1995). Adaptation and Learning Using Multiple Models, Switching and Tuning. IEEE Control Systems Magazine, June, 1995, pp. 37-51.

8. Brooks, R.A. (1986). A Robust Layered Control System for a Mobile Robot. IEEE Journal of Robotics and Automation, RA-2:14-23.

9. Gallinari, P. (1995). Modular Neural Net Systems: Training Of. In M.A., Arbib, editor, The Handbook of Brain Theory and Neural Networks, pp. 582-585. Bradford Books: MIT Press.

10. Hrycej, T. (1992). Modular Learning in Neural Networks. John Wiley, Chichester.

11. Pratt, L.Y., Mostow, J., and Kamm, C.A. (1991). Direct Transfer of Learned Information Among Neural Networks. In Proceedings of the Ninth National Conference on Artificial Intelligence (AAI-91), pp. 584-589. Anaheim, CA, 1991.

12. Ourston, D., Blanchard, D., Chandler, E., and Loh, E., (1995). From CIS to Software. In Proceedings of the Fifth Conference on Computer Generated Forces and Behavior Representation. Orlando, FL., May, 1995, pp. 275-285.

13. Henninger, A., and Gonzalez, A. (1997). Automated Acquisition Tool for Tactical Knowledge, In Proceedings of the 10th Annual International Florida Artificial Intelligence Research Symposium, Melbourne FL., May, 1997, pp. 307-311.

14. Hampshire, J.B., and Waibel, A.H. (1992). The Meta-P,I Network: Building Distributed Representations for Robust Multiource Pattern Recognition. IEEE Transactions on Pattern Analysis and Machine Intelligence, 14(7): 751-769, 1992.

15. Gonzalez, A., and Ahlers, R. (1995). Context-based Representation of Intelligent Behavior in Simulated Opponents. In Proceedings of the Fifth Conference on Computer Generated Forces and Behavior Representation, Orlando, FL., May, 1995.

16. Lin, K., and Ng, H. (1993). "Coordinate Transformations in Distributed Interactive Simulation (DIS)". Simulation, vol. 61, No. 5, Nov, 1993, pp. 326-331.

Context Dependency of Pattern-Category Learning

Martin Jüttner[1] and Ingo Rentschler[2]

[1] Neuroscience Research Institute, School of Life & Health Sciences – Psychology, Aston University, Aston Triangle, Birmingham B4 7ET, UK
m.juttner@aston.ac.uk
[2] Institut für Medizinische Psychologie, Universität München, Goethestr. 31, 80336 München, Germany
ingo@imp.med.uni-muenchen.de

Abstract. Despite its widely acknowledged importance context has remained a relatively vague concept in vision research. Previous approaches regard context primarily as a determinant for the interpretation of sensory information on the basis of previously acquired knowledge. In this paper we propose a complementary perspective, by showing that context also specifically affects *learning*, that is the acquisition of knowledge and the way in which such knowledge is mentally represented. In two pattern-category learning experiments we explored how complementary manipulations of context affect learning performance and generalization. In both experiments, generalization performance was measured as the ability to transfer acquired class knowledge to the contrast-inverted versions of the learning patterns. We then modelled the behavioural data in terms of evidence-based classification. Such an analysis allows to reconstruct combinations of non-relational and relational pattern attributes that provide potential solutions of a given classification problem. We show that 'context' in category learning affects the search within the search space of attribute combinations which underlie the production rules for the categories. Our results suggest a novel, context-based explanation for well-known phenomena of contrast-invariance in visual perception.

1 Introduction

Our visual perception of the world is highly adaptive to contextual information. Yet despite its widely acknowledged importance context has remained a relatively vague concept in vision research. Previous attempts have regarded context as part of a process of „unconscious inference" in vision - an idea that was first proposed by von Helmholtz and later rehabilitated by Bruner. Bruner's [1] notion of context as „readiness" of perception includes expectations and subject's knowledge. Such context effects have been shown to influence tasks as diverse as the recognition threshold of words as a function of familiarity [2] and predictability [3], or the critical exposure duration for the detection of anomalous versus regular playing cards [4]. The idea of a perceptual-cognitive continuum has not remained unquestioned. Pylyshyn [5] distinguishes between contextual effects as purely 'within-vision' or top-down effects (i.e., visual interpretations computed by early vision that affect visual interpretation) and effects of cognitive penetration, where the latter include influences from outside the visual system that affect the content of visual perception. A more pragmatic view prevails in artificial intelligence, where contextual information has been used to develop robust edge-finding schemes for extracting reliable features that could serve as a starting point for object recognition and scene analysis [6][7][8]. Such context-dependent influences eventually became subsumed under the more general label 'knowledge-based' and are considered to be essential both in human vision [9] and in computer vision [10].

The aforementioned approaches have in common that they regard context as important determinant of how previously acquired knowledge guides the interpretation of sensory experience. In this paper we pursue a complementary perspective, by showing that context also specifically affects *learning*, that is the acquisition of knowledge and the way in which such knowledge is mentally represented. For visual perception, such learning involves in particular the acquisition of object categories. Category learning has often been proposed, in cognitive science, as a basic mechanism of concept formation underlying object recognition [1][11]. Furthermore, readdressing the context problem within the paradigm of category learning has the advantage that context becomes a well-defined variable since it is given by the set of stimuli to be learnt.

In two classification-learning experiments we explored how complementary manipulations of context affect learning performance and the ability to generalize acquired class knowledge. In Experiment I, we changed the (local) context of the individual signals by changing the configuration of the learning set. In Experiment II, we varied the (global) context of a fixed signal configuration by changing the degree of signal accentuation. In both experiments, generalization performance was measured as the ability to transfer acquired class knowledge to contrast-inverted versions of the learning patterns. We then modelled the behavioural data in terms of evidence-based classification. In general, evidence-based systems (EBS) approach to pattern classification allows to reconstruct combinations of non-relational and relational attributes that provide potential solutions of a given classification problem [12]. In the present study, we use EBS computer simulations to show that 'context' in category learning affects the search within the search space of attribute combinations which underlie the production rules for the categories.

2 Behavioural experiments

In two category-learning experiments we explored how context influences learning speed and the ability for generalization to inversion of contrast. Our paradigm involves the classification of Compound Gabor patterns (cf. Fig.1). Such greylevel patterns result from the superposition of two sinewave gratings, a fundamental plus its third harmonic, within a Gaussian aperture. Only amplitude and phase of the third harmonic are parameters of variation (for details see ref. [13] [17]). Thus the signals may be represented within a two-dimensional Fourier feature space. Within this coordinate system each point uniquely specifies the appearance of a signal, and clusters of points are used to define the signal classes to be learned by the subject.

Gabor signals have the advantage that they may be regarded, on the one hand, as an elementary stimulus in early visual processing [14] [15] [16]. One the other hand, these patterns have been shown to be perceptually complex enough to stimulate category learning [13] [17] [18]. Furthermore. Gabor signals are completely unfamiliar for naive subjects. Hence there is no problem with prior knowledge and the learning process is entirely under experimental control.

In Experiment I we compared category learning and generalization with respect to two different class configurations (Fig. 1 top): A 3-class configuration defined by three clusters of five signals each (set 1). and a 4-class configuration composed of four clusters of three signals (set 2). In the first part of the experiment subjects were trained in a supervised-learning schedule to correctly classify all signals of one of the two learning sets. Learning was partitioned into learning units and each learning unit consisted of two phases, a training phase and a test phase. During training. each pattern was presented three times in random order for 200 ms, followed by the corresponding class number displayed for 1 sec. During testing, each pattern was presented once in random order and was classified by the observer. The learning criterion was reached when all signals had been correctly assigned in such a test. Otherwise the training continued with a further learning unit.

Once the subjects had reached the learning criterion they entered the second part of the experiment. It consisted of a generalization test where the observers ability was assessed to recognize contrast-inverted versions of the previously learned patterns. Each test pattern was presented and classified 30 times in random order. The timing parameters were the same as in the learning part of the experiment.

Two groups of five subjects with normal or corrected-to-normal vision participated. Fig. 2A shows for the two sets of learning patterns learning duration and generalization performance. The data reveals that the different learning context. as expressed by the two signal configurations, has distinct effects on both performance indices distinctly. The 3-class configuration is learned on average within 12 learning units, whereas the subjects need about 28 learning units to learn the 4-class configuration. For generalization, the response rate for correctly classifying the contrast-inverted images is about 0.8 for the 3-class configuration, and drops to 0.45 for the 4-class configuration.

In Experiment I we had changed the context *locally*, i.e. for the individual signal, by changing the configuration of the learning set. In contrast, Experiment II involved a *global* change of context, i.e. a manipulation of context for a complete signal configuration. This was achieved by modifying the degree of signal accentuation for a fixed configuration. Based on the 4-class configuration (set 2) of Experiment I. three further sets of learning patterns were generated by removing image parts via a non-linear threshold operation (Fig. 1 bottom). The samples of set 3 were obtained by removing all bright parts of the images. those of set 4 by removing all dark parts. and those of set 5 by removing parts with intermediate greylevel values. The thresholding led to a degraded, though more accentuated, physical stimulus representation than that of the original samples. With these new sets of stimuli we trained three groups of subjects to criterion and tested them for their ability to generalize to contrast inversion.

Experiment I

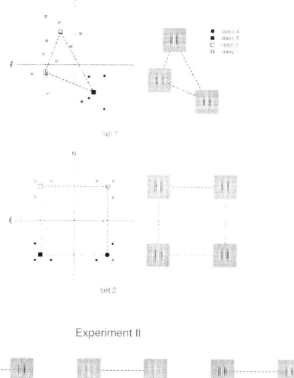

set 1

set 2

Experiment II

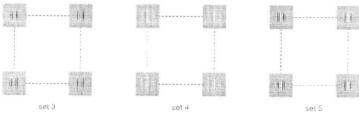

set 3   set 4   set 5

Fig. 1. Learning signals for Experiment I *(top)* and Experiment II *(bottom)*. For Experiment I two sets of signals were generated in an two-dimensional Fourier space (for details see ref. [13, 17]). Scale: 1 unit = 20 cd/m². Set 1 contained three clusters of five samples, set 2 four clusters of three samples. Each signal cluster defined one class to be learned by the subject. The large symbols connected by dashed lines denote the class means or prototypes. For illustration these class prototypes are depicted in their greylevel representation. For Experiment II, the 12 signals of set 2 were degraded by replacing parts of the grey levels by mean luminance (index value 127). Thus, in set 3 all bright parts of the image were removed (index value > 127), in set 3 all dark parts of the image (index values < 127), and in set 5 all intermediate values, defined by the interval [67,187] of grey level indices.

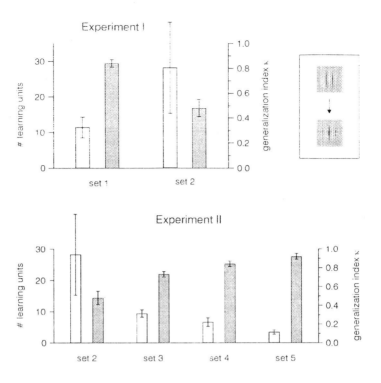

Fig. 2. Mean learning duration (bright bars) and generalization performance (dark bars) in Experiment I *(top)* and Experiment II *(bottom)*. Generalization was measured as the ability to classify the contrast-inverted versions of the learning patterns (see inset for an example).

As shown in Fig. 2B the accentuation brought about by the thresholding yields a drastic reduction of learning duration, from about 28 learning units for the original signals in set 2 to about 4 learning units for those of set 5. At the same time, generalization to contrast inversion improves, from about 0.45 in set 2 to about 0.95. Thus, the accentuated versions of the learning stimuli are much easier to learn and better to generalize than the original images.

3 Computer simulations

The variations of learning context introduced in Experiment I and Experiment II yielded distinct effects on both learning and generalization performance. To gain further insight into the nature of the underlying mental representations we modelled human performance in terms of evidence-based pattern classification. According to the evidence-based systems (EBS) approach to pattern recognition complex objects are best encoded in terms of parts and their relations. Originally developed in the area of machine learning and computer vision [19,20] we have shown that EBS also provides a framework for cognitive modelling of human perceptual classification and generalization [12].

In an evidence-based classification system a given pattern is first segmented into its component parts (Fig. 3). Each part is characterized by a set of part-specific, or unary, attributes (e.g. size, luminance, area), and each pair of parts is described by a set of relational, or binary, attributes (e.g., distance, angles, contrast). Thus, each part may be formally represented as a vector in a feature space spanned by the various unary attributes, and each pair of parts by a vector in a binary feature space. Within each feature space regions are defined that act as activation regions for rules. The rule regions are derived by clustering the feature spaces during the training phase of the system. During runtime, an attribute vector falling inside such a region will activate the corresponding rule (state 1), otherwise the rule remains inactive (state 0). A given object, then, is represented by a rule activation vector. Its components are assigned to the activation states of the individual rules. The activation of a given rule provides a certain amount of evidence for the class membership of the input object. The assignment of the evidence weights to the rules and their combinations is achieved within a neural network. Here each input node corresponds to a rule, each output node to a class, and there is one hidden layer. The relative activity of an output node provides a measure of the accumulated class-specific evidence. This activity may be probabilistically interpreted and related to a classification frequency.

An evidence-based classifier first has to be trained with patterns with known class membership are used. Given a reservoir of unary and binary attributes an attempt is made, for each attribute combination, to train the neural network via the backpropagation algorithm, in order to identify those attribute combinations that successfully allow to separate the classes. For the simulations of the present experiments, we taught the system similar to the human subjects to classify the patterns of the various learning sets. We supplied the classifier with a reservoir of four unary attributes (position, luminance, aspect ration and size) and three binary attributes (distance, relative size, contrast). We then tested, for which attribute combinations the training of the system converged, i.e. the system successfully learned to distinguish between the classes.

When used as a framework for cognitive modelling, EBS describes category learning as a successive testing of working hypothesis. Each working hypothesis corresponds to the selection of a subset of attributes which define a reference system for describing parts and their relations. Once chosen, the elaboration of such a working hypothesis will include the formation of rules and the tuning of evidence weights. Eventually, the elaboration process either results in a successful categorization, or the current working hypothesis is rejected and replaced by another one.

Each subset of attended attributes may be regarded as a state within a search space of possible working hypotheses defined by the set of all possible combinations of unary and binary attributes. Learning speed is determined by the time required to find a solution within that search space, i.e., a set of attributes, which allows to successfully distinguish between classes. If N_{FS} denotes the number of EBS solutions

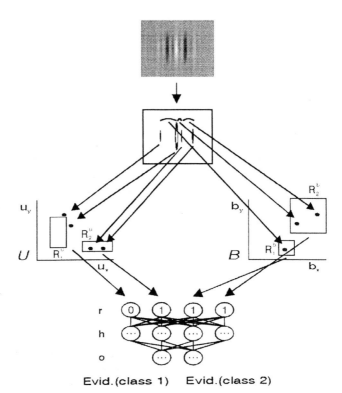

Fig. 3. Sample illustration of the various forms of representation involved in evidence-based pattern classification. For convenience, only two unary/binary attributes, four rules and two classes are considered. The input image is first decomposed into its components. Each part and each pair of adjacent parts then is described by a vector of unary (part-specific) and binary (relational) attributes, respectively. Within the corresponding feature spaces the attribute vectors trigger rules providing class-specific evidences. The evidence values are implicitly represented by the synaptic weights of a three-layer neural net which is trained during the learning stage of the system. The activity of the output nodes provides a measure of the total evidence concerning the class alternatives. See main text for further details.

then the higher the density $1/N_{FS}$ of solutions in search space the shorter the search time and, as a consequence, learning duration. If such a model accounts for human learning then any variation of context that affects learning difficulty (i.e., the density of EBS solutions), should be reflected in behaviour (i.e. the observed learning duration).

The model-predicted learning durations for the five sets of patterns are summarized in the dark bars of Fig. 4A. A comparison with the behavioural data shows that not only the ranking order of the empirical learning durations is preserved in the simulated values, but that also the ratios of learning durations are well approximated the latter. For instance, the estimate of the learning duration for signal set 2 is a factor

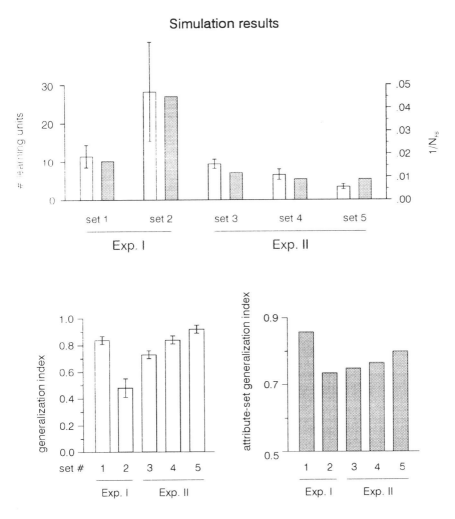

Fig. 4. *(top)* EBS-simulated learning durations (dark bars) and observed group means (bright bars, cf. Fig. 2) for learning set 1-5 in Experiments I and II. According to the proposed learning model the density $1/N_{\text{FS}}$ of solutions within the search space of possible working hypotheses provides a measure for the complexity of the learning task that should be linearly related to expected learning duration. *(bottom)* Empirical generalization performance (bright bars, cf. Fig. 2) and EBS attribute-generalization indices (dark bars) for set 1-5 in Experiments I and II.

of 2.6 longer than that for set 1, and a factor of 3.7 longer with respect to set 3. The ratios of the empirical values yield 2.6 and 3.0, respectively. Thus, the model provides a unified account for context effects induced by very different experimental manipulations - the alteration of class configuration (Experiment I) and variations of stimulus degradation (Experiment II).

The analysis in terms of EBS also allows predictions concerning the difficulty with which acquired class knowledge may be generalized to contrast inversion. For this purpose we computed an attribute-generalization index. It was defined as the ratio of the sum of contrast-independent attributes and the overall sum of all attributes appearing in the EBS solutions. As illustrated in Fig. 4B the ranking of this EBS generalization index mirrors the ranking in the observed generalization performance. Such a result suggests that the relative proportion of contrast-invariant attributes determines how well class concepts relying on these attributes may be generalized to contrast inversion.

4 Discussion

The learning of image categories implies a process of abstraction leading from the representation of sample patterns to the representation of an underlying class concept of these samples. In this paper we have shown that the kind of mental representation an image category can take is determined not only by the physical properties of the individual stimulus, but also by the learning context, i.e. the set of stimuli to be learnt. We demonstrated the effect of context on pattern-category learning in two behavioural experiments involving complementary manipulations of contextual information. The data of both experiments could be explained by an evidence-based classification model according to which pattern categories are learned by repeatedly generating and testing working hypothesis concerning the relevant part-specific and relational attributes of the learning patterns. Variations of context lead to variations in the density of solutions within the search space of feature combinations and thus to variations in learning speed.

In the present study we used the generalization to contrast inversion as an indicator for the context dependency of pattern category learning. This specific choice allows us to relate our findings to well-known phenomena of contrast-invariance in visual perception: Characters and simple geometric patterns are readily recognized even when seen as negative (i.e., contrast inverted) images, whereas it is much more difficult to recognize a contrast-inverted face (Fig. 5). The latter difficulty is not related to the presence of a grey-level spectrum *per se* as it persists in lithographic, binary-valued face representations [21]. Previous explanations of this phenomenon have regarded the spectral composition of images as critical [22]. According to this explanation low spatial frequencies are important for the identification of faces, whereas high spatial frequencies are critical for the recognition of characters and geometric patterns; but only contrast inversion for high spatial frequencies is easily achieved by the visual system.

In the light of the present experiments this explanation appears less convincing. First, the results of Experiment I clearly show that pattern sets with identical power spectrum may yield very different degrees in contrast-invariance (cf. Fig. 2A). Second, the results of the EBS computer simulations suggest that it is the relative proportion of contrast-invariant attributes that determines how well class concepts relying on these attributes may be generalized to contrast inversion. As a direct consequence, invariance to contrast is not a dichotomous property linked to certain

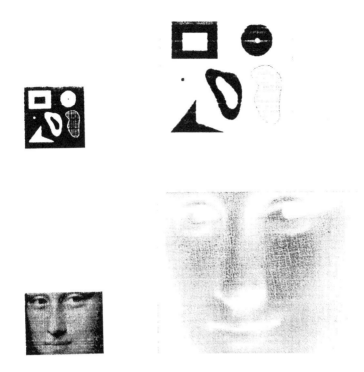

Fig. 5. Examples for contrast (in)variance in visual perception. Characters and simple geometric forms are readily recognized when seen as contrast inverted images, whereas the recognition of contrast-inverted portraits is exceedingly difficult.

physical features of certain stimuli. Rather it becomes manifest in a gradual, context-dependent way during the ontogenesis of internal representations for object categories. According to this view contrast information will only be evaluated if necessary for a certain (categorization) task, as specified by the context of the set of learning stimuli.

References

1. Bruner, J.: On perceptual readiness. Psychological Review 64 (1957) 123-152
2. Soloman, R.L., Postman, L.: Frequency of usage as a determinant of recognition thresholds for words. Journal of Experimental Psychology 43 (1951) 195-201
3. Miller, G.A., Bruner, J.S., Postman, L.: Familiarity of letter sequences and tachistoscopic identification. Journal of General Psychology 50 (1954) 129-139
4. Bruner, J., Postman, L.: On the perception of incongruity: a paradigm. Journal of Personality 18 (1949) 206-223

5. Pylyshyn, Z. : Is vision continuous with cognition? The case for cognitive impenetrability of visual perception. Behavioral and Brain Sciences 22 (1999) 341-423
6. Clowes, M.B. : On Seeing Things. Artificial Intelligence 2 (1971) 79-116
7. Shirai, Y.: Analyzing intensity arrays using knowledge about scenes. In: Winston, P.H. (ed.): Psychology of Computer Vision. MIT Press, Cambridge, MA (1975).
8. Freuder, E.C.: Knowledge-Mediated Perception. In: Nusbaum, H. C., Schwab, E. C. (eds.): Pattern Recognition by Humans and Machines: Visual Perception. Academic Press, Orlando (1986)
9. Riseman, E.M., Hanson, A.R.: A methodology for the development of general knowledge-based vision systems. In: Arbib, M.A., Hanson, A.R. (eds.): Vision, Brain, and Cooperative Computation. MIT Press, Cambridge, MA (1987)
10. Grimson, W.: The combinatorics of object recognition in cluttered environments using constrained search. Aritifical Intelligence 44 (1990) 121-165
11. Rosch, E.: Principles of categorization. In: Rosch, E., Lloyd, B. (eds.): Cognition and Categorization. Erlbaum, Hillsdale, NJ (1978) 27-48
12. Jüttner, M., Caelli, T., Rentschler, I.: Evidence-based pattern classification: a structural approach to human perceptual learning and generalization. Journal of Mathematical Psychology 41 (1997) 244-259
13. Rentschler, I., Jüttner, M., Caelli, T.: Probabilistic analysis of human supervised learning and classification. Vision Research 34 (1994) 669-687
14. Watson, A.B., Barlow, H.B., Robson, J. G.: What does the eye see best? Nature 302 (1983) 419-422
15. Rentschler, I., Caelli, T.: Visual representations in the brain: inferences from psychophysical research. In: Haken, H. (ed.): Synergetics of Cognition. Springer, Berlin (1990) 233-248
16. Westheimer, G.: Lines and Gabor functions compared as spatial visual stimuli. Vision Research 38 (1998) 487-491
17. Jüttner, M. , Rentschler, I.: Reduced perceptual dimensionality in extrafoveal vision. Vision Research 36 (1996) 1007-1021
18. Jüttner, M., Rentschler, I.: Scale invariant superiority of foveal vision in perceptual categorization. European Journal of Neuroscience 12 (2000) 353-359
19. Jain, A.K., Hoffman, D.: Evidence-based recognition of objects. IEEE Transactions on Pattern Analysis and Machine Intelligence 10 (1988) 783-802
20. Caelli, T. , Dreier, A.: Variations on the evidence-based object recognition theme. Pattern Recognition 27 (1994) 185-204
21. Phillips, R. J.: Why are faces hard to recognize in photographic negative? Perception & Psychophysics 12 (1972) 425-426
22. Hayes, A., Morrone, M.C., Burr, D.C.: Recognition of positive and negative bandpass-filtered images. Perception 15 (1986) 595-602

Simulating Context Effects in Problem Solving with AMBR

Boicho Kokinov[1,2]   Maurice Grinberg[2]

[1]Institute of Mathematics and Informatics, Bulgarian Academy of Sciences
Bl.8, Acad. G. Bonchev Str., Sofia 1113, BULGARIA
[2]Central and East European Center for Cognitive Science, New Bulgarian University
21 Montevideo Str., Sofia 1635, BULGARIA
e-mail: {bkokinov, mgrinberg}@nbu.bg

Abstract. This paper presents a computer simulation of context effects on problem solving with AMBR — a model of human analogy-making. It demonstrates how perceiving some incidental objects from the environment may change the way the problem is being solved. It also shows that the timing of this perception is important: while the context element may have crucial influence during the initial stages of problem solving it has virtually no effect during the later stages. The simulation also explores the difference between an explicit hint condition where the focus of attention is drawn towards a context situation which is analogous to the target problem and an implicit context condition where an arbitrary object from the environment makes us remind an old episode.

1. Context Effects: Psychological Data and Cognitive Models

Imagine you are sitting at your desk struggling with a difficult problem with a roving look. At some point your eyes incidentally fall on a steaming cup of tea or on a drawing in an open book and you are suddenly reminded of an old analogous problem and its solution that might be adopted to the current case as well. You may not realize that there was a relationship between the cup of tea and the old episode, you may even not notice that you have perceived the steaming liquid, finally, it is possible that you even do not remember that there was a cup of tea on the desk, but still the very fact of perceiving it may have had an influence on your problem solving process. We call this "context effect" on problem solving and we are interested whether such effects really exist and if yes, what might be the mechanisms responsible for that.

Context effects on language understanding [39], perception [36], decision-making [38], memory [9, 10, 27], concepts and categorization [4], affect and social cognition [3, 16, 33] have been extensively studied in psychology. Context effects on problem solving and reasoning are still not well explored. Gestalt psychologies have first demonstrated such effects [11, 29, 30]. Gick and Holyoak [12] have demonstrated how an explicit hint may influence the problem solving process. Lockhart [28] and Schunn and Dunbar [37] discuss the influence context may have on accessibility of concepts and therefore on thinking. Recently, Kokinov and his collaborators have studied in a systematic way the influence one incidental element from the environment may have on the problem solving process [25, 26].

In their first experiment Kokinov and Yoveva [26] have demonstrated that when solving a problem about boiling water in the forest in a wooden bowl, subjects, who have seen an illustration of a river by a forest with many rocks and stones around, tend to produce significantly more solutions using stones than control subjects, who have not seen the illustration. In a second experiment subjects received sheets of paper with two problems on each sheet, but they had to solve only the first one. The illustration accompanying the second problem and thus seeming to be irrelevant to the first problem played the role of an incidental environmental element. The results have clearly shown that this seemingly irrelevant picture may be crucial in the problem solving process and subjects may produce completely different solutions being exposed to different pictures, even though they claim they have not seen and used them. Being suspicious about participants' unawareness of the second picture on the page another experiment was carried out by Kokinov, Hadjiilieva, and Yoveva [25]. In this experiment the context condition described above was compared to an explicit hint condition in which the same picture was put on the sheet of paper, but an explicit instruction was given to subjects to try to use it when solving the target problem. The results were significantly different from the context condition which suggests that in the context condition subject have perceived and used the picture unconsciously. Moreover, in some cases, the same picture had opposite effect when used explicitly as a hint. This supports the hypothesis that different mechanisms are responsible for the picture influence and use in the context and in the hint condition.

Computational models of problem solving suggested by AI researchers tend to focus on the later case: when the external stimulus is intentionally and consciously perceived and used in the problem solving process [1, 5, 7, 8, 13, 14, 31, 32, 40]. Thus context is typically explicitly represented, moreover a complex structure is used for its representation (e.g. a schema or a frame [40], a feature vector [1], a logical constant [31, 32] or even a whole logical theory [5, 13, 14]) and a complex organization of contexts is introduced (hierarchy of contexts, network of bridges between different possible contexts, etc.). This was described as the "box metaphor": context is considered as a set of propositions grouped together and embedded in a box [14, 24]. This approach was criticized for not taking into account the possibility for automatic unconscious context influence and for the continuous dynamic changes in the context as reviewed in [24].

In an attempt to build a cognitive model of human problem solving and how it is influenced by the dynamically evolving context Kokinov [21, 24] has put forward a dynamic theory of context. According to it context is considered as the dynamic state of mind of the cognitive system and thus is not necessarily explicitly represented. This state may be reflected by the system itself and thus partially represented, but as seen above, other parts of the context may still have an influence on our behavior without our awareness of that fact. The theory was implemented in a general cognitive architecture, DUAL, and a model of problem solving, AMBR, has been built on it. The current paper describes some simulation experiments with AMBR demonstrating context effects.

2. A Context-Sensitive Model of Problem Solving

2.1. Dynamic Theory of Context

The essence of the dynamic theory [21, 24] is that context is considered as the dynamic state of human mind which state is crucial for all cognitive processes. If we paraphrase this in computational terms, the algorithms that compute a particular cognitive process and the data they are using are changing dynamically with the changes in the state of mind. Since the state evolves continuously the algorithms and data are never the same. That is why we can never replicate a given act of human thinking, perception, or learning fully — since the context will have been changed and the processes will change as well. Of course, in many cases the changes might be small and even unnoticeable, but it can also happen that even small changes turn out to be crucial for the computation and the generated behavior becomes radically different. This is analogous to the theory of catastrophes developed in mathematics.

According to the dynamic theory the state of mind is determined by the content of human working memory (WM) and the relative weight each memory element has in it. The WM elements are both operations and structures — thus changing the content of WM may result in changing the operations available for application or in changing the data we are currently using in the computation.

The dynamic theory of context is not bound to a symbolic computational interpretation, it can possibly be implemented in connectionist or dynamic systems terms where no differentiation between data and operations will be necessary.

2.2. DUAL: A Dynamic Context-Sensitive Cognitive Architecture

DUAL [19, 20, 22, 35] is a general cognitive architecture which has been developed with the dynamic theory of context in mind and it provides a basis for modeling context-sensitive cognitive processes. This is a massively parallel and highly decentralized system consisting of micro-agents each of whom represents a small piece of procedural and declarative knowledge. Thus all operations in DUAL are performed by some agents. The agents are connected via links (which can be dynamically changed) and exchange messages via these links. The overall behavior of the system, or what is being computed at the particular moment, is an emergent phenomenon which reflects the collective behavior of the acting micro-agents. There is no central mechanism which controls which agents to act and in what sequence. On the contrary, each agent acts independently and in parallel to the acting of other agents and it uses only local information coming from its neighboring agents.

Each agent has an activation level which is determined by the incoming activation from neighboring agents and its residual activation from earlier stages. This activation level determines the degree of availability of that agent in that particular moment. If the degree of activation of a given agent is below a certain threshold than the agent is "sleeping", i.e. it cannot take part in any computation. The higher the activation level, the more active the agent is and the faster its operations are performed. The connectionist activation is considered as a power supply for the symbolic operations performed by the agent [35].

Working memory in DUAL is considered to be the set of active agents in a particular moment of time. Thus the content of WM determines which agents will take part in the computation, how fast will each of them act, how they will compete, etc. and therefore it determines the outcome of the global emergent process that they generate. That is, in different contexts different sets of agents will act and with different levels of activation and therefore they will produce different outcomes. This is how context-sensitive behavior is implemented in DUAL.

The content of WM is determined by several factors: direct activation of agents from the environment via perception (modeled by connecting some of the agents to the INPUT node), direct activation of agents by internal motivational factors (modeled by connecting some of the agents to the GOAL node), residual activation of agents from previous memory states (modeled by a decay function of activation), and by receiving activation from neighboring agents via the links (modeled by a process of spreading activation).

Similar approaches to context modeling have been followed by John Anderson [2] where the semantic network has its internal dynamics, and by Douglas Hofstadter [15] where the Slipnet is also dynamically changing its structure as well as the codelets run with various probability depending on the context as represented in the workspace.

2.3. AMBR: A Context-Sensitive Model of Analogy-Making

AMBR [17, 18, 23, 34] is a model of human problem solving built upon the DUAL architecture. The program has semantic knowledge about various concepts and general facts as well as a number of past problem-solving episodes from everyday kitchen life. A target problem is presented to the program and it has to find its solution basically by analogy with one of the old episodes. There are many important differences between AMBR and other models of analogy-making. For example, mapping and retrieval are emergent processes based on the local computations and interactions of many micro-agents and thus they are running in parallel which makes it possible for mutual interaction between mapping and retrieval, including mapping guidance of retrieval. Since episodes are represented in a decentralized way (by a coalition of agents) they can be partially retrieved, they can be extended by intrusions from general knowledge or from other episodes, finally blending between episodes is possible. AMBR is sensitive to priming and context influences. The rest of this paper will present simulation data which demonstrate AMBR's context-sensitivity.

3. Simulation Experiments

The knowledge base (KB) of the system contains 570 agents representing about 270 concepts and 12 old episodes. Concepts include tea, milk, water, drinkable-liquid, liquid, temperature-of, high-temp, low-temp, made-of, color-of, cause, etc. The old episodes include the following ones (Table 1).

Table 1: Old episodes in the long-term memory of the system.

Short name of the episode	Short informal description of the episode
WTP	heating Water in a Teapot on a hot Plate
BF	heating water in a wooden Bowl on the Fire and burning the bowl
GP	heating water in a Glass on a hot Plate and breaking the glass
IHC	heating water by Immersion Heater in a Cup
MTF	cooling Milk in a Teapot in the Fridge
ICF	cooling Ice Cube on a glass in the Fridge
BPF	cooling Butter on a Plate in the Fridge
FDO	baking Food on a Dish in the Oven
STC	sweetening by putting sugar in the tea being in a cup
SFF	salting by putting salt into the food in the fridge
ERW	coloring an Egg put in Red Water
GWB	keeping a Glass in a Wooden Box

Here is a simple target problem HM: "How can you Heat some Milk which is put in a teapot?" This problem has to be solved by making analogy with one of the known episodes in the KB. A simplified propositional representation of this example is presented in Table 2. Each proposition is represented by a separate DUAL agent.

Table 2: Representation of the target problem HM — "heating milk". Content of input list, goal list, and primary WM are described.

Agent	External Activation	Propositional representaion
	Goal List	
T-of-HM	1.00	(temperature-of milk-HM high-T-HM)
high-T-HM	1.00	(inst-of high-T-HM high-temp)
milk-HM	1.00	(inst-of milk-HM milk)
	Input List	
in-HM	1.00	(in milk-HM tpot-HM)
tpot-HM	1.00	(inst-of tpot-HM teapot)
made-of-HM	0.50	(made-of tpot-HM mmetal-HM)
mmetal-HM	0.25	(inst-of mmetal-HM material-metal)
	Just in WM	
goalst-HM	0.0	(goal-state T-of-HM high-T-HM)
initst-HM	0.0	(init-state milk-HM tpot-HM in-HM made-of-HM)
to-reach-HM	0.0	(to-reach initst-HM goalst-HM)

In order to get statistical data 100 variations of the initial KB have been generated by randomly changing some associative links and instance links. This reflects the possibility that various people even sharing the general knowledge about this simple domain may have different associations for the same concepts, objects, or events. Someone may have richer experience with immersion heaters while someone else may have recently broken a glass on a hot plate.

3.1. AMBR's sensitivity to context

In order to test AMBR's sensitivity to context 100 simulations (with the 100 KBs) have been done within each of 6 different contexts using the same target problem HM. The context is changed by only one element: we simulate the incidental perception of one single object from the environment. We have run the simulations in the following conditions and the results are displayed in Table 3.

- control condition — without perception of any context elements
- "egg" condition — the system perceives an egg while solving the target
- "fridge" condition — the system perceives a fridge
- "immersion heater" condition — the system perceives an immersion heater
- "oven" condition — the system perceives an oven
- "sugar" condition — the system perceives sugar.

Table 3. Statistical results from 100 runs of AMBR with the target problem "Heating Milk" in 6 different conditions. Numbers in cells are the frequencies of making the analogy with the corresponding situation.

				Target: Heating Milk — Statistics of Solutions Found		
#	bases	no context	egg	fridge	immersion heater	oven	sugar
1	wtp	50	46	45	41	46	48
2	bf	3	1	0	0	0	1
3	gp	1	0	1	1	1	1
4	ihc	6	10	5	20	2	8
5	mtf	28	16	35	21	25	22
6	icf	1	1	0	1	0	1
7	bpf	0	0	0	1	0	0
8	fdo	6	3	3	2	13	7
9	stc	0	0	0	1	1	3
10	sff	1	0	1	0	0	1
11	erw	4	23	10	12	11	8
12	gwb	0	0	0	0	1	0
% Changes:		0%	32%	32%	37%	31%	24%
Total:		100	100	100	100	100	100

We can notice that in about one third of the cases we have changes due to the change of context element perceived, even when this element is not obviously related to the target and potential base for analogy. On the other hand, no drastic changes happen in the statistics. The most obvious base for analogy "heating water on the plate" is dominating in all conditions. As we can easily notice in Figure 1 the biggest changes are a facilitation effect for some rare remote analogies which in this context become relatively more probable. For example, in the "egg" condition the old episode "coloring an egg in red water" is more often retrieved and mapped than normally. In the "immersion heater" condition the case of heating water with an immersion heater is much more often retrieved and successfully mapped (20%) than normally (6%).

These results qualitatively correspond to the data obtained in an psychological experiment [17, 18] where subjects primed with "immersion heated" increased the solution of a target problem (a much more complicated one) involving an analogy to the immersion heater case from 14% to 44%.

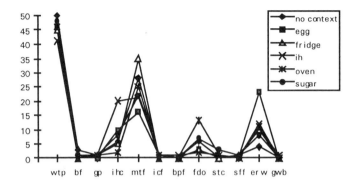

Figure 1. Statistical results from 100 runs of AMBR with the target problem "Heating Milk" in 6 different context conditions.

3.2. Control versus Hint versus Context Condition

The next simulation takes a closer look at the difference between a control condition (no perception of external elements), a context condition (perceiving a single incidental element from the environment without being aware of its relevance to the problem at hand), and an explicit hint condition (where a teacher provides another case and says it can help in solving the target problem — this may also be called a "forced-analogy" condition).

The target problem in this case was: "What will happen if you put an ice-cube in the coke which is in a glass?" In order to solve this problem the system should rely on its knowledge that "ice-cubes have low temperature" (a general fact which is part of the semantic knowledge of ice-cubes) and on an analogy with some of the old episodes in memory. All simulations are run with one single knowledge base — KB000— one of the randomly generated KBs as described in the previous section.

In the control condition the system finds an analogy between the target situation and the situation "Heating Water in a Teapot on a Plate". This is the most typical example of changing temperature (although it is heating instead of cooling) and is most easily retrieved. Table 4 presents the analogy found by the system — details of the established correspondences are shown.

Table 4: Correspondences established by AMBR in the control condition.

Situation "Ice-Cube in Coke"	Situation "Water in a Tea-pot"	Activation level of correspondence hypotheses
ice-cube	plate	1.74 winner
coke	water	1.75 winner
glass	tea-pot	1.82 winner
in(coke, glass)	in(water, teapot)	1.80 winner
temperature-of(ice-cube, low-temp)	temperature-of(plate, high-temp)	1.76 winner
low-temperature	high-temperature	1.76 winner
init-state-ICC	init-state-WTP	1.77 winner
end-state-ICC	end-state-WTP	1.29 mature
follows-ICC	follows-WTP	1.44 mature

In a context condition where an immersion heater is perceived for a while, i.e. when an arbitrary instance of "immersion heater" is put for a while on the input list without any relations to the target, without marking it as a target, etc. The only result of this is that this instance becomes active for a short period of time (25 time units) and starts spreading its activation to the network of agents via its link to the concept "immersion heater". As a result another base for analogy is found, namely — cooling water with an ice-cube is like heating water with immersion heater. The established correspondences are shown in Table 5.

Table 5: Correspondences established by AMBR in the context condition when perceiving an immersion heater.

Situation "Ice-Cube in Coke"	Situation "Immersion Heater in Water"	Activation level of correspondence hypotheses
ice-cube	immersion heater	1.82 winner
coke	water	1.80 winner
glass	cup	1.83 winner
table	saucer	1.72
in(ice-cube, coke)	in(immersion-heater, water)	1.81 winner
in(coke, glass)	in(water, cup)	1.79 winner
on(glass, table)	on(cup, saucer)	1.79 winner
temp-of(ice-cube, low-temp)	temp-of(imm-heater, high-temp)	1.78 winner
low-temp	high-temp	1.75 winner
Init-state-ICC	init-state-IHC	1.80 winner
End-state-ICC	end-state-IHC	1.28 mature
follows-ICC	follows-IHC	1.27 mature

In a hint condition we put a whole new situation of the type "heating water with immersion heater" on the input list and mark it as a target. This corresponds to an explicit hint to find an analogy between the two targets - a forced analogy case. The systems establishes the same correspondences as above, except that the elements are the ones provided by the input instead of the once retrieved from memory. The activation levels are a bit different, but the end result is the same.

Table 6: Correspondences established by AMBR in a context condition when perceiving "sugar".

Situation "Ice-Cube in Coke"	Situation "Sugar in Tea"	Activation level of correspondence hypotheses
ice-cube	sugar	1.82 winner
coke	tea	1.80 winner
glass	cup	1.80 winner
table	saucer	1.72 winner
in(ice-cube, coke)	in(sugar, tea)	1.81 winner
in(coke, glass)	in(tea, cup)	1.79 winner
on(glass, table)	on(cup, saucer)	1.79 winner
temp-of(ice-cube, low-temp)	taste-of(sugar, sweet)	1.77 winner
init-state-ICC	init-state-STC	1.80 winner
end-state-ICC	goal-state-STC	1.31 mature
follows-ICC	follows-STC	1.31 mature

Another example we have tried is to put some sugar to be perceived, i.e. to put an instance of the concept "sugar" on the input list for a while. In this context condition the system finds another analogy: cooling the coke with an ice-cube is like sweetening the tea with sugar. The correspondences found by the system are shown in Table 6.

Again in a forced analogy case where an externally perceived situation of sugaring tea is provided we obtain very similar results (only the activation levels differ).

Finally, as a third example of context condition we used an instance of an egg in the input. In this case the activation of the "egg" instance turned out not to be enough in order to retrieve the ERW episode from memory and the WTP episode got the power, i.e. we obtained the same result as in the control condition.

In a hint condition when a "coloring egg" situation is provided by a teacher, AMBR was trying to establish the analogy "cooling coke with an ice-cube is like coloring an egg in red water". In this case, however, AMBR failed to establish correct correspondences since in ICC the ice-cube is in the coke and it is the source of "coldness", while in the ERW situation the egg which is in the water is not the source of "redness", but the water is the coloring material in this case. This turned out to be too complicated for the system. AMBR was trying to color the water white using the color of the egg which contradicts the "follows" relationship in ERW. The established correspondences are presented in Table 7.

Table 7: Correspondence established by the system in the forced analogy case when presented with a coloring egg situation.

Situation "Ice-Cube in Coke"	Situation "Coloring Egg in Water"	Activation level of correspondenc e hypotheses
ice-cube	egg	1.79 winner
coke	water	1.66 winner
glass	tea-pot	1.08 mature
in(ice-cube, coke)	in(egg, water)	1.41 winner
temp-of(ice-cube, low-temp)	color-of(egg, white)	1.48 mature
low-temp	red	1.73 winner
init-state-ICC	init-state-ERW	1.80 winner
end-state-ICC	end-state-ERW	1.75 winner
follows-ICC	follows-ERW	1.75 winner

Finally, some of the others randomly generated variations of the KB have been tested. In the context condition when an egg is perceived it turned out that in many cases this context does change the solution found by the system. However, instead of making analogy with the "coloring case" AMBR found analogies to other episodes which somehow became available when "egg" is activated via the input list. Some of these analogies are, however, bizarre and inconsistent. With KB002 we obtained the following analogy: "cooling the coke with a ice-cube is like cooling the butter on the plate in a fridge" - this is a correct analogy, however, the correspondences found were inconsistent. With KB004 we obtained the analogy "cooling the coke with ice-cube is like putting a glass on the plate" which is extremely bizarre analogy. With KB006 we got "cooling the coke with ice-cube is like cooling the milk in the fridge" which is a fine analogy, but some of the correspondences were inconsistent. At the end, we tried the hint condition with KB011 and we obtained a perfect forced analogy which is presented in Table 8.

Table 8: Correspondence established by AMBR in the forced analogy case when presented with a coloring egg situation (KB011 used).

Situation "Ice-Cube in Coke"	Situation "Coloring Egg in Water"	Activation level of hypotheses
ice-cube	water	1.76 winner
coke	egg	1.74 winner
glass	tea-pot	1.75 winner
in(ice-cube, coke)	in(water, tea-pot)	1.74 winner
in(coke, glass)	in(egg, water)	1.77 winner
temp-of(ice-cube, low-temp)	color-of(water, red)	1.60 mature
low-temp	red	1.73 winner
init-state-ICC	init-state-ERW	1.77 winner
end-state-ICC	end-state-ERW	1.75 winner
follows-ICC	follows-ERW	1.77 winner

The results from the simulation presented in Table 7 seem to correspond to the finding in [25] that when the presented forced-analogy base is not obviously isomorphic, the hint hinders the problem solving process instead of facilitating it. In this case, a context condition might be a more effective facilitator since it may activate a completely different base for analogy.

3.3. Timing of Context Element Perception and its Relation to the Context Effect

Another experiment aimed at understanding the most effective timing of the context influence. We varied the onset of presentation of the context stimulus thus simulating various timing of perceiving of the incidental environmental element. It turned out that the effect is to a certain extent stimulus-specific. Thus in the case of "perceiving" sugar it has an effect only when perceived at the very beginning of the problem solving process, while in the case of "perceiving" immersion heater the effect lasts longer. For onsets less than 5 time units it has the effect of making the "immersion heater analogy", while for onsets greater than 5 time units it goes back to the "heating water on a plate" situation which is typical for the control condition. That is, when presented later than 5 time units after the problem solving process has started, the context does not have an effect.

This simulation makes a prediction that contextual clues can influence the problem solving process only if they are perceived at the very beginning, otherwise the reasoning process is too much preoccupied with its own commitments. We are not aware of psychological evidence in support of this prediction and are currently designing an experiment to test it. There is, however, an indirect support: Bransford and Johnson [6] have run an experiment on context effects on text understanding. They used a picture as a contextual element assisting the interpretation of a difficult paragraph. It turned out that the picture facilitates the understanding of the text only if provided before reading the text, but not after that. This seems coherent with our prediction, but is in the area of text understanding, not of problem solving.

4. Conclusions

The simulation experiments reported in this paper have demonstrated that the AMBR model of problem solving is context-sensitive and finds various solutions to the same problem (or fails to solve it) in different contexts. Still the internal knowledge and experience of the system dominates the type of solution found and only about 30% of the changes are due to the variations in the context.

It was shown that incidental environmental clues influence the process of problem solving only at its very early stages, in the later phases it does not change the solution produced. This is a prediction that needs to be experimentally tested.

Finally, a comparison was done between the incidental perception of an environmental element (context effect) and an explicit hint provided by a teacher which results in a forced analogy between the target and the provided situation. In some cases, both have the same effect, in others, the context does not have an effect while the hint does change the solution, and finally in third cases, the explicit and implicit hints have opposite directions of influence. This is coherent with psychological data [25], but needs further experimentation as well. What is important here is that AMBR offers an explanation of these opposite directions of influence, i.e. different mechanisms are responsible for them. While only spreading activation is involved in the context condition, the full sets of mechanisms are employed in the hint condition and explicit hypotheses for correspondence are formed with the context elements.

Acknowledgments

We would like to thank the AMBR research group for the stimulating environment and especially Alexander Petrov for his work on AMBR and the knowledge bases that are used in these simulations.

References

1. Abu-Hakima, S., Brezillon, P.: Principles for Application of Context in Diagnostic Problem Solving. In: Brezillon, P. Abu-Hakima, S. (eds.) Working Notes of the IJCAI'95 Workshop on Modelling Context in Knowledge Representation and Reasoning. IBP, LAFORIA 95/11 (1995)
2. Anderson, J.: The Architecture of Cognition. Harvard Univ. Press, Cambridge, MA (1983)
3. Bargh, J.: The Four Horsemen of Automaticity: Awareness, Intention, Efficiency. and Control in Social Cognition. In: Wyer, R. & Srull, Th. (eds.) Handbook of Social Cognition. vol. 1: Basic Processes. 2nd Edition, Erlbaum, Hillsdale, NJ (1994)
4. Barsalou, L. Flexibility, Structure, and Linguistic Vagary in Concepts: Manifestations of a Compositional System of Perceptual Symbols. In: Collins, A., Gathercole, S., Conway, M., & Morris, P. (eds.) Theories of Memory. Erlbaum, Hillsdale, NJ (1993)
5. Bouquet, P., Cimatti, C.: Formalizing Local Reasoning Using Contexts. In: Brezillon, P. Abu-Hakima, S. (eds.) Working Notes of the IJCAI'95 Workshop on Modelling Context in Knowledge Representation and Reasoning. IBP, LAFORIA 95/11. (1995)
6. Bransford, J., Johnson,. M.: Contextual Prerequisites for Understanding: Some Investigations for comprehension and Recall. Journal of Verbal Learning and Verbal Behavior, 61, 717-726 (1972)
7. Brezillon, P.: Context in Artificial Intelligence: I. A Survey of the Literature. Computers and Artificial Intelligence, vol. 18, 1999, No. 4, pp. 321-340.
8. Brezillon, P.: Context in Artificial Intelligence: II. Key Elements of Contexts. Computers and Artificial Intelligence, vol. 18, 1999, No. 5, pp. 425-446.
9. Davies, G. & Thomson, D.: Memory in Context: Context in Memory. John Wiley, Chichester (1988)
10. Davies, G. & Thomson, D.: Context in Context. In: Davies, G. & Thomson, D. (eds.) Memory in Context: Context in Memory. John Wiley, Chichester (1988)
11. Dunker, K.: On Problem Solving. Psychological Monographs, 58:5 (1945)
12. Gick, M. & Holyoak, K.: Analogical Problem Solving. Cognitive Psychology, 12 (1980) 306-355
13. Giunchiglia, F.: Contextual Reasoning. In: Epistemologia - Special Issue on I Linguaggi e le Machine, 16 (1993) 345-364
14. Giunchiglia, F. & Bouquet, P.: Introduction to Contextual Reasoning. In: Kokinov. B. (ed.) Perspectives on Cognitive Science, vol. 3, NBU Press, Sofia (1997)
15. Hofstadter, D.: Fluid Concepts and Creative Analogies. Basic Books, NY (1995)

16. Isen, A., Shalker, T., Clark, M., Karp, L.: Affect, Accessibility of Material in Memory, and Behavior: A Cognitive Loop? Journal of Personality and Social Psychology, 36 (1978) 1-12.

17. Kokinov, B.: Associative Memory-Based Reasoning: Some Experimental Results. In: Proceedings of the 12th Annual Conference of the Cognitive Science Society, Erlbaum, Hillsdale, NJ (1990)

18. Kokinov, B.: A Hybrid Model of Reasoning by Analogy. Chapter 5. in: K. Holyoak & J. Barnden (eds.) Analogical Connections, Advances in Connectionist and Neural Computation Theory, vol.2, Ablex Publ. Corp., Norwood, NJ (1994)

19. Kokinov, B.: The DUAL Cognitive Architecture: A Hybrid Multi-Agent Approach. In: A. Cohn (ed.) Proceedings of ECAI'94. John Wiley & Sons, Ltd., London (1994)

20. Kokinov, B.: The Context-Sensitive Cognitive Architecture DUAL. In: Proceedings of the 16th Annual Conference of the Cognitive Science Society. Erlbaum, Hillsdale, NJ (1994)

21. Kokinov, B.: A Dynamic Approach to Context Modeling. In: Brezillon, P. Abu-Hakima, S. (eds.) Working Notes of the IJCAI'95 Workshop on Modelling Context in Knowledge Representation and Reasoning. IBP, LAFORIA 95/11 (1995)

22. Kokinov, B.: Micro-Level Hybridization in the Cognitive Architecture DUAL. In: R. Sun & F. Alexander (eds.) Connectionist-Symbolic Integration: From Unified to Hybrid Architectures, Lawrence Erlbaum Associates, Hilsdale, NJ (1997)

23. Kokinov, B.: Analogy is like Cognition: Dynamic, Emergent, and Context-Sensitive. In: Holyoak, K., Gentner, D., Kokinov, B. (eds.) — Advances in Analogy Research: Integration of Theory and Data from the Cognitive, Computational, and Neural Sciences. NBU Press, Sofia (1998)

24. Kokinov, B.: Dynamics and Automaticity of Context: A Cognitive Modeling Approach. In: Bouquet, P., Serafini, L., Brezillon, P., Benerecetti, M., Castellani, F. (eds.) Modeling and Using Context. Lecture Notes in Artificial Intelligence, 1688, Springer, Berlin (1999)

25. Kokinov, B., Hadjiilieva, K., & Yoveva, M.: Explicit vs. Implicit Hint: Which One is More Useful? In: Kokinov. B. (ed.) Perspectives on Cognitive Science, vol. 3, NBU Press, Sofia (1997)

26. Kokinov, B., Yoveva, M.: Context Effects on Problem Solving. In: Proceedings of the 18th Annual Conference of the Cognitive Science Society. Erlbaum, Hillsdale, NJ (1996)

27. Levandowsky, S., Kirsner, K., & Bainbridge, V.: Context Effects in Implicit Memory: A Sense-Specific Account. In: Lewandowsky, S., Dunn, J., & Kirsner, K. (eds.) Implicit Memory: Theoretical Issues. Erlbaum, Hillsdale, NJ (1989)

28. Lockhart, R.: Conceptual Specificity in Thinking and Remembering. In: Davies, G. & Thomson, D. (eds.) Memory in Context: Context in Memory. John Wiley, Chichester (1988)

29. Luchins, A.: Mechanization in Problem Solving: The Effect of Einstellung. Psychological Monographs, 54:6 (1942)

30. Maier, N.: Reasoning in Humans II: The Solution of a Problem and it Appearance in Consciousness. Journal of Comparative Psychology, 12 (1931) 181-194.

31. McCarthy, J.: Generality in Artificial Intelligence. Communications of the ACM, 30 (1987) 1030-1035

32. McCarthy, J.: Notes on Formalizing Context. In: Proceedings of the 13th IJCAI, AAAI Press (1993) 555-560

33. Murphy, S., Zajonc, R.: Affect, Cognition, and Awareness: Affective Priming with Optimal and Suboptimal Stimulus Exposures. Journal of Personality and Social Psychology, 64 (1993) 723-739

34. Petrov, A., Kokinov, B.: Mapping and Access in Analogy-Making: Independent or Interactive? A Simulation Experiment with AMBR. In: Holyoak, K., Gentner, D., Kokinov, B. (eds.) Advances in Analogy Research: Integration of Theory and Data from the Cognitive, Computational, and Neural Sciences. NBU Press, Sofia (1998)

35. Petrov, A., Kokinov, B.: Processing Symbols at Variable Speed in DUAL: Connectionist Activation as Power Supply. In: Proceedings of the 17th IJCAI, AAAI Press (1999)
36. Roediger, H. & Srinivas, K.: Specificity of Operations in Perceptual Priming. In: Graf, P. & Masson, M. (eds.) Implicit Memory: New Directions in Cognition, Development, and Neuropsychology. Erlbaum, Hillsdale (1993)
37. Schunn, C. & Dunbar, K. Priming, Analogy, and Awareness in Complex Reasoning. Memory and Cognition, 24 (1996) 271-284
38. Shafir, E., Simonson, I. & Tversky, A.: Reason-Based Choice. Cognition, 49 (1993) 11-36
39. Tiberghien, G.: Language Context and Context Language. In: Davies, G. & Thomson, D. (eds.) Memory in Context: Context in Memory. John Wiley, Chichester (1988)
40. Turner, R. Context-Mediated Behavior for Intelligent Agents. Int. J. Human-Computer Studies, 48 (1998) 307-330

A New Method Based on Context for Combining Statistical Language Models

David Langlois, Kamel Smaïli, and Jean-Paul Haton

LORIA Laboratory, Campus Scientifique BP 239, 54506 Vandœuvre-Lès-Nancy, FRANCE,
phone: +33 (0)3 83 59 20 74, fax: +33 (0)3 83 41 30 79
{David.Langlois, Kamel.Smaili, Jean-Paul.Haton}@loria.fr

Abstract. In this paper we propose a new method to extract from a corpus the histories for which a given language model is better than another one. The decision is based on a measure stemmed from perplexity. This measure allows, for a given history, to compare two language models, and then to choose the best one for this history. Using this principle, and with a 20K vocabulary words, we combined two language models: a bigram and a distant bigram. The contribution of a distant bigram is significant and outperforms a bigram model by 7.5%. Moreover, the performance in Shannon game are improved. We show through this article that we proposed a cheaper framework in comparison to the maximum entropy principle, for combining language models. In addition, the selected histories for which a model is better than another one, have been collected and studied. Almost, all of them are beginnings of very frequently used French phrases. Finally, by using this principle, we achieve a better trigram model in terms of parameters and perplexity. This model is a combination of a bigram and a trigram based on a selected history.

1 Introduction

The aim of an automatic speech recognizer is to find the best sequence of words W which matches a sequence of speech observations O. This sequence is obtained by using the well known Bayes formula [2]:

$$W = \arg\max_{W} \frac{P(O|W)P(W)}{P(O)} \tag{1}$$

Because $P(O)$ is constant, (1) is reduced as follows:

$$W = \arg\max_{W} P(O|W)P(W) \tag{2}$$

The values of $P(O|W)$ and $P(W)$ are respectively provided by the acoustic component of the recognizer and the language model. One of the aims of a statistical language model is to capture recurrent structures in the natural language in order to accept or reject hypotheses from the recognizer. More precisely, the language model estimates the probability $P(W)$ of a sequence of words $W = w_1 w_2 \ldots w_N$ using the formula:

$$P(W) = \prod_{i=1}^{N} P(w_i|h_i) \qquad (3)$$

where h_i is the sequence of words $w_1 w_2 \dots w_{i-1}$.

Another aim of a statistical language model is to predict the word following its left context (classically, this context is called the history). In fact, the language model has to restrict the research space by proposing only the most likely words following a hypothesis h_i. In practice, this context h_i is not entirely used. One of the research areas in statistical language modeling consists in extracting from the context interesting information for prediction such as the partial syntactic structure [1], triggering words [2, 7], frequencies of words present in the history (cache model [2]) or the Part of Speech level from word level [9]. All these kinds of information are useful because lexical, syntactic, and semantic levels may be used in order to predict the word following a history.

Because the community working on statistical language modelling use large vocabularies and huge corpora, we have to care about the number of free parameters involved in a statistical language model by reducing it. A basic way to estimate the value $P(w_i|h_i)$ in (3) is to use the following formula:

$$P(w_i|h_i) = \frac{N(h_i w_i)}{N(h_i)} \qquad (4)$$

where $N(\cdot)$ is the frequency of a specified sequence of words in a text corpus called the training corpus. But, such sequences may be too rare in this corpus. Therefore, frequencies are not reliable. A way to prevent from this sparseness data is to cluster histories into several classes. These classes may be designed by hand [9] or retrieved automatically [14]. But, the first way to deal with sparseness data is to reduce the history to its $n-1$ last words, considering that only these last words are sufficient to predict the next word. This constitutes the n-gram language model:

$$P(w_i|w_{i-n+1} \dots w_{i-1}) = \frac{N(w_{i-n+1} \dots w_{i-1} w_i)}{N(w_{i-n+1} \dots w_{i-1})} \qquad (5)$$

To summarize, the aim of statistical language modeling can be thought as finding a compromise between the use of the entire history (and dealing with unreliable information) and clustering [9] the contexts (and so dealing with a possible less informative context). For example, for a trigram model ($n = 3$), there is no difference between the two histories "this man is falling in" and "this stone is falling in". Nevertheless, the word "love" could follow the former but not the latter. Trigram model can't make such a distinction: some information is lost by clustering[1].

---

[1] Note that reducing the history from $w_1 \dots w_{i-1}$ to $w_{i-n+1} \dots w_{i-1}$ can be thought as clustering this history: the class of $w_1 \dots w_{i-1}$ would be here $w_{i-n+1} \dots w_{i-1}$.

Another field of research consists in finding an effective way to combine several language models in order to take advantage of the predictive qualities of each one. In such a way, a linear interpolation is frequently used [4]:

$$P(w_i|h_i) = \alpha \cdot P_1(w_i|h_i) + (1 - \alpha) \cdot P_2(w_i|h_i) \qquad (6)$$

A drawback of this method is that it leads to a global mean between the models independently of the context. Since the models are often attributed a fixed set of weights $\{\alpha, 1 - \alpha\}$, the specific features of each language model are not used judiciously. Consequently, the contribution of a model is reduced. Actually, the best way to take into account each specific language model is to deal with a set of weights $\{\alpha_i, 1 - \alpha_i\}$ for each history h_i, but the number of parameters would be dramatically large. Moreover, using a set of weights for each cluster of histories does not solve the problem of selecting the best model for a particular history.

We claim that for a given history, it is generally possible to decide if one should use a model or another and not a combination of all the models.

For example, let consider the probability:

$$P(\text{music} \,|\text{the children are listening to})$$

Let use a bigram model ($n = 2$). With such a language model, the history is reduced to the word "to". But this word is semantically not useful to predict the following word. Actually, there is a strong relationship between "listening" and "music" *in the context* "listening to". This relationship is necessarily distant because the verb "to listen" must be used with a function word ("to", "in", "up"). So, a language model dealing with distant relationships (and not only contiguous relationships as classical n-gram models) should be used when the context is "listening to". We can remark that it is also possible to use the trigram model, but this solution involves a huger language model in terms of parameters and does not solve the problem when the distance is more important.

The maximum entropy principle [13] allows to merge several constraints and then to take advantage from each language model. But, it requires a huge computation and fuses together several parts of each model in a single one. Thus, the contribution of each model can not be qualitatively studied.

The aim of this paper is to propose a less expensive method for extracting from a corpus the histories for which a given language model is better than another one. This consists in evaluating each language model for each history. Histories are grouped into sets – one set for each language model – so that a history is classified in the language model set for which this model outperforms other ones for the same history. Then, during the test phase, for a given history, the language model used is the one which obtains the best evaluation. This method allows to make best use of each language model. Moreover, as histories become available, it is possible to study their linguistic features.

The paper is organized as follows: in Sect. 2 we present the measure used to evaluate the best language model for a given history. Then, we describe the method for extracting the histories for which a given model is better than another one. Sect. 3 presents the language models we used in our experiments, e.g. the bigram and the distant bigram in order to study the contribution of the second one. In addition, we applied the selected history principle to study the utility of a trigram model in relation to a bigram model in order to keep only the useful parameters of the trigram model. Then we present the experiments in terms of perplexity, Shannon game, and recognition in our dictation system (MAUD).

2 The Selected History Principle

2.1 Model Evaluation for a History

Statistical language models are often evaluated using the so called perplexity PP. The perplexity of a language model M defined by the distribution of probabilities $P(w|h)$ is computed on a text corpus C by:

$$PP = \exp^{-\frac{1}{N} \sum_{i=1}^{N} \log P(w_i|h_i)} \tag{7}$$

where N is the size of the corpus, and h_i is defined as in (3). PP results from Information Theory. Its value can be though as the mean difficulty to guess the word to a history in the corpus. It is as if this value was the mean size of the vocabulary if one assumes a uniform distribution of the possible words after each history [9]. Thus, the lower PP is, the better the language model is.

By grouping the $N(hw)$ occurences of the same sequences hw, we organize (7):

$$\log PP = -\frac{1}{N} \sum_{hw, \, hw \in C} N(hw) \log P(w|h) \tag{8}$$

where $N(hw)$ denotes the frequency of hw in the corpus C. In (8), h is common to several distinct sequences hw_i. Therefore, by splitting this sum in accordance to h, we obtain:

$$\log PP = -\frac{1}{N} \sum_{h \in C} \left(\sum_{w_i, \, hw_i \in C} N(hw_i) \log P(w_i|h) \right) \tag{9}$$

By defining $Q(h) = \sum_{w_i, \, hw_i \in C} N(hw_i) \log P(w_i|h)$, we get:

$$\log PP = -\frac{1}{N} \sum_{h \in C} Q(h) \tag{10}$$

$\log PP$ is thus written as a sum on the histories present in the corpus C. Then, minimizing $\log PP$ amounts to maximize $Q(h)$ for each h in C. Note that maximizing $Q(h)$ for a given history can be achieved independently of the other histories.

2.2 Combination of Two Models Based on the Selection of Histories

The idea consists in, for a given history h, choosing the model according to the value $Q(h)$. This one allows to select the contextually best language model.

Therefore, two language models, M_1 and M_2, defined by the distributions of probabilities P_1 and P_2, and a corpus $\mathcal{C}$, provide respectively two values of perplexity:

$$\log PP_1 = -\frac{1}{N} \sum_{h \in \mathcal{C}} Q_1(h) \tag{11}$$

and

$$\log PP_2 = -\frac{1}{N} \sum_{h \in \mathcal{C}} Q_2(h) \tag{12}$$

Histories h_i are then extracted from $\mathcal{C}$ and are grouped into a set $\mathcal{H}$. These ones constitute the histories for which a model is better than another one according to $Q(h)$. For instance, M_2 is better than M_1 if $Q_2(h) > Q_1(h)$. Then, we use M_1 and M_2 and the measures $Q_1(h)$ and $Q_2(h)$ in order to define a new language model M as follows:

$$P(w|h) = \begin{cases} P_2(w|h) & \text{if } h \in \mathcal{H} \\ P_1(w|h) & \text{otherwise} \end{cases} \tag{13}$$

Therefore, for each history, the model M uses the best of the two models M_1 and M_2 in terms of perplexity estimated on $\mathcal{C}$. So, the perplexity of M on the same corpus is necessarily better than the two other ones.

It is important to have a large $\mathcal{C}$ in order to be able to compare $Q_1(h)$ and $Q_2(h)$. Moreover, the larger $\mathcal{C}$ is, more histories are available to build $\mathcal{H}$.

To sum up, in the selected history method, each time when a history belongs to $\mathcal{H}$, M_2 is used instead of the baseline one.

3 Evaluated Models

In previous works [11, 12], we pointed out the importance of the distant bigram model. The linguistic motivation of these works is that the relationship between the history h_i and the word w_i does not deal, for all time, with the entire history but rather with distant and no contiguous components of h_i. In this framework, the method presented in the previous section allows to qualitatively study in which cases, the relationship between w_i and a part of h_i is distant and not necessarily contiguous.

In order to define precisely the model M, we have to give some details about M_1 and M_2. In our experiments, they correspond to a bigram and a distant bigram models, which are smoothed by Katz's method [4]:

$$P(w_i|w_{i-1}) = \begin{cases} fr^*(w_i|w_{i-1}) & \text{if } N(w_{i-1}w_i) > 0 \\ \alpha(w_{i-1})P(w_i) & \text{otherwise} \end{cases} \tag{14}$$

where fr^* denotes a discounting method, $P(w)$ is the unigram model and $\alpha(w_{i-1})$ is defined as below:

$$\alpha(w_{i-1}) = \frac{1 - \sum_{w \, , \, N(w_{i-1}w)>0} fr^*(w|w_{i-1})}{\sum_{w \, , \, N(w_{i-1}w)=0} P(w)} \tag{15}$$

Likewise, we define the distant bigram model as:

$$P(w_i|w_{i-2}) = \begin{cases} fr^*(w_i|w_{i-2}\cdot) & \text{if } N(w_{i-2} \cdot w_i) > 0 \\ \alpha_d(w_{i-2})P(w_i) & \text{otherwise} \end{cases} \tag{16}$$

where $N(w_{i-2} \cdot w_i)$ is the frequency of the distant bigram and:

$$\alpha_d(w_{i-2}) = \frac{1 - \sum_{w \, , \, N(w_{i-2}\cdot w)>0} fr^*(w|w_{i-2}\cdot)}{\sum_{w \, , \, N(w_{i-2}\cdot w)=0} P(w)} \tag{17}$$

In our experiments, we tested also a backoff trigram model. In all our experiments fr^* was the absolute discounting method:

$$fr^*(w|h) = \frac{N(hw) - b}{N(h)} \qquad (0 \le b < 1) \tag{18}$$

4 Experiments

4.1 Corpus

Our models are evaluated on a corpus of 24 months (a volume of 42M words) extracted from *Le Monde* French newspaper, 22 months (38M words) have been dedicated to train the bigram, distant bigram and trigram models. One month (2M words) has been used for the development and the remaining month (2M words) for the test set. The vocabulary is made up of the most frequent 20K words in the training corpus.

4.2 Experiments on Bigrams and Distant Bigrams

We compared the models built using the selected history principle with a bigram model, and a linear interpolation between a bigram and a distant bigram model [12]. The parameters of the linear interpolation are estimated using the Expectation-Maximisation algorithm [3] on the development corpus. Performance of these baseline models are given in Table 1.

The selected history model has been built considering respectively the bigram model and the distant bigram model as being M_1 and M_2. Thus, $\mathcal{H}$ is the set of histories h for which the distant bigram model achieves a better performance according to the measures $Q_1(h)$ and $Q_2(h)$.

Table 1. Performance of baseline models

Base Models	PP
bigrams	127.10
linear interpolation	121.87

4.3 Importance of the History Frequency on Retrieving the Best Selected Histories

The corpus $\mathcal{C}$ used to build $\mathcal{H}$ is a combination of two corpora: Tr (a subset of the training corpus) and Un (a corpus not included in the training one – Un is for Unseen because this corpus contains some events unseen in the training one). We used this last one in order to deal with unseen events. Since the quality of our model depends on the size of $\mathcal{C}$, we decided to increase Un by 6 years (6M words) of *Le Monde Diplomatique* a newspaper closely related to *Le Monde* French newspaper.

In order to build a reliable $\mathcal{H}$, a history is added to this set if and only if its frequency in $\mathcal{C}$ is higher than a fixed threshold. This is useful because of the weak trust put in $Q_1(h)$ and $Q_2(h)$ for rare histories.

Figure 1 shows the performance in terms of perplexity of the model for several combinations of Tr and Un and for several values of this threshold. Each curve corresponds to a combination of Tr and Un in terms of sizes.

First we notice that a better performance is obtained for large sizes of $\mathcal{C}$: the best value of the perplexity (118.1) is achieved for "Tr (38M words) + Un (8M words)" and a threshold of 30. This represents an improvement of 7.5% in comparison to the bigram model. Table 2 shows the number of histories in $\mathcal{H}$ for several values of the threshold with $\mathcal{C}$ = "Tr (38M words) + Un (8M words)". This table shows that the selected history principle leads to a significant improvement in terms of perplexity without dealing with a huge number of further parameters (only 28K).

Table 2. Size of $\mathcal{H}$ for $\mathcal{C}$ = Tr (38M words) + Un (8M words)

Threshold	size of $\mathcal{H}$	Threshold	size of $\mathcal{H}$
1	715689	8	81912
2	279708	9	74545
3	186775	10	68532
4	144402	20	39289
5	119527	**30**	**28135**
6	102863	40	22084
7	91043	50	18140

Second, for a given combination `Tr` and `Un`, performance decreases for high values of the threshold. Moreover, as seen above, Table 2 reveals the correspondence between high values of the threshold and small values of $\mathcal{H}$. So, we guess that performance depends strongly on the size of $\mathcal{H}$.

In addition, Table 3 presents the optimal value of the threshold for several sizes of $\mathcal{C}$, extracted from Fig. 1. We see that the higher the size of $\mathcal{C}$ is, the higher the value of the threshold is. This can be explained as follows: when the size of $\mathcal{C}$ increases (see curve 1.e. for a large size of $\mathcal{C}$), a given history h is followed by more distinct words w. As $Q_1(h)$ and $Q_2(h)$ are stemmed from perplexity, reliable statistics are required for each hw. Consequently, h must occur more frequently than it should for a small size of $\mathcal{C}$ (see curve 1.b. for a small size of $\mathcal{C}$). This corresponds to high values of the threshold.

Table 3. Optimal values of the threshold for several sizes of $\mathcal{C}$

Size of $\mathcal{C}$	Optimal value of the threshold
2M	5
26M	30
36M	40
46M	40

Last, let consider the two curves 1.a. and 1.b.; we notice that for the same size of $\mathcal{C}$, the figure shows better performance for the model using unseen events.

4.4 Qualitative Study of $\mathcal{H}$

We are interested in this section by the content of $\mathcal{H}$. Table 4 lists some histories in $\mathcal{H}$ corresponding to the best configuration "`Tr` (38M words) `Un` (8M words)". $\mathcal{H}$ shows that the distant bigrams contribution is very useful when the preceding word is a function word ("of", "by", "and", "on", "which"...), an article or a number etc...In general, $\mathcal{H}$ contains histories for which the last word is ambiguous for the prediction. Moreover, these histories reveal the semantic relationship between couples of distant words joined by a link-word. These link-words are emphasized in the following examples: "tremblements *de* terre"[2], "tirage *au* sort"[3], "saut *en* parachute"[4]...Thus, the histories selected by this method constitute generally the beginning of frequent natural language phrases.

4.5 Experiments on Shannon Game

The evaluation through Shannon game [8] consists in measuring the performance of the model in predicting the word which appears just after a randomly-position

---

[2] earthquakes
[3] drawing lot
[4] parachuting

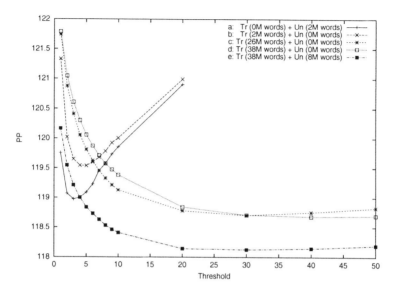

Fig. 1. Performance of selected history models

Table 4. Sample of selected histories from $\mathcal{H}$ for $\mathcal{C} = $ Tr (38M words) + Un (8M words)

French history	translation
voler en	fly by
quart d'	quarter of
rectifier le	to rectify the
limitation de	limitation of
barils par	barrels per
Jeanne d'	Joan of
forcés à	forced to
aprés_qu' il	after he
déguisé en	disguised as
noir et	black and

truncated sentence. In our experiment, the test was carried out with 10000 truncated sentences extracted from the *Le Monde Diplomatique* newspaper. For each truncated sentence the language model proposes the first potential 5000 best (in terms of probability) words. The proposed list is sorted in decreasing order of the probability. Then, several measures can be computed with these 10000 lists by estimating how well the true word which follows the truncated sentence in the corpus is ranked. Experimental results appear in Table 5 with the following meanings: "words in list" is the rate of discovered words; "mean rank" is the mean rank of the word to guess; "rank 1" (respectively "ranks 1–5") is the number of words observed at the first rank (respectively, in the five first ranks); Shannon Perplexity ("PP_{Sh}") is an adapted measure of the perplexity (for more details, see [12]).

We notice that the selected history model predicts more accurately than a bigram model in terms of mean rank. Besides, these words are better ranked. Moreover, the Shannon perplexity (high here, because the truncated sentences were randomly extracted from the corpus) has been improved. Last, in spite of these improvements, the number of words in list, almost by chance, has not changed.

Table 5. Experiments on Shannon game

	Bigram Model	Selected History Model
mean rank	275	266
rank 1	1212	1264
ranks 1–5	3166	3201
words in list	95%	95%
PP_{Sh}	277	261

4.6 Experiments on MAUD Dictation System

MAUD [5] is a 20K words continuous dictation system using an acoustic model trained on the French BREF database [10]. Each phoneme is modeled by a HMM2. The acoustic models used to construct the word lattice in a first step are context independent. This word lattice is obtained by combining an acoustic and a simple bigram language models. This first step is based on a Viterbi algorithm. In a second step, a high level language model is used to look for the best sentence.

We tested the combination of a distant bigram and a bigram models following the selected history principle on 300 sentences uttered by female and male speakers. As the first step is based on the Viterbi algorithm, it was only possible to incorporate our language model in the second step, because the basic Viterbi algorithm can only deal with a history of length one. For each input sentence, the model outputs one hypothesis. The evaluation was made using the SCLITE alignment tool[5] by comparing the reference sentence to the one proposed by our model. Unfortunately, due to the late intervention (only in the second step) of our language model, no significant improvement has been obtained. This is not due to a weakness of our model, but to the quality of the word lattices: even when we tried a classical trigram in this second step, only a slight improvement has been observed.

4.7 Experiments on Bigrams and Trigrams

In this experiment, we apply the selected history principle with M_1 and M_2 as being respectively the trigram and the bigram models. Our aim is to remove from the trigram model the trigrams for which histories are in $\mathcal{H}$. Now, this method allows to select trigram histories for which it is better or equivalent to use a bigram than a trigram model. Therefore, it is possible to remove these unuseful histories from the trigram model without loosing information. The baseline trigram perplexity is 89.1 on the same test corpus. We used "Tr (38M words) + Un (8M words)" to build $\mathcal{H}$. We found that a threshold equal to 1 leads to the best decrease of the perplexity (88.9). This is a non-significant improvement. The low value of the threshold shows that this is probably due to the relative weak size of $\mathcal{C}$ for a selected history trigram model: one must choose a low value for the threshold to obtain a reasonable size of $\mathcal{H}$. However, the histories of two words in $\mathcal{H}$ are involved in 400K distinct trigrams seen in the training corpus. Since for these histories we use only the bigram model, it is thus possible to remove these parameters from the trigram model. This leads to a less expensive model in terms of memory size: 2.7% in comparison to the baseline trigram.

The content of $\mathcal{H}$ for the selected history trigram shows that, in general, a history is selected because there is a strong linguistic relationship between the last word of this history and the words which follow it in $\mathcal{C}$. For example, the lexical unit "parce" constitutes the end of several histories in $\mathcal{H}$. In fact, this entry is never used alone: it is always followed by "que". Therefore, we do not need the whole trigram history to predict "que".

5 Conclusion and Future Work

In this paper we develop a selected history method which permits to build a set of histories for which a given model is better than another one. We applied this principle to study the contribution of a distant bigram model to a baseline bigram model. This selected combination outperforms the bigram model by 7.5%. Moreover the method reveals that the concerned histories have been selected because a strong semantic relationship links one of their words and distant words in the corpus. These relationships reveal sequences which could be a very interesting knowledge raw for linguists. They could study these sequences in order

---

[5] SCLITE is included in the Speech Recognition Scoring Toolkit distributed by the SNLP group (Spoken Language Natural Processing).

to select those which respect some constraints as: noun–verb, preposition–noun, or noun–noun, etc... In addition, this model makes the trigram model lighter by remaining the parameters for which a trigram model is less powerful than a bigram.

Therefore, the selected history principle is a good framework to extract linguistic features from a corpus and to keep only useful parameters for a model. Experiments on Shannon game show an improvement in terms of mean rank and Shannon perplexity. This method allows not only to measure the quality of the language model but also to understand why the model provides better results. We described the principle so that it can be applied to any kind of statistical language model.

One of our future work is to extend the experiment on selected distant bigrams to other language models in order to choose the best one for a given history. Our aim, for this part, is to find a cheaper alternative to the maximum entropy principle.

Another promising issue consists in incorporating the lexical units obtained by the selected history principle into a language model based on sequences [15, 6].

References

[1] Ciprian Chelba and Frederick Jelinek. Structured language modeling. *Computer Speech and Language*, 14(4):283–332, October 2000.

[2] Renato de Mori and Marcello Federico. Language model adaptation. In K. Ponting, editor, *Computational models of speech pattern processing*, volume 169, pages 280–303. NATO ASI, 1999.

[3] A. P. Dempster, N. M. Laird, and D. B. Rubin. Maximum-likelihood from incomplete data via the em algorithm. *Journal of Royal Statistic Society*, pages 1–38, 1977.

[4] Marcello Federico and Renato de Mori. *Spoken dialogues with computers*, chapter 7, pages 199–230. Academic Press, 1997.

[5] Dominique Fohr, Jean-Paul Haton, Jean-François Mari, Kamel Smaïli, and Imed Zitouni. Towards an oral interface of data entry: The maud system. In *Proceedings of the 3rd European Research Consortium for Informatics and Mathematics Workshop on "User Interface for All"*, pages 233–234, 1997.

[6] E. Giachin. Phrase bigrams for continuous speech recognition. In *Proceedings of the International Conference on Acoustics, Speech and Signal Processing*, pages 225–228, 1995.

[7] Zhou GuoDong and Lua KimTeng. Interpolation of n-gram and mutual-information based trigger pair language models for mandarin speech recognition. *Computer Speech and Language*, 13:125–141, 1999.

[8] M. Jardino, F. Bimbot, S. Igounet, K. Smaïli, and M. El-Beze. A first evaluation campaign for language models. In *Proceedings of the 1st International Conference on Language Resources and Evaluation*, volume 2, pages 801–805, Granada, Spain, 1998.

[9] Frederic Jelinek. Self-organized language modelling for speech recognition. In A. Waibel and K.-F. Lee, editors, *Readings in Speech Recognition*, pages 450–506. Kaufmann Publishers, San Mateo, CA, 1990.

[10] L. Lamel, J.-L. Gauvain, and M. Eskenazi. Bref, a large vocabulary spoken corpus for french. In *Proceeding of European Conference on Speech Communication and Technology*, volume 2, pages 505–508, Gênes, 1991.

[11] David Langlois and Kamel Smaïli. A new distance language model for a dictation machine: application to maud. In *Proceeding of European Conference on Speech Communication and Technology*, volume 4, pages 1779–1782, Budapest, Hungary, September 1999.

[12] David Langlois, Kamel Smaïli, and Jean-Paul Haton. Dealing with distant relationships in natural language modelling for automatic speech recognition. In *Proceedings of the SCI2000 conference*, volume 6, pages 400–405. International Institute of Informatics and Systemics, 2000.

[13] Ronald Rosenfeld. A maximum entropy approach to adaptive statistical language modelling. *Computer Speech and Language*, 10:187–228, 1996.

[14] K. Smaïli, A. Brun, I. Zitouni, and J.-P. Haton. Automatic and manual clustering for large vocabulary speech recognition: a comparative study. In *Proceeding of European Conference on Speech Communication and Technology*, volume 4, pages 1795–1798, September 1999.

[15] I. Zitouni, J.-F. Mari, K. Smaïli, and J.-P. Haton. Variable-length sequence language model for large vocabulary continuous dictation machine: the n-seqgram approach. In *Proceeding of the European Conference on Speech and Technology*, volume 4, pages 1811–1814, Budapest, Hungary, September 1999.

Experimental Pragmatics: Towards Testing Relevance-Based Predictions about Anaphoric Bridging Inferences

Tomoko Matsui

International Christian University, Division of Languages, 3-10-2 Osawa, Mitaka
Tokyo, 181-8585 JAPAN
matsui@icu.ac.jp

Abstract. Critics of relevance theory have charged that relevance theory provides no testable predictions, hence is unfalsifiable. This paper is an attempt to identify some testable relevance-theoretic predictions about anaphoric bridging inferences, and to show possible ways of testing these predictions. A relevance-based model of utterance interpretation is compared with Levinson's GCI model, and their contrasting views on how to divide explicitly communicated content and implicitly communicated content of utterance are discussed. Moreover, predictions following each theory about derivation of bridging inferences are compared before possible ways to test these predictions are suggested.

1. Introduction

One of the main on-going issues in post-Gricean pragmatics has been how best to tease apart different layers of utterance meaning. The best-known dichotomy in the debate is the distinction between 'what is said' and 'what is implicated' originally proposed by Grice (1975). More recent inquiries into the subject have centred on elucidating the notion of 'what is said' (e.g. Bach 1994; Gibbs & Moise 1997; Levinson 2000; Recanati 1989, 1993). Within the framework of relevance theory (Sperber & Wilson 1986/95), Carston has progressively sharpened an alternative notion, namely, 'explicature' proposed by Sperber & Wilson (Carston 1988, 1998, 2000a, b). The notion of explicature departs from the notion of 'what is said' in that it is claimed that context-dependent information plays an equally significant role in its full functioning, as is the case in the derivation of implicatures. Furthermore, Carston's notion of explicature is crucially different from Grice's notion of 'what is said' where derivation involves no maxims. In Carston's view, functioning of explicature is governed by the same principles as those which govern the derivation of implicatures, namely, the principles of relevance.

Few existing treatments of the distinction between 'what is said' and 'what is implicated' take into account cognitive structures or psychological processing. The relevance-theoretic distinction between explicature and implicature, in contrast, has its roots in fundamental assumptions about human cognition. Moreover, the derivation of explicature/implicature is claimed to be consistent with utterance processing. In this sense, at least in theory, its predictions ought to be testable for psychological validity.

The case of bridging inferences - typically inferences that introduce unmentioned antecedents (Clark 1977) - can provide an interesting testing ground for these predictions (Matsui 2000, Wilson & Matsui 1998). Before going into details of an experimental paradigm to show just how, brief explanation of the notion of relevance as it is understood in relevance theory and a presentation of the general outline of a relevance-based model of utterance processing are in order. My main aim in this research is to clarify predictions that the relevance-based model of utterance comprehension makes for generation and use of bridging inferences and contrast these predictions with those based on Levinson's GCI model (Levinson 2000). Furthermore, I hope to suggest ways of testing those contrasting predictions.

2. Relevance

Sperber & Wilson's relevance theory is a theory of ostensive communication, in which the recognition of a speaker's communicative intention is the starting point of the interpretation process. It inherits Grice's view that the nature of human communication is inferential, and at the same time, departs from Grice in claiming that what makes such inferential communication possible is some mechanism in our cognitive make-up that is responsive to 'relevant' inputs. 'Relevance' is a property of inputs to cognitive processes, and is assessed both by a positive function of cognitive benefit, i.e. improvements in one's knowledge, and a negative function of the mental cost of deriving such benefits. When an input contributes to improvements in one's knowledge, it interacts with the existing knowledge in one of the following three ways to yield cognitive effects: it may strengthen existing assumptions by providing further evidence for them; it may erase existing assumptions by providing contradicting evidence for them; or it may yield new implications, when combined with existing assumptions. Sperber & Wilson claim that the human cognitive system has a tendency to pursue inputs which are likely to maximise cognitive benefits and use its resources for processing such inputs. This is expressed as the First, or Cognitive, Principle of Relevance:

> *Cognitive Principle of Relevance*
> Human cognition tends to be geared to the maximisation of relevance.

Furthermore, it is claimed that this tendency is manifest enough to enable us to predict fairly well which inputs are likely to be perceived as relevant by an individual, and that we exploit such predictability in ostensive communication. For example, in verbal communication, a speaker should be aware that he needs to use an utterance which is relevant enough to attract the hearer's attention. But how relevant is relevant enough to attract the audience's attention? Sperber & Wilson provide the following definition of 'optimal' relevance:

> *Optimal relevance of an utterance*
> An utterance is optimally relevant to the hearer iff:
> (a) it is relevant enough to be worth the hearer's processing effort;
> (b) it is the most relevant one compatible with the speaker's abilities and
>   preferences.

Thus, if an utterance successfully attracts the audience's attention, it means that it has been perceived by the audience as conveying information likely to be optimally relevant. This idea is spelled out in the Second, or Communicative, Principle of Relevance:

Communicative Principle of Relevance
Every utterance communicates a presumption of its own optimal relevance.

The Communicative Principle of Relevance, together with the definition of optimal relevance, in turn suggests the following comprehension procedure:

Relevance-theoretic comprehension procedure
(a) test interpretive hypotheses (e.g. reference assignments, disambiguation, concept enrichment, implicature derivation) in order of accessibility, i.e. follow a path of least effort;
(b) stop when the expected level of relevance is achieved.

In what follows, this comprehension procedure will be illustrated in detail.

3. A Relevance-Based Comprehension Model and Bridging Inference

3.1. Mutual Parallel Adjustment of Explicature and Implicature

Utterance interpretation involves decoding of linguistically encoded information. The output of decoding is subpropositional and the process of developing this level to a fully propositional level has been the focus of recent pragmatic investigation (see, for example Carston 1998 for a detailed survey of different approaches). In relevance theory, the output of the decoding phase is called the 'logical form' of an utterance, and the enriched logical form to the level of full-fledged proposition is called 'explicature'. Explicature is thus related to the notion of 'what is said', but different from it in the following two ways. First, the derivation of 'what is said' typically involves reference assignment and disambiguation according to Grice, but it now looks likely that there are further pragmatic processes in explicature derivation, as Carston suggests (Carston ibid., 2000a, b). Second, both explicatures and implicatures of an utterance are seen as the output of the same pragmatic processes driven by the pursuit of relevance. This view is quite different from the standard view, taken, for example, by Grice, Levinson (2000) and Recanati (1989, 1993), in which the process of deriving an explicitly communicated proposition is distinct from that of deriving implicatures. According to Carston (ibid.), the only difference between explicature and implicature is derivational: explicatures are communicated propositions derived from both decoded information (the logical form) and inferences, whereas implicatures are communicated propositions derived from inferences alone. Typically, the standard view also assumes that explicature derivation precedes implicature derivation, and thereby, commits holders of this view to a sequential processing model. By contrast, a relevance-based comprehension model is not a sequential model: in relevance-driven processes, the implicature derivation may coincide with, precede, or follow, the explicature derivation, and the content of derived implicatures may affect the way explicatures are developed. In other words, a relevance-based comprehension model allows for parallel processing of explicatures and implicatures.

3.2 Bridging Inference as Implicated Premise

Sperber & Wilson (1986/95) claim that newly presented information is relevant if it improves one's belief, i.e. mental representation of the world. They go on to suggest that in the mind, new information is processed in a deductive device that yields a set of non-trivial implications. These non-trivial implications are standardly called 'implicatures' in pragmatics. However, Sperber & Wilson point out that some implicit assumptions are used as premises of deductive process rather than as a conclusion, and that it is equally important to include implicit assumptions which act as premises in the description of utterance understanding. Thus, they call an implicit assumption derived as the result of deduction an 'implicated conclusion', and an implicit assumption used as a premise of deduction to yield a conclusion an 'implicated premise'. In relevance theory, both types of implicit assumption are called 'implicature'. Both contribute to the relevance of an utterance, but they are qualitatively different in their contribution: while implicated conclusions directly yield cognitive effects, implicated premises are merely the means to bring about such effects, hence their contribution to the relevance of an utterance is rather indirect.

A bridging inference is regarded as an implicit premise in relevance theory. Typically, a bridging inference does not directly yield expected cognitive effects in its own right, but contributes to relevance by providing access to the intended explicature, which in turn yields cognitive effects. Recently, Wilson & Sperber (2000) and Carston (2000a) put forward schematic representations of a relevance-theoretic comprehension procedure. As they seem to be rather effective means to illustrate the details of the comprehension procedure, drawing on their approach, I will present a relevance-based comprehension model by using a simple conversational example below which involves the generation of a bridging inference. In particular, the illustration below provides a relevance-theoretic view of Peter's comprehension of Jane's second utterance in (1):

(1)   Peter: Did you enjoy the New Year's party at the Fairmont Hotel?
         Jane: No. The champagne was flat, and the music was awful.

Following Sperber & Wilson, I assume that new information communicated by an utterance is processed with a set of contextual assumptions intended by the speaker. In (1), it is assumed that the intended set of contextual assumptions, which are likely to have become highly accessible to Peter by the time he processes Jane's second utterance, includes the assumptions about the cerebration of the New Year and about a typical party, and most crucially, the assumption that Jane did not enjoy the New Year's party at the Fairmont Hotel, which was provided by the immediately preceding utterance. The last assumption may be considered as the trigger for the expectation of a particular cognitive effect generated in Peter's mind which is illustrated in (c) below. Note that no processing sequence is implied by the ordering of items in the illustration:

(a)   Jane has said to Peter "The champagne was flat, and the music was awful."
        [Linguistic decoding of Jane's utterance]
(b)   Jane's utterance is optimally relevant to Peter. [Presumption of relevance]
(c)   Jane's utterance achieves relevance by explaining why Jane didn't enjoy
        the New Year's party at the Fairmont Hotel.[Expectation of relevance
        raised by Jane's negative answer to Peter's question]
(d)   i. A party may involve the serving of champagne and the playing of music.
        ii. A good reason why someone may not enjoy a party is that the
        champagne served there is flat and the music played there is awful.
        [First accessible assumptions which might contribute to satisfying the
        expectation raised at (c). Accepted as *implicated premises* of Jane's
        utterance]
(e)   The New Year's party at the Fairmont Hotel involved the serving of
        champagne and the playing of music. [First accessible assumption which
        might combine with Mary's utterance to satisfy the expectation in (c).
        Accepted as an *implicated premise* of Jane's utterance]
(f)   The champagne served at the New Year's party at the Fairmont Hotel was
        flat and the music played there was awful. [First accessible *enrichment* of
        Jane's utterance which might combine with (dii) to satisfy the expectation
        of relevance in (c). Accepted as an *explicature* of Jane's utterance]
(g)   Jane didn't enjoy the New Year's party at the Fairmont Hotel because the
        champagne offered there was flat and the music played there was awful.
        [Inferred from (d), (e) and (f), and satisfying (c), and accepted as *an
        implicated conclusion* of Jane's utterance]
(h)   One shouldn't go to a New Year's party at the Fairmont Hotel in the
        future.
        [From (g) and background knowledge. One of several possible *weak
        implicatures* of Jane's utterance, which, together with (g) satisfy
        expectation (b)]

Notice here that a bridging inference is generated at (e), and is considered as an
'implicated premise' in this model. What is most significant in this processing model,
however, is that the derivation of bridging inference in (e) is complementary to the
derivation of another implicated premise in (dii) which is the assumption as to how
the utterance can achieve relevance. In other words, an expectation of particular
cognitive effects to be achieved by the utterance seems to have influenced generation
of the necessary bridging inference. It is worth pointing out here that in Levinson's
processing model, implicatures of the type illustrated by (dii) above are crucially
missing. This difference will also lead to different predictions about the processing of
anaphoric bridging implicatures.

3.3.   Expectation of Cognitive Effects and Assumption Schemata

In the illustration of the comprehension procedures presumably involved in fully
understanding Jane's second utterance above, it was taken for granted that Peter has
easy access to the assumption, or expectation, that her utterance will achieve
relevance by giving explanation for why Jane didn't enjoy the New Year's party at
the Fairmont Hotel. This, however, may raise several questions which require rather

careful consideration: Does the hearer *always* have an expectation of particular cognitive effects to be achieved by incoming utterances? Can such expectation of cognitive effects be strong or weak, and if so, what influences the strength of the expectation? Does the hearer expect one particular effect or several different effects for an incoming utterance?

There are several speculations one can make about these issues. For example, the hearer may not always have a strong expectation of particular cognitive effects to be achieved by an incoming utterance, as there are utterances which do not strongly discriminate the way the subsequent utterance may achieve relevance. However, recall here that relevance theory predicts that a good communicator and a good audience are more likely to exploit the fact that ostensive communication is relevance-based, rather than to ignore it. What follows from this are the following: (a) that it is natural for the speaker to formulate an utterance so that the hearer has easy access to the intended cognitive effects of the utterance; and (b) that it is natural for the hearer to infer the intended cognitive effects of the utterance at the earliest point possible.

Recently, Carston has offered an interesting discussion on this issue with regard to interpretation of juxtaposed utterances (Carston 1998:146-52) such as the following.

(2)   a. Max didn't go to school. He got sick.
        b. Max fell over. He slipped on a banana skin.
        c. Max can't read. He is a linguist.

Carston comments that the second utterances in (2) are understood as 'providing an explanation of some sort for the state of affairs described in the first, as if answering an implicit 'why?' or 'how come?' (146). It is striking that her comment is right even in the case of (2c), provided that we know well the fact that Max is a linguist is not an obvious explanation for his being poor at reading. Drawing on, for example, many psychological studies on text comprehension which suggest that causal inferences play the central role in understanding and remembering a text as a coherent whole, she concludes that this tendency to expect the explanation interpretation first for the second utterances in (2) stems from the organisational mechanism of our cognitive system: the mechanism 'requires that representation of individual states of affairs be embedded in a mesh of (broadly speaking) causal relations with other representation' (151). Relevant information for a cognitive system with such an organisational mechanism, therefore, is the information which can improve one's knowledge by being combined with other causally-linked representations in the system. She further speculates that our cognitive system may be equipped with some sort of assumption schemata (incomplete representations) ready to be filled/completed by relevant information. For example, she suggests that when we receive a new piece of information, P, typically, we construct an assumption schema, 'P because _____'. This assumption schema in turn creates the expectation that the missing information should be supplied.

While an explanation interpretation is seen as an answer to an 'implicit' question in the cases of the juxtaposed utterances discussed above, an assumption schema may be explicitly encoded in the case of wh—questions. In relevance theory, wh--questions have been analysed as an instance of assumption schema which (interpretively) represent missing information which the speaker considers relevant

(Sperber & Wilson 1988). For example, a 'why P?' question is understood as an assumption schema like 'P because _____'. Such an assumption schema is considered to indicate the expectation that an explanation of P would be relevant. On the other hand, yes-no questions are considered to express complete propositions for which confirmation or disconfirmation would be relevant. Note that this relevance-theoretic view of questions strongly suggests that questions are explicit ways of communicating the cognitive effects to be achieved by an incoming utterance. This, in turn, suggests that the person who asks a question is entitled to have rather strong expectation of particular cognitive effects to be achieved by the incoming utterance: namely, that it achieves relevance by providing an answer to his question. Later, I will return to these points when discussing the need to test these ideas.

4. Comparison: Levinson's GCI (Generalised Conversational Implicature) Model

The relevance-based model of the comprehension process illustrated above represents a clear contrast with the comprehension procedures envisaged in Levinson's neo-Gricean approach (Levinson 2000), which I call here the 'GCI model'. The GCI model differs from the relevance-based model in many ways, but here I will concentrate on the three following points. First, Levinson's model makes a sharp distinction between pragmatic processes of deriving the proposition expressed (i.e. explicature in relevance theory) and pragmatic processes of implicature derivation. As such, it commits to a theory of sequential processing rather than a theory of parallel processing as endorsed by relevance theory. Second, according to the GCI model, the initial, subpropositional, processes (our primary concern here), involve derivation of 'generalised conversational implicatures', which are context-independent, and hence, default, inferences based on streotypical assumptions stored in one's general knowledge. These are quite different from the inferences required to enrich the logical form to yield explicatures as envisaged in relevance theory. Relevance theory posits fully context-dependent, hence, non-default, inferences. Notice also that, being default inferences, generalised conversational implicature would be generated automatically across contexts, and would have to be cancelled when some contradiction arises during subsequent processing of the utterance. The third point is related to the second point: for Levinson, the derivation of generalised conversational implicatures is governed by default rules, and the derivation of particularised conversational implicatures, which are involved in post-propositional pragmatic processes, are governed by totally distinct rules. Here, the contrast with a relevance-based model, where both explicatures and implicatures are derived in the pursuit of relevance, is obvious.

Although bridging inferences are not the most typical GCIs (a prototypical GCI is scalar Q(Quantity)-implicature, which won't be discussed here), Levinson categorises them as examples of 'I(Informativeness)-implicature', which are inferences used to enrich the given information. I-implicatures are also characterized as 'minimum assumptions' to yield 'maximally informative' interpretation (Levinson 2000:183). Bridging inference is viewed as one of the prominent I-implicatures, required to preserve coherence when sentences are joined by parataxis (i.e. without being explicitly conjoined). The following are his examples of bridging I-implicature:

(3)   a. Harold bought an old car. The steering wheel was loose.
            I-implicature: The steering wheel of the car.
        b. Patience walked into the dining room. The French windows were open.
            I- implicature: The dining room had French windows.

Levinson says that typically, as in (3a) and (3b), the derivation of bridging I-implicaures is guided by stereotypical assumptions and highly accessible scripts or frames. He also suggests that even without such assumptions, bridging I-implicature can be derived (Levinson ibid. 127), although Levinson does not spell out exactly how it is derived. This at least indicates that there is more to his notion of 'minimal assumptions' than the accessibility of stereotypical assumptions. For the sake of argument, however, I will assume here that the existence of stereotypical assumptions is the necessary condition for derivation of bridging I-implicature.

5. Predictions of Two Pragmatic Models and Other Processing Models

Here, I will spell out concrete predictions regarding the derivation of bridging inferences which I believe follow from the assumptions of both pragmatic theories presented above. Let me start with relevance theory. As illustrated in Peter's comprehension procedure of Jane's second utterance above, relevance theory predicts that an expectation of particular cognitive effects influences the generation of implicated premises [(di) and (dii) in the illustration above] and that this is tested prior to, or concurrent with, the derivation of the bridging inference [(e) in the illustration], and that derivation of those two implicated premises [(di) and (dii)] precede or coincide with bridging reference assignment, which is part of the overall explicature construction. Thus, in the relevance-based comprehension model, the expectation of particular cognitive effects may constrain derivation of bridging inferences so that a bridging inference which contributes to deriving the expected cognitive effects will be generated.[1]

Levinson's GCI model, in contrast, predicts that when two juxtaposed utterances require a bridging inference, the most stereotypical one is always generated as a default, and 'tested' before finally being accepted or rejected. One of the reasons why I have chosen Levinson's GCI model as an alternative to a relevance-based model is

---

[1] One can take this position further and predict that a highly stereotypical bridging inference will not be generated if it will not be used as a premise in the deductive process. That is if the inference is not used to derive the intended implicature as a conclusion to yield the expected cognitive effects. However, the relevance-based model does not have to take this strong position, as it allows parallel activation of several competing assumptions, the most accessible one (in terms of both effort and effects) of which will be ultimately chosen. At the same time, it is also quite likely that even when such a highly accessible bridging inference is not used as a premise to derive the intended implicature, there may still be some sort of activation between the two (or more) semantically or encyclopaedically related concepts. If so, it will be an interesting challenge for the experimenter to come up with a way of distinguishing between such activation between closely related concepts and 'proper' bridging inferences in a relevance-theoretic sense which are generated and represented as the communicated proposition.

that the predictions his model makes are quite similar to other well-evidenced and widely-supported views on bridging inference in psycholinguistic research, and therefore, testing his predictions has wider implications. For example, Sanford & Garrod claim that subpropositional processing, which is the primary task of the language processor, is carried out via direct mapping between language input and background knowledge (Sanford & Garrod 1998). This direct mapping process is called 'primary processing'. It is automatic and rapid and is contrasted with more time-consuming 'secondary processing' which is only instigated after the primary processing fails (Sanford & Garrod 1981) (for a critical assessment of their approach, see Matsui 1998, 2000). Thus, both Levinson's model and Sanford & Garrod's model predict that when there is no obvious, stereotypical, route for mapping between linguistic input and background knowledge, the processor has to resort to secondary processing which is time-consuming.

To summarise, Levinson's model, as well as Sanford & Garrod's, envisages at least two possible stages in utterance processing: one is quick, automatic and default-based, and the other slow, conscious and strategy-based. This contrasts with a relevance-theoretic model, which claims that there is only a single overall "stage", which is quick, automatic and relevance-based. It seems that the major difference between the two models can be captured by two factors: first, the number of assumptions involved in constructing bridging implicature, and second, the expected time to construct bridging implicature. Recall that in the relevance-theoretic illustration of Peter's comprehension of Jane's second utterance in (1) above, the bridging implicature (e) had to be licensed by two other general assumptions, namely (di) and (dii). In Levinson's model, no such auxiliary assumptions are generated, and the bridging implicature alone is generated as the 'minimum' I-implicature. Hence, a relevance-theoretic model requires at least two more implicit assumptions in order to understand the second utterance in (1) than Levinson's. Generally, one may assume that the more assumptions are required to understand an utterance, the longer it takes to process it. However, the relevance-theoretic model predicts that no extra time is needed to understand the second utterance in (1). The question is how to test the prediction of the two models. In what follows, I will make some suggestions.

6. Testing the Predictions

Here, I will discuss the design of some of the experiments which Ray Gibbs and I have started in order to test predictions made by the two processing models discussed above. Although the experiments are still at the preliminary stage and the results are yet to be analysed fully, I will illustrate the expected experimental results according to the two contrasting models.

6.1. Testing the Effect of Expectation of Particular Cognitive Effects

Let us first consider one assumption in the relevance-based model which requires experimental scrutiny: namely, that the hearer tends to generate an expectation of particular cognitive effects to be achieved by an incoming utterance. Testing this assumption, which is completely ignored in the GCI model, is crucial in carrying out subsequent experiments to test the validity of relevance-theoretic predictions regarding the derivation of bridging inferences, since it is claimed that it is this expectation of particular cognitive effects that instigates a parallel explicature-implicature adjustment.

The best way to start testing the predicted effect of expectation of particular cognitive effect may be to observe the way answers to wh-questions are processed. If we adopt the view taken by Sperber & Wilson and Carston, which was briefly discussed above, a question is represented as an incomplete assumption schema in the speaker's mind which will be filled with the information provided by the relevant answer. An incomplete assumption schema then should be seen as being closely related to the strong expectation of particular cognitive effects. One can generalise that it is highly likely that the speaker who has asked a question has a very strong expectation of the cognitive effects to be achieved by what the hearer says next: namely, the relevant answer to his question. Compare the following two utterances both of which involve a classic example of bridging inference, namely, the beer was part of the picnic:

(4)   Mary: How was the picnic?
       John: The beer was warm.
(5)   John: I unpacked the picnic. The beer was warm.

It will be interesting to see if the comprehension of the utterance 'the beer was warm' is faster in (4) than (5), which would be the case if the relevance-theoretic view of questions are on the right track. Thus, our first experiment is designed to test this prediction by measuring the comprehension latency of two types of utterance pair such as (4) and (5), namely, the question-answer utterance pair and the narrative-utterance pair. If the expected difference in processing time is confirmed, it may be explained in terms of how highly accessible the implicature of each utterance is, which possibly facilitates explicature derivation as well as the overall interpretation process. Peter's utterance in (4), combined with other assumptions and Mary's expectation that Peter is providing an answer to her question, straightforwardly yields an implicature that the picnic was not totally successful (which provides an answer to Mary's question). By contrast, the second utterance in (5) does not seem to yield any strong implicature. Consequently, only in (4), the interpretation of the second utterance is likely to be facilitated by implicature/explicature adjustment. It is thus important to see if and when implicature is generated during reading for both types of utterance pair illustrated in (4) and (5). For this purpose, our first experiment includes a verification task in which subjects are asked questions, for example, "was the picnic successful?" for (4) and (5), and answers are assessed in terms of both latency and accuracy (see also Revlin & Hegarty 1999).

6.2. Bridging Implicature and Auxiliary Implicatures

The illustration of Peter's interpretation of Jane's second utterance in (1) shown above includes two implicated premises (di) and (dii) which support/warrant the bridging inference (e). These implicated premises are generated on the basis of what has been uttered, i.e. "the champagne was flat, and the music was awful", the given context, and the expectation of relevance raised by Jane's negative answer to Peter's question, namely, that Jane's utterance achieves relevance by explaining why Jane didn't enjoy the New Year's party at the Fairmont Hotel. In other words, the derivation of these implicated premises crucially depends on the existence of the expectation of this particular cognitive effect. Thus, by testing if the reader generates during comprehension an implicated premise such as (dii) in the illustration above, we may be able to confirm/disconfirm that the expectation of a particular cognitive effect which leads to the derivation of such implicated premises was actually raised or not. Thus, our first experiment also includes verification tasks in which subjects are asked to read statements such as "if the beer is warm, the picnic is not a success" and to choose whether they agree or disagree. A relevance-theoretic model predicts higher accuracy and shorter latency for the question-answer utterance pair than for the narrative-utterance pair. According to Levinson's GCI model, there are no auxiliary implicatures such as (di) and (dii) which lead to the bridging implicature such as (e), hence it should predict equally longer latency for both two types of utterance pair.

6.3. Bridging Cases with No Obvious Stereotypical Assumptions Available

Compare the following with (4) and (5):

(6)   Mary: How was the job interview?
        John: The beer was warm.
(7)   John: I had a job interview. The beer was warm.

Arguably, (6) and (7) are a less likely variation of (4) and (5). The crucial difference between (4) and (6), and (5) and (7), respectively, lies in the strength of association between the concept referred to by the bridging reference (i.e. 'beer') and another concept to be linked with it via bridging inference (i.e. 'picnic' or 'job interview'). While the relationship between 'picnic' and 'beer' is rather strong for most people, the connection between 'job interview' and 'beer' is extremely weak. As most existing accounts of utterance comprehension would predict, both the relevance-theoretic model and the GCI model predict that it will take longer to process (6) and (7) than (4) and (5) respectively. However, the predictions differ on another point concerning the related (i.e. (4) and (5)) and the unrelated (i.e. (6) and (7)) set. The GCI model predicts that there will be equal increase in comprehension latency for (6) and (7) in comparison with (4) and (5). The relevance-theoretic model, on the other hand, predicts that the increase in comprehension latency for (6) will be smaller than for (7). In other words, this model predicts that the influence of the weak connection of the two concepts linked via a bridging inference is relatively small in the question-answer utterance pairs. This would be explained along the following lines: the effect of the expectation of particular cognitive effect raised in the question-answer utterance pairs including (7) is strong enough to enable the hearer to construct the required bridging inference, e.g. 'the beer was offered during the job interview' for (7), even when the relation between the two concepts linked via such an inference is distant. In order to test the two predictions, the comprehension latency for the unrelated set including (6) and (7) are measured, and compared with the latency for the related set including (4) and (5).

6.4. Cases with Two Potential Bridging Inferences

Finally, let me discuss another experiment which we are currently planning. It involves examples where potentially more than one bridging inference can be made, one of which is stereotypical and the other much less so (Matsui 2000) as illustrated in (8) and (9). The pertinent questions are: which the two bridging inferences is chosen by the hearer, and why. An answer to the 'which' question is provided in Matsui (ibid.), where the results of an off-line experiment involving the utterance pairs such as (8) and (9) are reported. In the experiment, the subjects' final interpretation of the second utterance was elicited, and 100 percent of the subjects opted for the final interpretation which requires a non-stereotypical bridging inference, despite their judgment (which was also elicited) that the bridging inference is much less stereotypical than the more stereotypical alternative:

(8)   Mary moved from Brixton to St. John's Wood. The rent was less expensive. (NB. St. John's Wood is a upper-class residential area in London, and Brixton is the direct opposite)

Stereotypical bridging inference: The rent in Brixton is less expensive than that in St. John's Wood.
Non-stereotypical bridging inference: The rent in St. John's Wood is less expensive than that in Brixton.

(9)   I prefer the restaurant on the corner to the student canteen. The cappuccino is less expensive.

Stereotypical bridging inference: The cappuccino in the student canteen is less expensive than that in the restaurant on the corner.
Non-stereotypical bridging inference: The cappuccino in the restaurant on the corner is less expensive than that in the student canteen.

Notice that the GCI model would predict that for examples such as (8) and (9), the most stereotypical possibility should always be tested first, and accepted unless there is obvious conflict raised by the bridging inference in a later processing phase. Also, it seems reasonable to assume that the model predicts that the other, non-default, bridging inference, will be generated and tested only after the default option fails. Thus, this model predicts substantially longer latency for examples such as (8) and (9). By contrast, the relevance-based model predicts that the one which contributes to derivation of intended implicature will be tested first, independent of consideration of degree of stereotypicality, and that therefore such interpretations would require no extra processing time. The results of Matsui's off-line experiment indicate that it is possible that both bridging inferences are generated and tested in parallel, and that one was subsequently suppressed. However, this point remains to be tested by further on-line experiments.

7. Final Remarks

Critics have charged that relevance theory is an unfalsifiable theory. In this paper, as the title suggests, I have tried to move us towards a specific experimental paradigm that would permit testing claims made by relevance theory about processing of anaphoric bridging inferences. The work, of course, remains to be completed, but I hope that the present discussion helps further my ultimate goal of firmly placing relevance theory in the domain of cognitive science.

References

1. Bach, K. Conversational impliciture. *Mind and Language* 9, 124-162. 1994.
2. Carston, R. Implicature, explicature and truth-theoretic semantics. R. Kempson (ed.), *Mental Representations*. Cambridge: Cambridge University Press. 1988.
3. Carston, R. *Pragmatics and the Explicit-Implicit Distinction*. PhD thesis, University College London. 1998.
4. Carston, R. Cognitive pragmatics and explicit communication. Paper given at Mind & Language Pragmatics and Cognitive Science Workshop, Oxford. 2000a.
5. Carston, R. Explicature and semantics. *UCL Working Papers in Linguistics* 12, 1-44. 2000b.
6. Clark, H. Bridging. P. Wason & P. Johnson-Laird (eds), *Thinking: Readings in Cognitive Science*, 411-420. Cambridge: Cambridge University Press. 1977.
7. Gibbs, R. *The Poetics of Mind*. Cambridge: Cambridge University Press. 1994.
8. Gibbs, R. & Moise, J. Pragmatics in understanding what is said. *Cognition* 62, 51-74. 1997.
9. Grice, H. P. Logic and conversation. P. Cole & J. Morgan (eds), *Syntax and Semantics 3: Speech Acts*, 41-58. New York: Academic Press. 1975.
10. Levinson, S. *Presumptive Meaning*. Cambridge, Mass: The MIT Press. 2000.
11. Matsui, T. Pragmatic criteria for reference assignment: A relevance-theoretic account of the acceptability of bridging. *Pragmatics and Cognition* 6 (1/2): 47-97. 1998.
12. Matsui, T. *Bridging and Relevance*. Amsterdam: John Benjamins. 2000.
13. Recanati, F. The pragmatics of what is said. *Mind and Language* 4, 295-329. 1989.
14. Recanati, F. *Direct Reference: From Language to Thought*. Oxford: Blackwell. 1993.
15. Revlin, R. & Hegarty, M. Resolving signals to cohesion: two models of bridging inference. *Discourse Processes* 27/1, 77-102. 1999.
16. Sanford, A. & Garrod, S. *Understanding Written Language*. Chichester: John Wiley. 1981.
17. Sanford, A. & Garrod, S. The role of scenario mapping in text comprehension. *Discourse Processes* 26(2&3), 159-190. 1998.
18. Sperber, D. & Wilson, D. *Relevance: Communication and Cognition*. Oxford: Blackwell. 1986/95.
19. Wilson, D. & Matsui, T. Recent approaches to bridging: truth, coherence, and relevance. *UCL Working Papers in Linguistics* 10: 173-200. 1998.
20. Wilson, D. & Sperber, D. Mood and the analysis of non-declarative sentences. J. Darcy, J. Moravcsik & C. Taylor (eds), *Human Agency: Language, Duty and Value*, 77-101. Stanford, CA: Stanford University Press. 1988.
21. Wilson, D. & Sperber, D. Truthfulness and relevance. *UCL Working Papers in Linguistics* 12, 215-254. 2000.

Workflow Context as a Means for Intelligent Information Support

Heiko Maus

German Research Center for Artificial Intelligence
– DFKI GmbH –
P.O.Box 2080, 67608 Kaiserslautern, Germany
Heiko.Maus@dfki.de

Abstract. The paper presents Workflow Management Systems (WfMS) as valuable information sources for context information for accomplishing intelligent information support. First, the main advantages of WfMS for retrieving context are presented. Two projects from our research department show different approaches for retrieving workflow context and enabling an intelligent information support. However, they have to cope with the absence of a comprehensive representation concept for workflow context in WfMS. To overcome this, this paper presents a comprehensive classification scheme for workflow context.

1 Introduction

Systems supporting users in their daily work are becoming more and more important. There are several different approaches for information support, starting from simple web-based search engines with keyword search; continuing with systems using task-models for anticipating a user's actions and inferring relevant information [6]; up to approaches using context information from processes the user is involved in order to deliver relevant information.

In the case of business processes, a good starting point would be to consider Workflow Management Systems (WfMS) as information sources. WfMS automate processes according to process models, which define a process' activities, their order, under which conditions and when they will be carried out, by whom in the organization, with which tools, and define the 'flow' of data within the process (see [8, 11]). A popular description is: *Workflows deliver the right data to the right people with the right tools at the right time.*

Because of this, WfMS seem to provide an ideal environment to retrieve a user's process context in order to deliver relevant information, thus, enabling an intelligent information support. However, which kind of context information can be delivered depends highly on the properties of the used WfMS. Unfortunately, most (commercial) WfMS do not provide such an ideal environment.

In the following, the potentials of WfMS as context providers for intelligent information support are discussed. First, the main advantages of WfMS for retrieving context are presented, including the drawbacks of current (commercial) systems. Two projects from our research department show different approaches for retrieving workflow context (for a detailed comparison see [3]). After that, a comprehensive classification scheme for workflow context will be presented. An overview of related work and a summary conclude this paper.

2   WfMS as Source for Workflow Context

Driven by discussions about context, its nature and content, e.g., at the 2000 AAAI Spring Symposium [18], and by different notions of context depending on the application domain and its usage, this paper will give insight to the notion of workflow context as we use it at our research department. As already mentioned, WfMS provide an ideal environment for retrieving workflow context. This chapter addresses the properties of WfMS which contribute to workflow context, and also points out the limitations of current WfMS. However, this section should not be an introduction to workflow management, but rather give an overview of the valuable information sources for context which a WfMS provides. It is guided by a common understanding of workflow management as expressed by the standardisation efforts of the Workflow Management Coalition (WfMC)[1] [23] and several publications such as [8, 11].

Having a closer look on the architecture of WfMS, several sources can be found for comprising workflow context:

The *process model* or *workflow (process) definition*, specifies the constituents of the workflow. The workflow engine enacts a workflow instance according to this specification. The process model defines what, when, how, by whom, and with which data work has to be done. It consists of several objects:

- *Workflow activities* define how the work is actually done, e.g., by instructing the user or by invoking an application.
- The *control flow* defines the sequence of activity execution. Depending on the specific WfMS, several control constructs are available such as decision, alternative, parallelism, loops, start/exit conditions, or different kinds of constraints such as deadlines.
- The *data flow* specifies how data 'flows' through the workflow. Depending on the WfMS, different concepts exist such as input/output-container of activities or local/global variables.

The WfMC distinguishes in its glossary [23] three types of data:

workflow control data: *Data that is managed by the WfMS and/or a Workflow Engine. Such data is internal to the WfMS and is not normally accessible to applications.* Nevertheless, data such as instance or activity ids are usually accessible.

---

[1] the WfMC is a union of workflow vendors and institutions with the goal to provide standards for workflow management, www.wfmc.org

workflow relevant data: *Data that is used by a WfMS to determine the state transitions of a workflow instance, for example within pre- and post-conditions, transition conditions or workflow participant assignment.* Furthermore, this data can be *typed*, then the structure of the data is implied by its type and a WfMS will understand its structure and may be able to process it; and *untyped* - the WfMS will not understand the data structure, but may pass the data to applications.

application data: *Data that is application specific and not accessible by the WfMS.*

The *organizational model* represents the structure of an organization for declaring who actually should execute an activity. Again, depending on the WfMS, this ranges from rather simple models such as groups of users (Staffware[2]) up to complex ones with users, roles, competencies, occupation, resources, organizational hierarchy and enhanced declaration of potential workflow participants (WorkParty [16]).

The *audit data* represents the history of every workflow instance such as its execution log, state changes, or data changes. The audit data is an important archive for logging, performance analysis, or even legal purposes.

Considering intelligent information support, some concepts of workflow management are also worth to mention: Due to the process automation, workflows allow for invoking external applications. They provide access structures via APIs, data exchange, and even the possibility to access the workflow engine from external applications, requesting status information or control the workflow enactment. Thus, the WfMS also supports the task of information support by providing integration, monitoring, and manipulation capabilities.

Further, Jablonski et al. present in [8] *causality* originating from coordination theory, as a perspective worth considering in workflows, although it is not assumed essential for their workflow model. Nevertheless, causalities expressed by goals, business rules, and enterprise strategies are a valuable source for anticipating a user's behaviour or for providing information material. Therefore, causality should be considered in WfMS for intelligent information support.

Limitations with Respect to Workflow Context. Despite the existence of these various information sources, today's WfMS do not have a comprehensive representation concept for workflow context (see also [15]) and a convenient access of workflow context during runtime is not available. Therefore, one has to consider all information sources to retrieve context separately. Unfortunately, the capabilities mentioned only represent an ideal WfMS. Most of the WfMS do not provide the majority of the properties conveniently (at least from the point of view of intelligent information support). That means, some components have limited functionality as, for example, the audit data which logs only very coarse grained (e.g., start and finish of activities). Moreover, process models are often not very expressive to external applications, for instance, they only specify

---

[2] www.staffware.com

the control flow and a technical description of the activities to be performed, but do not provide the semantics of an activity. Therefore, an information need, necessary for information support, is hardly ever represented

To summarize, most (commercial) WfMS are not very helpful for the task of intelligent information support. But, it seems to improve due to demands resulting from introducing WfMS in heterogenous environments which require at least some powerful API. Furthermore, many research activities address limitations of WfMS (e.g., [8][7])

Considering research, a solution for intelligent information support should be generic, i.e., not depend on any specific WfMS. Despite the standardisation efforts of the WfMC, most vendors stay with their definition of workflow, their meta-models, architectures and API. Therefore, approaches trying to use context from workflows have to face several issues:

- generic vs. specific approach
- adapt workflow meta-models vs. no adaption, merely provide an add-on
- use commercial WfMS vs. research prototype

The following projects, which were conducted at our research center, show different approaches. Whereas *VirtualOffice* pursued a generic solution and considered only commercial WfMS, i.e., there is no chance to change any components, *KnowMore* built a new WfMS based on the WfMC standards, but enhanced it with concepts needed for intelligent information support.

3 *VirtualOffice* : **Workflow Context for Document Analysis and Understanding**

The DFKI project *VirtualOffice* had the goal to enhance document analysis and understanding (DAU) which deals with text recognition and information extraction from (paper) documents. DAU presents itself as a knowledge-intensive application when considering the information need of involved analysis tasks and the complexity of some application domains. Therefore, DAU systems started to also use external databases such as an address database for address verification. In addition, *VirtualOffice* pursued a comprehensive approach which considers all background knowledge on a document to be analysed. This knowledge can be found in a company's business processes, therefore, a generic integration into WfMS was accomplished.

The *VirtualOffice*-Scenario. As stated in [4], the efficiency of DAU will be significantly increased by using context information from business processes in which the documents to be analysed occur. A perfect domain for using context information is the one of business letters, which incorporates, for instance, different documents with different formats such as forms or free-form letters, with references to previous letters, open processes, or related persons. This domain distinguishes itself as having structured processes such as purchasing processes

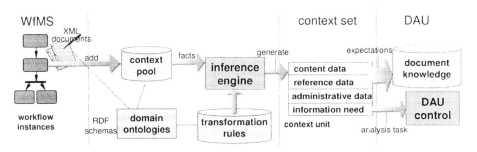

Fig. 1. Steps to retrieve context from workflows.

with their correspondence of orders, invoices, reminders, etc. These processes are ideal for automation by workflow management. Additionally, DAU is introduced into company's business processes placed in the business letter domain. Hence, with an integration of both systems context information from workflows is available for supporting DAU. Because a DAU system consists of several components, each having special tasks in the overall analysis process, the components benefit from the provided context by increasing their efficiency and precision. For example, the logo recogniser can reduce its search space to those logos of companies mentioned in the context. Moreover, the pattern matching component recognises text phrases and formulations typical for distinct message types in order to classify the document and to extract the contained information. Here, by knowing which names of clerks will be mentioned in which message types, the precision can be increased and the task contributes to a identification of the corresponding workflow instance [21]. For detailed information about the *VirtualOffice* project, the interested reader may refer to [22, 12].

Retrieving Context from Workflows. The retrieval of workflow context is split into two major steps, namely context collection within workflows and context transformation into context units and storage in the context set. These steps are shown in figure 1.

As mentioned, WfMS provide several sources which allow for the collection of context information. Because *VirtualOffice* is supposed to provide a generic integration into WfMS independent of any proprietary extension to the workflow model, *VirtualOffice* has to deal with the absence of a concept for workflow context. Therefore, the so-called *context pool* is introduced, a database where all valuable context information considered relevant can be collected throughout the workflow execution. This ranges from single information items such as a database reference to a supplier address, up to references to involved documents such as the order. Technically, if a WfMS does not allow access to all relevant information when needed (i.e., a context unit has to be generated), then special activities are modelled in the workflow definition storing relevant information in the context pool. Thus, the context pool also serves as an archive which guarantees the availability of workflow context when needed.

Now, in case an event occurs in the workflow which will cause a response by a document (e.g., sending an order and waiting for the invoice), i.e., the workflow is waiting for a specific document, the DAU has to be informed. Therefore, the workflow states its expectation by generating a context unit. A context unit is generated by an inference step which uses transformation rules and the context pool as a fact base. The task of these rules is twofold: First, they derive from the available workflow context a description of the expected document. Second, they accomplish a mapping between domain ontologies used in the WfMS and the DAU's domain ontology, represented by the document knowledge. The created context unit is stored in the context set. Given this, the resulting context is more than only a collection of available information, it is rather context tailored for DAU purposes.

If a document arrives in the company's in-box, the DAU performs a process identification whereby it takes into account all expectations of all workflow instances. Once a matching expectation is found, all requested information pieces are extracted and the document is assigned to the workflow instance stated in the context unit.

Workflow Context in *VirtualOffice*. The necessary context information for DAU consists of a description of the document to be analysed. But, it also includes information related to the originating workflow such as id or information need. Considering this, we get a definition for workflow context for DAU purposes used in *VirtualOffice* : *Workflow context includes all data related to a document with relevance to DAU and data required for the integration into the WfMS.*

Given this definition, a context unit consists of:

content data: includes everything known about the expected document such as sender (which can be inferred form the outgoing document's recipient), file number, or product list.

reference data: includes everything which could be referenced within the expected document, such as writing date of the outgoing order, responsible clerks, and the order number.

Both represent context information for DAU purposes and are handed over as so-called *expectations* to the document knowledge. An expectation states content and meaning of an expected document. The DAU uses expectations within several analysis strategies: they range from a closed world assumption restricting the DAU components only to consider expectations (i.e., only results which instantiate expectations are produced), up to the generation of both, results based on expectations and results based on more general concepts from the business letter domain at the same time.

And finally, a context unit consists of:

administrative data: used for the WfMS integration, consisting of data such as workflow instance id, or the event to trigger in the workflow in case the expected document had been assigned.

information need: it states the information the workflow needs from the document for further processing, e.g., as a list of information items to be extracted. From this the DAU dynamically infers its analysis task (i.e., it does not need to extract everything).

Besides using dynamic context from workflows, also more static context is used: so-called *standard context units*. These units serve two purposes: First, they describe documents not expected by a specific workflow instance such as adverts. Second, they serve as an exception handling: If there is no match between an incoming document and any context unit from the WfMS, a standard context unit is the default match (e.g., for documents of type 'invoice') and it defines the default handling, e.g., instantiation of a specific workflow definition.

VirtualOffice uses several sources for arranging its workflow context:

workflow control data: such as workflow instance id and activity id, to link a context unit to the specific instance and activity which stated it.

workflow relevant data: to fill the context pool with relevant information.

application data: also provides valuable information, e.g., the recipient's address entered into a text processor. Must also be stored in the context pool.

workflow definition: The name of a workflow definition to instantiate, in case a document had been assigned to a standard context unit.
The name of an event to trigger in case the expected document is assigned.

organizational model: is used to retrieve user-specific information which could occur in a document such as the telephone number. Furthermore, can also be used in standard context units to assign documents directly to users, roles, or departments instead of instantiating a workflow definition.

information need: the information need of an activity is explicitly modelled as a list of information items needed from the document, the DAU has to extract this information. These items correspond to a domain ontology.

4 *KnowMore* : Information Support for Knowledge-intensive Tasks

In contrast to *VirtualOffice*, the approach of the DFKI project *KnowMore* (Knowledge Management for Learning Organizations) aims at the support of workflow participants dealing with knowledge-intensive tasks (kiT). With the help of workflow context, *KnowMore* retrieves relevant knowledge from an *organizational memory* (OM). This OM combines a company's information sources. The contents of these sources are modelled using formal ontologies describing conceptual knowledge.

The *KnowMore* -Scenario. The information support in *KnowMore* is a proactive (i.e., without explicit request from the user), context-sensitive delivery of relevant information. More detailed, if a workflow participant has to perform an activity which involves a kiT, the workflow engine invokes an information

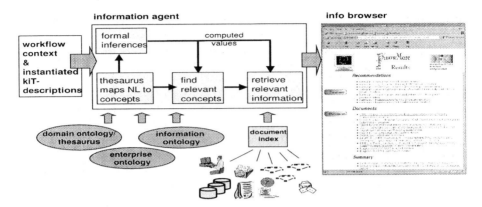

Fig. 2. *KnowMore*: Information Support using Workflow Context.

agent in the background. Given a *kiT-description* and the corresponding context from the workflow activity, the agent accomplishes an extended, ontology-based information retrieval to satisfy the user's information need by presenting relevant information (see figure 2). The information provided includes everything relevant from the company's organizational memory such as problem-related documents, best practice reports, or emails from intranet discussion forums. Furthermore, references to previous workflow instances with the same problem and involved documents or information pieces. And finally, references to users involved in these workflows, or with experience because of their profile. A webpage is presented which lists links to all found information grouped by categories.

The OM considered in *KnowMore* contain a variety of knowledge and information sources to be searched and retrieved for information support. These sources are of different nature, resulting in different structures, access methods, and contents. To enable precise-content retrieval from heterogeneous sources, a representation scheme for uniform knowledge descriptions is needed. To this end, structure and metadata, information content, and information context are modelled on the basis of formal ontologies [2]. *KnowMore* uses three types of ontologies, namely

domain ontology: contains the concepts used to model the contents of information sources.

enterprise ontology: comprises the concepts used in WfMS; it is based upon the ADONIS meta-model [9] and close to the notions of the WfMC [23].

information ontology: describes the different kinds of information sources with their respective structure, access, and format properties. Furthermore, it contains generic concepts such as author, or statement types.

Retrieving Context from Workflows. In order to provide a pro-active information support, *KnowMore* uses an extended workflow model supporting information agents. The kiT-descriptions extend the conventional definition of a workflow activity with a support specification. It specifies the information need as generic queries together with the responsible information agent. During runtime, the agent delivers relevant information by instantiating the queries.

In order to instantiate the queries with current context, the agent must have access to workflow context suitable for the necessary reasoning for intelligent retrieval. But, as mentioned earlier, this goes beyond what is modelled in a conventional workflow definition. Hence, *KnowMore* introduces *kiT-variables* which are embedded into a domain ontology (i.e., their values must be of types defined as ontology concepts). The kiT-variables extend a workflow's data flow and represent the relevant context of the knowledge-intensive tasks at runtime.

Because of this, one can say that the kiT-variables extend the conventional data flow to an *information flow* which incorporates information pieces necessary for information retrieval. That means, the concept of workflow context is introduced by explicitly modelling the desired context in the information flow.

KnowMore also uses context-aware storage, whenever a workflow activity results in the creation of an information item worth preserving, an agent retrieves the current workflow context from all available sources such as workflow control data. Then, this context is stored in the document index and linked to the information piece to enable a context-aware retrieval later on.

Workflow Context in *KnowMore.* *KnowMore* uses several sources for its workflow context for intelligent information support, namely

workflow control data: such as workflow instance id, activity id, and current user, to link an information piece (e.g., a document) to the specific instance and activity where it was created. Furthermore, it is used within the information retrieval, e.g., to retrieve the workflow participant's profile.

workflow relevant data: *KnowMore* introduces kiT-variables to provide the necessary context to instantiate the generic queries.

application data: specific agents observe applications used in the workflow such as forms and, for instance, try to propose data to be filled in.

workflow definition: use of workflow definition and activity ids, to link information pieces to them. This allows for proposing related material to all instances of these definitions or activities. Moreover, activities are extended by kiT-descriptions.

audit data: used to find other workflow instances or activities with comparable kiT-descriptions

organizational model: workflow participants have competencies, interest profiles, and are part of the organizational model with its department and project hierarchies, therefore, a user-specific view on a workflow instance can be derived.

5 A Classification Scheme for Workflow Context

Due to the absence of a comprehensive concept for workflow context, the presented projects introduced their own solutions for retrieving workflow context. However, both use available WfMS sources.

The DFKI follow-up project *Frodo* (Framework for Distributed Organizational Memories, [1]) pursues – among other things – a workflow support for knowledge work. Therefore, a new WfMS will be designed which will allow us to overcome the limitations of current WfMS also with respect to workflow context (the vision is given in [17]).

Given all the limitations, the different architectures, and understanding of workflow, *Frodo* needs as a starting point a generic and extensible approach for classifying workflow context. In the following, a workflow modelling methodology will be presented, which will serve as a basis for the classification scheme.

Perspective-oriented Workflow Modelling. Jablonski et al. propose in [8] a comprehensive workflow model based on perspectives used in information system development. As a continuation, Stein proposes in [19] the corresponding methodology for developing workflow applications. These perspectives originate from methodologies of different research areas, such as business management, enterprise modelling and architecture, software process modelling, and coordination theory. The identified perspectives which are basic for the workflow model are in detail: function, behaviour, organization, information, and operation. Furthermore, but not assumed basic, history and causality. Additionally, several perspectives concerning more technical issues such as security or integrity. The different perspectives are used in the analysis and implementation phase of the workflow management application. This can be easily done, because the components of the proposed WfMS address each of these perspectives.

Workflow Context as Design Concept for WfMS. Considering the aforementioned basic perspectives including history and causality as dimensions, the required classification scheme can be derived. The resulting workflow context space is shown in figure 3 along with the properties of WfMS identified in chapter 2. Taking the perspectives as dimensions of the workflow context space provides several benefits:

- workflow context is embedded in a methodology and can be considered right from the beginning of system design.
- the specific WfMS components are responsible for different perspectives, thus, contributing to the respective dimension in the workflow context space.
- different agents need different parts of workflow context, thus, agents can easily specify the desired workflow context dimensions, therefore, enabling a more precise context delivery.
- as well as the methodology, the workflow context space stays extensible. If new perspectives are becoming important in the system, they can also be added to the workflow context space.
- the same holds the other way around: the workflow context space can be tailored to the perspectives of a specific WfMS.

Fig. 3. The Dimensions of the Workflow Context Space.

The presented workflow context space serves as guideline for *Frodo* to consider in the WfMS architecture. That means, to enable workflow context for intelligent information support, the workflow context space will be represented as a formal ontology along with the relations to the specific components of the WfMS. Thus, all information sources of the WfMS are also accessible via the workflow context space. Furthermore, these sources will be semantically enriched by using formal ontologies. For example, the workflow definition will be represented using RDF (resource description framework[3]). RDF allows for expressing properties of resources, their relationships, and defining standardised models of meta-data, i.e., provides means for representing formal ontologies.

Based on this, the workflow definition can be used, e.g., to infer goals of the workflow participants. Moreover, workflow activities will be grounded in an ontology consisting of concepts describing generic tasks, thus, the activities will have some kind of semantics for external applications. Furthermore, *Frodo* now fully introduces the information flow concept of *KnowMore*. Given these properties, the audit data repository will be a valuable source for all kinds of information retrieval and for offering context information on a task based on previous workflow instances.

Furthermore, *Frodo* introduces a comprehensive organizational model for integration into OM, with user and role profiles, consisting of skills, experience (level of prior knowledge about a topic), and interests. These ideas are detailed in [20]. Given this, workflow context can be enriched by user-specific views on workflow instances. We believe that the *Frodo* WfMS will profit from this comprehensive model of workflow context.

6 Related work

Information Support. The Watson-system [6] is an example for a *Information Management Assistant (IMA)* which observes users interacting with applications and then anticipates their information needs using a task model. The Watson-system then retrieves documents from the internet by specifying detailed queries.

---

[3] www.w3c.org/RDF

Such systems could benefit from workflow context which provides an explicit process model with a user's tasks and goals. And vice versa, instead of modelling the information need during workflow design-time, as done in *VirtualOffice*, it could also be dynamically inferred by such IMA.

The COI IntelliDoc-system [5] provides an integration of document analysis and their WfMS BusinessFlow. In contrast to *VirtualOffice*, no dynamic workflow context is used, but keywords occurring in specific document types. According to these keywords, documents are routed to the specified in-boxes/worklists (*VirtualOffice* achieves this with the standard context units).

Context from Workflows. WoMIS (Workflow Memory Information System) [7] links the WfMS CSE Workflow with a web-based information system. It organizes documents involved in the workflows, as well as supporting material (recommendations, best practice reports,...), and information on the workflow model-level (e.g., discussion about workflow definitions) in so-called *contexts*. A context is a tree-structure relating all involved workflow objects to information pieces such as reports about a customer to the workflow instance dealing with her credit request. The user can browse from his worklist through these contexts. New documents are manually inserted into contexts.

Context in Organizational Memories. Klemke provides in [10] a context framework for OM in order to identify, store, and retrieve information within OM according to context models. Therefore, he introduces a context agent which observes the user's current context. In case this context changes (context shift) the agent contacts a context service to retrieve relevant information according to the new context. In his context typology, he identifies three main dimensions: physical, personal, domain/content-based, and organizational. Because processes are a part of of the organizational dimension, workflow context would fit into this typology and provide additional information for other dimensions.

Context. As a representative for related work on context, we refer to Pomerol et al. who define in [14] *contextual knowledge* as "all the knowledge which is relevant for one person in a given situated decision problem and which can be mobilized to understand this problem and explain the choice of a given action." The rest of the context is called *external knowledge*. Further, they define *proceduralized context* as the proceduralized part of the contextual knowledge which has been invoked, structured, and situated according to a given focus. The proceduralization is triggered by an event which focused the attention of the user on parts of the contextual knowledge.

Comparing the *VirtualOffice*-scenario with this definition, one can say that external knowledge becomes contextual knowledge if inserted into the context pool. The context units represent parts of the contextual knowledge, because only these parts can be 'mobilized'. An event which will cause a response triggers the proceduralization (done by the inference engine) of parts of the context pool to expectations. Thus, expectations are the representation of the proceduralized context for DAU purposes.

The scenario described by Pomerol et al. is close to the one of *KnowMore*, because both are user centered. In *KnowMore*, contextual knowledge is available in the organizational memory. The generic kiT-descriptions together with the kiT-variables provide a means to obtain the necessary proceduralized context. Their instantiation and the following information retrieval represent the proceduralization. Its result is proceduralized context because the user is supported with context information relevant in her current situation.

7 Conclusion

Workflow management systems automate a company's business processes. In order to achieve this, the processes have to be modelled including tasks, business rules, data, users, and applications. Because workflows are the place where a company's work is done, they are subject to various additional services such as information support. The paper pointed out that a WfMS's environment is a valuable information source and showed different components contributing to workflow context.

Two projects conducted in our research department showed in different approaches, that – although not supported by WfMS – workflow context is a reasonable concept and a valuable source for enabling intelligent information support.

However, current WfMS neither have a comprehensive representation concept for context, nor do they provide convenient access structures. Therefore, the paper presented a comprehensive approach for workflow context which builds the basis for a new WfMS designed to support knowledge work. This WfMS is supposed to overcome the limitations of current WfMS and to provide several concepts to enable workflow context as a means for intelligent information support.

Acknowledgment. This work was supported by the German Ministry for Education and Research, bmb+f (Grant: 01 IW 901, FRODO: A Framework for Distributed Organizational Memories).

References

1. A. Abecker, A. Bernardi, A. Dengel, L. van Elst, M. Malburg, M. Sintek, S. Tabor, A. Weigel, and C. Wenzel. FRODO: A Framework for Distributed Organizational Memories. Project Proposal, DFKI GmbH Kaiserslautern, 2000. URL http://www.dfki.uni-kl.de/frodo/.
2. A. Abecker, A. Bernardi, K. Hinkelmann, O. Kühn, and M. Sintek. Toward a Technology for Organizational Memories. *IEEE Intelligent Systems*, June 1998.
3. A. Abecker, A. Bernardi, H. Maus, M. Sintek, and C. Wenzel. Information Supply for Business Processes – Coupling Workflow with Document Analysis and Information Retrieval. *Knowledge-Based Systems, Special Issue on AI in Knowledge Management, Elsevier*, 13(5), 2000.
4. S. Baumann, M. Ben Hadj Ali, A. Dengel, T. Jäger, M. Malburg, A. Weigel, and C. Wenzel. Message extraction from printed documents - a complete solution. In *4th Int. Conf. on Document Analysis and Recognition (ICDAR 97), Ulm, Germany, August 18-20*, 1997.
5. R. Bleisinger, M. Müller, P. Hartmann, and T. Dörstling. Intelligente Eingangspostverarbeitung mit wissensbasierter Dokumentanalyse. *Wirtschaftsinformatik*, (8), 1999.

6. J. Budzik and K.J. Hammond. User interactions with everyday applications as context for just-in-time information access. In *Proc. of Intelligent User Interfaces 2000*. ACM Press, 2000.
7. Th. Goesmann and M. Hoffmann. Unterstützung wissensintensiver Geschäftsprozesse durch Workflow-Management-Systeme. In *DCSCW 2000*. Springer, 2000.
8. S. Jablonski and Ch. Bussler. *Workflow Management. Modeling Concepts, Architecture and Implementation*. International Thomson Computer Press, 1996.
9. D. Karagiannis, St. Junginger, and R. Strobl. Introduction to Business Process Management Systems Concepts. In B. Scholz-Reuter et al., editors, *Business Process Management*, LNCS. Springer, 1996.
10. R. Klemke. Context Framework - an Open Approach to Enhance Organisational Memory Systems with Context Modelling Techniques. In *PAKM-00: Practical Aspects of Knowledge Management. Proc. 3rd Int. Conf., Basel, Switzerland*, 2000.
11. F. Leymann and D. Roller. *Production Workflow - Concepts and Techniques*. Prentice Hall PTR, Upper Saddle River, New Jersey, 2000.
12. H. Maus. Towards a functional integration of document analysis in workflow management systems. In R. Becker and M. zur Mühlen, editors, *Workflow Based Applications, Proc. of Workflow Management '99, Münster, Germany*, 1999.
13. H.-J. Müller, A. Abecker, K. Hinkelmann, and H. Maus, editors. *Workshop 'Geschäftsprozeßorientiertes Wissensmanagement' at WM'2001, Baden-Baden, Germany*. http://sunsite.informatik.rwth-aachen.de/Publications/CEUR-WS/Vol-37/ , 2001.
14. J. Pomerol and P. Brezillon. Dynamics between contextual knowledge and proceduralized context. In P. Bouquet et al., editors, *Modeling and Using Context. Proceedings CONTEXT'99, Trento, Italy*, number 1688 in LNAI. Springer, 1999.
15. U. Remus and F. Lehner. The Role of Process-oriented Enterprise Modeling in Designing Process-oriented Knowledge Management Systems. In *[18]*, 2000.
16. W. Ruppietta and W. Wernke. *Umsetzung organisatorischer Regelungen in der Vorgangsbearbeitung mit WorkParty und ORM*. 1994.
17. S. Schwarz, A. Abecker, H. Maus, and M. Sintek. Anforderungen an die WorkflowUnterstützung für Wissensintensive Geschäftsprozesse. In *[13]*, 2001.
18. St. Staab and D. O'Leary. *AAAI Spring Symposium: Bringing Knowledge to Business Processes*. 2000. http://www.aifb.uni-karlsruhe.de/~sst/Research/Events/sss00/.
19. K. Stein. *Integration von Anwendungsprozeßmodellierung und Workflow-Management*. PhD thesis, Department of Computer Science, University of Erlangen-Nürnberg, July 1999.
20. L. van Elst and A. Abecker. Integrating Task, Role, and User Modeling in Organizational Memories. In *14 Int. FLAIRS Conference, Special Track on Knowledge Management, Key West, Florida, USA*, May 2001.
21. C. Wenzel. Integrating information extraction into workflow management systems. In *Natural Language and Information Systems Workshop (NLIS/DEXA 98), Vienna, Austria*, 1998.
22. C. Wenzel and H. Maus. Leveraging corporate context within knowledge-based document analysis and understanding. *Int. Journal on Document Analysis and Recognition, Special Issue on Document Analysis for Office Systems*, 2001.
23. WfMC. Terminology and Glossary, issue 3.0. Technical report, Workflow Management Coalition, 1999.

The Role and Modeling of Context in a Cognitive Model of Rogers' Person-Centred Approach

Renate Motschnig-Pitrik[1] and Ladislav Nykl[2]

[1]Department of Computer Science and Business Informatics
University of Vienna,
Rathausstr. 19/9, 1010 Vienna, Austria
email: Motschnig@ifs.univie.ac.at

[2]Person-Centred Approach, Lederergasse 17/7, 1080 Vienna, Austria
email: Nykl@aon.at

Abstract:
Since the American psychologist Carl R. Rogers founded the person-centred approach to counseling, his way of approaching the individual by creating a facilitating relationship has helped thousands of clients, as proved by numerous empirical studies. While Carl Rogers himself described all aspects of the process of improvement in scientific, precise detail, a model to explain the functioning of the approach has not yet been formulated. The purpose of this paper is to propose an abstract, cognitive model to serve two purposes. First, to provide insight into some aspects of the way Rogers' approach works and second to argue, that one distinguishing criterion underlying Rogers' theory can be traced to the notion of context. This is in so far, as the person-centred approach is unique in having an individual solve problems within his personal context, as opposed to other approaches, where the counselor searches for problems to provide advice from his/her context and perspective. It will be argued that problem solving within an individual's context is particularly effective, since it most closely matches the living, sensing, and experience of this individual and has the highest potential for disposition and reuse of the individual's experience.

The best vantage point for understanding the behavior is from the internal frame of reference of the individual himself. [1] p 494

1 Introduction

The basic hypothesis underlying C. Rogers' approach is very simple: given a warm and facilitating atmosphere, governed by the principle of acceptance for the individual, every person is moving to a state that C. Rogers characterizes as:

"The other individual in the relationship:
will experience and understand aspects of himself which previously he has repressed;
will find himself becoming better integrated, more able to function effectively;
will become more similar to the person he would like to be;
will be more self-directing and self-confident:
will become more of a person, more unique and more self-expressive;
will be more understanding, more acceptant of others;
will be able to cope with the problems of life more adequately and more comfortably.

[2] p 37-38

The preconditions as well as the process of personal growth are precisely described by the founder of the Person-Centred (PersC) Approach, Carl R. Rogers, whose scientific attitude towards counseling, personal relationships, psychotherapy and freedom to learn is well documented at several places [2, 3, 4, 1] etc. Rogers' Theory of Personality and Behavior comprises 19 propositions [1]. A model to explain the functioning of the PersC Approach, however, has, to the best of the authors' knowledge, not been proposed yet. The motivation to construct such a model is threefold: firstly it should allow one to precisely distinguish the peculiarities of the PersC Approach as compared to other theories, secondly, it should explain the success of the thousands of cases examined, and finally it should improve understandability of the approach to improve its application and point to possible enhancement.

The psychology of counseling and psychotherapy is in the state of heavy debate and contest on various schools. In particular, the classical psychoanalysis by S. Freud is incompatible with C. Rogers' humanitarian approach. The incompatibility can be traced to the basically positive attitude and capacity of growth ascribed to the human being by C. Rogers, as opposed to the basically destructive attitude held by S. Freud. More recent approaches such as games theory and transaction analysis [5, 6, 7], to name just two, share the fact that they offer rules to explain maladjustments. While it is outside the realm of this paper to compare the individual theories, focusing on the notion of context helps us to clearly distinguish the PersC Approach from all others: In Rogers' Approach, all problem solving and change, due to insight, is performed by an individual within a single frame of reference, the inner frame or context of that individual himself. The outer necessary context to *facilitate* the changes is that of an accepting, understanding partner or therapist who provides the climate necessary for change in the direction described in Rogers' words above.

Assuming that an individual's mind is supposed to assimilate and provide for disposition this individual's experience and learning better than any other mind, leads us to conclude that the PersC Approach, in many respects, should be superior to other approaches. These share the feature of making use of "foreign" contexts and techniques to solve problems. We argue that one reason why the PersC Approach is highly effective is the fact that it focuses on the whole individual: His inherited properties, his learning, sensing, and most important, his particular experience.

In order to communicate our ideas, we use a simple, abstract model of human memory and rely on its undisputed basic properties only. This model, extended by the notion of context and represented using the UML (Unified Modeling Language, [8]) is employed to illustrate our reasoning. This is done by tracking a sample dialogue and thereby examining individual memory structures (i.e. subcontexts) as they pop up as the result of the conversation.

The primary goals of this research are twofold. First, we aim to use a cognitive model, extended by contexts, to explain several effects of Rogers' PersC Approach and point to the consequences. Second we want to show the role of contexts [9, 10, 11, 12, 13, 14] and their representation not only in the model itself, but also in the process of arguing about the role of the PersC Approach as compared to its competitors [15], [16].

In the next section we introduce the Abstract cognitive model of Human Associative Memory (AHAM), along with our view on the notion of context. Further, we give a glimpse on selected aspects of UML, the modeling notation used to represent the model. In Section 3, which takes the role of the core Section of this paper, we start by outlining a few key theses of Rogers' Theory of Personality. We proceed by giving the motivation, scope and construction of our model, present a sample dialogue to serve as a guiding example, and track the PersC Process using the terminology of our model. Section four validates the model and states the results. In the final section we discuss potential consequences of our findings and point to questions for further research.

2   Preliminaries

2.1   The Abstract Model of Human Associative Memory

The key idea behind our model for the PersC Approach is to implant a simple, abstract model for the human associative memory (AHAM) as a part or aspect of Rogers' construct of the Total Personality in Rogers' Theory of Personality and Behavior. The cognitive AHAM model and its representation in UML (Unified Modeling Language) is intended to serve as a vehicle to explain and to visualize the resolution of conflicts via the problem-solving process of PersC communication, given a facilitating interpersonal relationship in a proper atmosphere. The task here is to find a model that is as simple and as generic as possible for meeting our goal. The authors are well aware of advanced cognitive, linguistic, and other models stemming from areas such as cognitive science, AI, cognitive psychology and linguistics [17, 18, 19, 20, 21]. For ease of understanding and for our striving on consensus about the basic issues we employ a strongly simplified cognitive model relying on undisputed features. Further research will be directed towards specializing and the model.

According to J. R. Anderson [Anderson90] there is a broad consensus on the two-concept theory of memory. One concept refers to some transient factor that determines the momentary availability of the memory trace, referred to as *activation*. The other, called *strength*, refers to the long-term durability of the memory. Activation is defined in terms of our access to memories and is characterized by the fact that it can decay from a high level to a low level in seconds. In contrast, it takes some memories years to decay in their strength.

The memories that are currently active are often referred to as *working memory* (WM) [22]. The latter is loosely comparable with a processor of a computer. Knowledge in working memory is the only knowledge, which we can currently work with, i.e. think about, compare, match, or restructure. A well-known fact is that the working memory is constrained to hold a limited number of information units referred to as *chunks*, whereby a chunk can be as small as a single proposition, a concept, a structure, and as large as a whole picture.

Memories having sufficiently strong encoding that they can be reactivated at long delays are called *long-term memory* (LTM). LTM can loosely be compared with a computer's store. Several experiments prove that LTM is structured as an *associative network* with nodes being concepts or *chunks* and associations interconnecting the nodes. Although to the authors the model of a propositional network of concepts looks most appealing, in this paper we want to stay more generic such that we postulate only an associative network of chunks. This is due to the fact that we want to leave the exploration of intranode structure and content (like concept plus emotions plus values, etc.) to further research. Also, talking about chunks sufficiently serves our goals in modeling the functioning of the PersC Approach.

In the AHAM model associations between chunks play a vital role for the *spread of activation* that is necessary to activate knowledge to be available in working memory [17]. It is comparable to water running through an irrigation system. We assume the following to hold for the spread of activation [21]:

- Activation spreads in LTM from active chunks to other chunks and this spread takes time.
- The spread-of-activation has *limited capacity*. A source node has a certain fixed capacity for emitting activation.
- To determine the amount of activation that is spread from a node N to an associated node N', the branching level of the node N in the network is important in determining the number of alternative associations (paths) leaving this node. One can imagine that activation needs to be partitioned such that only a fraction is spread to each associated node N'. This phenomenon is called the *fan-effect*. It is so named because the increase in reaction time is related to an increase in the fan of nodes emanating from N.
- The spread-of-activation process is not entirely under an individual's control. Numerous association experiments have shown that, for a given concept (say, dog), certain concepts tend to be stronger associated (e.g. meat) than others (e.g. flower). Such unconscious priming is referred to as *associative priming*. Also, associations learned first or repeated more often tend to be stronger encoded and thus faster recalled than associations learned later or repeated less often.
- Various factors can affect the *amount* of activation that is spread to a knowledge structure. As argued above, more strongly encoded information receives greater activation and is faster recalled.
- *Recognition* is more accurate than *recall* [19]. For the sake of recognition, activation can be imagined to spread from both sides and hence the conclusion can be drawn faster.
- The term *interference* is used to convey the fact that additional information about a concept or chunk interferes with memory for a particular piece of information. Interference from other information associated with a chunk can slow down the speed with which the information can be retrieved. In the extreme case, subjects even fail to remember information under some second condition! Note that this effect will play a particular role in discussing PersC communication, since the latter aims to provide workarounds for interference by shifting context.
- An immediate consequence of inference is that *forgotten information* is still in memory but it is too weak to be activated in the face of the interference from other associations.

2.2   Contexts in Person-to-Person Communication

In accordance with [9], we refer to an object that denotes a situation in a model as a *context*. Thus, a context typically is a meaningful slice of the model or, in a special case, represents the universal context, such as some universe of discourse. Note that we chose to characterize a context in the first place by its contents, i.e. the set of objects or chunks it includes, Further, we associate contexts with features, such as relativized naming, authorization, channels for the propagation of changes between contexts, and ownership [11]. Since contexts are objects in their own right, in other words first-class citizens in the model, they can be classified, associated with state and behavior, enclosed in contexts, and dealt with like ordinary objects, resulting in a powerful mechanism [14].

In a nutshell, using object-oriented terminology, contexts are instances of the class 'Context'. They are special objects representing the decomposition of some object base. The class Context includes (amongst others) the following property functions [13], [14]:

- **Contents**: associating each context with a set of unique object identifiers (oid's);
- **Lexicon**: associating each object identifier of the context's contents with a local name;
- **Authorization**: associating each context with an authorization predicate, based on users and transactions, saying which users may perform what transactions (atomic operation sequences);
- **Change Propagation**: associating each context with a set of change propagation links, based on the partner context(s), users, and transactions, in order to describe, how changes in one context affect other contexts;
- **Owner**: user owning the context and having by default all access rights to its contents.

Interestingly and, frankly, also surprisingly, the object-oriented context model was found well suited to describe the contexts relevant for explaining the functioning of the PersC approach, as will be illustrated below. Perhaps the only adaptation needed is to take a broader view on the concept of an object. While in the object-oriented model objects are associated with properties and behavior, in our model (AHAM) we suggest to think of objects as general, thinkable entities, including ordinary objects but also concepts like goals, feelings, emotions, beliefs, pictures, rules, plans, etc. Sticking with the terminology we introduced for the AHAM model (see Section 2.1), we refer to these thinkable entities as *chunks*.

Leaving further formalization for a subsequent paper, Figure 1 sketches the contexts that play a role in interpersonal communication between, say, a person C and a person T. Note that the topology (and generic content structure) of a person's context and its subcontexts is analogous across individuals. Hence, for a static view, it suffices to discuss the topology of an arbitrary person's, e.g. person C's context. The overall structure is such that the two subcontexts, WMC (working memory of C) and LTMC (long term memory of C) have as common intersection those chunks that have been activated from LTM. WMC may contain, in addition to the common intersection chunks relating to current experience that are not yet encoded in LTM. While the contents of WMC and LTMC are represented as chunks, in our model we chose to abstract from the nature of the units in the enclosing context personC, calling them plainly information units. Exploring the nature of these units definitely constitutes a thrilling research question we cannot further expand on here.

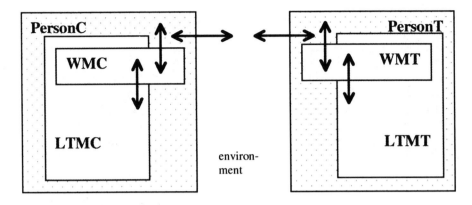

Fig. 1. A sketch of the topology of contexts relevant in person-to-person communication

The arrows in Figure 1 denote communication- or propagation links between contexts or between a context and its environment, as is the case for PersonC. For example, the bi-directional arrow between WMC and LTMC means that changes to chunks in WMC may be propagated to corresponding chunks in LTMC and vice versa. Representing the sketched contexts in our object-oriented context model leads to the following extended description that, for brevity, is represented in a semiformal way. I

context personC
    contents: {WMC, LTMC, informationUnitSet }
      /* each information unit and the contexts WMC and LTMC are associated with unique identifiers */
    lexicon: /* every information unit from the contents is associated with a name according to a language spoken by C */
    authorization: authorP(u, t) = C(u) /* C may perform any transaction */
    propagateFrom: propagateFrom(c, u, t) = (environment(c) and WMC(c))
    propagateTo: propagateTo(c, u, t) = (environment(c) and WMC(c))
    owner: C

context WMC
    contents: {chunkSet from current experience $\cup$ activated chunkSet from LTMC}
    lexicon: /* naming of chunks according to a language spoken by C*/
    authorization: authorP(u, t) = C(u)
    propagateFrom: propagateFrom(c, u, t) = (personC(c) and LTMC(c))
    propagateTo: propagateTo(c, u, t) = (personC(c) and LTMC(c))
    owner: C

context LTMC
    contents: {chunkSet from LTMC /*conscious as well as unconscious*/}
    lexicon: /* naming of chunks according to language spoken by C*/
    authorization: authorP(u, t) = C(u)

propagateFrom:	propagateFrom(c, u, t) = WMC(c)
propagateTo:	propagateTo(c, u, t) = WMC(c)
owner:	C

The context representation above adds the following to the description of Figure 1. From considering the lexicon, it follows that the naming of contexts or chunks proceeds in the language of the client. The authorization predicates say that only the client C himself is allowed to update his contexts. From the propagation predicates note, in particular, that the LTM of the client can only be updated via the actualization in the working memory of the client, which holds chunks depending on the client's current experience (e.g. in the PersC conversation). While Figure 1 depicts contexts in general person-to-person communication, Section 3 will explain a special feature of the PersC Approach that is targeted on those LTM reorganizations that are based on a client's personal experience and insight facilitated by Person-Centred conversation[1].

2.3   UML: Static Structure Diagrams

Due to the fact that we want to emphasize the notion of abstractness of our model and the resulting design decision to interpret nodes as chunks of arbitrary size, we refrain from using any of the prepositional network notations proposed in the literature. Instead, we model structural aspects by using the Unified Modeling Language [8], a general modeling notation used as a standard in computer science. Only few features of the UML diagramming techniques will be used in this paper laying the focus on structural modeling. Nodes correspond to classes or instances, the intranode structure consists of a name, the structural -, and the behavioural properties ("methods") of the node. Note that, due to UML's *extensibility* via the *stereotype* mechanism, nodes could be complemented to hold other kind of information such as emotional values, beliefs, etc. Nodes are interconnected by associations, whereby part-of relationships [23] are distinguished by drawing a diamond at the side of the 'whole' concept (compare Figure 2). Generalization links between concept are associated with the mechanism of property inheritance.

3   A Model for Rogers PersC Approach

3.1   Towards a Model to Explain the Effects of Rogers' Person-Centred Approach

The hypothesis underlying our research is that substitution of a part or *aspect* of *Self* in Rogers' Theory of Personality and Behavior by a cognitive model with context will throw light and explain the way Rogers' approach works. In order to provide at least some imagination of Rogers' Theory, let us discuss just two of his 19 propositions. Proposition IV, for example, states that "The organism has one basic tendency and striving -- to actualize, maintain, and enhance the experiencing organism." This *actualization tendency* involves movement in the direction of greater independence,

---

[1] Note, though, that the reorganizations typically actually take place between interviews.

self-responsibility, self- regulation and autonomy, and away from heteronymous control, or control by external forces. Proposition VII, the one most closely related to the notion of context says that "The best vantage point for understanding the behavior is from the *internal frame of reference of the individual himself.*" The consequent implementation of this thesis makes Rogers' direction different from all other developments in psychology, which tend to view a person's behavior from an *external frame* of reference.

3.2   A Sample Dialogue

The following dialogue between a therapist (T) and a client (C) is intended to provide the reader with a concrete instance of person-centred communication. It will be used throughout as a running example that has been constructed for didactic purpose. Note that in this example any understanding partner willing to help could substitute the therapist who in more recent terms would be called a *facilitator*.

(1) C: The door closed with a snap and she was gone. I felt miserable, I was very desperate.
(2) T: Her behavior must have caused you pain.
(3) C: Yes, my eyes got full of tears running down my cheeks, I had to weep and I felt like a little child.
(4) T: You really felt lonely and helpless.
(5) C: I did. I felt like a helpless creature, a something, in no case did I feel like a man!
(6) T: You mean, you did not want to weep, but equally you could not stop the tears. Tears by no means fit your conception of a real man.
(7) C: Exactly, but I could not suppress the tears. A real man does not weep.
(8) T: ...and in this situation of deep despair you wept anyway.
(9) C: Yes, I did. - And soon I even felt relieved, but also such as if I did something I was supposed not to do.
(10) T: You clearly felt better, but at the same time you feel like having done something that was not allowed.
(11) C: Exactly: My mother often used to tell me: "A real man does not weep."
(12) T: That was your mother's opinion, but in your case, as you just told me, weeping caused relief.
(13) C: Precisely this was my sensation.
(14) T: Personally, should you be interested, I am quite familiar with situations where one's mood is such that tears are the only fair response. ...

3.3   Characterizing and Tracking the Process

The purpose of this section is to describe the way in which the model introduced above can be used to explain the cognitive facets of the PersC Approach. Hence, we proceed by characterizing the PersC process in action by interpreting it in terms of our model. We use the dialogue from Section 3.2 to make the discussion more concrete.

C. Rogers states the overall hypothesis on the relationship he aims to establish during counseling or therapy as follows: [Rogers 1961, 33-35] "If I can provide a certain type of relationship, the other person will discover within himself the capacity to use that relationship for growth, and change and personal development will occur." Rogers describes the relationship that, naturally, depends of the seeking of help of the other person and his willingness to participate in the process, as consisting of three major phrases. We interpret them as three iterative and incremental phases of the accompanying process targeted at establishing and maintaining the relationship.

Realness, Transparency. "I have found that the more that I can be genuine in the relationship, the more helpful it will be. [...] Being genuine also involves the willingness to be and to express, in my words and my behavior, the various feelings and attitudes, which exist in me. It is only by providing the genuine reality which is in me, that the other person can successfully seek for the reality in him. [...]." [2], p. 33.

Being real requires the therapist (intuitively) to search for the proper, in the sense of best matching, subcontexts within the context of his own memory, allowing him to activate related chunks for comparing and matching with the respective chunks of the client's working memory while the client recalls his experience. For communicating his realness in his responses to the client, the therapist holds in his working memory those chunks that provide the best matches to the client's utterances. Being open on the topic of conversation in a supportive way helps the client to open up in turn and activate associated concepts and to access paths that otherwise, due to the interference effect, may be too week to follow. Note that the above will be possible only, if the client feels save. This can be achieved by the therapist's unconditional positive attitude towards the client to be discussed below.

Turning to the dialogue about weeping, activation and communication of related concepts can be observed in lines (1) - (3) in particular and generally throughout the dialogue. The client first mentions his despair and then, facilitated by the therapists reflection of similar concepts, mentions tears and weeping. This is illustrated using UML structure diagrams in Figures 2 - 3. While Figure 2 represents the LTM context holding chunks on the topic of feelings of distress - assumed to be shared on a general level by both client and therapist -, Figure 3 shows sample activated subcontexts (WMs) of the client and the therapist, respectively.

LTM subcontext of therapist to be searched for activation of suitable chunks:

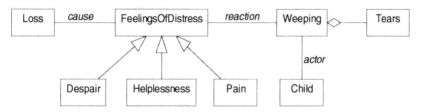

Fig. 2. Subcontext of LTM on the topic of feeling miserable, assumed to hold similar concepts in both therapist and client.

Acceptance, Positive Regard. "I find that the more acceptance and liking I feel toward this individual, the more I will be creating a relationship which he can use. By acceptance I mean a warm regard for him as a person of unconditional self-worth, of value no matter what his condition, his behavior, his feelings. It means a respect and liking for him as a separate person, a willingness for him to possess his own feelings in his own way." [2] p 34.

Trying to interpret positive regard in terms of contexts and the AHAM model, it means firstly the effort to create an environment where the client feels safe and reassured to proceed in freely exploring his LTM and communicating activated concepts to the therapist. The therapist can make the client feel safe if the former succeeds in communicating his *unconditional positive regard* towards the client[2]. Secondly it means the effort on the side of the therapist to understand the relevant subcontext of the other person as part of the other person's LTM context or mind. This definitely is harder to achieve than realness, since the therapist has kind of try to step temporarily into the context of the other person and yet remain in his context.

In our dialogue, steps (4) - (9) reflect positive regard, although the borderline to the next phase is hard to draw viewing the transcript only. The LTM subcontexts that form the basis for activations to achieve *positive regard in response to the particular situation* of the client are sketched in Figure 4.

Subcontexts from the WM of the client and the therapist:

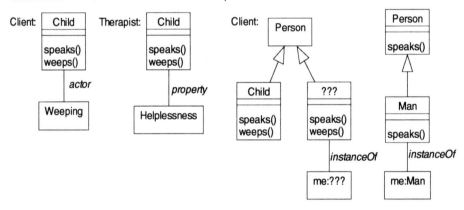

Fig. 3. Activations in response to searching the LTM subcontext depicted in Figure 2. The right side depicts the conflict in the client's WM. (At that time the LTM subcontext being searched is assumed to be extended by concepts like Person and Man (not yet shown in Figure 2).

Understanding, Empathy. "[...] I feel a continuing desire to understand - a sensitive empathy which each of the client's feelings and communications as they seem to him at that moment. Acceptance does not mean much until it involves understanding. It is only that I understand the feelings and thoughts which seem so horrible to you, or so weak [...] - it is only as I see them as you see them and accept them and you, that you feel really free to explore [...] your inner and often buried experience. [...] There is

---

[2] We are not sure yet which of the multiple options for the encoding of this effect is the proper one.

implied here a freedom to explore oneself at both conscious and unconscious levels."
[2] p 35.

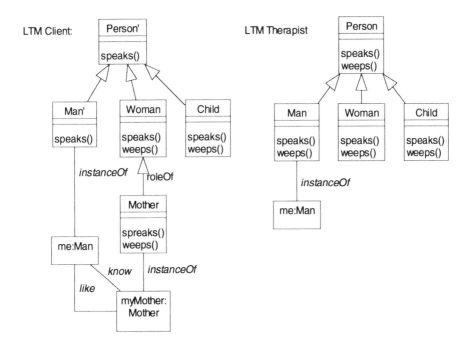

Fig. 4. LTM subcontexts surrounding the concept of Man in the LTM of the client (left) and the therapist (right)

Considering the cognitive projection of empathy, this deep way of understanding is accompanied by and directed towards matching the assumed subcontext of the other persons LTM context with one's own LTM subcontext on the topic of which chunks have been activated in the previous phases. It means to explore and to communicate matches in order to reveal buried experience and activate chunks from the unconscious levels. In this step, in particular, the therapist looks for ways to work around inference effects in order to help activate associated concepts on the side of the client that he thinks may be useful for the client to help him find his solution. He aims to see his world through his eyes. Steps (10) - (14) can be viewed as expressions of empathy in our sample dialogue. The restructuring to be performed by the client as a result of the dialogue is depicted in Figure 5.

Summarizing, one can clearly observe that *reflection* from the therapist's side supports the activation of associated concepts on the client's side that otherwise, due to *inference*, may have been to week to be activated. Thus, more concepts from any focused subcontext are represented in the client's WM and hence the matching and comparison use broader information that without reflecting conversation. The atmosphere of personal acceptance definitely contributes to more open, non-blocking conversation that perhaps is the crucial factor for the thorough explorations of one's self as a precondition to reorganisation. We conjecture that unconditional positive regard towards the client generally improves the spread of activation, be it by strengthening associations or by an increase of the amount of activation available. Besides reflection, the phenomenon of empathic understanding seems to play an enormous role in activating unconscious memories. Since the therapist tries to live the experience of the client, he is likely to talk about concepts that the client *recognizes* in himself. Recognition being more accurate than recall easily explains that information previously denied to consciousness can be activated.

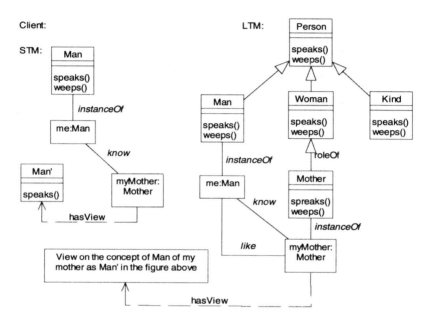

Fig. 5. LTM subcontext of the reorganized LTM of the client (right). This is the result of the matching between the concept Man' and that of Man in STM as a consequence of the dialogue.

In a nutshell, given the willingness of the client - enabled by establishing the proper PersC atmosphere, mainly cognitive and context-based considerations completely suffice to explain the benefits of the PersC approach.

4 Validation of the Model

Model construction. The theory of spread of activation in the AHAM model allows to explain that persons, in a facilitating atmosphere established by a facilitating partner, principally are able to recall and hence think about, compare, match, focused information they may find useful to solve their problems. The cognitive model so far does not touch on means other than cognitive to explain its cognitive effects. The creation of a proper emotional atmosphere is taken as a precondition here, such that our model is intended solely to explain the cognitive aspects of the approach. More than surprisingly, these cognitive aspects as described above play such an essential part in the PersC process, that their understanding explains the working of Rogers approach fairly completely, given Rogers' preconditions are met.

Necessity of Rogers' Three Variables of the PersC Approach: Realness, Acceptance, Empathy. Section 3.3 has shown that all three components of the process postulated by C. Rogers are really required in our model and have cognitive projections. The latter, respectively, are the search for a proper (i.e. suitable for the topic at hand) subcontext of one's LTM context, the virtual reconstruction of the other person's LTM subcontext on that topic, and the virtual transfer of the other person's subcontext into one's own WM for the sake of empathy.

Addressing Areas Denied to Consciousness. Due to Rogers's Theory of Personality (e.g. thesis XIV) there exist situations in which the organism hides certain experiences from consciousness. In order to remove tensions, PersC communication needs means to address these areas. In our model, chunks not being conscious can be reached in two ways: Firstly, reflection can be used to activate conscious chunks that are associated with ones not being conscious and empathic understanding can be employed to extinguish inference effects. Secondly, empathically understanding and reflecting utterances of one's partner, such that he just needs to recognize chunks instead of recalling them, is known to require less activation.

Eliza Effect. Weizenbaum [24] observed that when using a program called ELIZA that reflects the utterances of persons who communicate with that program, these persons like the program, feel well understood and are inclined to carry on the conversation, at least up to the point where the program "acts strangely" due to incompetence on some topic. This observation strongly supports our model that uses and requires the technique of reflection as a precondition to insight and reorganisation. It shows that no "magic" is in action and that cognitive aspects are essential, given a person feels sufficiently secure and accepted.

In brief, the major result of this paper is the provision of a model that uses contexts and core ideas from cognitive psychology and modeling in order to understand and to visualize psychic tensions on the one hand and explain the effect of personal growth in PersC communication on the other hand, given the proper preconditions are met. With this work, in particular, we aim to reduce some of the mysticism that many psychologists allocate to C. Rogers' approach.

5 Conclusions, Discussion, and Further Research

This paper aimed to model and explain aspects of Self from C. Rogers' Theory of Personality and Behavior by employing an abstract, cognitive model on human memory (AHAM) and by applying the notion of context, as proposed by one of the authors [14]. The latter led to a significant observation, namely that Rogers Person-Centred Approach differs from other developments in psychology by addressing the inner context of an individual rather than by occupying some other, external context, in order to explain a person's behavior. Another significant result of this work is the fact that, using our model, problems or psychic tensions can explicitly be represented and visualized. The same holds true for the reorganizations necessary to resolve the problems, always staying in the inner context of an individual himself. This explains the effectivity of Rogers' psychology as far as the cognitive dimension is concerned. We want to emphasize, however, that the preconditions for success, namely the proper climate of empathic understanding and, of course, the willingness of the persons involved, can only very incompletely be expressed in the cognitive dimension.

Further research will concern the investigation of the precise structure of chunks, the possibility of labelling associations with values measuring the strength of encoding, and in researching more rigorously the effects of empathy on creativity and on mental achievement. A complementary research direction should address applications of the Person-Centred Approach to areas of individual as well as corporate creative problem solving, such as in requirements engineering, goal analysis, or situational project management. Influence on the provision of content in telelearning is seen as another fruitful direction to follow. Currently we are in the process of visually modeling effects like introjections and assimilation. Further, we experiment with UML sequence diagrams for modeling dynamic issues inherent in the Person-Centred Approach.

It is our hope that this work helps to more clearly understand the effects of the PersC Approach and hence can contribute to the renaissance of C. Rogers' Approach that is so human, so genuine, and so real. To end with C.Rogers' words: "If they [these hypotheses] prove to be a stimulation to significant study of the deeper dynamics of human behavior, they will have served their purpose well." [1] p 532.

Acknowledgements: Sincere thanks are due to Michael Trimmel for his insightful discussions and comments on an earlier draft of this paper.

Comment: In reverence to C. Rogers and for the purpose of forceful writing we use the masculine form throughout. In the spirit of C. Rogers we note that each masculine form could equally well be stated in its feminine equivalent.

References:

1. Rogers C., R.: "Client-Centered Therapy"; (First printed in 1951), Constable, (1995)
2. Rogers C., R.: "On Becoming A Person - A Psychotherapists View of Psychotherapy"; Constable, (1961)
3. Rogers C., R.: "Freedom to Learn for the 80's"; Charles E. Merrill Publishing Company, A Bell&Howell Company, (1983)
4. Rogers C., R.: "Die Nicht-Direktive Beratung (Non-Directed Counseling)"; Fischer Taschenbuch Verlag, Frankfurt am Main, 6th Ed., (1985)
5. Berne E.: "Transactional Analysis in Psychotherapy"; New York, (1961)
6. Berne E : "Games People Play"; (first published in 1964), Penguin Books, (1984)
7. Harris T., A.: "I'm OK – You're OK, Pan Books London and Sydney, (1970)
8. Rumbaugh J., Jacobson I., Booch G.: The Unified Modeling Language Reference Manual; Addison-Wesley, (1999)

9. Schneider, P., F.: "Contexts in PSN"; Proc. of the AI-CSCSI-SCEIO Conference, Victoria, B.C., Canada, (May 1980) 71-78

10. Motschnig-Pitrik R.: "An Integrating View on the Viewing Abstraction: Contexts and Perspectives in Software Development, AI, and Databases"; *Journal of Systems Integration*, Kluwer, 5 (1), April (1995) 23-60

11. Mylopoulos J., Motschnig-Pitrik R.: "Partitioning Information Bases with Contexts"; Proc. of the 3rd International Conference on Cooperative Information Systems, Vienna, (May 1995)

12. Motschnig-Pitrik R., Mylopoulos J. : Semantics, Features, and Applications of the Viewpoint Abstraction, Proc. of CAiSE'96, 8th Internat. Conference on Advanced Information Systems Engineering, Springer LNCS 1080, (June 1996) 514-539

13. Motschnig-Pitrik R.: "Contexts and Views in Object-Oriented Languages, in: P. Bouquet, P. Brezillon and L. Serafini, eds. 2nd International and Interdisciplinary Conf. on Modeling and Using Context, CONTEXT'99, Lecture Notes in Artificial Intelligence No 1688; Springer Verlag, (1999) 256 - 269

14. Motschnig-Pitrik R.: "A generic framework for the modeling of contexts and its applications"; *Data & Knowledge Engineering* 32, (2000) 145-180.

15. Nykl L.: "Psychological Contexts in Rogers' Psychotherapy in Relation to the Theory of Personality - a Comparison with Behaviorism"; (in German) PhD-Thesis, Karlova Universita, Prague, (1999)

16. Nykl L.: "Psychological Contexts in Rogers' Psychotherapy - The Self in the Focus of the Theory of Personality" (in German)"; Virya - Zeitschrift für Psychotherapie und Kommunikation, L. Nykl: editor; No. 4, Vienna, (September 2000) 1 - 108

17. Quillian M., R.: "Word Concepts: A Theory and Simulation of some Basic Semantic Capabilities"; Behavioral Science 12, (1967) 410 - 430

18. Schubert L., Goebe lR., Cercone N.: "The Structure and Organization of a Semantic Net for Comprehension and Inference"; in Findler N. (ed.): Associative Networks; Representation and Use of Knowledge by Computers, Academic Press, (1979)

19. Sowa J., F.: "Conceptual Structures: Information Processing in Mind and Machine"; Addison Wesley, (1984)

20. Brachman R. J., Levesque H., J. (editors): "Readings in Knowledge Reprsentation"; Morgan Kaufmann Publ., Inc., (1985)

21. J. R. Anderson: "Cognitive Psychology and its Applications"; 3rd ed., Freeman, New York, (1900)

22. Baddeley A. D.: "Working Memory"; Oxford: Oxford University Press, (1986)

23. Motschnig-Pitrik R., Kaasboll J.: "Part-Whole Relationship Categories and Their Application in Object-Oriented Analysis"; IEEE TSE 11(5), (Sept./Oct. 1999) 779-797

24. Weizenbaum J: "Die Macht der Computer und die Ohnmacht der Vernunft"; suhrkamp taschenbuch wissenschaft, (1976)

Local Holism

Carlo Penco

Department of Philosophy, University of Genoa (Italy)
penco@unige.it

Abstract. This paper is devoted to discuss a general tendency in contextualism which is known as "radical contextualism". In the first part I state the well known paradox of semantic holism, as discussed in philosophy of language: if meaning is holistic there is no possibility to share any meaning. In the second part I present the different answers to this paradox, from atomism to different forms of holism. In the third part I give a criticism of the traditional interpretation of Wittgenstein as a supporter of global holism. I stress some similarities between Wittgenstein's thought and Multi Context theories in artificial inteligence. In the last part I give some argument against a rigid interpretation of "local holism": I claim the need to give restrictions to local holim and to develop a study of the connections between "default" properties and high level rules which are studied in Multi-Context theories.

1 The paradox of semantic holism

The work of Wittgenstein is apparently characterized by a strong attitude towards an holistic view of language. Even in *Tractatus logico-philosophicus* - considered as a program for logical atomism - we find reference to Frege's context principle: names have meaning only in the context of a sentence (TLP 3.3). Names do not have meaning in isolation; only when *used* to refer to something they are meaningful. Wittgenstein subsequent work seems to be a progressive generalization of the context principle. The Fregean principle is quoted as such at the beginning of *Philosophical Investigation* in order to show that words do not have denotation in isolation, but only when used inside a language game, a social environment of speech and action. If the sentence is the basic move in a language game, like a move in the game of chess, a language (game) itself is taken to be the basic unit in linguistic activity:

«To understand a sentence means to understand a language. To understand a language means to be master of a technique» [Wittgenstein 1953, § 199]

Quine and Davidson interpret the sentence quoted above as an expression of a radical holism. Quine refers to it in *World and Object* (§16) to stress the radical dependence of any individual sentence from the entire language. Davidson endorses this holistic attitude in his seminal essay "Truth and Meaning" where he says that «we can give the meaning of any sentence (or word) only by giving the meaning of every sentence (and word) in the language. Frege said that only in the context of a sentence does a word have meaning; in the same vein he might have added that only in the context of the language does a sentence (and therefore a word) have meaning» (p.22). Davidson's original theory of meaning gives a picture of language as a fixed set of sentences whose meaning can be systematically given by their truth conditions.

However the extreme holistic viewpoint has a disastrous consequence, clearly denounced by Dummett 1973 in his comment to Quine's work. Assuming a definition of meaning as inferential role, the paradox could be expressed as such: if the meaning of an expression is its inferential role, the meaning is the set of inferences connected with the given expression; however, given that there is no distinction between analytic and synthetic sentences, we cannot define a restricted set of relevant inferences which defines meanings (as e.g. analytical sentences given in the form of meaning postulates). If meanings depends on the entire language and on the entire system of beliefs of a speaker, given that there are no two individuals with the same identical set of beliefs, no two individuals may give the same meaning to an expression. But if two individuals do not give the same meanings to the same expressions, then they can neither agree nor disagree. Hence communication becomes impossible. The apparent paradox is therefore that if meaning is defined holisticaly, .there is no meaning to be used in communication.

Dummett sees clearly that this criticism of holism is a criticism on its consequences, and then it is not a proof of the falsity of semantic holism; however it is an evidence in favour of a methodological stance against holism (Dummett 1993,p.21). Certainly, if holism holds, we could find it difficult to explain language learning and communication. But not being able to explain language learning and communication can be read both as evidence against holism and as evidence against traditional explanations of learning an communication. Dummett follows the first horn of the dilemma; others will follow the second one.

2   Alternative solutions

Given the paradox of radical holism, we have the following option: either abandoning holism and finding a viable version of atomism (Fodor) or molecularism (Dummett, Perry, Marconi) or, on the other hand, keeping holism and abandoning the traditional view of communication as sharing common meanings or contents (Davidson, Brandom, Stalnaker). I will treat some of these solutions to hint at their limitations which seem to point towards an alternative: local holism.

2.1   The atomistic option

The *atomistic option* has been taken by Fodor. A basic argument against any form of holism has been developed in Fodor-Lepore 1992. They claim that alternative options are almost impossible to accept without either falling into holism or accepting a principled analytic-synthetic distinction, which has been shown untenable by Quine. If you accept the idea that in order to communicate you need to share some belief you fall into holism, because there is no principled distinction which permits to decide *which* beliefs are the relevant ones (unless you accept a not welcome principled distinction between analytic and synthetic).

A way out is to accept that meanings are atomistic: each concept is an atom which is causally activated in our mind (in our innate language of thought). Authors like Fodor 1998 claim that the atomistic option is the only one which permits to overcome the problem of holism. The atomistic stance had received a strong theoretical support with the publication of Wittgenstein's *Tractatus logico-philosophicus*. However the logical atomism vivid in the early period of analytic philosophy received also strong criticism by most philosophers, including Wittgenstein himself. The new version of atomism given by Fodor seems a psychological adjustment of a already untenable position. Strange enough Fodor and Lepore accept the Quinean criticism of the analytic-synthetic distinction, forgetting that the main target of the criticism is the atomistic theory of language (the idea that sentences has a meaning in isolation from other sentences). The dismantling of the atomistic theory of language implies the dismantling of the idea of the atomistic theory of the meaning of single words (which had already been definitely destroyed by the results of structuralist linguistics). The new claims for atomism are more supported with the negative criticism of alternative options than with positive arguments. I will leave therefore the atomistic option as it is, to verify the robustness of the alternative options.

2.2   The molecularist option

The *molecularistic option* is normally considered the stance where you have some basic beliefs (or some basic semantic properties) which are definitory of the meaning of words and sentences. This option falls under the criticism of Fodor and Lepore who claim that any attempt to build up a molecularist stance (we share only some beliefs) drives you directly either into holism or into the acceptance of the analytic/synthetic distinction (either meaning is given by all beliefs or it is given by analytic definitions). However Perry 1994 and others claim that there is a weak form of molecularism which escapes this criticism. We have therefore to distinguish a strong and a weak molecularism, where the distinction is given by the scope of the quantifier (I use here Marconi 1997):

- the *strong molecularism,* which is supposed to lead to holism or to A/S distinction, might be expressed as such:

$$\forall p \, \exists q \, (q \neq p \, \& \, \text{Nec} \, (p \text{ is shared} \rightarrow q \text{ is shared})$$

that is, if two people share a belief p, there is some other belief q which must also be shared. Fodor and Lepore claim that, unless you give a class of privileged sentences, you have no idea of how to choose the sentences q to be shared. But to isolate a class of privileged sentences is to come back to the idea of a set of beliefs analytically connected with p, therefore to come back to the analytic/synthetic distinction, which is to be rejected.

What is wrong, however, with analytic/synthetic distinction? Quine himself was certainly aware of the apparent utility of a weak distinction between analytic and synthetic, or theoretic and observation sentences. He claims that there is no "principled" distinction, universally valid; however, for practical purpose a distinction of the kind is needed. We might therefore accept a relatively innocuous distinction of the kind linguistic/factual (practically most of the knowledge representation systems accept one, since the distinction between assertional and descriptional in the KL-ONE semantic networks). Certainly strong molecularism (which seem the position still hold by Dummett 1991) is a stable position and coherent with the traditional view of communication. However, for the sake of the argument, we grant a suspicion on the appeal to any kind of distinction between analytic and synthetic sentences. Is it possible to build a molecularist position completely free from this danger?

- the *weak molecularism*, which is supposed to avoid both holism and the A/S distinction, might be expressed as such:

$$\forall\, p \text{ Nec } (p \text{ is shared} \rightarrow \exists\, q\ (q \neq p\ \&\ q \text{ is shared})$$

that is, necessarily, if you share p, there are other beliefs that are also shared. However there is no privileged class of beliefs; there must be other shared beliefs if p is shared, but there is no reason why these beliefs should belong to a class of analytic or privileged sentences. It is easy to see how the weak molecularist option is different both from the strong molecularist one and from the holistic one. Certainly you do not need to understand all the language in order to understand a sentence; on the other hand this option maintains the classical view that communication is based on sharing some common content (which content, is not relevant at all; if you say to a hearer that your ring is gold, maybe you share just the wrong belief that gold is yellow, or the belief that gold is a metal; who cares?). However the position is highly unstable. To assert that you need to have some shared beliefs q if you hold a belief p cannot avoid the question of which *kind* of beliefs we expect to be shared. If two people may share few beliefs, certainly they are *expected* to hold some beliefs which are relevant to the matter. Maybe they do not share all the relevant beliefs, but we, speakers of a language, must distinguish what is relevant and what is not. Sharing beliefs is on one hand an individual matter, on the other hand a social matter; there are beliefs shared in the society, even if not shared by all the individuals. Idealized individual competence is neither a universal encyclopedia nor a set of casual beliefs. If communication is, on this view, a sharing of contents, we cannot avoid the normative problem of *which* contents are the best to be shared to improve successful communication.

2.3   The holistic option

The *holistic option* is bound to reject the traditional view of communication if it wants to avoid the criticism of Dummett. Radical holism has bee expressed clearly in Davidson's theory of meaning based on the concept of interpretation and on Tarski's theory of truth. Not much has been said about communication in the early papers by Davidson. And radical or global holism is the typical target of Dummett's criticism. But if we change the picture of communication, maybe holism could be saved. This stance is well expressed in Davidson's "Nice derangement of epitaphs", in Stalnaker's *Context and Content* and in Brandom's *Making it Explicit*. Recently Hinzen 1999 has give further support to the idea that "shared linguistic knowledge is no precondition for communication".

The main point in Davidson is exactly to give a different view of what communication is: not a sharing of the same contents (meanings) but a work of *convergence* between two different idiolects, and the formation of a "passing" theory during the dialogue, provoked by the utterances of the other speaker. This passing theory is what a speaker is able to build on the ground of what he expects the speaker is thinking and of what she actually says.

A similar stance, in a different framework, has been developed by Robert Stalnaker in *Content and Context*. While Davidson keeps Quine's attitude of using canonical extensional first order language, Stalnaker's framework is given by model theoretic semantics in the tradition of Carnap's and Montague's modal languages. In Stalnaker the expectations of a speaker are framed in terms of "presuppositions"; the context is what is given by the (probably different) presuppositions of the speakers, by what they assume for granted: «context dependence means dependence on certain facts, but the facts must be available, or presumed to be available, to the participants in the conversation. So I propose to identify a context (at a particular point in a discourse) with the body of information that is presumed, at that point, to be common to participants in the discourse» (p.98). Given that the context is "constantly changing as things are said" (p.101), a dialogue is a constant adjustments of the presuppositions prompted by the sentences which are uttered by the speakers.

The main problem with Davidson's proposal is that it reduces language to a set of idiolects of speakers; further criticism given by Dummett 1992 is mainly devoted to the lack of analysis of language as social institution and social practice; even if communication is important, to restrict the function of language to communication is to give a fairly incomplete view of language, which is also a vehicle of thought in a community.

If I have well understood Stalnaker's proposal, every proposition, relevant or not, that is taken for granted by the speakers contributes to the definition of the context. The difficulty with this proposal is that the context so conceived is "too big". A context embeds all the presuppositions of the speakers in the dialogue; while they change subject, the presuppositions are still there and we have to take them into account to ascertain the validity of the context set. Therefore the overall project seems bound to a computational complexity which is beyond any reasonable formal treatment.

There is another form of holism developed in the tradition of semantic networks. For Quillian 1967 each node of a semantic network activates the nearest nodes following some path in the network and is indirectly connected with every other node. Meaning can be computed at different degrees, depending on the number of nodes activated, and similarity of meaning is computed as similarity in activation of nodes starting from the node under consideration. However the idea that, given any system, the elements of the system are in principle connected is an aspect of holism which does not necessarily imply meaning holism; in fact the claim behind semantic networks does not entail that that to compute the meaning of an expression we have to run through the entire semantic network, even if there is no clear assumption about restrictions in the numbers of nodes activated for individuating meaning.

3   Sharing rules, contexts and language games

The solutions given above of the paradox of holism have been all criticized for some relevant aspects. We might doubt that the solutions given above exhaust the varieties of possible solutions. I suggest that Wittgenstein's ideas, which seem to be at the heart of most of these solutions, have been partly misunderstood. When Quine quotes Wittgenstein as a heir of an holistic position, he quotes from the *Blue Book*. However the complete quotation from *Philosophical Investigations* says not only that "to understand a sentence is to understand a language", but also that "to understand a language is mastering a technique". How is to be interpreted the first sentence? Is this second assertion relevant to our discussion?

To answer the first question we should take care to understand "a language" not as "the" language. In Wittgenstein's perspective language itself, as a universal representation, disappears. We are left with a multifarious interconnection of language games, situations in which language and action are interwoven. Therefore if we want to give a definition of meaning, we have to give it always relative to a language game. And if we want to define meaning holistically, we cannot define meaning relative to the entire language, but relative to single and specific language games.

As far as the second sentence is concerned, a *technique* is something which is given by a social practice - we master a technique if we follow some common rules. Therefore understanding a language is ability to follow rules (social practices). This passage suggests a shift from sharing contents to sharing rules. What do we share? Not mainly contents but rules; Brandom 1994 tries to develop a similar point in speaking of "sharing the structure, not the content". The picture of communication as *sharing of contents* can be abandoned with a picture of communication as *sharing of rules*.

Which kind of rules? Here there is no clear answer in Wittgenstein; however his overall picture of the working of language avoids postulating a unique set of rules; apparently different rules apply in different language games. Language itself is a highly abstract idealization; you may postulate a language instinct and a language faculty, but the varieties of linguistic activities cannot be embedded in a unique formal representation. Wittgenstein's attitude is a reaction against a unique representation of language as a single unit; language is a social enterprise and different aspects are developed in different ways; but if there cannot be a unique representation of the working of language, there can be a careful description of different language games. Their description must be completed by an analysis of the connections and transformations from one language game to another. In Wittgenstein's *Philosophical Investigations* the study of the relationships among language games is left to a very general level of programmatic remarks. This point seems to me the place where artificial intelligence may give some suggestion to philosophy. There is an apparent similarity between the Wittgenteinian picture of language games and the basic ideas of multi-context theories in artificial intelligence. In multi-context theories you cannot develop a single formalization for "the" language, but you are bound to describe different contexts as different theories, each one with its language, axioms and rules.

Somebody might ask whether it is sensible to make a comparison between an old-fashioned philosopher of the beginning of the last century and the work of contemporary a.i. I can only suggest that the *motivations* of the formal treatment of context in a.i. are similar to the motivation behind Wittgenstein's philosophy. The answers are partly different. The motivation is the problem of generality: at any time you may find people interpreting what you say in an unexpected way.

McCarthy 1987, 1993 says that, given any sentence, you may always find, with some ingenuity, some axioms where the sentence can be interpreted as false or however different from the intended interpretation; his answer insists on the importance of relativizing any assertion to a specific context and studying the rules which permit operations among contexts. Wittgenstein 1953 says that given any sentence (or any rule) you may always find an interpretation different from yours. Wittgenstein's answer insists on the difference between interpreting a rule and following a rule. Rules are social practices which are *followed* before being *interpreted*; therefore in understanding language you cannot rely only on interpretations, but you have to rely on social practice. Social practices are laid down in language games.

The detailed study of the rules which work across contexts is exactly what is missing in Wittgenstein's approach, even if his philosophy clearly go towards this clarification. This kind of study is also what is missing in the different attempts to face the problem of holism. All attempts to solve the problem of holism end up with a search of shared contents: communication is either the sharing of meanings or a convergence towards some shared meanings or contents. No question has been posed on the means to attain this aim; Davidson 1986 (p. 445) speaks of the "mysterious" aspect of the communicative success. On the contrary, the suggestion stemming from artificial intelligence is that there is no mistery at all: we share and we may explicitly study general rules to navigate across contexts. For a communication being successful, we need to share these high level rules, and the formal study of this kind of rules may help to understand exactly the strategies used in successful communication.

There are many presentations of rules for navigating across contexts; Mc Carthy 1993 speaks of rules of entering and exiting contexts, or of lifting a sentence from one context to another; Giunchiglia 1993 speaks of bridge rules which permit to draw a conclusion in a context from a premise in another context; Fauconnier 1997 (ch.6) speaks of rules for blending concepts from different contexts; Benerecetti et alia

2000 summarize most of the research in three kinds of mechanisms of contextual reasoning: localized reasoning, push and pop, shifting. These three mechanisms correspond to three basic aspects of a contextual representation as *partial, approximated* and *perspectival*. While the first aspect works *inside* contexts, the two other aspects work *on* contexts.

We find here a distinction between two different kinds of rules: using a Wittgensteinian terminology we might speak of rules governing the working *of* language games, and the rules governing relations *among* language games. How shall we define rules defining contents *inside* different contexts? In order to blend concepts we need concepts to be blended; in order to lift an inference from a context to another we need an inference to be performed. While we are beginning to study a new level of rules among contexts, we run the risk to find inside each context the same problem of semantic holism we have found at the beginning. Do the discovery of new kinds of rules which run across contexts have some impact on this problem? I will come back on these question after some remarks on one last solution on the market: local holism.

4 Local Holism and the meaning of the words

After the different solutions of the problem of holism, with their limitations, one last alternative is still to be discussed, a solution which seems lurking behind the Multi Context theories: "local" holism, a label which fits also some of Wittgenstein's remarks. While there is a general tendency to criticize global holism, local holism is nowadays considered a viable option (see for instance Peacocke 1997). However the label is still vague, and many interpretations of what "local holism" is are available. A first basic definition of local holism should give restrictions to the meaning of linguistic expressions relative to specific contexts in which they are used. A further specification might claim that the meaning of a word or a sentence depends on a "local" theory, and that - given no difference in principle between analytic and synthetic sentences - it depends on all the possible beliefs or inferences enclosed in that theory.

There is an ambiguity here. (Cognitive) contexts may be used to represent the sets of beliefs of individuals. Given that each person has her personal touch or that semantic twins do no exist in principle (at least when both say "I" they refer to different persons), there will be no possibility to have two cognitive contexts identical with one another. Representing cognitive contexts as sets of beliefs of individuals may have some advantage to solve some problems (differences of points of view, and so on). However contexts may also represent collective activity or shared information and action, may be given as representations of what is going on in a typical situation (as frames or scripts). In this case it is not always necessary to represent the point of view of the individual, but the point of view of the "social setting", the result of the interactions among individuals. Think for instance of a "restaurant" script and think of the concept "dish"; I don't care if the waiter believes that her aunt has a set of dishes with golden stripes. I care that the waiter beliefs that dishes are to be used for food, and that they are fragile. Are we going back to some form of atomism inside each contexts? Actually this is not the case. I am not suggesting to define each concept in isolation; however I think it important not to forget the basic core of the "typicality" or "default" reasoning, applied to meaning.

There is a solid core which is represented by the typical situations in which, as Wittgenstein says, "a word is at home", or in which a concept is typically used. The great lesson of frame nets is that we don't need a strict definition or strict (necessary & sufficient) meaning postulates, but just defeasible ones. The point is that if we abandon the principles behind the analytic-synthetic distinction, we may still find some pragmatic principles which justify the distinction between two sorts of inferences, the one defining basic uses of words, the other defining occasional applications of them. A philosophical attitude of this kind is well followed in the practice of A.I.: any "viable" (=which can be implemented in a system) representation of meaning as inferential role is bound not to include all (or most) possible inferences. Many A.I. programs may be considered as attempts to respect this restriction in defining meaning and understanding. There are many examples since the beginning of a.i.: McCarty ("advice talker") defines the concept of "immediate inference": in order to understand a situation we do not need to make explicit all the inferences from the relevant premises, but only their immediate consequences, beginning with the inferences which require just one step in the deductive process. The idea is barely sketched; however, it does point to the necessity of controlling the risk of combinatorial explosion of inferences; Norvig 1989 designed an algorithm computing a limited set of proper inferences quickly, without computing all types of inferences. Proper inferences are defined as plausible, relevant, and easy. Quick computation of a small set of proper inferences yields a *partial* interpretation, which can be used as input for further processing. In many frame systems we find a distinction between assertional and definitional part. The definitional part is not linked to the analytic-synthetic definition, but it is prompted by the necessity of the system to run properly. We may use the idea of frame (which can be represented as a set of default inferences) as a substitute of the idea of "basic" or "literal meaning".

On Gricean lines many authors suggest that the literal meaning is to be computed before any possible and possibly deviant interpretation. Grice's hypothesis has been criticized on the ground of psychological plausibility and other experimental results (see Gibbs 1993) which in principle make it dubious to speak of a unique "literal" meaning of a word. Reinforced also from the fact that each word and each concept may have many different uses and interpretations in different contexts, the concept of basic or literal meaning has been therefore challenged. The extreme alternative choice is to say that the meaning of a word is *always* relative to the specific context in which it is uttered, and therefore we have to decide the context before deciding which meaning is at stake. Searle 1979 has been one of the first authors to insist of the underdetermination of meaning in respect to context (or backgound), assuming that literal meaning does not exist, but only contextual determination permits to avoid ambiguity. Other author (see Bianchi 1999) has developed to the extreme this radical contextualism tending to abolish the divide between typicality and variation. This point is really hard to swallow (see appendix 1). Studies on typicality suggest that there is a solid core in meaning: basic inferential competence is construed in typical situations together with basic referential competence.

A solid core of procedures lies behind the possibility of variations of the uses of words in contexts. This procedural aspect of meaning together with the idea of typicality or default values is also the heritage of the first period of artificial intelligence, with the procedural paradigm of toy words and the development of frame systems with default values. We may point out that even in early toy words menings as procedures were assured compositionality (see Penco 1999). Criticisms on absence of compositionality in prototype theories (see Fodor 1998) do not exrtend to the procedural paradigm of meaning. Granting contextual restrictions to compositionality, we may accept a deveopment of the concept of meaning as procedure in both aspects pertaining to inferential and referential competence (see Marconi 1997, who tries to avoid speaking of "meaning", and tries to explain the dual aspect of lexical competence). This solid core of procedural meaning can be an explanation of the relative invariance of the conceptual lexicon (invariance also among languages and cultures) which is a datum we cannot avoid, and which can be evidences supporting it in many cases as, for instance:
- the slots to be filled in a frame for most of typical situations and the referential competence connected with basic ontology.
- the linguistic rules associated with indexicals and with reports of indirect speech [If I report her speech, I will say "she..."; if you report my speech, you will say "he...", and so on].
- the coherence of sets of words whose meaning is inter-definable or co-defined as a system like logical constants or words for colors.

A good test to choose between accepting the relative autonomy of the conceptual lexicon or following local holism in a "radical" contextualist way is comparing two expressions belonging to two different contexts. Are we allowed to speak of *identity of meaning* through contexts? Here identity of meaning may signify identity of inferences correlated to the expressions. We have an alternative:

(a) we decide to have some stable contexts, or definitional contexts, where an expression takes its most basic meaning, given by typical inferences and recognitional abilities. Clark 1992 speaks of "introductory scripts", referring to contexts appropriate to introduce a new linguistic expression. These definitional contexts should be able to be lifted in different contexts in which the word is used. We might therefore speak of sameness of meaning when a word used in two different contexts belongs to a definitional context which has been lifted in the two contexts without much change on the defauls values.

(b) we decide to allow only compatibility relations between expressions. We might say that two expressions are compatible if they may be intersubstitutable in the same contexts. But two expressions, even of the same type, can never have the same meaning if they are used in different contexts; in different context they will produce different inferences, and their inferential power or meaning will be different.

Following (a) ensures a safe way towards a theory of meaning which uses the concept of "basic meaning" of an expression to be a stereotypical representation which can be shared among contexts. The measure in which the values of the frame are shared gives the measure of similarity of meaning between the two concepts. The lexicon of a language might *partly* depend on the definitions in a "definitory" vocabulary, which should take into account partitions and levels of knowledge. We still maintain the relevance of cognitive contexts to decide the final interpretation of the meaning, but we still keep some starting points. On the other hand, if we follow (b), we may hold a point of view of radical local holism and we have either to give up speaking of meaning, or to define meaning each time, relatively to the context in which the expression is used. In this case it is not possible to define identity of meaning, unless we have identity of context. We might have no definitory vocabulary (or vocabularies), but just a list of expressions to be interpreted each time in each context.

Following a radical form of local holism we run the risk of missing something deeply embedded in our linguistic practice: the comparison of meanings, or of our sets of inferences and beliefs. The ability to say "you do not understand what I mean" or "you have got exactly the meaning of my words" relies on our social practice of converging on stable sets of typical inferences; their defeasable character is one of the peculiarity we have discovered in the past century. Defeasibility means also possibility to shift context, but also ability to recognize tipicality and normativity.

A misunderstanding seems to run through the discussion on cognitive contexts and it is the not always clear distinction between *kinds* of context (definitory contexts, working contexts, procedural contexts, belief contexts,...). When we treat contexts as sets of beliefs of individual agents, particular inferences drawn in each individual context will be unique for that context. Therefore we cannot think that individuals may share conceptual contents intended as exactly the same sets of inferences; as I said before no two persons could share that. But we all at least share basic rules to navigate across contexts; one of the most used is to pick up (import, lift) definitional contexts in different dialogues and actions. We may then change what is normally assumed for granted, but the change comes after a *prima facie* assumption of typicality. A new field of study is open to us: the study of the interaction between rules "external" to contexts, and what is defined "inside" contexts.

A working hypothesis which is emerging from different fields fo research is that at least *part* of the definition of our conceptual machinery derives from the convergence of high level rules among contexts, convergence which represents the agreement of individuals regarding basic information and action. The overlapping of uses and the relative stability of definitional contexts is anchored to the common acceptance of relations of compatibily among contexts. The difference between an extreme and a weaker form of local holism depends on the wheight given to this hypotesis: an extreme and radical form of local holism would suggest to abandon the concept of conceptual content and to recontruct it completey from these practices of converging (Brandom 1994 seems to go in this direction); a weaker form would insist on the relative persistence of conceptual structures which emerge in typical situations and are basic for our language learning and understanding. I have give some very programmatic remarks about the danger of following the radical form of local holism; this does not mean that this project deserves careful attention; any serach to put it to work may certainly reveal new dimensions of the contextual dependence of meaning and understanding. Local holism is however not necessarily so radical as that.

Appendix 1:

A note on the difficulty of "literal meaning"

"Alice finished the book"

The example is suggested by Pustejovsky: to interpret "Alice finished the book" you are compelled, in Pustejovsky's argument, to generate two readings, depending on the restrictions on "book" (a physical object which is read and written):
- Alice finished reading the book and
- Alice finished writing the book.
Apparently, if Alice is a goat and not a woman, you cannot accept *prima facie* these interpretations (unless the goat Alice is in a fantasy novel). Which answer could be given? Pustejovsky could specify that the "reading/writing" selection are linked to humans. "x finished the book" means "x finished reading/writing the book" if x is a human. This step might make the structure heavier and heavier. A simpler alternative might be to read "x finished y" as

"*x* terminated a process *z* regarding *y*",

where z is unspecified, depending on other information of the context. This would not count against the theory that the first interpretation to be computed is the "literal meaning". The reason is as follows: Pustejovsky claims that the "literal" meaning of "to finish" in the co-text of "to finish a book" is dependent on the object and its relevant properties. We may either abandon this choice or to weaken it. The option suggested above is not an abandon but a weakening. In Pustejovsky's semantics there is a distinction between two kinds of properties of a book: (i) a physical object (ii) something which can be read or written. We might restrict the basic definition of "to finish" to the first level. The more radical alternative is to abandon every link with the object. In this case "to finish" is computed even before arriving at the word "book": "to terminate an operation *z*". Which operation? It is not really important. Alice has brought to an end some operation. This is the literal meaning of "to finish", to be completed before deciding further specifications given by the context.

Appendix 2:

A short summary of the different stances on communication and meaning

"The cat is on the mat"

* *atomism:*
cat and mat are concepts causally imposed in our mind.

The meaning of the sentence is given by the language of thought and corresponding causal relation with reality.

* *strong molecularism*

a speaker and a hearer have to know definitions of:

cat (x) -> animal (x) and feline (x) and makes "miau" (x)

mat (x) -> made of wool (x) and on the floor (x) and used for

* *weak molecularism*

a speaker and a hearer have to share, by chance:

some property of cat and mat, not necessarily the so called definitions; for instance: "cats like mice", and "mats are made of wool"

* *global holism*

a speaker and a hearer have to share the entire system of the meaning theory:

in the form: " 'the cat is on the mat' is true iff the cat is on the mat"

* *convergence holism*

a speaker and a hearer have to converge towards a common passing theory:

the hearer has to intend the intentions of the speaker, who - for instance - may intend with "cat" what hearer means with "dog" and with "mat" what the hearer means with "blanket". The corresponding inferences follow.

* *local holism*

"cat" and "mat" are words which take their meaning from the use of these words in a context with given axioms and rules of inferences. Unless you specify the cognitive context, the words have no meaning at all.

* *weak local holism*

"cat" and "mat" are word which are defined in typical definitory contexts, and their basic frame structure (a set of inferences) is lifted in any context, waiting for a verification of compatibility. Changes are made afterwards.

References

1. Benerecetti M., Bouquet P., Ghidini C. 2000, "Contextual Reasoning Distilled", *Journal of Theoretical and Experimental Artificial Intelligence*, 12(3), 279- 305.
2. Bianchi C. 1999, "Three forms of Contextual Dipendence" in P. Bouquet, P. Brézillon, L. Serafini, F. Castellani eds. *Modeling and Using Context*, Springer, Berlin (67-76).
3. Brandom R. 1994 *Making it Explicit*, Harvard U.P., Cambridge (Mas)
4. Clark H.H. 1992, *Arenas of Language Use*, The University of Chicago Press, Chicago.
5. Davidson D. 1967, "Truth and Meaning" reprinted in D. Davidson 1984, *Inquiries into Truth and Interpretation*, Clarendon Press, Oxford.
6. Davidson D. 1986, "A Nice Derangement of Epitaphs", in E. Lepore (ed.) *Truth and In terpretation. Perspectives in the Philosophy of D. Davidson*, Blackwell, Oxford (433-446).
7. Dummett M. 1973, *Frege, Philosophy of Language*, Duckworth, London
8. Dummett M. 1992, *The Logical Basis of Metaphysics*, Duckworth, London.

9. Dummett M. 1993, *The Seas of Language*, Clarendon, Oxford.
10. Fauconnier, G. 1997, *Mappings in Thought and Language*, Cambridge University Press, New York.
11. Fodor J. 1998, *Concepts*, Clarendon Press, Oxford.
12. Fodor J., Lepore E. 1992, *Holism*, Blackwell, Oxford.
13. Gibbs R. W. 1993, "Process and products in making sense of tropes", in A. Ortony (ed.) Metaphor and Thought, Cambridge University Press, Cambridge.
14. Giunchiglia F. 1993, "Contextual reasoning", in C.Dalla Pozza-C. Penco(eds.) "Linguaggi e Macchine" Special Issue of *Epistemologia*.
15. Hinzen 1999, "Contextual Dependence and the Epistemic Foundations of Dynamic Semantics", in P.Bouquet, P. Brézillon, L. Serafini, F. Castellani eds. *Modeling and Using Context*, Springer, (186-199).
16. Marconi D. 1997, *Lexical Competence*, MIT Press, Cambridge (Mass.).
17. McCarthy J. 1968 "Programs with Common Sense" in M.Minsky (ed) *Semantic Information Processing* MIT Press, Cambridge.
18. McCarthy J. 1987, "Generality in A.I.", reprinted in McCarthy, *Formalizing Commonsense* (edited by V. Lifschitz), Ablex, 1990.
19. McCarthy J. 1993, "Notes on Formalizing Contexts" in *Proc.13 IJCAI*, Chambery (555-560).
20. Norvig P. 1989, "Marker Passing as a Weak Method for Text Inferencing" in *Cognitive Science* (469-620)
21. Peacocke C. 1997, "Holism", in B. Hale and C. Wright, *A Companion to the Philosophy of Language*, Blackwell, Oxford (227-247).
22. Penco C. 1999, "Holism in Artificial Intelligence?" in Language, Quantum, Music edited by M.L.Dalla Chiara, Laudisa and Giuntini, Kluwer.
23. Perry J. 1994n "Fodor and Lepore on Holism", in *Philosophical Studies*, 73 (123-138).
24. Pustejovsky J. 1995, *The Generative Lexicon*, MIT Press, Cambridge (Mass).
25. Quillian M.R., 1967 "Word Concepts: a Theory and Simulation of some Basic Semantic Capabilities", in *Behavioral Science*, 12 (410-430).
26. Quine W.V.O. 1960, *Word and Object*, MIT Press, Cambridge (Mass).
27. Searle J., 1979, *Expression and Meaning*, Cambridge U.P., Cambridge.
28. Stalnaker R. 1999, *Context and Content*, Oxford U.P., Oxford.
29. Wittgenstein L., 1953 *Philosophical Investigations*, Blackwell, Oxford.
30. Wittgenstein L., 1958, *The Blue and Brown Books*, Blackwell, Oxford.

Whom Is the Problem of the Essential Indexical a Problem for?

Isidora Stojanovic

Institut Jean Nicod, 1bis avenue Lowendal, F-75007 Paris, France, and
Stanford University, Dept. of Philosophy, Stanford, CA 94305-2155, USA
isidora.stojanovic@free.fr

Abstract. Philosophers used to model belief as a relation between agents and propositions, which bear truth values depending on, and only on, the way the world is, until John Perry and David Lewis came up with cases of *essentially indexical belief*; that is, belief whose expression involves some indexical word, whose reference varies with the context. I shall argue that the problem of the essential indexical at best shows that belief should be tied somehow to what is subsequently acted upon, and must make room for other relations than those properly predicated. But it does not show that belief cannot be modeled as a binary relation between an agent and some suitable object (*pace* Perry), nor that this object cannot be a proposition (*pace* Lewis).

1   The Problem

It is prima facie plausible to have the account of the notion of belief rely on these assumptions: A_1 Belief corresponds to a relation between an agent and an abstract object, called a *proposition*; A_2 Propositions are true or false depending on, and only on, the way the actual world is. However, it has been argued, most persuasively by John Perry and David Lewis, that such an account could not handle beliefs that are essentially indexical; that is, beliefs that one naturally expresses with the help of indexical expressions, such as "this", "today" or "I", which are known for being able to stand for different things in different contexts, without turning ambiguous thereby.

What has been under attack is not the claim that some beliefs cannot be *expressed* without indexicals, but the claim that propositions provide an apparatus powerful enough to model belief, granted that belief helps in accounting for behavior. Here is a situation, borrowed from Perry [4], which illustrates the problem. Suppose that I went hiking, and had previously gathered from guides and other sources all possible information on the area where I went hiking. But I got lost. I know that to leave the wilderness I should take the Mt. Tallac trail, but I do not know whether it is the trail right in front of me, or some other one. Suddenly, I realize: "This is the Mt. Tallac trail! This is the trail I should take!" And so I move onto the trail. Now, it seems that I have gotten here a new piece of information, but of what sort can that information be? What distinguishes my beliefs before I figured out which trail I was looking at, from my beliefs afterwards?

If one could show that there can be no proposition that I only came to believe when I figured out which trail I should take, and none that I ceased to believe either, one would be right to reject A_1 or A_2 – assumptions that I shall call the *naive* doctrine about belief. The naive doctrine holds that in every situation of the sort, it is always possible to come up with some suitable proposition. One who wants to refute it, then, must be able to dismiss every proposition came up with as inadequate. What I shall do is offer, one after another, propositions that provide the ground for a potential difference in behavior, and consider, as I go along, possible reasons to doubt that the difference has been made, until I reach a proposition against which there is neither empirical nor theoretical evidence.

The aim of the present paper is to show that propositions are tools good enough to classify beliefs, whether or not their expression involves indexicals. I shall not suggest that these should be the only available tools, or even the best ones – all I wish is to show that the naive doctrine stands the challenge that has been taken to undermine it. Now clearly, that challenge must not hinge upon the question of how propositions happen to be conceived. Whatever bears a truth value relative to, and only to, the way the world is, ought to be able to count as a proposition. But for the sake of expedience, I shall avail myself of the distinction between *general* and *singular* propositions. If propositions are thought of as being structured, general ones will be structured only out of relations, which include properties, and of second-order relations between relations. On the opposite side, singular propositions will also have particulars among constituents. If propositions are rather thought of as corresponding to sets of possible worlds, general ones will be sets closed under isomorphism (that is to say, if some world belongs to the set, every other world isomorphic to that one will belong to the set too), while singular ones will distinguish among isomorphic worlds as well.[1] Now, if it turned out that, for every particular, there were a class of properties that together hold of, and only of, that particular, the distinction between general and singular propositions would simply vacuous. Still, it may be helpful to maintain it, and to relate it to the distinction, found in the framework of predicate logic, between a closed sentence, and an open sentence endowed with an assignment of values to variables. Singular propositions, as against general ones, presuppose that a structure of interpretation has been previously settled upon.

The notion of singular proposition implies that it should be possible to refer to something *directly*, without having to individuate it as whatever uniquely falls under this-and-such description. It is an open issue what secures direct reference. There certainly ought to be some non-trivial relation to the object directly referred to. Russell used the relation of acquaintance to that effect: "I say that I am *acquainted* with an object when I have a direct cognitive relation to that object, that is when I am directly aware of the object itself."[2] What matters to the present discussion is that singular propositions belong among the tools available to the naive doctrine. Essentially indexical belief, it has been argued, cannot be accounted for in any propositional framework, be it provided or not with singular propositions or any

---

[1] In philosophical milieus, it is widely agreed on that the apparatus of structured propositions is more fine-grained than that of sets of possible worlds, but this difference in grain is in fact irrelevant to the issues that I shall be dealing with.

[2] [9], p. 16.

other device of direct reference. Perry wrote: "The problem is not solved merely by replacing or supplementing [the view that belief is a relation between subjects and propositions conceived as bearers of truth and falsity] with a notion of *de re* belief."[3] For our purposes, it will be safe to identify belief *de dicto* with belief that only takes general propositions as arguments, and analogously belief *de re* with belief some of whose arguments are singular propositions.

Let me clarify what the issue is. Suppose that, under the same circumstances, one behaves differently only if one entertains different beliefs. Then how sophisticated a machinery do we need to articulate those differences in belief? There might be more differences than general propositions allow us to make. In the hiking situation e.g., my promptness to move onto a particular trail can hardly, if at all, be accounted for by de dicto beliefs. But are there more differences than singular propositions allow us to make? That is the question I shall focus on. So, the moment I could say "This is the trail I should take", did I not acquire a de re belief about the Mt. Tallac trail, to the effect that I should take *it*? Well, philosophers seem to agree that I could have had that same belief all along, which leaves my change in behavior unexplained. Perry thus went on to suggest that there need be no change in *what* I believe, that is, in the conditions under which my beliefs are true. Instead, the difference in behavior would stem from the way in which I believe whatever it is that I believe. Thus when I think of the Mt. Tallac trail as of "this trail", nothing changes within my beliefs, only do I come to entertain my de re belief about the Mt. Tallac trail, to the effect that I should take it, under a different guise, picturing the "res" that my belief is about, as the trail that I am looking at.

The view just sketched sees the structure of belief as essentially bipartite: *what* is believed is not the only thing that matters; it also matters *how* that is believed. In what follows, I shall argue that there are no compelling reasons to go bipartite. The strategy, in a nutshell, will be to incorporate everything imparted upon the guise under which I entertain some belief, into the belief itself. Then the problem of the essential indexical turns out not to be a problem for the naive doctrine, as long as it takes care of the fact that beliefs, in the sense of the conditions under which beliefs are true, had better be tied to the particulars acted upon as a result of those beliefs; and also, of the fact that some relations, like of demonstrating or of looking at when perceptual demonstratives are used, are not limited to their heuristic role, but matter to what is believed as well.

2 In Quest of the Best Analysis of "This"

Once again, here is the situation. I know that, to leave the wilderness, I should take the Mt. Tallac trail, but am unsure as to which trail it is. Then, say at 6 p.m. sharp, I am ready to say: "This is the Mt. Tallac trail! This is the trail I should take!" Now, what is the belief that I come to express? It had better be a belief I must have lacked, if my action of moving onto the trail is to be explained by a change in beliefs. Perhaps what I got out of the hiking guides were not beliefs de re, but de dicto, with

---

[3] [4], p. 34.

respect to the Mt. Tallac. I would have merely believed that there existed some outward trail, named after Mt. Tallac, which I should have taken. Let that belief be glossed as:

$$\exists x \, (\delta x \,\&\, \text{I should take } x) \qquad\qquad p_0$$

where δ stands for some suitable description (e.g. x is an outward trail, x's name is "Mt. Tallac", x is mentioned in guides, etc.) In contrast, identifying the Mt. Tallac trail deictically would earn me a de re belief to the effect that I should take *it*:

$$\text{I should take } x \text{ [the Mt. Tallac trail} \to x] \qquad\qquad p_1$$

The worry with p_1 is that I could have believed that proposition all along – or so it seems. For suppose that I had taken the Mt. Tallac trail on my way to the wilderness. The trail must have become familiar enough to me to have de re beliefs about it, in particular p_1. But again, I could get lost, so p_1 would not account for my moving onto the trail only once I could say "This is the trail I should take."[4]

2.1 *"This"* as *"the Thing that I Am Looking at"*

In hope of avoiding overstrong constraints on the cognitive relation borne to the constituents of the propositions believed, let us seek a better candidate than p_1. It is crucial that my change in behavior occurred precisely at the moment at which I started looking at a certain trail *as* at the trail that I should take. So why not say that I simply came to have a de re belief about the Mt. Tallac trail, to the effect that it was not only the trail that I should take, but also the trail that I was looking at, glossed as:

$$\text{I should take } x \,\&\, \text{I look at } x \text{ at } t \text{ [the Mt. Tallac trail} \to x, 6 \text{ p.m.} \to t] \qquad p_2^{\cdot}$$

The worry, quite as before, is that it seems that I could have believed $p_2^{\cdot}$ all along. The case is somewhat harder than the previous one, for it is not clear what secures direct reference to some time, especially when the time referred to belongs to the future or to the past. But still, let us suppose that I had taken the Mt. Tallac trail on my way in, and that at some time earlier than 6 p.m., say at 5.57 p.m. sharp, I came to believe that I would be looking at the Mt. Tallac trail at 6 p.m., of which time I was directly aware somehow – e.g. I might have thought of it as of the time which was going to occur in exactly 3 minutes. But meanwhile, I have lost track of time, and have found myself in the same situation as before, knowing that I should take the Mt. Tallac trail, but not knowing which trail it was. Then $p_2^{\cdot}$, having already been among my beliefs, cannot account for my change in behavior.[5]

---

[4] One could still deny, however, that I continued to have de re beliefs about the Mt. Tallac trail, such as p_1, after I got lost. One could thus hold that we must continuously bear a direct cognitive relation to every constituent of the singular propositions we believe. At some point, I would have ceased believing p_1 to the detriment of a more general proposition, viz. that there existed some trail, named after Mt. Tallac, which I had taken on my way into the wilderness, and should take now to get out.

[5] Again, one could suggest that when I lost track of time, I also lost my grip on the relevant time, 6 p.m., losing thereby all my de re beliefs about it.

There is another worry with p_2, related to the contribution of the indexical "I". Assume that when I say "This is the trail I should take", I express a proposition that involves myself together with the Mt. Tallac trail, and is true depending on whether *I* should take *it*. Analyzing "this" further down, we come up with this alternative to p_2^-:

$$y \text{ should take } x \text{ \& } y \text{ looks at } x \text{ at } t \qquad\qquad p_2$$
$$[\text{Isidora} \rightarrow y, \text{ the Mt. Tallac trail} \rightarrow x, 6 \text{ p.m.} \rightarrow t]$$

Now, suppose that you also came hiking with me, but you do not want to get out of the wilderness. You also come to believe p_2. For the sake of the argument, we may even go as far as to suppose that our beliefs and desires are exactly the same – where desires, just as beliefs, are seen as *propositional* attitudes, i.e. as relations between agents and propositions –. Then both you and I have a de re desire about me, to the effect that I leave the wilderness, and a de re desire about you, to the effect that you do not leave the wilderness. Yet, we behave differently, since only I move onto the trail. How come?

In relation to the same issue, Ruth Millikan wrote: "It is trivial that if I am to react in a special and different way to the knowledge that I, RM, am positioned *so* in the world, a way quite unlike how I would react knowing anyone else was positioned so in the world, then my inner term for RM must bear a very special and unique relation to my dispositions to act. *But what does that have to do with indexicality?* My inner name 'RM' obviously is not like other names in my mental vocabulary. It is a name that hooks up with my know-hows, with my abilities and dispositions to act, in a rather special way."[6] What I find insightful in Millikan's remark has nothing to do, in turn, with inner names. The point, as I would put it, is that if some agent believes a proposition with himself as a constituent, he may act otherwise than someone else who believes that same proposition, simply because his behavior is attuned to the presence of himself in the propositions he believes or desires, and not to the presence of other agents. Thus my dispositions to act are attuned to beliefs about myself, yours to beliefs about yourself, and so on. This "reflexive" feature may be taken care of through the way in which action relates to beliefs and desires, so there need be no inner names, or anything alike.

2.2 Believing About without Attending To

I have just been brought upon an issue which, if left unsettled, may later cast doubt on the viability of the naive doctrine. The issue has to do with the cognitive relation we must bear to the constituents of the propositions that we have attitudes toward. Russell wrote: "Every proposition which we can understand must be composed wholly of constituents with which we are acquainted."[7] But if acquaintance implies "direct awareness", then some may find it questionable that when I say to myself "This is the trail that I should take", I need to be aware at all of the time, 6 p.m., at which the thought came down on me, and which has been made a constituent of p_2. The intuitions are that when, at 6 p.m., I come to think "This is the way I should go",

---

[6] [3], p. 273.
[7] [9], p. 23.

I am not reflecting on the relevant time, nor do I need to be attending to that time, or even to conceptualize it. Moreover, my behavior will not be different if the thought occurs to me a minute earlier or later, a day before or after, and so on. Insofar as the time is a constituent of my thought, it is an "unarticulated constituent", as Perry might have put it in [5]. The question, then, is whether grasping a proposition requires having articulated all of its constituents. If the answer were affirmative, something like Millikan's inner names would be called for, and opposite intuitions would have to be explained away. But clearly, there is nothing inherent to the notion of singular proposition that should force an affirmative answer upon us. Regardless of what Russell himself had in mind, the cognitive relation that we need for direct reference should not require any attentive reflection on the things referred to. So we might simply say that to grasp some proposition, one must *potentially* be directly aware of all of its constituents, the idea being that one who is not attending to some constituent of his belief, could always do so if he wanted to.

2.3 "*This*" as "the Object of This (Mental) Event"

With p_2, the worry was that I could have believed that proposition before I decided to move onto the Mt. Tallac trail. So why not try to tie the proposition that I came to believe then not only to the moment at which I started looking at the Mt. Tallac trail as at the trail I should take, but also to my action of so looking at it? Events such as looking at something, reflecting on it, invoking it in memory, etc., may be plausibly considered as particulars also. Indeed, we refer to them, ascribe them properties, and relate them to other particulars. Given that events generate singular propositions just as other worldly things do, to explain my moving onto the trail, we simply need some suitable proposition among whose constituents is the event that corresponds to my looking at the Mt. Tallac trail, at 6 p.m., as at the trail I should take. Let ε stand for that event. When I got ready to say "This is the trail I should take" and to move onto the trail, I came to have, inter alia, a de re belief about ε, to the effect that the Mt. Tallac trail was the object of *it*. Then what I expressed may be glossed as:[8]

$$y \text{ should take } x \text{ \& } y \text{ looks at } x \text{ at } t \text{ \& } x \text{ is the object of } z \qquad p_3$$
$$[\text{Isidora} \rightarrow y, \text{ the Mt. Tallac trail} \rightarrow x, \text{ 6 p.m.} \rightarrow t, \varepsilon \rightarrow z]$$

There are two worries with p_3 worth addressing. One comes from our layman's intuitions on the matter, and holds that there is just no plausibility to the idea that if I say "This is the trail I should take", I should ever express a belief about any mental event, in particular the one that I am undergoing. The other worry comes from the feeling that particulars corresponding to our mental events should, in principle, be possible to apprehend under different guises. Chances are then that the same agent could be endowed with the same de re beliefs about the same mental event, while still assuming different attitudes to it, therefore behaving differently.

The worry about the plausibility of using propositions such as p_3 proves spurious in the light of the observation that to have a de re belief about something, one does not have to be attending to it. The naive doctrine cannot be accused of letting action

---

[8] An option is to take "y undergoes z at t" instead of "y looks at x at t."

hinge upon the ability to conceptualize thoughts and other mental events, for it does not. The issue, once again, is whether the naive doctrine has got tools powerful enough to account for different behaviors under the same circumstances. Its having recourse to the mental events that the agent happens to undergo cannot commit it to the idea that every action of ours involves company of fully articulated thoughts about those thoughts themselves.

Now, does the other worry go through? Is it possible, for instance, to so modify the hiking situation as to let me have believed p_3 all along, even before I figured out, at 6 p.m., which the Mt. Tallac trail was, even before ε came into existence? That seems hard. There is a more general question, though: is it possible to bear a direct cognitive relation to some mental event, of the sort required to have de re beliefs about it, without actually undergoing that mental event? In particular, can anyone else than the person undergoing ε, grasp propositions about ε, such as p_3?

I shall not try to settle that question. What I shall do instead is argue that neither way will the naive doctrine come under threat. In other words, I shall argue to the conditional: even *if* it should turn out that one can directly refer to mental events that one does not undergo, there are ways for the naive doctrine to account for the change in behavior.

As with any conditional, let us suppose the antecedent, namely, that it is possible to refer to mental events directly, without undergoing them. To lend the idea a speck of plausibility, let us think of some case that makes this sort of direct reference possible. For instance, could you, my hiking companion, come to think, while I am undergoing ε, "*this* mental event of hers must be such-and-such"? Would the object of your thought be a singular proposition about ε, to the effect that *it* must be such-and-such? No, for it might have happened that I were not undergoing any mental event. The object of your thought would be at best a singular proposition about *me*, to the effect that the mental event I am undergoing, if any, must be such-and-such.

Since it is dubious that in everyday life we come to be directly aware of other mental events than the ones we ourselves undergo, it may be worthier to look at the case, say, of a neuroscientist who is working on mental processes. Suppose that a study is being carried out on several subjects, and that our neuroscientist is able to isolate particular mental events on the subjects' brain scans. Wouldn't he then be able to have de re beliefs about those mental events themselves, rather than de dicto ones? Whatever the answer to this question should be, let us assume, for the sake of the argument, that isolating a mental event on a brain scan secures direct reference to the event, and let us use this assumption to try to set out a pair of cases in which my beliefs, de dicto and de re, would be exactly the same, yet I would behave differently.

Engaging in something of a science-fiction, suppose that, unbeknownst to me, I am constantly brain-scanned, as part of a study carried out on several subjects by a team of neuroscientists. As before, I decide to go hiking, and I get lost. At 6 p.m. sharp, as I stare at the Mt. Tallac trail, it dawns down on me that *this* is the trail that I should take, and so I move onto the trail. At the same time, ε appears on my brain scan, so that everyone looking at my brain scan may now refer to ε directly, and form de re beliefs about ε. In particular, let us assume that, knowing me wishful to leave the wilderness, all of our neuroscientists come to believe p_3 itself:

y should take x & y looks at x at t & x is the object of z p_3
[Isidora $\rightarrow y$, the Mt. Tallac trail $\rightarrow x$, 6 p.m. $\rightarrow t$, $\varepsilon \rightarrow z$]

Now, add to the situation that I also happen to be part of the team, and have access to the brain scans of some of the subjects. So let us consider two versions of this situation. On one version, the subject whose brain scan I have access to is not myself, whereas on the other, it is myself – although, of course, I am ignorant of that. Suppose furthermore that I had been instructed, were I to isolate on the brain scan some mental event having the Mt. Tallac trail for object, I should remain still until further instruction. So here is what we get: I go hiking, get lost, but end up figuring out which trail I should take. Now, on one of the two tokens, as usual, I move onto the trail. But on the other, ε appears on the brain scan, and no later than I have spotted it do I decide to remain still, as instructed.

Despite its fictional nature, the situation is challenging in that, if we give credit to the naive doctrine, it seems that we will end up endowing the agent (me) with exactly the same beliefs. But in the case in which I happen to have access to my own brain scan, one may be inclined to say that I came to believe p_3 "twice", under different guises: once in a genuine token-reflexive manner, another time in a deictic manner, as every other neuroscientist. There is an intuitive difference between those manners of coming to believe p_3, which might explain the difference in my behavior. But how can the naive doctrine make use of that difference, if it is to be a difference in *how* I believe things, and not in *what* I believe?

The bet of the naive doctrine was that whenever the same agent assumed different behaviors under the same circumstances, there would be some proposition that he or she believed in one case only. Here we have one and the same agent – me, and the circumstances seem to be the same. I do not behave in the same manner, yet there seems to be no proposition to distinguish between my beliefs. And if this is how things are, the naive doctrine has clearly lost its bet… But this is *not* how things are! For there are propositions to distinguish between my beliefs. In the case in which I do not move onto the trail, I have an additional de re belief about ε, to the effect that it is the mental event that I have isolated on the brain scan.[9]

---

[9] There are two more worries with the view that uses propositions such as p_3. One, concerning infinite regress, rests on the assumption that every occurrence of "this" must be further analyzed in terms of the complex "this mental event". But clearly, nothing commits to this assumption, nor does anything prevent one from taking "this mental event" for a primitive term. The other worry, concerning circularity, rests on the assumption that it is possible to individuate beliefs by their contents; so, how could the content of some belief have the belief itself as a constituent, since one would then have to individuate the belief itself in order to individuate its content, yet this content is necessary to individuate the belief? Without rejecting the assumption, one may simply define contents of beliefs inductively. Let s stands for the belief that I would express by saying "This φs" in reference to some b. As any mental episode, s extends through time, say from t_i to t_j. Suppose that the interval [i, j] is well-ordered by its linear order, and let the content of s at t_i be empty by definition, and for every k: $i<k\leq j$, let the content of s at t_k consist of b's φing and of b's being the most salient thing relative to the belief individuated by the sum of the contents of s at t_l, for every l: $i\leq l<k$. In spite of sketchiness, this hint at a definition reveals that the worry should not be paid great attention.

3 What Has Been Objected to the Naive Doctrine

Let us see what Perry and Lewis were upset for. Perry's conviction that the notion of de re belief cannot handle the problem of the essential indexical is partly due to focusing on only one way of associating de re beliefs with the "essentially indexical" ones. An essentially indexical belief, recall, is a belief one naturally expresses with the help of indexicals. Thus, in the atomic case, let P be some predicate and ι some indexical term. Perry seemed to think in [4] that the only singular proposition some utterance of "Pι" was likely to express, was: $\mathbf{P}x$ [b $\rightarrow x$], with $\mathbf{P}$ the property denoted by "P" (ignoring tense, for the sake of simplicity), and b the individual referred to with "ι" in the context of the utterance. For instance, if, in reference to the Mt. Tallac trail, I say "This is an outward trail", I shall be assigned only the de re belief that consists in the property of being an outward trail ascribed to the Mt. Tallac trail. It comes then as little surprise that such "atomic" de re beliefs are not powerful enough to account for behavior. As Stalnaker noted: "the lesson of the examples of essentially indexical belief – the examples that motivate Perry's account – is that indexicals are essential to the information itself and are not just part of the means used to represent it."[10] A sentence built out of some predicate and the demonstrative "this" need not be limited to ascribing only the predicated property to what the demonstrative stands for. There is no reason it should not encompass the property of being currently looked at, e.g. So to sum up, Perry would have been right to say that the problem of the essential indexical is not solved merely by supplementing de dicto beliefs with a certain fairly restricted class of de re beliefs. But this is clearly not to say that *no* de re belief may supply a solution to the problem.

To see what Lewis was upset for, we must imagine two "omniscient" hikers wishful to leave the wilderness. One hiker is looking at the Mt. Tallac trail, while the other happens to be looking at some *inward* trail instead. Now, for every proposition, the hikers know, ex hypothesi, whether it is true or not. In terms of possible worlds, they know exactly which world is theirs. But neither knows, claims Lewis, whether he should move or not onto the trail, because neither knows *which* of the two hikers he is, nor which trail he is looking at.

Now, unless it may be shown that mental events cannot be considered as a sort of particulars, this argument is flawed. Indeed, at least one of the assumptions that it rests on is false. If it is not the assumption that the hikers know all true propositions, i.e. know exactly which world is theirs, then it is the assumption that they are unsure as to what to do. Here is why. At some point, each hiker comes to wonder whether he should move onto the trail that he is looking at. Let ε_0 and ε_1 stand respectively for the mental events that consist of their looking at those trails. Then the proposition, call it q_0, about ε_0, to the effect that its object is an outward trail, is true, while an analogous proposition about ε_1, call it q_1, is false. The hikers, being omniscient, are deemed to know that q_0 is true and q_1 false. The problem, it is argued, is that neither knows *which* mental event, q_0 or q_1, he himself has undergone.

Now, one cannot just stipulate, without further ado, that each hiker knows q_0 to be true and q_1 to be false, yet cannot identify the mental event that he has undergone as

---

[10] [11], p.148.

ε_0 or ε_1 respectively. First of all, the hiker who undergoes ε_0 bears a direct cognitive relation to ε_0, as does to ε_1 the hiker who undergoes ε_1. So, to give the argument its chance, one must stipulate that the hikers did not come to know q_0 to be true and q_1 false via the most direct relation they respectively bear to ε_0 and ε_1. But then, could they acquire that knowledge and yet be unable to reidentify ε_0 and ε_1, as they occur in q_0 and q_1, as the mental events they have undergone respectively? I do not see how they could. Take the hiker who has undergone ε_0. He is directly aware of it in virtue of having undergone it, and is again directly aware of it in virtue of whatever has earned him the knowledge of q_0's truth. Is it then possible for him not to realize that these are one and the same mental event? No, if he is omniscient. For if he failed to realize that, there would be a proposition – an identity proposition, to wit – whose truth he would be ignorant of.

The fact is that each hiker must be directly aware of the mental event that he has undergone. Furthermore, the way in which the hiker who has undergone ε_0 came to know q_0 to be true must, modulo his omniscience, allow him to realize that q_0 is about the mental event that he has undergone. *Idem* for the hiker who has undergone ε_1 and the way in which he came to know q_1 to be false. So it cannot be the case that the hikers are unsure as to what to do – unless, again, they are ignorant of q_0, q_1, or even worse, of some identity proposition.

Lewis's argument proves flawed in the framework of possible worlds as well. Let w be the actual world (that is, actual to the hikers), and v a possible world exactly like w, except for the fact that ε_0 and ε_1 had switched places, so to say. According to Lewis, the hikers know exactly which world is theirs – w, to wit. But if they are still unsure whether to take the trails that they are looking at, then it cannot be the case that they know w to be the actual world. They can only know that either w or v is the actual world, but they cannot decide between the two. Only when they figure out which are the trails that they are looking at will they sway from the knowledge that the actual world is either w or v, to the knowledge that it is w and not v. The point, in one word, is that the hikers cannot distinguish w from v, unless they are already able to distinguish ε_0 from ε_1.[11]

4 Conclusion

When Perry and Lewis questioned it, the naive doctrine was seen as the received view. Since then, the idea that propositions are not powerful enough to model belief and account for behavior, has become something of a received view itself. I have argued here that the problem of the essential indexical does not refute the naive doctrine. Every time we came upon an agent who, under the same circumstances,

---

[11] Stalnaker made a similar point: "The case of the two gods (...) is also a case of ignorance of which of two indiscernible possible worlds is actual. (...) The gods are not really omniscient with respect to propositional knowledge, although they are omniscient with respect to purely qualitative features of the world." See [11], p.143. Note that w and v are perhaps qualitatively distinguishable – perhaps mental events that switch places, as ε_0 and ε_1 have done, must instill qualitative differences to the world. If true, this would just break the argument even further.

assumed different behaviors, we were able to distinguish his beliefs by means of some proposition.[12] Propositions about ordinary things, like you, me or the Mt. Tallac trail, most often do the trick. When they do not, others, whose truth depends on things such as mental events, do. Note that the naive doctrine does not have to put special constraints on the cognitive relation borne to mental events propositions about which are to grasped. The conditions for referring to things directly, remain the same regardless of whether the things referred to happen to be mental events, other sorts of events, or other sorts of particulars. Now, it is not excluded that the mental events that allow for direct reference should be *de facto* the same events as the ones that are undergone at the time of reference – that is an empirical question.

Two lessons have emerged from the problem of the essential indexical. One has to do with ensuring that a given agent will act upon a certain thing rather than another. For this, we need tools analogous to those supplied by the notion of de re belief. To be sure, what a belief is about, and what the believer will be led to act upon, does not need to play an explanatory role in the account of the nature of the resulting action. Views on which belief is modeled as a relation to things other than propositions, like the view that belief relates agents to properties, defended by Lewis, are perhaps more attractive on this point. But this tells us nothing against the naive doctrine. For some complex may well be the object of belief, even if some constituents of the complex do not affect behavior.

The other lesson has to do with the relationship between indexicals, which are linguistic devices for expressing beliefs, and the beliefs expressed. It has emerged that the role of an indexical often goes beyond the thing that the indexical stands for in a given context. Key roles may be conferred on the agent's relation to that thing, rather than to the thing itself. Now many, including Perry, Kaplan or Recanati, seem to think that such relations must fall outside what is properly believed, and only qualify the way in which that is believed.[13] But there is no compelling reason, I have argued, to think that those relations should not be part of what is believed.

The problem of the essential indexical is not an insuperable problem for the naive doctrine. True, it shows that heed should be paid to what is acted upon as a result of some belief. Singular propositions allow us to do that, as does any mechanism of direct reference. The problem also shows that care is to be taken not only of the relations that come with the predicate, but also of the relations that come with the indexicals with whose help some belief is expressed. To take care of them, we need nothing more than propositions *tout court*.[14]

---

[12] To be sure, I did not show that for every single possible case of the sort, there existed some suitable proposition. However, the burden of the proof is now again on the opponent's side. Ideally, the naive doctrine should come up with a method of construing a suitable proposition upon the parameters of the case. Since problematic cases appear to arise only when something has been identified under different guises, the clue lies, I believe, in turning those guises into relations proper, which may then be incorporated into the proposition under construal.

[13] See [6], pp. 529-540 of [1], and Part I of [8], respectively. I ought to emphasize that Perry's current view (as in [7] e.g.) has changed in certain important aspects. I can only regret having been unable to take the relevant changes into account in the present paper.

[14] I am indebted to David Chalmers for helpful suggestions, as well as to John Perry, François Recanati, Philippe Schlenker and two anonymous reviewers for comments on an earlier draft.

References

1. Kaplan, D.: Demonstratives, in *Themes About Kaplan*, Oxford UP (1989)
2. Lewis, D.: Attitudes *De Dicto* and *De Se*, in *Collected Papers*, Oxford UP (1993)
3. Millikan, R.: The Myth of the Essential Indexical, Noûs **24** (1990)
4. Perry, J.: The Problem of the Essential Indexical, Noûs **13** (1979), reprinted in [6]
5. Perry, J.: Thought without Representation, Supplementary Proceedings of the Aristotelian Society **60** (1986), reprinted in [6]
6. Perry, J.: *The Problem of the Essential Indexical*, Oxford UP (1993)
7. Perry, J.: *Knowledge, Possibility, and Consciousness*, The MIT Press (2001)
8. Recanati, F.: *Direct Reference*, Blackwell Oxford (1993)
9. Russell, B.: Knowledge by Acquaintance and Knowledge by Description, Proceeding of the Aristotelian Society **11** (1919), reprinted in [10]
10. Salmon N., Soames S. (eds.), *Propositions and Attitudes*, Oxford UP (1988)
11. Stalnaker R.: Indexical Belief, Synthese **49** (1981)

Contextual Categorization and Cognitive Phenomena

Charles Tijus

Laboratoire CNRS- ESA 7021 de Cognition et Activités Mentales Finalisées,
Université de Paris 8.
http://www.ipt.univ-paris8.fr/~psycog/

Université de Paris 8, 2, rue de la Liberté,
93526 Saint-Denis Cedex 02 FRANCE
Tel: 00 33 1 49 40 64 79
Fax: 00 33 1 49 40 67 54
tijus@univ-paris8.fr

Abstract. Contextual Categorization theory (CC-T) is introduced as a theory based on Galois lattices that are used to capture the organization of current situations. It is shown how the objects and their properties are processed to simulate cognitive phenomena related to context effects: denotation, description, explanation, similarity judgement, analogy, non-literal language understanding and reasoning.

Introduction

Contextual categorization is a component of diverse theories or models about human cognition that comprises perceptual categorization (1; 2), categorization for text understanding (3), or task oriented categorization (4). The aim of this paper is to describe how Contextual Categorization Theory (CC-T) works and how it can help explaining some cognitive phenomena.

CC-T can be seen as founded by a basic and simple mechanism which is applied to process environmental inputs of any kind. It is of interest because it has two main results: (i) it shows the organization of both present objects and of present properties, more precisely how properties are distributed to form objects and (ii) it reflects the organization of the world.

Contextual categorization model (CC-M) operates on Galois Lattices to create the one hierarchy of categories with transitivity, assymetry and irreflexivity, when given the O_n X P_m boolean matrice which indicates for each of the n objects, O, if it has, or if it has not, each of the m properties, P. The maximum number of categories is either 2^{n-1}, or m if $m < 2^{n-1}$, in a lattice whose complexity depends on the way properties are distributed over objects (figure 1). Consider three objects (o1, o2, o3) having some of a set of properties (p1, p2, p3, ..., p7), as in the boolean table of figure 1.

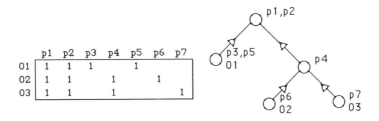

Figure 1. Binary descriptions of 3 objects and its corresponding Galois Lattice.

The corresponding Galois lattice is shown in figure 1 as a hierarchy of Categories. Let us label X the categorie defined by properties p1 and p2 and Y the category defined by properties p3 and p5. Object o1 is an instance of the category Y which has category X as superordinate. The link between Y and X is a "KIND-OF" link: Y is a kind of X. Due to the inheritance principle, category Y includes properties p1 and p2, the properties of categorie X. This can be seen in the boolean table of figure 1.

Let's take as a simple example the set of objects depicted in figure 2 : "A a 1 b 2". These objects can be described with the following list of properties (or features, or descriptors) : "character, letter, number, vowel, consonant, upper-case, lower-case, order in the set (place 1 to 5), /a/, /one/, /b/, /two/, ...". The Galois Lattice (5, 6) can be used to build the hierarchy of categories that merges when factorizing the properties (figure 2). In this case, the categories are contextual categories because categorization is a function of what objects are in the current situations and not on pre-existing categories in long term memory.

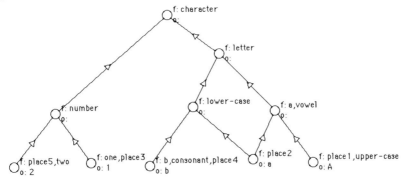

Figure 2. The Galois lattice for a set of five objects " "A a 1 b 2" formed with the following properties : "character, letter, number, vowel, consonant, upper-case, lower-case, order in the set (place 1 to 5), /a/, /one/, /b/, /two/, ...". in this graph, "o" means "object", "f" means "feature", nodes represent categories that are hierarchically linked by "is a kind of" association. Thus "o : 1" (object "1" is an instance of [category f: one, place3] which is subordinate to [category f: number] which in turn is a kind of [category f: character]

First, the hierarchy of categories provides a circumstantial and contextual structure of the presented objects : all objects are characters, there are letters and numbers, and so on. Note that increasing the number of already existing objects will not change the number of categories neither the structure of the network : for instance, the following set of objects "A A 2 b a 1 2 1 1 a 1 b 2" will display the same network of categories (nodes and links).

Second, the Galois lattice renders explicit for instance that "lower-case" and "upper-case" do not apply to numbers, that "number" and "letter" are kind of "character", and that each object has a proper place, which is its ontological property. These relations between properties and between categories of objects and properties can be due to the sample in hand, but it might also reflects the structure of the world, which is to say that all letters are characters and that we will never met numbers in lower or upper-case or two objects having the same place. The world permanence of one relation can be confirmed or dismissed with more experience with the objects of the world.

In addition, and what is fundamental to CC-T, is that contextual categorization computes each unique object in the context of all the other objects which form its unique context.

It is known, for instance that processing in context provides a number of interesting cognitive phenomena. For instance, when properties are related to each other in this way, there are also semantic effects. Thus, "racoons" and "snakes" are judged to be more dissimilar when they are not placed in an animal context (7). This is probably because the relational properties that are brought about by the presentation context depend on the objects that are presented (8, 9, 10). These are referred to as "extension effects" by Tversky (11), who has shown that South-American countries are judged to be more similar to each other when they are presented alongside European countries than when they are presented on their own. This is mainly the kind of cognitive phenomena CC-T adresses.

We first present the basic computing assumptions of contextual categorization Theory. Then, we show how a number of phenomena such as denotation, description and explanation, similarity, analogy, metonymy, metaphor, tautology and reasoning can be derived from the processing of contextual categories.

2. Computing relations for contextual categories

Let us take two terms, X and Y, to represent two values of a property, two properties, two sets of properties or two objects or categories of objects. Inferences with regard to the relationship between X and Y can concern the nature of the relation in intension (*part-whole* and *kind of*), its nature in extension (independence, exclusion, implication and equivalence) and the orientation of the relation (non-oriented, oriented and the opposite of this).

2.1. Known intensional relation

In intension, X and Y may already have a known relation. For instance a *part-whole* or *a kind of* relation. The *part-whole*-type relation does not only concern structural properties of a physical nature (e.g. "X : has skin, Y : has a body"), but also properties linked to action : "taking hold of its handle" is part of "transporting a saucepan"; for instance the participants studied by Rips & Conrad (12) interpreted "imagining" as "a part of", "dreaming". The *kind of-* type relation, which is a complex one because it requires an abstraction, does not only concern relations between categories. It also applies to *property lines* (13), in that "vermilion" is a sort of "color".

We should note that it is not always easy to distinguish between *part-whole* and *kind of*, in that if X is a part of Y, Y is a kind of object of which X is the property (leaves are part of a tree and a tree is a sort of leafy object). Moreover, if Y is a sort of X, the description of X forms part of the description of Y (14, 15). CC-T takes these intensional relations[1] for granted.

2.2. Computing occurrences

In extension, i.e. basing ourselves on the observation of occurrences, it is possible to envisage a Boolean logic[2] based on the absence (0) vs the presence (1) of X and Y. Between X and Y, there is
- independence, when the presence of one does not allow us to infer the presence of the other,
- equivalence, when the presence of one brings about the presence of the other and vice-versa.
- exclusion, when the presence of one precludes the presence of the other,
- implication, when the presence of one brings about the presence of the other, though the reverse is not necessarily true,

Lastly, for implication, the relation can be non-oriented, oriented, converse or reciprocal. The non-oriented relation is a relation which can flow just as easily from X to Y as it can from Y to X. The oriented relation is only valid in one direction, for example, X to Y ,but not Y to X. A converse relation is an implication between types of relation. Accordingly, if there is an A-type relation from X towards Y, then we will observe a B-type relation from Y towards X, though the opposite will not necessarily be true. Lastly, the reciprocal relation is a doubly converse relation, in that an equivalence between implications of types of relations is recorded : if we observe an A-type relation from X towards Y, from Y towards X we will observe a B-type relation, and vice-versa (if it is from Y to X, it will be a B-type relation, so if it is from X to Y, it will be an A-type relation). Thus, by definition, the relation of equivalence is non-oriented and the *sort of* relation is oriented. The *part-whole* relation is a converse relation in instances where, in the presence of the whole, the part composing this whole is necessarily present, whereas when we have the part, we do

---

[1] How intensionnal relations could be learnt through contextual categorization, what we think, is not considered as a topic of this article.

[2] We should note that fuzzy logic (the work of Zadeh, or of Bouchon-Meunier) allows us to take imprecise values into account, while Bayesian inferences allow us to taken into consideration the probabilities of the presence/absence of X and Y together with the notion of quasi-implication (c.f., the work of Bernard & Charron). Their use is not under the topic of this article.

not necessarily have the rest needed to form the whole. Lastly, in terms of describing object categories, we can record a reciprocal relation between *part-whole* and *sort of*. Thus, if the X category is a sort of Y category, the description of Y will form part of the description of X. And if the description of Y forms part of the description of X, X must be a sort of Y (15).

When it is applied to the values that a property can take, this computation allows us to make distinctions between different properties. For example, certain properties can have inclusive values, others not. Certain properties can be exclusive and others not. Accordingly, the *number of years* versus the *number of tokens*, or then again the *place* as opposed to the *size* are properties that are not equivalent with regard to the inferences they enable us to make. Thus, Peter who is 6 years old is not 5 (exclusion), whereas if he has 6 tokens, he has 5 tokens (implication). Similarly, although two objects cannot occupy the same place (exclusion of values), they can be of the same size (non exclusion). In this respect, according to Tijus (16), many classic problems in psychology arise out of the inadequate inferences that subjects make on the basis of values that object properties can take. A simple illustration of this would be to imagine a problem where the solution is to draw lines that joins two dots, people will draw lines that start from one point and end at the second dot while the solution requires drawing lines going beyond the dots, or a problem where the solution is a square, though a rectangle is mentioned in the wording of the problem. While the unequal nature of the sides does not form part of the subject's definition of the rectangle, the subject will base all his or her attempted solutions on the exclusion of the equality of the sides.

Certain relations allow us to characterize properties as separable (e.g. color and shape) or integral (e.g. saturation and brightness combine to form the inseparable whole that is color). Separable relations can arise from empirical observation if they frequently co-occur (small, light) or then again from implications of a causal nature (push, move), a semantic nature (blue, color) or a structural nature (has an edge, shape). If these kind of relations can be sought directly between the properties (in intension), they can also be inferred via the objects in question (in extension). We can look for these relations in extension by considering the scope of the property. Thus, for example, in a situation where Peter announces that he is "going to have the furniture moved" and Marie that she is "going to polish it", we understand that a "polished piece of furniture" will be a "moved piece of furniture", but that a "moved piece of furniture" will not necessarily have been polished. In a way, *to polish* implies *to move* here. However, the relation brought about here by the extension is an ad-hoc relation, a contextual relation, not a significant one. *Polishing* is not a sort (or manner) of *transporting*.

2.3. Inferring relations

Relations also exist between different property types according to their type. A fundamental relation exists between structure, function and procedure, in that functional and procedural properties are in some ways secondary properties of the structural properties on which they depend. We can use a functional object (F) to act on a "patient" object (P) providing that F has the structural properties that will allow it to be used as a functional object for P. Moreover, the way in which the procedure integrates F and P will also depend on the structural properties of F and P. It is easy to see that in order to cut a sheet of paper (P) with a pair of scissors (F), the structural properties of the scissors (which enable them to cut) must be capable of applying to the structural properties of the paper (which make it "cuttable") according to a procedure which will also depend on other structural properties of the scissors (can be held by the handle).

However, the structural properties of F and P may be either visible or hidden. In the case of the former, by matching up the properties of the "patient" object P and the structural properties of F, we can generate the functional properties of F and the procedural properties of F and P. Thus, if I want to "transport water", perceiving the structural properties of the saucepan (container and handle) enables me to infer the function (can be used for) and the procedure (how to do it), even if I am seeing the saucepan for the very first time. We believe that this matching up is at the root of the "affordances of the environment" described by Gibson and based on the notion of "Aufforderungscharakter" used by Kurt Lewin in his motivation theory. For Lewin, there is a correspondence between the state of the subject (his or her target) and the valence (Aufforderungscharakter) of the objects within his or her scope. For instance, there is a correspondence between hunger and edible objects. Affordances correspond to that which the environment offers in the way of opportunities for action. We are looking here at relations between the environment and the subject's possibilities for action which can be perceived as such. "Perceiving" the presence of the floor allows us to envisage moving from one point to another, whereas the absence of the floor will not allow us to do so. "Perceiving" an object as a container allows us to envisage placing something within it.

As for the relations that structural, functional and procedural properties can have with surface properties, if the structural properties are masked as is often the case, the functional and procedural ones must be discovered and learnt[3].

Certain inferences based on values concern the new value that an attribute acquires following a particular event or action. Objects must also be placed in relation to each other, for while the conceptualization of the situations influences the selection of the properties to be considered in the light of the transformations to be carried out (17). We make use above all of relations between properties – those properties that an object has "in relation" to other objects either in terms of location (to the right of, above, etc.) or in terms of surface properties (same color) or structural properties (identical parts, method of assembly, etc.), or then again in terms of action (X and Y carry out something together) or agent-patient intentional causality (X acts on Y) arising from functional and procedural properties. These relational properties are properties that are extrinsic to the object, (in that they do not concern the object on its own but in relation to others) and which change as the situation evolves.

---

[3] With experience, if certain surface properties are found to have a strong correlation with the structural properties, they can be used to trigger action. This could correspond to the "putting into place of affordances".

3. Cognitive phenomena under the light of contextual categorization

Our general hypothesis is that many cognitive abilities can take advantage of contextual categorization. Among the kind of human cognitive phenomena under investigation there are (i) denotation which is the ability to use context to designate without ambiguity an object, (ii) description which is the ability of summarizing data at many levels of precision depending on the purpose of the description, (iii) explanation to make someone understand what is under question, (iv) similarity to judge how one object looks like another one or looks like a set of objects, (v) analogy which is the capacity to use similarity to use what is known from one object (or a set of objects) and that can be transferred to another object (or to a set of objects), (vi) non-literal language which is used to talk about objects using a part of this object (metonymy), name of other objects or nomes of properties of other objects (metaphor), and tautology to say something about one object (or a set of objects) while saying virtually nothing (e.g., London is London), and finally (vii) the ability of making inferences.

3.1. CC-Denotation

The ability to designate an object is the more evident characteristic of contextual categorization. It explains why objects are so differently named. Having the set of objects "A a 1 b 2", "A" could be designated by a number of names : "character, letter, vowel, upper-case, object at the first place, /a/, ...". It could be named as "character" in " - A - - -", as "letter" in " 8 5 A 9", as "vowel" in "7 9 b A B", as /a/ in "A E p 3" and as "upper-case" or "object at the first place" in "A a 1 b 2" but not in this last case as "character", "letter", "vowel" or "/a/". The solution of how to name "A" in "A a 1 b 2" is given in the Galois lattice of figure 2 corresponding to this set of objects: to designate an object, or a group of objects, without ambiguity, consider the properties linked to the most specific category of this object. Thus "A a" can be called "vowel" or "/a/" because there any other vowels, "a b" can be called "lower case", and so on.. In our example, "place" can be used for designating any object. But if this is not possible (for instance if the set of objects were displaying at random in a two dimensional space), how to name "a" in "A a 1 b 2" ?. Contextual categorization shows that one property is not enough to name without ambiguity "a". The conjonction of the two terms "lower-case vowel" should be used.

3.2. CC-Description

Providing a short, but complete, or a more deep description of a situation is another of the cognitive abilities that can be supported by CC-T. Generating sentences such as "This is a set of characters", "This is a set of numbers and "letters", "This is a set of numbers and of letters that are either in lower-case or upper-case", are levels of description from general to more and more specific which summarize the data. The chosen level would depend on the purpose of the description. Note that, contrary to denotation, which is a bottom up path from specific to general categories, description is computed top-down, from general to specific categories.

3.3. CC-Similarity

Similarity between objects is directly processed by CC-T Galois lattice, since objects are grouped in categories given their commonalties and differences. But this is not sufficient to support contextual similarity. One of the other main results of CC-T for similarity is that objects that do not share any of their properties may be judged very similar according to the whole context. For instance, a book and the moon can be considered has being per se very dissimilar (figure 3, left panel), but in the context of other objects, they can be judged similar for instance when they both differ from the other objects (figure 3, right panel). For instance, they can be judged as similar as being "intruders" or as "being of other kinds". This is directly represented in the Galois lattice since all the characters of figure 3 will be grouped in a sub-category of the top category "object" while "moon" and "book", being rejected, will be instances of other categories. Thus, with contextual categorization, similarity is computed considering the whole network of categories.

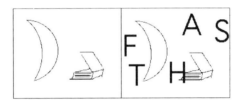

Figure 3. A book and the moon are judged more similar between letters (right panel) than when seen alone (left panel).

3.4. CC-Analogy

Analogy makes use of similarity for transferring properties. For instance, an analogue set of "A a 1 b 2" would be "E e 2 c 3". It could be "B b 2 c 3" if consonant and vowel were not retained properties. It could be "E e 3 c 4" if "even" and "odd" were to be considered as properties. How to solve the analogy problem is how to transfer the set of relations. The set of relations is provided by the network of categories. The target and the source should be aligned and alignment is provided by the hierarchy of properties in the Galois lattice. Similarly, having "A a 1 b 2" as a source, what can be put at the X place in "E e 2 X 3" ? The answer can be easily induced. For same reasons, the moon can be said being "as the book" in the right panel of figure 3. In contextual categorization paradigm, analogy is nothing more than recognition. Saying that "b" in "A a 1 b 2" is a lower-case as "a" but is a consonant is a proposition produced by the same process that generates "c" (lower case, consonant) for answering the question "gimme another letter instead of "b".

324

3.5. CC-Explanation

Explanation is the process of providing information to someone who already does have some prerequisite knowledge (which should be first evaluated). For instance, in order to explain what is a duck, "a duck" can be defined as being an "animal", like a "chicken", but going in the water making a "coin-coin" sound (which is the french duck call). This explanation will be provided for instance to a child which is supposed to know what are "animal, chicken, water and animal call". Facing "A a 1 b 2", a child could ask "what is the fourth object ?". Answering "this is a lower case letter as the second letter but a consonant while this second letter is a vowel" can be automatically produced by computing the Galois Lattice of figure 2 for "A a 1 b 2".

Such explanation-based verbalization were collected by Faure & McAdams (in preparation) with participants having to judge similarity between two sounds (sound 1 and sound 2) and to explain their judgement. To do so, twelve sounds were presented in couples providing 12 X 11 verbalizations by each of 20 listeners. Collaborating with Faure and McAdams, we reasoned that if explanation-based verbalization were computed as predicted by CC-T, then participants should provide properties in their description in a strict order.

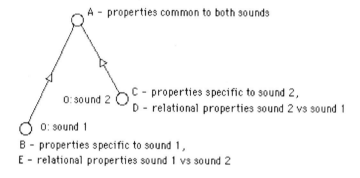

Figure 4. Contextual categorization when listening sounds.

We labelled "A" the properties common to both sounds (as in the sentence "the two sounds are soft"), "B" the properties describing sound 1 (as in the sentence "the first sound is rich and hot"), "C" the properties describing sound 2 (as in the sentence "the second sound is dry"), "D" the relational properties used to compare sound 2 to sound 1 (as in the sentence "but the second sound is more brilliant than the first") and "E" the relational properties used to compare sound 1 to sound 2 (as in the sentence "the first sound was longer than the second"). An explanation such as "I found the two sounds dissimilar because if they are both quite hot, the second is brilliant and longer than the first" was then coded an "ACD" explanation while an explanation such as "the second sound was dry but shorter than the first which was soft and the two are low" was then coded as a "CDBA" explanation (figure 4).

CC-T and listening order from first to second sound predict that participants should build their explanation in a "A then B then C then D then E" order, which means than the following structured explanation based verbalization "ABCDE",

"ADE", "AC", "A", "DE", "D" are compatible with predictions while "BA", "CDBA", "ACBDE", "ED" are not predicted by CCM-explanation.

Although only 31 of 325 types (9 %) of possible verbalizations were compatible with CC-T, 53 % of the verbalizations corresponded to our strict predictions. More over, the more frequent verbalization was of the ABC form (10%), followed by ABCD (6%), by A (5.2 %), AD (5%) and BC (4.2. %). Each of the predicted form was six times more frequent than the non-predicted form. In addition the 13 most frequent forms of explanation were 54% of the total amount of verbalization. Among them, ten were predicted (unpredicted were AED, BCA and ABDA) and corresponded to 78 % of them. In summary CC-T appears to be a good approximation of modelling human explanation.

3.6. CC-literal language : metonymy, metaphor and tautology

Natural language appears to be much more non-literal than literal (18). "The pizzas have forgotten their changes" is metaphoric when it designates a group of persons in a restaurant, one of their parts being the pizzas. As "part of" are properties used in CC-T, metonymy is predictable when such a property is what is specific to the objects going to be designated. Conversely, having the "part of" property, it is possible to understand the sentence by deriving who is depicted in the Galois Lattice. The solution is the denotation solution.

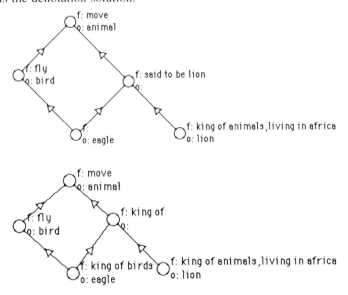

Figure 5. The creation of an attributive category as said in the sentence "eagles are lions" render possible to generalize and to specify "king of" to eagles. Note that the knowledge about the vehicle is also changed. Lions are not any more the only sort of king.

Metaphor is much more problematic given that an object (vehicle) is used to designate another target object (topic). However, note that facing "A a 1 b 2", someone could be told to "underline the b vowel". This could be considered as contradictory since "b" is not a vowel. This metaphor is easily solved with CC-metaphor. Starting from "b", we search what is common to both "b" and "vowel", "lower-case" is found. So the sentence can be understood as being "underline the lower-case vowel" which is "a". The process is quite similar to Glucksberg theory (19) of attributive category. "Among the birds, eagles are lions" can be solved by categorizing "birds", "eagles" and "lions". The attributive category built for what is common to eagles and lions makes generalizing the properties of lions that can be attributed to eagles (figure 5, top panel). Among candidates, we found for instance "living in Africa" and "king of animals". The last property can be generalized and attributed to eagles with the adjustment that makes eagles being "king of birds", since there is already a king of animals (figure 5, bottom panel).

Understanding tautology arises from the same kind of processing Contextual categories. If we agree that tautology focuses on the more specific properties of a repeated term X in a sentence such as "X_2 is X_1" and that specific properties are precisely what is linked to a specific category, then placing X_2 as a contextual and circumstantial sub-category of X_1 makes X_2 inherit the specific properties of X, which is to say what X does not share with other things like X. However a context is necessary to filter between the specific properties which ones correspond to the situation at hand. In a *rainy day*, "London is London" will meant "London is a capital as others, but you know it has this specific property of having, as a difference with others great towns, a lot of rainy days". When *crossing the street* and facing gentle drivers, "London is London" will meant that "London is a capital as others, but you know it has this specific property of having a lot of gentle drivers".

3.7. CC-Reasoning

With CC-reasoning, inferences are not made from true/false propositions but on objects and on properties in hierarchical networks of categories. Connectors such as AND (the object "2" has the property "place5" and the property "/two/"), OR ("consonant" XOR "upper case"; "lower-case" OR "vowel"), find their resolution in Galois lattices. "If ... then" implication in modus-ponens (as in "if "a" then "vowel") corresponds precisely to the Galois lattice structure, as well as modus-tollens (as in if "non-vowel" then "non-a"). However, note that to verify modus-tollens ("if "a then vowel), it is impracticable because, - as there is no reason to limit the search to "consonant" category given that "non-vowel" is not restricted to "consonant" -, searching if "a" is an instance of other non-vowel categories will provide that "a" belongs to the "lower-case" category.

CC-T can light other human reasonning phenomena. In a group of experiments (120 participants), we used the following materials :
- e<u>B</u>u and E<u>B</u>u, for condition 1 and condition 2 respectively, with the statement "Someone was said "If among the letters, there are many vowels, then underline an uppercase" and did so. Do you agree ? answer Yes or no."
- Ba<u>M</u> and Ba<u>E</u>, for condition 3 and condition 4, respectively with the statement "Someone was said "If among the letters, there are many uppercases, then underline a vowel" and did so. Do you agree? answer Yes or no."

Note that the four problems are isomorphic problems, except that vowel and uppercase were changing place in the statements (condition 1 and 2 vs condition 3 and 4) and that the materials were reversed (lower-case vowels became uppercase consonants and vice-versa). In addition, in the set from which a letter was to be underlined, there was either only one target (one "B" for uppercase in condition 1, one "a" for vowel in condition 3) or two targets (one "E" and one "B" for uppercases in condition 2, one "a" and one "E" in condition 4 for vowel).

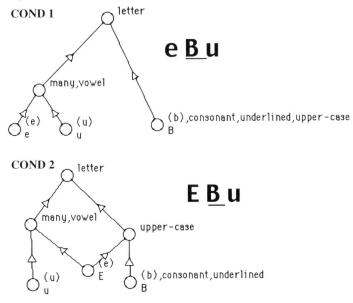

Figure 6. Contextual Categories for "e B u" (CONDITION 1) and for "E B u" (CONDITION 2) that were materials for participants of an experiment that should answer if "yes" or "no" someone was right to underline "B", as he did, following the statement "If among the letters, there are many vowels, then underline the uppercase".

With so simple problems, one could expect some kind of similar results (100% yes responses in the four problems). This was not the case. Underlining "B" as in eBu to follow the statement "If many vowels, then underline an uppercase" was agreed by 75 % of the participants, while only 40 % agreed underlining "B" as in EBu. In fact, with "eBu", 25 % of the participants understood that the letter to be underlined should be an upper-case vowel. With "EBu", they were 60 %. Solving the problem seems to be as follows : "consider the vowels and, if many, among them find an upper-case and underline it". This procedure can be easily proceeded in the network of figure 6 (bottom graph). In opposite, with "eBu", there is no uppercase as a sub-category of "many, vowel" (figure 6, top graph). Thus, these results show a strong effect of context on reasoning.

However, Underlining "a" in BaM to follows the statement "If many upper-cases, then underline a vowel" was agreed by 85 % of the participants, while only 65 % agreed underlining "B" in EBu . Although the main results was found to be repeated, with significant differences, upper-class seems less able to determine a category in which to found the letter to be underlined than vowel. Decontextualized categories have also their specific effect on reasoning in interaction with contextual categories.

4. Conclusion

Researchers have many tools at their disposal when it comes to identifying relations between descriptors in context and setting out the implication relations between categories and between properties. These include methods of classificatory statistics (e.g. ones based on geometrical methods), multidimensional methods, probabilistic methods that are adapted to handle the frequency of property occurrence, methods for measuring similarity (11), methods of hierarchical classification based on common properties, such as HICLUS (20) and ADCLUS (21), methods based on distinctive properties, such as EXTREE (22) and ADDTREE (23), methods for representing networks of category inclusion, such as the HICLAS model (24) and the PROCOPE model (13), both based on the Galois lattice (5). Lastly, the STONE model (13), enables us to represent relations between properties in the form of property lines.
    These tools can be used to study contextual categorization effects on cognition if they are used to model the very precise state of affairs of current situations and how the mind interact with the very detailed world of objects at hand.

References

[1] Zibetti, E., Hamilton, E., & Tijus C.A. (1999). The role of Context in Interpreting Perceived Events as Action. In J.G. Carbonell & J. Siekmann (eds), *Lectures Notes in Artificial Intelligence, vol. 1688, Modeling and Using Context,* (pp. 431-441). New-York: Springer.

[2] Schyns, P., Goldstone, R.L., & Thibaut, J.-P. (1998). The development of features in Sjoberg, L. (1972). *A cognitive theory of similarity.* Goteborg: Psychological Reports, 2 (10).

[3] Tijus, C.A., Moulin, F. (1997). L'assignation de signification à partir de textes d'histoires drôles. *L'Année Psychologique, 97,* 33-75.

[4] Barsalou, L.W., 1995. "Deriving Categories to Achieve Goals". In A. RAM & D.B. LAKE (eds.), *Goal-Driven Learning.* Cambridge: The M.I.T. Press.

[5] Barbut, M., & Monjardet, B. (1970). *Ordre et classification: algèbre et combinatoire.* Paris : Hachette.

[6] Poitrenaud, S. (1995). The Procope Semantic Network: an alternative to action grammars. *International Journal of Human-Computer Studies, 42,* 31-69.

[7] Barsalou, L. W. (1982). Context-independent and context-dependent information in concepts. *Memory and Cognition, 10,* 82-93.

[8] Nosofsky, R. M. (1991). Stimulus bias, asymmetric similarity, and classification. *Cognitive Psychology, 23,* 94-140.

[9] Sjoberg, L. (1972). *A cognitive theory of similarity.* Goteborg: Psychological Reports, 2 (10).

[10] Thibaut, J.P. (1986). Classification et représentativité d'objets. Rôle des attributs constitutifs. *Cahiers de Psychologie Cognitive, 6,* 41-60.

329

[11] Tversky, A. (1977). Features of similarity. *Psychological Review, 84,* 327-352.

[12] Rips, L.J., & Conrad, F.G. (1989). Folk Psychology of Mental Activities. *Psychological Review, 96,* 187-207.

[13] Poitrenaud, S. (1998). *La représentation des PROCédures chez l'OPErateur: Description et mise en oeuvre des savoir-faire.* Thèse de Doctorat. Université de Paris 8.

[14] Smith, E.E. & Medin, D.L. (1981). *Categories and Concepts.* Cambridge, M.A. Harvard University Press.

[15] Rips, L.J., & Conrad, F.G. (1989). Folk Psychology of Mental Activities. *Psychological Review, 96,* 187-207.

[16] Tijus, C.A. (1997). *Assignation de signification et construction de la représentation.* Habilitation à Diriger des Recherches. Université de Paris VIII.

[17] Richard, J.F., & Tijus, C.A. (1998). Modelling the Affordances of Objects in Problem Solving, *Special Issue of Analise Psicologica about Cognition and Context,* 293-315.

[18] Lakoff, G., & Johnson, M. (1980). *Les métaphores dans la vie quotidienne,* Paris : édition de minuit.

[19] Glucksberg, S., McGlone, M.S., & Manfredi, D. (1997). Property attribution in metaphor comprehension, *Journal of Memory and Language, 36,* 50-67.

[20] Johnson, S. C. (1967). Hierarchical clustering schemes. *Psychometrica, 32,* 241-254.

[21] Arabie, P., & Carroll, J., D. (1980). MAPCLUS model : a mathematical programming approach to fitting the ADCLUS model. *Psychometrica, 45,* 211-235.

[22] Corter, A., & Tversky, A. (1986). Extended similarity trees. *Psychometrica, 51,* 429-451.

[23] Sattath, S., & Tversky, A (1977). Additive similarity trees. *Psychometrika, 42,* 319-345.

[24] Génoche, A., & Van Mechelen, I. (1993). Galois approach to the induction of concepts. In I. Van Mechelen, J. Hampton, R.S. Michalski, & P. Theuns (Eds.), *Categories and concepts: Theoretical and inductive data analysis* (pp.287-308). London: Academic Press.

Representing the Graphics Context to Support Understanding Plural Anaphora in Multi-Modal Interfaces[*]

Elise H. Turner[1] and Roy M. Turner[1]

Computer Science Department
University of Maine
Orono, ME USA 04468-5752
{eht,rmt}@umcs.maine.edu

Abstract. Previous communication provides important context for new communication in an interaction. In natural language interfaces, the discourse context represents and maintains information about what has been said before. When other modes of communication are also used, they must also contribute to the context. In this paper, we describe how information about the graphics can be represented and maintained in the graphics context. We are particularly interested in how the graphics context can be used to support finding referents for plural anaphora.

1 Introduction

Understanding plural anaphoric references is a difficult problem for natural language interfaces. To understand anaphora, a discourse context that represents the entities that have been referred to in the discourse must be maintained. To find the correct referent, the system must create a set with the proper membership. Some sets that can serve as referents are clearly indicated in the discourse by a plural head noun (e.g., "the dogs") or the use of a conjunction (e.g., "Lassie and Clifford"). Others are not so clearly marked and must be pieced together from distinct noun phrases. This requires knowledge gained from reasoning about the world which may be time-consuming and may be difficult to focus.

In multi-modal interfaces, when users are allowed to communicate using graphics as well as natural language, correctly understanding plural anaphora can still be difficult. As with discourse, the graphical communication itself can provide important clues to the membership of the set. However, because the graphics remains visible throughout the interaction, sets can be formed from related icons that are entered into the graphics over time. Unlike relationships between entities that are added over time in the discourse, these relationships

---
[*] This work was funded in part by grant IIS-9613646 from the National Science Foundation. The authors would also like to thank Shawnee Treadwell for her work on transcibing videotapes and the anonymous reviewers for their helpful comments on an earlier draft of this paper.

do not require time-consuming general purpose reasoning to be identified. Instead, they are relationships such as sharing the same icon that can be easily and quickly perceived when viewing the graphics. This means that, unlike the discourse context, the graphics context must support relationships between entities that may only be known much after the first entity is drawn.

In this paper, we will describe how the graphics context can be represented to support finding the proper referent of "these." We begin in Section 2 by discussing how understanding "these" in natural language interfaces differs from understanding "these" when graphics are also used. In Section 3 we illustrate how "these" can be understood with an example from a videotaped session of a speaker describing a location. We present our representation of the graphics context in Section 4.

Before we begin our discussion, we need to specify how some terms will be used throughout the paper. We will use *anaphora* for expressions that refer to entities that have been referred to previously, either in discourse or graphics. We will use *discourse* to refer only to spoken or written communication. We will use *communication* to include both discourse and graphics. We will call the extended multi-modal communication between the user and the system the *interaction*.

2   Understanding "These" in Multi-Modal Interfaces

In order to understand plural anaphora, a system must have two types of information about entities that have been referenced in the communication. First, it must know which entities are currently *available* as referents to anaphoric expressions. Second, it must know the *membership criteria* that identifies which of the available entities belong in the referent set.

In natural language systems, entities that have been referenced in the discourse are stored in the *discourse context*. Many systems use simple history lists for the discourse context [1]. Entities are placed on the list in the order in which they are referenced in the discourse. When the system must find the referent for an anaphoric expression, it searches the history list, considering the most recently referenced entities first. Items are removed from the history list after a specified period of time. This is useful because people have limited short term memory and may not remember entities referenced much earlier. However, when a set must be formed with entities that have been mentioned throughout the discourse, they may not all be available at the time the plural anaphora is used. Similar problems occur with methods of representing the discourse context that are designed to better reflect the structure of the discourse (e.g., [2–4]). These methods document the progress of the discourse by way of its topics. Entities referenced while the topic is being discussed are associated with the topic in the discourse context. Some schemes distinguish certain entities as being in higher focus than others. Only entities that are in high focus can be referenced by a pronoun. As the discourse moves from topic to topic, the entities referenced in some previous topics may be referred to anaphorically. Other previous topics may be closed in such a way that prohibits anaphoric reference to their entities.

Although a speaker can return to a closed topic, it is unclear whether and for how long entities associated with a topic can be referenced anaphorically.

Entities do not become unavailable over time in the graphics context. Discourse is ephemeral. Speech "goes away" as it is spoken, leaving the hearer with only a mental representation of what was said. Although written text does not actually disappear as it is read, the reader is not expected to have to re-read passages in order to understand anaphoric references. Graphical communication, on the other hand, remains accessible throughout the entire interaction. In our videotaped examples, graphical communication was only made inaccessible if it was erased. Although we have not studied erasures, we believe they effectively eliminate the erased entity from the graphics context. In other communication, graphics may be occluded (e.g., covered by other windows in the system) or otherwise made temporarily unavailable. However, to communicate by pointing, the speaker must believe that the hearer will be able to access the graphics (e.g., by moving the window). In these ways, graphics are available for the user to refer to, and to reinterpret, at any time later in the interaction. Consequently, the system's representation of the graphics in the graphics context cannot simply point to entities in the system's knowledge base, but must store the information that will allow the system, like the user, to reinterpret those graphics.

Because the graphics can be viewed and reinterpreted throughout the interaction, it is easy for speakers to add new entries to existing sets. By a simple pointing gesture the speaker is able to draw the user's attention to all of the entities in an area. The speaker can then add entities to the area and relate them to nearby entities – no matter how distant the last reference to those entities or how unrelated their associated topic. The graphics is also repository for shared knowledge for the interlocutors who can see it and who have understood as it was built. As a result, with graphics a speaker can point to an icon and say "these" and expect the user to be able build a set of all similar items that have been referenced throughout the interaction. Using discourse alone, the speaker would have to refer to the same set of X's using an expression like "all of the X's".

In addition to differences in availability of entities, the graphics context also differs from the discourse context in the ways that entities can be identified as members of certain sets. Both can rely on general purpose knowledge and reasoning to make the connections that group entities into sets. However, this requires significant effort and can easily lead to miscommunication. Membership criteria can be interpreted more efficiently and more effectively if they rely on standard relationships that can be easily apprehended from the communication.

For discourse, this is through the use of plurals and conjunctions. Sets derived from these sources can be added immediately to the discourse context. It is more difficult to add new entities to these sets, requiring that the set be available and that the hearer recognize, usually with the aid of additional reasoning, that the new entity should be a set member. For graphics, the mode of communication increases the ease of creating sets. As discussed above, all entities remain available throughout the interaction. More important, entities can be grouped together in several ways that are easily perceived by looking at the graphics. Specifically, entities can be related by location and by icon. In addition, a speaker can refer to a set by pointing to one of its members in the graphics, but relying on the discourse context to help understand the referent. For example, among many buildings, a speaker might draw several buildings using the same icon while saying "There are some new buildings in this area." She might next point to one and say "These are all up to code." The referent set can be best identified as the new buildings using information from the discourse.

In the current work we are more interested in constructing the proper set for a plural reference than in the deictic nature of "these." Consequently, we have focused our work on gestural usages when a speaker is pointing to a member of a set and when information from the graphics context is needed to find the proper referent. We believe the graphics context that we are developing to support creating appropriate sets can provide a foundation for handling deixis in multi-modal interfaces. Specifically, we believe that the support for relating entities by location will be useful for understanding gestural usages of "here." In the future, we will focus more on "these" as a deictic expression. In particular, we would like to explore how the gesture used (e.g., pointing to a single object vs. pointing to several objects vs. a sweeping gesture) helps to indicate the breadth of the set in terms of the relationships that we have identified.

3 Example

Our work on context will be used to support Sketch-and-Talk, a multi-modal interface to geographical data being developed by the Department of Spatial Information Science and Engineering at the University of Maine. With Sketch-and-Talk, users will describe locations using speech and graphics. To begin understanding the role of context in these interactions before the system was implemented, we examined videotaped sessions of humans describing locations. Descriptions were provided by students and faculty from a research seminar class studying the use of context for understanding multi-modal communication. Class participants chose a location and described it using a chalk board for graphics. This gave the participants greater flexibility than they would have with existing software for recognizing graphical input.

The following example includes communication that helped motivate our representation of the graphics context, including a gestural usage of "these." It was transcribed from our videotaped sessions and is representative of them. A fragment of the discourse is shown in Fig. 1. The letters appearing in the text correspond to the labels on icons in the figures showing the graphics. These labels were not included in the original drawing. Labels appear after the word that was being said as the speaker began to draw the corresponding icon.

The speaker has chosen to describe Appledore Island, which is the home of the Shoals Marine Laboratory. He first introduces the topic and draws the island (Utterance 1, Icon A). Next, he draws many of the buildings that house the Shoals Marine Laboratory, starting with Kiggins Commons (Icon B, and

1. (A) The Shoals Marine Lab out on Appledore Island down south.
2. And Appledore is an island that's kind of got a wasp waist to it.
3. It's going to be two islands in a few years if they're not careful.
4. Um, we have the Kiggins (B) Commons here which has a nice porch (C) out back overlooking like a little ravine (D) are and the rest, the rest of the island is out here.
5. There's a laboratory (E) over here and classroom (F,G) buldings.
6. And (H) there (I) are dorms (J) back here.
7. And (K) also out here.
   discussion of particular buildings that were discussed above
8. Ok, um, we would do a lot of our work over in this lab.
9. It was a big nature lab.
10. It had a couple of nice features.
11. One is it (L) overlooked, ah, across the little, the little area over here overlooked Starr Island which (M) had some of the old hotel era uh era huge hotels on it.
12. It was essentially a resort, not really a resort, a retreat run by the Unitarians and Congregationalists.
13. So, you could look over there and see that.
14. You could also see the sunsets, that was nice.
15. Portsmouth's down here. Portsmouth, New Hampshire, six miles that way.
16. Across there was also another (N) building here, uh, and here (O) or so.
17. Across the ravine there was some...
18. Most of what we were interested in was the inter-tidal which was all around.
19. Um, down here on this part, um, there's a harbor here, too, sorry, Kinsb the ship, the boat would park here, the Kingsbury.
20. And, us, then they divided the area up into transects, places where people would do their experiments.
    discussion of transects
21. Ok, this is low, high, very low, and back up to pretty high.
22. There are some cliffs down here.
23. Uh, around here was an area that people had started building a cairn (P) on, this is a ritual sort of thing, people take rocks up there.
24. But this is where Celia Thaxter, I don't know if you know who that was,
    discussion of Celia Thaxter
25. She's sit up here and she'd look out at Portsmouth down here.
26. Across the way here was where (Q) people would play volleyball.
27. And then around here was the remains of Celia Thaxter's garden (R), or Celia Thaxter's garden and the remains of her (S) house.
    discussion of area around Celia Thaxter's house
28. There were trails back between all these (T–X) through the scrub.

Fig. 1. Discourse example.

porch Icon C) in Utterance 4. When the first square (Icon B) is drawn, a set for entities represented by a square is formed. Each time a new entity is drawn as a square icon, it is added to this set.

In the same utterance after discussing the Commons, he draws a "ravine area" and notes that it separates the Lab from "the rest of the island...out here". This indicates that a set should be formed for this area. This set should contain all entities currently in this area as well as those that will be added later. The speaker then goes on to talk about the buildings of the Lab. Fig. 2 shows the graphics at this point.

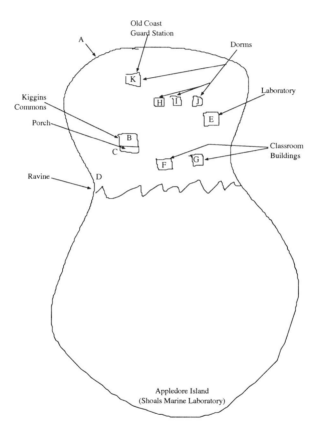

Fig. 2. Drawing through discussion of the lab buildings.

Next, the speaker talks about and draws two areas that provide interesting views from the lab. This includes a description, in Utterance 11, of Starr Island (Icon L) and the hotel on it (Icon M). The icon for the hotel is clearly a rectangle instead of a square, so a new set is created for icons that are large rectangles. The speaker then returns to the topic of the buildings at the lab and adds two more (Utterance 16, Icons I and O). The icons, the locations of the buildings, and the

fact that only Laboratory buildings have been discussed so far all lend evidence
to understanding these buildings to be laboratory buildings. Recognizing that
only laboratory buildings have been discussed would require some reasoning
by the hearer. However, this is the only means of establishing the connection
between the buildings using only speech.[1] In that mode, no set would be formed
that contained all of the buildings at the time of understanding. With graphics,
both the icons and the locations would cause the newly-referenced buildings
to join sets containing the existing buildings. The icon set that these buildings
join is the one created at Utterance 4, and the location set is the one created
at Utterance 16. Though identified as related by icon or location instead of by
organization, these sets will allow us to accurately understand a future reference
to the buildings of the Laboratory.

The speaker next discusses the part of the island across the ravine. This
includes a discussion of Celia Thaxter's garden and house (Utterance 26) and a
discussion of the volleyball courts (Utterance 27). These are drawn with square
icons like those used for the laboratory buildings, but larger (Icons O–S). Fig. 3
shows the graphics at this point.

At Utterance 28, the speaker draws trails between some Lab buildings, as
shown in Fig. 4. He begins drawing trails as he says "these," at that point drawing
the trail (Icon T) between two buildings. He does not connect all buildings with
the trail, yet two independent reviewers of the videotape understood "these"
to refer to all laboratory buildings. When asked, the speaker reported that he
intended that interpretation.

The speaker has linked two square icons (Icons B and N). We would expect
"these" to indicate an existing set, and the set of entities drawn as square icons
has already been formed. "These," as opposed to "all these" or "those," also
indicates that the entities in the set are near to each other. The ravine area is
the smallest identified area that contains the linked icons. We find the referent
to "these" by taking the intersection of these sets.

The set of Laboratory buildings could also be created by reasoning about the
information given in the discourse about the buildings. However, the icons can
so the same work more efficiently. We believe the icons that a speaker chooses
indicates how he or she is dividing up the world. In general, entities that are
seen by the speaker as related in an important way are drawn using the same
icon. It is also possible for slight, but regular, variations in the icon to represent
subclasses in the icon class. Icons often reflect the shape of the entity, but more
often are used for this sort of grouping. There are exceptions to this. Speakers may embellish an icon. For example, the porch (Icon C) added to Kiggins
Commons (Icon B) is an embellishment. It should not change the type of icon
for Kiggins Commons and should only be included in an icon set with similar
icons that are also used as embellishments. Some speakers changed icons when
drawing more of an often repeated type of entity. Speakers usually changed from

---

[1] We assume the buildings would be referenced by speech only. However, that
speech might include additional information that would more easily link the newly-
referenced buildings to the other Lab buildings.

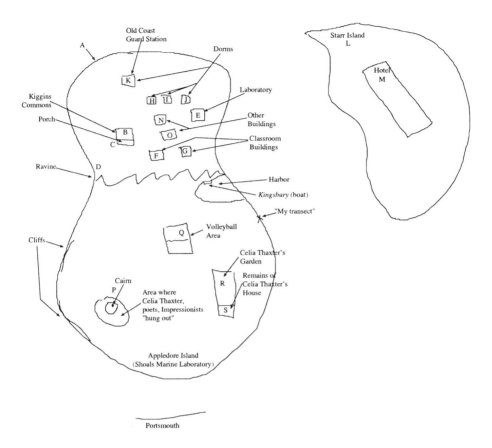

Fig. 3. Drawing just prior to trails being added.

a complicated icon or one that was more time-consuming to draw to X's or dots. When speakers did this, they also were not as precise about the objects in other ways. Specifically, they were often not precise about the number of objects or their exact location. In this way, entities drawn as X's or dots had a diminished status. Speakers also reused icons. The separate uses were usually clearly identified in the discourse. Occasionally, there was a clear point in the discourse when the icon changed meaning. More often, either none of the entities represented by the icon were so important that they needed to be identified in the graphics (i.e., the icon created the set of "other things"), or all but one use of the icon followed a standard interpretation of that icon (e.g., two parallel lines to designate roads and to designate inter-tidal regions).

The general rule is upheld in our example. Squares were used to indicate "the places lab members frequented." Smaller squares represented buildings and larger squares represented other areas. In discussing understanding "these," we did not divide the square icon class into subclasses. This would have made understanding no harder because the buildings alone would form a group. A different icon was used to indicate the cairn area (Icon P), which was a place of special

338

significance; no icons were used to indicate transects, each of which was only frequented by a few lab members. The speaker also used a different icon for buildings that lab members did not visit. In Utterance 11, the speaker uses a rectangle (Icon M) instead of a square to indicate a hotel. After the fragment shown in the figure, the speaker refers to houses that were owned by lobstermen and that were not part of the Lab. He draws squares for these houses and then draws X's over the squares.

4 Representing the Graphical Context

In addition to the drawing itself, the interface needs to represent two kinds of information about the graphics context: the graphical objects present and various ways of grouping those objects into sets that could be the referents for plural references.

Graphical objects can be thought of as augmented icons. A graphical object is the icon drawn by the user plus additional information that is either given by the user or derived by the system, including information about what object in the world the icon stands for. In Fig. 4, graphical objects include the dormitories,

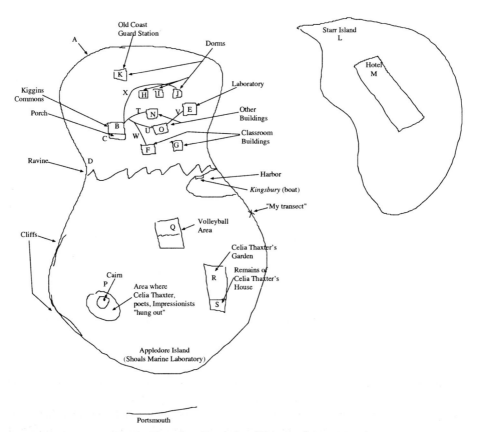

Fig. 4. Drawing for entire discourse fragment.

the laboratory, Kiggins Commons, the cairn, and the ravine. In drawings of other kinds of locations, graphical objects such as roads, rivers, lakes, and so forth, would be expected.

Fig. 5 shows a graphical object represented as a frame. The *icon* slot holds a frame-based representation of the icon that was drawn. In addition to the bitmap of the icon, that frame will contain information about the shape (e.g., a square), the approximate size, the icon's location, and the legend used to interpret the icon.

The *legend* is an aspect of the current context that the system tracks (see [5]). It contains information that, like a map legend, links icons to meanings. The legend contextual aspect may contain information that is user- and task-independent, such as the fact that squares often denote buildings. It may also contain information about the way icons are used in the current task. For example, as mentioned above, in some drawings in our protocols, both squares and X's were used for buildings; this information would be stored in the legend.[2] Iconography that is idiosyncratic for the user will come from contextual information having to do with the user [5].

```
^g-dorm1:
    isa: ^graphical-object
    icon: ^icon1
    object: ^dormitory1
    inferences: nil
```

Fig. 5. A graphical object representing one of the dormitories.

The *object* slot contains a pointer to the frame representing the object this graphical object stands for. In the figure, the graphical object refers stands for a particular instance of "dormitory".

The *inferences* slot contains any inferences that were made in order to fill in the other slots.

In order to resolve plural anaphoric references, candidate referent sets must be constructed and considered. In our approach, these sets are created and maintained as objects are added to the drawing based on relationships that are likely to be useful and that make set creation and maintenance relatively easy. The sets are explicitly represented and associated with the graphics context. At the time a plural reference is made, they can be quickly examined to determine the referent. In our approach so far, we are considering three kinds of sets: location sets, icon sets, and discourse-related sets. Function sets and class sets may be added if there is sufficient support for them in the discourse or graphics. However, since there is support for class sets in the knowledge base, they may be created only when needed.

---

[2] In such cases, the use of one kind of icon rather than the other may indicate that the user considers there to be two distinct sets of the same kind of object.

A *location set* is based on spatial relationships between icons in the drawing. These are comprised of graphical objects that are all within regions of the drawing that have either been explicitly identified or that have been inferred. Regions in the drawing of the Laboratory include the island itself, Starr Island, the region north of the ravine, the region south of the ravine, the area of cliffs, the area where poets and Impressionists "hung out", and the cluster of dorms near the laboratory building. Each of these regions would correspond to a location set containing all the graphical objects contained within that region.

The system only creates location sets that have been marked by the user through discourse or graphics. For example, a location set is created for dorms H–J at Utterance 6 when the user indicates this set with the words "back here".

Spatial regions can nest and overlap; their corresponding location sets will have similar subset-superset and intersection relationships. For example, as shown in Fig. 6, it is possible to derive several location sets in the area near the three dorms. One is comprised of the three graphical objects representing the dorms and another, larger set consists of those objects and the graphical object representing the laboratory. Others include sets consisting of all graphical objects in the northern half of the island and of all graphical objects on the island. When the user points near the dorms and says "these", the system should consider all of these regions as possibilities for possible referents.

Most of the work of location set creation and maintenance will be done using simple heuristics as new icons are added. This will speed the process of finding referents for plural references. However, there may be times when new location sets need to be created based on gestures or utterances by the user. For example, the user might use a sweeping gesture while saying "around here"; the system

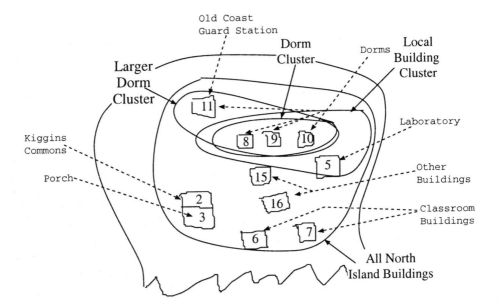

Fig. 6. Several different regions of the Shoals Marine Laboratory sketch.

may interpret this as the definition of a new region, figure out what that region encompasses, then create a new location set to represent graphical objects within that area.

Location sets are represented as frames. Fig. 7 shows a representation of a location set that includes the three dorms by the laboratory. The representation of a location set includes the graphical objects that are members, the region that corresponds to the set, any label supplied by the user, any inferences that led to filling other slots, and a list of related sets. The related sets in this case are other location sets that are spatially related to this one. For example, the location set shown would be related to the set containing the three dorms and the laboratory; both sets would be based on clustering icons, but the latter would be a larger cluster.

```
^locset1:
  isa: ^location-set
  members: (^dorm1 ^dorm2 ^dorm3)
  region: ^region1
  label: "dorms"
  inferences:
  related-sets:  (^locset2 ...)
```

Fig. 7. A location set containing the three dorms by the laboratory.

The second kind of set is the *icon set*. For now, an icon set is a set of graphical objects that have the same icon. The problems noted above of using the same icon for different objects, or different icons for the same object, are a subject for future work. We also leave for future work the problem of determining when icon subsets should be formed (e.g., when there should be separate sets for small squares and large squares as well as for all squares). The current representation of an icon set is consequently simple: just a slot for the icon class itself (e.g., "squares") and a slot containing the members of the set, that is, the graphical objects that were drawn using icons that match the icon class (e.g., graphical objects representing buildings, etc.). These icon sets are easy to create and maintain.

The third kind of set is the *discourse-related set*. This set is based on the discourse context in which the objects were introduced or discussed. For example, if the user talks about being attacked by a gull while walking along the path from Kiggins Commons to the laboratory, the corresponding discourse-related set would include the graphical objects mentioned. Later, if the user says "that bird attacked me around here" and gestures near the path, the discourse could be used to determine what "that bird" refers to, and the appropriate discourse-related set from the graphics context could be used to determine what "around here" means—in this context, somewhere along the path, and not just somewhere near where the user pointed.

The representation of discourse-related sets is simple: just the members of the set and a pointer to the discourse context that defined the set. Although in principle the information contained in discourse-related contexts could be generated from the discourse context, as we have mentioned, that is ephemeral, while the graphics context is not. It makes sense to have graphical objects that were grouped by the discourse remain grouped together for later anaphora resolution.

5 Conclusion

When discourse and graphics can be used for communication in a multi-modal interface, both must contribute to the context. In this paper, we have described our work on creating a graphics context. The graphics context differs from the discourse context because the graphics are visible throughout the interaction and because a much richer set of relationships between objects can be readily apprehended from the graphics. These relationships often become the membership criteria for sets that serve as the referents for plural anaphora. We have discussed the need for a graphics context that is separate from the discourse context and have shown a representation for the graphics context that will support finding referents for plural anaphora such as "these."

References

1. J. Allen. *Natural Language Understanding*. The Benjamin/Cummings Publishing Company, Inc., Reading, Mass., 1987.
2. B. J. Grosz. The representation and use of focus in a system for understanding dialogs. In *Proceedings of the Fifth International Conference on Artificial Intelligence*, pages 67–76, Los Altos, California, 1977. William Kaufmann, Inc.
3. R. Reichman. *Getting Computers to Talk Like You and Me: Discourse Context, Focus, and Semantics (An ATN Model)*. The MIT Press, Cambridge, Mass, 1985.
4. B. J. Grosz and C. L. Sidner. Attention, intention, and the structure of discourse. *Computational Linguistics*, 12(3):175–204, 1986.
5. E. H. Turner, R. M. Turner, J. Phelps, C. Grunden, M. Neale, and J. Mailman. Aspects of context for understanding multi-modal communication. In *Lecture Notes in Artificial Intelligence 1688: Modeling and Using Context* (Proceedings of the 1999 International and Interdisciplinary Conference on Modeling and Using Context (CONTEXT-99), Trento, Italy). Springer–Verlag, 1999.

Using Explicit, A Priori Contextual Knowledge in an Intelligent Web Search Agent

Roy M. Turner[1], Elise H. Turner[1], Thomas A. Wagner[1], Thomas J. Wheeler[1], and Nancy E. Ogle[2]

[1] Department of Computer Science, University of Maine, Orono, Maine 04469 USA
{rmt,eht,wagner,wheeler}@umcs.maine.edu
[2] School of Performing Arts, University of Maine, Orono, Maine 04469 USA
Nancy_Ogle@umit.maine.edu

Abstract. The development of intelligent Web search agents will become increasingly important as the amount of information on the Web continues to grow. Intelligently searching the Web depends on the searcher understanding not only the context of the query, including the person for whom the search is being done, but also the context of the results, including the information sources and the retrieved information itself. Consequently, intelligent Web search agents will need to have mechanisms for representing and using contextual knowledge. In this paper, we discuss the kinds of contexts and contextual knowledge such an agent will encounter. We use as an example a Web search agent we are beginning to develop, FERRET, that will search for scholarly information about music. We then propose some ways in which explicitly represented, *a priori* contextual knowledge can be used by the search agent, and we discuss directions for future research.

1   Introduction

The World Wide Web is increasingly being relied upon as a source of scholarly information for serious users. However, searching the Web for useful information can be frustrating and time-consuming. The user must devise a search strategy that takes into account the locations of search engines and their characteristics, including the reliability of their results, determines what form the queries must take, and estimates which keywords are most likely to garner the desired results. The user must then evaluate the potentially large set of results with respect to relevance and usefulness. Often the process is one of trial and error, with the user submitting a search, then refining the keywords based on the results obtained and submitting a new search, and so forth. Searching the Web thus effectively requires not only knowledge of the domain of the search, but also a great deal of knowledge about properties of the search engines and content sites that are available. To search efficiently, the user is forced to become an expert on the process of searching. As noted in a recent review of intelligent information agents: "Far from being the answer to everyone's information dreams, distributed sources of online information [...] often turn into an information nightmare" [5].

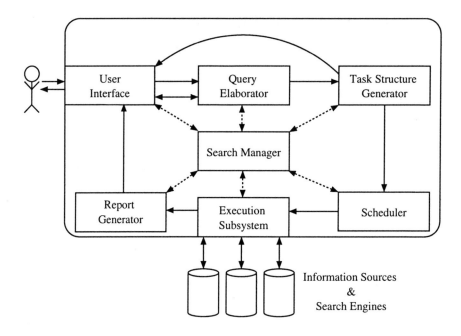

Fig. 1. Planned structure of FERRET.

The object of the FERRET (Facilitated Elaboration and Retrieval for Researchers' and Experts' Tasks) project is to create an intelligent search agent that will ease the task of finding scholarly information on the Web. FERRET's domain will be 20th-century music, and the target users will be musicians and musicologists. The agent itself will be an expert in searching the Web, freeing its users from the need to become such experts themselves.

Figure 1 shows the structure of FERRET. The user will enter a query in English. For example, a singer who is interested in finding material for a recital might submit the query: "musical settings of Emily Dickinson's poems". The agent will then use its knowledge of the user, the domain, and how to search the Web to carry out the search. The *query elaborator* module will examine the query and create a more useful query, based on its knowledge. A *task structure generator* will then take the elaborated query and create a TAEMS [3] task structure, a plan-like representation of different ways the appropriate results might be obtained. This will be passed to the Design-to-Criteria *scheduler* [17], which will examine the task structure and select the best way of carrying out the query, given the constraints given by the user and those imposed by the agent itself, based on its knowledge. An *execution subsystem* will then actually carry out the search by interacting with search engines and known knowledge sources (e.g., Web sites). A *report generator* will filter out extraneous results and summarize the remainder for the user. A *search manager* will coordinate and control the entire process, interacting with the user as necessary via the user interface to restrict or expand the search and to assess the quality of the results.

An intelligent agent such as FERRET needs contextual knowledge to behave appropriately for situations in which it finds itself. In general, an agent can use its knowledge of kinds of situations to handle ambiguity of input, to determine situation-specific meaning, to handle unanticipated events, and to determine how best to achieve its goals [14]. By recognizing the context it is in, the agent can use *a priori* knowledge about the context to guide its perception, reasoning, and action. In the particular case of a Web search agent, paying attention to the context can help the agent determine what its user really means by his or her query, how to elaborate the query effectively, how best to plan for and schedule search actions, how to behave to effectively interact with various Web search engines and content sites, how to construct a coherent set of results, and how to control the overall search process.

In the remainder of this paper, we will examine the role of context in intelligent Web searching, then discuss how we intend to make use of explicitly-represented contextual knowledge in the FERRET search agent. We briefly examine some related work, then conclude with a discussion of future work.

2   Context in Intelligent Web Searching

Before examining the role of context in Web searching, we must first define what a context is. By "context", we mean the *kind* of situation in which an agent finds itself. That is, it is the class of known situations the current situation has been recognized as being a member of. It is the agent's knowledge about the class of situation it is in—its context—that aids it in behaving appropriately. Thus context recognition is a key process for a context-sensitive agent.

In general, recognizing the context enables an agent to quickly bring to bear a wealth of knowledge about how to behave in that context. Recognizing the kind of user, for example, can tell the agent much about what the user's query really means, what he or she is likely to want for results, and constraints on the search.

Context has many components or dimensions, what we have called elsewhere *contextual aspects* [12]. For a Web search agent, an important component of the context is the user. Different kinds of users behave differently when using the system, and they require different results. For example, a singer and a composer of electronic music may each ask the system to find "music based on Emily Dickinson's poems", but the agent should use its knowledge of the user to determine what kind of music to search for. It is also likely that different kinds of users will use different vocabularies, or that they will phrase search queries differently. For example, one would expect an expert in the area of late 20th-century music to use a more technical vocabulary than a beginning music student. By recognizing the category of user, the agent may be able to make the distinction between a novice user using non-technical terms because he or she has no other option and an expert user using such terms to indicate the level of formality he or she wants in the results.

In addition to obvious categories of users such as novice or expert, singer or composer, there may be more subtle distinctions that the agent should make. For example, some users will be more impatient than others. If the agent can identify the user as being usually impatient, then it can generate appropriate time constraints for the search. Particular users will have idiosyncrasies. For example, a scholar may consider some types of music "serious"; a query such as "find serious music related to the work of Edna St. Vincent Milay" should thus, for this user, restrict the results to the kind of music he or she considers serious, even if the information found is not in any way described as "serious" by its author.

The user may provide information to the agent that the agent can use to recognize other aspects of the context. For example, if the user tells the agent that he or she is in a hurry, then the agent should recognize the context as "time constraints present". Knowing this, the agent might decide to give preference to Web sites and search engines that are fast. The user could similarly tell the agent that he or she does not wish to pay more than x for the search, or provide other task-related information.

The search query itself can also provide an indication of the context which can provide predictive information to guide the agent. For example, some kinds of queries may lead to more hits than others; if the agent expects, based on this aspect of the context (i.e., the kind of query), there to be more hits than there are, then it should suspect that something has gone wrong in the search. The semantics of portions of the query might also establish a context. For example, in the query, "musical settings of Emily Dickinson poems", "musical settings" establishes a context in which the agent should know that it should look for the poems themselves (among other things), as opposed to criticism of the poems, discussions of musical imagery used in the poems, etc.

Features of the results found may also establish a context that can guide the agent. For example, the situation of finding a very large number of hits relative to what is expected might be recognized itself as a kind of context, namely one in which the agent should do further query elaboration. Recognizing this would allow the agent quickly to determine how to handle the problem. As another example, it may be possible to recognize a context analogous to the situation of a piece swap in chess, in which a game-playing program's static evaluation function applied halfway through the swap would give a drastically different value than when the swap is completed. An example of this in the Web search domain might be the case where the hit rate for the search was initially low, but ramped up exponentially as the time allotted for the search expired. This kind of situation may occur frequently enough that it makes sense recognize it as a distinct context. Knowledge about this context would allow the agent to predict that if it devoted just a little more time to the search, it would drastically improve its chances of obtaining a good answer for the user.

There may also be features of the search engines and content sites that define a context with predictions useful to the agent. For example, searching some sites may require particular vocabularies or ontologies. Recognizing this would facilitate query elaboration and search, as well as the summarization process. In addition, some sites may be more or less scholarly than the language in which the query was expressed by the user. In this case, the agent may need to do some translation of terms between the user's query and the site. It would know to do this based on recognizing the aspects of the context corresponding to the user and the site or search engine being used.

Contextual knowledge can also help a Web search agent handle unanticipated events. This includes such things as the user interrupting the agent to give it additional information or to change the search constraints, unexpected responses from search engines or content sites, or failure of some portion of the agent's search plan. Contextual knowledge would help here by providing information about how important the event is likely to be in the current context, what may have caused it, and how to handle it. For example, if the agent has decided to use a particular search engine to find examples of Dickinson's poems, but there is a time-out while contacting the agent, it may decide to respond differently based on whether its context includes a time constraint. In that case, it may opt to try a different search engine rather than to retry this one.

Summarization of results can also benefit from contextual knowledge. The agent's knowledge of its context can help it determine what to present to the user, based on what it predicts the user already knows. It can help it select the level of detail to give to the user and the kind of language to use (e.g., expert vocabulary versus novice vocabulary). It can help the agent decide what to rate highly or filter out based on knowledge about the kind of Web site or author that produced the result.

3 Using Contextual Knowledge in the Web Search Agent

Our approach to using contextual knowledge is *context-mediated behavior* (CMB) [14, 15]. In this approach, contexts with some predictive worth for the agent's behavior are identified, either by the agent's designers or by the agent itself (e.g., via learning), and these contexts are explicitly represented as knowledge structures called *contextual schemas* (c-schemas). Each c-schema represents a context or significant aspect of a context that, if recognized, provides important information about how to behave in the context. C-schemas can be thought of as generalizations of cases of problem solving, and consequently, they are similar to the internal knowledge structures generated by some case-based reasoners (e.g., [10, 11]).

Explicitly representing contextual knowledge is important. It allows the agent to compare the representation to the current situation to determine the degree of fit. It allows the agent to recognize a context, then have immediate access to all the knowledge it has about that context. It also facilitates knowledge acquisition, learning, and maintenance by making all knowledge about a context readily available to the agent and the maintainers.

A first step toward representing contextual knowledge is to determine what kinds of contexts, or contextual aspects, there are. Basically, contextual aspects are the components or dimensions of the overall context that can be individually identified, then whose knowledge can be blended to generate a coherent picture of the overall context. In this domain, these aspects would include:

- user context: what kind of user is using the system?
- query context: what is subject of the query? what is the form of the query (e.g., scholarly, colloquial, etc.)?
- task context: what constraints are there on the task (e.g., time, cost)?
- search plan context: are there properties of the search plan selected that can be used to make predictions about the results?
- execution context: what is the status of the execution of the plan? have queries to search engines failed?
- result context: are the results what was expected (quality and quantity)?

There will be many c-schemas representing each kind of context. For example, there will be c-schemas for various user contexts corresponding to particular users, kinds of users, and so forth. Although in general the agent's current situation will be represented by finding and combining different kinds of c-schemas, there will be some some c-schemas that directly represent combinations of kinds of contexts, for example, a particular kind of user making a particular kind of query. The general rule will be that unless such a combination makes predictions for behavior that cannot be generated by combining the components, then only the components will be represented. This will allow a large number of context representations to be generated from a relatively few c-schemas. It also allows novel contexts to be represented by composing existing c-schemas.

The agent will need to recognize its initial context and to monitor the situation to detect changes in the context. We will use a separate context manager module for this purpose. This will be a version of ECHO, the Embedded Context-Handling Object, which is discussed elsewhere [14]. Briefly, ECHO will watch the agent's evolving problem-solving situation and use features of that situation to recognize the aspects of the current context by a diagnostic reasoning process. The c-schemas "diagnosed" as fitting the current situation will be merged, and knowledge from them will be given to the agent's other modules. When the situation changes sufficiently, ECHO will adjust its notion of what the context is to correspond to the new situation.

In order to get the contextual knowledge to the modules that need it, we plan to treat the agent itself as a kind of multiagent system, with each of its modules corresponding to an agent. Each module/agent will register when it starts with ECHO. It will tell ECHO how it can get information from the module about what it is currently doing and how the module would like to access the contextual knowledge. For example, the module might request ECHO to simply notify it when the context changes; the module could then ask for information as it needs it. Alternatively, it could request that ECHO send it all relevant information when the context changes.

When it registers, a module would also tell ECHO what kinds of information it is interested in receiving. The user interface, for example, would request knowledge related to understanding the user's commands and constraints and building an initial query. The query elaborator would need knowledge about how to elaborate or refine the query in the current context; this information could come from the user context as well as the query context. The task structure generator would need information to allow it to create an appropriate set of plans for the context; this would include constraint information from the user context and hints about search engines to use from the query context. The Design-to-Criteria scheduler might request information about search constraints from the user context as well information about likely success from the search plan context. The execution subsystem might request information related to detecting and handling unanticipated events as well as information about search engines and Web sites it needs to interact with. The report generator might request information from the user context so that it can tailor the report to the user. The search manager would need a variety of information from all the different aspects of the context in order to insure that the overall agent is behaving appropriately for the context. For example, it might request knowledge, perhaps from a c-schema representing the result context aspect, that allows it to decide to devote a little more time than it intended to the search in order to get better results.

The agent's context manager will watch the evolving problem-solving situation to decide when the context has changed. For ECHO, a context change occurs when the set of c-schemas matching the current situation changes. When the context changes, ECHO will notify the other modules and, depending on how they registered with it, send them knowledge about the new context.

In the short term, the agent's knowledge will be provided by humans. In the longer term, however, we would expect the agent to be augmented with the ability to modify its contextual knowledge based on its own experience, including learning about new contexts. Although their discussion is beyond the scope of this paper, context-mediated behavior has some features that should make it relatively easy to acquire knowledge from the sort of similarity-based generalization done in some case-based reasoning systems (e.g., [10]). This sort of learning might be augmented with explanation-based learning mechanisms to allow the agent to modify its contextual knowledge base over time.

4   Related Work

There are many existing intelligent information retrieval (IR) systems for the World Wide Web and other distributed information sources, for example, BIG [6], WebACE [1], InfoSpiders [7], OySTER [8], and WebMate [2]. Of these, BIG is most similar to FERRET. We will use some of the same components and technologies, in particular TAEMS task structures and the Design-to-Criteria scheduler.

Although context is taken into account by some of these systems, it is usually narrowly defined and plays a relatively minor role. The most common contextual knowledge that is represented and used by intelligent IR systems is user profiles. Generally, the profiles are learned by the system based on observing the user's behavior as he or she uses the system or from explicit user feedback. For example, various clustering and other machine learning techniques are used by WebACE, OySTER, and WebMate. In some cases (e.g., WebMate), the user model is as simple as a set of vectors describing "domains of interest". In these approaches, the vectors hold weighting information for words in documents based on how often a word occurs in a document matching that domain of interest and how often such documents contain the word.

Some systems do attempt to model and use other aspects of context. For example, the SINGLESOURCE system [4] has a simple representation of the task context that various tools use to aid selection of documents and for other purposes. Another system, InfoSpiders [7], uses neural net agents in an evolutionary model to create connectionist representations of the local context of individual documents. Some information filtering systems, such as Ringo [9], use a kind of extended user context by incorporating information from other users' preferences to suggest documents (or music, in Ringo's case) the user might find interesting.

Our approach to representing and using contextual knowledge, context-mediated behavior, was first developed in the MEDIC and Orca projects [13], and its development continues in Orca. MEDIC was a medical diagnostic system, and Orca is an intelligent mission controller for autonomous underwater vehicles (AUVs). CMB is an active focus of research in our laboratory. In addition to the AUV and Web search agent domains, it is being considered for use in intelligent multiagent system control [16].

5   Conclusion and Future Work

Context is important in all facets of an intelligent Web search agent's activities. Its context includes aspects relating to user or the kind of user, the search query itself, other elements of the task, the information sources it is considering using, and the results so far obtained. By explicitly representing knowledge about the contexts in which the agent may find itself, the agent can compare its current situation to its contextual knowledge to determine what its current context is, then use its contextual knowledge to determine how behave appropriately for the situation. This should help the agent search more efficiently, as well as provide better results for the user.

We are just beginning the FERRET project, which aims to build a context-sensitive, intelligent Web search agent. The project builds on current work by some of the authors on intelligent Web searching and context-sensitive reasoning. FERRET will be designed along the lines described above to create a tool for serious musicians and musicologists to use to search the Web.

The project provides a rich testbed for our work on context-sensitive reasoning. During the project, we will examine the question of which aspects of context are important to identify and represent in this domain, which will complement earlier work [12]. Another research topic will be the contextual knowledge in these aspects of context: what knowledge does it make sense to represent given the Web search task, and how should it be represented? A version of the context manager, ECHO, is currently being developed in the Orca project. This will be extended and tested in FERRET's domain. Context diagnosis and merging contextual knowledge from different aspects will be important topics in this work. Contextual knowledge maintenance will also be very important. Ultimately, techniques from case-based reasoning and similarity-based and explanation-based learning will need to be brought to bear to allow the search agent to update and maintain its own knowledge about contexts.

References

[1] D. Boley, M. Gini, R. Gross, E. Hong Han, K. Hasting, G. Karypis, V. Kumar, B. Mobasher, and J. Moore. Document categorization and query generation on the World Wide Web using WebACE. *Artificial Intelligence Review*, 13(5):365–391, 1999.

[2] L. Chen and K. Sycara. WebMate: A personal agent for browsing and searching. In *Proceedings of the 2nd International Conference on Autonomous Agents and Multi Agent Systems*, Minneapolis, MN, May 1998.

[3] K. Decker. Task environment centered simulation. In M. Prietula, K. Carley, and L. Gasser, editors, *Simulating Organizations: Computational Models of Institutions and Groups*. AAAI Press/MIT Press, 1996.

[4] K. D. Fenstermacher and C. A. Marlow. Supporting consultants with task-specific information retrieval. (Presented at the AAAI-99 (National Conference on Artificial Intelligence) Workshop on Intelligent Information Agents. On the WWW as `http://people.cs.uchicago.edu/~fensterm/writing/AAAI-workshop99.pdf`, accessed January 18, 2001.), 1999.

[5] D. S. Haverkamp and S. Gauch. Intelligent information agents: Review and challenges for distributed information sources. *Journal of the American Society for Information Science*, 49(4):304–311, 1998.

[6] V. Lesser, B. Horling, F. Klassner, A. Raja, T. Wagner, and S. X. Zhang. BIG: A resource-bounded information gathering agent. *Artificial Intelligence*, 118(1–2):197–244, 2000.

[7] F. Menczer and R. K. Belew. Adaptive retrieval agents: Internalizing local context and scaling up to the Web. *Machine Learning*, 39(2/3):203–242, 2000.

[8] M. E. Müller. Machine learning based user modeling for WWW search. In Workshop on Machine Learning for User Modeling, 7th International Conference on User Modeling, 1999.

[9] U. Shardanand. Social information filtering for music recommendations. Master's thesis, Massachusetts Institute of Technology, 1994.

[10] H. S. Shinn. The role of mapping in analogical transfer. In *Proceedings of the Tenth Annual Conference of the Cognitive Science Society*, pages 738–744, Montreal, Canada, 1988.

[11] K. Sycara. Arguments of persuasion in labour mediation. In *Proceedings of the International Joint Conference on Artificial Intelligence (IJCAI-85)*, pages 294–296, Los Angeles, 1995.

[12] E. H. Turner, R. M. Turner, J. Phelps, C. Grunden, M. Neale, and J. Mailman. Aspects of context for understanding multi-modal communication. In *Lecture Notes in Artificial Intelligence 1688: Modeling and Using Context* (Proceedings of the 1999 International and Interdisciplinary Conference on Modeling and Using Context (CONTEXT-99), Trento, Italy). Springer–Verlag, 1999.

[13] R. M. Turner. *Adaptive Reasoning for Real-World Problems: A Schema-Based Approach.* Lawrence Erlbaum Associates, Hillsdale, NJ, 1994.

[14] R. M. Turner. Context-mediated behavior for intelligent agents. *International Journal of Human-Computer Studies,* 48(3):307–330, March 1998.

[15] R. M. Turner. A model of explicit context representation and use for intelligent agents. In *Lecture Notes in Artificial Intelligence 1688: Modeling and Using Context* (Proceedings of the 1999 International and Interdisciplinary Conference on Modeling and Using Context (CONTEXT-99), Trento, Italy). Springer-Verlag, September 1999.

[16] R. M. Turner and E. H. Turner. Organization and reorganization of autonomous oceanographic sampling networks. In *Proceedings of the 1998 IEEE International Conference on Robotics and Automation (ICRA'98),* pages 2060–2067, Leuven, Belgium, May 1998.

[17] T. Wagner, A. Garvey, and V. Lesser. Complex goal criteria and its application in Design-to-Criteria scheduling. In *Proceedings of the Fourteenth National Conference on Artificial Intelligence (AAAI-97),* pages 294–301, July 1997.

Contexts and Philosophical Problems of Knowledge

Nicla Vassallo

University of Genova, Dept. of Philosophy, via Balbi 4, I-16126 Genova, Italy
nicla@nous.unige.it
http://www.lettere.unige.it/sif/strutture/9/epi/hp/vas/hpv.htm

Abstract. The following paper analyzes three traditional epistemological problems – the problem of justification, the problem of knowledge and the problem of skepticism – and considers the virtues and the difficulties of contextualism in treating them. The main virtue is its compatibility with our everyday epistemic practices. The main difficulty is the risk of relativism. I will conclude that contextualism is superior to invariantism. According to the former justification and knowledge attributions legitimately vary with context, while the latter denies it.

1 Introduction

Plato [40, 97e-98a] was the first to consistently face the problem of knowledge. It is present throughout the entire history of philosophy. The key concepts to understand this problem are the concept of justification, the concept of skepticism, and, of course, the very concept of knowledge itself. We can not but recognize that this history has been dominated by invariantism.[1] According to this thesis there is one and only one epistemic standard, and therefore it is wrong to claim – for the same cognitive subject S and the same proposition p – that it is true that "S knows that p" or "S is justified in believing that p" in one context, and that it is false that "S knows that p" or "S is justified in believing that p" in another context. The contextualist thesis is quite recent. It admits the legitimacy of several epistemic standards that vary with context of use of "S knows that p" or "S is justified in believing that p". So according to that thesis it is right to claim – for the same cognitive subject S and the same proposition p – that it is true that "S knows that p" or "S is justified in believing that p" in one context, and that it is false that "S knows that p" or "S is justified to believe that p" in another context. The contextualist thesis is quite interesting and appealing because, compared to invariantism, promises epistemological theories more compatible with our everyday epistemic practices and solutions more alluring to the problem of skepticism.

---

[1] The term is due to [48].

2 Contexts and justification

We do not want beliefs obtained by mere conjectures to count as knowledge. This is why justification is a necessary condition for propositional knowledge.[2] Foundationalism is the more traditional theory of justification. It has been maintained by Aristotle, Descartes and Locke – to mention some of the outstanding philosophers. Its central idea is that beliefs are divided into basic ones and derived ones. The former do not need any inferential justification, but have an immediate one. The latter are founded on the former and derive their justification from them through deductive and inductive inferences.

Basic beliefs are useful to stop the regress of justification. Aristotle [2 I(A), 3] was the first clearly to individuate the problem. It consists in the fact that regress: (i) can go on ad infinitum; (ii) can stop with unjustified beliefs; (iii) can be circular; (iv) can stop in immediately justified beliefs. Foundationalists choose (iv), and judge (i), (ii), and (iii) as disappointing: (i) is disappointing because the human mind is finite and, therefore, is not able to consider and infinite number of beliefs; (ii) is disappointing because the regress stops in something which is substantially arbitrary; (iii) is disappointing because the circle is nothing but vicious.

Rationalists and empiricists do not agree about the content of basic beliefs. For example, Descartes considers the *cogito ergo sum* as a basic belief, while for empiricists it is something of the form "I see red", "I redly see" or "I am experiencing a visual sensation of red". But, once content has been chosen, rationalists and empiricists agree that basic beliefs are fixed and given forever. Different objections have been raised against this conception. The main two are the following: the existence of basic beliefs is a myth (the myth of the given), and their content is so slight (or trivial) that it is unable to constitute the starting point of all those derived beliefs which we intuitively assume to be justified[3].

Annis [1] thinks contextualism superior to foundationalism because the former is able to face the regress problem in a satisfactory way, since it does not postulate beliefs given forever, and therefore it is not subject to objections raised against the latter. One important point in the debate about contextualism is the ability of the cognitive subject to reply to objections couched in terms of precise epistemic aims, i.e. achieving true beliefs and avoiding false beliefs. Concerning a proposition p, the epistemic claims of a cognitive subject S may be objected to in two different ways: (A) S is not in a position to know that p is true; (B) p is false. Because we do not want to have conditions so strong that S can not satisfy them, not every objection is possible or, at least, S is not required to answer every objection. Objections must be «based on the current evidence available»,[4] and «must be a manifestation of a real doubt where the doubt is occasioned by a real life situation».[5] It may be said that S «is not required to respond to an objection if *in general* it would be assigned a low

---

[2] This is widely accepted, but not by everybody. For example, not by [33] who, however, espouses contextualism.

[3] For these and other objections, cf. [43], [5], [6, ch. 2], [31].

[4] Cf. [1, p. 207].

[5] Cf. [1, p. 207].

probability by the people questioning S».[6] Obviously, these people must pursue the above epistemic aims – looking for truth and avoiding falsity – because, otherwise, their objections will not be appropriate, and S must reply in such a way to produce a general agreement that the force of objections entirely collapses or, at least, that it is considerably decreased. It is however obvious that S can also reply by noting that the objections are not appropriate, because they are not based on the actual available evidence, or because they are not the result of a real doubt, or because they do not pursue epistemic aims, or because they do not belong to the types (A) or (B).

The main question is: is S justified in believing that p is true? According to Annis, this question is always relative to an issue-context or to a conversational context. Let us suppose that we are going to decide if Flora – an ordinary person in an ordinary context – is justified in believing that the genetic secret of Down's syndrome has been discovered. We ask Flora: "Why do you believe it?" We are satisfied if she answers that she has read it in a newspaper and that newspapers are generally reliable, because we apply a rather relaxed epistemic standard – we are in an ordinary context. Of course the same answer is not accepted if the context changes. In fact let us suppose that Flora is taking her bachelor examination in genetics. We do not judge her justified at all in her believing if she appeals to her reading the newspaper, because in this new context we apply a rather elevated epistemic standard. So, with regard to an issue-context a person can be justified in believing a proposition p, and with regard to another issue-context the very same person may not be justified at all in believing the very same proposition. It is evident that the issue-context «determines the level of understanding and knowledge that S must exhibit, and it determines an appropriate objector-group».[7] So, while in an ordinary context, the appropriate objector-group is constituted by ordinary people, and not by geneticists, in the above bachelor examination it is surely constituted by geneticists.

Given a certain issue-context, if the appropriate objector-group asks S reasons for her belief, this belief is not a basic one in that context, because it will be derived from reasons and, therefore, from beliefs that are meant to support it. In the above ordinary context Flora's belief is obviously derived because the basic belief is: "the newspapers are generally reliable". But in a context where newspapers' reliability is in question, the belief "the newspapers are generally reliable" will not be basic anymore.

For a better understanding, let us see another example. There is Annabel. She is in perfect psycho-physical conditions and would like to buy a pair of red shoes. She goes into a shoe store, sees a pair of red shoes and says: "These shoes are red". Is she justified in believing that the shoes are red? The issue-context is an ordinary situation, and it is neither a physics examination, where Annabel would be requested to have a good knowledge of light transmission, nor a cognitive science examination, where Annabel would be requested to have a good knowledge of colour perception. The shoe store is an ordinary context where the objector-group is constituted by ordinary people with good perceptive abilities, and cognition of standard perceptive conditions and of causes of perceptive mistakes. In such a familiar context, objections are not usually raised: Annabel's belief is considered immediately justified and, as such, is to

[6] Cf. [1, p. 207].
[7] Cf. [1, p. 208].

be regarded as contextually basic. But suppose that someone, who knows that the shoe shop is illuminated by a red light, raises the following objection: "The shoes might appear red just because of the red light ". If Annabel does not find a way to reply, her belief is to be regarded as unjustified. However she might answer: "Yes, I know of the red light, but the shop assistant guaranteed to me that the shoes are red also under a normal light". Her belief would be justified in virtue of this answer and, therefore, the justification for "These shoes are red" would be derived. The regress problem seems solved, without the necessity to postulate basic beliefs given forever and so without the possibility to refer to them as the myth of the given. In fact, according to contextualism, contextually basic beliefs vary with issue-context.

I said that the regress problem seems solved, and not that it is solved. It is not solved because there is at least one problem to face.[8] According to Annis, contextually basic beliefs are able to stop the regress. Like foundationalists, he opts for the solution (iv): regress stops with immediately justified beliefs. In virtue of what are these beliefs immediately justified? For foundationalists, they are immediately justified in virtue of their content. For contextualists, they are immediately justified in virtue of the issue-context or of the topical, disciplinary and dialectical constraints. More precisely they are immediately justified because they are not brought into question or doubt. The problem is: does the absence of objections constitute a good reason to be confident in the truth of contextually basic beliefs? Foundationalists would certainly maintain that their absence is not a good reason at all, and therefore that contextually basic beliefs do not solve the regress problem, because the regress stops with unjustified beliefs. So, from their point of view, the contextualist answer to the problem is not (iv), but (ii), which is a disappointing one because the regress stops in something that is substantially arbitrary. Contextualists can reply quoting a well known Wittgensteinian remark: «At the foundation of well-founded belief lies belief that is not founded».[9] They can interpret it as following: at the foundation of justified beliefs lie always unjustified beliefs. Wittgenstein was not a naive philosopher, so it would be quite silly to attribute him the view that all unjustified beliefs are arbitrary.[10] As Moser [38, p. 10] claims, not all unjustified beliefs can be put on the same level. There are unjustified beliefs which are true or not contradictory, and there are unjustified beliefs which are false or contradictory. Therefore contextualists need to «avoid the implausible view that *any* unjustified belief, however obviously false or contradictory, can yield justification in certain contexts». This means that contextualists need to show that some unjustified beliefs, i.e. contextually basic beliefs, can yield justification to derived beliefs. It is a task yet to be carried out.

3 Contexts and Knowledge

I have analyzed the contextualization of justification. Let us now turn to that of knowledge. The traditional definition of knowledge – it is justified true belief – was

---

[8] For another problem, cf. [7].

[9] Cf. [53, par. 253].

[10] The interpretation of [53] is however controversial. Cf., for example, [44] and [37].

doubted by Gettier's counterexamples. One of the original counterexamples is the following:

> Let us suppose that Smith has strong evidence for the following proposition: (f) Jones owns a Ford. Smith's evidence might be that Jones has at all times in the past within Smith's memory owned a car, and always a Ford, and that Jones has just offered Smith a ride while driving a Ford. Let us imagine, now, that Smith has another friend, Brown, of whose whereabouts he is totally ignorant. Smith selects three place names quite at random and constructs the following three propositions: (g) Either Jones owns a Ford, or Brown is in Boston; (h) Either Jones owns a Ford, or Brown is in Barcelona; (i) Either Jones owns a Ford, or Brown is in Brest-Litovsk. Each of these propositions is entailed by (f). Imagine that Smith realizes the entailment of each of these propositions he has constructed by (f), and proceeds to accept (g), (h), and (i) on the basis of (f). Smith has correctly inferred (g), (h), and (i) from a proposition for which he has strong evidence. Smith is therefore completely justified in believing each of these three propositions. Smith, of course, has no idea where Brown is. But imagine now that two further conditions hold. First, Jones does *not* hold a Ford, but is at present driving a rented car. And secondly, by the sheerest coincidence, and entirely unknown to Smith, the place mentioned in proposition (h) happens really to be the place where Brown is. If these two conditions hold, then Smith does *not* know that (h) is true, even though (1) (h) is true, (2) Smith does believe that (h) is true, and (3) Smith is justified in believing that (h) is true.[11]

Many agree on the fact that the outcome is the following: the three conditions – truth, belief, and justification – are necessary, but insufficient, and are to be integrated with other conditions.[12] So, if you adhere to contextualism at the level of justification, the strength of your position at the level of knowledge concerning a proposition p partially depends on the strength of your justification for believing p. In this case, the concept of knowledge is contextualized in virtue of the contextualization of the concept of justification. This means that if you espouse a contextualized concept of justification, you must also espouse a contextualized concept of knowledge. However, after Gettier's counterexamples, if you espouse a contextualized concept of knowledge, you do not need to espouse also a contextualized concept of justification, since you can espouse a contextualized concept of those other conditions that comprise the traditional definition of knowledge. Given that several different conditions have been devised,[13] I will generally speak of standards for knowledge, and take for granted that they concern those conditions, not justification.

---

[11] Cf. [23].

[12] It worth noting in passing that [33] suggests a contextualist solution to Gettier's problem. [12] contests it. I assume here that contextualism does not offer such a solution.

[13] For several of these conditions, cf. [45] and [50].

First of all it is important to distinguish between subjective contextualism and attributive contextualism. According to the former, contextual factors are those concerning the cognitive subject and her surroundings: the elements of the context are substantially extra-evidential factors that depend on the situation in which the subject is in and on the situation of her environment. According to the latter, it is essentially the conversational context of attributor, i.e. whoever describes the cognitive subject as a knower or a nonknower. DeRose [17, pp. 187-188] offers a good definition of attributive contextualism:

> As, I use it, and as I think the term is most usefully employed, "contextualism" refers to the position that the truth-conditions of knowledge ascribing and knowledge denying sentences (sentences of the form "S knows that p" and "S doesn't know that p" and related variants of such sentences) vary in certain ways according to the context in which they are uttered. What so varies is the epistemic standards that S must meet (or, in the case of a denial of knowledge, fail to meet) in order for such a statement to be true. In some contexts, "S knows that p" requires for its truth that S have a true belief that p and also be in a *very* strong epistemic position with respect to p, while in other contexts, the very same sentence may require for its truth, in addition to S's having a true belief that p, only that S meet some lower epistemic standards.

The idea that there are two senses of "know" – a weak or ordinary sense and a strong or philosophical sense – is not completely new. More recently that idea has been defended by Malcolm [35, p. 183]:

> When I use "know" in the weak sense I am prepared to let an investigation (demonstration, calculation) determine whether the something that I claim to know is true or false. When I use "know" in the strong sense I am not prepared to look upon anything as an *investigation*; I do not concede that anything whatsoever could prove me mistaken; I do not regard the matter as open to any *question*.

Malcolm maintains that there are two different epistemic standards for knowledge attributions. This surely is a contextualistic thesis, but it is mild, since contemporary contextualism allows that there are several standards. To say that there are several standards is nothing but to recognize the indisputable fact that we apply different standards in different conversational contexts, so that it happens that we are willing – for the very same proposition and the very same subject – to attribute knowledge in contexts where low standards count and to deny knowledge in contexts where high standards count. This is certainly true for knowledge in the situations which I have already presented, when I talked of justification. Concerning the question whether Flora knows that the genetic secret of Down's syndrome has been discovered, we apply low standards in an ordinary context and high standards in a bachelor examination of genetics. Concerning the question whether Annabel knows that the shoes are red, we apply low standards in an ordinary context and high standards in a bachelor examination of physics or cognitive sciences. However it is worth noting that we can apply different standards also in ordinary contexts. For a better understanding, let us consider the following two cases:

(a) It is Saturday afternoon. Bertha and I are walking around in the town. We stop in front of the chemist's shop. I would like to go in to buy some aspirins. But I realize that the chemist's shop is too crowded and I hate the crowds. I tell Bertha: "Tomorrow I will come back to buy some aspirins". She says: "It is better to do it now. Perhaps tomorrow the chemist's shop is closed. Several chemist's shops are closed on Sunday". I answer her: "I know that the chemist's shop will be open tomorrow. It is open on Sunday. I personally saw it two weeks ago."

(b) It is Saturday afternoon. Bertha and I are walking around in the town. We stop in front of the chemist's shop. I would like to go in to buy some aspirins, because I need it to cure my bad cold. But I realize that the chemist's shop is too crowded and I hate the crowd. I tell Bertha: "Tomorrow I will come back to buy some aspirins". She says: "It is better to do it now. Perhaps tomorrow the chemist's shop is closed. Several chemist's shops are closed on Sunday". I answer her: "I know that the chemist's shop will be open tomorrow. It is open on Sunday. I personally saw it two weeks ago." She replies: "You have to buy some aspirins, otherwise your bad cold will get worse and worse. The chemist's shop might have changed its opening days during the last two weeks. Do you really know that it will be open tomorrow?". I admit: "Perhaps I do not know. It is better that I go in the shop and ask which days it is open".

From a contextualistic perspective, the statement "Nicla knows that the chemist's shop will be open tomorrow" is true in case (a), and false in case (b), taking however for granted that the three traditional conditions are satisfied in both cases, i.e. that: it is true that the chemist's shop will be open tomorrow; Nicla believes that the chemist's shop will be open tomorrow; Nicla's belief is justified. In order to secure her perspective, the contextualist only needs to underline the important contextual differences between the two cases:[14]

(1) there is the problem of needing to be right because of the cold, which is important in (b), but not in (a).[15]

(2) there is the relevance of a possibility or a doubt. In (b) Bertha mentions the possibility that the chemist's shop might have changed its opening days during the last two weeks. Once this possibility has been mentioned, it becomes relevant,[16] so that, in order to attribute knowledge to Nicla, it is no longer sufficient that Nicla knows that the chemist's shop was open on Sunday two weeks ago. It is also necessary that Nicla is able to rule out that possibility. In (a) it is not mentioned and, therefore, Nicla does not need to rule it out.[17]

---

[14] Cf. [14, pp. 914-915]

[15] Cf. [3, p. 76, n. 1] on this point.

[16] Cf. [24], [46], [11], [14], [9], [16], [26] for the contextualist debate on relevant possibilities or alternatives.

[17] Cf. [32] on this contextual factor.

(3) there is the consideration of such a possibility. Given that it is mentioned in (b), Nicla is compelled to consider it relevant, before she can assert "I know that the chemist's shop will be open tomorrow". If Nicla does not consider it, it will be very difficult to attribute knowledge to her. In (a), the possibility is not mentioned, and so Nicla need not to consider it.[18]

In both cases the cognitive subject, to whom knowledge is attributed or denied, is present at the conversation or, in other words, is inside the conversational context. Some contextualists consider also the hypothesis that she is not present and, in doing so, embrace a radical form of attributive contextualism.[19] Let us see an example of this form. Camilla and Emma are discussing a very important matter m. Given that m is important, they are applying quite high standards by mutual consent. M is true, they believe that m is true and have such an evidence for m that in a more ordinary context – where the standard would be more relaxed – they would attribute knowledge to themselves without any hesitation. But, since m is important, they are in a context where they do not judge that evidence sufficient, and so deny knowledge to themselves by mutual consent. Let us suppose now that Geraldine is not present at their discussion. She is in an ordinary context and has just that evidence for m that in an ordinary context nobody would deny knowledge to her. Camilla and Emma are well informed about Geraldine's epistemic situation and get it into their heads to ask if she knows that m. Given that they deny knowledge to themselves, it seems obvious to deny knowledge also to Geraldine. The radical form of attributive contextualism agree with Camilla and Emma, because it requires that the applied standards are those of attributor's context. Of course this is not always necessary. For certain aims or purposes it is also possible to apply standards of the subject's context. Contextualism does not preclude it.

To sum up, according to contextualism, the truth value of knowledge attributions varies on the basis of certain characteristics of the conversational context. For subjective contextualism, they are the characteristics of the context of the cognitive subject, while for attributive contextualism they are the characteristics of the context of the attributor. However, both forms of contextualism allow the possibility of truly asserting that "S knows that p" in one context and that "S does not know that p" in another context, because different contexts call for different epistemic standards – lower or higher, weaker or stronger – that S must satisfy.

4 Contexts and Skepticism

At the beginning I said that there are three key notions of the philosophical problem of knowledge: justification, knowledge, and skepticism. Until now I have analyzed the contextualist treatment of the first two notions. It is time now to consider the third one.

---

[18] Cf. [24] on this contextual factor. Other contextual factors can be the topic under discussion – it is clear in [51] and [52] – and the elements of the situation that affect the cognitive subject's reliability.

[19] Cf. [17, p. 191].

There are partial forms of skepticism. They concern specific sectors of knowledge: for example, moral knowledge, religious knowledge or mathematical knowledge. They are called partial, because they do not doubt the entirety of knowledge, but only some particular areas of it. On the contrary, global forms of skepticism doubt, or deny, all, or almost all, knowledge. They come as hypotheses. Descartes' hypotheses of the dream and of the malicious demon [19, p. 13 and p. 15] are well-known. The contemporary version of them is the hypothesis of a brain in a vat. This is its scenario. Unknown to me, I was abducted and taken to a far away planet. My brain was extracted, put in a vat full of nutritional liquids, and connected to a computer which is managed by an extraterrestrial – malicious or not, depending on what you like. The extraterrestrial completely manages my brain, and, in particular, makes me believe everything I would believe if I were not a brain in a vat.[20]

What do I believe now? I believe I am in my study. I believe that there is a Compaq machine in front of me. I believe that I am writing a paper entitled "Contexts and Philosophical Problems of Knowledge". I believe that my body exists. I believe that I am listening to some music from my CD. I believe that I have two hands. And so on. But if I were dreaming or being deceived by a demon or an extraterrestrial, everything I believed would be false and, therefore, could not be knowledge. Could I know I was not in a dreaming or deceiving situation? No, I could not, because, as Descartes wrote, «there are never any sure signs by means of which being awake can be distinguished from being asleep», and the same is true for the possibility to distinguish deception from not deception. In Nozick's words [39, p. 201]:

> ... how could we know we are not being deceived that way, dreaming that dream? If those things *were* happening to us, everything would seem the same to us. There is no way we can know it is not happening for there is no way we could tell if it were happening; and if were happening we would believe exactly what we do now – in particular, we still would believe that it was not. For this reason, we feel, and correctly, that we don't know – how could we? – that it is not happening to us.

But, if we do not know that it is not happening to us, we must admit that we know almost nothing of what we believe to know, and, therefore, that we almost never succeed in truly attributing knowledge to ourselves and to the others. This is at least the skeptic's conclusion.

Contextualism has been often developed in order to face the skeptic's challenge.[21] Hume [28, p. 316] surely was a precursor:

> Most fortunately it happens, that since reason is incapable of dispelling these clouds, nature herself suffices to that purpose, and cures me of this philosophical melancholy and delirium, either by relaxing this bent

---

[20] Cf. [41, ch. 1].

[21] Cf. [20], [21], [22], [49], [10], [11], [12], [13], [15], [16], [32], [33], [51], [52] for contextualist approaches to the problems of skepticism. Cf. [42] e [47] for criticisms of these approaches.

of mind, or by some avocation, and lively impression of my senses, which obliterate all these chimeras. I dine, I play a game of backgammon, I converse, and am merry with my friends; and when after three or four hour's amusement, I wou'd return to these speculations, they appear so cold, and strain'd, and ridiculous, that I cannot find in my heart to enter into them any farther.

This Humean suggestion is that there is a philosophical, or skeptical, context and an ordinary context. The skeptical hypotheses are normally raised in the former, while in the latter they are so obliterated that they appear cold and ridiculous, when we come back to the philosophical context.

Contemporary contextualism elaborates something similar, maintaining that the skeptic modifies by her hypotheses the ordinary epistemic standards, and, in particular, elevates them in order to create a context in which we can not truly attribute knowledge to ourselves and to others. In Goldman's words [25, p. 148], «the skeptic … exercises an aberrant pattern of possibility exploration». Once the standards are elevated, or, if you prefer, strengthened, even if aberrantly, we must admit that we feel all the force of skepticism, and concede that we accept its conclusion: we know almost nothing. In this way we recognize, of course, that skepticism has its valid reasons.

What does the skeptic do? He mentions a skeptical hypothesis, and so confers relevance to it, and so compels us to consider it.[22] Let us see an example. I am talking to Naomi and telling her about my winter holidays: "I have been on the Alps, I skied, I ate polenta". She interrupts me: "Do you know that you to have really been on the Alps, etcetera?". We are in an ordinary conversational context, and, therefore, her question seems inappropriate to me. I reply a little irritated: "Yes, of course I know it. Are you perhaps doubting my mental or mnemonic abilities?". Perhaps worse because she has in mind the skeptical doubt: "I am only thinking that you might have dreamed that you have been on the Alps or that you might have been deceived by a demon or by an extraterrestrial into falsely believing that you have been on the Alps. Perhaps even now you might dream or be deceived. Perhaps you might always dream or be deceived". Naomi has mentioned a skeptical possibility and I am compelled to consider it. She has changed the context: now we are in a skeptical context.[23] In order truly to state I now know something, i.e. that I have been on the Alps, I must rule out such a possibility. But, as Descartes and Nozick rightly decreed, I can not. So I must realize the triumph of skepticism. And none of us would do otherwise.

But then why do we not espouse skepticism straight away and forever? Because the damage would be huge: almost all we believe we know would not be knowledge at all. How can we avoid it? We can simply go back to more ordinary conversational contexts, where the epistemic standards are more relaxed, because the skeptical possibilities are not normally mentioned, and so we are not compelled to consider and rule out them. And, in any case, when they are mentioned, we are not anymore in an ordinary context, since the epistemic standards are elevated in order to create a

---

[22] Lewis speaks of "Rule of Attention", Cohen speaks of "Rule of Salience", DeRose speaks of "Rule of Sensitivity".

[23] See (2) and (3).

skeptical context in which we can not truly attribute knowledge to ourselves and to the others. Once we are back in more ordinary conversational contexts, we apply their more relaxed standards and realize that we can truly attribute knowledge to ourselves and to the others. In DeRose's words [17, p. 194]: «As soon as we find ourselves in more ordinary conversational contexts, it will not only be true for us to claim to know the very things that the skeptic now denies we know, but it will also be *wrong* for us to *deny* that we know these things». The fact that the skeptic employs high standards in her context can not show at all that we do not satisfy the weaker standards of ordinary contexts. So there is not any contradiction between saying that we know and that we do not know. Given that there are some standards in the ordinary contexts and other standards in the skeptical context, the skeptical negation of knowledge is perfectly compatible with ordinary knowledge attributions.

It is possible to object that the contextualist approach to skepticism is not new at all, since Moore elaborated it. He writes [36, p. 144]:

> I can now give a large number of different proofs, each of which is a perfectly rigorous proof; and ... at many other times I have been in a position to give many others. I can now prove, for instance, that two human hands exist. How? By holding up my two hands, and saying, as I make a certain gesture with the right hand, "Here is one hand", and adding, as I make a certain gesture with the left, "and here is another".

Like the contextualist, also Moore surely wants to safeguard our ordinary knowledge attributions. In an ordinary context nobody would doubt that Moore knows he has two hands, if, obviously, he has two hands. Better still, in such a context, we feel that the statement "I know I have two hands" is rather bizarre, because it is a type of knowledge that we take for granted: it is obvious. However, contrary to the contextualist, Moore wants to defeat the skeptic, saying "here is one hand and here is another". This means that he does not admit other epistemic standards than those of ordinary contexts. In other words, he does not recognize that the skeptic elevates the standards so much to create a special context in which we can not anymore truly attribute knowledge to ourselves and to the others. Consequently Moore is not a contextualist and does not share with her the good point of acknowledging the epistemic force, the legitimacy, of the skeptical challenge and, at the same time, the force, the legitimacy, of our ordinary epistemic practice or life. If we want to find a precursor of contextualism approach to skepticism, it is, as I said, Hume, and not Moore.

5 Advantages and problems

Moore is an invariantist: the only standards which count are the more relaxed ones. At his extreme, there is the invariantist who claims that the only standards which count are the higher ones. The obvious advantage of contextualism over invariantism is its compatibility with everyday epistemic practice. In fact it is evident that, contrary to what invariantism claims, we legitimately apply different epistemic standards in different contexts. Contextualism theorizes this point and bridges the gap between epistemological reflection and ordinary practice. Moreover it has other advantages in looking at traditional problems in a new way. Though it may be compatible with foundationalism, contextualism offers a different solution to the regress problem. It accepts the result of Gettier's counterexample that it is necessary to integrate the traditional definition of knowledge with other conditions, and proposes to contextualize these other conditions. It recognizes the validity of skepticism and, at the same time, the validity of our ordinary knowledge attributions. Of course, as any other philosophical theory, contextualism has not only advantages, but also its own problems. The most serious one – at least for the attributive form – is the problem of relativism about truth.[24] The point is that the truth of statements like "S knows that p" or "S does not know that p" is relative to the context of the attributor. So it seems that "S knows that p" or "S does know not that p" can not be true *tout court*, but only true for somebody or for a point of view. This problem disappears if statements containing "know" are considered in the same way as statements containing indexicals. The result is that the truth of "S knows that p" «is relative to the attributor's context, but the notion of truth is preserved by treating knowledge claims as having an indexical component».[25]

The interpretation of statements containing indexicals depends on the characteristics of contexts in which they are uttered. This means that the interpretation varies with context of use. "I am English" is false if uttered by Giustina (who is an Italian), while it is true if uttered by Justina (who is an English). According to Kaplan [29 and 30], we need to distinguish the "character" from the "content": in different contexts of use, the character of a statement containing indexicals is constant, while the content changes; such a character is the linguistic meaning or, better, a function from contexts of utterance to contents, while the content is the sense or what is said.[26] What is the character of "S knows that p?". According to DeRose [14, p. 922], for example, it is roughly the following: «S has a true belief that p and is in a *good enough* epistemic position with respect to p». What is the content of "S knows that p"? It is «how good an epistemic position S must be in to count as knowing that p»[27], and this shifts from context to context.

Let us consider the statement (s) "Lucy knows that there is some good pesto sauce in the dish". The character of "knows" in (s) is always constant: there is some good pesto sauce in the dish, Lucy believes it and she is in a good enough epistemic position with respect to "there is some good pesto sauce in the dish". The content varies with the context of attributor, and, in particular, with the epistemic position she requires for the cognitive subject. If I am not a chef, but a normal person, I may truly state that (s) is true, if there is some good pesto sauce in the dish, Lucy believes it, and Lucy is in a certain epistemic position: for example, it is clear to her that pesto sauce is made with basil, that it does not taste of garlic too much, that it is palatable. Of

---

[24] Cf. [8, p. 649] and [17, pp. 195-203] for other problems and their solutions.
[25] Cf. [8, p. 648].
[26] On Kaplan, and, more in general, on contextualism in philosophy of language, cf. [4].
[27] Cf. [14, p. 922].

course such a position is not judged good enough, if I am a chef, and so in this case I may state that (s) is false. It is obvious that the way in which the truth conditions of (s) vary with context is not different at all from the way in which the truth conditions of "I am English" vary with context[28].

References

1. Annis D.B.: A Contextualist Theory of Epistemic Justification, *American Philosophical Quarterly*, 15, (1978) 213-129. Now in Moser P.K. (ed.): Empirical Knowledge. Readings in Contemporary Epistemology, Rowman & Littlefield, Lanham, Maryland, (1996) 205-217.
2. Aristotle: Posterior Analytics, Clarendon Press, Oxford, (1975).
3. Austin J.L.: Other Minds, in Philosophical Papers, Oxford University Press, Oxford, (1961) 44-84.
4. Bianchi C.: La dipendenza contestuale. Per una teoria pragmatica del significato. Edizioni Scientifiche Italiane, Napoli, (2001)
5. Bonjour L.: Can Empirical Knowledge have a Foundation?, *American Philosophical Quarterly*, 15, (1978) 1-13.
6. Bonjour L. : The Structure of Empirical Knowledge, Harvard University Press, Cambridge, Mass, (1985)
7. Brady M.S.: Can Epistemic Contextualism Avoid the Regress Problem?, *The Southern Journal of Philosophy*, XXXVI, (1998) 317-328.
8. Brower B.W.: Contextualism, Epistemological, *Routledge Encyclopedia of Philosophy*, Routledge, London, (1998) 646-650.
9. Brueckner A.: The Shifting Content of Knowledge Attributions, *Philosophy and Phenomenological Research*, LIV, (1994) 123-126.
10. Cohen S.: Knowledge, Context, and Social Standards, *Synthese*, 73, (1987) 3-26.
11. Cohen S.: How to be a Fallibilist, *Philosophical Perspectives*, 2, (1988) 91-123.
12. Cohen S.: Contextualist Solutions to Epistemological Problems: Scepticism, Gettier, and the Lottery, *Australasian Journal of Philosophy*, 76, (1998) 289-306.
13. DeRose K.: Knowledge, Epistemic Possibility, and Scepticism, UCLA Doctoral Dissertation (1990).
14. DeRose K.: Contextualism and Knowledge Attributions, *Philosophy and Phenomenological Research*, LII, (1992) 913-929.
15. DeRose K.: Solving the Skeptical Problem, *The Philosophical Review*, 104, (1995) 1-52.
16. DeRose K.: Relevant Alternatives and the Content of Knowledge Attributions, *Philosophy and Phenomenological Research*, LVI, (1996).
17. DeRose K.: Contextualism: An Explanation and Defence, in Greco J e Sosa E. (eds.), *Epistemology*, Blackwell, Oxford, (1999) 187-205.
18. Descartes R.: Discours de la méthode, Leida, (1637)
19. Descartes R.: Meditationes de Prima Philosophia, Michel Soly, Paris, (1641). En tr.: Meditations on First Philosophy, in The Philosophical Writings of Descartes, vol. II, Cambridge University Press, Cambridge, (1984).
20. Dretske F.: Epistemic Operators, *Journal of Philosophy*, 67, (1970) 1007-1023.
21. Dretske F.: Conclusive Reasons, *Australasian Journal of Philosophy*, 49, (1971) 1-22.
22. Dretske F.: The Pragmatic Dimension of Knowledge, *Philosophical Studies*, 40, (1981) 363-378.

---

[28] I would like to thank Claudia Bianchi, Lory Lemke, Carlo Penco, and three anonymous reviewers who helped me in writing the final version of this paper.

23. Gettier E.L.: Is Justified True Belief Knowledge?, *Analysis*, 23, (1963) 121-123.
24. Goldman A.I.: Discrimination and Perceptual Knowledge, *The Journal of Philosophy*, 73, (1976) 771-791. Now in Goldman A.I.: Liaisons, The Mit Press, Cambridge, Mass., (1992) 85-103.
25. Goldman A.I.: Psychology and Philosophical Analysis, *Proceedings of the Aristotelian Society*, 89, (1989) 195-209. Now in Goldman A.I.: Liaisons. Philosophy Meets the Cognitive and Social Science, Mit Press, Cambridge, Ma, (1992) 143-153.
26. Heller M.: The Proper Role for Contextualism in an Anti-Luck Epistemology, in Tomberlin J.E. (ed), *Philosophical Perspectives, Epistemology*, 13, (1999) 115- 129.
27. Henderson D.K.: Epistemic Competence and Contextualist Epistemology: Why Contextualism is not just the Poor Person's Coherentism, *The Journal of Philosophy*, XCI, (1994) 627-649.
28. Hume D.: A Treatise of Human Nature, Penguin, London, (1969).
29. Kaplan D.: On the Logic of Demonstratives, *Journal of Philosophical Logic*, 8, (1970) 81-98.
30. Kaplan D.: Demonstratives, in Almog J., Perry J. and Wettstein H.K. (eds), *Themes from Kaplan*, Oxford University Press, Oxford, (1989).
31. Kornblith H.: Beyond Foundationalism and the Coherence Theory, *The Journal of Philosophy*, LXXVII, (1980) 597-612.
32. Lewis D.: Scorekeeping in a Language Game, *Journal of Philosophical Logic*, 8, (1979) 339-359.
33. Lewis D.: Elusive Knowledge, *Australasian Journal of Philosophy*, 74, (1996) 549-567.
34. Locke J.: An Essay concerning Human Understanding, London, (1690)
35. Malcolm N.: Knowledge and Belief, *Mind*, 51, (1952) 178-189.
36. Moore G.E.: Philosophical Papers, Collier Books, New York, (1962).
37. Morawetz T.: Wittgenstein and Knowledge, University of Massachusetts Press, Amherst, Mass, (1978).
38. Moser P.K.: Empirical Knowledge, in Moser P.K. (ed), *Empirical Knowledge*, Rowman & Littlefield, Lanham, (1996) 1-34.
39. Nozick R.: Philosophical Explanations, Harvard University Press, Cambridge, Ma, (1981).
40. Plato: Meno, in The Collected Dialogues of Plato, Princeton University Press, Princeton, (1961).
41. Putnam H.: Reasons, Truth and History, Cambridge, (1981).
42. Schiffer S.: Contextualist Solutions to Scepticism, *Proceedings of the Aristotelian Society*, XCVI, (1996) 317-333.
43. Sellars W.F.: Science, Perception and Reality, Routledge, London, (1963).
44. Shiner R.: Wittgenstein and the Foundations of Knowledge, *Proceedings of the Aristotelian Society*, 78, (1977) 102-124.
45. Shope R.K.: The Analysis of Knowing, Princeton University Press, Princeton, NJ, (1983).
46. Stine G.: Skepticism, Relevant Alternatives, and Deductive Closure, *Philosophical Studies*, 29, (1976) 249-261.
47. Stroud B.: Epistemological Reflection on Knowledge of the External World, *Philosophy and Phenomenological Research*, 56, (1996) 345-358.
48. Unger P.: Philosophical Relativity, University of Minnesota Press, Minneapolis, (1984).
49. Unger P.: The Cone Model of Knowledge, *Philosophical Topics*, 14, (1986) 125-178.
50. Vassallo N.: Teorie della conoscenza filosofico-naturalistiche, Angeli, Milano, (1999).
51. Williams M.: Unnatural Doubts. Epistemological Realism and the Basis of Scepticism, Blackwell, Oxford, (1991)
52. Williams M.: Skepticism, in Greco J e Sosa E. (eds.), *Epistemology*, Blackwell, Oxford, (1999) 35-69.
53. Wittgenstein L.: On Certainty, Basil Blackwell, Oxford, (1969).

Practical Context Transformation for Information System Interoperability

Holger Wache, Heiner Stuckenschmidt

Center for Computing Technologies
University of Bremen,
P.O.B.: 33 04 40, D-28334 Bremen, Germany
{wache, heiner}@tzi.de

Abstract. This paper discusses the use of contextual reasoning, i.e. context transformation for achieving semantic interoperability in heterogeneous information systems. We introduce terminological contexts and their explication in terms of formal ontologies. Using a real-world example, we compare two practical approaches for context transformation one based on transformation rule, the other on re-classification of information entities in a different terminological context. We argue that both approaches supplement each other and develop a unifying theory of context transformation. A sound and complete context transformation calculus is presented.

1 Introduction

Mediators [5] are middleware components that provide a flexible integration of several information systems such as database management systems, geographical information systems, or the World Wide Web. A mediator combines, integrates, and abstracts the information provided by the sources [20] tackling the same problems which are discussed in the federated database research area, i.e. *structural heterogeneity* (schematic heterogeneity) and *semantic heterogeneity* (data heterogeneity) [13]. Structural heterogeneity means that different information systems store their data in different structures. Semantic heterogeneity considers the content and its semantics of an information item. In rule–based mediators [6], rules are mainly designed in order to reconcile structural heterogeneity. Discovering semantic heterogeneity problems and their reconciliation play a subordinate role. But for the reconciliation of the semantic heterogeneity problems, the semantical level also has to be considered [11, 4]. *Contexts* are one possibility to capture this semantical level. A context [12] contains "meta data relating to its meaning, properties (such as its source, quality, and precision), and organization" [16]. A value has to be considered in its context and may be transformed into another context (so–called *context transformation*).

In this paper, we review two approaches to the implementation of context transformation in mediators, namely functional context transformation and context transformation by re-classification. We discuss their use for providing semantic interoperability among heterogeneous information systems. We propose a unifying theory of practical context transformation and present a sound and complete context transformation calculus. The paper is structured as follows: Section 2 introduces the problem of semantic heterogeneity and motivates the use of contextual knowledge. In section 3 we illustrate an integration process using an example from a real application. The use of the different transformation approaches is discussed in section 4. In section 5 we present the unifying theory of context transformation and the transformation calculus including sketches of the soundness and completeness proofs.

2   Context, Ontologies and Information Systems

In principle there are two possible solutions to achieving semantic interoperability between heterogeneous information systems [7]: the tight coupling strategy that creates a new information system with a unified semantics and the loose coupling approach that does not touch the individual semantics and instead provides transformations on a semantic level. There are strong arguments in favor of the loose coupling approach [12]. First of all the use of individual semantics allows small representations and efficient reasoning within the individual system. Second, the semantics in a multi-context system is much more flexible and can be used to handle inconsistencies that would become threatening when trying to create a single context with a global semantics.

2.1   Contexts and Semantic Heterogeneity

In order to achieve semantic interoperability in a heterogeneous information system, the *meaning* of the information that is interchanged has to be understood across the systems. Semantic conflicts occur, whenever two contexts do not use the same interpretation of the information. Goh identifies three main causes for semantic heterogeneity [7].

- *Confounding conflicts* occur when information items seem to have the same meaning, but differ in reality, e.g. due to different temporal contexts.
- *Scaling conflicts* occur when different reference systems are used to measure a value. Examples are different currencies or marks.
- *Naming conflicts* occurs when naming schemes of information differ significantly. A frequent phenomenon is the presence of homonyms and synonyms.

It has been argued that semantic heterogeneity can be resolved by transforming information from one context into another. In [16] and [7] context transformation methods are developed. The scope of these approaches is mainly on the conversion of different scaling conflicts. In our work we address the problem of providing practical solutions for the context transformation problem that is not only capable of converting between different scales, but also covers the transformation of application-specific vocabularies. We therefore argue for a semantic interoperability approach that is based on transformations between individual terminological contexts.

2.2   Ontologies as Contextual Information

Ontologies have set out to overcome the problem of implicit and hidden knowledge by making the conceptualization of a domain explicit. This corresponds to one of the definitions of the term ontology most popular in computer science [8]: *"An ontology is an explicit specification of a conceptualization."* An ontology is used to make assumptions about the meaning of a term available. It can also be seen an an explication of the context a term is normally used in.

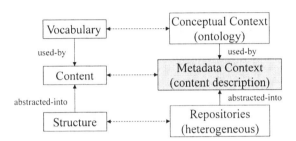

Fig. 1. The Role of Context in Information Systems Interoperability. (adapted from [12])

Kashyap and Shet [12] discuss the role of contexts and ontologies for semantic interoperability (compare figure 1). According to their view, contexts are used to abstract from the content of an information repository. So-called *metadata contexts* describe the information content of a repository and therefore allow to decide whether a repository contains relevant information. Additionally *conceptual contexts* are introduced, which are ontologies that define the meaning of terms used in the metadata context and the repository. While Kashyap and Shet define relationships between the ontologies, our approach relies on the use of shared basic vocabulary that is used to derive inter-ontology relationships.

We propose to use formal ontologies in order to capture and explicate the assumptions made by each context, because they can be used as a basis for automatic translations between vocabularies that preserve the intended meaning of the translated vocabulary.

3   Context-Based Semantic Integration

We illustrate the need for context modeling and transformation by a real–world example that also serves to illustrate our approach. Two sources — CORINE and ATKIS — provide geological information.

The first source CORINE [3] stores its data in two tables[1]. The first table is called clc_ns2. Every entry represents one geological item. clc_ns2 contains

---

[1] For readability reasons the tables of both sources are simplified. Some attributes are omitted.

the attributes CLC_NS2_ID (identifier), AREA (size in *ha*), and NS (classification). Especially the last attribute NS refers to catalog, wherein all items are classified. In CORINE, the catalog contains more than 64 concepts. The second table clc_ns2_pol stores polygons describing the area of an item. The attributes are CLC_NS_ID (reference to clc_ns2), VERT_ID (identifier of a vertices), and NEXT_V_ID (identifier of the following vertices).

In the second source ATKIS [1] a geological item is stored in one table atkisf with the attributes id, fl (size in m^2), and folie (classification). Analogously to CORINE the last attribute folie refers to a classification catalog containing more than 250 terms.

But the catalogs of CORINE and ATKIS are different. Further, both catalogs use different conceptualizations. The task of this example is that the data of CORINE database has to be converted in the ATKIS database. Of course, this transformation can be viewed as a special case of an integration task demonstrating all the problems that can occur. Besides the obvious structural heterogeneity problems, the main problem relies on the reconciliation of the semantic heterogeneity: both geological information sources classify the common areas in different catalogs. A mediator system that tries to query information from one system in terms of the other will fail or return wrong results, because it will not be able to unify the land-use classifications and will not recognize that the returned size of an area refers to a different scale. Consequently, the classification of the CORINE has to be converted into the ATKIS catalog. Moreover, the size has to be converted according to their different currencies. Both conversions are the challenge for the semantic integration and are handled by the both kinds of context transformation.

3.1 A Minimal Modeling Language

In order to capture the semantics of the different land-use classifications used in the systems we want to integrate, we have to describe ontologies of land-use classes. We use description logic in order to build these ontologies. The features of this language are described below.

Description logics are a family of logic-based representation formalisms that cover a decidable subset of first-order logic. Description logics are mostly used to describe terminological knowledge in terms of concepts and binary relation (slots) between concepts that can be used to define a concept term by necessary and sufficient conditions that have to be fulfilled by all instances of the concept. We use a minimal description logic that consists of conjunction, disjunction, and negation as well as existentially and universally qualified range restrictions on slots. These language elements can be used to describe concept expressions with the following syntax and semantics:

syntax	semantics
concept-name	$\mathcal{I}(C) \subseteq \mathcal{D}$
top	$\mathcal{I}[\text{top}] = \mathcal{D}$
bottom	$\mathcal{I}[\text{bottom}] = \emptyset$
(and concept$^+$)	$\mathcal{I}[(\text{and } C_1\, C_2)] = \mathcal{I}[C_1] \cap \mathcal{I}[C_2]$
(or concept$^+$)	$\mathcal{I}[(\text{or } C_1\, C_2)] = \mathcal{I}[C_1] \cup \mathcal{I}[C_2]$
(not concept)	$\mathcal{I}[(\text{not } C)] = \mathcal{D} - \mathcal{I}[C]$
(all role concept)	$\mathcal{I}[(\text{all } r\, C)] = \{x \in \mathcal{D} | \forall y \in \mathcal{D} : \langle x, y \rangle \in \mathcal{I}[r] \Rightarrow y \in \mathcal{I}[C]\}$
(some role concept)	$\mathcal{I}[(\text{some } r\, C)] = \{x \in \mathcal{D} | \exists y \in \mathcal{I}[C] : \langle x, y \rangle \in \mathcal{I}[r]\}$

Class expressions are used to define concepts. A concept is defined using the keyword **concept** followed by the name of the concept and a concept expression that restricts the set of entities belonging to the concept to a subset of the whole domain of discourse. The meaning of a concept definition is defined by an interpretation. The Tuple $\langle \mathcal{D}, \mathcal{I} \rangle$ is an interpretation, if $\mathcal{D}$ is a domain and $\mathcal{I}$ is an extension function that maps concept names into subsets of $\mathcal{D}$ and role names into $\mathcal{D} \times \mathcal{D}$. Using this interpretation, the semantics of the language constructs is given by the equations in the table above. This Tarskian-style semantics offers a formal framework for the comparison of different terminologies.

3.2 The Integration Process

Step 1:Authoring of Shared Terminology Our approach relies on the use of a shared terminology in terms of properties used to define different concepts. This shared terminology has to be general enough to be used across all information sources to be integrated but specific enough to make meaningful definitions possible. The top-level concept *parcel* is defined below:

```
(concept parcel (and
        (all ground ground-type)
        (all coverage structure)
        (all cultivation plant)
        (all vegetation plant)
        (all use use-type)))
```

For the given integration task the shared terminology mainly consists of ontologies that define concepts a parcel can be related to, namely ground types, artificial structures built on a parcel, different kinds of plants that may grow on a parcel and general types of land use.

Step 2: Annotation of Information Sources Once a common vocabulary exists, it can be used to annotate different information sources. In this case annotation means that the inherent concept hierarchy of an information source is extracted and each concept is described by necessary and sufficient conditions using terms from the vocabulary defined in the share terminology. The result of this annotation process is an ontology that contains a definition of the terminological context. The meaning of land-use classes from both classifications is formally defined by further restricting the range of the slots attached to the general parcel concept. Here is an example:

```
(concept broad-leaved-forest (and parcel
        (all coverage no-stuctures)
        (all ground land)
        (all vegetation (or trees shrubs))
        (some vegetation broad-leaved-trees)))
```

The above example is taken form one of the entries in our CORINE data set used in the case study. This entry is classified as 'broad-leaved-forest', which is a subclass of parcel that can be identified by the absence of water, a lack of artificial structures and vegetation that may consist of trees and shrubs where some of the vegetation consists of broad-leaved trees.

We use so-called templates to assign a contextual description to data structures in a repository. A template is a fifth-ary predicate:

$$T = \langle name, context, type, value \rangle @source$$

A template has a *name*, a *context* addressing the semantics of the concept. The name of the context refers to the corresponding ontology that explicated the terminological context. Further elements of a template are: *type* determining the data type, the *value* referencing the information item itself, and the last identifier *source* denoting which source the template belongs to. The value can be a simple value, e.g. a number, or a string, or a list of attributes. An *attribute* consists of a name and a template the attribute refers to. In the last case the type is `complex`. In case of simple values the type slot contains the basic data type.

Templates with attributes can represent tables (relations) in a relational data structure model. The attributes of the template are the attributes of the relation. The values of the template attributes are templates encapsulating the basic data types of the relation attributes[2]. An example template for the ATKIS table is given below. The template contains variables and therefore describes a set of instances found in the database.

```
<atkisf,?LA,complex, {
    id ->     <id,?LI,string,?ID>,
    fl ->     <fl,?LS,real,?S>,
    folie ->  <folie,?LC,int,?C>
    }>@ATKIS
```

Step 3: Semantic Translation of Information Entities The purpose of the steps described above was to lay a base for the actual translation step. The existence

---

[2] For readability reasons the source is omitted in the nested templates

of a terminological context model for all information sources to be integrated enables a translation method to work on the contextual knowledge. Two different types of translation by context transformation have been investigated:

- Rule-based functional transformation [19]
- Classification-based transformation [17].

We argued that these two kinds of context transformation supplement each other in the sense that functional transformation is well suited to resolve scaling conflicts while classification based transformation can be used to resolve non-trivial naming conflicts [18]. The transformation step is discussed in more detail in the next section.

4 Context Transformation

A conceptual model of the context of each information source builds a basis for integration on the semantic level. We call this process context transformation, because we take the information about the context of the source (in our case CORINE) and re-interpret this information in the terms of a target (ATKIS) providing a new context description for that entity within the new information source. We compare two different approaches for context transformation namely rule-based context transformation and context transformation based on classification and show how these two approaches can be used to integrate the example data.

4.1 Context Transformation with Rules

Context Transformation Rules (CTR's) define a context transformation between two templates. Operationally they have to *exchange* information. More precisely CTR's replace one template by another. An important aspect of CTR's is that they can be applied to templates, which are nested in the structure of a top–level template i.e. to a template in an attribute. This aspect simplifies the formulation of CTR's and improves the scalability and the flexibility of context transformation. A CTR is represented as follows:

$$a \rightsquigarrow b \leftarrow d_1, ..., d_m$$

The head of the rule defines the relation $\rightsquigarrow$ — the so called context transformation relation. The relation describes which template a can be transformed into template b. The other terms in the body $d_1, ..., d_m$ are required to support or to restrict the context transformation. Normally the body terms are expressions but can also be templates, e.g. if further information for the context transformation is needed.

We illustrate the use of CTR's in our example. The surfaces in ATKIS and CORINE are stored with different measures of size, namely square-meters and hectares. Therefore the surface value of CORINE cannot be copied but has to be converted dividing the number of square-meters by the factor 10000. The conversion is done during the context transformation. The appropriate CTR looks like:

```
<?N,surface,?T,?V_HA>@CORINE -> <?N,surface,?T, ?V_M2>@ATKIS
    :- ?V_M2 := ?V_HA / 10000.
```

In the templates the contexts and the sources are specified but the names, types, and values are replaced by variables. Such a CTR is applicable to all templates with the specified context, where an appropriate substitution for the variables exists, including those templates which are hidden in the structure, e.g. to the template AREA stored in the attribute AREA of template clc_ns2.

4.2   Context Transformation by Classification

Context transformation rules cover a lot of semantic heterogeneity problems, i.e. we were able to integrate the diverging measures and units e.g. used to determine the size of area. However, the integration of the different kinds of type information is more difficult. Representing this by CTR's would lead to very large set of trivial CTR's. For maintainability and scalability reasons, this demands for more sophisticated mechanisms for context transformation. We solve this problem by automatically deriving type transformation rules using the inference capabilities of the description logics we use to represent conceptual contexts.

The main inference mechanism used in description logics is subsumption checking. A concept is said to subsume another concept, if the membership of the latter implies membership in the former. Following the semantics defined above the subsumption relation between two concepts is equivalent to a subset relation between the extensions of the concept definition. Given two concept definition A and B subsumption is tested by checking if $A \sqsubseteq B \iff \mathcal{I}[(\textbf{and } B\,(\textbf{not } A))] = \emptyset$. Subsumption checking can be seen as a special classification method, because it returns a list of classes B_i (concepts) a member of a given concept A belongs to. In terms of subsumption reasoning a context transformation task can be defined as follows:

Definition 1. *Let S and T be two terminological contexts represented by sets of concept definitions with subsumption relations $\sqsubseteq_S$, $\sqsubseteq_T$ and concept membership relations $\in_S$, $\in_T$. Let further S be a concept from one terminological context S ($S \in S$). Then the transformation of a data set s from context S into the context T is described by*

$$(s \in_S S \implies s \in_T T) \iff (S \sqsubseteq_T T)$$

In general, it is not decidable, whether the condition ($S \sqsubseteq_T T$) holds, because the subsumption relation is only defined for the context T while the concept definition S is taken from context S and is therefore used by a different subsumption relation. At this point, the shared vocabulary comes into play. Provided, that the concepts from both contexts are defined using the same basic vocabulary, we get a unified subsumption relation defined as:

$$\sqsubseteq = \sqsubseteq_S \cup \sqsubseteq_T$$

We can compute $\sqsubseteq$ using available subsumption reasoner that support the language. The result of the context transformation is now given by

$$class_T(S) = \{T_i | S \sqsubseteq T_i \wedge T_i \in T \wedge \not\exists V \in T : V \sqsubset T_i\}.$$

Having determined the result set $class_T(S)$ we can use its elements for defining a set of new context transformation rules in the following way:

$$s \rightsquigarrow t \leftarrow s \in_S S, t \in_T T, T \in class_T(S)$$

These new rules supplement the rule base used for context transformation and integrate classification-based and rule-base transformation.

In the case study we used the FaCT reasoner [10] in order to compute the unified subsumption relation for the ATKIS and the CORINE context. The derived direct subsumers of 'broad-leaved-forest' from the CORINE context are FORESTS-AND-SEMI-NATURAL-AREAS and FORESTS. In the case of 'broad-leaved-forest' we also get the correct result for the ATKIS context. The direct subsumers from the target hierarchy are: VEGETATION-AREA and FOREST-AREA.

5 A Unifying Model of Context Transformation

In the previous section we describe the two kinds of context transformations from an informal point of view and give an impression how context transformation rules are represented and context classification is defined. The context classification can be transformed into a set of CTR's. Therefore the calculus only must handle CTR's. In this section we present a formal context transformation calculus, which explains how context transformation rules can be implemented.

5.1 A Theory of Context Transformation

As shown in the examples above the context transformation is indicated by the binary relation $\rightsquigarrow$. The expression $s \rightsquigarrow t$ means that term s is context transformed into the term t. We give an axiomatic specifying the meaning of $\rightsquigarrow$. The set of axioms establish a unifying theory $\mathcal{T}_C$ of context transformation. They require that for all values x_i, y_i and z the following implications hold:

$$x \rightsquigarrow x \tag{CT1}$$

$$x \rightsquigarrow y \wedge y \rightsquigarrow z \implies x \rightsquigarrow z \tag{CT2}$$

$$\forall f : x \rightsquigarrow y \implies f(..., x, ...) \rightsquigarrow f(..., y, ...) \tag{CT3}$$

$$\forall P : x_1 \rightsquigarrow y_1 \wedge ... \wedge x_n \rightsquigarrow y_n \wedge P(x_1, ..., x_n) \wedge P \neq \rightsquigarrow \implies P(y_1, ..., y_n) \tag{CT4}$$

The first two axioms show the reflexivity and the transitivity of context transformation relations. The next two axioms are known as the substitution axioms and allow the application of context transformation on sub-terms. The first axiom allows the exchange of x by y in the functional term f. The second substitution axioms substitutes all arguments $x_1, ..., x_n$ by $y_1, ..., y_n$ in the n-ary predicate P.

If the theory of context transformation is compared to other theories the similarity to the equality theory is conspicuous. Only the symmetry is missed in the context transformation theory. The $\rightsquigarrow$ is obviously not symmetric because a term s can be transformed into a term t but not vice versa (e.g. if during the transformation s is abstracted to t). On the other hand, in general $\rightsquigarrow$ is not asymmetric because sometimes a term t can be retransformed in s (e.g. if there is a bijective functional dependency).

The substitution axioms are formulated in second order predicate logic. It is possible to reformulate these axioms in first order predicate logic by giving one axiom for every functional symbol f and every predicate symbol P. But this reformulation would lead to an infinite number of axioms which is not be possible to handle practically.

5.2   A Transformation Calculus

In principle, the theory of context transformation can be implemented using standard logical inference, i.e. deduction. However this turns out to be extremely inefficient. We therefore develop a more efficient calculus and show that it follows the general theory. The calculus determines the context transformation relation without referring to the satisfiability conditions, which are checked during the integration task (see section 5.4).

Due to the similarity to equality theory the calculus is similar to a term reduction system. The difference is that a context transformation is only applicable on the right side of the goal $\leftarrow s \rightsquigarrow t$ (reflecting the missing of the symmetry). The transformation eliminates the goal $\leftarrow s \rightsquigarrow t$ if the left side is unifiable with the right side of $\leftarrow s \rightsquigarrow t$ (cf. the reflexivity axiom). The two inference rules of the context transformation calculus are:

Definition 2. *Let CT be a set of context transformations and $\leftarrow s \rightsquigarrow t$ a goal state, then the following deduction rules apply:*

1. **Context Transformation Inference Rule (CTIR)**
   Let $a \rightsquigarrow b \in CT$ be a context transformation and let the term s at position p contain the sub-term u ($s|_p = u$). If there is a most general unifier σ exists in such a way that $\sigma u = \sigma a$ then

$$\frac{\leftarrow s[u]_p \rightsquigarrow t \qquad a \rightsquigarrow b}{\leftarrow \sigma(s[b]_p \rightsquigarrow t)}$$

The expression $s[b]_p$ denotes the replacement of the sub-term at position p in term s by term b.

2. **Elimination Inference Rule (EIR)**
   If there is a most general unifier σ in such a way that $\sigma s = \sigma t$ then the empty clause $\square$ can be inferred. I.e. $\leftarrow s \leadsto t \vdash \square$

5.3 Correctness and Completeness of the Calculus

In the following we prove theorems about the correctness and completeness of calculus with respect to the context transformation axioms (see 5.1). The correctness theorem states that for every (negated) goal for which a refutation exists the (positive) goal is a logical consequence of the set of context transformations.

Theorem 1. *Correctness of the Context Transformation*
Let CT be a set of context transformations and $\leftarrow s \leadsto t$ a goal state. Assume that for $\leftarrow s \leadsto t$ there exists a refutation in n steps ($CT \cup \{\leftarrow s \leadsto t\} \vdash \square$). Then every interpretation which satisfies CT and the context transformation axioms in T_C, also satisfies $s \leadsto t$.

$$CT \cup \{\leftarrow s \leadsto t\} \vdash \square \implies CT \cup T_C \models s \leadsto t$$

Due to the limit of paper length we only give a proof sketch of the theorem above:

Proof sketch. The proof is an induction over the length of the refutation. Suppose that the resolvent R of a deduction is a logical consequence. In the induction step ($n \rightarrow n+1$) it is show that the goal G from which R is inferred is also a logical consequence depending on which inference rule of the calculus is applied. For example[3] if the CTIR is used the context transformation $a \leadsto b$ is applied on $G = s[u]_p \leadsto t$ with $a = u$ resulting in $R = s[b]_p \leadsto t$. Every interpretation I which satisfies $a \leadsto b$ must also satisfy $s[a]_p \leadsto s[b]_p$ because I has to satisfy the substitution axioms (CT3). Applying the transitivity axiom (CT2) on $s[a]_p \leadsto s[b]_p$ and $R = s[b]_p \leadsto t$ leads to $s[a]_p \leadsto t$. Because $u = a$ it can be concluded that I also satisfies $s[u]_p \leadsto t = G$. The proof of the induction start for EIR can be reduced to the reflexivity axiom (CT1). ∎

The completeness theorem states that for every goal which is a logical consequence of CT there exists a refutation for the (negated) goal. Here we only give the completeness result for terms without any variable (ground terms). A lifting lemma extends this result to terms with variables.

Theorem 2. *Completeness of the ground Context Transformation*
Let CT be a set of ground context transformations and $\leftarrow s \leadsto t$ a ground goal. If there exists no interpretation which satisfies $CT \cup \{\leftarrow s \leadsto t\}$ and the context transformation axioms in T_C then there exists a refutation for $CT \cup \{\leftarrow s \leadsto t\}$.

$$CT \cup T_C \models s \leadsto t \implies CT \cup \{\leftarrow s \leadsto t\} \vdash \square$$

---

[3] For brevity the substitution which normally is needed is omitted.

Proof sketch. We show that every term from the minimal Herbrand model $M_\mathcal{P}$ is refutable. It can be proven that $M_\mathcal{P}$ is the union of $M_0 = CT$ and $M_{n+1} = M_n \cup \{s \rightsquigarrow t \mid s \rightsquigarrow t \leftarrow \overline{B} \in \mathcal{T}_C \wedge \overline{B} \subseteq M_n\}$ for $n > 0$. By induction over n we prove that for every $s \rightsquigarrow t \in M_{n+1}$ there exists a refutation. By induction hypothesis for every $s_i \rightsquigarrow t_i \in M_n$ there already exists a refutation.

The main idea of this prove is that the refutations for $s_i \rightsquigarrow t_i$ are combined into one refutation for $s \rightsquigarrow t$ according to $s \rightsquigarrow t \leftarrow s_1 \rightsquigarrow t_1, ..., s_k \rightsquigarrow t_k$ With respect to the theory $\mathcal{T}_C$ there are four possibilities how $s \rightsquigarrow t$ can be constructed. Suppose that $s \rightsquigarrow t$ is generated by the transitivity axiom (CT2) $s \rightsquigarrow t \leftarrow s \rightsquigarrow u, u \rightsquigarrow t$. The two refutations of $s \rightsquigarrow u$ with length $m + 1$ and $u \rightsquigarrow t$ with length $l + 1$ can be combined in a refutation of length $m + l + 1$ as follows:

$$
\begin{array}{ll}
\leftarrow s \rightsquigarrow u & \qquad\qquad \leftarrow s \rightsquigarrow t \\
\underline{\quad a_1 \rightsquigarrow b_1 \quad} & \qquad\qquad \underline{\quad a_1 \rightsquigarrow b_1 \quad} \\
\leftarrow s_1 \rightsquigarrow u & \qquad\qquad \leftarrow s_1 \rightsquigarrow t \\
\vdots & \qquad\qquad \vdots \\
\leftarrow s_{m-1} \rightsquigarrow u & \qquad\qquad \leftarrow s_{m-1} \rightsquigarrow t \\
\underline{\quad a_m \rightsquigarrow b_m \quad} & \qquad\qquad \underline{\quad a_m \rightsquigarrow b_m \quad} \\
\leftarrow s_m \rightsquigarrow u & \qquad\qquad \leftarrow s_m \rightsquigarrow t \\
\square \;\; (\text{with } s_m = u) & \qquad\qquad \equiv \quad (\text{because } s_m = u) \\
(\text{appl. of EIR}) &
\end{array}
$$

$$\Longrightarrow$$

$$
\begin{array}{ll}
\leftarrow u \rightsquigarrow t & \qquad\qquad \leftarrow s_m \rightsquigarrow t \\
\underline{\quad a_{m+1} \rightsquigarrow b_{m+1} \quad} & \qquad\qquad \underline{\quad a_{m+1} \rightsquigarrow b_{m+1} \quad} \\
\leftarrow u_1 \rightsquigarrow t & \qquad\qquad \leftarrow s_{m+1} \rightsquigarrow t \\
\vdots & \qquad\qquad \vdots \\
\leftarrow u_{m-1} \rightsquigarrow t & \qquad\qquad \leftarrow s_{m+l-1} \rightsquigarrow t \\
\underline{\quad a_{m+l} \rightsquigarrow b_{m+l} \quad} & \qquad\qquad \underline{\quad a_{m+l} \rightsquigarrow b_{m+l} \quad} \\
\leftarrow u_l \rightsquigarrow t & \qquad\qquad \leftarrow s_{m+l} \rightsquigarrow t \\
\square \;\; (\text{with } u_l = t) & \qquad\qquad \square \;\; (\text{with } s_{m+l} = u_l = t)
\end{array}
$$

The other axioms can also be proven in the same way. ∎

5.4 Integrating context transformation into query decomposition

The main task of a mediator [20, 6]) is to receive a global query and to decompose the query in a set of sub-queries, which are understandable by the sources. From a logical point of view query decomposition is simply unfolding the global query with respect to query decomposition rules corresponding to the well-known resolution principle. Integrating the context transformation calculus into the query decomposition needs an extension of the classical resolution principle. In the following we present a theory hyper-resolution — the CT-resolution — where the theory corresponds to the context transformation theory $\mathcal{T}_C$. The basic idea of the extension of the CT-resolution is to substitute the unification by the context transformation and to collect the conditions for the context transformation.

Definition 3. *Let* $P(s_1, ..., s_n) \leftarrow B$ *a query decomposition rule from the set* $\mathcal{R}^{QD}$, $\{(a_j \rightsquigarrow b_j \leftarrow G_j^{CT}) \in \mathcal{R}^{CT} \mid j \in \{1, ..., m\}\}$ *a set of context transformation rules and* $\leftarrow P(t_1, ..., t_n), G$ *a goal, where the symbols* B, G *and* G_j^{CT} *represents a set of literals. If a most general unifier* σ *exists with* $\sigma(a_1 \rightsquigarrow b_1, ..., a_m \rightsquigarrow b_m) \models_{\mathcal{T}_C} \sigma(s_1 \rightsquigarrow t_1, ..., s_n \rightsquigarrow t_n)$ *then* $\sigma(\leftarrow G, B, G_1^C, ..., G_m^C)$ *is the resolvent of the CT-resolution.*

The correctness and the completeness of the CT-resolution can also be shown.

6 Discussion

We presented a context-based approach for the resolution of semantic conflicts among heterogeneous information sources. The approach preserves the individual contexts of the repositories involved and achieves interoperability by context transformations on the basis of explicit models of the terminological context of an information source.

The approach presented is a practical one; therefore it does not cover all aspects of context transformation investigated in theoretical work (e.g. [14],[9]). However it extends the capabilities of working system (e.g. [2, 15]) by providing a calculus for rule-based and classification-based context transformation that has been implemented in the MECOTA System [19] and is guaranteed to be correct and complete.

The integration allows us to cover two types of semantic conflicts mentioned by Goh, namely scaling and naming conflicts. The integration of methods for resolving confounding conflicts involving reasoning about space and time are a major topic for further research.

References

1. AdV. Amtliches Topographisch Kartographisches Informationssystem ATKIS. Technical report, Landesvermessungsamt NRW, Bonn, 1998.
2. S. Bressan, C.H. Goh, K. Fynn, M. Jakobisiak, K. Hussein, T. Lee, S. Madnick, T. Pena, J. Qu, A. Shum, and M. Siegel. Demonstration of the context interchange mediator prototype. Technical report, Sloan School of Management, MIT, 1997.
3. EEA. Corine land cover. Technical guide. Technical report, European Environmental Agency. ETC/LC, European Topic Centre on Land Cover, 1997-1999.
4. P. Frankhauser, M. Kracker, and E. Neuhold. Semantic vs. structural resemblance of classes. *SIGMOD Record*, 20(4), December 1991.
5. Hector Garcia-Molina, Joachim Hammer, Kelly Ireland, Yannis Papakonstantinou, Jeffrey Ullman, and Jennifer Widom. Integrating and accessing heterogeneous information sources in tsimmis. In *Proceedings of the AAAI Symposium on Information Gathering*, pages 61–64, Stanford, California, March 1995.
6. Hector Garcia-Molina, Yannis Papakonstantinou, Dallan Quass, Anand Rajaraman, Yehoshua Sagiv, Jeffrey Ullman, and Jennifer Widom. The tsimmis approach to mediation: Data models and languages. In *Next Generation Information Technologies and Systems (NGITS-95)*, Naharia, Israel, November 1995. Extended Abstract.

7. Cheng Hian Goh. *Representing and Reasoning about Semantic Conflicts in Heterogeneous Information Sources.* Phd, MIT, 1997.

8. T.R. Gruber. A translation approach to portable ontology specifications. *Knowledge Acquisition*, 5(2), 1993.

9. R.V. Guha. *Contexts: A formalization and some applications.* PhD thesis, Stanford University, 1991.

10. I. Horrocks. The FaCT system. In H. de Swart, editor, *Automated Reasoning with Analytic Tableaux and Related Methods: International Conference Tableaux'98*, number 1397 in Lecture Notes in Artificial Intelligence, pages 307–312. Springer-Verlag, Berlin, May 1998.

11. V. Kashyap and A. Sheth. Schematic and semantic semilarities between database objects: A context-based approach. *The International Journal on Very Large Data Bases*, 5(4):276–304, 1996.

12. Vipul Kashyap and Amit Sheth. Semantic heterogeneity in global information systems: The role of metadata, context and ontologies. In M. Papazoglou and G. Schlageter, editors, *Cooperative Information Systems: Current Trends and Applications.* 1996.

13. W. Kim and J. Seo. Classifying schematic and data heterogeinity in multidatabase systems. *IEEE Computer*, 24(12):12–18, 1991.

14. J. McCarthy. Notes on formalizing context. In *Proceedings of the thirteenth international joint conference on artificial intelligence IJCAI'93*, 1993.

15. E. Mena, V. Kashyap, A. Sheth, and A. Illarramendi. Observer: An approach for query processing in global information systems based on interoperability between pre-existing ontologies. In *Proceedings 1st IFCIS International Conference on Cooperative Information Systems (CoopIS '96)*. Brussels, 1996.

16. Edward Sciore, Michael Siegel, and Arnie Rosenthal. Using semantic values to facilitate interoperability among heterogeneous information systems. *ACM Transactions on Database Systems*, pages 254–290, June 1994.

17. Heiner Stuckenschmidt and Ubbo Visser. Semantic translation based on approximate re-classification. In *Workshop on Semantic Approximation, Granularity and Vagueness*, Breckenridge, Colorado, 2000.

18. Heiner Stuckenschmidt and Holger Wache. Context modelling and transformation for semantic interoperability. In Mokrane Bouzeghoub, Matthias Klusch, Werner Nutt, and Ulrike Sattler, editors, *Knowledge Representation Meets Databases, Proceedings of the 7th Intl. Workshop KRDB'2000.* 2000.

19. Holger Wache. Towards rule–based context transformation in mediators. *Proceedings of the International Workshop on Engineering Federated Information Systems (EFIS 99)*, 1999.

20. Gio Wiederhold. Mediators in the architecture of future information systems. *IEEE Computer*, 25(3):38–49, March 1992.

Explanation as Contextual

R. A. Young

Philosophy Department, University of Dundee, Scotland
r.a.young@dundee.ac.uk

Abstract. There is a view that *all explanation is contextual*. An explanation answers questions that are relevant in a context and that are open to solution in that context. In another context, there might be no such questions, or they might not be open to solution. Van Fraassen has used a contextual account of explanation to argue in favour of what he calls 'constructive empiricism' and against what he calls 'scientific realism'. On his account, both empiricists and realists search for theories that are empirically adequate. These will explain the relevant observable phenomena, but differ on the unobservable phenomena, for example quantum states. For the realist, science aims to provide a literally true account of the unobservables. For the empiricist, science aims at no more than empirical adequacy. One argument in the realist armoury is the following. The best philosophical explanation of how the best scientific explanation does explain the observables requires that it is true about the unobservables. An empiricist response to this is that all explanation is contextual, so there is no globally best scientific explanation. The present paper explores the empiricist line by reference to formal learning theory and a logic of questions. Van Fraassen's contextual theory of explanation does not employ learning theory. The present paper is a step towards a more developed theory, differing from van Fraassen in some respects.

1 Introduction

On one view, a consistent axiomatisation of a model that combines a scientific theory together with contingent initial conditions can provide an explanation of a fact. This is so when a proof of a description of the fact to be explained can be deduced. In practise, in empirical science, theories often remain unaxiomatised, and proofs remain relatively informal. Nevertheless, on this view of explanation, genuine explanations are ones that can be articulated formally. Stated thus, the account is incomplete. This is because there can be deductions of descriptions of events which are not accepted as explanatory of those events.

Take a road accident. The police may be able to deduce the speed and the position of the car as it came around the bend from descriptions of skid marks and damage, together with a theory of mechanics, a theory of the properties of sheet metal and so forth. However, we would not normally think that the skid marks and damage, together with the background theories, explain the speed and position of the car. They are the effects of the speed, not part of its explanation. Even when we consider conditions that are prior in time to the event to be explained and that we take to be part of the causal background to the event, it varies from case to case what we take to be explanatory. In some cases, we may give an explanation by citing the driver's choice of speed, but in another situation we might cite the state of the car's brakes, the fact that the bend was hidden by the brink of a hill or the fact that the sign indicating the bend was obscured by foliage, or that the car's headlights were feeble because they were dirty. There are many diverse causes that might be considered explanatory of the car's speed when it began to skid. The range of causes which we take to be relevant will vary from case to case, and will depend upon our interest in the matter. In other cases of explanation, our explanations may not be causal; we may explain in terms of tendencies towards equilibrium, in terms of considerations of symmetry, or even in teleological terms. When we employ these different forms of explanation, the range of alternatives to our preferred explanation will vary.

As well as thinking of the contingent conditions as explanatory, we can think of a theory as explanatory. Thus we can think that Newton's theory explains the tides. However, we can also think that there are other phenomena which Newton's theory fails to explain correctly. Thus Newton's theory is false. This illustrates how we can think that even a theory we recognise to be false does explain some phenomena in its domain[10, p. 98]. When we put forward Newton's theory as explanatory, we consider a range of alternative theories, perhaps including Aristotelian physics, but not including relativity theory as an alternative under consideration.

Thus, as well as a theory with means of expressing it, background conditions with ways of describing them, and a deductive apparatus, it seems that we need to consider something else which determines what is to constitute an explanation in the given instance. We can think of this further factor as *the context*, and perhaps we can think of it as consisting in a set of classes of models for our incomplete description of the situation to be explained, a set of classes from which which we need to choose, if we are to identify an explanation. Thus, in the case of the car accident, we might think that there is a class of models in which the car driver chose to travel at too great a speed for the conditions, a class in which the brakes fail and so on. For each class of model, let us suppose, descriptions can be articulated from which we can deduce a description of the event to be explained. As we have noted, the classes of models need not be entirely exclusive. The chosen speed might be too fast for the conditions, but the brakes might also fail.

The notion of *a context of explanation* plays a part in the grand debate between realism and non realism in philosophy of science. This debate concerns explanation in terms of unobservables, for example quantum states. We may identify some set of classes of models which include unobservables, as the set from which we are to select an explanation of events. As scientists, if we do aim to identify an explanation in this way, are we thereby committed to holding that one of the models in our context of explanation is realised in the world, and therefore some of our propositions about unobservables are literally true? Are we committed to thinking that our aim as scientists is to find the best explanation in our set and thereby to find the true explanation? Non realists, such as van Fraassen do not think that we do need to commit ourselves to the literal truth of explanatory theories. Thus they need to criticise the claim that we can make inferences to the best explanation and thereby identify literally true theories. In van Fraassen's critique of *inference to the best explanation* he says [9, pp.142-3]:

> ...it is a rule that only selects the best among the historically given hypotheses. We can watch no contest of the theories we have so painfully struggled to formulate, with those no one has proposed. So our selection may well be the best of a bad lot. To believe is *at least* to consider more likely to be true than not. So to believe the best explanation requires more than an evaluation of the given hypothesis. It requires a step beyond the comparative judgement that this hypothesis is better than its actual rivals. While the comparative judgement is indeed a 'weighing in the light of the evidence', the extra step — let us call it the ampliative step — is not. For me to take it that the best of the set X will be more likely to be true than not, requires a prior belief that the truth is already more likely to be found in X, than not.

A non realist position is that all explanation is contextual, and that therefore we do not aim at any globally best explanation which we need take to be true of unobservables. Thus, even when we talk of a theory as explaining an event, that theory only explains given a certain background. In order to sustain this position, the non realist needs an account of our attitude towards a context of explanation that does not require commitment to the literal truth of any proposition about unobservables. Instead of thinking that a context of explanation includes a true theory, the non realist can think it includes an empirically adequate theory, or even a theory which, like Newton's, is empirically adequate for some restricted domain, such as the observable properties of the tides.

2 Van Fraassen on Explanation and Context

Van Fraasen offers us a non realist account and it is a contextual one. The realism that he opposes declares that the aim of science is to discover literally true theories, which are true even about the non observables. In contrast, for him, the aim of science is only to construct theories that are empirically adequate. He has a semantic account of what a theory is, that is to say a theory is a model, or class of models. It is a mathematical structure which can used to provide an interpretation that will make our scientific statements true. The realist thinks that science aims to construct models that are entirely instantiated in the world. For van Fraassen, the non realist ('he would say "constructive empiricist"') aims to construct models whose observables are instantiated in the world.

On van Fraassen's account, there is no difference between the formal semantics of the realist and the non realist. Thus van Fraassen's position is not like that of Dummett, where non realism goes with a semantics of warranted assertability as opposed to a semantics based upon the correspondence theory of truth. His position on semantics may be compared with the account of semantics provided by one school of thought on context, namely that of Giunchiglia et al at Trento [4]. They think of contexts as consisting of sets of local models. Each agent has a different set of local models, and there is no assumption of one shared model which is the model that is instanced in reality. Like van Fraassen, they do not develop a semantics of warranted assertability in order to express non realism. Both they and van Fraassen express their non realism by arguing that it is unnecessary to commit to any one one model.

Van Fraassen's account of explanation is a particular kind of contextual account, because it conceives of explanations as answers to questions. Thus van Fraassen says [10, p.134]

'I shall now propose a new theory of explanation. An explanation is not the same as a proposition, or an argument, or list of propositions; it is an answer. An explanation is an answer to a why-question. So, a theory of explanation must be a theory of why-questions.'

Van Fraasen argues that context is required in order to specify what is requested by a question [10, p.156].

'The discussion of explanation went wrong at the very beginning when explanation was conceived of as a relationship like description: a relation between theory and fact. Really it is a three-term relation, between theory, fact and context ... Since an explanation is an answer, it is evaluated vis-a-vis a question, which is a request for information. But exactly what is requested, by means of the question 'Why is it the case that P?', differs from context to context. In addition the background theory plus data relative to which the question is evaluated, as arising or not arising, depends on the context. And even what part of that background information is to be used to evaluate how good the answer is, qua answer to the question, a contextually determined factor. So to say that a given theory can be used to explain a certain fact, is always elliptic for: there is a proposition which is a telling answer, relative to this theory, to the request for information about certain facts (those counted as relevant for this question) that bears on a comparison between this fact which is the case and certain (contextually specified) alternatives which are not the case.'

His position on the the general structure of why questions is that they are of the following form [10, p.127].

Why (is it the case that) P in contrast to (other members of) X?

However, the 'why' is governed by a relevance relation and therefore an 'abstract question' may be, 'at least in a preliminary way', identified with a triple $< P_k, X, R >$, where P_k is the topic (what is to be explained), X is the contrast class $\{P_1, \ldots, P_k, \ldots\}$ and R is the relevance relation [10, p.143]. For van Fraassen part of what is determined by the context is the contrast class, X. Also the relevance relation is determined by context.

What constitutes an answer to a 'why' question? Van Fraassen gives the following definition of a direct answer [10, p.144].

> B is a *direct answer* to question $Q = < P_k, X, R >$ exactly if there is some proposition A such that A bears relation R to $< P_k, X >$ and B is the proposition which is true exactly if P_k; *and* for all $i \neq k$; *not* P_i; and A is true.

Of course, according to van Fraassen, when a non realist gives or accepts an answer to such a question, where the answer describes non observables, then the non realist is not committed to the literal truth of the answer, but only to its empirical adequacy.

The set of direct answers to a question is called the set of *alternatives*. The context needs to determine this set, as well as determining the contrast class and the relevance relation. Let XA be the set of alternatives. Then we can think of a context as determining a class of models in each of which P_k holds, for all $i \neq k$ not P_i holds; and for some $A_i \in XA$ holds such that A_i bears relation R to $< P_k, X >$.

However, what is a context for van Fraassen? Here, at least, is a characterisation of what it does [10, p.137]:

> 'The context will generally select the proposition expressed by a sentence A via a selection of referents for the terms, extensions for the predicates and, and functions for the functors ... But intervening contextual variables may occur at any point in these selections. Among such variables there will be the assumptions taken for granted, theories accepted, world-pictures or paradigms adhered to, in that context. A simple example would be the range of conceivable worlds admitted as possible by a speaker.'

An obscurity here is just what the context is. According to what he says here, in the simple example, it can be identified with a set of conceivable worlds that is being used to determine an interpretation for a language in which an explanation is being given. I shall work with this simple account in the rest of this paper.

3 Explanations and illocutionary acts

On van Fraassen's account, an explanation, is an answer to a question, and a question is a request for information. I propose to understand a request for information as an illocutionary act. In that case we need to distinguish between the illocutionary act of questioning, and what van Fraassen's calls the 'abstract question', which, on his view, is the triple $< P_k, X, R >$. Indeed, perhaps we should not follow van Fraassen in using the term 'question' for both the illocutionary act and the 'abstract question'. Perhaps the best terminology is that the illocutionary act is simply that of 'asking' a question.

If we say, this then we follow Austin, who has 'ask' in his list of expositives [1, p.162], together with 'explain' [1, p.163]. Both the asking of questions and the giving of explanations are placed in a category of clarification of reasons, arguments and communications. If the asking of a question is, at least when it is felicitous, a step in clarification, then it need not be a request for information. The asking of a question might, at least on some occasions, be more like a step in a deductive proof. In a deductive proof, all the information necessary to prove a theorem is already present, nevertheless it requires a proof to make clear that it is a theorem. Admittedly, on some occasions, no one agent may have all the information required to answer a question, and asking it may serve as a request for information from one agent to another. On yet other occasions, none may have the information required and the posing of a question may determine a field of research which we can consider pursuing if it is feasible, not too expensive and so forth. On Austin's view the giving of an explanation is also, at least when felicitous, a step in clarification. As an illocutionary act, it is one that can be performed by uttering a sentence, where that sentence, in virtue of certain conventions or rules, and the surrounding context, constitutes an act. Sometimes, of course, one can perform conventional acts in a non-linguistic way. Nevertheless, clarification would seem to be a linguistic matter. Therefore, on this view, the giving of an explanation would seem to be a linguistic matter. If this is right, then how linguistic is an explanation itself?

Let us go back to van Fraassen. In defining the class of direct answers he defines them in terms of propositions, that is in a way that abstracts from language. Thus part of his definition is 'there is some proposition A such that A bears relation R to $< P_k, X >$' (see p. 5). On the other hand, when he explains the role of a context we get, 'The context will generally select the proposition expressed by a sentence A via a selection of referents for the terms, extensions for the predicates and, and functions for the functors' (see p. 5). Thus at least part of the role of a context is to select the proposition expressed by a sentence. Furthermore he argues, as we have seen, that an explanation is a three part relation between theory, fact and context. On his view, theories and facts are not directly linguistic entities (theories are classes of models and facts feature in models). Nevertheless, since the role of context is at least in part linguistic, it would seem that the relation of explanation is in part a linguistic, or if you like a formal relation. So just how linguistic is an explanation? Or, if you will, just how formal is its role in clarification? If one thinks in a non formal way about explanation, then one can think that an explanation has been given, when a proposition has been identified that bears the right relation to the right element of the contrast class. If one thinks in a formal way about it, then one can think that an explanation has only been given when a sentence has been identified as a premiss from which it is possible to deduce a description of the right element in the contrast class.

Suppose we think at the level of illocutionary acts. Is it a condition of an explanation having been given that the recipient is able formally to deduce some description of what is to be explained? Or is it at least a condition of the felicitous giving of explanations that the recipient of the explanation be able to make such a deduction? If we pose the question like this, then we put it as if we may presuppose some preexisting clear conventions about explanation. Perhaps this is the wrong approach. Instead we should think of proposing norms for explanation and, in particular, of proposing norms for scientific explanation in particular. It would be too much to require that all scientific explanations consist of formal derivations, but is it too much to require that a scientific explanation be given so articulately that its recipients should be able to construct a formal derivation from it if necessary? I think it is not too much, also that if we are to think in this way, then we need to think of explanations not just contextually, but linguistically.

Thus, I shall agree with van Fraassen that explanation is not a two-place relation between theory and fact, that it is at least three-place, because context is involved as well. However, I shall think that, if theory and context are conceived of semantically and are arguments of the relation, then we need the relation to be at least four-place, because *descriptions* of theory, fact and context are involved, and these are given in a language whose syntax, set of rules and conventions for deduction and for illocutionary acts are intrinsic to explanation. I shall also argue that we can conceive of explanation as an answer to a 'which' question. Thus, I shall think that, when a 'why' question is asked, some set of candidate models of what happened is identified, together with a set of descriptions. The explanation or answer to the question selects a subset of these candidate models. Consider explanation of events. A rough approximation to my view is that a good explanation selects a model from a set of alternatives together with a description of it in language that enables, indeed facilitates, (1) deduction of a description of the events to be explained. (2) deduction of the absence of the other members of the contrast class. Each model in the set of alternatives is such that, in it, some proposition is true that bears a relevance relation to the topic and the contrast class. A refinement is that the deduction may be of a probability of the events to be explained. Thus we may think of an explanation as: a relation between the elements of the tuple

$$< T, F, C, L >$$

where:

> T is the theory conceived of semantically and with specific initial conditions
> F is the fact to be explained
> C is a context, conceived of as a set of models (NB, on the semantic view of theories, according to which theories are models, each of these is a theory)
> L is a linguistic system, that is to to say a syntactic system with rules of logic and illocutionary conventions.

In a full account of the illocutionary act of giving a scientific explanation, we would need to ask whether the explanatory theory that the recipient of the explanation accepts needs to be the same as that employed by the person giving the explanation. I am inclined to think that this need not be so. The two people may have different models in mind, yet, so long as there are appropriate relations between the two models, the person giving the explanation may have an adequate explanation, and so may the person receiving it. Indeed, where we have different scientific communities, it is often the case that they employ different models. Yet often one community may offer another community an explanation which needs to be transposed from the model of the exporting community into the model employed by the importing community. Thus aspects of quantum physics may explain aspects of chemical bonding, aspects of chemical bonding may explain aspects of biochemistry, and aspects of biochemistry may explain aspects of cellular biology, but, despite all that, we should not expect the same model to be employed in all these sciences. To analyse the relationship between different communities, I would propose to use a version of the 'Distributed First Order Logic' under development by Ghidini and Serafini [3].

4 Explanation and Formal Learning Theory

We can better understand both the debate about explanation between realism and non realism in science and the role of context, if we refer to formal learning theory. Formal learning theory is concerned with identifying explanations for whole data streams, even though those data streams continue indefinitely, and even though, at any given time, a learning system only has information about a finite sequence in the data stream. In the preceding section, we began by considering an explanation of a car speeding and skidding. However, a scientific explanation of any such event is an explanation that purports to apply to an indefinitely large set of events and we can, at least to begin with, think of that set in terms of a data stream. If we consider the matter in this way, then the non realist needs to give an account of what it is that justifies us in thinking that a theory is empirically adequate for a whole data stream. The aspiration of a realist for science is that it should succeed in finding a theory that is literally true about even the unobservable properties of the world. Perhaps this aspiration is too ambitious. However, is the non realist, who aspires to empirical adequacy, really better placed?

I adopt Kelly's approach to Formal Learning Theory [7]. In Kelly's logic of reliable inquiry, we have a data stream (S) consisting of a denumerable infinity of instances of elements from some set (D), a set of assumptions (A) about the data stream, and a denumerably infinite set of hypotheses (H) about how the data stream is generated. Let us relate this to our discussion in the previous section. We can ask, 'Why do we have the actual data stream S instead of any other data stream (ie. any other denumerably infinite sequence of elements from D)?' Thus our contrast class consists of the set of denumerably infinite sequences of elements from D. A direct answer to our question consists of an hypothesis from the set of hypotheses, H.

For Kelly, there is a question of whether we can prove that there is a reliable method, amongst some set of methods M, for selecting an hypothesis such that from it we can deduce a true and complete description of the data at any time in the data stream. A method is reliable for finding such an hypothesis if, for any data stream consistent with A, the method results in such an hypothesis within finite time. NB. it is not necessary for reliability that there is one finite bound within which, for all instances of D consistent with A, the method results in a predictive hypothesis. All that is necessary is that, for each data stream, there is some finite time t within which a predictive hypothesis will be found.

It is standard to let M be the set of computable methods. However one can also consider methods for oracle machines, for example an oracle machine with a module for solving the halting problem for Turing machines. Kelly's [7] work derives from earlier work by [8], [5] and formal learning theorists such as t[6]

To provide us with a simple example for discussion let us consider a finite state machine paradigm. Let A consist of the assumptions that

I the set D consists of characters in a finite alphabet
II s is generated by some finite state machine

Note that the states of finite state machines are not in the data stream and therefore are not observable states. The realist can take it that assumption 2 is literally true whereas the non realist will take it to be an empirically adequate hypothesis, albeit not one that is falsifiable in any finite time.

Let h_i be the hypothesis that s is generated by some specific finite state machine. This hypothesis is not decidable for both a yes and no answer in finite time. Instead it is *decidable in the limit*. Or rather it is:

– for a no answer decidable in finite time
– for a yes answer *decidable in the limit*

A procedure for *deciding in the limit* is to hypothesise h_i, but to retract h_i if h_i is proved false in finite time. If h_i is true, then we are left holding h_i for all time.

Note that, even though any finite state machine will eventually loop, it is not possible to decide on a yes answer after noticing that the machine loops for amy finite number of times. This is because the data stream might be generated by a machine that generates the observed loop forever, but in any finite time, it could just be that a finite state machine with a sufficient number of states is mimicking the behaviour of smaller machine, whilst, in effect, counting upwards through its states, ultimately coming to a state with a new effect. In this case, the large finite state machine behaves like a time bomb. Eventually it breaks out of the loop.

Take any alphabet and language capable of describing all finite state machines which input and output elements of our data stream. Take an algorithm m_1 that will, given any list of finite state machines,append a member not in the list, and that will (if successively given its own output as input) eventually include in its output a description of any finite state machine describable in the language.

There is an algorithm m_2 guaranteed to identify in the limit a finite state machine which will generate the entire data stream:

1 hypothesise that the data stream would be generated by the first member of m_1's current list not yet falsified by the data stream
2 hold that hypothesis until it is falsified
3 if it is falsified, run m_1 on its previous output, and repeat1

Note that we can have a reliable method for identifying a finite state machine capable of generating the whole of s, even though it is not possible to prove of any specific h at any specific time t that it enables deduction of all further data. For a reliable method all we need to prove is that, at *some* t, *some* h selected by the method will enable deduction of all future data.

The finite state machine model may be simple, but we can use it to criticise the argument against the realist's use of inference to the best explanation quoted on page 3. In that argument van Fraassen argues that the best explanation can only be selected from amongst the historically given, already formulated hypotheses. However, in the finite state machine model one can see that there can be a reliable method for selecting the best (according to some ordering) from a potential infinity of hypotheses which have certainly not all been formulated even though their class has been identified.

Now let us consider how the realist and the non realist might justify this algorithm. The non realist conception is that it is justified because of the assumption that the data stream is generated by some particular finite state machine. The non realist's assumption is simply that the data stream is computable by a finite state machine, or by any other equivalent machine. Indeed, in the case of one data stream, the non realist can simply make the assumption that the data stream finitely loops. Thus, in the case of one data stream, the non realist need not even state a justifying hypothesis in terms of finite state machines. We can think of the contrast between the realist and the non realist here as exemplifying a difference on a fundamental scientific principle. Often scientists seek a spatio-temporally local explanation. The finite state machine explanation is local, because it explains a state of the data stream at time $t + 1$ just in terms of the state of the data stream and the state of the finite state machine at the preceding time t. An explanation in terms of a cycle of looping avoids non observables, however it fails to be a local explanation. This is because, in the absence of a counter in the data stream, it ceases to be a local explanation, because it is necessary to describe the history of the data stream in order to identify which phase of the loop has been reached at t+1. Thus the demand for local explanations can motivate assumptions about hidden properties.

However it is not realistic to think of science as being concerned with one data stream that is the output of just one system. Instead we may think that a science will typically study many varying experimental situations, but take them all to exemplify the same theory, with their variation occurring because of different initial conditions. A simple model for this is a set of data streams all of which are generated by exactly the same type of finite state machine, but which vary because that machine begins in different initial states. Each pair of finite state machine and initial condition gives us what we may call a *closed finitely determined experimental situation.* Here the realist takes it as literally true that there is such a machine. The non realist does not, but can still have a motive to adopt such a model. The motive can be to have a concise representation of the data streams. Thus the non realist could refrain from hypothesising any hidden states, and simply hypothesise that each data stream is an element of a finite set of cyclical data streams. However, this would not be a concise representation of the set of data streams. For the non realist, use of a particular model of computation can be justified because it can be concisely described. Thus in order to provide a model of science in this paper, we may conceive of science as seeking explanations for experimental situations, where each experimental situation is describable as the output of a finite state machine.

Of course, such a model is not adequate to an entire world which includes scientists. At least, not if scientists are capable of holding hypotheses about arbitrarily large finite state machines. If they are, then we need to think of them as being the equivalents of Universal Turing Machines, not of finite state machines generating data streams, but unable to operate on a tape.

It might be thought that, in order to give an account of science, we need to move to models in which there are real numbers and not even natural numbers, let alone elements from a finite alphabet. Perhaps the data stream can be modelled with natural numbers, because of limitations on human data input. However, what explains it might need to be modelled by real numbers, that is physical reality might be analogue. A reason for resisting this move is that we are concerning models that we can manage to identify. However, any language that we can use for this purpose will have only a denumerable infinity of sentences or well-formed formulae. Indeed we have the Lowenheim Skolem theorem for first order languages. The version proved by Skolem in 1919 tells us that if a denumerable set of sentences is satisfiable, then there is an interpretation that satisfies it in a universe of discourse with only a denumerable infinity of objects. Thus any such theory can be modelled using the natural numbers.

In considering the algorithm above we considered as hypotheses ones which postulate that some one finite state machine generates the data stream. It is not necessary to think in this way. Instead, one can think of each hypothesis as consisting of the claim that the data stream is generated by a specific finite state machine *or by any of the infinity of finite state machines that, given the same initial condition, and initial internal state would generate the same data stream*. If one thinks in this way, then in making an hypothesis, one selects from the denumerably infinite set M a denumerably infinite subset. If one makes the assumption that experimental situations are repeatable, except that there may be variation in the initial state of the data stream, and also that there may be variation in the internal state of the finite state machine, then one can envisage selecting a subset of H after observing other data streams.

We can use the case of closed finitely determined experimental situations, with a potentially infinite data stream, to elucidate the contrast between the non realist and the realist as follows. The non realist argues that in science we do not aim to hold that data streams are generated by a certain finite state machine instead of by any of the infinity of finite state machines (or other equivalent machines) that, given the same initial condition, and appropriate internal state, would generate the same data stream. In contrast, the realist argues that it is (at least sometimes) correct to hypothesise that a specific finite state machine is generating the data stream.

Our excursion into formal learning theory, in this section illustrates how, on the non realist view, we begin with the question. 'From which description (of a pair of Finite State Machine and initial state) is the data stream deducible', and our answer concerns an infinite subset of the finite state machines. We can take this infinite subset to identify a question about which of the remaining finite state machines will explain experimental situations which are a repetition of our experimental situation with variations in initial conditions. Since the set M of machines includes machines that can generate data streams in alphabets which extend the alphabet of the actual data stream,there is even scope for considering variation in observable or measurable parameters of which we have not yet conceived. On the non realist view, in the case of potentially infinite data streams, this will go on indefinitely. However finitely many variations on experimental situations we explore the answer that we have to our question about which machines generate the data stream will still consist in an hypothesis about a deunumerably infinite set of finite state machines.

5 Contexts and Questions

In his discussion of questions, van Fraassen cites Belnap and Steel. However, in that work there is only a small discussion of 'why' [2, p.86-7] questions, which is inconclusive, and yet these are the questions to which van Fraassen takes explanations to be answers. My personal approach is to regard these questions as equivalent to a certain kind of 'which' question and 'which' questions are extensively discussed in Belnap and Steel, but I feel that their work is not an adequate basis for understanding the role of questions in science. This is because Belnap and Steel's approach to erotetic logic (logic of questions) is to give an account of the syntax and semantics of questions, not a theory of inference for them [2, p.7]:

> Absolutely the wrong thing is to think it is a logic in terms of a deductive system, since one would thus be driven to the pointless task of inventing an inferential scheme in which questions, or interrogatives, could serve as premises and conclusions ... what one wants of erotetic logic is not its proof theory but rather its other two grand parts, grammar (syntax) and semantics.

Therefore, I prefer to turn to Wisniewski's [12] work on erotetic logic [11, p.176]. He does have an account of inference:

> if an initial question has a true direct answer and all the auxiliary premises are true, then the arising question must have a true direct answer as well. (By a direct answer to a question we mean a possible and just sufficient answer to the question).

He proposes the following requirements on implying and implied questions in his account [11, p.177].

(*) If an implying question has a true direct answer and the auxiliary premises are all true, then the implied question must have a true direct answer as well.

(**) For each direct answer B to an implied question there exists a non-empty proper subset of the set of all the direct answers to the implying question which must contain at least one true direct answer if B is true and all the auxiliary premises are true.

When we considered closed finitely determined experimental situations, it was suggested that we begin with the question. 'from which finite state machine hypothesis is a description of the data stream deducible', and that our answer concerns an infinite subset of the finite state machines. It was suggested that we took this infinite subset to identify a question about which of the remaining finite state machines will explain experimental situations that are a repetition of our experimental situation with variations in initial conditions. It was also suggested that, even when we explored variations on our experimental situation, we would still have an hypothesis about an infinite subset of finite state machines.

In his account of the logic of questions, Wisniewski makes use of multiple conclusion logic[11, p.178-9]

> It seems to be natural to think of some questions in terms of set of possibilities, among which some selection should be made. And when we are going to analyze the relation between questions and the contexts of their appearance, some notion of, to speak generally, "entailing a set of possibilities" would be needed. There is a logic, however, within which such notion is elaborated on: it is multiple-conclusion logic ...Let us then introduce the concept of multiple-conclusion entailment. We say that a set of declarative formulas X of L multiple-conclusion entails a set of declarative formulas Y of L ...if and only if the following condition holds:
>> whenever all the formulas in X are true in some normal interpretation of L, then there exists at least one formula in Y which is true in the interpretation of L.

Wisniewski supplies us with an account not only of implication between questions, but also of the raising of questions by declarative sentences. A set of declarative sentences D 'weakly generates' a question Q if D mc-entails the set of direct answers to Q, but does not entail a unit subset of these direct answers. In that case the question is sound and an answer to it is informative.

Consider an answer to the question 'From which finite state machine hypothesis can we deduce a description of the data stream'. According to the non-realist, a justifiable answer will identify a machine that can generate the data stream, but which uses that machine to specify an infinite set of finite machines that could also generate the data stream. Both the question and the answer that is given to it, given the background assumption that the experimental situation is repeatable with variations, raise questions about which finite state machines will explain the data stream in each variation of the experimental situation.

6   Conclusion

In this paper it has been argued that a non realist and contextual account of science can be developed by beginning from van Fraassen's work and extending it using formal learning theory and a logic of questions. On this account, the non-realist in science holds that

- explanation is contextual, in a sense in which context is specified by a set of alternative models
- the scientific reason for choosing one set of models rather than another is pragmatic (eg. economy of representation) not metaphysical
- the explanatory hypotheses that we are justified in employing invariably themselves entail open questions about further experimental situations.

References

1. J.L. Austin. *How to do things with words.* OUP, 2nd. edition, 1975.
2. N.D. Belnap and T.B. Steel. *The Logic of Questions and Answers.* Yale University press, 1976.
3. C. Ghidini and L. Serafini. Distributed first order logics. In D.M. Gabbay and M. 'De Rijke', editors, *Frontiers of Combining Systems.* Research Studies Press, 2000.
4. F. Giunchiglia and C. Chidini. Local models semantics, or contextual reasoning = locality + compatibility. In *Proceedings of the Sixth International Conference on Principles of Knowledge Representation and Reasoning,* 1998.
5. Gold. Limiting recursion. *Journal of Symbolic Logic,* 1965.
6. S. Jain. *Systems that Learn.* MIT, 1987.
7. K. Kelly. *The Logic of Reliable Inquiry.* OUP, 1996.
8. Putnam. Recursive predicates and the solution to a problem by moskowski. *Journal of Symbolic Logic,* 1965.
9. B.C. van Fraassen. *Laws and Symmetry.* OUP, 1980.
10. B.C. van Fraassen. *The Scientific Image.* OUP, 1980.
11. A Wisniewski. Erotetic implications. *Journal of Philosophical Logic,* 1994.
12. A Wisniewski. *The Posing of Questions.* Kluwer, 1995.

Contextual Categorization: A Mechanism Linking Perception and Knowledge in Modeling and Simulating Perceived Events as Actions

Elisabetta Zibetti [1], Vicenç Quera [2], Francesc Salvador Beltran[2], Charles Tijus[1],

[1]Laboratoire CNRS- ESA 7021 de Cognition et Activités Mentales Finalisées,
Université Paris 8.
2, rue de la Liberté,
93526 Saint-Denis Cedex 02 FRANCE
http://www.ipt.univ-paris8.fr/~psycog/
ezibetti@univ-paris8.fr
tijus@univ-paris8.fr

[2]GTICC (Grup de Tecnologia Informàtica en Ciències del Comportament),
Departamento de Metodología de las Ciencias del Comportamiento,
Facultad de Psicología
Universitat de Barcelona
Passeig de la Vall d'Hebrón,171
08035 Barcelone
http://www.ub.es/comporta/gticc.htm
vquera@psi.ub.es
fsalvador@psi.ub.es

Abstract. The specific objective of this paper is to introduce the computer model ACACIA (Action by Contextually Automated Categorizing Interactive Agents) capable of simulating the way in which context is taken into account for the interpretation of perceived actions elaborated by a number of autonomous moving agents in a bidimensional space. With this in mind, we will examine some different modeling approaches in Artificial Intelligence and Artificial Life and emphasize the strong and weak points of each approach in relation to the set of issues addressed by our theory based on Contextual Categorization. Second, we provide a theoretical explanation of how contextual categorization accounts for temporal and environmental context to interpret ongoing situations in terms of perceived action. Finally, we describe the computer implementation of ACACIA, and we propose a preliminary simulation of a simple situation using StarLogo software.

Introduction

The question we address here is the manner in which context intervenes in the interaction between agents, which is to say, when each agent perceives and interprets the actions of other agents in order to take action on its own. To this end, we will first present the interpretation of perceived action, followed by a discussion of different models developed in the Cognitive Sciences. Lastly, we will present our approach based on Contextual Categorization and Artificial Life which takes the form of the computer model, ACACIA (Action by Contextually Automated Categorizing Interactive Agents) a joint development of the GTICC team (Computer Technology for the Behavioral Science Research Group, University of Barcelona) and the research team at the Laboratoire CNRS- ESA 7021, *Cognition et Activités Mentales Finalisées*, (University of Paris 8).

1. The interpretation of perceived action

What mechanisms and processes do we need in order to model the understanding of seen events in terms of action? The interpretation of perceived action is one of the highest and most complex activities carried out by the human brain. It involves both basic and higher-level functions (e.g., detection of objects and events vs. verbalizing actions which are not directly perceived in the environment but inferred), and it requires inter-relating different kinds of knowledge to the perception of an environment that continues changing.

In terms of bottom-up processing, understanding a situation of daily life such as a person crossing a busy street consists in being able to interpret the spatiotemporal relations between the objects in the world (e.g., a person, a vehicle, a street and its sidewalks) as actions done by agents [28, 29, 30].

In terms of top-down processing, understanding such daily situations requires a number of cognitive components such as the observer's attribution of goals and intentions to the other agents, drawing causal links between the different events, predicting future events, and thus activating knowledge. Finally, this understanding allows the observer to anticipate action and perhaps interact (e.g., to help a visually handicapped person cross the street).

How can the problem of matching the bottom-up perceptual input data and the top-down knowledge data be solved? Because the world is not made up of a set of objects and events with conceptual counterparts in the mind, the notions of "object" and "event" need defining in the context of the interaction between the observer and the changing environment in which its stands, in order to account for the observer's ability to understand and interpret new situations. But, what kind of knowledge can be matched to a changing and somewhat unpredictable world?

Our stand, like Barsalou's "ad hoc categories" [3], is based on the idea that actions are interpretations based on perception: we place ourselves in a perspective which accords a decisive role to the physical properties of objects and to the perceived relations between objects in a context (environmental and temporal) in order to interpret events as actions. The mechanism we hypothesize as being responsible for the emergence of action from events is *contextual categorization*.

The process of building contextual categories creates a circumstantial representation, which can be seen as a short-term database. Contextual categories are then used in order to infer new properties. These properties are goals from which action can be derived and attributed to agents. Consider for instance the perception of someone moving through space. This person will not simply be seen as someone moving but instantiated in the contextual category of "walking persons". In contrast, a moving ball will be instantiated as a "rolling ball". "Walking persons" are people that have the goal "of going somewhere", whereas "rolling balls" "move in the direction they were kicked". If the direction in which the object is moving is toward a parked car, instantiated as being a "car", then a superordinate contextual category will be built to catch the two objects "walking person" and "car" or "rolling ball" and "car". This superordinate category will factorize what is common to subordinate categories which, respectively, are "to drive" or "to be under". Thus, the "walking person" can be attributed the goal of "using the car", whereas the "rolling ball" can be attributed the property "will disappear under the car".

Note that this process of contextual categorization is neither construed as a learning process, nor as a form of organizing and storing knowledge in long term memory, but as an active process that allows making inferences while adapting to the current state of the situation. This extension of the concept of categorization to include a "mechanism linking ongoing perception and knowledge structures" is what we believe will allow accounting economically and ecologically for dynamic spatial and temporal contextual effects.

In our approach based on categorization, context is central. Our definition of context is Turner's [26] definition of "the world state", which is to say, "the state of the agent's world at some particular time: i.e., all features of the world, including all objects in existence, their properties and internal states, and the relationships between them" (p.376). Also central to our approach, is the fact that we do not separate the target from the context as is usually done: the target emerges from the contextual categories. Each objet is processed in relation to the other objects in the context. Thus, all objects are similarly processed and instantiated in circumstantial categories which are, in turn, grouped into superordinate categories. As concerns our topic, spatial and temporal coordinates are determining factors in understanding what is taking place.

Let us now present and discuss some of the existing Artificial Intelligence models which are, to our knowledge, the only kind of model proposed for simulating the interpretation of perceived action. We will then provide a theoretical explanation of how contextual categorization accounts for the role of temporal and environmental context in interpreting ongoing situations in terms of perceived action. Finally we will describe a computer implementation of our model, ACACIA, and propose a preliminary simulation of a simple situation using StarLogo software [18].

2. Some existing models for interpreting perceived actions

As far as we know, few models have been proposed for modeling the interpretation of perceived action. A first type of computation model arises at least in two major subareas of Artificial Intelligence (AI), (i) natural language processing [e.g.; 22] and (ii) computer vision techniques for object and movement recognition [e.g.; 1, 9, 10] and probabilistic plan recognition [9, 10]. These models, like other models traditionally developed in AI., adopt a primarily top down perspective for studying cognitive processes. These are closed systems using pre-defined knowledge for building representations of a situation which is often posited without the constraints constituted by a changing spatial (environmental) and temporal context. In contrast, a second type of computational model arises from the Artificial Life (AL) paradigm [e.g.; 11, 5, 12, 16, 17]. This more recent approach takes an evolutionist, situated and bottom-up perspective in which the data furnished by the environment have the priority for studying the adaptive capacities of living beings and robots. In this section, we will briefly present three existing AI models intended for simulating perceived action and their limits as we see them. We then introduce the Artificial Life approach and what it can contribute to the discussion.

2.1. The Thibadeau model: a faitfhful mapping of natural laguage theory

One of the first propositions for modeling perceived action was put forward by Thibadeau [22]. His model is derived from Miller and Johnson-Laird's "componential" theory [13] in which complex actions are built up from primitive ones (*action primitives*) with the addition of traits such as direction, agent, intentionality, manner, etc. This model takes the transformations rather than the nature of actions into account. But Thibadeau does not consider the fact that changing the objects involved in the situation may change the interpretation of the action. If the processing of the objects present in the situation where events take place is secondary to comprehension, then how does one explain that the same series of events in a different context can result in interpretations that differ in terms of action? [28, 30]. In fact, we believe that the physical and functional properties of the objects that are involved in a perceived situation are determining factors for comprehension. The functional properties of an object, inferred from the relational properties established between the objects in the context, are the ones that allow accessing predictions as to the actions the object can carry out or be submitted to as well as the manner in which it can be interacted with [4, 20, 25, 21, 27, 6].

2.2. The Ayes & Shah model based on object and movement recognition

In order to account for contextual properties, Ayes and Shah [1] developed a system capable of recognizing the actions of different persons acting within a defined environment (e.g., an office). Their system represents an innovation in the field of AI because it uses context for recognizing actions that are difficult to model, such as "picking up the phone", "using a computer", etc. The context in which the events take place is stored in the form of a knowledge base relative to the scene: where the entrances are located, the objects present and the manner in which they are usually used. What we believe is relevant and to be emphasized in this approach is that information about the function of objects is fundamental for allowing the system to recognize changes in space and time concerning one or several objects as an action.

Nonetheless, the information carried by the function of an object and its relation to the environmental context is not always obvious or enough for furnishing correct interpretations. The interpretation of events as actions is also heavily dependent on the goals attributed to the actors and to the temporal context.

2.3. The Intille & Bobick probabilistic model based on object and movement recognition and probabilistic plan recognition.

The probabilistic model for the representation and visual recognition of complex action presented by Intille and Bobick [10] and Intille [9] includes a particularly interesting formalization of the effects of temporal context. Action is represented using temporal graphs. "The primitive in these graphs are agent-based belief networks that can recognize agent goal by probabilistic integration of visual evidence" (p.80).
Intille and Bobick simulated representation and recognition of complex actions in American football. They developed algorithms that integrate contextual domain knowledge and computer vision feature detection in order to interpret and describe events in video sequences. Their system automatically labels states and actions such as "passing" and "blocking" using probabilistic models. Their studies are among the most comprehensive in the field of modeling and simulating perceived action. However, like most AI models, theirs requires a pre-defined knowledge base, very well defined as to the variables involved in football. This is why the model can not explain how someone who knows nothing about this sport may begin to understand merely by watching, start attributing goals to the players, extract the rules and eventually anticipate the players' strategies.

2.4. Limitations of this kind of system from a psychological point of view

What is indisputably fascinating about the models developed in AI is that they work so well in some well defined domains. Indeed, by applying astute methods for solving problems such as the detection of objects and movements, they are fairly efficient in surveillance tasks in pre-coded environments. However, when the spatial and temporal variables of a context can not be completely mastered and coded beforehand, their performance levels decline drastically due to their lack of psychological relevance.

What, from a psychological point of view, is probably the most "bothersome" limitation of this kind of system, particularly for the proponents of the importance of contextual data (temporal and visual-perceptive), is their heavily top-down approach to what goes into a representation. In the "closed system" paradigm, context tends to be defined as static and predetermined. This is why these systems, unlike human observers, are so difficult to adapt to a world which is only partially predictable.

2.5. Bottom-up and top-down approaches to interpreting perceived actions

A perspective emphasizing bottom-up processing would seem to be more adequate for accounting for context. In this respect, our approach is similar to Artificial Life's [11, 5, 12, 16, 17]. AL postulates that the mechanisms underlying adaptive behavior must necessarily be studied and conceived in situ, in other words, the goals the agent is trying for and the opportunities the environment affords for doing so must be accounted for. This kind of approach is highly ecological and parsimonious. Though our approach has much in common with AL's (i.e., parsimony, active learning as a function of goal, adaptability, etc...), it is obvious that simulating the "adaptive behavior" of an observer and potential agent would involve making our system capable of acquiring knowledge about objects in the world and successfully linking contextual data to acquired knowledge.

According to our conception, an observer's representation is not internal, stored, complete and activated for purposes of comprehension (I.A.). Neither is it absent nor is it distributed throughout the successive algorithms which allow the agent to show adaptive behavior without prior knowledge of the objects it will encounter (AL). In our approach, representations are put together in an "ad hoc" and dynamic manner in an interface which allows access to stored knowledge through the physical properties of objects and their reciprocal relationships to the other objects in the environment. In this way, the role of knowledge is reduced, it comes into play in processing objects as a source of information, it is not a knowledge base activated all at once by top down processes. Additionally, because comprehension is highly dependent on a constantly changing context, an adaptive agent should be capable of economically assimilating the changes as they occur.

For the problem at hand, it is necessary to postulate the existence of a mechanism linking actual-perception and knowledge structures at each moment of a current situation. The mechanism should account for temporal context by providing comparisons between the past perceptual configurations of the environment (t-1), the current configuration of the world (t), plus inferences about the future activated in the mind of the observer (t+1) which also modify the representation of the situation.

In contrast to fishing in a knowledge base that is previously organized and structured and which contains information about actions, the construction of contextual categories seems to offer the link between actual perception and knowledge that allows activating inferences based on a set of actions relevant to understanding a given situation.

3. A Contextual Categorization Approach

If perception is a purposeful activity involving the pick-up of relevant environmental patterns [7, 8], then all the components leading to an action are not necessarily actually perceived: they may be inferred from other temporal and spatial contextual components as well as from knowledge about the properties of objects. We interpret this principle of inference by proposing that the construction of a representation of a perceived evolving situation is a sequential process during which objects are categorized on line. As objects appear and disappear and as their properties change, contextual categories are created and modified. The categorization, both of objects and of events, generates inferences through the implication of categories and is thus responsible for goal attribution and the emergence of a specific interpretation. For instance, if an object that occupies place A, disappears and appears at place B, then it can be categorized as a moving object, either animate or being pushed or propelled. If animate, then the movement is intentionally directed. If the movement is in the direction of another object, then the object can be instantiated in the category of an animate object approaching another object, for instance "following" or "chasing" [28, 30].

The mechanisms involved in this process are modeled using the Dynamic Allocation of Meaning Model (C.A.D.S., *Categorisation et Assignation Dynamique de Signification*) [23, 24, 29]. This model proposes an explanation of the manner in which temporal information and the perceived properties of a situation interact by constructing contextual categories. Through an approach based on contextual categorization that is heavily dependant on the spatiotemporal properties of objects, the representation is no longer centralized but distributed across a dynamic interface between the observer and the world context being experienced.

3.1. On line contextual spatial categorization using a Galois lattice

On line contextual categorization using a Galois lattice[1] is a new research topic that we have applied to perceived action [29]. Consider the four frames of a short movie involving three objects (figure 1). The Galois Lattice (figure 2) of frame 1 has four categories, whereas the lattice of frame 2 has six categories. In the four frames, object *a* does not change (same shape, color and place). However, in the Galois lattice of frame 1, object *a* belongs to two categories and in the Galois lattice of frame 2, it belong to three categories. Notice that object *a* is not moving (figure 1) but is nevertheless affected to contextual categories because of relational and contextual properties (figure 2).

---

[1] The Galois lattice [2] is a hierarchy of categories with transitivity, assymetry and irreflexivity, when given the O_n X P_m boolean matrice which indicates for each of the n objects O, whether or not it has each of the m properties P. The maximum number of categories is either 2^{n-1}, or m if $m < 2^{n-1}$, in a lattice whose complexity depends on the way properties are distributed over objects. The hierarchy of categories has the inheritance principle of taxonomies: for one object, to belong to one category is to belong to the superordinate ones, having the properties of one category means having the properties of the superordinate categories. In order to build the Galois lattice network of object 'properties, objects are on the first colum and properties on the first line of a binary table. When the object posses this properties it is coodied by "1" in a boolean table, when it does not posses that properties it is coodied by "0". The Galois lattice are automatically constructs by STONE software [15]

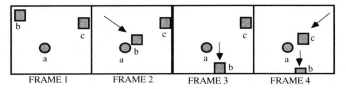

Figure 1. Four frames of a short animated film which shows two rectangles approaching a circle, touching it and then leaving the scene one after the other.

Though the semantic context of the animation is poor, observers of the four frames of figure 1 will often interpret the displacement of the two squares as a story of intentional action [28, 30] such as, for instance, "Before leaving, two boys (the squares) go tell their mum (the circle) goodbye." How can such an interpretation emerge from contextual categorization? C.A.D.S. models perceived action by building a contextual network of categories for each of the successive frames.

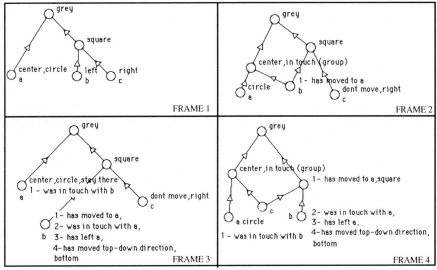

Figure 2. The Galois lattices of C.A.D.S.: successive networks of contextual categories provide support for action attribution (see text for a detailed explanation).

Frame 1: The network of frame 1 corresponds to a participant's description: there are three gray figures: *a*, *b*, and *c* (the most superordinate category is "gray"), two squares: *a* and *b*, (subordinate category: "square"), one on the left (subordinate category "left" of which object *b* is an instance) and one on the right (subordinate category "right" of which object *c* is an instance), and a circle in the center (category "center, circle" of which object *a* is an instance).

Frame 2: Comparing lattices of frame 1 and of frame 2, the new perceptual data is that objects *a* and *b* are now "touching in the center" (a position). From object *b*'s change in space and time it can be inferred that *b* "has moved toward" object *a*. This is an inference derived from contextual categorization. "Moving toward" object *a* is a new property attributed to *b*. In addition, C.A.D.S. noticed that object *c* "did not move". It noticed this because objects belonging to the same category (squares) should have the same properties. This is a principle of contextual categorization that has two effects: the economy of simple lattices and the attribution of features not perceived. So, object c is attributed the property "hasn't moved". At this point, perceptions and inferences (b moved to a, c did not move) may interface with knowledge in long term memory about action (b "moved toward" a: b "went to meet" a, c "did not move" while b "went toward" a: c "watched b moving toward" a; ...). In addition, action attribution furnishes kinds of objects that can do the action (animated objects, persons, for instance male and female because of their size difference, ...).

Frame 3: What is new in frame 3 is that the group in the center no longer exists because object b has moved to the bottom (its place has changed from center to bottom). So b has left a and a is staying put. Now an observer can summarize and compare the changes in time and space having occurred from frames 1 to 3, and say that "one of the two squares has gone to see the circle and left it".

Frame 4: Processing frame 4 with C.A.D.S. yields the interpretation that that c has moved toward a just as b did earlier. Then C.A.D.S. will predict that c will touch a, leave a, and move downwards, because of the generalizing procedure that helps infer unseen features. Successive interpretations such as "before leaving, two boys go say goodbye to their mum" can be inferred from "going toward somebody who doesn't change his/her place, touching, going away from him/her, etc". Notice that the property "gray" common to all three objects is filtered out by location in the most superordinate category, an observer might not even mention it.

Our point of view is that C.A.D.S.'s modeling of action perception may be a relevant representation of psychological process. The main idea is that perceived action is in the scope of on-line contextual categorization: networks of contextual categories are built from what is perceived at each moment; inferences concerning actions are produced from comparing categorical changes of objects in space and time. This approach is new and so is the idea that the variation in space and time of the properties of objects is what leads to the attribution of action to objects seen as agents [28].

3.2. On line contextual temporal categorization in Galois lattices

As seen in the preceding section, information already activated (t-1) and current properties (t) feed into a process that creates contextual categories by activating properties of the relationships of the objects to each other (in the previous example, the two squares). The hierarchical structure of the contextual categories allows the system to eliminate current state properties that are not considered relevant to the goals attributed [2] (future).

---

[2] The predictive ability that comes into play during understanding of actions performed by others, is based on the possibility of attributing goals to agents [e.g.; 14]. This allows excluding or considering action possibilities as well as facilitating comprehension of what is taking place. However, though most models agree on the fundamental role played by attributing goals to agents in order to recognize and determine the type of action that is being carried out, they do not explain how the prerequisite role of agent or patient is attributed to objects in the situation [30].

Thus contextual properties appear in the network and the selection of relevant properties is mainly guided by the data furnished by the temporal context. In this way, the observer is in a position to infer a set of possible and imaginable actions, compatible with the properties already activated as the event has unfolded (t-1), with the properties of the current state of the situation (t) and with the properties anticipated through the attribution of goals to agents (t+1). For instance, the agent moving in the direction of a car could be seen as "going to use the car", but if this agent was previously seen "leaving the car", and is now seen "moving back to the car", it might be categorized as someone having forgotten something in the car. In thise case, the goal attributed will be "going to get something" instead of "going to drive the car".

Through temporal contextual categorization, the observer establishes coherence between different sequential events and adapts her perception of the current situation (bottom up process) according to the goals she has attributed to the agents (top-down process). In order to test the plausibility of our hypothesis about contextual categorization and the psychological relevance of the C.A.D.S. model, we are currently conducting a computer simulation using StarLogo software which takes the form of the computer model, ACACIA (Action by Contextually Automated Categorizing Interactive Agents)

4. Simulating ACACIA's Contextual Categorization with StarLogo Software

According to AL's basic principles, StarLogo[3] language makes it possible to populate a microworld with large numbers of autonomous agents. Agents (or *"turtles"*, in StarLogo jargon) have properties, like their positions in a two-dimensional world, their headings, or any variable that the programmer wants to define for them, (e.g., their "closeness" to other agents). An *"observer"* controls how the system is set up, and is in charge of displaying the global properties of the agents. Thus, the *"observer"* may "spy on" the properties of each individual agent. Also, individual agents may have access to the properties of other individual agents, and act in consequence. For example, if agent A knows that agent B is now closer to A than before, then A could react by increasing its distance from B. The agents are then set loose to interact with each other, leading to complex emergent behavior.

We are presenting a simple situation to illustrate the programming rationale we are developing for simulating the emergence of interpretation in terms of action based on the temporal and spatial displacements of agents. We have defined three agents represented by three squares of three different colors. For each time unit, the agents move in space and construct a representation of perceived events in an output file. The knowledge in terms of action that each agent acquires is coded by a list of properties. These properties are relative to the agent's own position in space, the other agent's positions and their respective relational positions at each instant.

---

[3] StarLogo is a software developed at the MIT Media Lab by Resnick, [18], specifically aimed to the simulation of decentralized, leaderless, and parallel multi-agent sytems, in which the interaction among the agents makes emerge global properties that are not specified in (and cannot derived analitically from) their local interaction rules.

Representations are updated for each agent and for each time unit according to certain probabilistic rules. Thus, at each instant, each agent has its own representation of the situation in accordance with what it "has learned" up to that point. This allows showing that changes in simple spatial coordinates can produce inferences in terms of perceived action such as "touching" and "approaching" through successive contextual categorization and applying probabilistic rules.

4.1. Building the knowledge network

In order to implement contextual categorization based on the Galois lattice in our StarLogo simulation (called ACACIA: Action by Contextually Automated Categorizing Interactive Agents), one linked data list is defined for each agent. At the outset, that is, before interpretation of action starts, the data lists are empty. As interpretation progresses, elements are added to the list or updated, resulting in a list with as many elements as properties of the agents are considered (see also footnote 1). Taking all the agents altogether, the lattice is represented as a matrix of n rows (one per agent) and m columns (one per property). When the agent has a certain property (e.g., "being on the left"), then it is coded as "1" in the corresponding column, and for all the other agents not sharing that property (i.e., "not being on the left") it is coded "0". By using linked data lists it is possible to add, delete, insert, and update elements to the list, and so we can simulate how the Galois lattice grows when knowledge about other agents and their interaction with the environment is acquired by each agent.

At each time unit, the data list for an agent is compared with its own data list at the preceding time unit, in order to check for changes in the properties. For instance, if at t-1 the value for the properties "being on the left" and "being on the right" are "1" and "0" respectively, but they are "0" and "1" at t, then a new property is added (if not already present), i.e., "moved from left to right", and an "1" is assigned for the agent. All the other agents not sharing that new property at t are assigned "0" (i.e., "not moved from left to right"). In this way, new interpretations are added to the knowledge network, which are superimposed on previous or more primitive ones. For a given set of possible locations (left, right, center), movements (from left to right, etc.), and relative movements among agents (approach, leave, in touch, etc.), the number of possible properties, and the rules used for generating upper level interpretations from lower level ones can be specified in advance.

The agents' interpretations are obtained in an "*output*" file listing the contents of the semantic network in the form of the properties that each agent has recorded. This simultaneously represents its knowledge and interpretation of the situation at each instant.

The process of contextual categorization operates at different levels of specificity. It operates in parallel for each agent's construction of the representation at each moment and it works sequentially and locally in activating emerging properties (including what an object can do) as a function of what an agent has learned from its context. For more sophisticated simulation of action interpretation using our ACACIA model, we are currently developing computer models 1) of the probability of perceived events and properties in the situation, and 2) to refine the simple rules defining basic displacements in space (i.e. walking at random, chasing each other, approaching and leaving all the other agents, as in the P-Space model) [16,17].

4.2. Probability, noise and generalization

When modeling the interpretation of actions, it is not always necessary to assume that the information gathered by the agents, and the rules they apply in order to produce interpretations, are error free. In fact, more realistic simulations can be achieved by allowing for some noise in the data. When an agent perceives other agents' actions, it might perceive them incorrectly, or it even might not perceive them at all. Thus, in some cases the perceptions can be incomplete or absent. This may be true for some of the interacting agents but not for others. For example, if we define a scope of perception for each agent by specifying some area in front of it to which it can pay attention, then, depending on its current heading, the actions of the agents lying outside its current scope will be missing from the agent's current knowledge network; that is, neither a "1" nor a "0" can be assigned to a property the agent is unaware of. Consequently, whereas some agents could reach interpretations based on "correct" perceptions, others may interpret using incomplete ones. The rules for using perceived actions for interpretation should thus be probabilistic.

Probability plays yet another role. In order to generalize (e.g., "all blue agents move from left to right, except if they are approached by a red agent, in which case they move from top to bottom"), an agent can either perceive the actions once, or perceive them many times. In the former case, a generalization that is based on one or several actions will have a low prediction power (that is, when applied in the future it will fail most of the time), while in the latter, powerful predictions will be possible. The agents can then make generalizations, test them, and assign them a degree of success in prediction. This way, the agents learn to categorize and generalize. The process of categorization and generalization is thus an emergent property of the agent's individual rules of movement and interpretation.

4.3. Adaptation and Prediction

Initially, the agents move according to a few simple pre-specified rules (i.e., agents may walk at random, chase each other, approach and leave all the other agents,...) [16,17]. However, as the simulation progresses and they learn how to predict other agents' actions through generalization, they become capable of reacting to or even anticipating these actions. Their movement is no longer governed by "blind rules" but by prediction and anticipation built on repeated series of interpretations of the other agents' actions. As a consequence, ACACIA uses the knowledge network specified in a Galois lattice for coordinated actions in a group of agents. Each agent acts as an observer and interpreter of all the other agents' actions, and it is the interaction of their interpretations and predictions that can be considered as an emerging property of group behavior.

5. Conclusions

As ACACIA integrates bottom-up (perceptual components) and top-down (cognitive components) processing to account for environmental and temporal context through successive constructions of contextual categories, the model can interpret the behavior of other agents without a knowledge base necessarily pre-defined by its designer. Its comprehension emerges from active situated cognition, organized in the form of semantic property networks in which actions are represented as properties inferred from modifications in the network's own "ad hoc" categories. As the situation evolves and creates spatiotemporal changes, the system is capable of changing its current representation of the situation as well as associating perceived events to the set of properties that constitute an object involved in the event through probabilistic calculations. In this way it is capable of interpreting but also of anticipating what is going to happen as a function of acquired knowledge about the action "possibilities" for other agents.

The system accounts for context (environmental and temporal) through: (i) comparing contextual category networks constructed at "t" and "t+1" to detect changes, (ii) a generalization process based on past categorization experience, a feature which endows it with predictive capacities. It is important to emphasize that the probabilistic rules which give ACACIA its predictive power are not contained in activated contextual schemas as in Intille and Bobick's [9, 10] model, rather they are highly dependant on knowledge recently acquired by the system in its context.

Acknowledgments: The research reported herein was supported by the CNRS (France) Grant:00N92/1247, the Direcció General de Recerca (Catalan Autonomus Government) Grants 1997SGR-00344 and 2000BEA/400085, and the Secretaria de Estado de Universidades e Investigación (Spanish Government) Grant PFE2000-00014. The authors are grateful to Elizabeth Hamilton for her reviewing of this paper, suggestions and critical comments.

6. References

[1] Ayes, D., & Shah, M. (1998): Monitoring Human Behavior in an Office Environment. In *Proceeding of the IEEE Computer Society Workshop: The Interpretation ofVisual Motion, CVPR'98, Santa Barbara, CA, June 22.* 65-72.
[2] Barbut, M., & Monjardet, B. (1970). *Ordre et Classification: algèbre et combinatoire.* Paris. Hachette.
[3] Barsalou, L.W. (1983). Ad Hoc Categories. *Memory and Cognition, 11,* 211-227.
[4] Barsalou, L.W. (1991). Deriving categories to achieve goals. In G.H. Bower (Ed.), *The psychology of learning and motivation: Advances in Research and Theory, Vol. 27,* (1-64). New York: Academic Press.
[5] Brooks, R.A. (1991). Intelligence without representation. *Artificial Intelligence, 47,* 139-159.
[6] Cordier, F., & Tijus, C. A. (2000). Propriétés d'Objets: Typologie et Organisation. *Actes du XXVI/ Congrès International de Psychologie, Montréal, 26-29 juillet 2000.*
[7] Gibson, J. (1977). *The Theory of affordance* . In R.E. Shaw, & J. Brandsford (Eds.) Perceiving, acting, and knowing. Hillsdale, N.J.: Erlbaum
[8] Gibson, J. (1979). *The Ecological Approach to Visual Perception.* Boston, M.A.: Houghton Mifflin.
[9] Intille, S. S. (1999). *Visual recognition of Multy-Agent action.* Ph.D. Thesis, Massachusetts Institute of Technology.

[10] Intille, S. S., & Bobick, A.F. (1998). Representation and Visual Recognition of Complex, Multi-agent Actions using Beliefs Networks. In *Proceeding of the IEEE Computer Society Workshop: The Interpretation ofVisual Motion, CVPR'98, Santa Barbara, CA, June 22. 73-80.*

[11] Langton, C.G. (1989). Artificial life. In C.G. Langton (Ed.), *Artificial life. The proceedings of an interdisciplinary workshop on the synthesis and simulation of living systems* (pp.1-47). Redwood City, Ca: Addison-Wesley.

[12] Maes, P. (1998). Modeling adaptive autonomous agents. In C.G. Langton (Ed.), *Artificial life. An overview* (pp. 135-162). MIT Press.

[13] Miller, G. A., & Johnson-Laird, P. N. (1976). *Language and Perception.* Cambridge, MA: Harvard Univ. Press.

[14] Oatley, K. & Yuill, N. (1985) Perception of personal and interpersonal action in a carton film. *British Journal of Social Psychology 24,* 115, 124.

[15] Poitrenaud, S. (1995). The Procope Semantic Network: an alternative to action grammars. *International Journal of Human-Computer Studies, 42,* 31-69.

[16] Quera, V., Solanas, A., Salafranca, L., Beltran, F.S., & Herrando, S. (2000). *A dynamic model for inter-agent distances.* In Meyer, J.-A., Berthoz, A., Floreano, D., Roitblat, H.L., Wilson, S. (Eds.), From Animals to Animats 6, SAB2000 Proceedings Supplement. Honolulu (Hawaii): USA.

[17] Quera, V., Solanas, A., Salafranca, Ll., Beltran, F.S., & Herrando, S. (2000). P-SPACE: A program for simulating spatial behavior in small groups. *Behavior Research Methods, Instruments, and Computers, 32 (1),* 191-196.

[18] Resnick, M. (1994). *Turtles, Termites, and Traffic Jams: Explorations in Massively Parallel Microworlds.* Cambridge, MA: MIT Press.

[19] Richard, J.F., & Tijus, C. A. (1998). Modeling the Affordances of Objects in Problem Solving. In A.C. Quelhas & F. Pereira (Ed.), *Cognition and Context.* Lisboa ISPA, 293-315.

[20] Ross, B.H. (1996). Category learning as problem solving. In D.L. Medin (Ed.), *The Psychology of Learning and Motivation: Advances in Research and Theory, Vol. 35* (165-192). San Diego, CA: Academic Press.

[21] Schyns, P., Goldstone, R.L., & Thilbaut, J.-P. (1998). The development of features in object concepts. *Behavioral and Brain Sciences 21 (1):* 1-54.

[22] Thibadeau, R. (1986). Artificial Perception of Actions, *Cognitive Science, 10,* 177-149.

[23] Tijus, C. A., & Moulin, F. (1997). L'assignation de signification étudiée à partir de textes d' histoires drôles. *L'Année Psychologique, 97,* 33-75.

[24] Tijus, C. A., & Poitrenaud, S. (1997). Modeliser l'Affordance des Objets. *Actes du 6ème colloque: Sciences Cognitives, Individus et Société,* p 57-65.

[25] Tijus, C.A., (1996). *Assignation de signification et construction de la réprésentation.* Habilitation à diriger les recherches. Université de Paris 8.

[26] Turner, R. M. (1999). Model of Explicit Context Representation and Une for Intelligent Agents. In J.G. Carbonell & J. Siekmann (eds), *Lectures Notes in Artificial Intelligence, vol. 1688, Modeling and Using Context,* (pp. 375-388). New-York: Springer.

[27] Yamauchi, T., & Markman, A. (1998). Category Learning by Inference and Classification. *Journal of Memory and Language , 39,* 124-148.

[28] Zibetti, E., Hamilton, E. & Tijus, C.A. (under revision). Contextual Categorization in Interpreting Perceived Actions: The Role of Objects Properties. *Cognitive Science.*

[29] Zibetti, E., Hamilton, E., & Tijus C.A. (1999). The role of Context in Interpreting Perceived Events as Action. In J.G. Carbonell & J. Siekmann (eds), *Lectures Notes in Artificial Intelligence, vol. 1688, Modeling and Using Context,* (pp. 431-441). New-York: Springer.

[30] Zibetti, E., Poitrenaud, S., & Tijus, C.A. (in press). La construction de la représentation de l'action perçue. *Intellectica.*

The Motivational Context

William A. Adams[1]

[1]Adjunct Associate Professor of Psychology, Chapman University, Washington Academic Center, PO Box 2120, Silverdale, WA 98383, USA.
badams@halcyon.com.

Abstract. This paper suggests a psychological approach to the problem of context management in intelligent software. The user's motivational context is taken by the agent as its own motivational context. While traditional task-specific context problems still must be dealt with, the agent can use its semi-autonomous motivation to navigate these problems on the user's behalf. An implementation strategy is suggested.

1 Introduction

AI applications are notoriously brittle, unable to adapt when context changes, but people are remarkably adaptable, possibly because humans maintain two different kinds of context while AI applications have only one. Humans make contextual assumptions about their physical environment, but also have the ongoing context of their own motivation. The motivational context subsidizes the other one. It is this linked, dual-context system that makes humans resilient under conditions of change. The paper defines the two kinds of context then suggest how an AI application might incorporate them both.

When context changes, the validity of descriptions and the truth of assertions about a situation may be lost. Who has not been startled when doing a word-processing task to see out of context results. If you want to change instances of the word "as" to "like," you do not expect the software to change "Christmas" to "Christmlike." We can call that kind of context "environmental context." Another kind of context is "motivational context." An example is a context-sensitive help system. It operates on an inference about the user's motivation, though not on knowledge of her actual motivation.

Because human purposes are indefinitely variable, a cup can be a paperweight if that is one's wish, and a coin can be a screwdriver. Searle[1] handles this relationship between objects and motivation by identifying a class of "socially constructed objects." A screwdriver used as a doorstop is still really a screwdriver, he says, while as-a-doorstop it is merely a "socially constructed" object. That formula isn't much help for designing AI systems since we cannot tag every environmental object for an unbounded set of potential uses. Instead we need to be more clear about the motivational context which determines the environmental context of objects, for each person, in each situation. The context problem is actually a problem of alignment between motivation and the objects that satisfy it. No amount of elaboration of environmental context alone can solve it.

2 Motivation and the Frame Problem

Minksy[2] gives this exemplar AI context problem: "Fred told the waiter he wanted some chips" (p. 68). Minsky lists a dozen or so inferences, adapted from Lenat [3], that can be made from that sentence, such as "Fred wants potato chips, not wood chips, cow chips, or bone chips." This is followed by a generalized hierarchical "Architecture of Representations" which describes "levels" of detail from which these inferences might be drawn. Minsky proposes that the problem of changed environmental context can be managed by representing the environment in ever larger, more inclusive, more abstract propositions.

But there is no limit to the detail that might be needed, and no sides to the breadth of interconnections among details. It is not hard to imagine a fellow named Fred pursuing industrial espionage who asks his co-conspirator restaurant employee for stolen microprocessor chips. Is Fred is hungry or is Fred a thief? An elaborate hierarchy of frame-based environmental context is no help. Understanding of the environmental context depends entirely on knowledge of Fred's motivation.

In some formal system of language, perhaps the word, "waiter" constrains "chips" to the category "food products," so we could infer that "chips" refers to potato chips. But natural language is not a closed system and the polysemy of "chips," can only be disambiguated by reference to context. Minsky suggests that an agent could infer from the sentence that "Fred and the waiter speak the same language. Fred and the waiter are both human beings. Fred is old enough to talk (2+ years of age). The waiter is old enough to work (4+ years, probably 15+)" (pp. 68-69). The example invokes an imaginary frame much larger than the explicit representation, in which we assume that Fred is a person just like us. We also implicitly assume a parallel frame of motivation. We feel we can say, "I know what I would intend in that situation, therefore I know what Fred intends."

But isn't the whole point of the context problem the fact that this approach produces errors? In fact we don't know much about other people's motivation nor really, about our own. Minsky has seduced us into believing we understand far more about the situation than we actually do and therefore that we could program an AI agent to understand as much. But we cannot effectively represent an environment to our agent without an analysis of the agent's motivation.

3 An Intelligent Agent is Motivated

An intelligent agent should have an explicit motivational context as a person does. The obvious source and model of motivation for the agent is the user. As the user's literal agent, the software agent would be motivated as the user is. The agent would make decisions based on both its own mental state and its understanding of the mental state of the user [4]. The user's relationship to the agent would not be one of machine operator to device, as it is today. Rather, it would be a social relationship, like any based on mutual consideration. The user would ask the agent to adopt her goal as its own [5]. If the user is trying to find and buy a consumer product, she might ask an agent to search for her. The motivated agent attempts to understand what the user is trying to accomplish, not just what the user is trying to buy and is less likely to return choices that are irrelevant to the user. By taking on the user's motivation as its own, the agent's behavior is grounded across changing environmental contexts.

4 Implementation Ideas

In a simple strategy for a well-motivated agent, a program would ascertain and adopt the user's motivation as its own, something a person would not do. A person or an agent can adopt another's goals as his own, but goals are merely the objects of motivation. A person's motivation is intrinsic. However, a software agent can copy a user's motivation, becoming a semi-autonomous motivational clone of the user with respect to the objects in the environment and goals related to them.

A series of dialog boxes could define the user's motivation and inform the user about the agent's capacities. The dialog must be general and recurrent rather than singular and task-specific, aimed at making explicit the user's needs and expectations. The agent interviews the user as if considering the user for employment. The interface need not be natural language. The user might select germane questions from lists and type in words and phrases that the agent can maintain in lists. The point of the transaction is for the agent to establish a model of the user's motivation. Task-specific parameters still must be set for the environmental context, but the agent can embed these in the context of the user's motivation.

Any user has short-term, task-specific intentions, a medium-term ("project-sized") motivational context and a long-term (personal development) motivational context. This is the framework of the user's motivation, which becomes the agent's own motivational context. Within that temporal framework (short, medium, and long-term), the agent might classify the user's bodily interests (e.g., in comfort, health, beauty, skills, tools, strength), social interests (e.g., in love, power, status, family, things and information, community, affiliation, achievement), or philosophical/intellectual interests (e.g., spiritual, scientific, literary, self-help). That tripartite division of motivation is adapted from the ancient Greek theory of education, but other schemas are possible. The sophistication of the motivational schema determines the ultimate effectiveness of the agent. It is an abstract taxonomy of the user's motivation, not a classification of goods and services that the user might want.

Each environmental object that might be encountered or retrieved by the agent must be tagged with a set of motivational identifiers that connect to the user's and agent's motive taxonomy. Since the taxonomy is much broader than any specific task, the object tags are also at a high level of generality. The motive tags are in addition to the ordinary feature list that defines a retrievable item. They allow the agent's search of the environmental context to be guided by the fit between the user's motivation and objects' motive tags.

The most direct source of object tags is the user. For example, the user could execute a rating scale on an object or class of objects. It would ask for reactions to or impressions of the object's features. The user might indicate if she associates an item more with strength or weakness; goodness or badness; activity or inertia, etc. The resulting user reaction profile for the object, similar to a semantic differential [6], constitutes the set of motivational tags for an object. This method addresses the fact that most people do not articulate their own motivation very well. A well designed reaction profile would be suitable for a large range of objects, yet map determinately to the agent's representation of its user's motivation. The user could create reaction profile ratings for the key terms of a particular search request, or for entire categories of items.

Alternatively, each object's motivational tags could be been defined by whoever offers the object for retrieval, according to some standard set of categories. While less specific to a user's transient reactions, this would characterize the specific kinds of satisfaction offered by the object for specific kinds of consumers. Consumers would have power of active selection based on their own motivation as implemented in an agent.

5 Conclusion

An agent is someone who acts in my behalf. An intelligent agent must understand my motivation, for even I do not know exactly what I want. "Understanding" then means 'able to connect my motivation to a set of objects which could satisfy it.' This is the rationale from the user perspective for motivated software agents. From the engineering perspective, rather than try to map all possible environmental context frames to each other, we might take a cue from human psychology, where the context of a person's motivation is her portable disambiguator of environmentally bound object definitions.

References

1. Searle, J.R. (1995). The Construction of Social Reality. NY: The Free Press.
2. Minsky, M. (2000). Commonsense-based interfaces. Communications of the ACM, Vol. 43, No. 8, pp. 67-73.
3. Lenat, D.B. (1990). The Dimensions of Context-space. www.cyc.com/publications.htm.
4. Rosis, F., Covino, E., Falcone, R., & Castelfranchi, C. (1999). Bayesian cognitive diagnosis in believable multiagent systems. International Workshop on Belief Revision, Trento. http://aos2.uniba.it.8080:/papers/cogdia.ps.
5. Conte, R., & Castelfranchi, C (1995). Cognitive and Social Action. London: UCL Press.
6. Osgood, C.E., Suci, G.J., & Tannenbaum, P.H. (1957). The Measurement of Meaning. Urbana, Ill.: University of Illinois Press.

An Approach to Anaphora Based on Mental Models

Guido Boella and Leonardo Lesmo
email: {guido, lesmo}@di.unito.it

Dipartimento di Informatica and Centro di Scienza Cognitiva
Università di Torino
Cso Svizzera 185 10149 Torino ITALY

Abstract. Structural approaches to anaphora try to solve it at the level of the formal language used for representing the meaning of sentences. But we believe that it must be approached by referring to the extension of the sentences. In this paper, we show that Johnson-Laird's Mental Models provide an adequate tool for coping with extensional representations and anaphora in a cognitively plausible way.

1 Introduction

Anaphora is a complex phenomenon. It has proven difficult to analyze at a syntactic level, so that structural approaches as DRT [6] or semantic ones as Dynamic semantics [3] enriched the formal language used to represent the meaning of sentences. However, no approach is completely satisfactory and, often, they appear to adopt *ad hoc* solutions to widen their coverage. We believe that most anaphors can be resolved in a more natural way by making direct reference to *extensional* representations [4]. In other words, the representation of the context where the anaphora must find its referent should put at disposal all elements of the situation which the anaphora could refer to (we do not consider here *generic* readings).

An extensional approach which has been shown to be cognitively plausible is the one of *mental models* [5]. With respect to anaphora, let's consider a simple example. In the following pairs, the first sentence introduces the context where the anaphora must be solved. In the first pair there is number agreement between the (intended) referent and the pronoun, while no agreement is enforced in the second pair. However, acceptability is guaranteed just for the non-agreeing pair:

Fig. 1. *Every farmer owns a donkey.*

[1] **Every farmer owns a donkey. It is pink.*

[2] *Every farmer owns a donkey. They are pink.*

A mental model contains a finite number of tokens (placeholders for individuals, here farmers f and donkeys d) and relations among tokens. In particular, the first sentence of the two pairs appears as shown in Fig.1.

Given the model shown below, which donkey, out of the represented ones, can we relate to the singular *it*, appearing in the second sentence of [1]? On the contrary, the plural pronoun in [2] can be interpreted as referring to the set of donkeys appearing in the model, without the need of any choice.

2 The interpretation of logical connectives

As a starting point, we must recall the mental model representation of logical connectives. A negation is represented by means of an horizontal line, which keeps apart the items appearing in the model. For instance, Fig.2 represents the sentence:

[3] *John does not own a car.*

Conjunction is simply represented by inserting the representations of the conjoined sentences in the same subplane. As the last connective, we consider disjunction[1]; it involves the construction of two distinct models, one for each disjunct. The two models are alternative, so the two disjuncts are taken into account separately. Each of them is incomplete because, as all mental models, it includes only the focused information. But, when necessary, a model can be extended (*fleshed out*) with more information, provided that it is compatible with the existing one. So, in

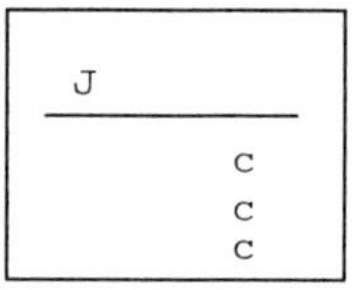

Fig. 2. Negation.

[4] *John went to the restaurant or to the cinema.*

we get one model where John went to the restaurant and a second, distinct, model where John went to the cinema. But if one considers all possible extensions of the two original models, the three classical interpretations of logical *inclusive or* come out: (1) [restaurant + cinema] (2) [restaurant + not cinema] (3) [not restaurant + cinema].

Another important point concerns indefinites: when an indefinite expression is encountered, only one token is introduced: it represents an entity with the given property, but it is marked (with three dots) to represent the fact that, if needed, more tokens of the same type may be introduced.

Let's now see how the mental models representation of logical connectives affects the analysis of anaphors. The first example involves negation:

[5] **No farmer has a car. It is red.*

Examples as this one present some difficulties for other representation frameworks (in particular, DRT), because the main verb (*has*) does not include an explicit negation (which appears just in the subject NP), so that the object NP still constitutes a potential antecedent. In the mental models approach, the first sentence produces a model where farmers appear in the subplane of existing entities and owned cars in the other subplane, so that no referent for 'a red thing' can be found in the subplane of existing entities.

Another interesting anomaly is related to conjunction and disjunction:

[6] *John owns a car$_i$ and Fred washes it$_i$*

[7] **John owns a car$_i$ or Fred washes it$_i$*

In the two examples above, the syntactic structure is identical, but the acceptability is not. Since the mental model representation of a conjunction involves the inclusion in the same model of the conjoined sentences, no problem arises with [6]. But disjunction requires the construction of two *separate* models, and in the second model there is no available referent for the pronoun. When an error (e.g. impossibility of understanding a sentence) occurs, the model can be fleshed out; when applied to the second model,

---

[1] In this paper we do not discuss implication because of space constraints.

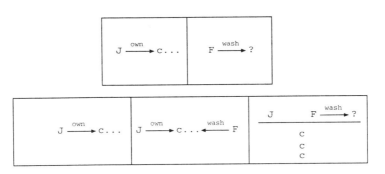

Fig. 3. Implicit and explict models of sentence [7].

this process could produce two alternatives: John owns a car, or he does not. The first extension seems to solve the problem: John owns a car and Fred washes it. In Fig.2 the lower part shows the three resulting models where the second one includes the first and the third is discharged However, from any disjunction at least two distinct models must be constructed, and that none of them must be included in the other: otherwise, the common part of the two models would be necessarily true and according to Grice, the speaker should not have use a disjunction to express such a meaning.[2].

3 Donkey sentences

Donkey sentences, so called after the example:

  [8] *Every farmer who owns a donkey beats it*

are difficult to interpret in standard approaches, because of some problems associated with the scoping of the quantifiers. In principle, the NP *Every farmer who owns a donkey* can be interpreted (as we did) with the universal having wider scope than the existential or with reversed scope. In this example this second reading is excluded by pragmatic principles (the same donkey cannot be owned by different farmers). So, it is the preference for the wide-scope reading of the universal, and the plurality of donkeys implied by that reading, which makes [8] acceptable and *Every farmer owns a donkey. *It is pink* unacceptable. Then, it is the absence of any connection between the predicate in the second sentence and the universal quantifier that blocks the interpretation process.[3]

  When faced with [8], the procedure first interprets the subject phrase, thus obtaining, in the wide-scope reading of the universal, the representation on the left side of Figure 4; then it extends the representation by searching a referent through each complex token

---

[2] An example that supports the previous analysis is: *John does not own a car or he washes it* In this case, there are two separate non-overlapping models. In the first one John does not own a car, while the second one can be fleshed out to put at disposal the required car (which he washes).

[3] Pragmatics can enter into play by establishing the bridge between different sentences. In *Every farmer owns a donkey. He needs it for carrying heavy loads*, the antecedent of *he* is *a farmer*; because of the rhetorical relation of "justification" between the two sentences, *it* can be assumed to refer to *the donkey of that farmer* [7].

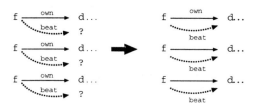

Fig. 4. Resolution of anaphoric pronouns

$f \rightarrow d$; so, for each farmer, a different referent for *it* is found, i.e. the donkey owned by him. The possible antecedent satisfies the restriction carried by the singular number (cfr. *Every farmer who has two donkeys beats it*). So, the sentence is interpreted successfully, as shown in Fig.4.

4 Conclusion

Mental models are a cognitively plausible model of human reasoning; so, they can be useful in finding an explanation of linguistic phenomena (see [2] and [1]). In this paper we have shown that a mental model approach to anaphora is not only plausible from a cognitive point of view, but provides also a general and elegant explanation to some complex anaphoric phenomena.

   Some problems remain open. We want to mention here just intensional anaphora, as exemplified by *The leopard is difficult to see. It is a shy animal.* Since, as we have shown, the phenomena discussed in the paper are best faced from an extensional point of view, it is clear that some different machinery is required here. However, the basic logical framework on which the mental models construction process is based already accounts for the difference. It is another piece of research to verify that mental models are also suited to cope in a perspicuous way with intensional entities.

References

1. G. Boella, R. Damiano, and L. Lesmo. Beating a donkey: a mental model approach to complex anaphorical phenomena. In *Proc. of European Congress of Cognitive Science of ECCS'99*, Pontignano, 1999.
2. G. Boella, R. Damiano, and L. Lesmo. Mental models and pragmatics: the case of presuppositions. CogSci99 Conference, 1999.
3. G. Chierchia. Anaphora and dynamic binding. *Linguistics and Philosophy*, 15:111–183, 1992.
4. D. A. H. Elworthy. A theory of anaphoric information. *Linguistics and Philosophy*, 18:207–332, 1995.
5. P.N. Johnson-Laird. *Mental Models*. Cambridge University Press, Cambridge, 1983.
6. H. Kamp. A theory of truth and semantic representation. In P. Gardenfoers, editor, *Formal Methods in the Study of Language*. Mathematisch Centrum, Amsterdam, 1981.
7. J. Moore and C. Paris. Planning texts for advisory dialogues: capturing intentional and rethorical information. *Computational Linguistics*, 19(4):651–695, 1993.

Context and *Multi-media Corpora*

Cristina Bosco[1], Carla Bazzanella[2]

[1] Department of Computer Science - University of Turin
C. Svizzera 185 - 10149 - Turin, Italy
bosco@di.unito.it
[2] Department of Philosophy - University of Turin
V. Sant'Ottavio 20 - 10124 - Turin, Italy
bazza@cisi.unito.it

Abstract. In the recent research work on *multi-media corpora* the notion of context appears to be crucial both on the theoretical level and the applied level. The aim of this paper is to analyze the three levels which are relevant to the treatment of contextual information in *multi-media corpora* (i.e. *annotation, storage, retrieval*), and the different solutions which are resorted to in recently implemented systems to meet the need for a multi-layered, multi-linked annotation, and a hierarchically organized retrieval of contextual *data*.

1 Introduction

As a consequence of the recognition of the multi-modality of communication and of the relevance of context to comprehension in spoken language [1], the usage of *multi-media* technologies in spoken language *corpora* is increasing. In the recent research work on *multi-media corpora* the notion of context appears to be crucial both on the theoretical level (*what context is*), and on the applied level (*how context should be annotated and referred to*), particularly in *multi-media corpora*, where different sources of information can be recorded and associated with verbal communication [2]. We will refer to an 'integrated' [3] notion of context, which includes both a *global* level (i.e. *a priori* features and sociolinguistic parameters independent of the ongoing conversational interaction), and a *local* level (i.e. the parameters selected because of their relevance and *activated* by the ongoing interaction itself).

2. Contextual data in multi-media corpora

The problem of how to make *multi-media corpora* flexible, extensible, and reusable, in order to meet a variety of needs, has already been discussed within the "Language resource community" [4], and the notion of context appears to be an unavoidable crossroads in this landscape. More specifically, the treatment of contextual information in *multi-media corpora* involves three levels which will be distinguished for the sake of analysis: annotation, storage, retrieval.

2.1 Annotation

Annotation "[...] is any multi-media information explicitly added to a 'document'. This information can be deduced from the content and made explicit or represented in some form different from the original one (audio, video ...)." [5, p. 76]. Annotation can be used to characterize the corpus and also to generate information about it; more specifically, four layers of information are included: information about the recordings (where they came from, how they were made, with what equipment, under what conditions, etc.), about the interlocutors (sex, age, level of education, i.e. the sociolinguistic parameters referred to above), about the way in which the *data* were processed, and cross-reference information with regard to *data* available from other projects or in other forms. This kind of *data* can play a very important role by making it possible to access precisely the subset of *data* of interest (see 2.3.).

In accordance to the literature [6] we will refer to all the information included in the annotation as *meta-data*. *Meta-data* annotation describes in detail the context in which the communication took place in a multi-layered, multi-modal, multi-linked way. A case in point is the treatment of anaphora, and the complex inference processes of interpretation of pronouns or proper nouns which can often be avoided by correlating these terms with some explicit annotation of non-linguistic objects [7, p. 53]. Starting from the idea that the availability of non-linguistic context often allows the interpretation of pronoun and other references, the DAMSL scheme [8], designed to annotate human-human task-oriented conversation, has been extended by introducing a *graphical context* [7]; an algorithm for correlating linguistic terms with the graphical referents in the graphical context is available in this schema.

In the *data* annotation, both the *global* and *local* levels of context (see 1), should be taken into account, by registering global level *data* at the beginning of the transcription, and by signaling local level *data* whenever they occur. This 'double' annotation of context is particularly convenient when one is reusing *corpora*: global context annotation makes *data* more identifiable even in larger *corpora* or in sets of *corpora* on the web; local context annotation facilitates the parametrical selection of *data* (see 2.3).

Another 'double' annotation of context which has recently been introduced relies on the basic distinction between the *mandatory/optional data*, or *primary/secondary data*, corresponding to the distinction between *main* information and *ancillary* information, and partly to the distinction between *primary* and *secondary* context [9]. An example of this distinction is provided by the CHILDES format, where the annotation tiers are divided into *main* and *dependent*; similarly, [10] distinguishes information concerning *permanent* characteristics from that concerning *temporary* characteristics (e. g. voice quality). *Optionality* is also useful in *data* retrieval: if the *corpus* is structured hierarchically, any scholar can elicit only the required information (see 2.3).

In the transcription and analysis of *corpora* of spoken language another problem is constituted by the complex relationship between speech and gesture: MATE, an abstract *meta*-model for referential annotation in multimodal dialogues, makes possible the annotation of gestures and links between gestures and universe elements (<universe> and <kinesic>; http://mate.mip.ou.dk/).

2.2 *Data* organization and storage

In general, organizing contextual *data* can be important in distinguishing different kinds of information, in increasing the accessibility and flexibility of a *corpus*, and in modeling granularity in the extraction of information by using a hierarchical organization. The organization of *meta-data* is also useful in distinguishing factual information (e. g. the speaker's place of residence) from derived information (e.g. the fact that the speaker lives in a town instead of a small village), and in distinguishing information concerning permanent characteristics (e. g. the date of birth) from that concerning temporary characteristics (e. g. age) [10].

The necessary interface between extra-linguistic and linguistic *data* has been introduced in the form of *meta-description*, which is defined as "structured sets of meta-*data* which describe a certain resource (or a group of such resources) in a way that it is meaningful to the user community" [4]. *Meta-descriptions* are usually distinguished from resource content by including them in the header of the resource file, or storing them in separate header files, which are linked to resources [11].

There are two ways of associating *meta-descriptions* with a language resource which relates to the two above-mentioned levels of context (*local* and *global*):

- all *meta-descriptions* are attached to resources as a whole: all them are global and stored in files separate from resources,
- some *meta-descriptions* are assigned to regions in a resource: also *meta-*descriptions which are valid for some specific parts of the resource are made possible and stored in the same file as the resource.

2.3 Accessibility and retrieval

To facilitate implementation and make query execution more efficient, a basic hierarchical organization of *meta-data* should be extended and more attributes and qualifiers should be used. The flexibility of the *meta-data* system can also be useful in the possible extension of existing *corpora*. For example longitudinal *corpora* are extendable to *multi-media corpora*; transcriptions in terms of episode/event may be more precisely annotated to describe the internal structure of episodes and micro-events such as gestures.

The problem of organizing *meta-data* in video resources[1] is usually solved in *multi-media* non-linguistic material by using hierarchical structures. For example, in the MPEG7 initiative (http://drogo.cselt.stet.it/mpeg/standards/mpeg-7/mpeg-7.htm), which uses XML representation to describe movies, the user can hierarchically order descriptions starting at the top with the whole video and ending with single frames [4].

Many efforts have been devoted to representing the *continuum* between the redundant and complementary use of speech and gesture: MATE includes facilities not only for creating, acquiring and maintaining large *corpora* (see 2.2), but also for treating spoken dialogue at multiple levels of representation. The *Smartkom project* [13, p.

---

[1] The problems raised by video resources can find a better solution in the same theoretical framework (see 2), and by resorting to *multiple* tiers cf. ATLAS (http://www.nist.gov/speech/atlas/; [12])

49], which is meant to develop an intelligent human-machine interface, provides another way of treating the natural speech and gestures of users.

Similar problems are treated with a different approach in a system developed for modality integration in the interaction between human and virtual reality: the *Staging project* [14]. Usually in spoken language corpora the integration of gestures is speech-driven, on the assumption that verbal production has precedence over hand movements. For instance if the user said 'Give the cow an apple' the reference for 'cow' is searched for first in the text and only if that fails it is searched for in deictic movements. The *Staging* approach, by contrast, points out the relevance of all modes of communication which are considered equal.

The flexibility which is available in recent technological development should be exploited, as it is already in systems as MATE, with regard to the complexity of contextual *data*, so as to meet the needs of reuse by a variety of users for a variety of purposes.

References

1.   Bazzanella C.:. The significance of context in comprehension. The *'we* case'. Special issue of *FOS* , *Context in context*, B. Edmonds and V. Akmand eds. (forth.)
2.   Wittemburg, P.: About annotation schemes and terminology. In: LREC2000 (2000) 39-45
3.   Bazzanella, C.: On Context and Dialogue, in: S. Cmejrkovà *et al.* (eds.): Dialogue in the Heart of Europe. Niemeyer, Tübingen (1998) 407-416
4.   Wittemburg, P., Broeder, D., Sloman, B.: Meta-description for language resources. In: LREC2000 (2000) 1-11
5.   Ballim, A., Fatemi, N., Ghorbel, H., Pallotta, V.: A knowledge-based approach to semi-automatic annotation of multi-media documents via user adaptation. In: LREC2000 (2000) 76-79
6.   LREC2000: Proceedings of LREC2000 Workshop on Meta-descriptions and Annotation Schemes for Multimodal/Multi-media Language Resources, University of Athens Press, Athens, Greece (2000).
7.   Villasenor, L., Massé, A., Pineda, L. A.: A multimodal dialogue contribution coding scheme. In: LREC2000 (2000) 52-56
8.   Allen, J., Core, M.: Drafts of DAMSL: dialog act markup in several layers (1997) (http://w ww.cs.rochester.edu/research/cisd/resources/damsl/RevisedManual/)
9.   Dey, A., Abowd, G. D.: Towards a Better Understanding of Context and Context-Awareness. (2000) (http://www.gvu.gatech.edu/gvu/reports/2000/abstracts/00-18.html)
10. Oostdijk, N.: Meta-*data* in the Spoken Dutch Corpus project. In: LREC2000 (2000) 21-25
11. Berman, S., Evert, S., Heid, U.: Searchable metaspaces. In: LREC2000 (2000) 13-19
12. Bird, S., Day, D., Garofolo, J., Henderson, J., Laprun, C., Liberman, M.: ATLAS a flexible and extensible architecture for linguistic annotation. In: LREC2000 (2000) 68-75
13. Steiniger, S.: Transliteration and labeling of emotion and gestures in SmartKom. In: LREC2000 (2000) 49-51
14. Paggio, P., Jongejan, B.: Representing multimodal input in a unification-based system: the Staging project. In: Holmqvist *et al.* (eds.) Integrating information from different channels in multi-media contexts. Birmingham (2000) 20-26

Belief Expansion, Contextual Fit and the Reliability of Information Sources

Luc Bovens[1] and Stephan Hartmann[2*]

[1] CU at University, Dept. of Philosophy, CB 232, Boulder CO 80309, USA,
`bovens@spot.colorado.edu`
[2] University of Konstanz, Dept. of Philosophy, 78457 Konstanz, Germany,
`stephan.hartmann@uni-konstanz.de`

Abstract. We develop a probabilistic criterion for belief expansion that is sensitive to the degree of contextual fit of the new information to our belief set as well as to the reliability of our information source. We contrast our approach with the success postulate in AGM-style belief revision and show how the idealizations in our approach can be relaxed by invoking Bayesian-Network models.

1 The Success Postulate

The success postulate is one of the central dogmas of AGM-style belief revision: if new information comes in, then it must be incorporated into our belief set [5]. But we often do not integrate new information in our belief set. We find the information too implausible relative to what we already believe. Or we do not find the information source sufficiently reliable. So what are we to make of this postulate? Certainly we could defend the postulate by pointing out that it is an idealization: it is being assumed that the information sources are fully reliable. But notice that the challenge in AGM-style belief revision is how we should revise our beliefs once an inconsistency occurs in our belief set. How is it that an inconsistency can enter into our belief set when our information comes from fully reliable information sources? We have met with a range of responses from belief revisionists against this challenge and will not enter into this discussion here. There is also a literature on non-prioritized belief revision in which the success postulate is actually dropped. According to Hansson [6], we may not be willing to accept the new information because"it may be less reliable (...) than conflicting old information." Makinson [7] writes that "we may not want to give top priority to new information (...) we may wish to weigh it against old material, and if it is really just too far-fetched or incredible, we may not wish to accept it." Indeed, the question of belief expansion has something to do with the reliability of the information source as well as with my background beliefs, i.e. the context of beliefs in which this new information

---
* The research was supported by a grant of the National Science Foundation, Science and Technology Studies (SES 00-80580) and grants of the Transcoop Program and of the Feodor Lynen Program of the Alexander von Humboldt Foundation.

is supposed to be inserted. Newly presented items of information have a certain degree of contextual fit: they are more or less plausible given our background beliefs, they fit in with our background beliefs to a greater or lesser degree. The more reliable the information source is, the less contextual fit is required for me to be justified to add the belief to my belief set. The more contextual fit the new item of information has, the less reliable the information source needs to be given my context of beliefs, for me to be justified to add the belief to my belief set. The challenge is: can a precise account of this relationship be provided? In the literature on non-prioritized belief revision, the reliability of the sources does not enter into the model itself, unlike in our model; Furthermore, the lack of contextual fit of a new item of information with the belief set is understood in terms of logical inconsistency, which is only a limiting case in our model. Our model has both theoretical and practical virtues: By introducing some idealizations of our own, viz. that the information sources are independent and equally unreliable, we reach some elegant results; At the same time, these idealizations can be readily relaxed by implementing a Bayesian Network that is responsive to the particulars of the situation. To introduce our approach, we address the simple question of belief expansion. We believe that our model also carries a promise to handle belief revision in general, but this project is beyond the scope of this paper.

2 A Model for Probabilistic Belief Expansion

Suppose that there are n independent and relatively unreliable background sources and each source i informs us of a proposition R_i, for $i = 1, \ldots, n$, so that the belief set is $\{R_1, \ldots, R_n\}$. Furthermore, there is one independent and relatively unreliable new source [2] informing us of a proposition R_{n+1}, so that the expanded belief set would be $\{R_1, \ldots, R_{n+1}\}$. For each proposition R_i (in roman script) in the information set, let us define a propositional variable R_i (in italic script) which can take on two values, viz. R_i and $\bar{R}_i$ (i.e. not-R_i), for $i = 1, \ldots, n+1$. Let $REPR_i$ be a propositional variable which can take on two values, viz. $REPR_i$, i.e. after consultation with the proper source, there is a report to the effect that R_i is the case, and $\overline{REPR_i}$, i.e. after consultation with the proper source, there is no report to the effect that R_i is the case. We construct a joint probability distribution P over $R_1, \ldots, R_{n+1}, REPR_1, \ldots, REPR_{n+1}$, satisfying the constraint that the sources are independent and relatively unreliable. We model the independence of the sources by stipulating that P respects the following conditional independences:

$$\{REPR_i\} \perp\!\!\!\perp \mathcal{M}_i \mid \{R_i\} \tag{1}$$

with $\mathcal{M}_i = \{R_1, REPR_1, \ldots, R_{i-1}, REPR_{i-1}, R_{i+1}, REPR_{i+1}, \ldots, R_{n+1}, REPR_{n+1}\}$ for $i = 1, \ldots, n$, or, in words, $REPR_i$ is probabilistically independent of $R_1, REPR_1, \ldots, R_{i-1}, REPR_{i-1}, R_{i+1}, REPR_{i+1}, \ldots, R_{n+1}, REPR_{n+1}$, given R_i, for $i = 1, \ldots, n+1$. We model the idealization of equal unreliability by specifying that $P(REPR_i|R_i) = p$ and $P(REPR_i|\bar{R}_i) = q$ for $i = 1, \ldots, n+1$

under the constraint that $p > q > 0$. Following a tradition in epistemology that goes back to John Locke, we let belief correspond to a sufficiently high degree of confidence [4]. The degree of confidence in the background information before the new report has come in is the posterior joint probability of this information after all the relevant reports have come in:

$$P^*(R_1, \ldots, R_n) = P(R_1, \ldots, R_n | REPR_1, \ldots, REPR_n). \qquad (2)$$

Since it is assumed that we believe this information, we let $P^*(R_1, \ldots, R_n)$ exceed some threshold value t for belief. We are justified to expand our belief set from $\{R_1, \ldots, R_n\}$ to $\{R_1, \ldots, R_{n+1}\}$ just in case $P^{**}(R_1, \ldots, R_{n+1})$ exceeds t. It can be shown that, for any set of propositions $R_1, \ldots, R_m$, given the constraints on P in (1),

$$P^*(R_1, \ldots, R_m) = \frac{a_0}{\sum_0^m a_i x^i}, \qquad (3)$$

in which the *likelihood ratio* $x := q/p$ and a_i is the sum of the joint probabilities of all combinations of values of the variables $R_1, \ldots, R_n$ that have i negative values and $n - i$ positive values. For example, for an information triple containing the propositions $R_1, R_2,$ and R_3, $a_2 = P(\bar{R}_1, \bar{R}_2, R_3) + P(\bar{R}_1, R_2, \bar{R}_3) + P(R_1, \bar{R}_2, \bar{R}_3)$.

It is easy to construct examples that have the following structure. Take an information set $\{R_1, R_2\}$ and construct a probability distribution P over R_1 and R_2. Set the likelihood ratio x so that $P^*(R_1, R_2)$ exceeds the threshold value t. Now compare two scenarios. On scenario S the new information R_3 is rather probable given R_1 and R_2 while on scenario S' the new information R'_3 is rather improbable given R_1 and R_2. Let the probability distributions P_S^* and $P_{S'}^*$ represent these two scenarios. Given a judicious choice of parameters, $P_S^*(R_1, R_2, R_3)$ will exceed t - and may even exceed $P^*(R_1, R_2)$ - whereas $P_{S'}^*(R_1, R_2, R'_3)$ will drop below t. Hence we are justified to expand our beliefs with R_3 but not with R'_3 on grounds of the difference in contextual fit, although the witnesses are equally reliable in both scenarios. Subsequently, we can raise the reliability of the witnesses by lowering the value of the likelihood ratio x: in this case $P_{S'}^*(R_1, R_2, R'_3)$ may come to exceed t again: with sufficiently reliable witnesses, we are also justified to expand our beliefs with new information that has low contextual fit. Hence, our model shows how the interplay between contextual fit and witness reliability affects the rationality of belief expansion in the face of new information.

So far, our model makes various idealizing assumptions, which may not be realized in practical applications. The theory of Bayesian Networks permits us to relax these idealizations. A Bayesian Network allows for an economical representation of a joint probability distribution over a set of variables by organizing the variables into a *Directed Acyclical Graph* (DAG) reflecting the *Parental Markov Condition*, i.e. each variable in a *child node* in the network is independent of all the variables in its *non-descendant nodes* in the network, conditional on the variables in its *parent nodes* [8]. In [1] we suggested a Bayesian Network model for belief expansion, based on the assumptions made in this section. This model still contains various idealizations which can, however, be relaxed in a straightforward manner. Suppose that there are more and less reliable sources in play:

424

it is easy to adjust the $P(\text{REPR}_i|R_i)$ and $P(\text{REPRi}|\bar{R}_i)$ for particular values of i. Suppose that two or more propositions came from the same source: we can let one report variable be parented by multiple fact variables. Suppose that the sources are not fully independent: If a source is influenced in its report by other facts than the one that it is meant to report on, we can add arrows from these other fact variables to the report variable in question and define the appropriate conditional probabilities; If a source is influenced by what other sources have to report, we can add arrows from these report variables to the report variables in question and define the appropriate conditional probabilities.

3 Conclusion

In AGM-style belief revision, the success postulate states that new information must be integrated in our belief set. This postulate is at best an extremely strong idealization. In reality, the following is the case: whether we integrate new information in our belief set is typically determined by the degree of contextual fit of this new information, i.e. by how plausible this new item of information, is given what we already believe, and by our assessment of the degree of reliability of the information sources. Similarly, in philosophy of science, the question whether new data are accepted or not within a scientific community is a function of its contextual fit as well as of the reliability of the sources for these data. We construct a probabilistic model for belief expansion that incorporates both types of considerations. Although our model is also subject to certain idealizations, we show how these idealizations can readily be relaxed by invoking Bayesian Networks.

References

1. Bovens, L., Hartmann, S.: Coherence, Belief Expansion and Bayesian Networks. Proceedings of the 8th International Workshop on Non-Monotonic Reasoning, NMR'2000 Breckenridge, Colorado, USA, April 9-11, 2000. (http://www.cs.engr.uky.edu/nmr2000/proceedings.html) (2000)
2. Bovens, L., Olsson, E.: Coherentism, Reliability and Bayesian Networks. Mind **109** (2000) 685–719
3. Duhem, P.: The Aim and Structure of Physical Theory. Princeton University Press, Princeton (1954)
4. Foley, R.: The Epistemology of Belief and the Epistemology of Degrees of Belief. American Philosophical Quarterly **29** (1992) 111-121
5. Gärdenfors, P., Rott, H.: Belief Revision. In: Gabay, D.M. et.al. (eds.): Handbook of Logic in Artificial Intelligence and Logic Programming, Vol. 4 - Epistemic and Temporal Reasoning. Clarendon, Oxford (1995) 35-132
6. Hansson, S.O.: Editor's Introduction: What's New Isn't Always Best. Theoria **63** (1997) 1–13
7. Makinson, D.: Screened Revision. Theoria **63** (1997) 14–23
8. Pearl, J.: Probabilistic Reasoning in Intelligent Systems. Morgan Kaufmann, San Mateo (1988)
9. Quine, W.V.: Two Dogmas of Empiricism. Philosophical Review **60** (1951) 20–34

The Role of the Context in the Acquisition and in the Organisation of Knowledge: Studies from Adults and from Children

Aline Chevalier[1] and Laure Martinez[2]

[1] Research Center in Psychology of Cognition, Language and Emotion (PsyCLE)
[2] Laboratory of Cognitive Psychology (LPC)
29, avenue Schuman, University of Provence F-13621 Aix-en-Provence Cedex 1
aline.ch@up.univ-aix.fr   laure.m@up.univ-mrs.fr

Abstract. For a few years, partisans of two theoretical approaches have debated about the role attributed to the context concept in the acquisition and the organization of knowledge. The first one is the symbolic information processing system which focuses on the symbolic structures of the mind. The second one is the "situated cognition" theory which postulates that all the action of subject proceeds according to social and physical context in which it appears. Although these two approaches appear *a priori* conflicting, several authors get to connect certain characteristics of these two theories. These authors propose the intervention of two forms of context in cognition. The purpose of this paper is to present this new approach and illustrate it with experimental studies.

When knowledge of subject is not sufficient to solve any given problem, he/she has to modify his/her knowledge according to the situational context and tests again the elaborated reasoning [6]. Thus, knowledge is linked with the context, that leads to distinguish two types of knowledge [2]. The "rational knowledge", that is met in training courses and/or in books of specific fields. It is structured by general principles and must be presented in an accessible format for everyone. The "functional knowledge", that has a contextual organization, *i.e.* it is structured by the subject according to the goal(s) to reach. The functional knowledge is activated as soon as a similar problem arises. Repetition of similar situations allows development of strategies adapted to solve certain problems, by transforming rational knowledge in functional knowledge and schemas. The acquisition of knowledge brings about a structuring or a reorganization of knowledge representation according to situations in which it is used. The context cannot be separated from knowledge: knowledge is organized according to the context in which it appears, *i.e.* contextual constraints play a determining role in the acquisition and in the (re)organization of the subject's knowledge [7]. So, the context can be considered as a means which delimits the whole of knowledge mobilized and used to deal with the current situation [2]. This approach of Richard [1, 2, 14] about the role allocated to the context brings an interesting innovation and allows a compromise between the symbolic information processing symbolic system theory [12, 16] and the SC theory [8, 9, 15]. For Bastien [2] and Richard [14], the context is fundamental in cognition, but its effects cannot be reduced to external elements (*i.e.* to stimuli from current situation), as the partisans of the situated cognition (SC) theory affirm. In all domains, an internal environment defines the active subject's knowledge and more generally the state of his/her cognitive system at any given time. Therefore, these authors [2, 14] formulate the existence of two forms of context: *(1) External Context* corresponds to stimuli from current situation. For instance, to solve a problem the external context corresponds, at least partially, to information from problem's statement. *(2) Internal Context* represents subject's knowledge state stored and organized in memory at any given time.

In order to illustrate this dichotomy, we have chosen to present a study [5] conducted in the design of web sites. In this work, we appreciate on the hand, the role of the internal context by varying the level of knowledge of designers of web sites. On the other hand, we determine the role of the external context by varying the specification's degree of the schedules of conditions (or problem's statement) attributed to designers (the schedule of conditions represents, partially at least, the expectations of the costumer for the future web site). In this study, the authors ask professional designers of web sites (working for approximately three years in companies) and novice designers (who have just trained to design web sites) to elaborate a sketch of web site. Designers are confronted with two different schedules of conditions according to their degree of specifications: a well defined schedule of conditions – WDS (with many constraints) and an ill defined schedule of conditions – IDS (with very few information). The results obtained show the influence of the two forms of context on the amount and on the nature of the constraints taken into account by designers, and on their cognitive effort:

(1) Influence of the internal context: whatever the schedule of confitions, professional designers take into account more constraints than novices and professional designers' cognitive effort is more important than novices' cognitive effort. Therefore, the internal context seems to have an influence on the problem's understanding: schemas of knowledge acquired by professionals (or functional knowledge) allow to infer and to add new information to solve the problem. On the other hand, specific knowledge of professionals does not enable them to obtain a cognitive effort less important than novices. Indeed, this domain of activity necessitates for designers a certain part of creativity, since the web sites must be more and more original. Creativity necessitates the taking into account of constraints and it develops in a "constrained cognitive environment" [4]. So, innovative solutions produced by designers necessitate an expensive activity for cognitive system.

(2) Influence of the external context: the nature of the schedule of conditions has an influence on the cognitive effort of designers and on the amount of constraints taken into account. The IDS requires a cognitive effort more important than the WDS and it has an influence on the amount of constraints taken into account, only for professionals. This last result is surprising: professionals, dealing with the IDS, take into account more constraints than other professionals. We could have expected contraries results, *i.e.* designers dealing with the WDS take into account more constraints than the others, since they already have to satisfy the constraints presented in the WDS. No significant difference is observed for novices: they take into account as many constraints whatever the nature of the schedule of conditions.

This study allows us to appreciate the role of previous knowledge to solve a design problem and also shows that the external contex influences the designers' activity, and more particularly knowledge mobilized. The external context makes possible to define conditions of knowledge activation and has a different influence according to the subjects' level of expertise. Thus, the context can be considered as a component of knowledge. It defines the conditions of the knowledge activation, the links between knowledge and limits the validity of this knowledge: knowledge is only valid for and in a particular context [2]. Rappaport [13] talks about "contextuality", which he defines as the interaction of the system with its internal environment and its external environment. The comprehension and the interpretation of any given problem depend on information from the external environment and from the subject's specific knowledge [7]. We can illustrate this viewpoint with experimental results from studies about children's knowledge acquisition.

According to the classical view of the cognitive structures' development, knowledge is organized in a general form, an universal and hierarchical stage, common to all domains of learning. So, learning consists to elaborate cognitive general structure applicable in all situations and domains. In this perspective, subject's answer in any given context depends on degree of his/her knowledge's organization. To critic this theory, we can wonder if child obtains a "know-how" restrict for the situation met or if the apprenticeship allows him/her to grasp definite property of the concept, *i.e.* construction of knowledge that could be generally applied to overall situational contexts. Opposite to this classical perspective, the suggestions of the psychology of development [10] and the cognitive psychology [2, 3, 14] propose a theoretical approach specific to each learning. The cognitive development emerges as an internal "self-organizer" system directly affected by its interactions with environment. Karmiloff-Smith defines a theoretical model in which acquisition fulfils itself by cycles within each domain [10]. Knowledge is specific for a domain and consequently it is contextualized. For Karmiloff-Smith, the changes result from the external environment and from the internal "self-organizer" system. Cognitive development is not homogenous and each knowledge is linked with the context in which it has been constructed. This view explains the contextualized character of knowledge and the role of the internal context in knowledge acquisition.

An experimental study [11] conducted with 6,5 year-olds children stands in this trend of psychology and defends the idea that knowledge is constructed in and for specific domains. In this study, two kinds of task are proposed: (1) children must ordinate various materials in a pragmatic and in a temporal order. Then, in order to evaluate children's knowledge on order of letters in a word, (2) the authors propose a second task that consists in reading 32 non-sense words. The results do not show any correlation in the capacity to produce an order in a pragmatic or temporal context and in the capacity to respect the letter's order in the word. Children seem to deal with letters as they would do with objects, *i.e.* without taking into account letter's order. So, children's general knowledge about temporal and pragmatic order is ineffective in the reading domain: children have to construct a specific and contextualized knowledge that is "a order change, that does not modify the identity of other object, affects the identify of the word". Children have to take awareness that the letters' order in a word is distinctive and relevant feature in this specific domain. This study gives an experimental argument to the roles played by the two kinds of context: previous knowledge in a particular context is not it effective in another situation. Knowledge organization suggests that knowledge is both determined by activation of child's internal context and by information from external context. Children cannot transfer a previous knowledge acquired in a particular situation to another one without any contextualization of this knowledge in a new domain. Therefore, according to Weil-Barais [17], knowledge must be contextualized, de-contextualized and re-contextualized in variety of domains to become a general structure.

The context can be considered according to two main dimensions and not only in its first sense (information from environment): Internal Context and External Context. What kept our attention, in our experimental studies, is the self-construction aspect of the cognitive system in interaction with the external context. When an external stimulation occurs, activation of knowledge and answer causes bu it are guided in the cognitive system by the internal context. Thus, the context can be considered as a component of knowledge: it defines the conditions of knowledge activation, links between knowledge and limits the validity of knowledge used: knowledge is only valid for and in a particular context. Therefore, the dichotomy "internal context *vs.* external context " appears relevant and adapted to study and to explain, on the hand, inter-individual differences, by the organization and the mobilization of knowledge, according to the subjects' level of expertise. On the other hand, this dichotomy can explain also intra individual differences, by the acquisition and the reorganization of previous knowledge according to situations/domains in which it is acquired and used.

1. Akman V (2000) Rethinking context as a social construct. Journal of Pragmatics 32: 743-759.
2. Bastien C (1998) Does context modulate or underlie human knowledge ?. In: Quelhas, A.C., Pereira, F. (eds): Cognition and Context, ISPA, Lisboa, pp 13-25.
3. Bastien-Toniazzo M (1997) Tutorials in domain-specific acquisition. International Journal of Psychology 32: 129-138.
4. Bonnardel N (2000) Towards understanding and supporting creativity in design: Analogies in a constrained cognitive environment. Knowledge-Based Systems Journal 13: 505-513.
5. Bonnardel N, Chevalier A (2000) The role of constraints in creativity: A study on the design of Web sites. Oral Communication presented at the XXVII International Congress of Psychology, Stockholm, Sweden (July), pp 23 – 28.
6. Brézillon P, Pomerol J-CH, Saker I (1998) Contextual and contextualized knowledge: An application in subway control. International Journal of Human-Computer Studies 48: 357-373.
7. Butterworth G (1998) Context and cognition in models of cognitive growth. In: Quelhas, A.C, Pereira F. (eds): Cognition and Context, ISPA, Lisboa, pp 27-44.
8. Clancey W J (1993) Situated action: A neuropsychological interpretation response to Vera and Simon. Cognitive Science 17: 87-116.
9. Clancey W J (1997) The conceptual nature of knowledge, situations, and activity. In: Feltovich, P., Hoffman, R., Ford, K. (eds): Human and Machine Expertise in Context. Menlo Park, CA, The AAAI Presse, pp 247-291.
10. Karmiloff-Smith A (1992) Beyond modularity : A developmental perspective on cognitive science. Cambridge, MA, MIT Press.
11. Martinez L, Genisio V (1999) Le concept d'ordre : connaissance générale ou connaissance spécifique. Proceedings of the National Congress of the French Society of Psychology. Aix-en-Provence, France.
12. Newell A, Simon H A (1972) Human problem solving. Englewood Cliff. New Jersey : Prentice Hall.
13. Rappaport A T (1998) Constructive cognition in a situated background. International of Human-Computer Studies 49: 927-933.
14. Richard J-F (1995) Les activités mentales : comprendre, raisonner, trouver des solutions. Paris, Armand Colin.
15. Suchman L A (1987) Plans and situated action: The problem of human-machine communication. New York, Cambridge University Press.
16. Vera A H, Simon H A (1993) Situated Action : A Symbolic Interpretation. Cognitive Science 17: 7-48.
17. Weil-Barais, A (ed) (1999) L'homme cognitive. France, Presse Universitaire de France.
Acknowledgments: we acknowledge the participants of our experiments. These studies have been supported by the Conseil Régional Provence Alpes Côte d'Azur.

VC-Dimension of a Context-Dependent Perceptron

Piotr Ciskowski

Institute of Engineering Cybernetics,
Wrocław University of Technology,
Wybrzeże Wyspiańskiego 27, 50 370 Wrocław, Poland
cis@vectra.ita.pwr.wroc.pl

Abstract. In the paper, we present the model of a context-dependent neural net - a net which may change the way it works according to the external conditions. The information about the environmental conditions is fed to the net through the context inputs, which are used to calculate the net's weights, and as a consequence modify the way the net reacts to the traditional inputs.
We discuss the Vapnik-Chervonenkis dimension of such a neuron and show that the separating power of a context-dependent neuron and multilayer net grows with the number of adjustable parameters. We present the difference in the way traditional and context-dependent nets work and compare the input space transformations both of them are able to perform. We also show that context-dependent nets learn faster than traditional ones with the same VC-dimension.

1   Introduction

The notion of context in computer science appeared some time ago, first in the area of formal languages. Now it is introduced to many areas of machine learning, classification, robotics and neural nets [5]. Medical applications seem to be an intuitive example of decisions' dependence on external parameters. One of the first medical applications of context-sensitive neural networks was presented in [9], where a neural network is tuned to the parameters of a monitored patient.

The paper presents a model of a context-dependent neural network - a network which may change the way it works according to the environmental conditions. In other words, such a network may react differently for the same values of inputs, depending on external conditions, later called context variables.

The problem of defining and identifying primary, context-sensitive and irrelevant features among the input data is presented well in [1]. In the paper we assume that the division of the net's inputs into primary and context-sensitive ones (for simplicity called context inputs) has already been done.

Different strategies of managing context-sensitive features are presented in [2]. The neural network model presented in the paper corresponds to the strategy 3 (contextual classifier selection or strategy 5 (contextual weighting).

⋆ Paper supported by Wrocław University of Technology grant no. 332291

2 Model of a Context-Dependent Neuron

Consider a neuron model of the form:

$$y = \varPhi\left[-w_0\left(\overline{Z}\right) + \sum_{s=1}^{S} w_s\left(\overline{Z}\right)x_s\right] = \varPhi\left[\sum_{s=0}^{S} w_s\left(\overline{Z}\right)x_s\right] = \varPhi\left[\overline{W}^T\left(\overline{Z}\right)\overline{X}\right], \quad (1)$$

where y is the neuron's output, w_s is its weight on the x_s input and w_0 is the threshold (which is included in the weight vector, while the input vector includes the bias $x_0 = -1$). $\varPhi$ is the neuron's activation function - for example a sigmoidal function: $y\left(u\right) = \frac{1}{1+e^{-\beta u}}$.

The dependence of the neuron's weight on the context vector is modeled by:

$$w_s\left(\overline{Z}\right) = \overline{A}_s^T \overline{V}\left(\overline{Z}\right) = [a_{s1}, a_{s2}, \ldots, a_{sM}]\left[v_1\left(\overline{Z}\right), v_2\left(\overline{Z}\right), \ldots, v_M\left(\overline{Z}\right)\right]^T, \quad (2)$$

where $\overline{V}\left(\overline{Z}\right)$ is the vector of M linearly independent base functions spanning the weights' dependence on the context vector $\overline{Z}$, and $\overline{A}$ is the vector of coefficients approximating the s-th weight's dependence on the context. The number of adjustable parameters in each neuron is $M\left(S+1\right)$ (for the traditional neuron the number of parameters equals the number of weights: $S+1$). This number is crucial for estimating the Vapnik-Chervonenkis dimension of the context-dependent perceptron.

3 The VC-dimension of a Context-Dependent Neuron

Vapnik-Chervonenkis dimension is the main quantity used for measuring the capacity of a learning machine, its generalization abilities or the number of learning examples needed to obtain the required accuracy of predictions. In the following we shall compare the results for the traditional and the context-dependent neuron. For more details on the VC-dimension of neural nets, see [6].

Theorem 1. [6] *Consider a standard real-weight perceptron with $S \subseteq N$ real inputs and denote the set of functions it computes by H^{stand}. Then a set $S^{\mathrm{stand}} = \left\{\overline{X}_1, \overline{X}_2, \ldots, \overline{X}_n\right\} \subseteq \mathrm{R}^S$ is shattered by H^{stand} iff S^{stand} is affinely independent, that is iff the set $\left\{\left(\overline{X}_1^T, -1\right), \left(\overline{X}_2^T, -1\right), \ldots, \left(\overline{X}_n^T, -1\right)\right\}$ is linearly independent in R^{S+1}. It follows that:*

$$\mathrm{VCdim}\left(H^{\mathrm{stand}}\right) = S + 1 \quad (3)$$

For the lack of space we omit the proofs of the following theorems, which may however be reconstructed by analogy to those presented in [6].

Theorem 2. *Consider a context-dependent real-weight perceptron with $S \subseteq N$ real inputs, $P \subseteq N$ real context inputs and $P \subseteq N$ base functions. Denote the set of functions it computes by H^{cont}. Then a set $S^{\mathrm{cont}} = \{\overline{X}_1, \overline{Z}_1, \overline{X}_2, \overline{Z}_2, \ldots, \overline{X}_n, \overline{Z}_n\} \subseteq \mathrm{R}^S$ is shattered by H^{cont} only if in the subsets of S^{cont} containing* points with the same value of context, e.g. $\overline{Z} = z$: $\left\{ \left(\overline{X}_{z,1}^{T}, -1 \right), \left(\overline{X}_{z,2}^{T}, -1 \right), \ldots, \left(\overline{X}_{z,n_z}^{T}, -1 \right) \right\}$, all points are linearly independent in R^{S+1}. It follows that:

$$\mathrm{VCdim}\left(H^{\mathrm{cont}} \right) = M\left(S + 1 \right) \tag{4}$$

It is known [6] that for standard feed-forward linear threshold networks with a total of W weights the VC-dimension grows as $O\left(W^2 \right)$.

Theorem 3. *Suppose N^{cont} is a context-dependent feed-forward linear threshold network consisting of context-dependent neurons given by (1), with a total of W weights, where each weight is given by a combination of M coefficients and base functions as in (2). Let H^{cont} be the class of functions computed by this network. Then*

$$\mathrm{VCdim}\left(H^{\mathrm{cont}} \right) = O\left[(MW)^2 \right] \tag{5}$$

The difference in the way traditional and context-dependent nets work can be seen in the following example. Suppose we have a traditional neuron with $S + 1$ inputs (including bias) and add another P contextual variables as traditional ones. We therefore expand the neuron's input space from R^{S+1} to R^{S+1+P} (the same expansion is done with its parameter space) and the transformation done by the neuron $\mathrm{R}^{S+1+P} \to \mathrm{R}$ is still hyperplane, but in a higher-dimensional input space. When we add these P inputs as context ones and expand the base function vector with M functions (M may be greater than P), the neuron's input space remains R^{S+1}, while its parameter space growths to $\mathrm{R}^{M(S+1)}$ and the division $\mathrm{R}^{S+1+P} \to \mathrm{R}$ done by the neuron is not a hyperplane but a hypersurface, the more complicated, the more M is, remaining a hyperplane for a fixed value of context - this is the reason why the separating power of a context-dependent net is greater for sets of points in different contexts.

4 Learning of Context-Dependent Nets

An interesting learning algorithm for context-dependent nets is presented in [7]. It uses the properties of the Kronecker product and allows to train the net using all examples from different contexts during training. It is a gradient descent algorithm, in which the gradient of the quality function:

$$Q\left(\overline{A} \right) = E_{\left(\overline{X}, \overline{Z}, \overline{Y} \right)} \left[\Phi^{-1}\left(\overline{Y} \right) - \overline{W}^{T}\left(\overline{Z} \right) \overline{X} \right]^2 = \tag{6}$$

$$= E_{\left(\overline{X}, \overline{Z}, \overline{Y} \right)} \left[\Phi^{-1}\left(\overline{Y} \right) - \overline{A}^{T} \overline{X} \otimes \overline{V}\left(\overline{Z} \right) \right]^2 \tag{7}$$

is given by

$$grad_{\overline{A}} = -E_{\left(\overline{X}, \overline{Z}, \overline{Y} \right)} \left[\Phi^{-1}\left(\overline{Y} \right) - \overline{A}^{T} \overline{X} \otimes \overline{V}\left(\overline{Z} \right) \right] \overline{X} \otimes \overline{V}\left(\overline{Z} \right) \tag{8}$$

It should be emphasized that the neuron's output is calculated directly from the input vector $\overline{X}$ and the vector of base functions $\overline{V}\left(\overline{Z} \right)$ without having to calculate the neuron's weight. The same Kronecker product is then used for calculating the target function's gradient w.r.t. the coefficient vector $\overline{A}$. If all the net's layers have the same base functions vectors this calculation is also done once per epoch. These facts result in much less calculations in each learning epoch of the context-dependent net. This estimation may be slightly disturbed by the necessity of calculating the weights for backpropagation algorithm - but in this case it is only necessary to calculate the weight of neurons in all layers except the first one, which usually contains most neurons.

5 Conclusions

The model of a context-dependent perceptron has been presented in the paper, as well as learning algorithms. It has been shown, that similarly to the traditional neurons, the Vapnik-Chervonenkis dimension of a context-dependent neuron (and net) grows with the number of adjustable parameters but, as this number is greater than that of a traditional one, the separating power of such a neuron is much greater and depends not on the context variables, but on the way the network designer uses them by choosing the base functions $v\left(\overline{Z}\right)$. The growth of the Vapnik-Chervonenkis dimension is both a benefit and a problem - the number of examples needed for the learning algorithm to achieve the desired error is larger. The advantage of context-dependent nets over the traditional ones is that when comparing the nets with the same number of parameters (the same VC-dimension), the context-dependent ones learn faster and this difference gets more significant with the growth of the nets' size.

References

1. Turney P.: The Identification of Context-Sensitive Features: A Formal Definition of Context for Concept Learning, Proc. of 13th International Conference on Machine Learning (ICML96), Workshop on Learning in Context-Sensitive Domains, Bari, Italy, 1996
2. Turney P.: The Management of Context-Sensitive Features: A Review of Strategies, Proc. of ICML96, Bari, Italy, 1996
3. Turney P.: Exploiting context when learning to classify, Proc. of ICML93, Springer-Verlag
4. Harries M., Sammut C., Horn K.: Extracting hidden contexts, Machine Learning 32
5. Yeung D.T., Bekey G.A.: Using a context-sensitive learning to robot arm control, Proc. IEEE Int. Conf. on Robotics and Automation, pp 1441-1447, 1989
6. Anthony M., Bartlett P.L.: Neural Network Learning: Theoretical Foundations, Cambridge University Press, 1999, Cambridge
7. Rafajłowicz E.: Context Dependent Neural Nets - Problem Statement and Examples (Part 1), Learning (Part 2), Proc. of 3rd Conference Neural Networks and Their Applications, Zakopane, Poland, 1999
8. Ciskowski P., Rafajłowicz E.: Context Dependent Neural Nets - Structures and Learning, to be published in IEEE Trans. on Neural Networks
9. Watrous R.L., Towell G.: A Patient-Adaptive Neural Network ECG Patient Monitoring Algorithm. In Proc. Computers in Cardiology 1995, Vienna, Austria.

A Framework for Context-Driven Web Resource Discovery

Christo Dichev

Department of Computer Science, NC A&T State University
Greensboro, N.C. 27411, USA
dichev@ncat.edu

Abstract: In practice, few of the documents returned by a search engine are valuable to a user. Which documents are valuable depends on the *context* of the query. In this paper we propose a framework for dynamic conceptual clustering of web documents based on clusters of users that share common interests. It can support personalization of a search based on a search engine that 'knows' the context of the user information needs and uses it to tailor the search results.

1 Introduction

Web is huge and ubiquitous, unstructured, diverse in quality, dynamic and distributed, which makes searching for information principally difficult. Which documents will be valuable to the user depends on the *context* of the query. Search engines, however, treat each request independently from previous requests of the same user and of other web users making similar requests. Therefore the ranked list of documents received in response to the same queries is typically the same and depends neither on the user nor on the context in which the query is made. The question is how to infer context information and how to use this context information for selecting relevant documents?

Web users typically search for diverse information. Some searches are sporadic and irregular while others might be related to their interests and have more or less regular nature. An important question is then how to filter out these sporadic, irregular searches and how to combine regular searches into groups identifying topics of interest by observing the user behavior on the web. If we are able to identify *topics of interest* for a given user we can infer relevant contextual information associated with that user. Such contextual information when available to search engines could support personalized searches. Our approach to topic identification on the web is based on observations of the searching behavior of large groups of users rather than of a single user. The basic intuition is that a topic of interest can be determined by identifying a collection of web objects (articles, documents) that is of common interest to a sufficiently large group of web users.

In the present paper we present a resource discovery framework based on a contextual topology. Such partitioning of the web information space would reflect the presence of groups of users that share common interests and possibly some common patterns of behavior. Thus the partitioning of the web *user space* into groups of users generates a corresponding partitioning of the web *information space* into matching groups of objects. From these user groups we could derive the individual interests of their members and model the context of user's information needs.

The framework for modeling context of user information needs suggested in this paper is based on the identification of collections of documents being viewed by web users. For a given group of users we refer to the collection of objects that are of common interest to all users of that group as a *matching group of objects*. Assume now that on the web there are user groups, from one side, and matching groups of web objects, from another. Then a user, who is a member of a given group and is searching the web for specific information can view the web as a *huge* list of objects beginning with the ranked list of objects corresponding to her/his group. A practical implication of such a view is that it enables us to select that portion of the web information space, for which there is a kind of consensus on the relevance of the objects. The remaining objects not belonging to the "interesting" category might be filtered out. By synthesizing a conceptual context structure on the web specific to the interests of user groups, this framework provides a ground for a context-based resource discovery.

Since the topic of interest shared by a community is paired with the members of the community, they can be used in turn as "recommendation partners. Once the collection for a particular topic has been gathered and organized, different users with interest in that topic would be able to share the information. In many cases the user is not certain of what information exactly to look for and needs to learn more about the content of the information space. In such cases browsing a collection of articles generated on the base of the current context can be a good navigational strategy.

2 A Formal Perspective

Given a set of users U, a set of articles A and a binary relation uFa (user u is interested in article a) determine a pair of subsets $U_I \in Pow(U)$ and $A_J \in Pow(A)$ such that

$$U_I = \{u \in U | (\forall a \in A_J) \, uFa\}, \quad A_J = \{a \in A | (\forall u \in U_I) \, uFa\}$$

That is, a topic of interest (U_I, A_J) is defined by a binary relation uFa (*interested_in(u,a)*) and is characterized by the set of all articles A_J that are common objects of interest to all users in U_I.

From a formal point of view, the suggested contextual structure on the web can be interpreted as a binary relation between a set of users (U) and a set of articles (A), called *context*. Thus a context is a triple (U,A,F), where $F \subseteq U \times A$. Based on an analogy with formal concept analysis (FCA) [1,3], a topic of the context (U,A,F) can be defined to be a pair (U_I, A_J) where $U_I \subseteq U$, $A_J \subseteq A$ and,

$$U_I = \{u \in U | (\forall a \in A_J) \, uFa\}, \quad A_J = \{a \in A | (\forall u \in U_I) \, uFa\}$$

that is U_I is the set of all users interesting in all articles in A_J and A_J is the set of all articles that are common objects of interest to users in U_I. Exploiting further the analogy with FCA, A and U can be interpreted also as a set of *objects* and a set of *descriptors* correspondingly. Then A_J is the set of all objects possessing all the descriptors in U_I and conversely U_I is the set of descriptors held by all objects in A_J. We may think of the set of articles A_u associated with a given user $u \in U$ as represented by a bit vector. Each bit i corresponds to a possible article $a_i \in A$ and is on or off depending on whether the user u is interested in article a_i. The advantage of this interpretation is that now we can characterize the binary relation between the set of users and the set of articles in terms of *topic lattice*. Let us denote the set of all topics of the context (U,A,F) by $T(U,A,F)$. An ordering relation is easily defined on this set of topics by

$$(U_1, A_1) \leq (U_2, A_2) \leftrightarrow U_1 \subseteq U_2 \text{ or } (U_1, A_1) \leq (U_2, A_2) \leftrightarrow A_1 \supseteq A_2.$$

The set $T(U,A,F)$ along with "$\leq$ " relation form a partially ordered set that can be characterized by a *concept lattice* (referred here as *topic lattice*). Each node of the topic lattice is a pair composed of a subset of the articles and a subset of the corresponding users. In each pair the subset of users contains just the users sharing common interest to the subset of articles and similarly the subset of articles contains just the articles sharing overlapping interest from the matching subset of users. The set of pairs is ordered by the standard "set inclusion" relation applied to the set of articles and of users that describe each pair. The partially ordered set can be represented by a Hasse diagram, in which an edge connects two nodes if and only if they are comparable and there is no other node-intermediate topic in the lattice, i.e. each topic is linked to its maximally specific more general topics and to its maximally general more specific topics. The ascending paths represent the subclass/superclass relation. The bottom topic is defined by the set of all users, the top topic is defined by all articles and the users (possibly none) sharing common interest in them. A very simple example of user and information spaces is presented in Table 1. The corresponding lattice is presented in Figure 1. (The bottom is omitted due to a lack of space).

	a_1	a_2	a_3	a_4	a_5	a_6	a_7	a_8	.
u_1	1	1	1	1	1	1	1	1	.
u_2	1	1	1	1	1	0	1	0	.
u_3	1	0	0	0	0	1	0	1	.
u_4	0	1	0	0	1	0	1	0	.
u_5	0	0	1	1	0	0	1	0	.
u_6	1	0	1	1	0	0	1	0	.
u_7	0	0	0	0	1	0	1	0	.
u_8	0	0	0	0	0	1	0	1	.
.	.	.	.	.	.	.	.	.	.

Table 1

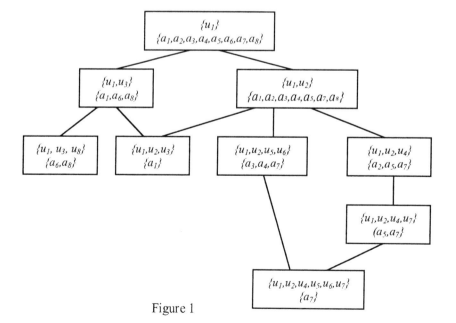

Figure 1

In contrast to conceptual clustering [1] where the descriptors are static, in the suggested approach the users who play a role of descriptors are "dynamic": in general, a user interest in can not be specified completely and his topical interests change over time. Hence, the lattice describing the topical structure is dynamic too. This entails the following assumptions. A collection of articles A_J from an existing topic (U_I, A_J) can only be expanded. This is due to the assumption that documents that are interesting for a user u remain interesting. Therefore, an expansion of the collection of articles with respect to a topic (U_I, A_J) will not impose any change of existing links, since $A_J \subseteq A_K \rightarrow (U_I, A_J) \leq (U_J, A_K)$. That is, an expansion of an existing collection of articles preserves the structure of the lattice. Next assumption is that for a given topic (U_I, A_J) the collection of articles that are likely to be interesting to a user $u \in U_I$ are the articles interesting to the other members of the group U_I. These are collections of articles $A_u \subseteq A_K \setminus A_J$ where A_K is a set of articles of the topic (U_M, A_K), such that $U_M \subset U_I$, $u \notin U_M$ and $A_J \subseteq A_K \subseteq A$. This fact is a formal support of our intuition that the search domain relevant to the user $u \in U_I$ includes a subset of articles $A_u \subseteq A_K \setminus A_J$ to which other members of the group U_I have demonstrated interest.

An important characteristic of this method is that it does not require explicit representation of the web objects, due to the fact that it exploits "membership" relations. The set of objects A_u are identified based on their relevance to the context "interesting to the user u", rather than on specific syntactic properties of their representations. An additional advantage of the presented approach is that it can cover objects behind the conventional search forms, such as pdf files, images, music files, and compressed archives. This observation suggests also an ordering relation $(\angle)$ for ranking articles a_1, a_2 returned in a response to a request from a user $u \in U_I$, where (U_I, A_J) is a topic: $a_1 \angle a_2$ if there exist user groups $U_I \subseteq U_1 \subseteq U_2$, such that $a_1 \in A_1, a_2 \notin A_1, a_2 \in A_2$, and $(U_1, A_1) \leq (U_2, A_2)$. From an "active users" perspective this approach enables us to recognize a community of users for which a given article is most likely to be interesting.

3 Conclusion

In this paper we have presented a framework for information retrieval on the web. Our framework is close in spirit to the application of FCA [3]. The basic assumption is that the results of a search would be more relevant to a given user when provided within the context of semantically related objects marked as "interesting" by their peers. In addition, a contextual structure would help users in getting better insight about the scope of their search and optimizing the search strategy [2]. By partitioning web users into groups it would be possible to make useful predictions about some other shared features and patterns of users' behavior and derive some correlating properties regarding the web information space. Moreover, the identification of groups of users with similar interests can help producers of information to reach interested consumers in a timely manner.

References

1. Carpineto C., Romano G. A lattice conceptual clustering system and its application to browsing retrieval. *Machine Learning* 24, 1996, pp. 95-122.
2. Lawrence S. Context in Web Search. *IEEE Data Engineering Bulletin*, 23(3), 2000, pp. 25-32.
3. Wille R. Restructuring lattice theory: an approach based on hierarchies of concepts. In: I. Rival (ed.): *Ordered sets*. Reidel, Dordrecht-Boston, 1982, pp 445-470.

Specifying Contexts for Coordination Patterns

Patrick ETCHEVERRY, Philippe LOPISTÉGUY, Pantxika DAGORRET

L.I.U.P.P.A., IUT de Bayonne – Pays Basque, Université de Pau et Pays de l'Adour
Château Neuf – 64100 Bayonne – France
[Patrick.Etcheverry], [Philippe.Lopisteguy], [Pantxika.Dagorret]@iutbayonne.univ-pau.fr

Abstract

This paper focuses on coordination problems resolution. We state that contexts delimit environments where coordination problems are recurrent. Thus, identification of coordination contexts is necessary to propose solutions that solve coordination problems. We propose a pattern catalogue where each pattern describes how to apply a coordination form to manage a given coordination context. Contexts and problems are described using the terminology of the concerned area; patterns describe how to apply a solution to a specific problem.

1. Introduction

This paper deals with the problem of coordination specification, which is a recurrent problem in numerous domains (e.g. human organizations, multi-agent systems). More generally, coordination difficulties exist within every society composed by entities which are able to act in an autonomous way.

The problem we point out is the difficulty to describe and, therefore, to solve coordination problems within a complex process. The difficulty is often proportional to the complexity of the process, which depends on the number of tasks to be performed, and the number of actors to perform the tasks.

The paper is structured as follows: firstly, we present coordination contexts as a structural axis of coordination patterns. Secondly, we specify coordination contexts and their related coordination problems. Thirdly, we present coordination forms that can be applied in previously identified contexts. In order to illustrate our purpose, we present one coordination pattern. Finally, we present an approach for pattern utilization.

2. Specifying Coordination Contexts

We aim to elaborate patterns that help coordination within human or software processes. Consequently, contexts and coordination forms specification has to be performed in terms of elements that belong to the process (activities, actors, resources, ...). Then, it is necessary to define a vocabulary for process description.

We consider that a *process* is basically composed of a set of *activities* that combine and use *resources*. An activity corresponds to an action of the process. It can be elementary, or composed of other activities. A resource is an identified entity belonging to the activities environment needed for activities progress. We define three types or resources : actors (human being or software, and more generally, any component of the organization able to process an activity), devices and documents. Moreover, activities and resources have interactions, like resource utilization (by an activity) and temporal constraints (between activities).

Our typology definition of coordination contexts relies on [7]. This work studies the recurrent and interdisciplinary character of coordination problems. Thus, the presented typology of coordination contexts is generic. Coordination is defined as "the management of dependencies between activities" where the main types of dependencies are: production-expenditure of resources, resource sharing, simultaneity constraints and tasks - sub-tasks relationships.

3. Coordination Contexts

Subsequently, we define a coordination context as a situation where one of the former four dependencies can be identified between activities of a given process. So, we will consider four coordination contexts:

- *Production-expenditure of resources*: This context arises when an activity produces a resource which is used by another activity. The production - expenditure relation is not limited to material flows, it also extends to informational flows.

- *Simultaneity constraints*: This context arises when activities must satisfy one or more temporal constraints among the following ones [5]: "A activity *before* B activity", "A activity *starts* B activity", "A activity *overlaps* B activity", etc.

- *Tasks and Subtasks Relationships*: This context happens when the goal to reach is divided into sub-goals and the associated activities are distributed to several actors.

- *Sharing Resources*: This context arises when activities must share a limited resource. It is necessary to have a resource allocator which manages the resource requests formulated by the activities.

4. Coordination Forms

The study of various works [8], [3], and [1] points out that all detailed coordination forms are enclosed in coordination forms described in [8]. Thus, we rely upon this nomenclature for identifying coordination forms. Any coordination is expressed according to three basic mechanisms:

- *Supervision*: It is the coordination form where an activity (called supervisor) controls the execution of a set of activities. The supervisor activity gives instructions to the supervised activities and controls the carried out work.

- *Standardisation*: It is the coordination form where activities have to respect norms that focus on: coordination unfolding's behavior (process standardization), results to reach (results standardization), qualifications to have or standards to respect.

- *Mutual adjustment*: This mechanism carries out the activities coordination by informal communication. It is a particularly suitable mechanism for complex contexts where numerous activities interact.

5. Coordination Patterns: one Example

Each pattern results from the connection of one of the coordination contexts and one of the coordination forms we have introduced in the former section. The set of patterns is organized as a catalogue of patterns. The pattern catalogue is composed of the whole possible combinations of coordination contexts and coordination forms.

For example, mapping a standardization process mechanism upon the simultaneous access problem leads to specify a pattern which focuses on solutions for access conflicts thanks to standardization techniques. Let us consider such a pattern.

Our patterns are described according to a framework derived from those given in [4]. We present an abstract description of each clause. The formal part of the "Context" and "Solution" clauses details models that allow an easier pattern programming.

Pattern name: Resource sharing by process standardization

Examples:
- If several employees want to use a photocopier, the employee which has less photocopies to do uses the photocopier first.
- If two patients arrive at the same time at the urgencies service, the worst affected one is treated first.

Context: This pattern can be used each time a resource has to be shared between several activities.

Problem considered by the pattern: The pattern deals with problems of simultaneous access. These problems occur when a shared resource is not usable simultaneously by an unlimited number of users. It is necessary to have a mechanism to define who can use the resource.

Solution: The solution consists in defining a standardized procedure to establish who can use the shared resource. The procedure can be formalized with: instructions manuals, internal regulations, algorithms, etc. Any procedure articulates with the events that characterize the context: *resource released, request done, request accepted* and *request cancelled*. The procedure can be centralized or distributed. The entities in charge of the procedure are not necessarily elements of the context.

Strengths and compromises: This pattern is effective in contexts where individuals cannot or do not have to communicate. For example, urgencies situations must to favour action rather than communication. The pattern weak point appears in strongly dynamic contexts prone to unforeseen and not standardized events.

6. Using the Catalogue to Solve Coordination Problems

We present in this section an approach that uses the catalogue in a process modelling context [6]. This approach aims to provide a thread and tools to specify activities coordination. It is composed of four steps:

1) *Describing activities according to a process approach.* The aim of this step consists in describing the various activities that must be carried out in order to achieve the process goal. The description is done thanks to a semi-formal language [2]. It does not focus on how activities are carried out but on how activities are connected to achieve the final goal.

2) *Identifying contexts that generate coordination problems.* The goal of this stage consists in analysing the described process and detecting the contexts that need coordination forms. Identification of these contexts is carried out thanks to the contexts typology defined in the pattern catalogue.

3) *Choosing a coordination form for each coordination problem.* It consists in associating each identified coordination problem with a coordination form. The choice of a coordination form relies upon the coordination form models defined in the catalogue. A coordination problem can be solved by different coordination forms.

4) *Carrying out coordination.* After having selected the coordination form, implementation of coordination consists in applying the corresponding pattern. The pattern is used as guidelines for carrying out the coordination form in the given context.

7. Conclusion

The coordination problem is a recurrent problem which appears in various domains such as software agents design or companies organization. Our contribution deals with coordination improvement in domains that can be modelled in terms of processes.

Our contribution is materialized by defining a pattern catalogue where each pattern describes a way to apply a coordination form to solve a coordination problem of a given coordination context. The description of each pattern includes the circumstances, strengths and compromises of its application.

Currently, we are working on formal models corresponding to the context and solution clauses of the patterns for their application to the multi-agent domain.

References

1. Keith S. Decker, Environment Centered Analysis and Design of Coordination Mechanisms, Department of Computer Science, University of Massachusetts, UMass CMPSCI Technical Report, 1995.

2. Patrick Etcheverry, Pantxika Dagorret, Philippe Lopistéguy, A multi-agent architecture to validate organisational coordination know-how, The 2000 International Conference on Artificial Intelligence (IC-AI'2000), ISBN: 1-892512-56-4, June 26-29, 2000, Monte Carlo Resort, Las Vegas, Nevada, USA.

3. Jacques Ferber, Multi-Agent Systems - Towards a collective intelligence, InterEditions – ISBN: 2-7296-0665-3, 1997.

4. E. Gamma, R. Helm, R. Johnson, J. Vlissides, Design Patterns - Elements of Reusable Object-Oriented Software, Addison-Wesley publishing company - ISBN: 0-201-63361-2, 1995.

5. T.D.C. Little, A. Ghafoor, Interval-Based Conceptual Models for Time-Dependent Multimedia Data, In IEEE Trans. on Knowledge and Data Engineering (Special Issue: Multimedia Information Systems), Vol. 5, N°4, August 1993, pp 551-563, 1993.

6. Philippe Lorino, The value development by processes, in French Review of Management, June 1995.

7. Thomas W. Malone and Kevin Crowston, The Interdisciplinary Study of Coordination, Appeared in ACM Computing Surveys, 1994 (March), 26 (1), 87-119, November 1993.

8. H. Mintzberg,, Management. Travel Toward Organisations Centre, Organisations Editions, Paris, 1990.

Looking at "Situated" Technology: Differences in Pattern of Interaction Reflect Differences in Context

Anne-Laure Fayard[1], Austin Henderson[2]

[1] INSEAD, Technology Management Dept, Bld de Constance, F-77305 Fontainebleau Cdx
Tel.: +33 1 60 72 41 47/Fax: +33 1 60 74 61 58
anne-laure.fayard@insead.fr

[2] Rivendel Consulting & Design, Inc., PO Box 334, La Honda, CA 94020, USA
+1 650 747 9201
henderson@rivcons.com

Abstract. Technology cannot be considered as a stand-alone element; it is always situated in a spatial and organizational context. To understand technology usage, we must focus on the context in which this usage takes place. We conducted two field studies of everyday interactions with and around copier machines. This paper describes these two studies and the interaction patterns that we observed. We found some variations in these interaction patterns. These variations can be interpreted as reflecting differences in contexts – both spatial and organizational.

1 Introduction

Most of the studies looking at the impact of technologies in office work focus on the human-machine dyad. However, some studies consider the social situational context in which machine usage takes place as a crucial element (e.g. [1], [4], [6], [8], [9]). This paper examines the everyday social interactions that take place among co-workers around copier machines in two office environments. Our observations show variations in the patterns of interactions of people with and around the technology. We claim that these differences can be accounted for by reference to the differences in the social and organizational structure and the spatial configuration.

2 Technology is Embedded in a Social Situational Context

Technology is often considered as one element that can be studied as a stand-alone "decontextualized" system (e.g. ([2], [7]). However, some scholars ([1], [3], [4], [6], [8], [9]) have stressed the importance of looking at the social situational context in which machine use takes place. They claim that technology is part of a larger system of people, practices and values situated in a particular local environment.

In this paper, we use the situated perspective to observe and analyze interactions in copier rooms. We argue that copier machines are one element of a complex situated system involving users, people maintaining the machines, the organizational structure and the physical layout.

3 Two Field Studies

Our observations at the two sites showed very different patterns of interactions. We tried to understand these differences by analyzing the structural differences (organizational, spatial and social structures) existing between these two settings.

3.1 Methodology

The study of socially situated action requires a specific methodology that provides a rich detailed description of behaviors in specific settings ([1], p.198; [4]; [5]; [6], p.14 sq.; [9] p. 109 sq.). Formal structured interviews and questionnaires do not provide relevant information on what people really do, i.e. the informal practices and the unobtrusive work styles. Thus, we chose to have a research strategy that included on-site field observations, videotaping and in situ questioning. We did observations and videotaped several hours (6 hours at the Business School; 12 hours at the Research Center) in each setting.

3.2 What We Saw

Our observations of people interacting with, and around, copier machines were carried out at two different office sites in France:
- *The Business School*, an international educational institution located near Paris,
- *The Research Center* of a public institutional bureaucracy.
At each site, the group we observed was small (10-20 people), composed mostly of professionals, and included some administrators. At both sites, the copier was located in a "copier room" which also contained a fax machine, a shared printer and a supply cabinet (e.g., for pens, pencils). In both settings, the copier was casually operated, i.e. operating the copier was not the main job function of the individuals observed .

Patterns

We noticed different patterns of interactions around the copiers.
At the Business School, we recorded only a few interactions around the copier. We found no multi-person interactions either with the copier, or around the machine. The only people who made copies were the secretaries, and they were nearly always alone in the copier room.
At the Research Center, many of the records captured interactions involving two or more people. These interactions were of two sorts: interactions between people around the copier and interactions with the copier.

We assume that these distinct patterns reflect different ways of supporting the needs for supporting the copying, and that many of these differences can be explained in terms of contextual differences.

4 Differences in Interaction Patterns Reflect Differences in Context

We tried to understand this difference of interaction patterns by analyzing the contextual differences (spatial and organizational structures) existing between these two settings.

4.1 Differences in the Spatial Context

Space –as a setting and a medium where external representations are displayed- is an important element for analyzing interaction patterns with and around the machine. The activity around the copier takes place in a physical space that provides a set of resources and constraints that have an impact on the interactions between people and machines.

In our studies, the location of the copier room can explain why there were more interactions at the Research Center than at the Business School. At the Research Center, the copier room was located near the elevator, near to the coffee room and the mailboxes, and at the beginning of the corridor. Thus, people always passed by the copier room to go to their office, to pick up their mail or take a coffee. The copier room was an encounter space located near to other encountering places where social gatherings occur. In contrast, at the Business School, the copier room was rather isolated: it was at the far end of the corridor, and people went there only if they had to make copies, pick up printed jobs, or send faxes.

4.2 Differences in the Organizational Context

Variations in the interaction patterns not only reflect differences in the spatial layout, but they also reflect differences in the organizational structure. One major difference between the two sites was the organizational structure: in one case, the organizational structure was very strong, while in the other case the organizational structure was rather loose. The number of interactions seems to be linked to the nature of the organizational structure: the stronger the organizational context, the fewer interactions you find.

The Business School had quite a strong organization structure with well-assigned roles. We noticed that with few exceptions only the secretaries made copies. In fact, at the Business School, making copies (for courses, as well as for administrative documents) was part of the administrators' jobs, and they were skilled at it. Moreover, there was a person in charge of the functioning of all the copiers, Michael. He had a certain expertise, he was able to either fix the problem, or diagnose that it needed repair, and knew whom to call.

The Research Center had a rather flat organizational structure. There were only two administrators for the whole group, and they were explicitly instructed not to be supporters for the individuals. Both researchers and administrators did their own copying.

As the infrastructure was rich at the Business School, it was relatively easy to find the resources and to get information on how to operate the machine, how to modify it, or how to repair it. As there were few users of the copiers (mainly the administrators), there were few opportunities for interactions around the copier. As roles were well-assigned, people did not need to build a social network on which to rely for seeking information, advice and help. On the contrary, at the Research Center, the infrastructure was weak and the roles not clearly defined. Thus, "who you know" became crucial in the managing of basic resources as well as in the solving of problems. People heavily used social interaction to find resources. These social interactions are either a way of using the social web, or of building a social network on which to rely later.

5 Conclusion

These two comparative studies show how variations in the interaction patterns of people in a copier room reflect differences in the spatial and organization context. We argue that the differences in overt social activity around the copier can be explained by reference to the differences in location of the copier room and its use as an encountering place, and on the strength of the organizational infrastructure.

References

1. Blomberg, J., 1987, Social Interaction and Office Communication: Effects on User's Evaluation of New Technologies. Technology and the Transformation of White Collar Work. R. Kraut. Hillsdale, New Jersey, Lawrence Erlbaum Associates: 195-210.
2. Card, S.K., Moran, T., and Newell, A., 1983, The Psychology of Human-Computer Interaction, Hillsdale, NJ: Earlbaum.
3. Hutchins, E., 1995, Cognition in the Wild, MIT Press.
4. Jordan, B., 1993, Ethnographic Workplace Studies and Computer Supported Cooperative Work, Proceedings of the Interdisciplinary Workshop on Informatics and Psychology, Dan Shapiro, M. Tauber & R. Traunmüller, eds., Amsterdam: North Holland.
5. Jordan, B., and Henderson, A., 1995, "Interaction Analysis: Foundations and Practice." The Journal of Learning Sciences, 4(1): 39-103.
6. Nardi, B. and O'Day, 1999, Information Ecologies.
7. Norman, D., 1993, Things That Make Us Smart, Perseus Books.
8. Orr, J., 1996, Talking about Machines, ILR Cornell University Press.
9. Suchman, L., 1987, Plans and Situated Action: The Problem of Human-machine Communication. New York, NY, Cambridge University Press.

A Context-Driven Approach for Knowledge Acquisition: Application to a Leukaemia Domain

J. T. Fernández-Breis[1], Rafael Valencia-García[1], Rodrigo Martínez-Béjar[1], & Pascual Cantos-Gómez[2]

[1]Departmento de Ingeniería de la Información y de las Comunicaciones
Universidad de Murcia. Campus Universitario de Espinardo
30071 Espinardo (Murcia). Spain
Tel: 34-968-364634   Fax: 34-968-364351
E-mail: jfernand@perseo.dif.um.es, rodrigo@dif.um.es
[2] Departamento de Filología Inglesa,
Universidad de Murcia, Campus de La Merced (Murcia), Spain
Tel: 34-968-364365 Fax:34-968-363185
E-mail: pcantos@um.es

Abstract: Knowledge acquisition processes (KAPs) could be simplified by means of extracting knowledge directly from natural language texts. This would simplify the KAP as knowledge engineers would become redundant in this process and knowledge could be acquired straight from experts. The approach presented here uses techniques from both knowledge acquisition and natural language recognition research areas. The KAP described is represented by means of ontologies and has been applied to the leukaemia domain.

1.Introduction

Extracting knowledge directly from natural language text is a challenging task as it would allow to extract knowledge easily and, what is more, without the intervention of knowledge engineers. This paper presents a technique for generating knowledge from text. This work combines knowledge acquisition and natural language recognition, two disciplines that have been following opposite roads. Knowledge is introduced by experts into the system; these have to specify first where knowledge resides in the text. The system's charge is to associate text and knowledge. The whole process can be divided into two main steps: (1) the *search phase*: this previous stage is completely human-guided: an expert reviews a text and knowledge is generated from scratch; (2) the *setting in a context phase*. The main task of this phase is to store knowledge found by the expert in order to be able to automatically identify this knowledge when it reappears.

Knowledge has been represented in this work by means of ontologies. In the literature, ontologies are commonly defined as specifications of domain knowledge conceptualisations ([4]). An advantage of ontologies is the possibility of making a mathematical study on their properties (see [2]). The operators formalised in [2] are implemented in this work in order to build a domain ontology.

2. Overview of the approach

The aim of this work is to extract knowledge from natural language texts. More precisely, building an ontology from a *text*, whose content might be about some specific application domain. The ontology is built by an *expert*. Ontologies divide knowledge in (knowledge) entities such as concepts, attributes, relationships, rules, etc. These knowledge entities can appear explicitly in the text although sometimes knowledge is only referred to implicitly. Thus, the process attempts to find only explicit knowledge of the text. The starting point is an empty *knowledge base*. In this phase, the system is unable to find any knowledge in the text and the expert has to introduce knowledge manually. The expert identifies all the knowledge entities of the fragment and (s)he also tells the system the *expressions* in which they appear. These *expressions-knowledge* associations are stored by the system in order to be used for new knowledge findings thereafter. The expert has only to identify these associations once, and from that moment on the system will perform automatically, and the expert's task will just be to confirm the results given by the system.

3. Parsing the text to look for knowledge

The first goal of this phase is to find expressions with associated knowledge in the knowledge base. Next, it has to decide what to do whenever an expression has more than one associated knowledge to it. The result of the search process is a list containing all the expressions of the fragment already contained in the knowledge base. New expressions are not associated to any knowledge, but are "potentially associated" to a knowledge list. The initial set of fragment expressions with associated knowledge is empty, and the iterations of the algorithm finish once all words of the current fragment have been analysed. Next, it takes the remaining non-analysed word of the text fragment (current word) and looks for *similar* words in the already existing expressions in the knowledge base. Then, for each expression of the knowledge base similar to the current word, if it is considered to be an *acceptable* expression, these actions are performed: (1) obtaining and sorting the associated knowledge to the expression present in the knowledge base; (2) creating a new expression that matches the knowledge base expression and associate to it as possible knowledge to the previously sorted one; and (3) adding the new expression to the list of fragment expressions with its associated knowledge. Let us suppose that the current word is "mortality". When looking up the database, two expressions are identified as similar: "mortality rate" and "mortality risk". If the word that follows "mortality" in the current fragment is "rate", then the first expression will be considered acceptable whereas if it is "risk", the second one will be accepted. Else, none will be considered as acceptable.

4. Context assessment

Once the search phase has been performed, the system is fitted with a list of associated knowledge expressions. However, the system's task has not finished yet, unless the inferred knowledge is a concept, else, some operations still need to be performed: (1)

current fragments are processed backwards from the current expression on, until an expression which is labelled as a concept is found; (2) the system looks for expressions for which knowledge has already been inferred from in the current working session. In this way, if the user had inferred the concept, the system would find it and would associate the concept to the attribute; (3) if no expressions with associated knowledge on the left of the attribute are found, then the system searches the database for the corresponding concept. All relations are assumed to be binary. The search phase is a semantic process: words are selected from a text and their meanings are looked up in a database. The database and the knowledge contained are of paramount importance for correctly associating knowledge to expressions. Whereas, context setting is a syntactic process: this phase starts once all knowledge has been found in the database. Furthermore, this knowledge will only be used once a context has been found, derived from the former. Concepts are associated to attributes and participants to relations through a simple linear search method.

5. Implementation of a software tool

A tool based on the approach described above has been designed and implemented for acquiring knowledge from texts (text needs to be specified in a text file, i.e., in ASCII format). Text length is irrelevant as it can be split into minor fragments. Text samples might belong to one or more specific domains or tasks. The distinction of domains is important as word meanings depend heavily on the domain they occur in. The final user of the tool is an expert. Each expert is acquainted with knowledge of one or more domains. The system also accounts for the associations between experts and tasks. The KAP is performed in sessions. A knowledge expert on a specific task specifies the file to work with and a new session is created and associated to this expert, task and file. While processing the fragments, the expert finds or recognizes knowledge, which can appear explicitly or implicitly in the fragment. If knowledge appears explicitly in the fragment, then the expert has to identify the expression in which this knowledge appears, associating expressions to knowledge or inferring knowledge from expressions.

The tool is fitted with two distinct working modes: (1) the *query mode* and (2) the *maintenance mode*. In the maintenance mode, users are provided with the full functionality of the tool (adding new experts and tasks, associating experts to tasks; saving the work/session(s) in the database, loading previously saved work, etc). The query mode has a reduced functionality. The user cannot perform management activities nor save work/sessions in the database. The ontological categories of the system are only five out of the six categories of CommonKADS ([3]) are used, namely: (1) concepts; (2) attributes; (3) values; and (4) relations (IS-A, PART-OF, ASSOCIATION and INFLUENCE). The tool visualises ontologies as trees with three branches: (1) one for concepts, (2) one for relations and (3) another one for axioms. Each concept has branches for its attributes and each attribute has branches for its values. The relations are branches of the "relationships" node, and the instances of the relations can be viewed on the right side of the screen.

The tool has been applied to a specific domain, namely, leukaemia. It allows the user to visualise the acquired knowledge and to view the learning diagram curve for the ontological entities discussed here relative to text fragments analysed. Additionally, the user can also decide whether (s)he wants to see the knowledge associations found/identified by the user, by the system or by both. As a result of the knowledge acquisition process in this domain, an ontology was obtained with the following number of knowledge entities: 167 concepts, 30 (valued) attributes, 181 relationships and three axioms.

6. Discussion and conclusion

In the work explained here, an approach that combines knowledge acquisition and natural language recognition techniques has been used for implementing a system capable of extracting knowledge from natural language texts. The techniques for acquiring natural language presented in this work offer a different and interesting method within natural language acquisition. The way we approach knowledge structuring differs from the one presented in [1]: our knowledge entities are concepts, attributes, values, relations, and rules whereas in [1], the discussion is about concepts, roles, individuals and axioms. Another difference with [1] is that the concept acquisition process is performed in a different way, too: the system's suggestions are hypotheses the user accepts or rejects, whereas in [1], the process is structured in three phases: (1) generating quality labels for hypotheses; (2) estimating the credibility of the hypotheses; and (3) computing the order of preference of the hypotheses.

We believe to have shown that our approach can be easily adapted to new requirements. The system has been used within the leukaemia domain and an ontology with almost two hundred concepts and relationships has been built by applying the framework described in this paper to a set of natural language texts on leukaemia. We are confident that this approach of recognizing natural language offers some advantages with respect to pure linguistic methods as: (1) ambiguity is taken into account (i.e., person dependency, spatial location, domain dependency); (2) implicit knowledge can be identified and added by the user; and (4) the system is incremental and automatic.

Acknowledgements:The first author is supported by the Fundación Séneca (Centro de Coordinación para la Investigación), through the Program Séneca (FPI).

References

[1] Hahn, U. & Schnattinger, K.: An Empirical Evaluation of a System for Text Knowledge Acquisition. In Proceedings of the European Knowledge Acquisition Workshop (1997), 129-144, Spain.
[2] Martínez-Béjar, R. & Martín-Rubio, F.: A mathematical functions-based approach for analysing elicited knowledge. In Proceedings of the Ninth International Conference on Software Engineering and Knowledge Engineering (1997), Madrid.
[3] Schreiber, A. T., Akkermans, J. M., Anjewierden, A. A., De Hoog, R., Shadbolt, N. R., Van de Velde, W. & Wielinga, B. J.: CommonKADS. Engineering and Managing Knowledge. The CommonKADS Methodology. University of Amsterdam, 1998.
[4] Van Heijst, G., Schreiber, A. T., & Wielinga, B.J. Using explicit ontologies in KBS development. International Journal of Human-Computer Studies, 45 (1997): 183-292.

Context in Natural-Language Communication: Presupposed or Co-supposed?

Anita Fetzer

University of Stuttgart
Institute of English Linguistics
D-70174 Stuttgart
Germany
anita@ifla.uni-stuttgart.de

Abstract. The role of context is investigated in natural-language communication by differentiating between cognitive, linguistic and social contexts. It is firmly anchored to a dialogue framework and based on a relational conception of context as structured and interactionally organised. It adopts bottom-up and top-down perspectives and argues for natural-language communication as a dialogical, cooperative and collaborative endeavour, in which local meaning is negotiated in context. In the case of an acceptance, an utterance and its presuppositions are allocated to the dialogue common ground and assigned the status of co-suppositions. In the case of a non-acceptance, a negotiation-of-validity sequence is initiated. The adaptation of both micro and macro perspectives requires a differentiation between unilateral speech acts and collective dialogue acts, individual I-intentions and collective WE-intentions, individual presuppositions and collective co-suppositions, and individual sense-making and collective coherence.

1 Linguistic, Social and Cognitive Contexts

Natural-language communication is a rather complex endeavour and generally described as interlocutors exchanging utterances in context in order to transmit information. But do interlocutors really just exchange utterances in context? And what do the concepts of interlocutor, utterance and context stand for? In a simplified dialogue framework, interlocutors consist of a speaker, who produces one or more utterances, and a hearer, who interprets and ratifies the utterances by producing further utterances which s/he directs at the previous speaker. Thus, an interlocutor is assigned the status of a coparticipant. But which status is assigned to an utterance? Analogous to speech act theory, an utterance represents the minimal unit of communication. Contrary to the ideal notion of a speech act, however, an utterance refers the speaker's actual linguistic output, which is not realised in a void but anchored to linguistic, social and cognitive contexts, as is manifest, for instance, in the employment of an indexical expression [1], whose local meaning is retrieved through a process of inferencing. What does the concept of context refer to?

In Relevance Theory, context is no longer represented by a diffuse entity, but by an infinite number of interdependent layers, to employ the onion metaphor [12], or by interdependent frames, to employ Goffman's terminology from his seminal work on frame analysis [7]. This also applies to the dynamic outlook on context in ethnomethodology, where coparticipants reconstruct social context in and through the process of communication. If this ethnomethodological premise is adapted to a pragmatic outlook on the production and interpretation of utterances in a context, the social context and the utterance's local meaning are reconstructed in communication. But is this bottom-up approach also valid for the construction of a linguistic context? If the ethnomethodologcial premise of accountability of social action, which states that social agents know, at some level, what they say and what they mean by their social actions [6], Recanati's availability principle, which is based "on a specific cognitive hypothesis, according to which what is said is consciously accessible" [9:28], and Searle's principle of expressibility, stating "whatever can be meant can be said" [10:68], are adapted to the production and interpretation of local meaning in a context, the issue of how a coparticipant designs their utterance to realise their communicative intention can no longer be based on a random selection of linguist items and structures because social and linguistic contexts have to compatible with the coparticipant's communicative intention. Yet compatibility is only a necessary condition as the relation between communicative intention and linguistic and social contexts also has to be appropriate [5]. For this reason, the reconstruction of local meaning in communication requires intentionality to already manifest at the level of the production of an utterance in a context which manifests in the employment of a specific sentence type, word order, style, lexical item and phonological realisation.

Thus, a relational conception of context is based on multiple embeddedness: cognitive context is represented by interdependent layers, linguistic context by adjacent utterances, and social context by the coparticipants' shared physical environment. Naturally, the immediately shared cognitive, linguistic and social contexts are embedded in larger, more remote cognitive, linguistic and social contexts and their macro constraints, such as a cognitive script [12], a communicative project [8] or institutional communication.

2 Unilateral Speech Acts vs. Collective Dialogue Acts

In speech act theory, sociopragmatics and ethnomethodology, rational agents perform social actions intentionally. Thus, the premise of rationality manifests on the micro level in the meaningful and purposeful production and interpretation of local meaning in a context. As has been argued above, coparticipants do not just exchange speech acts but rather a direct or an indirect linguistic representation of a specific speech act in a specific context. Moreover, the exchange is ratified by an acceptance or rejection. For this reason, an analysis of context in natural-language communication has to be based on the lower-order concept of an utterance and account for how the underlying speech act is represented linguistically and how it is ratified. As soon as the ratification of a communicative contribution is assigned the status of a necessary condition for felicitous communication and thus the status of a social action, a framework based on unilateral speech acts can no longer be sustained as it has accommodate the constraints of dialogue, such as cooperation and collabortion which manifest in the postulation and ratification of a communicative contribution regarding the appropriateness of the linguistic representation and social action. That is, the social actions of postulation and ratification do no longer represent two unilateral speech acts. Instead, they are constitutive parts of collective action anchored to a set of coparticipants who are no longer defined by their individual I-intentions only, but also assigned a collective WE-intention.

3 Individual I-Intentions vs. Collective WE-Intentions

In ordinary-language communication, communicative intentions are hardly ever represented explicitly but are retrieved from context. As a consequence of this, communicative intentions are not simply anchored to the individual participants and their subjective worlds. Rather, they manifest in the surface phenomenon of an utterance and its immediate linguistic and social contexts. This is also implicit in Ducrot's principle of *why this to me now* [3], where 'why' refers to the individual communicative intentions, 'this' to the communicative contribution, 'to me' to the reception format, and 'now' to the sequential slot in time, place and discourse. As has been argued above, coparticiants do not generally postulate and ratify single speech acts, but rather a dialogue act. Adapting the premise of embeddedness, this collective action is not produced in a void either, but anchored to a larger-scale communicative project which is reconstructed in context by the coparticipants [5]. And it is this premise of embeddedness which requires coparticipants to collaborate with regard to (at least) one collective communicative intention. Again, this collective WE-intention [11] does not exist in a void but is anchored to the collective category of a communicative project.

Thus, the reconstruction of a communicative intention, or individual sense-making, is framed by the collective concept of a dialogue act, which is embedded in a commmunicative project defined by a collective WE-intention. For this reason, the construction of coherence goes beyond the attribution of sense by individual speakers. Instead, it is anchored to the set of coparticipants, to their communicative project and their collective WE-intention. As a consequence of this, communicative contributions are not only accepted or rejected with regard to their local meaning, but also with regard to the collective WE-intention. In the case of an acceptance, the communicative contribution and its presuppositions are allocated to the already exisiting common ground. Contrary to an acceptance, a non-acceptance initiates a negotiation-of-validity sequence, in which the non-accepted references, presuppositions, propositions or force are made explicit. Only then is it possible to negotiate their communicative status and modify or reject them [4]. Once agreement has been reached about their status, it is possible to re-establish the common ground. But what is actually being re-established: the default-context notion of a common ground, or the context-dependent notion of a dialogue common ground?

4 Dialogue Common Ground and Co-Suppositions

In an interactional-organisation outlook, cognitive, linguistic and social contexts are constitutive parts of natural-language communication, and natural-language communication and other semiotic systems are constitutive parts of cognitive, linguistic and social contexts. As a consequence of this embeddedness, communicative contributions do not exist in an void but are anchored to an already existing common ground which subcategorises into the domain of personal common ground and the domain of cultural common ground [3]. Furthermore, context is represented by an infinite number of interdependent layers or interdependent frames. Since these frames presuppose one another, they can only be accessed with regard to the order of inclusion [12]. As has been argued above, communicative intentions are interdependent on both social antecedents and social consequences and thus a basic prerequisite for achieving coordinated social action. For these reasons, dialogue is progressive, viz. the coparticipants instantiate a dialogue common ground or build onto an already exisiting dialogue common ground. In the case of an acceptance, the dialogue act and its presuppositions are allocated to the dialogue common ground and assigned a co-suppositional status. And it is this co-suppositional status which makes the dialogue act and its co-suppositions irreversible, viz. whatever is added to the dialogue common ground can not simply be deleted from it. In the case of a rejection, a negotiation-of-validity sequence is initiated in order to secure the dialogue common ground with regard to the collectively shared co-suppositions and the indvidual presuppositions which are not shared.

To conclude, dialogue does not consist of indiviudal speakers exchanging unilateral speech acts. Instead, it is based on cooperation and collaboration, which manifest in the collective categories of coherence, communicative project, collective WE-intention, coparticipant, dialogue act, co-supposition and dialogue common ground.

5 References

1. Bar-Hillel, Y.: Indexical expressions. In: Kasher, A. (ed.): Pragmatics: critical concepts. Routledge, London (1998) 23-40
2. Clark, H.H.: Using language. CUP, Cambridge (1996)
3. Ducrot, O.: Dire et ne par dire. Hermann, Paris (1972)
4. Fetzer, A.: Non-acceptances: re- or un-creating context. In P. Bouquet, P. Brezillon, L. Serafini (eds.): 2nd international and interdisciplinary conference on modeling and using context (Context'99). Springer, Heidelberg (1999) 133-144
5. Fetzer, A.: Negotiating validity claims in political interviews. Text 20(4) (2000) 1-46
6. Garfinkel, H.: Studies in ethnomethodology. Polity Press, Cambridge (1994)
7. Goffman, E.:. Frame analysis. North Eastern University Press, Boston (1974)
8. Linell, P.: Approaching dialogue. Benjamins, Amsterdam (1998)
9. Recanati, F.: The pragmatics of what is said. Mind & Language 4/4 (1989) 295-329
10 Searle, J.: Speech Acts. CUP, Cambridge (1969)
11 Searle, J.: Conversation. In J. Searle et al. (eds.): (On) Searle on conversation. Benjamins, Amsterdam (1992) 137-147
12 Sperber, D. & Wilson, D.: Relevance. Blackwell, Oxford (1996)

Using Contexts Competition to Model Tactical Human Behavior in a Simulation

[1]Avelino J. Gonzalez, [2]Shinya Saeki

[1]School of Electrical Engineering and Computer Science
University of Central Florida Orlando, FL
gonzalez@pegasus.cc.ucf.edu

[2]Mitsubishi Research Institute, Inc.
Tokyo, Japan
saeki@mri.co.jp

Abstract. This article describes an innovative approach for representing tactical decision-making in *Autonomous Intelligent Platforms*, or AIP. The *Competing Context Concept,* is associated with the *Context-Based Reasoning* (CxBR) modeling paradigm, and represents an improvement thereof. CxBR uses as its basis an intuitive structure called a *Context*. One specific context is always in control of the AIP, and it contains all the information required to control that AIP when in that situation. When the situation changes, a new context must be found that properly addresses the new situation. Upon finding such a new context, it becomes activated, and the old context deactivates itself. An AIP, therefore, can be controlled intelligently through a sequence of transitions among various (pre-existing) contexts. The Competing Context Concept introduces a means to control the transition process without the need to pre-determine the next contexts. This paper briefly describes the CxBR paradigm and the competing context concept extension. Results from prototype testing will also be discussed.

1 Introduction

In military training systems, trainees often have to fight opponents who will resist their assigned mission. These exercises are often executed in complex simulators, and the opposing forces are simulated representations of real enemies. In order to reduce the staffing required to support such exercises, software agents called *Computer Generated Forces* (CGFs) are instead employed to represent the enemy (as well as friendly) forces. CGFs display the behavior of a real enemy under the conditions of the exercise, and can react to the actions of the trainees in a realistic manner. One single element of a CGF ensemble (a single tank, aircraft or vessel) is referred to as an *Autonomous Intelligent Platform*, or AIP.

Context-based Reasoning (CxBR) is a paradigm used to model tactical human behavior simply and effectively through an intuitive structure called a *Context*. Each contexts contains all the necessary knowledge and functionality for the AIP to successfully address the situation which that context specifically addresses. Behaviors are controlled through a sequence context activations and de-activations that are driven by the changing tactical situation. However, this behavior control of an AIP is currently based on pre-defined criteria for transitioning between such contexts. In complex tactical situations, such as those involving typical military tactics, it can be difficult to predefine these transition criteria. Therefore, it is necessary to implement a real-time decision-making function that more effectively represents realistic human performance in complex situations.

The literature describes many different ways to represent the real-time decision-making process of AIPs. They suffer from many disadvantages such as high complexity, difficulty of use, inefficiency for real time operation and others [1]. In this research, we propose, describe and test the *competing context concept*, as an enhancement to the basic CxBR paradigm [2], which we feel addresses many of the drawbacks of other approaches.

2 The Competing Context Concept

It would be advantageous to define the current situation as a set of *needs* to be addressed by the AIP in order to accomplish its mission and/or survive. The possible next contexts then can be said to *compete* for the right to become the next activated context to control the AIP. The winning context would ideally be the one that best addresses the identified needs of the new situation faced by the AIP.

We use a tire blowout event in a freeway as an example to describe how the competing context approach can be used to determine the best next active context. Assume a **freeway-driving** context that has four compatible next Main Contexts: **exit-ramp**, **enter-rest-area**, **fix-tire**, and **abandon-car**. If a tire blowout event occurs, **fix-tire** and **abandon-car** contexts are the relevant ones, and they would compete for the right to become the next activated context. Let's assume that there are two situations and two immediate goals as shown below.

Goal 1: Reach the destination as soon as possible at any cost.
Goal 2: Reach the destination driving the car.

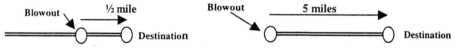

In the leftmost situation above, the blowout occurs near the destination (0.5 mi.). In situation 2 above (rightmost one), the blowout occurs far from the destination (5 miles).

If it takes 30 minutes to fix tire, the speed limit of this highway is 60 mph and walking speed is 2.5 mph, the relationship between each situation and each competing context can be easily determined. With respect to the goals, the "best" context depends on the goal as well as the situation. In the case of Situation #1 and Goal #1, it is preferable to abandon the car and walk the rest of the way. Under these conditions/goals, the **abandon-car** context would be selected for activation. However, for the three remaining combinations, **fix-tire** is the clearly the right thing to do.

To implement the Competing Context Concept, we propose a multi-faceted approach that contains four processes: (1) Generation *of Situation Interpretation Metrics*, (2) Relevant Context group selection, (3) Context attribute matching and (4) *Time-warp simulation*. Due to space limitations, only the first of these steps is described below.

In order to select the best next context, the situation must somehow be represented in finite terms. Such a definition needs to consider things that are static in nature (state of the car, weather, etc.), as well as those that change with time (distance to destination, time to arrive, etc.). *Situation interpretation metrics* (SIM) is the element that characterizes the situation being faced by the decision-maker.

Some examples of SIMs are 1) The `Time-to-accomplish-objective` SIM is, as the name suggests, the time available to accomplish the objective; 2) The `Weather` SIM has the following list of variables - sunny, rain, snow, visibility range, etc. In this process, these SIMs would be generated and presented to the context competition.

It is necessary to briefly define the types of SIMs and how the SIMs are generated. A SIM that describes the status of an AIP such as, for example, `operational` and `non-operational`, is called a *static SIM*. On the other hand, a SIM that is specifically related to time, such as `Time-to-accomplish-objective`, is called a *time-related SIM*. While a static SIM only needs to obtain its status from the current situation, the time-related SIM needs a formula or a simulation in order to be defined.

SIMs are generated only when they are required by an AIP. Some SIM's may need to be monitored at every time step, while others need only be monitored at a designated time step or event. Furthermore, some SIM's may only be checked as a result of the Time-warp simulation (to be discussed later). According to the pre-defined manner described above, the value of each SIM is checked and generated with respect to the monitoring requirements at every time step in the simulation. The value of a SIM may be unchanged from one time step to the next. If so, it does not trigger any competition among contexts, as it is assumed that the critical parameters of the situation have not changed. Otherwise, the situation is regarded as having changed, and the context competition process begins.

The *immediate goal* is important inasmuch as it describes how the current situation changes to accomplish the ultimate goal, the so-called "mission". Thus, these immediate goals can be expressed by a priority list of some combinations of the SIMs. This priority list represents a variable whose value is of primary importance. It will also define the desired value of the variable. The context that is most likely to cause this variable to achieve the desired value is then sought. The order of this list indicates the priority. The notation about the immediate goal can be defined as follows:

{<SIM1>, <desired value1>}
{<SIM2>, <desired value2>}

In the tire-blowout example above, immediate goal 1 might be to work towards setting the value of the applicable variable to desired values. For example,

{Time_to_destination, minimum}
{Car_status, operational}

The "Time to destination" immediate goal is ranked higher than "Car status". Therefore, the **abandon-the-car** context better addresses the needs of the situation and should be selected. This is because the driver can reach the destination earlier by walking than by driving the car after fixing the tire.

3 Summary and Conclusion

The work briefly described in this paper was tested and evaluated in a military simulation involving a small land battle. The results show that it is a very workable concept for representing human behavior in a tactical situation. However, more work needs to be done to better represent the SIM's, and to make them more general. This will be the subject of future work by the authors.

References

1   Funge, J.:Cognitive Modeling for Computer Generated Forces. Proceedings of the 8th Computer Generated Forces and Behavioral Representation Conference. Orlando, FL., (1999)
2   Gonzalez, A. J. and Ahlers, R.: Context-Based Representation of Intelligent Behavior In Training Simulations. Transactions of the Society for Computer Simulation International 15(4), (1998) 153-166

Case Studies in Developing Contextualising Information Systems

Roland Klemke, Achim Nick

GMD – German National Research Center for Information Technology
Schloß Birlinghoven
D-53754 Sankt Augustin
Roland.Klemke@gmd.de, Achim.Nick@gmd.de

Abstract. Contextualisation of information is done for at least two different purposes: (1) contextualisation approaches address problems of information overload by filtering information appropriate in a certain context. (2) The presentation of information enriched with contextual information supports the recognition of its relevance and guides its understanding. We review four approaches to contextualisation and develop a framework of guidelines for the development of information systems that make use of contextualisation.

1. Introduction

Increasing amounts of information available online lead to problems of information overload and to a perceived decrease of information quality. However, the availability of high quality information as a key factor for the success of an organisation is more important than ever. Information contextualisation is an important technique to cope with information overload as contextualised information is better comprehensible and may be presented in appropriate contexts only. We present four approaches performed focussing on the role of contextualisation, compare these and derive guidelines helping to use contextualisation techniques.

2. Contextualisation Approaches

COBRA. During the COBRA project we developed an information brokering environment supporting brokers at the Economic Information Centre of Milan Chambers of Commerce (EIC). These brokers provide customers with information about organisations in the Milan area. Their work is a mixture of routine tasks (querying online information sources and databases), and intellectual tasks (understanding ambiguous client needs and transforming them into formal queries using complex categorisation and classification schemes). It was our goal to automate routine tasks (see [4]) and support the intellectual tasks.

One of the core aspects of the brokers situation is that they have to work for several clients simultaneously, meaning, that they are often forced to switch contexts. We support this situation by contextualising all information objects along a visualisation of the brokering processes performed for clients. When a broker switches from one client to another, she can see, in which stage the corresponding process is and how many open requests are waiting at which respective stages.

Our evaluation of the system showed that the contextualisation of information guided retrieval and reuse of information objects. Also, the permanent availability of an overview over the state of the work simplified the work of the brokers.

ELFI. ELFI is an information brokering system for research funding. Funding agencies offer information about funding programs to researchers with a funding need. About 2000 German researchers currently use the system (see [6]).

ELFI's brokering process is in three stages: (1) the ELFI service provider sets up the initial ELFI domain model, resulting in domain concepts and classification terms. (2) Automatic processes contextualise documents gathered from funding agencies and a human broker conceptualises and categorises the contextualised documents updating the domain model. (3) Funding agents at the different universities personalise this information to the researcher's need specifying interest profiles that filter appropriate items out of the available information.

We can observe two contextualisation steps: (1) incoming documents are contextualised along the domain model, i.e. they are enriched with occurrences of domain terms. This contextualisation helps the broker to decide about information relevance. (2) The domain model is contextualised along interest profiles filtering information items relevant to a specific researcher. Thus, the first contextualisation step enriches information while the second one reduces its amount.

A survey of ELFI users yielded that interest-based information contextualisation helps to save time in the searching process. The ELFI service provider team reports, that document contextualisation accelerates the specific domain modelling tasks.

CRUMPET. CRUMPET realises services for nomadic users targeting towards tourists visiting a town. Tourists explore cities guided and supported by personalised handheld devices combined with GPS or infrared sensors determining their position. Information is tailored to the position and interests. E.g. for a tourist interested in churches the CRUMPET system may generate a description of a trip to a nearby cathedral, showing a map with the actual position and the path to follow. Users access the system with different devices (e.g. mobile phones, handheld devices, desktop PC) to which the presentation is adapted. The actual network bandwidth is used for further adaptation. CRUMPET uses three forms of contextualisation: the topical filtering context, the actual physical context of the user and device characteristics.

WINDS. The WINDS project contributes to the reorganisation of the pedagogical, cultural and functional aspects of design education at universities. The traditional approach to design teaching shows some frequent problems which increase learning time and reduce knowledge retention. WINDS aims at creating support instruments favouring a pedagogically more adequate approach to design teaching.

Learning course materials following predefined structures is called *expository learning* as opposed to *exploratory learning*, where students explore learning materials on their own, based on interests and current needs. WINDS offers support for both learning styles based on contextualised learning materials. Three contextualisation strategies are used to guide the student's learning process: structure-based, content-based, and experience-based contextualisation.

The *structure-based contextualisation* of learning materials sets up paths through courses and is mainly used to support expository learning. Structural models put single units into the context of a course. *Content-based contextualisation* uses graphs of concepts and relations to offer an exploitable structure of information units. Concepts are linked to learning units and relations between different concepts support an exploratory learning style. *Experience-based contextualisation* uses a learner model to keep track of concepts and learning units a student worked with, offering a way to monitor individual progress and propose individual learning paths.

3. Contextualisation Framework

Table 1 summarises the approaches, identifying the modelled contextual feature, the contextualised information, and the contextualisation purpose. From the table we can observe that the contextual dimensions modelled vary with the presented information. However, the purpose of contextualisation is either filtering and/or enrichment.

Table 1. Contextual features, contextualised information and contextualisation purpose of different approaches.

	COBRA	ELFI	CRUMPET	WINDS
Feature taken as Context				
• "dynamic" process knowledge	X			
• "static" domain knowledge		X		X
• "static" personal interest		X	X	X
• "dynamic" location			X	
• "dynamic" device characteristics			X	
• "dynamic" user experience				X
Contextualised Information				
• "dynamic" process artefacts	X			
• "dynamic" news articles and other resources		X		
• "dynamic" domain knowledge		X		X
• "static" tourism related information & services			X	
• "static" learning materials				X
Contextualisation Purpose				
• Presentation Enrichment / Navigation Support	X	X		X
• Information Filtering		X	X	X

Based on our experience from the presented approaches, we present a framework for the development of contextualising information systems. The first step in designing such a system is to understand the nature of the information dealt with. Are huge amounts of items to be presented? Is the information structured or heterogeneous? Is the amount of items growing or do we have a stable set? These questions show whether the information systems task is to reduce the amount of information or to support its comprehension by enriching the presentation.

Having clarified this, we can select contextual dimensions identifying the context of use of the information system. Are these contexts changing (and do we have to detect these changes) or is there a stable set of contexts? Which contextual dimensions are relevant? Do we need to automatically observe these dimensions? From these questions we can learn whether we can use pre-modelled contexts or whether we have to handle dynamically changing contexts.

The next step is to design appropriate filtering mechanisms which reduce the available information to the amount relevant in context. How flexible shall these filter mechanisms be? Should filtering be done automatically or under user control (there is a trade-off here between comfort of use and flexibility)? Should information that is considered irrelevant be hidden or should we use ranking mechanisms?

Finally, a visualisation approach is needed that allows to present information together with contextual enrichments. Here, the envisioned users of the system have to be considered: what kind of contextual information will they need? Which contextual information is obvious (and would overload the interface)? Will they need detailed contextual annotations or do they just need contextual hints?

4. Conclusion and Future Work

The presented system development guidelines focus on contextual filtering and presentation issues and complement existing frameworks for context-aware systems, that focus on technological aspects (e.g. [1], [2]). We plan to extend the guidelines towards a context modelling framework (see [5]). An important goal is to guide designers to reflect on contextual information and to define the contextualisation purpose before developing a system.

References

1. P. J. Brown. *"Some lessons for location-aware applications"*, in: Proc. 1st Workshop on HCI for Mobile Devices, Glasgow University, May 1998.
2. A. K. Dey, G. D. Abowd. *"Towards a Better Understanding of Context and Context-Awareness"*, Tech. Rep. GIT-GVU-99-32, College of Computing, GIT, 1999.
3. M. Jarke, R. Klemke, A. Nick. *"Broker's Lounge - An Environment for Multi-Dimensional User-Adaptive Knowledge Management "*, in: Proc. 34th Hawaii Int'l Conf. on System Sciences, Hawaii, 2001.
4. R. Klemke, J. Koenemann. *"Supporting Information Brokers with an Organisational Memory"*, in: XPS-99, 5th German Conf. on Knowledge-Based Systems, Workshop on KM, OM and Reuse, Würzburg University, March 1999.
5. R. Klemke. "Context Framework - an Open Approach to Enhance Organisational Memory Systems with Context Modelling Techniques", in: PAKM2000: Basel, Switzerland, 2000.
6. A. Nick, J. Koenemann, E. Schalueck. *"ELFI: Information Brokering for the domain of research fundingt"*, Int'l Journal of Computer Networks and ISDN systems, 1998.

About Some Relationships Between Knowledge and Context

J.-Ch. POMEROL and P. BRÉZILLON

LIP6, Case 169, University Paris 6, 4 place Jussieu, 75252 Paris Cedex 05, France
E-mail: {Jean-Charles.Pomerol, Patrick.Brezillon}@lip6.fr

Abstract. Many attempts have been made to capture, on the one hand, the very nature of knowledge, and on the other hand, the nature of context. In this paper, we compare the two concepts of context and knowledge which, obviously, share some common aspects. We review the main characteristics of both concepts and while we conclude to a large overlapping of the two concepts, we also emphasize their differences as regards decision making and action. We start by reviewing the most famous views and definitions of knowledge. Then we give some characteristics of knowledge that appear important to us. We also introduce the notion of context with its main components. Then, we stress the differences between knowledge and context.

1 Introduction

On the one hand, many attempts have been made to capture the very nature of knowledge. These analyses come from different fields: philosophy, cognitive science, artificial intelligence, etc. On the other hand, there is now a renewal of the studies on context and several proposals to represent and implement the context in "intelligent" systems.

Up to now, there were, as far as we know, few attempts to compare the two concepts of context and knowledge, while they obviously share some common aspects. In this paper, we review the main characteristics of both concepts and, while we note a large overlapping of the two concepts, we also emphasize their differences as regards decision making and action.

This paper represents a viewpoint in artificial intelligence. As such, it is certainly open to criticism, but can also bring some new insights and fields applications.

Our contribution is the object of a full paper available from http://www-poleia.lip6.fr/~brezil/Pages2/Publications/CXT01/index.html .

2 Different types of knowledge

We first introduce the classical distinction between data, information and knowledge. Data are the stimuli that enter an interpretation process. Information is then data with meaning. Information is also the input to a knowledge-based process of decision making. Knowledge is used: (1) to transform data into information, (2) to derive new information from existing ones, and (3) to acquire new knowledge pieces. It follows that knowledge is both a means and a result of this complex process.

Across domains, there are different forms of knowledge:

• *know how* versus *know that*. The term *know how* refers to the knowledge that people use to operate or behave as opposed to *know that* which is related to the profound, ultimate and often hidden causes of the on-going phenomenon.

• *deep* versus *surface knowledge*. *Deep knowledge* refers to models and causal explanations that goes back to nature laws, whereas the *surface knowledge* is represented by practical rules that can be acquired from people performing efficiently a given task (human experts).

• *procedural versus declarative knowledge*. *Procedural knowledge* is a knowledge which is expressed, in expert systems by rules or, in organizational life, by procedures. *Declarative knowledge* refers to more descriptive knowledge represented by objects or agents in the new programming languages.

• *tacit* versus *explicit knowledge*. *Explicit knowledge* is easily shared whereas *implicit knowledge* is highly personal. (Nonaka [2] describes four types of movement between the two types of knowledge: socialization, externalization, combination and internalization.)

Comparisons among the different forms of knowledge are made in the full paper. Note only that the AI approach is close to many approaches in cognitive science.

3 Context

There is already a large amount of discussion about context (see Brézillon [1] for a survey in AI). We suggested to consider three types of contextual knowledge [4], namely external and contextual knowledge, and proceduralized context. The *contextual knowledge* is a backstage knowledge whereas *proceduralized context* is immediately useful for the task at hand. In our representation of context, the *contextual knowledge* is largely tacit, mainly because it is the context that everybody knows without expressing it.

An important issue is the passage from *contextual knowledge* to *proceduralized context*. This proceduralization results from the focus on a task. Thus, it is task-oriented just as *knowing how*; it is often triggered by an event or primed by the recognition of a pattern. We also observed that the construction of the *proceduralized context* from *contextual knowledge* is often a process of communication in the operator community.

Ozturk and Aamodt [3] proposed a quite similar distinction between external context (our *contextual knowledge*) and internal context (our *proceduralized context*). The main difference is that they do not consider the dynamics between the two types of context but only inside the internal context. In a similar spirit, Hewitt (see Tiberghien [5]) distinguishes between *intrinsic* and *extrinsic* context, the former denoting a synthetic interaction and the latter denoting surroundings of the effective stimulus.

4 Discussion

To sum up the discussion presented in the full paper, the differences and analogies between context and knowledge, are:

- context and knowledge can be *explicit* or *implicit*, but both can be explicited except for some parts of *know how*
- context can contain *deep* and/or *surface knowledge*,
- the *contextual knowledge* is loosely task-oriented not reduced to *know how*, because it may contain *deep knowledge*
- the *contextual knowledge* is mainly concerned with this part of knowledge which is useful for describing the nature state preceding decision making or action; as such a given *contextual knowledge* may have several realizations.
- the proceduralization of a *contextual knowledge* piece is a process which may take place in a community of practice and is anyway a mandatory step on the road to action. As such, it has a role in priming action or practice. In some sense, it is the preliminary step for the activation of *knowing how*.
- the *proceduralized context* is task-oriented or/and recognition-primed and subjective like *know how* or *situated knowledge*,
- the link between *proceduralized context* and action is either explicit or implicit (compilation of the *proceduralized context*). As such, the *proceduralized context* is relevant to the so-called externalization process. This externalization process is a more or less a social process.
- whereas the knowledge is fixed, the *proceduralized context* changes during action.

Finally, we do believe that knowledge is a too vague concept to be really operant in the analysis of decision making and of task undertaking. On the contrary, the notion of context which is entirely task oriented offers a shrewder concept to model the relationships between knowledge and action.

Conclusion

The *contextual knowledge* is certainly not all the knowledge. The notion of context offers an alternative view to *knowing how* to capture that part of knowledge which is related to decision making and action. *Contextual knowledge* is subjective and yet can be shared by many individuals. One of the main difference between context and knowledge is that context and its proceduralization offer a model to understand the links between decision making and/or action and the backstage knowledge. The notion of context does certainly not explain *know how*, but it help to understand how experienced people with a recognized *know how* adapt their behavior according to the circumstances. In some sense, context is knowledge about the instantiation of *know how*, it is the framework which reveals *know how*.

References

1. Brézillon P. and Pomerol J.-Ch. (1996) Misuse and nonuse of knowledge-based systems: The past experiences revisited. In: *Implementing Systems for Supporting Management Decisions*, Humphreys P. *et al.* (Eds.), Chapman and Hall, London, 44-60.
2. Nonaka I. and Takeuchi H. (1995) The *Knowledge-Creating Company*. Oxford University Press, New York, NY.
3. Ozturk, P. and Aamodt, A. (1998) A context model for knowledge-intensive case-based reasoning. *Special Issue on Using Context in Applications. International Journal on Human-Computer Studies*, 48(3): 331-355.
4. Pomerol J.-Ch. and Brézillon P. (1999) Dynamics between contextual knowledge and proceduralized context. *Modeling and Using Context* (CONTEXT-99). In: Lecture Notes in Artificial Intelligence, N° 1688, Springer Verlag, 284-295.
5. Tiberghien, G. (1986) Context and cognition: Introduction. *Cahier de Psychologie Cognitive*, 6(2): 105-119.

Combining Cases and Rules to Provide Contextualised Knowledge Based Systems

Debbie Richards

Department of Computing,
Division of Information and Communication Sciences,
Macquarie University, Sydney
richards@ics.mq.edu.au

Abstract: Providing contextualised knowledge often involves the difficult and time-consuming task of specifying the appropriate contexts in which the knowledge applies. This paper describes the Ripple Down Rules (RDR) knowledge acquisition and representation technique which does not attempt to define up front the possible context/s. Instead cases and the exception structure provide the context and rules provide the index by which to retrieve the case/s. KA is incremental. The domain expert locally patches rules as new cases are seen. Thus, RDR is a hybrid case-based and rule-based approach. The use of Formal Concept Analysis to translate the RDR performance system into a *formal context* and uncover an explanation system in the form of an abstraction hierarchy further strengthens our emphasis on the combined use of cases and rules to provide contextualised knowledge.

1. The Role of Context in Knowledge Based Systems

The issue of context has been recognized as an important factor in the reuse and sharing of knowledge (e.g. [1,14]). A situated view of knowledge places even greater emphasis on the role of context [2]. Situated cognition involves taking into account interaction between the individual's inner state and the external environment and trying to record all the influencing factors. However, specification of the context in which the knowledge applies is difficult, time consuming and error-prone. The knowledge acquisition and representation technique described in this paper, known as ripple-down rules (RDR) avoids the need for complete specification as our goal is not to build global rules or large-scale common ontologies but to capture local contextualised knowledge from which we can retrospectively generate domain-specific ontologies.

2. What are Ripple Down Rules ?

RDR is a hybrid case-based and rule-based approach. RDR are developed online and incrementally by the domain expert who is responsible for knowledge acquisition (KA), validation and maintenance, which are indistinguishable from one another in the approach. KA proceeds as follows. The expert performs an inference on a case. If they disagree with the conclusion given they specify the correct conclusion and pick some features in the case to justify the new conclusion. These features must differentiate the current case from the case associated with the rule that misfired [5]. The new rule is added as an exception.

RDR non-monotonically reasons over a list of ordered rules with exceptions. RDR belong to a class of representation schemes that provide modularity through the use of exceptions. While this class includes other approaches, RDR are 'the most general for attribute-value based representations and most strongly structured" [18, 279]. Interest in exception structures is due to a number of factors including: the naturalness and comprehensibility of the representation by human experts; the support they offer for incremental change; the use of context and maintainability of the knowledge due to localization of changes [7,13]. Exceptions also provide a compact representation and accounts for the use of exceptions as output structures for some machine learners [19]. The cases and exception structure work together to provide the context.

The approach seeks to draw on the benefits of cases and rule-based systems but avoid the limitations. Rule based systems do not provide context or grounding in the real world. CBR suffers from the indexing problem associated with retrieving appropriate cases and deciding how best to adapt cases. The use of cases in RDR is similar to the use of cases in CBR. Cases are used to:

- assist the user to develop rules,
- provide the appropriate context of the new rule being entered through storage of *cornerstone case* (the case that prompted a rule to be added) and
- validate the entered rule by ensuring the current case is differentiated from other cases associated with the incorrect rule.

When the expert picks the salient features in the case (which form the rule conditions) they are in effect selecting the index by which to retrieve the case. The creation of indexes is one of the major problems in CBR because most approaches try to generate these automatically to some extent. Getting the expert to provide this index as a natural part of their duties substantially simplifies the task. The way that a Ripple-Down rule is used to differentiate between cases combines the approaches of difference and checklist-based indexing and the failure-driven nature of learning in RDR makes it similar to explanation-based indexing. See [12] for description of these three main approaches to indexing cases. While RDR does place importance on the role of cases, each case provides a local context and there is no attempt to define generally applicable rules or landmark cases. CBR techniques usually try to identify important cases that are used to classify new cases.

RDR were first developed to handle single classification tasks. An exception structure in the form of a binary tree with true and false branches is used to provide rule pathways, see an example in Figure. We have developed multiple classification RDR (MCRDR) to handle classification tasks where multiple independent classifications are required [10,11]. The method builds n-ary trees and consists only of exception branches. A better description may be sets of decision lists joined by exceptions. In contrast to single classification RDR all rules attached to true parents are evaluated against the data. An MCRDR is defined as the quadruple <rule,P,C,S>, where P is the parent rule, C are the children/exception rules and S are the sibling rules within the same level of decision list. Every rule in the first list is evaluated. If a rule evaluates to false then no further lists attached to that rule are examined. If a rule evaluates to true all rules in the next list are tested. The list of every true rule is processed in this way. The last true rule on each path constitutes the conclusions given. Current empirical evaluations of a commercial system using MCRDR have shown that experts can build systems with 3- 4,000 rules in about one person week. Even KBS with 7,000 rules do not suffer from maintenance problems. Thus the RDR approach is not only rapid but also highly scalable. Simulation studies [10] have shown MCRDR to be a superior representation to the original RDR structure by producing knowledge bases that mature more quickly and are more compact even for single classification domains. It is conjectured that this occurs because more use is made of expertise rather than depending on the knowledge base structure [11]. The simulation studies showed that although the order of cases seen and the quality of the cases (stereotypical or landmark cases can be viewed as higher quality) will affect the compactness of the knowledge base and how quickly it matures, a similar and equally effective set of rules will be developed regardless of the order or nature of the cases.

We have recently applied ideas from Formal Concept Analysis (FCA) [20] to MCRDR so that the implicit concepts, both primitive and more abstract, in an MCRDR assertional KBS can be found and structured into a terminological KBS. The RDR assertions provide a performance system and the concept lattice derived using FCA provides an explanation system. This enhancement is important as minimal analysis of domain knowledge was a strength of the KA technique but it meant that it was not possible to show higher level models of the domain knowledge. The abstraction hierarchy that FCA automatically develops offers a retrospective model that is based on the MCRDR rules. While the MCRDR approach does not require a model for KA or inferencing we are interested in providing the user with a model since models can assist instruction [17] and explanation [3].

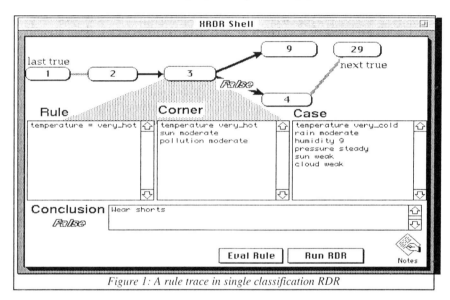

Figure 1: A rule trace in single classification RDR

3. Discussion and Conclusion

Providing contextual knowledge to the user is a high priority in the RDR approach. Cases, the exception structure and local patching have made it possible to offer contextualised explanations and KA, detection of erroneous or missing knowledge; a critique of the user's plan in the form of an explanation of the system's plan; and increased depth of knowledge by showing abstracted concepts not obvious directly from the rule pathways. The FCA option also provides the structure of the knowledge by showing the sub, super and matching concepts.

Others (e.g. [4, 9]) have found the combination of rule-based and case-based reasoning to be beneficial. In [4] C5 is used initially to classify the cases and a typicality measure is used next to rank the cases. The use of a similarity measure is seen to provide global knowledge based on all the cases whereas the C5 rules generate more local knowledge. [9] also applies rules to get a first approximation and then uses cases when an exception to the rules is seen to be compellingly similar. They see that the use of cases can overcome deficiencies in the rule set. As we found, cases are often more readily available and easier to acquire than rules. However, our combined use of cases and rules is a little more holistic in that the relationship between cases and rules are more intertwined. Our rules are developed based on cases which are then stored with that rule and used in further knowledge maintenance. In the other two approaches cases are used as a second step to supplement the rule-based knowledge.

Mainstream KBS research is focused on *knowledge level* modelling [15] and the use of ontologies to assist development of these models. Kolodner [12] argues that in domains where models are not well understood, that is causal knowledge is not known, cases can be used to capture knowledge about the domain. We go further and argue that models by their very nature are problematic [3, 8,], both in their definition and validation, and that cases can be useful to alleviate these problems. By letting the domain expert run cases and assign conclusion/s, which is what they are expert at, we easily and rapidly capture a performance system with minimal *a priori* analysis of the domain. By translating the rules into a formal context we can use FCA to uncover an explanation system in the form of an abstraction hierarchy. Thus the user is able to capture, validate, apply, manipulate and explore contextualised knowledge through the combined use of rules and cases.

Bibliography

[1] Chandrasekaran, B. and Johnson, T. (1993) Generic Tasks and Task Structures In David, J.M., Krivine, J.-P. and Simmons, R. (eds), *Second Generation Expert Systems* Springer, Berlin, 232-272.

[2] Clancey, W.J., (1992) Model Construction Operators *Artificial Intelligence 53*:1-115.

[3] Clancey, W.J., (1993) Situated Action: A Neurological Interpretation Response to Vera and Simon *Cognitive Science*, 17: 87-116.

[4] Coenen, F, Swinnen, G., Vanhoof, K., and Wets, G. (1999) The Improvement of Response Modelling: Combining Rule-Induction and Case-Based Reasoning In J. Zytkow & J. Rauch (eds) *Principles of Data Mining and Knowledge Discovery, 3rd European Conference, PKDD'99, Prague, Lecture Notes in AI,* Vol 1704, Springer, 301-308.

[5] Compton, P. and Jansen, R., (1990) A Philosophical Basis for Knowledge Acquisition. *Knowledge Acquisition* 2:241-257.

[6] Compton, P., Preston, P. and Kang, B. (1995) The Use of Simulated Experts in Evaluating Knowledge Acquisition, *Proceedings 9th Banff Knowledge Acquisition for Knowledge Based Systems Workshop* Banff. Feb 26 - March 3 1995, Vol 1:12.1-12.18.

[7] Gaines, B.R., (1991) Induction and Visualization of Rules with Exceptions In J. Boose & B. Gaines (eds), *Proceedings of the 6th Banff AAAI Knowledge Acquisition for Knowledge-Based Systems Workshop.* Banff, Canada,Vol 1: 7.1-7.17.

[8] Gaines, B. R. and Shaw, M.L.G. (1989) Comparing the Conceptual Systems of Experts *The 11th International Joint Conference on Artificial Intelligence,* 633-638.

[9] Golding, A. and Rosenbloom, P. (1991) Improving Rule-Based Systems through Case-Based Reasoning In *Proceedings of AAAI'91,* Anaheim, CA.

[10] Kang, B. (1996) *Validating Knowledge Acquisition: Multiple Classification Ripple Down Rules* PhD Paper, School of Computer Science and Engineering, University of NSW, Australia.

[11] Kang, B., Compton, P. and Preston, P. (1995) Multiple Classification Ripple Down Rules: Evaluation and Possibilities *Proceedings 9th Banff Knowledge Acquisition for Knowledge Based Systems Workshop* Banff. Feb 26 - March 3 1995, Vol 1: 17.1-17.20.

[12] Kolodner, Janet (1993) *Case-Based Reasoning* Morgan Kaufman Publishers Inc., CA.

[13] Li, X. (1991) What's so bad about rule-based programming ? *IEEE S/W*, Sept., 103-105.

[14] McCarthy, J. (1991) *Notes on Formalizing Context* Technical Report. Computer Science Department, Stanford University.

[15] Newell, A. (1982) The Knowledge Level *Artificial Intelligence* 18:87-127.

[16] Richards, D and Compton, P. (1997) Combining Formal Concept Analysis and Ripple Down Rules to Support the Reuse of Knowledge *Proceedings Software Engineering Knowledge Engineering SEKE'97*, Madrid 18-20 June 1997, 177-184.

[17] Schon, D.A. (1987) *Educating the Reflective Practitioner* Jossey-Bass, San Francisco, CA.

[18] Scheffer, T. (1996) Algebraic Foundation and Improved Methods of Induction of Ripple Down Rules Repetition In Compton, P., Mizoguchi, R., Motoda, H. and Menzies, T. (eds) *Proceedings of Pacific Knowledge Acquisition Workshop PKAW'96*, October 23-25 1996, Coogee, Australia, 279-292.

[19] Vere, S. A. (1980) Multilevel Counterfactuals for Generalizations of Relational Concepts and Productions *Artificial Intelligence* 14:139-164.

[20] Wille, R. (1982) Restructuring Lattice Theory: An Approach Based on Hierarchies of Concepts In I. Rival (ed), *Ordered Sets* Reidel, Dordrecht, Boston, 445-470.

Author Index

Lecture Notes in Artificial Intelligence (LNAI)

Lecture Notes in Computer Science